Carbonyl Compounds

for JEE Main & Advanced

Study Package for

Chemistry

Includes Past
JEE & KVPY Questions

Useful for Class 12,
KVPY & Olympiads

Fully Solved

Dr. O. P. Agarwal

□ Corporate Office : 45, 2nd Floor, Maharishi Dayanand Marg, Corner Market, Malviya Nagar, New Delhi-110017

Tel. : 011-49842349 / 49842350

Typeset by Disha DTP Team

DISHA PUBLICATION

For further information about the books from DISHA,
Log on to www.dishapublication.com or email to info@dishapublication.com

PREFACE

REVISED EDITION

It gives us immense pleasure and satisfaction to bring out the thoroughly revised and updated edition of the book **"Disha's Carbonyl Compounds"** The book has been designed to give a better look & feel and to make the text more lucid. The new pattern of JEE Main & Advanced has been kept in mind throughout.

The exercises at the end of each chapter have been designed in the flavour of the new pattern of JEE Main & Advanced. The questions from the previous JEE papers have been incorporated in the different exercises. A separate section having past JEE questions is also provided at the end.

1. **Exercise 1 - MCQ with One correct option :** This exercise contains a collection of question, which has been very carefully selected and it is ensured that there is no repetition. The exercise contains a collection of questions, which has been very carefully selected and it is ensured that there is no repetition. The exercise has been designed so as to cover all the concepts involved in the chapter.

2. **Exercise 2 :** This exercise contains all the four new variety of questions which have been asked in the last 3-4 JEE examinations. These variety of questions are-

   (i) **MCQ's with one or more than one correct answers :** Around 20-30 well selected problems introduced in each chapter.

   (ii) **Comprehension based questions :** More than 50 passages which tests the student's comprehension and analytical ability have been added. All these are newly framed problems.

   (iii) **Matching type question :** Match the following type of question with multiple matching have been introduced in each chapter. These are unique and newly framed problems which will definitely pose a big challenge to the student. I feel that this type of problem is the best way to check a student's concepts.

   (iv) **Assertion & Reason type questions :** Assertion and Reason type of questions have been incorporated in each and every chapter.

3. **Exercise 3 - Subjective Problems :** This exercise contains a unique collection of subjective problems which will not only give practice to the students but will also help in revising the complete chapter.

In the end, We would like to request all readers to highlight the printing errors and come forward with suggestions for further improvement of the book.

DR. O.P. AGARWAL

CONTENTS

CHAPTER 14
ALDEHYDES AND KETONES
671-744

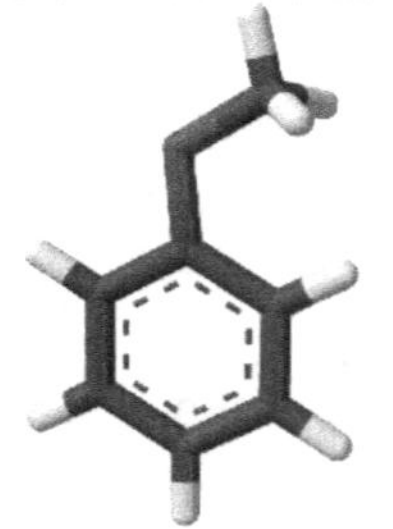

CHAPTER 15
CARBANIONS
745-766

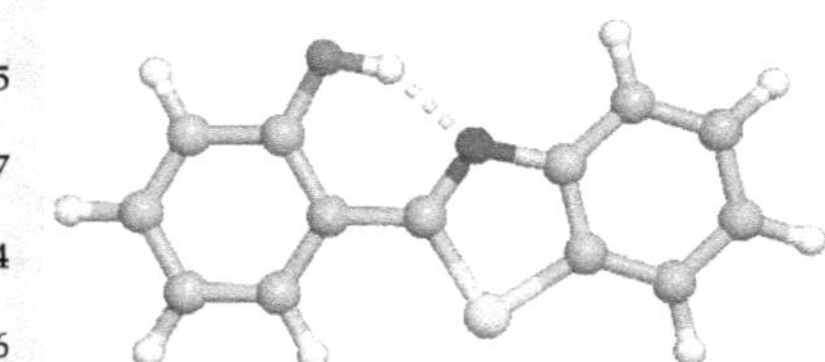

CHAPTER 16
α,β-UNSATURATED CARBONYL COMPOUNDS
767-788

CHAPTER 17
CARBOXYLIC ACIDS
789-846

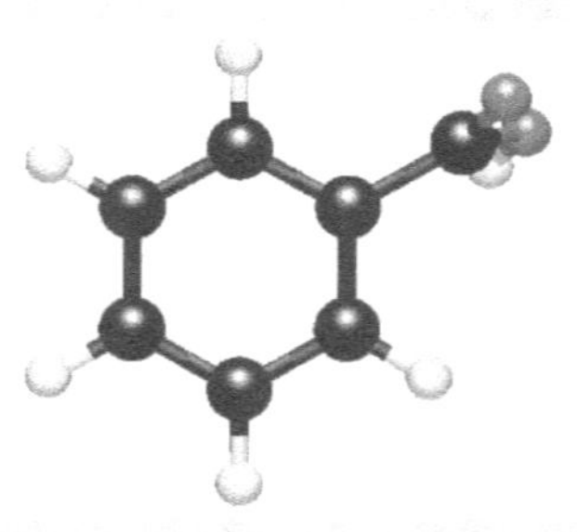

CHAPTER 18
FUNCTIONAL DERIVATIVES OF CARBOXYLIC ACIDS
847-900

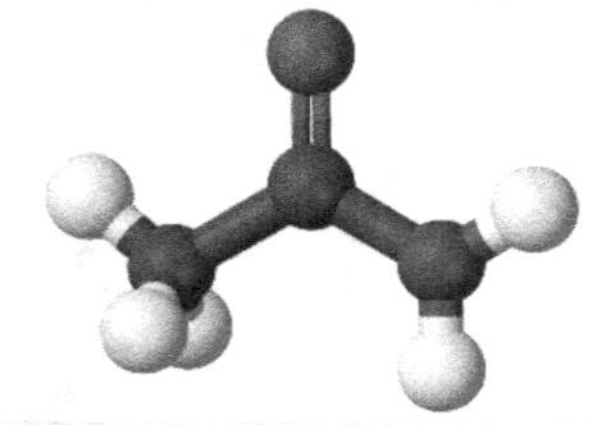

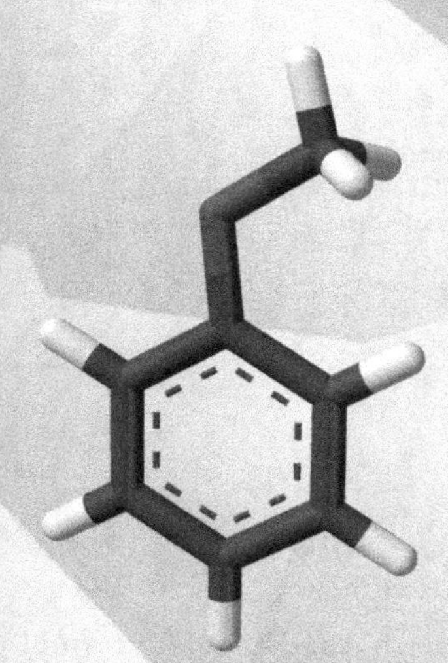

14 Aldehydes and Ketones

CHAPTER HIGHLIGHTS

14.1 Nomenclature and Isomerism

Aldehydes and ketones are the compounds containing a carbonyl group, > C=O. They have the same general formula, $C_nH_{2n}O$. The general structure of aldehydes is R—CHO, except for formaldehyde where R=H ; and that of ketones is RR′CO ; the groups R and R′ may be aliphatic, aromatic or alicyclic.

The *common names of aldehydes* are derived from the names of the corresponding carboxylic acids by replacing -*ic acid* by -*aldehyde*. In IUPAC system, aliphatic aldehydes are named as **alkanals**.

$$\underset{\text{Methanal (Formaldehyde)}}{H-\overset{O}{\overset{\|}{C}}-H} \qquad \underset{\text{Butanal }(n\text{-Butyraldehyde})}{CH_3CH_2CH_2\overset{O}{\overset{\|}{C}}-H} \qquad \underset{\text{3-Chloropropanal }(\beta\text{-Chloropropionaldehyde})}{ClCH_2CH_2\overset{O}{\overset{\|}{C}}-H} \qquad \underset{\text{Phenylethanal (Phenylacetaldehyde)}}{C_6H_5CH_2\overset{O}{\overset{\|}{C}}-H}$$

Aldehydes in which the —CHO group is attached to a ring system are named as substitutively by adding the suffix *carbaldehyde*.

Benzenecarbaldehyde (Common name : Benzaldehyde) — Cyclohexane-carbaldehyde — 2-Naphthalenecarbaldehyde

Common name for ketones are obtained simply by adding the word ketone to the name of the two alkyl groups. In IUPAC system, these are named as **alkanones**.

$CH_3CH_2\overset{O}{\overset{\|}{C}}CH_3$ — Butanone (Ethyl methyl ketone)

$CH_3COCH_2CH{=}CH_2$ — 4-Penten-2-one (Allyl methyl ketone)

$C_6H_5CH_2COCH_3$ — 1-Phenyl-2-propanone (Benzyl methyl ketone)

A ketone in which the carboxyl group is attached to a benzene ring is named as a - *phenone.*

$COCH_3$ — Acetophenone

$COCH_2CH_2CH_3$ — *n*-Butyrophenone

COC_6H_5 — Benzophenone

NO_2, CH_3 — 3-Nitro-4′-methylbenzophenone

When it is necessary to name the —CHO and —COR groups as prefix, these are named as **methanoyl (or formyl) and alkanoyl (or acyl) groups** respectively.

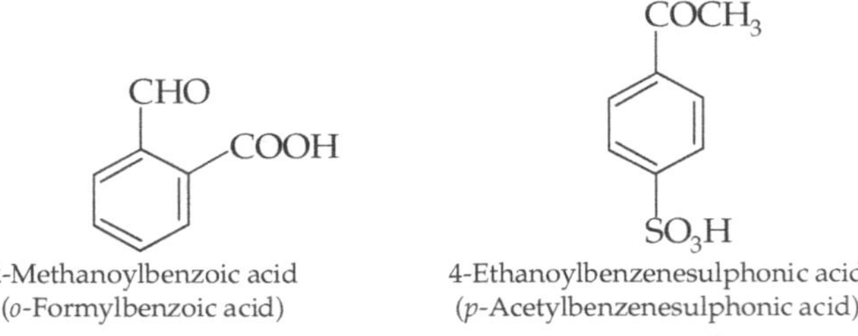

2-Methanoylbenzoic acid (*o*-Formylbenzoic acid)

4-Ethanoylbenzenesulphonic acid (*p*-Acetylbenzenesulphonic acid)

Aldehydes show **chain** and **functional isomerism.**

Chain isomers. $CH_3CH_2CH_2CHO$ — *n*-Butanal; $(CH_3)_2CHCHO$ — 2-Methylpropanal (iso-Butanal)

Functional isomers.

CH_3CH_2CHO	CH_3COCH_3	$CH_2 = CHCH_2OH$	$CH_3CH—CH_2$ (bridged by O)	$CH_2 = CH.O.CH_3$
Propanal	Acetone	Allyl alcohol	α, β-Propylene oxide	Methyl vinyl ether

Ketones show **chain, functional and metamerism.** *Examples of functional isomerism is given above in aldehydes.*

Chain isomers. $CH_3CH_2CH_2—\overset{O}{\overset{\|}{C}}—CH_3$ — Methyl propyl ketone; $(CH_3)_2CH—\overset{O}{\overset{\|}{C}}—CH_3$ — Methyl isopropyl ketone

Metamers. $CH_3CH_2CH_2—\overset{O}{\overset{\|}{C}}—CH_3$ — Methyl propyl ketone; $CH_3CH_2—\overset{O}{\overset{\|}{C}}—CH_2CH_3$ — Diethyl ketone

TEST YOUR UNDERSTANDING - 14.1

1. Give IUPAC names of the following compounds :

(*a*) OHC–(CH₂)₃–CHO (b) C_6H_5–CH=CH–CHO (*c*) HO–C₆H₃(OCH₃)–CHO (*d*) $C_6H_5–CH_2COCH_2–C_6H_5$

(*e*) C_6H_5–CH.CHO with CHO (*f*) cyclopentyl–CHO (*g*) $C_6H_5CH{=}CHCOC_6H_5$

2. Write down the structural formulas for (*a*) the seven carbonyl compounds of formula $C_5H_{10}O$, (*b*) the five carbonyl compounds of formula C_8H_8O having a benzene ring.

14.2 Structure of the Carbonyl Group (*Cf. carbon-carbon double bond*)

Like the carbon-carbon double bond of alkenes, the carbon-oxygen double bond of the carbonyl group is composed of one σ and one π bond.

In the carbonyl group, carbon atom is in a state of sp^2 hybridisation. The C—O σ bond is produced by overlap of an sp^2 orbital of carbon with a *p* orbital of oxygen. On the other hand, the C—O π bond is formed by the sideways overlap of *p* orbitals of carbon and oxygen. The remaining two sp^3 orbitals of carbon form σ bonds with the *s* orbital of hydrogen or sp^2 orbital of carbon of the alkyl group. Now since the three σ bonds of the carbonyl carbon utilize sp^2 orbitals, they lie in one plane and are 120° apart (*similarity with* C = C).

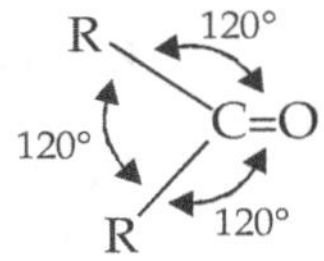

R, R, C=O, 120°, 120°, 120°

However, it is important to note that the carbon-oxygen double bond is different from carbon-carbon double bond. Due to greater electronegativity of oxygen atom, the π electron cloud is attracted towards oxygen. Consequently, oxygen attains a partial negative charge and carbon a partial positive charge. This polar nature of the carbonyl group causes intermolecular attraction in aldehydes or ketones and hence accounts for their higher boiling points than that of hydrocarbons and ethers of comparable molecular weight. Moreover, polar nature of the carbonyl group also explains the dipole moment in aldehyde and ketones. However, the high values of dipole moments (2.3 – 2.8 D) of aldehydes and ketones can't be accounted for only by inductive effect ; this can be accounted for if carbonyl group is a resonance hybrid of the two structures.

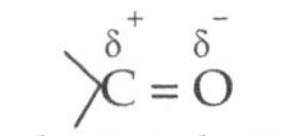

$>\overset{\delta^+}{C}=\overset{\delta^-}{O}$ Polarity due to inductive effect

$>C=\ddot{O}: \longleftrightarrow >\overset{+}{C}-\overset{-}{\ddot{O}}:$ Polarity due to resonance

Other important difference in carbon-oxygen and carbon-carbon double bonds lies in the fact that the carbonyl group undergoes nucleophilic addition reactions, while olefinic bond undergoes electrophilic addition reactions.

14.3 Preparation of Aldehydes and Ketones

1. **By oxidation of primary and secondary alcohols.** Discussed in the chapter on "Monohydric Alcohols".

$$RCH_2OH \xrightarrow{\text{pyridinium chlorochromate, } CH_2Cl_2} RCHO$$

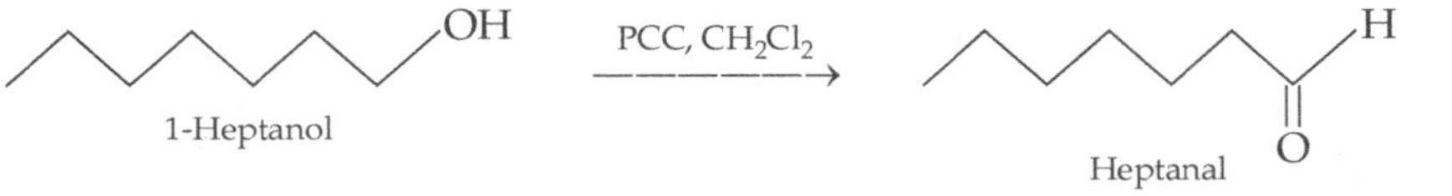

1-Heptanol $\xrightarrow{PCC,\ CH_2Cl_2}$ Heptanal

Cyclohexanol $\xrightarrow[\text{or } K_2Cr_2O_7 + H_2SO_4]{CrO_3 \text{ in glacial acetic acid}}$ Cyclohexanone

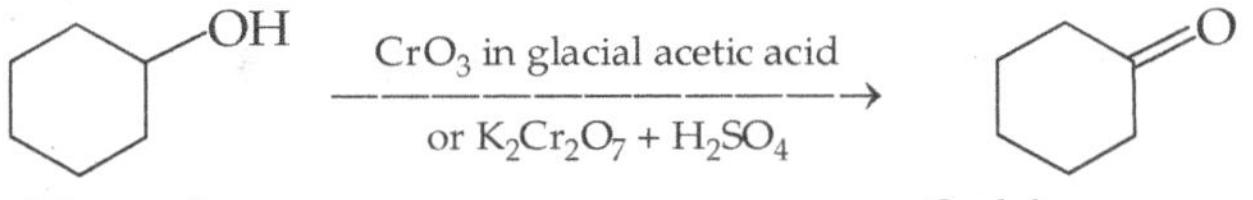

Since ketones are oxidised with difficulty, so these can be easily prepared by oxidizing 2° alcohols with acidic dichromate (difference from aldehyde preparation).

Recall that solution of chromic anhydride in pyridine is known as **Sarett's reagent**, while solution of chromic anhydride in water, acetone and sulphuric acid is known as **Jone's reagent**.

Primary and secondary alcohols may also be oxidised to aldehyde and ketones respectivley by heating with copper at about 250–300°C (dehydrogenation of alcohol).

Ketones can also be prepared by oxidizing 2° alcohols with aluminium *tert*-butoxide (**Oppenauer oxidation).**

$$R_2CHOH \xrightarrow{(tert\text{-}BuO)_3Al} R_2CO$$

OH ⟶ O

TEST YOUR UNDERSTANDING - 14.2

1. Can an aldehyde be prepared by oxidation of a 1° alcohol with acid dichromate ? If, yes mention the condition.

2. **By reduction of acid chlorides, esters, and nitriles (only for aldehydes).** Theoretically, we may think that aldehydes can be prepared by reducing carboxylic acids with lithiumaluminium hydride ($LiAlH_4$ or LAH). However, LAH is a very powerful reducing agent and hence aldehydes formed as intermediate are very readily further reduced to primary alcohols.

$$RCOOH \xrightarrow{LiAlH_4} [RCHO] \xrightarrow{LiAlH_4} RCH_2OH$$

However, a modified version of the reaction is used for preparing aldehydes. For this,

(*i*) a derivative of a carboxylic acid, which is more easily reduced than the carboxylic acid itself is taken as a starting material. Three such acid derivatives are acid chlorides, esters and nitriles ; which in turn are easily prepared from carboxylic acids.

(*ii*) a less reactive aluminium hydride derivative than $LiAlH_4$ is used. Two such derivatives are lithium tri-*tert*-butoxyaluminium hydride (**LBAH**) and diisobutylaluminium hydride (**DBAH**).

$$Li^+\left[H{-}Al(OC(CH_3)_3)_3\right]^- \qquad HAl(CH_2CH(CH_3)_2)_2$$

Lithium tri-*tert*-butoxyaluminium hydride — Diisobutylaluminium hydride

These two hydrides are less reactive than $LiAlH_4$ as they are much more sterically hindered and, therefore, face difficulty in transferring hydride ions. Reduction by these reagents is brought about by the transfer of a hydride ion from the aluminium atom to the carbonyl carbon (in case of acid chlorides and esters) or the nitrile carbon (in case of nitriles). Subsequent hydrolysis of the intermediate liberates the aldehyde.

(*a*)
$$R{-}\overset{O}{\overset{\|}{C}}{-}Cl \xrightarrow[\text{ether, }-78°C]{LiAlH(OCMe_3)_3} R{-}\underset{Cl}{\underset{|}{\overset{O\,\bar{Al}(OCMe_3)_3}{\overset{|}{C}}}}{-}H\ \ \overset{+}{Li} \xrightarrow{H_2O} R{-}\overset{O}{\overset{\|}{C}}{-}H + LiCl + Al(OCMe_3)_3$$

$$O_2N{-}C_6H_4{-}COCl \xrightarrow[(ii)\ H_2O]{(i)\ LiAlH(OBu\text{-}t)_3} O_2N{-}C_6H_4{-}CHO$$

Acid chlorides may also be reduced to aldehydes by catalytic hydrogenation (H_2/Pd)

$$RCOCl + H_2 \xrightarrow{Pd/BaSO_4} RCHO + HCl$$

over deactivated (by sulphur or quinoline) palladized barium sulphate or carbonate. (**Rosenmund reduction**).

$$RCOCl + H_2 \xrightarrow[\text{S or quinoline}]{Pd/BaSO_4} RCHO$$

Partial deactivation of the catalyst is necessary to check further reduction of the product aldehyde.

(*b*)
$$CH_3(CH_2)_{10}\overset{O}{\overset{\|}{C}}{-}OC_2H_5 \xrightarrow[\text{hexane, }-78°C]{(iso\text{-}Bu)_2AlH} CH_3(CH_2)_{10}\underset{OC_2H_5}{\underset{|}{\overset{OAl(iso\text{-}Bu)_2}{\overset{|}{CH}}}} \xrightarrow{H_2O} CH_3(CH_2)_{10}CHO$$

(*c*)
$$CH_3CH{=}CHCH_2CH_2C{\equiv}N \xrightarrow[\text{hexane}]{(iso{-}Bu)_2AlH} CH_3CH{=}CHCH_2CH_2\overset{NAl(iso\text{-}Bu)_2}{\overset{\|}{CH}} \xrightarrow{H_2O} CH_3CH{=}CHCH_2CH_2CHO$$

Ketones can't be prepared by this method.

3. **By hydration of alkynes** (Discussed in alkynes).

$$HC \equiv CH \xrightarrow{H_2SO_4, Hg^{2+}} CH_2 = CHOH \rightleftharpoons CH_3CHO$$

$$CH_3CH_2C \equiv CH \xrightarrow{H_2SO_4, Hg^{2+}} CH_3CH_2COCH_3$$

4. **Hydroboration of alkynes** (Discussed in alkynes). Hydroboration of terminal alkynes followed by oxidation of the intermediate (vinylboranes) with alkaline hydrogen peroxide gives aldehydes.

$$\underset{\text{Propyne}}{CH_3C \equiv CH} \xrightarrow{BH_3.THF} \underset{\text{Vinylborane}}{[CH_3CH = CH]_3B} \xrightarrow{H_2O_2/\bar{O}H} CH_3CH = CHOH \rightleftharpoons \underset{\text{Propanal}}{CH_3CH_2CHO}$$

Similar reaction with non-terminal alkynes gives ketones

$$\underset{\text{Butyne-2}}{CH_3C \equiv CCH_3} \xrightarrow{BH_3.THF} [CH_3CH{=}\underset{\displaystyle CH_3}{\underset{|}{C}}]_3B \xrightarrow[\bar{O}H]{H_2O_2} CH_3CH = \underset{\displaystyle CH_3}{\underset{|}{C}}OH \longrightarrow \underset{\text{Butanone-2}}{CH_3CH_2COCH_3}$$

To get good yield of vinylboranes and hence aldehydes, sterically hindered alkylboranes should be used instead of borane itself.

$$CH_3C \equiv CH \xrightarrow{R_2BH.THF} (CH_3CH = CH)BR_2 \xrightarrow{H_2O_2/OH^-} CH_3CH = CHOH \rightleftharpoons CH_3CH_2CHO$$

TEST YOUR UNDERSTANDING - 14.3

1. Write structures for A and B in the following reactions :

$$B \xleftarrow[0°C]{LBAH} CH_3CH(CH_3)COCl \xrightarrow{LAH} A$$

2. Prepare $CH_3CH_2CH_2CHO$ from (*a*) an ester, (*b*) a nitrile, and (*c*) an acid chloride.
3. Give an outline of the scheme for preparing 3-phenylpropanal from benzene and oxirane.
4. Use hydroboration method for preparing following aldehydes or ketones.

(*a*) Pentanal (*b*) Cyclohexanone (*c*) *n*-Butyl cyclopentyl ketone (*d*) Dicyclohexyl ketone.

5. **From organometallic compounds.**

(*a*) Aldehydes are obtained by the reaction of (*i*) Grignard reagent with hydrogen cyanide, or (*ii*) Grignard reagent with alkyl formate in equimolar amounts. For details, consult chapter on Grignard reagents.

(*i*) $HC \equiv N + \text{(cyclopropyl)MgBr} \xrightarrow{\text{ether}} \text{(cyclopropyl)}HC = NMgBr \xrightarrow{H_2O} \text{(cyclopropyl)}CHO + MgBrNH_2$

(*ii*) $$H{-}\overset{\displaystyle O}{\overset{||}{C}}{-}OC_2H_5 + CH_3MgBr \longrightarrow H{-}\overset{\displaystyle \bar{O}}{\overset{|}{\underset{\displaystyle CH_3}{\underset{|}{C}}}}{-}OC_2H_5 \xrightarrow{H_3O^+} CH_3{-}\overset{\displaystyle O}{\overset{||}{C}}{-}H + C_2H_5\bar{O}$$

(*b*) **Ketones from Grignard reagents** (Details discussed earlier).

(*i*) $$\underset{\text{A nitrile}}{R{-}C \equiv N} + R'MgX \xrightarrow{\text{ether}} R{-}\overset{\displaystyle R'}{\overset{|}{C}} = NMgX \xrightarrow{H_2O} R{-}\overset{\displaystyle R'}{\overset{|}{C}} = O$$

$$CH_3C \equiv N + C_6H_{11}MgBr \xrightarrow[(ii)\ H_2O]{(i)\ ether} C_6H_{11}\text{-}\overset{O}{\overset{\|}{C}}\text{-}CH_3$$

Cyclohexyl methyl ketone

(*ii*) $$\underset{\text{An acid chloride}}{RCOCl} + CH_3MgBr \xrightarrow[(ii)\ H_3O^+]{(i)\ ether} RCOCH_3 + MgBrCl$$

(*iii*) $$\underset{\text{An acid anhydride}}{(RCO)_2O} + CH_3MgBr \xrightarrow{-70°C} RCOCH_3 + RCOOMgBr$$

(*iv*) $$\underset{\text{Ethyl ethanoate}}{CH_3COOC_2H_5} + C_2H_5MgBr \xrightarrow[(ii)\ H_3O^+]{(i)\ ether} CH_3COC_2H_5$$

(*c*) **Ketones from organolithium compounds**

$$CH_3C \equiv N + CH_3CH_2CH_2Li \xrightarrow[(ii)\ H_3O^+]{(i)\ ether} CH_3COCH_2CH_2CH_3$$

Even though a nitrile has a triple bond, addition of the Grignard or lithium reagent takes place only once because addition of second molecule of the reagent would place a double negative charge on the nitrogen.

$$RC \equiv N \xrightarrow{R'Li} \underset{R'}{\underset{|}{R\text{—}C}} = N^-Li^+ \xrightarrow{R'Li}\!\!\!\!\not\;\; R\text{—}\overset{R'}{\overset{|}{\underset{R'}{\underset{|}{C}}}}\text{—}N^{2-}\,2Li^+$$

Alternatively, organolithium reagents react with carboxylic acids in the following way to form ketones.

$$R-\overset{O}{\overset{\|}{C}}-OH \xrightarrow{LiOH} R-\overset{O}{\overset{\|}{C}}-O^-Li^+ \xrightarrow{R'Li} R-\overset{O^-Li^+}{\overset{|}{\underset{R'}{\underset{|}{C}}}}-O^-Li^+ \xrightarrow{H_3O^+} \left[R-\overset{OH}{\overset{|}{\underset{R'}{\underset{|}{C}}}}-OH\right] \xrightarrow{-H_2O} R-\overset{O}{\overset{\|}{C}}-R'$$

Or $$RCOOH + 2R'Li \longrightarrow R-\overset{O^-Li^+}{\overset{|}{\underset{R'}{\underset{|}{C}}}}-O^-Li^+ \xrightarrow{H_3O^+} \left[R-\overset{OH}{\overset{|}{\underset{R'}{\underset{|}{C}}}}-OH\right] \xrightarrow{-H_2O} R-\overset{O}{\overset{\|}{C}}-R'$$

(*d*) **Ketones from lithium dialkylcuprates**, also known as **Gilman reagent** (*Organocopper compounds*).

$$\underset{\text{Lithium dialkylcuprate}}{R_2CuLi} + R'COCl \xrightarrow[-78°C]{ether} R'COR + RCu + LiCl$$

$$(CH_3)_2CuLi + C_6H_{11}COCl \xrightarrow[-78°C]{ether} C_6H_{11}COCH_3 + CH_3Cu + LiCl$$

Cyclohexyl methyl ketone

$$n\text{-}C_4H_9Br \xrightarrow{Li} n\text{-}C_4H_9Li \xrightarrow{CuI} \underset{\text{Lithium di-}n\text{-butylcuprate}}{(n\text{-}C_4H_9)_2CuLi} \xrightarrow{2(CH_3)_2CHCOCl} \underset{\text{2-Methyl-3-heptanone}}{2\ n\text{-}C_4H_9COCH(CH_3)_2}$$

Organocopper reagents (lithium dialkylcuprate) are less reactive than Grignard reagents and organolithium compounds toward the carbonyl group of ketones, hence the reaction stops at the ketonic stage whereas in other reagents, *tert*-alcohols are usually formed because ketones are more reactive than acid chlorides. Although organocopper compounds are more reactive than Grignard reagents toward alkyl halides, however, these do not react with many of the functional groups (*e.g.* $—NO_2$, —CN, —CO—, —COOR, etc.) with which Grignard reagents and organolithiums do react. In short, organocopper compounds are highly selective toward different functional groups.

$$CH_3OOC.CH_2CH_2COCl + [(CH_3)_2CHCH_2CH_2]_2CuLi \rightarrow CH_3OOC.CH_2CH_2COCH_2CH_2CH(CH_3)_2$$

Lithium diisopentylcuprate — Methyl-4-oxo-7-methyloctanoate

(*e*) **Ketones from organocadmium compounds**

$$RCOCl + R'—Cd—R' \longrightarrow RCOR' + R'CdCl$$

Dialkyl cadmium

Like organocopper compounds, organocadmium compounds are also less reactive than Grignard reagents and organolithiums.

TEST YOUR UNDERSTANDING - 14.4

1. Account for the difference in behaviour of RMgX and R_2CuLi.
2. (*a*) Identify the compounds A and B.

(*i*) Br—C_6H_{10}=O + $(CH_2{=}CH)_2CuLi \longrightarrow$ A (cyclohexanone with Br at position 4)

(*ii*) $O_2N—C_6H_4—COCl$ + B $\longrightarrow O_2N—C_6H_4—COCH_2CH_3$.

(*b*) Would it be feasible to prepare *p*-nitroacetophenone in the following way ?

$$(O_2N—C_6H_4)_2CuLi + CH_3COCl \longrightarrow O_2N—C_6H_4—COCH_3$$

Lithium di (-*p*-nitrophenyl) cuprate — *p*-Nitroacetophenone

6. **Ozonolysis of alkenes.** Alkenes and ozone react readily at low temperatures to yield ozonides which on decomposition with a reducing agent yield aldehydes or ketone depending upon the structure of the alkene.

$$RCH = CH_2 \xrightarrow{O_3} \text{R—CH—CH}_2 \text{ (ozonide: O bridge above, O—O below)} \xrightarrow{H_2O,\ Zn} RCHO + CH_2O$$

$$\underset{\text{1, 3-Butadiene}}{CH_2 = CH\,CH{=}CH_2} \xrightarrow[\text{(ii) } H_2O/Zn]{\text{(i) } O_3} \underset{\text{Glyoxal}}{\begin{matrix} CHO \\ | \\ CHO \end{matrix}} + 2HCHO$$

$$(CH_3)_2C = CHCH_3 \xrightarrow[\text{(ii) } H_2O/Zn]{\text{(i) } O_3} (CH_3)_2CO + CH_3CHO$$

7. **By the hydrolysis of *gem*-dihalides.**

$$CH_3CH_2CHCl_2 \xrightarrow{OH^-} CH_3CH_2CH(OH)_2 \longrightarrow CH_3CH_2CHO + H_2O$$

$$CH_3CCl_2CH_3 \xrightarrow{OH^-} CH_3C(OH)_2CH_3 \longrightarrow CH_3COCH_3 + H_2O$$

8. **By the reduction of nitriles.** This method is used only for aldehydes.

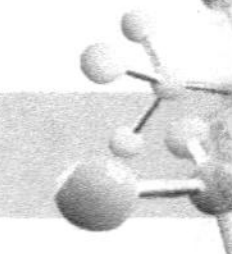

(*a*) $CH_3C \equiv N \xrightarrow[HCl]{SnCl_2} CH_3CH = NH \xrightarrow{H_2O} CH_3CHO$ (**Stephen reduction**)

(*b*) $CH_3C \equiv N \xrightarrow[(ii)\, H_3O^+]{(i)\, (iso\text{-}Bu)_2AlH_2,\ -40°C} CH_3CHO$

9. **By dry distillation of calcium salts of fatty acids.** Calcium formate, on pyrolysis, gives formaldehyde ; calcium formate mixed with calcium salt of any other fatty acid gives aldehydes; calcium salts of fatty acids other than calcium formate yield ketones.

$$\begin{matrix} H|COO \\ H|COO \end{matrix} \!\!>\! Ca + Ca \!<\!\! \begin{matrix} O|OCH \\ O|OCH \end{matrix} \longrightarrow 2HCHO + 2CaCO_3$$

Calcium formate (2 moles) Formaldehyde (2 moles)

$$\begin{matrix} CH_3COO \\ CH_3COO \end{matrix} \!\!>\! Ca + Ca \!<\!\! \begin{matrix} OOCH \\ OOCH \end{matrix} \longrightarrow \begin{matrix} CH_3CHO \\ + \\ CH_3CHO \end{matrix} + 2CaCO_3$$

Cal. acetate Cal. formate Acetaldehyde

$$\begin{matrix} CH_3COO \\ CH_3COO \end{matrix} \!\!>\! Ca + Ca \!<\!\! \begin{matrix} OOCCH_3 \\ OOCCH_3 \end{matrix} \longrightarrow \begin{matrix} CH_3.CO.CH_3 \\ + \\ CH_3.CO.CH_3 \end{matrix} + 2CaCO_3$$

Calcium acetate (2 moles) Acetone (2 moles)

When calcium salts of dicarboxylic acids are heated, cyclic ketones are formed.

$$\text{Calcium succinate } (Ca^{2+}) \xrightarrow{heat} \text{Cyclopropanone} + CaCO_3$$

Calcium succinate Cyclopropanone

$$\text{Calcium adipate } (Ca^{2+}) \xrightarrow{heat} \text{Cyclopentanone} + CaCO_3$$

Calcium adipate Cyclopentanone

Instead of using calcium salts of an acid, vapours of acid or mixture of acids can be passed over heated MnO at 300°C.

$$CH_3COOH + HCOOH \xrightarrow[300°C]{MnO} CH_3CHO + CO_2 + H_2O$$

$$2CH_3COOH \longrightarrow CH_3COCH_3 + CO_2 + H_2O$$

$$CH_3COOH + CH_3CH_2COOH \longrightarrow CH_3COCH_2CH_3 + CO_2 + H_2O$$

PREPARATION OF AROMATIC ALDEHYDES

1. **Gattermann aldehyde synthesis.**

$$C_6H_6 + HCN + HCl \xrightarrow{AlCl_3} C_6H_5CHO$$

Mechanism

$$H-C\equiv N+HCl\longrightarrow ClCH\equiv NH\xrightarrow{AlCl_3}\underset{\text{Electrophile}}{\overset{+}{C}H=NH}+AlCl_4^-$$

$$C_6H_6\xrightarrow{\overset{+}{C}H=NH}\overset{\oplus}{C_6H_6}(H)(CH=NH)\xrightarrow{-H^+}C_6H_5CH=NH\xrightarrow{H_2O}C_6H_5CHO$$

2. **Gattermann Koch aldehyde synthesis.**

$$C_6H_6+CO+HCl\xrightarrow{AlCl_3}C_6H_5CHO$$

3. **Oxidation of toluene.**

$$C_6H_5CH_3\xrightarrow{CrO_2Cl_2}C_6H_5CHO$$

$$C_6H_5CH_2CH_3\xrightarrow{CrO_2Cl_2}C_6H_5CH_2CHO$$

Etard reaction

Industrial methods.

(*a*) Formaldehyde, a starting material for a number of plastics, is prepared by oxidation of methanol over a silver or iron oxide-molybdenum oxide catalyst at elevated temperature.

$$CH_3OH+\frac{1}{2}O_2\xrightarrow[500°C]{\text{Catalyst}}HCHO+H_2O$$

(*b*) Acetaldehyde can be prepared by (*i*) hydration of acetylene, or (*ii*) more economically by aerial oxidation of ethylene in presence of palladium chloride and copper (II) chloride as catalysts (**Wacker process**).

$$CH_2=CH_2+\frac{1}{2}O_2\xrightarrow[H_2O]{PdCl_2,\,CuCl_2}CH_3CHO$$

Similarly,

$$CH_3CH=CH_2\xrightarrow[H_2O]{PdCl_2,\,CuCl_2}CH_3CH_2CHO$$

$$CH_3CH=CHCH_3\longrightarrow CH_3-\overset{O}{\overset{\|}{C}}-CH_2CH_3$$

(*c*) Aldehydes can also be prepared by **hydroformylation**, a reaction in which alkenes are converted to aldehydes containing an additional carbon atom by reaction with carbon monoxide and hydrogen in presence of a suitable cobalt– or rhodium-based catalyst.

$$RCH=CH_2+CO+H_2\xrightarrow{Co_2(CO)_8}\underset{\text{(Major)}}{RCH_2CH_2CHO}+\underset{\text{(Major)}}{R-\underset{\underset{CH_3}{|}}{CH}.CHO}$$

14.4 Physical Properties

(*i*) The carbonyl group is a polar group, therefore, the dipole-dipole attractive forces between molecules are stronger and hence aldehydes and ketones have higher boiling points than hydrocarbons (non-polar) of comparable molecular weight. However, aldehydes and ketones cannot have strong hydrogen bonds between their molecules, hence they have lower boiling points than the corresponding alcohols.

(*ii*) The carbonyl oxygen atom of aldehydes and ketones form hydrogen bonds to water molecules, hence lower aldehydes and ketones show appreciable solubility in water.

(*iii*) Formaldehyde is a gas (b.p. – 21°C), and is handled either as an aqueous solution (**formalin**), or as one of its solid polymers : **paraformaldehyde**, $(CH_2O)_n$, or **trioxane**, $(CH_2O)_3$. When dry formaldehyde is desired (as in reaction with a Grignard reagent), it is obtained by heating paraformaldehyde or trioxane. Similarly, acetaldehyde is usually generated by heating its higher-boiling trimer with acid.

$—CH_2OCH_2OCH_2O—$
Paraformaldehyde

Trioxane (cyclic: H_2C, O, CH_2, O, CH_2, O)

Paraldehyde (cyclic: CH_3CH, O, $CHCH_3$, O, CH(CH_3), O) $\underset{}{\overset{H^+}{\rightleftharpoons}}$ $3CH_3CHO$

TEST YOUR UNDERSTANDING - 14.5

1. Identify A to C in the following reactions :

(*a*) $[B] \xleftarrow{CO,\ H_2} CH_3CH = CH_2 \xrightarrow[CuCl_2,\ H_2O]{O_2,\ PdCl_2} A$ (*b*) $(CH_3)_2C = C(CH_3)_2 \xrightarrow{CO,\ H_2} C$

2. Which of the components of each of the following pair has higher boiling point ?

(*a*) Hexane or hexanal (*b*) Hexanal or 1-hexanol (*c*) 2-Pentanol or 2-pentanone

(*d*) Benzaldehyde or benzyl alcohol (*e*) 2-Phenylethanol or acetophenone.

3. *n*-Butanol boils at 118°C and *n*-butanal boils at 76°C, although their molecular weights are nearly similar. Explain.

14.5 Chemical Properties

The carbonyl group, C = O governs the chemistry of aldehydes and ketones in two ways : (*a*) by providing a site for nucleophilic addition, and (*b*) by increasing the acidity of the hydrogen atoms attached to the alpha carbon. Both of these effects is due to the ability of oxygen to accommodate a negative charge.

(A) Carbonyl group as a site for nucleophilic addition

The mobile π electrons of the carbon-oxygen double bond are pulled strongly towards oxygen, which makes carbonyl oxygen electron-rich and carbonyl carbon electron-deficient. Further, since carbonyl group is flat, it is relatively open to attack from above or below. The positive charge on the carbonyl carbon atom means that it is especially susceptible to attack by a nucleophile. On the other hand, the negative charge on the carbonyl oxygen atom means that nucleophilic addition is susceptible to acid catalysis.

$R'R\overset{\delta+}{C}=\overset{\delta-}{\ddot{O}}:$

Thus nucleophilic addition to the carbon-oxygen double bond occurs in either of two general ways.

1. When the reagent is a *strong nucleophile*, addition usually takes place in the following way, in which trigonal planar aldehyde or ketone is converted into a tetrahedral product.

$$\underset{\text{Reactant (Trigonal)}}{R'R\text{C=O} + :Z} \longrightarrow \underset{\text{Transition state* (Becoming tetrahedral)}}{\left[R'R\text{C}(\cdots Z)\cdots O^{\delta-}\right]} \longrightarrow \underset{\text{Product (Tetrahedral)}}{R'R\text{C}(Z)O^-} \xrightarrow[\text{or nucleophile}]{H_2O} R'R\text{C}(Z)OH$$

Note that as the nucleophile is forming a bond through its electron pair with the carbonyl carbon atom, the electron pair of the carbon-oxygen π bond shifts out to the carbonyl oxygen (as indicated by full negative charge on oxygen) and thus oxygen gets a negative charge which it can accommodate easily. Thus **the ability of oxygen to carry a negative charge is the real cause of reactivity of carbonyl group toward nucleophiles.** (The polarity of the carbonyl group is not the cause of the reactivity, it is simply another manifestation of the electronegativity of oxygen).

2. When the reaction is acid-catalysed, nucleophilic addition on carbonyl group takes place in the following way.

$$R'R\text{C=O} \underset{}{\overset{H^+}{\rightleftharpoons}} \underset{\text{An oxonium cation}}{R'R\text{C=}\overset{+}{O}H} \xrightarrow{:Z} \left[R'R\text{C}(\cdots Z)\cdots \overset{\delta+}{OH}\right] \longrightarrow R'R\text{C}(Z)OH$$

(*i*) The oxonium cation is highly reactive toward nucleophilic attack at the carbonyl carbon atom because the carbonyl carbon atom carries more positive charge than it does in the unprotonated compound.

(*ii*) Prior protonation of the carbonyl group lowers the E_{act} for nucleophilic attack, because it permits oxygen to acquire the π electrons without having a negative charge.

(*iii*) This mechanism operates when carbonyl compounds are treated with *strong acids* (sometimes Lewis acids) in presence *weak nucleophiles.*

Relative reactivity of aldehydes and ketones toward nucleophilic addition. The reactivity of the carbonyl group toward the nucleophilic addition reactions depends upon the magnitude of the positive charge on the carbonyl carbon atom (**electronic factor**) and also on the crowding around the carbonyl carbon atom in the transition state (**steric factor**). Both these factors predict the following order

$$H-\overset{O}{\overset{\|}{C}}-H \quad > \quad R-\overset{O}{\overset{\|}{C}}-H \quad > \quad R-\overset{O}{\overset{\|}{C}}-R$$

(*i*) Formaldehyde has no alkyl group, whereas other aldehydes and ketones contain one and two alkyl groups respectively. Since an alkyl group is larger than the hydrogen atom, greater the number of alkyl or aryl group more will be crowding in the transition state which has four groups on C (sp^3) and lesser will be its stability.

(*ii*) Aldehydes have only one electron-releasing group to partially neutralize, and thereby stabilize, the positive charge at their carbonyl carbon atom. Ketones have two electron-releasing groups and are thus stabilized more. Greater stabilization of the ketone (the reactant) relative to the product means lesser reactivity.

$$H-\overset{O^{\delta-}}{\overset{\|}{C^{\delta+}}}-H \qquad R\rightarrow\overset{O^{\delta-}}{\overset{\|}{C^{\delta+}}}-H \qquad R\rightarrow\overset{O^{\delta-}}{\overset{\|}{C^{\delta+}}}\leftarrow R$$

Carbonyl carbon atom becomes lesser positive, successively increasing stability of the compound

In short, any substituent in the carbonyl compound that decreases the positive charge on the carbonyl carbon will increase the stability (or decrease the reactivity) of the molecule toward nucleophilic addition and *vice versa*. Thus, the decreasing order of reactivity of certain carbonyl compounds is

(*a*) $NO_2CH_2CHO > ClCH_2CHO > CH_3CHO > CH_3CH_2CHO$

(*b*) $CH_3COCH_3 > CH_3-\overset{O}{\overset{\|}{C}}-C_2H_5 > CH_3-\overset{O}{\overset{\|}{C}}-CH(CH_3)_2 > CH_3-\overset{O}{\overset{\|}{C}}-C(CH_3)_3$

* Note that this transition state is relatively roomy as compared to the transition state for an S_N2 reaction in which carbon is pentavalent.

(*iii*) An alkyl group releases electrons, and thus destabilizes the transition state by intensifying the negative charge developing on oxygen.

(*iv*) An aryl group has an electron-withdrawing inductive effect, and thus it is expected to destabilize the reactant or stabilize the transition state and thus should speed up the reaction. However, it seems to stabilize the reactant even more, by resonance and thus causes net deactivation.

$$R—C=\ddot{O}: \longleftrightarrow R—C—\ddot{O}:^- \longleftrightarrow R—C—\ddot{O}:^- \longleftrightarrow R—C—\ddot{O}:^- \equiv R—C—\ddot{O}:^-$$

Addition of water, alcohols, hydrogen cyanide, sodium bisulphite, ammonia derivatives, hydride ion (in the form of $LiAlH_4$ and $NaBH_4$), organometallic compounds, etc. are examples of nucleophilic addition on carbonyl group.

1. **Addition of water (*gem*-diol formation)**. Aldehydes and ketones react with water in presence of acid or base in a rapidly reversible equilibrium.

$$R—\overset{O}{\overset{\|}{C}}—R' + H_2O \xrightleftharpoons{\text{fast}} R—\underset{OH}{\overset{OH}{C}}—R'$$

Like the general nucleophilic additions, hydrate formation follows the following order :

	HCHO	>	CH_3CHO	>	$(CH_3)_3CCHO$	>	CH_3COCH_3
% of hydrate formed	99.96		50		19		0.14

TEST YOUR UNDERSTANDING - 14.6

1. Arrange the following compounds in decreasing order of reactivity toward nucleophilic addition.
   (*a*) RCHO, CH_2O, R_2CO and RCOY : (*b*) R_2CO, Ar_2CO, ArCOR and $ArCH_2COR$.
2. In contrast to negligible hydration of acetone, hexafluoroacetone is completely hydrated. Explain.
3. Account for the isolation of $CH_3CO^{18}CH_3$ from a solution of $CH_3CO^{16}CH_3$ in excess of H_2O^{18}.
4. Ninhydrin has three ketonic groups, which one of them is likely to be hydrated easily ?

   (structure: ninhydrin with carbonyls labelled *a*, *b*, *c*)

5. Arrange the following in decreasing ease of hydration to form *gem*-diol.

   (*a*) MeO–C₆H₄–CO–C₆H₄–NO₂ (A); C₆H₅–CO–C₆H₅ (B); O₂N–C₆H₄–CO–C₆H₄–NO₂ (C); MeO–C₆H₄–CO–C₆H₄–OMe (D)

   (*b*) CH_3CH_2CHO (A); $CH_3CHFCHO$ (B); $CH_3CHClCHO$ (C); CH_2ClCH_2CHO (D)

2. **Addition of alcohols** (*Acetal formation*). Anhydrous alcohols add to the carbonyl group of aldehydes in the presence of anhydrous hydrogen chloride to form **acetals** via **hemiacetals**.

$$\underset{H}{\overset{R}{}}\!>C=O + R'OH \xrightleftharpoons{\text{dry HCl}} \underset{H}{\overset{R}{}}\!>C<\underset{OR'}{\overset{OH}{}} \xrightleftharpoons{R'OH,\ H^+} \underset{H}{\overset{R}{}}\!>C<\underset{OR'}{\overset{OR'}{}}$$

Hemiacetal (an alcohol, as well as an ether) — Acetal (an ether) (stable to alkalies)

(i) With a few exceptions, open-chain hemiacetals are too unstable to be isolated. However, cyclic hemiacetals with five- or six-membered rings are usually much more stable.

(ii) All steps in the formation of an acetal from an aldehyde are reversible.

(iii) Acetal formation is not favoured when ketones are treated with simple alcohols and gaseous HCl (remember that the usage of hemiketals and ketals have been replaced by hemiacetals and acetals respectively). However, cyclic acetal formation is favoured when a ketone is treated with an excess of a 1, 2-diol and a trace of acid.

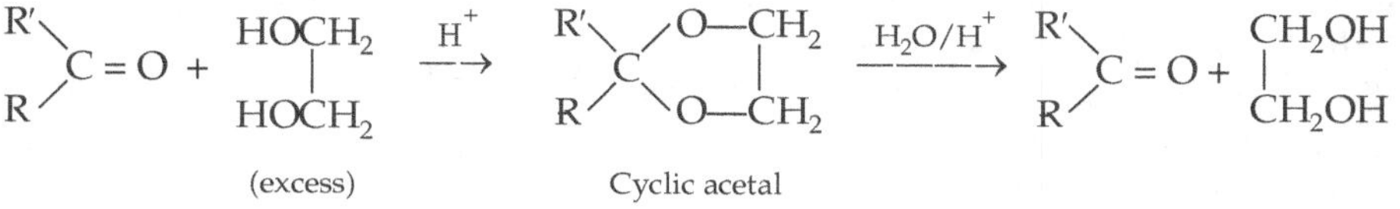

$$\begin{matrix} R' \\ R \end{matrix}\!\!>C=O + \begin{matrix} HOCH_2 \\ | \\ HOCH_2 \end{matrix} \xrightarrow{H^+} \begin{matrix} R' \\ R \end{matrix}\!\!>C\begin{matrix} O-CH_2 \\ | \\ O-CH_2 \end{matrix} \xrightarrow{H_2O/H^+} \begin{matrix} R' \\ R \end{matrix}\!\!>C=O + \begin{matrix} CH_2OH \\ | \\ CH_2OH \end{matrix}$$

(excess) Cyclic acetal

(iv) Like ethers, acetals are cleaved by acids and are stable toward bases. However, acetals differ from ethers, in the extreme ease with which they undergo acidic cleavage, actually acetals are rapidly converted into aldehydes and alcohols by dilute mineral acids even at room temperature. Thus acetal formation may be used to protect the aldehydic and ketonic group against undesired reactions in basic solutions.

Thus we can reduce only ester group in the following group by protecting ketonic group.

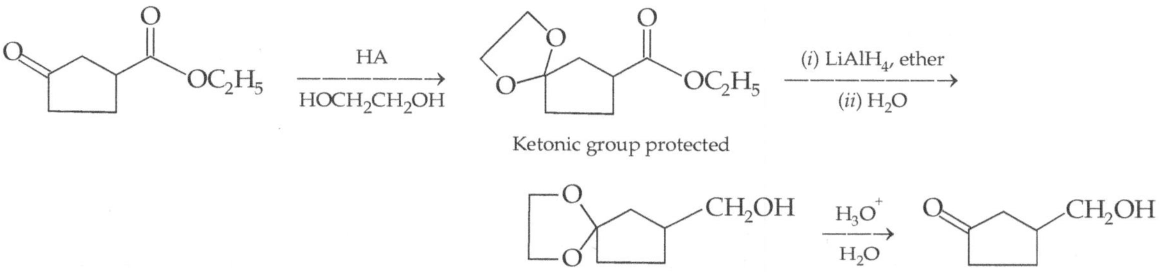

3-oxocyclopentyl–$COOC_2H_5$ $\xrightarrow[HOCH_2CH_2OH]{HA}$ (ethylene ketal of 3-oxocyclopentyl)–$COOC_2H_5$ $\xrightarrow[(ii)\ H_2O]{(i)\ LiAlH_4,\ ether}$ (ethylene ketal)–CH_2OH $\xrightarrow[H_2O]{H_3O^+}$ 3-oxocyclopentyl–CH_2OH

Ketonic group protected

Several other examples have been discussed in ethylene glycol in the chapter on "Polyhydric Alcohols".

TEST YOUR UNDERSTANDING - 14.7

1. 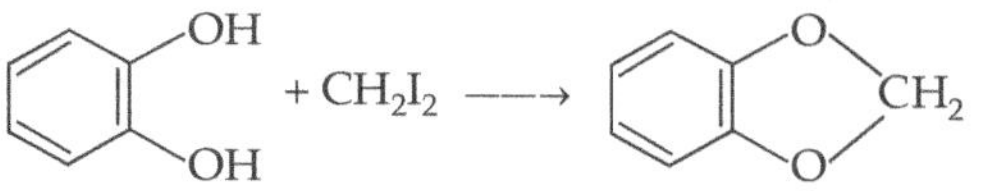 Catechol (1,2-dihydroxybenzene) $+ CH_2I_2 \longrightarrow$ 1,3-benzodioxole (benzene ring fused with $-O-CH_2-O-$)

Answer the following with reference to above reaction.

(a) The above reaction is an example of which familiar synthesis ?

(b) To what family of compounds does the product belong ?

(c) Give the reaction of the product with acid, and base.

2. Account for the fact that anhydrous acids bring about formation of acetals while aqueous acids bring about hydrolysis of acetals.

3. Give the structure of the acetal formed in each of the following reactions.

(a) 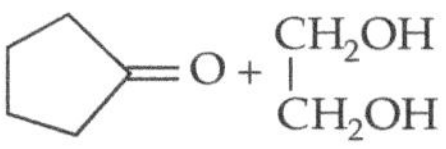 Cyclopentanone $+ \begin{matrix} CH_2OH \\ | \\ CH_2OH \end{matrix}$ (b) Butanal + 1, 3-propanediol (c) $BrCH_2CH_2COCH_3 + CH_2OH.CH_2OH$.

4. Give steps involved in the conversion of each of the following.

(a) $CH_2{=}CHCHO \longrightarrow CH_2(OH)CH(OH)CHO$ (b) 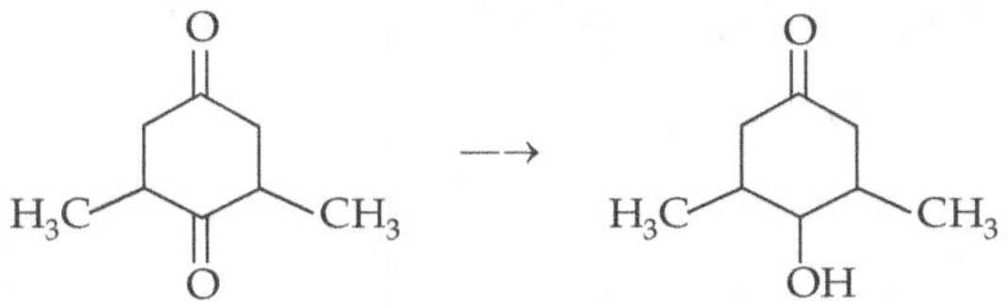 2,6-dimethylcyclohexane-1,4-dione (H_3C, CH_3) $\longrightarrow$ 4-hydroxy-3,5-dimethylcyclohexanone (H_3C, CH_3, OH)

(c) $HOCH_2CH_2CH_2CH_2CHO \longrightarrow$ 2-methoxytetrahydropyran (six-membered ring with O, OCH_3)

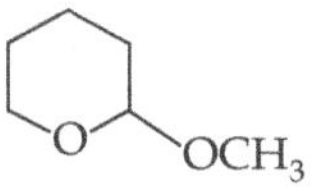

3. **Addition of hydrogen cyanide.** Hydrogen cyanide adds to the carbonyl groups of aldehydes and *most ketones* to form **cyanohydrins.** Ketones in which carbonyl group is highly hindered do not undergo this reaction.

$$>C=O + HCN \longrightarrow >C(OH)(CN)$$

(*i*) Addition of hydrogen cyanide itself takes place very slowly because HCN is a poor source of the nucleophile, CN^-. However, addition of potassium cyanide, or any base that can generate cyanide ions from the weak acid HCN, causes a dramatic increase in the rate of reaction. The cyanide ion, being a stronger nucleophile, is able to attack the carbonyl carbon atom much more rapidly than HCN itself, and this is the source of its catalytic effect. Bases stronger than cyanide ion catalyze reaction by converting HCN (pK_a = 9) to cyanide ion.

(*ii*) Liquid hydrogen cyanide can be used for this reaction (HCN is a gas at room temperature), but since HCN is a very toxic and volatile, it is generally produced in the reaction mixture for which an acid (generally H_2SO_4) is added to a solution of the aldehyde or ketone and aqueous sodium or potassium cyanide.

$$2,4\text{-}Cl_2C_6H_3\text{-}CHO \xrightarrow[\text{then HCl}]{\text{NaCN, ether, water,}} 2,4\text{-}Cl_2C_6H_3\text{-}CH(OH)C\equiv N$$

2, 4-Dichlorobenzaldehyde → 2, 4-Dichlorobenzaldehyde cyanohydrin

$$CH_3-\overset{O}{\overset{\|}{C}}-CH_3 \xrightarrow[\text{then } H_2SO_4]{NaCN,\ H_2O,} CH_3-C(OH)(CN)-CH_3$$

Acetone → Acetone cyanohydrin

Cyanohydrins are useful intermediates in organic synthesis. A cyano group may be hydrolysed to an α-hydroxy carboxylic acid or to an α, β-unsaturated acid (depending upon the condition used) or may be reduced to a primary amine.

$$CH_3CH_2-C(CH_3)=O \xrightarrow{CN^-,\ H^+} CH_3CH_2-C(CH_3)(OH)-CN \xrightarrow[\text{heat}]{HCl,\ H_2O} CH_3CH_2-C(CH_3)(OH)-COOH$$

2-Butanone → 2-Hydroxy-2-methylbutanoic acid

$$CH_3CH_2-C(CH_3)(OH)-CN \xrightarrow{\text{Conc. } H_2SO_4,\ \text{heat}} [CH_3CH_2-C(CH_3)(OH)-COOH] \longrightarrow CH_3CH=C(CH_3)-COOH$$

2-Methyl-2-butenoic acid

$$\text{Cyclohexanone} \xrightarrow{HCN} C_6H_{10}(OH)(CN) \xrightarrow[(ii)\ H_2O]{(i)\ LiAlH_4} C_6H_{10}(OH)(CH_2NH_2)$$

A β-amino alcohol

TEST YOUR UNDERSTANDING - 14.8

1. Arrange the following compounds in decreasing ease of formation of cyanohydrin.

I: $C_6H_5COCH_3$ II: $C_6H_5CH_2CHO$ III: $p\text{-}NO_2C_6H_4COCH_3$ IV: $p\text{-}CH_3OC_6H_4COCH_3$

2. Can you draw a scheme for converting acetone to methacrylonitrile, $CH_2=C(CH_3)CN$, an industrial chemical used in the production of plastics and fibres ?

3. Following compounds are converted into their corresponding cyanohydrins. Predict the number of fraction and their optical activity status in each case.

(a) CH_3CHO (b) $(CH_3)_2CO$ (c) R –(+)– $CH_2OHCHOHCHO$ (d) (±)– $CH_2OHCHOHCHO$.

4. (a) In cyanohydrin formation, an optimum pH of 9—10 is recommended. Explain.

(b) Which is the more favourable equilibrium situation for cyanohydrin formation ?

$$RCHO + NaCN \quad \text{or} \quad RCHO + HCN \text{ (both in water).}$$

4. **Addition of sodium bisulphite.** Aldehydes, methyl ketones and cyclic ketones (not aromatic) react with sodium bisulphite in presence of ethanol to give solid adduct.

$$\underset{H}{\overset{R}{>}}C=O + Na^+ HSO_3^- \longrightarrow \underset{H}{\overset{R}{>}}\overset{+}{C}—OH + :SO_3^{2-} + Na^+ \longrightarrow \underset{H}{\overset{R}{>}}C<\underset{OH}{\overset{SO_3^-Na^+}{}}$$

Sodium bisulphite (adduct) (solid)

NOTE.

(i) A C—S bond is formed rather than C—O because S has more nucleophilic site than O.

(ii) Sulphite ion, SO_3^{2-} is a large ion and hence reacts only if C = O is not sterically hindered ; as in the case for RCHO, $RCOCH_3$, and cyclic ketones.

The solid adduct is filtered from the ethanolic solution and then decomposed by acid or base to regenerate the carbonyl compound. Hence *this reaction is used for the purification and separation of carbonyl compounds.*

$$\underset{H}{\overset{R}{>}}C<\underset{OH}{\overset{SO_3^-Na^+}{}} \xrightarrow{H^+ \text{ (or } OH^-)} \underset{H}{\overset{R}{>}}C=O + SO_2 \text{ (or } SO_3^{2-})$$

(Extracted with ether)

Separation of RCHO from unreacted RCH_2OH.

$$RCH_2OH \longrightarrow RCHO \xrightarrow[C_2H_5OH]{NaHSO_3} RCH(OH)SO_3Na\downarrow \xrightarrow{H^+} RCHO$$

Separated from unreacted RCH_2OH

5. **Addition of derivatives of ammonia.** Certain compounds related to ammonia (such as hydroxylamine, NH_2OH; phenylhydrazine, $H_2NNHC_6H_5$; and semicarbazide $H_2NNHCONH_2$, etc.) react with carbonyl compounds to form compounds, having carbon-nitrogen double bond, known as **imines**. The reaction is acid catalyzed and involves two stages : addition of the ammonia derivative to form *carbinolamine* followed by dehydration to yield imine which is a mixture of *E*- and *Z*-isomers

$$>C=O + H_2NG \xrightarrow[\text{(addition)}]{H^+} >\underset{OH}{\underset{|}{C}}—NHG \xrightarrow[\text{(elimination)}]{-H_2O} >C=NG$$

Imine

Like ammonia, these derivatives of ammonia are basic and hence form salts with acids, viz. hydroxylamine hydrochloride $N^+H_3OHCl^-$, phenylhydrazine hydrochloride, $C_6H_5NHNH_3^+Cl^-$; and semicarbazide hydrochloride, $NH_2CONHNH_3^+Cl^-$. These salts are less easily oxidized by air than the free bases, and hence these ammonia derivatives are best used in the form of their salts. When used, the parent reagents are liberated from their salts in the presence of the carbonyl compound by adding a base, generally sodium acetate.

$$\underset{\text{Stronger acid}}{GNH_3^+Cl^-} + \underset{\text{Stronger base}}{CH_3COONa} \rightleftharpoons \underset{\text{Weaker base}}{GNH_2} + \underset{\text{Weaker acid}}{CH_3COOH} + NaCl$$

Imine formation requires a moderate pH (between 4–5), because very low as well as very high pH retards the reaction. To know why it is so, we must know the steps involved during the reaction

$$>C=O \overset{H^+}{\rightleftharpoons} >C=\overset{+}{O}H \xrightarrow{:NH_2G \text{ (free base)}} >C<\underset{\overset{+}{N}H_2G}{\overset{OH}{}} \longrightarrow >C<\underset{NG—H}{\overset{\overset{+}{O}H_2}{}} \longrightarrow >C=NG + H_3O^+$$

From the above steps, it is obvious that an acid is essential to protonate the carbonyl oxygen which makes carbonyl carbon more susceptible to nucleophilic attack. Hence *protonation of the carbonyl group is favoured by high acidity*. However, in presence of strong acid, the ammonia derivative ($H_2\ddot{N}$—G) can also undergo protonation to form the ion, H_3N^+—G lacking the unshared electrons which thus will no longer be nucleophilic. Hence *the addition of reagent* (H_2NG) *will be favoured by low acidity*. Thus optimum acidity is the compromise between the two steps to carry out the reaction successfully, *i.e.* the solution must be acidic enough for an appreciable fraction of the carbonyl compound to be protonated, but not so acidic that the concentration of the free nitrogen compound is too low. The exact conditions used depend upon the basicity of the reagent, and upon the reactivity of the carbonyl compound.

Reaction of aldehydes and ketones with derivatives of ammonia, (H_2NG)

$$>C=O + H_2N\text{—}G \longrightarrow >C=NG$$

Reagent H_2NG and its name	Name of product with specific example
H_2NR, 1° Amine	$(C_2H_5)(CH_3)C=O \xrightarrow{H_2NC_2H_5} (C_2H_5)(CH_3)C=NC_2H_5$ An **Imine** (A Schiff 's base)
H_2NOH, Hydroxylamine	$(CH_3)(H)C=O \xrightarrow{H_2NOH} (CH_3)(H)C=NOH$ Acetaldoxime **oxime**
H_2NNH_2, Hydrazine	$(CH_3)(CH_3)C=O \xrightarrow{H_2NNH_2} (CH_3)(CH_3)C=NNH_2$ Acetone **hydrazone**
$H_2NNHC_6H_5$, Phenylhydrazine	$(C_6H_5)(CH_3)C=O \xrightarrow[H_3\overset{+}{O},\ CH_3COOH]{H_2NNHC_6H_5} (C_6H_5)(CH_3)C=NNHC_6H_5$ Acetophenone **phenylhydrazone**
$H_2NHN\text{—}C_6H_3(NO_2)\text{—}NO_2$,	$(CH_3)(H)C=O \xrightarrow[\text{phenylhydrazine}]{\text{2, 4-Dinitro-}} (CH_3)(H)C=NNH\text{—}C_6H_3(NO_2)\text{—}NO_2$ Acetaldehyde **2, 4-dinitrophenylhydrazone**
$H_2NNHCONH_2$, Semicarbazide	$C_6H_{10}=O \xrightarrow{H_2NNHCONH_2} C_6H_{10}=NNHCONH_2$ Cyclohexanone **semicarbazone**

The products of the reaction of aldehydes and ketone with hydroxylamine, phenylhydrazine, 2, 4-dinitrophenylhydrazine and semicarbazide are usually insoluble solids with sharp characteristic melting points. Moreover, oximes and hydrazones when refluxed with dil HCl, they regenerate the parent aldehyde or ketone. Hence, formation of oximes and hydrazones is used for the detection and purification of aldehydes and ketones

$$>C=O + H_2NOH \longrightarrow >C=NOH \xrightarrow[\text{reflux}]{\text{HCl}} >C=O + NH_2OH.HCl$$

$$>C=O + H_2NNHPh \longrightarrow >C=NNHPh \xrightarrow[\text{reflux}]{\text{HCl}} >C=O + H_2NNHPhHCl$$

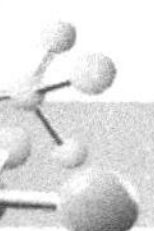

Unlike, 2, 4-dinitrophenylhydrazones, simple hydrazones have low melting points and are hence occasionally used to identify carbonyl compounds. However, they form the basis for a useful method to reduce carbonyl group to methylene group (**Wolf-Kishner reduction**).

$$>C=O + H_2NNH_2 \xrightarrow[\text{heat}]{\text{base}} \left[>C=NNH_2\right] \longrightarrow >CH_2 + N_2$$

Hydrazone

Ammonia reacts with formaldehyde, other aldehydes and ketones in different ways.

$$6HCHO + 4NH_3 \longrightarrow (CH_2)_6N_4 + 6H_2O$$

Hexamethylene tetramine (Urotropine)

$$CH_3(H)C=O + NH_3 \longrightarrow CH_3C(H)(OH)NH_2$$

Acetaldehyde ammonia

$$(CH_3)_2C=O + HNH_2 + HCH_2COCH_3 \longrightarrow (CH_3)_2C(NH_2)CH_2COCH_3$$

Diacetoneamine

Secondary amines, R_2NH add to aldehydes and ketones to form carbinolamines which are dehydrated easily to form **enamines**

$$>C=O + R_2NH \longrightarrow >C(OH)NR_2 \longrightarrow >C=NR_2$$

Enamine

Cyclopentanone + Pyrrolidine ⟶ N-(1-Cyclopentenyl)-pyrrolidine + H_2O

6. **Addition of organometallic compounds.** Organometallic compounds, such as Grignard reagents, alkyllithiums and organozinc compounds provide nucleophile which add on carbonyl group to form alcohols.

$$>C=O \xrightarrow{\overset{\delta-}{R}:\overset{\delta+}{M}} -\overset{R}{\overset{|}{C}}-\ddot{\underset{..}{O}}:^- M^+ \xrightarrow{H_3O^+} -\overset{R}{\overset{|}{C}}-O-H$$

Such reactions with Grignard reagents and alkyllithiums have already been discussed at length, so here we will confine only to addition of organozinc compounds.

In short, it can be summarised that *Grignard reagents* (M = MgX) *or alkyllithium* (M = Li) *react with formaldehyde, other aldehydes and ketones to form 1°, 2° and 3° alcohols respectively.*

Addition of organozinc compounds (The Reformatsky reaction). Reformatsky reaction involves the reaction of an aldehyde or ketone with an α-bromoester in presence of zinc metal to form β-hydroxy ester.

$$>C=O + BrCH_2COOR \xrightarrow[\text{benzene}]{Zn} -\overset{OZnBr}{\overset{|}{C}}-CH_2COOR \xrightarrow{H_3O^+} -\overset{OH}{\overset{|}{\underset{\beta}{C}}}-\underset{\alpha}{CH_2}COOR$$

α-Bromoester β-Hydroxy ester

Actually an organozinc compound is first formed as an intermediate which then adds to the carbonyl group in a manner analogous to that of a Grignard reagent.

$$BrCH_2COOC_2H_5 + Zn \xrightarrow{\text{benzene}} \overset{\delta+\ \delta-}{BrZn\ CH_2COOC_2H_5}$$

Organozinc compound

Since organozinc reagent is less reactive than a Grignard reagent, it does not add to the ester group.

$$CH_3CH_2CH_2CHO + BrCH_2COOC_2H_5 \xrightarrow[\text{(ii) } H_3O^+]{\text{(i) Zn}} \underset{\beta\text{-Hydroxy ester}}{CH_3CH_2CH_2\overset{OH}{\overset{|}{C}}HCH_2COOC_2H_5}$$

The β-hydroxy esters produced in the reaction are easily dehydrated to α, β-unsaturated esters because the resulting product contains a more stable conjugated system.

$$CH_3CH_2CH_2\overset{OH}{\overset{|}{C}}HCH_2COOC_2H_5 \xrightarrow[\text{heat}]{H_3O^+} CH_3CH_2CH_2CH = CH—\overset{O}{\overset{||}{C}}—OC_2H_5 + H_2O$$

TEST YOUR UNDERSTANDING - 14.9

1. What are Schiff bases. Give the structure of the product of the following reactions :
   (*a*) Cyclohexanone + *tert*-Butyl amine
   (*b*) $CH_3COCH_3 + H_2NCONHNH_2$
   (*c*) 2-Butanone + $[H_3N^+OH]Cl^-$, CH_3COONa
   (*d*) Acetophenone + Cyclohexyl amine
   (*e*) $CH_3COCH_2C_6H_5$ and HN (piperidine ring)
   (*f*) $CH_3CH_2COCH_2CH_3$ + HN (pyrrolidine ring)
   (*g*) Cyclohexanone + Morpholine (O-containing ring with N–H)
   (*h*) o-Phenylenediamine ($C_6H_4(NH_2)_2$) + $\overset{CHO}{\underset{CHO}{|}}$
2. Explain the following :
   (*i*) Reaction of hydroxylamine with acetone gives a single oxime, while similar reaction with an aldehyde or a methyl ethyl ketone forms two isomeric oximes.
   (*ii*) Oximes are more acidic than hydroxylamine.
   (*iii*) Although semicarbazide has two NH_2 groups, only one of them reacts with an aldehyde or ketone.
3. (*a*) How would you prepare following compounds using Reformatsky reaction ?
   (*i*) $(CH_3)_2\overset{OH}{\overset{|}{C}}CH_2COOCH_2CH_3$
   (*ii*) 1-Hydroxycyclohexyl with $\underset{CH_3}{\underset{|}{C}}HCOOCH_2CH_3$ (OH and CHCOOCH₂CH₃ on the same ring carbon)
   (*b*) Why is Mg or Cd not used in place of Zn in the Reformatsky reaction ?

7. **Cannizzaro reaction.** *Aldehydes containing no α-hydrogen atom, when treated with concentrated alkali, (aqueous or alcoholic), undergo self oxidation-reduction* (also known as disproportionation) *to yield a mixture of an alcohol and a salt of a carboxylic acid.* This reaction, known as **Cannizzaro reaction,** is carried out at room temperature ; remember that under these conditions, aldehydes having α-hydrogen atom undergo aldol condensation.

$$2HCHO \xrightarrow{50\%\ NaOH} \underset{\text{Methanol}}{CH_3OH} + \underset{\text{Sodium formate}}{HCOONa}$$

$$2(CH_3)_3CCHO \xrightarrow{50\%\ NaOH} (CH_3)_3CCH_2OH + (CH_3)_3CCOONa$$

In general, a mixture of two aldehydes (each having no α-hydrogen atom) undergo Cannizzaro reaction to form a mixture of all possible products. However, if one of the aldehydes is formaldehyde, reaction always yields sodium formate as one of the products and the alcohol (second product) corresponding to the other aldehyde. Cannizzaro reaction between different aldehyde molecules is known as **crossed Cannizzaro reaction.**

$$\underset{\text{Benzaldehyde}}{C_6H_5CHO} + \underset{\text{Formaldehyde}}{HCHO} \xrightarrow{\text{conc. NaOH}} \underset{\text{Benzyl alcohol}}{C_6H_5CH_2OH} + \underset{\text{Sod. formate}}{HCOONa}$$

Mechanism.

The reaction involves two successive nucleophilic addition, of course at different carbonyl groups.

Step 1. $Ar—\overset{H}{\overset{|}{C}}=O + OH^- \rightleftharpoons Ar—\underset{\underset{I}{OH}}{\overset{H}{C}}—O^-$

Step 2. $Ar—\overset{H}{C}=O + Ar—\underset{OH}{\overset{H}{C}}—O^- \longrightarrow Ar—\underset{H}{\overset{H}{C}}—O^- + Ar—\underset{OH}{C}=O$

(Second molecule) I

$\xrightarrow{H^+} ArCH_2OH \qquad \xrightarrow{-H^+} ArCOO^-$

Intramolecular or Internal Cannizzaro reaction

$\underset{CHO}{\overset{CHO}{|}} \xrightarrow{\text{conc. NaOH}} \underset{COONa}{\overset{CH_2OH}{|}}$; $C_6H_5—\overset{O}{\overset{||}{C}}—CHO \xrightarrow{\text{conc. NaOH}} C_6H_5—\overset{OH}{\overset{|}{C}}H—COONa$

Remember that keto group can only be reduced, not oxidised, in internal Cannizzaro reaction.

Although aldehydes having α-hydrogen atom do not undego Cannizzaro reaction, they along with all their aldehydes can be made to undergo such reactions in presence of aluminium ethoxide. The reaction is now known as **Tischenko reaction** and here esters are isolated instead of alcohol and carboxylic acids.

$$2RCHO \xrightarrow{Al(OC_2H_5)_3} [RCH_2OH + RCOOH] \longrightarrow \underset{\text{Ester}}{RCOOCH_2R}$$

8. **Addition of ylides (The Wittig reaction).** An ylide is a neutral molecule having a negative carbon adjacent to a positive hetero atom (*e.g.* P or S), each atom has an octet of electrons and directly bonded to each other. Aldehydes and ketones react with phosphorus ylides to yield *alkenes* and triphenylphosphine oxide. The reaction, known as Wittig reaction, has proved to be a valuable method for synthesizing alkenes.

$$>C=O + (C_6H_5)_3P=C\langle^R_{R'} \text{ or } \underset{\text{Phosphorus ylide}}{(C_6H_6)_3\overset{+}{P}—\overset{-}{C}\langle^R_{R'}} \longrightarrow \underset{\text{Alkene}}{>C=C\langle^R_{R'}} + \underset{\text{Triphenylphosphine oxide}}{O=P(C_6H_5)_3}$$

Thus the net result of the reaction is the replacement of carbonyl oxygen, = O, by the group = CRR′. The reaction is carried out under mild conditions and in presence of solvents like tetrahydrofuran (THF) and dimethyl sulfoxide (DMSO).

$$C_6H_{10}=O + (C_6H_5)_3\overset{+}{P}—\overset{-}{C}H_2 \xrightarrow{DMSO} C_6H_{10}=CH_2 + (C_6H_5)_3P^+—O^-$$

Wittig reaction has a great advantage over most other alkene syntheses in that *no ambiguity exists as to the location of the double bond in the product.*

Mechanism. The ylide acting as a nucleophile attacks the carbonyl carbon of the aldehyde or ketone to form an unstable intermediate *betaine* followed by *oxaphosphetane* which then spontaneously loses triphenylphosphine oxide to form an alkene. The driving force for the Wittig reaction is the formation of the very strong P—O bond (DH° = 540 kJ mol^{-1}).

$$>C=\ddot{O}: + :\overset{R\ R'}{C}—\overset{+}{P}(C_6H_5)_3 \longrightarrow \underset{\text{Betaine}}{\left[—\underset{:\ddot{O}:^-}{C}—\underset{^+P(C_6H_5)_3}{\overset{R}{C}}—R'\right]} \longrightarrow \underset{\text{Oxaphosphetane}}{—\underset{:O}{C}—\overset{R}{C}—R' \atop \quad —P(C_6H_5)_3} \longrightarrow \underset{\text{Alkene}}{>C=C\langle^R_{R'}} + \underset{\text{Triphenylphosphine oxide}}{:\ddot{O}=P(C_6H_5)_3}$$

TEST YOUR UNDERSTANDING - 14.10

1. Give the structure of the product(s) obtained in each of the following reactions.

   (a) Furan-2-CHO $\xrightarrow{\text{conc. NaOH}}$ (b) $C_6H_5COCHCl_2 \xrightarrow{\text{conc. NaOH}}$ (c) $ArCDO \xrightarrow{\text{conc. NaOH}}$

   (d) $D_2C{=}O \xrightarrow{OH^-}$ (e) $D_2C{=}O \xrightarrow{OH^-}$

2. In the crossed Cannizzaro reaction, formaldehyde is always oxidised. Explain.
3. Which of the following intermediate (I or II) is considered as a better hydride donor to an aldehyde ?

   I: $R{-}CH(OH){-}O^-$ II: $R{-}CH(O^-){-}O^-$

4. Identify the alkene produced in each of the following Wittig reactions :

   (a) Benzaldehyde + $Ph_3P^+{-}\overset{\ominus}{C}$(cyclopentylidene) (b) Butanal + $Ph_3P^+\ \ddot{C}^-HCH=CH_2$

   (c) Cyclohexyl methyl ketone + $Ph_3P^+ = \ddot{C}^-H_2$

5. Give the structure of an ylide and a carbonyl compound from which each of the following could be prepared.

   (a) $CH_3CH_2CH_2CH = C(CH_3)CH_2CH_3$ (b) $C_6H_5CH = CHC_6H_5$ (c) Cyclopentylidene$=CHCH_3$

(B) Acidity of α-hydrogens of carbonyl compounds

In addition to nucleophilic addition reactions, carbonyl compounds exhibit the unusual acidity of α-hydrogen atoms. Actually, in the first type of properties carbonyl group acts as a functional group, while in the second type carbonyl group acts as a substituent and exerts its effect on the adjacent (alpha) carbon atoms.

$$R{-}\overset{O}{\overset{\|}{C}}{-}\underset{H}{\underset{|}{C}}{-}\underset{H}{\underset{|}{C}}{-}$$

α-Hydrogen, acidic ($pK_a = 19 - 20$)   β-Hydrogen, not acidic ($pK_a = 40 - 50$)

The unusual acidity of the α-hydrogens of carbonyl compounds is due to its strong electron-withdrawing nature which in turn makes α-carbon also electron-withdrawing. Hence in presence of base, it easily loses hydrogen as proton and itself converted into carbanion. Once the anion (carbanion) is formed, it is stabilized by resonance.

$$B:^- + H{-}C{-}C{=}O \underset{}{\overset{-BH}{\rightleftharpoons}} \ddot{C}^-{-}C{=}\ddot{O}: \longleftrightarrow C{=}C{-}\ddot{O}:^- \equiv \overset{\delta-}{C}{=\!=}C{=\!=}\overset{\delta-}{O}$$

Carbanion   Enolate anion (larger contribution)

Resonance stabilized anion

Thus the carbonyl group affects the acidity of α-hydrogens in just the same way it affects the acidity of carboxylic acids, *i.e.* by helping to accommodate the negative charge of the anion.

$$-C(=O)-O-H \rightleftharpoons \left[-C(=O)-O^- \longleftrightarrow -C(-O^-)=O \right] + H^+ \quad \text{or} \quad -C\{O,O\}^- + H^+$$

Resonance stabilized carboxylate anion
(Equivalent contributing structures)

$$-C(=O)-C-H \rightleftharpoons \left[-C(=O)-C^- \longleftrightarrow -C(-O^-)=C \right] + H^+ \quad \text{or} \quad -C\{O,C\}^- + H^+$$

Resonance stabilized enolate anion
(Non-equivalent contributing structures)

Although α-hydrogen atoms of an aldehyde or ketone are very weakly acidic than the hydrogen atom of a —COOH group, they are considerably more acidic than hydrogen atoms anywhere else in the molecule and they are acidic enough for producing carbanions in significant concentration. It is interesting to note that the two important properties of a carbonyl group : (*a*) susceptibility to nucleophilic attack, and (*b*) acidity of α-hydrogens, is due to the *ability of oxygen to accommodate the negative charge.*

TEST YOUR UNDERSTANDING - 14.11

1. Account for the following facts.
   (*a*) (+)—$C_6H_5CH(CH_3)CHO$ undergoes reacemization, when treated with base.
   (*b*) The diketone 2, 4-pentanedione is almost as acidic as phenol, and much more acidic than acetone.
   (*c*) γ-Hydrogens of α, β-unsaturated carbonyl compounds are acidic.
2. Write down the structure of the product in the following reactions.

   (*a*) Cyclopentanone $=O + 4\,D_2O \xrightarrow{KOD}$

   (*b*) $CH_3-C(CH_3)=CH-C(=O)-CH_3 + NaCN\,(\text{aqueous}) \longrightarrow$

Reactions of carbonyl compounds due to acidic hydrogen atom, i.e. *due to enols and enolate anions.*

9. **Aldol condensation.** Two molecules of an aldehyde or a ketone, containing at least one α-hydrogen atom, when treated *with dilute base* (like NaOH, $Ba(OH)_2$, K_2CO_3, etc.) at room temperature (or below) combine to form a β-hydroxyaldehydes or β-hydroxyketones. This reaction is called **aldol condensation**. In every case, it is the α-carbon and α-hydrogen atoms of one molecule that add to the carbonyl carbon and oxygen atoms respectively of the second molecule.

(*i*) $CH_3-CH=O + CH_3.CHO \xrightarrow{OH^-} CH_3-CH(OH)-CH_2CHO$

3-Hydroxybutanal

(*ii*) $CH_3CH_2-CH=O + H_3C^{\beta}-CH_2^{\alpha}-CHO \xrightarrow{OH^-} CH_3CH_2-CH(OH)-CH(CH_3)-CHO$

Propionaldehyde (2 moles) 3-Hydroxy-2-methylpentanal

(*iii*) $CH_3-C(CH_3)=O + CH_3.CO.CH_3 \xrightarrow{OH^-} CH_3-C(CH_3)(OH)-CH_2-C(=O)-CH_3$

4-Hydroxy-4-methyl-2-pentanone

Mechanism.

Step 1. $CH_3CHO + OH^- \rightleftharpoons [CH_2CHO]^- + H_2O$ (Carbanion, I)

Step 2. $CH_3-\underset{}{\overset{H}{\overset{|}{C}}}=O + [CH_2CHO]^-$ (I (Nucleophile)) $\rightleftharpoons CH_3-\overset{H}{\overset{|}{\underset{O^-}{\underset{|}{C}}}}-CH_2CHO$ (Alkoxide ion, II)

Step 3. $CH_3-\overset{H}{\overset{|}{\underset{O^-}{\underset{|}{C}}}}-CH_2CHO + H_2O \rightleftharpoons CH_3-\overset{H}{\overset{|}{\underset{OH}{\underset{|}{C}}}}-CH_2CHO + OH^-$

Remember that presence of α-hydrogen in aldehyde or ketone is the essential condition for aldol condensation, since only such carbonyl compounds can form carbanions, the actual nucleophile, which then attacks the carbonyl carbon to form the product. Hence, aldehydes or ketones, not having α-hydrogen atom, do not undergo aldol condensation.

$$ArCHO,\ HCHO,\ (CH_3)_3CCHO,\ ArCOAr,\ \text{or}\ ArCOCR_3 \xrightarrow[OH^-]{\text{dilute}} \text{No reaction}$$

However, in presence of concentrated base, above compounds undergo Cannizzaro reaction.

Dehydration of aldol products. The β-hydroxy aldehydes and β-hydroxy ketones obtained from aldol condensation are very easily dehydrated, on heating, to form α, β-unsaturated carbonyl compound (conjugated system).

$$\underset{\text{Aldol}}{CH_3-\overset{H}{\overset{|}{\underset{OH}{\underset{|}{C}}}}-\underset{H}{\underset{|}{CH}}-\overset{H}{\overset{|}{C}}=O} \xrightarrow[\text{heat}]{H^+ \text{ or } OH^-} \underset{\text{2-Butenal}}{CH_3-\overset{H}{\overset{|}{C}}=CH-\overset{H}{\overset{|}{C}}=O} + H_2O$$

Dehydration under acidic conditions follows a mechanism similar to those of other acid-catalyzed alcohol dehydration. The steps involved in *base-catalyzed dehydration* of aldol are summarised below.

$$CH_3-\underset{OH}{\underset{|}{CH}}-\underset{H}{\underset{|}{CH}}-\overset{O}{\overset{||}{CH}} \underset{}{\overset{\bar{O}H,\ (-H_2O)}{\rightleftharpoons}} \underset{\text{Enolate ion}}{CH_3-\underset{OH}{\underset{|}{CH}}-\ddot{C}H-\overset{O}{\overset{||}{CH}}} \rightleftharpoons \underset{\text{Conjugated system}}{CH_3-CH=CH-\overset{O}{\overset{||}{CH}}} + OH^-$$

Note that in the second step, **hydroxide ion which is not a good leaving group in an E2 elimination is removed** However, here OH^- can serve as a leaving group in a strongly exothermic step leading to a highly stable (conjugated) compound.

In some cases, especially when the double bond produced is conjugated with an aromatic ring, dehydration of the aldol product occurs so readily that we cannot isolate the product in the aldol form.

$$C_6H_5-\overset{O}{\overset{||}{C}}-CH_3 + CH_3-\overset{O}{\overset{||}{C}}-C_6H_5 \xrightarrow{C_2H_5ONa} \left[C_6H_5-\overset{CH_3}{\overset{|}{\underset{OH}{\underset{|}{C}}}}-\underset{H}{\underset{|}{CH}}-\overset{O}{\overset{||}{C}}-C_6H_5\right]$$

Acetophenone (Hypnone)

$$\xrightarrow{-H_2O} C_6H_5-\overset{CH_3}{\overset{|}{C}}=CH-\overset{O}{\overset{||}{C}}-C_6H_5$$

1, 3-Diphenyl-2-buten-1-one (Dypnone)
(a fully conjugated system)

Synthetic applications. (*i*) Aldol reaction is a general reaction given by aldehydes and ketones having an α-hydrogen atom.

(*ii*) Further, aldol reaction gives us a product by introducing a new carbon-carbon bond between two molecules.

(*iii*) Aldol products contain two functional groups, —OH and —CHO, each of which can be used to carry out a number of subsequent reactions.

$$2RCH_2CHO \xrightarrow{OH^-} RCH_2CH(OH)-CH(R)CHO \xrightarrow{NaBH_4} RCH_2CH(OH)CH(R)CH_2OH$$

Aldehyde; An aldol; A 1, 3-diol

$$RCH_2CH(OH)CH(R)CHO \xrightarrow{H^+, (-H_2O)} RCH_2CH=C(R)CHO$$

$$RCH_2CH_2CH(R)CH_2OH \xleftarrow[\text{high P}]{H_2/Ni} RCH_2CH=C(R)CHO \xrightarrow{LiAlH_4} RCH_2CH=C(R)CH_2OH$$

A saturated alcohol; An α, β-unsaturated aldehyde; An allylic alcohol

$$RCH_2CH=C(R)CHO \xrightarrow{H_2,\ Pd-C} RCH_2CH_2CH(R)CHO$$

A saturated aldehyde

Acid-catalyzed aldol condensations. Aldol condensation can also be brought about with acid catalysts. The enol serves as a weak nucleophile to attack an activated (protonated) carbonyl group. Steps involved in the acid-catalyzed aldol condensation of acetaldehyde are given below.

$$CH_3-\overset{+OH}{\overset{\|}{C}H} + CH_2=\overset{:\ddot{O}H}{\overset{|}{C}H} \rightleftharpoons \left[CH_3\overset{OH}{\overset{|}{C}H}-CH_2\overset{OH}{\overset{|}{\overset{+}{C}H}} \longleftrightarrow CH_3\overset{OH}{\overset{|}{C}H}-CH_2-\overset{+O-H}{\overset{\|}{C}H}\right]$$

protonated acetaldehyde; enol form of acetaldeyde

$$\underset{RO^+H_2}{\overset{ROH}{\rightleftharpoons}} CH_3\overset{OH}{\overset{|}{C}H}-CH_2\overset{O}{\overset{\|}{C}H} \overset{H^+}{\rightleftharpoons} CH_3CH=CH\overset{O}{\overset{\|}{C}H} + H_2O$$

Aldol

Similarly acetone, when treated with hydrogen chloride gives 4-methyl-3-penten-2-one. Here, the aldol formed undergoes dehydration to form 4-methyl-3-penten-2-one.

$$2CH_3-\overset{O}{\overset{\|}{C}}CH_3 \xrightarrow{HCl} CH_3\overset{OH}{\underset{CH_3}{C}}CH_2\overset{O}{\overset{\|}{C}}CH_3 \xrightarrow[(-H_2O)]{} CH_3\underset{CH_3}{C}=CH\overset{O}{\overset{\|}{C}}CH_3$$

Acetone (2 mole); Diacetone alcohol; 4–Methyl–3–penten–2–one (Mesityl oxide)

Mesityl oxide may further undergo crossed aldol condensation to form phorone as final product.

$$CH_3\underset{CH_3}{C}=CH\overset{O}{\overset{\|}{C}}CH_3 + \underset{\text{(3rd mole)}}{CH_3\overset{O}{\overset{\|}{C}}CH_3} \xrightarrow[\text{Crossed aldol condensation}]{} \left[CH_3\overset{OH}{\underset{CH_3}{C}}CH_2\overset{O}{\overset{\|}{C}}CH=\overset{CH_3}{\overset{|}{C}}CH_3\right] \xrightarrow{-H_2O} CH_3\underset{CH_3}{C}=CH\overset{O}{\overset{\|}{C}}CH=\overset{CH_3}{\overset{|}{C}}CH_3$$

2, 6-Dimethyl-2, 5-heptadien-4-one (Phorone)

Crossed aldol condensation. An aldol condensation between two different carbonyl compounds each having at least one α-hydrogen atom (**crossed aldol condensation**) gives a mixture of the four possible products, hence it is not always feasible in the laboratory. For example, reaction of acetaldehyde and propanal in presence of dilute NaOH gives a mixture of four products.

$$CH_3CHO + CH_3CH_2CHO \xrightarrow{OH^-} CH_3CH(OH)CH_2CHO + CH_3CH_2CH(OH)CH(CH_3)CHO$$

Ethanal, Propanal; 3-Hydroxybutanal (from 2 molecules of ethanal); 3-Hydroxy-2-methylpentanal (from 2 molecules of propanal)

$\downarrow OH^-$

$$CH_3CH(OH)CH(CH_3)CHO + CH_3CH_2CH(OH)CH_2CHO$$

3-Hydroxy-2-methylbutanal, 3-Hydroxypentanal
(from 1 molecule of ethanal and 1 molecule of propanal)

(Ethanal as a carbonyl group and propanal as a nucleophile) (Propanal as a carbonyl group and ethanal as a nucleophile)

Intramolecular aldol condensation (*Cyclization via aldol condensation*). A dialdehyde, a keto aldehyde, or a diketone undergoes aldol condensation to form five and six-membered (sometimes even longer) cyclic compounds, *e.g.*

OHC–(CH$_2$)$_4$–CO–CH$_3$ $\xrightarrow{OH^-}$ [cyclopentenyl–CO–CH$_3$]

1-Cyclopentenyl methyl ketone

In the above keto aldehyde, three different enolates are possible, however it is the enolate from the ketone side of the molecule that adds to the aldehyde group leading to the product. The reason being greater reactivity of aldehydes toward nucleophilic addition than the ketones due to electronic as well as steric factors.

TEST YOUR UNDERSTANDING - 14.12

1. Write structural formulas for the products obtained by the aldol condensation of following compounds:

(*a*) cyclohexanone (=O) (*b*) C_6H_5–$COCH_3$ (*c*) C_6H_5–CHO + CH$_3$CH=CHCHO

(*d*) cyclodecane-1,6-dione (*e*) C_6H_5CHO + cyclopropyl–$\overset{O}{\overset{||}{C}}$–$CH_3$

Other reactions related to aldol condensation

There are large number of condensations that are closely related to the aldol condensation, each of these reactions has its own name, viz. Claisen-Schmidt, Knovenagel, Perkin (given only by aromatic aldehydes), etc. At first glance each may seem to quite different from the others, closer examination shows that each of these involves attack by a carbanion on a carbonyl group. In each case carbanion is generated like that in aldol condenstion, *i.e.*, hydrogen α-to the carbonyl group is abstracted by base.

(*a*) **Claisen-Schmidt reaction.** A crossed aldol condensation in which an aromatic aldehyde reacts with an enolizable aldehyde, ketone or ester, eg $CH_3COOC_2H_5$ to form α, β-unsaturated carbonyl compound is known as **Claisen-Schmidt reaction**.

$$C_6H_5CHO + RCH_2COR' \xrightarrow{OH^-} C_6H_5CH = \overset{R}{\overset{|}{C}}\overset{O}{\overset{||}{C}}R' + H_2O$$

(R′ = H or alkyl) α, β-Unsaturated carbonyl compound

$$C_6H_5CHO + (CH_3)_3C\overset{O}{\overset{||}{C}}CH_3 \xrightarrow{OH^-} C_6H_5CH = CH\overset{O}{\overset{||}{C}}C(CH_3)_3$$

4, 4-Dimethyl-1-phenyl-1-penten-3-one

(*b*) **Knoevenagel reaction.** Condensation between an aldehyde or ketone with compound containing active methylene group* in the presence of ammonia, amines, pyridine, piperidine etc. to form α, β-unsaturated compound is known as **Knoevenagel reaction.**

(*i*) $CH_3CHO + H_2C(COOH)_2 \longrightarrow CH_3CH = C(COOH)_2 \xrightarrow[-CO_2]{heat} CH_3CH = CHCOOH$

Malonic acid — Crotonic acid

(*ii*) $C_6H_5CHO + H_2C(COOH)_2 \xrightarrow[(ii)\ -CO_2]{(i)\ heat} C_6H_5CH = CHCOOH$

Cinnamic acid

Note that in Knoevenagel reaction, enol (or enolate ion) is provided by molonic acid and not by aldehyde.

TEST YOUR UNDERSTANDING - 14.13

1. Give the structure of the mixed aldol condensation product of the following.

(*a*) $C_6H_5CHO + C_6H_5COCH_3$ (*b*) C_6H_5–CHO + O=(cyclohexanone) (*c*) (substituted cyclohexenyl)–CHO + acetone

2. Give the final product in each case.

(*a*) $CH_3CHO + CH_3NO_2 \xrightarrow{KOH}$ (*b*) $C_6H_5CHO + C_6H_5CH_2CN \xrightarrow{C_2H_5ONa}$

(*c*) $C_6H_5CHO + CH_3COCH_2COOC_2H_5 \xrightarrow{NH_3}$

10. **α-Halogenation of aldehydes and ketones.** Aldehydes and ketones having α-hydrogen atom react with halogens to form α-haloaldehyde or ketone.

$$-\overset{H}{\underset{|}{\overset{|}{C}}}-\overset{O}{\overset{\|}{C}}- + X_2 \xrightarrow[base]{acid\ or} -\overset{X}{\underset{|}{\overset{|}{C}}}-\overset{O}{\overset{\|}{C}}- + HX$$

The reaction is *regiospecific* for substitution of an α-hydrogen.

Cyclohexanone $+ Cl_2 \xrightarrow{H_2O}$ 2-Chlorocyclohexanone $+ HCl$

Cyclohexanecarbaldehyde $+ Br_2 \xrightarrow{CHCl_3}$ 1-Bromocyclohexanecarbaldehyde $+ HBr$

$C_6H_5COCH_3 + Cl_2 \longrightarrow C_6H_5COCH_2Cl$

Acetophenone — Phenacyl chloride

Phenacyl chloride is a relatively harmless but powerful **lachrymator** or *tear gas* and is used by police to disperse mobs.

---

* A methylene group flanked on both sides by negative groups is known as active methylene group, *e.g.*,

$CH_2(COOH)_2$ Malonic acid; $CH_2(COCH_3)(COOC_2H_5)$ Ethyl acetoacetate; $CH_2(CN)(COOC_2H_5)$ Ethyl cyanoacetate

(i) α-Halogenation of aldehydes and ketones can be carried out in a variety of solvents like water, chloroform, acetic acid and diethyl ether.

(ii) The reaction is quite different from the free-radical halogenation of alkanes and involves the formation of resonance stabilized enols.

(iii) Unlike ketones, aldehydes are easily oxidized, and since halogens are strong oxidizing agents, halogenation of aldehydes usually results in oxidation to carboxylic acids.

$$RCH(=O) + X_2 + H_2O \longrightarrow R-C(=O)-OH + 2HX$$

(iv) Since one of the reaction products is hydrogen halide, the process when catalyzed by acids is said to be **auto-catalytic**. However, halogenation promoted by base is more important and discussed here.

Mechanism. The rate of reaction depends upon the concentration of acetone and of base, but is independent of bromine concentration.

Step 1. $$CH_3-C(=O)-CH_3 + :B^- \xrightleftharpoons{\text{slow}} \left[CH_3-C(=O)-\bar{C}H_2 \longleftrightarrow CH_3-C(-O^-)=CH_2\right] + H:B$$

Step 2. $$CH_3-C(=O)-\ddot{C}H_2 + Br-Br \xrightarrow{\text{fast}} CH_3-C(=O)-CH_2Br + Br^-$$

Since base is not regenerated during the reaction, halogen of ketones in presence of base is called **base-promoted**, rather than *base-catalyzed reaction*. As we will discuss below in haloform reaction, multiple halogenation of aldehydes and ketones having more than one α – H occurs.

Mechanism of acid catalyzed α-halogenation of ketones. The ketone is dissolved in acetic acid, which serves as both the solvent and the acid catalyst. In contrast with basic halogenation, acidic halogenation can selectively replace just one hydrogen or more than one if appropriate amounts of the halogen are used.

In the first step, the carbonyl oxygen is protonated to form enol which reacts with the halogen (electrophile).

$$CH_3-C(=O)-CH_3 \xrightarrow{H^+} CH_3-C(=\overset{+}{O}H)-CH_3 \xrightarrow[\text{(say } H_2O)]{\text{Base}} \underset{\text{enol}}{CH_3-C(OH)=CH_2}$$

$$\xrightarrow[(-Br^-)]{Br-Br} \left[CH_3-\overset{+}{C}(\ddot{O}H)-CH_2Br \longleftrightarrow CH_3-C(=\overset{+}{O}-H)-CH_2Br\right] \xrightarrow{Br^-} CH_3-C(=O)-CH_2Br + HBr$$

11. **Haloform reaction.** When methyl ketones (or acetaldehyde) react with halogen in the presence of base, multiple halogenation of the α-methyl group takes place because introduction of the first halogen (due to its electronegativity) makes the remaining α hydrogens on the methyl carbon more acidic. Actually, introduction of the first halogen is slowest, while that of last (*i.e.* third) is fastest.

$$CH_3-C(=O)-CH_2X \xrightarrow{X_2,\ OH^-} CH_3-C(=O)-CHX_2 \xrightarrow{X_2,\ OH^-} CH_3-C(=O)-CX_3$$

In short,

$$CH_3-C(=O)-CH_3 + 3X_2 + 3OH^- \xrightarrow{\text{base}} CH_3-C(=O)-CX_3 + 3X^- + 3H_2O$$

When methyl ketones react with halogens in aqueous sodium hydroxide (*i.e.* hypohalite solutions), an additional reaction takes place. Hydroxide ion attacks the carbonyl carbon atom of the trihaloketone (*nucleophilic addition*) and causes a cleavage of the carbon-carbon bond between the carbonyl group and the trihalomethyl group ($:CX_3^-$), the latter, being a *good leaving group**, departs easily forming a carboxylic acid and the trihalomethyl anion.

$$CH_3-\overset{\overset{\ddot{O}:}{||}}{C}-CX_3 \xrightarrow{OH^-} CH_3-\underset{OH}{\overset{:\ddot{O}:^-}{|}}{C}-CX_3 \longrightarrow CH_3-\underset{OH}{\overset{O}{||}}{C} + \overset{\ominus}{:}CX_3$$

$$\downarrow OH^- \qquad \downarrow H_2O$$

$$\underset{\text{Carboxylate anion}}{CH_3-\overset{O}{\overset{||}{C}}-O^-} \qquad \underset{\text{Trihalomethane}}{HCX_3}$$

Since haloform ($CHCl_3$, $CHBr_3$ or CHI_3) is produced in the reaction, it is known as **haloform reaction** (*reaction of methyl ketones with alkaline halogen to form haloform, CHX_3*).

Importance of haloform reaction.

1. Haloform reaction is used as a means of preparing carboxylic acids from methyl ketones. For this, chlorine and bromine are most commonly used as the halogen component because resulting haloform (chloroform and bromoform) are water immiscible liquids and hence are easily separated from the aqueous solution containing the carboxylate anion.

$$\underset{\text{3, 3-Dimethyl-2-butanone}}{(CH_3)_3C-\overset{O}{\overset{||}{C}}-CH_3} + Br_2 + OH^- \longrightarrow \underset{\text{2, 2-Dimethylpropanoic acid}}{(CH_3)_3C-COOH} + CHBr_3$$

2. Haloform reaction, particularly iodoform reaction is used as a laboratory test for identifying methyl ketones, acetaldehyde and methyl secondary alcohols which are first oxidized to methyl ketones under the reaction conditions.

$$\underset{\text{Methyl sec. alcohol}}{-\underset{OH}{\overset{H}{|}}{C}-CH_3} \xrightarrow{I_2} \underset{\text{Methyl ketone or acetaldehyde}}{-\underset{O}{\underset{||}{C}}-CH_3} \xrightarrow{3I_2 + 3OH^-} \underset{\text{Triiodoketone}}{-\underset{O}{\underset{||}{C}}-CI_3} + 3I^- + 3H_2O$$

$$-\underset{O}{\underset{||}{C}}-CI_3 + OH^- \longrightarrow -\underset{O}{\underset{||}{C}}-O^- + \underset{\text{Yellow precipitate}}{CHI_3\downarrow}$$

TEST YOUR UNDERSTANDING - 14.14

1. Give the product of the reaction of 1 equivalent of Br_2 in H_3O^+ with
   (*a*) propanal (*b*) acetophenone (*c*) cyclopentanone.
2. Arrange the following in decreasing ease of bromination.
   CH_3COCH_3, CH_3COCH_2Br, CH_3COCH_2Cl, $CH_3COCHBr_2$.
3. Explain the following.
   (*a*) Ketone I undergoes racemization in basic solution, but ketone II does not.

$$\underset{\text{I}}{C_6H_5-\underset{O}{\underset{||}{C}}-\underset{CH_3}{\underset{|}{CH}}-C_6H_5} \qquad \underset{\text{II}}{C_6H_5-\underset{O}{\underset{||}{C}}-\underset{C_2H_5}{\overset{CH_3}{\underset{|}{\overset{|}{C}}}}-C_6H_5}$$

   (*b*) ArCHO, HCHO and RCH_2CHO ($R \neq H$) do not undergo haloform reaction.

(C) Other reactions of aldehydes and ketones.

12. **Oxidation.** Aldehydes are much more easily oxidized, than ketones, to carboxylic acids. Aldehydes are oxidized not only by the same reagents that oxidize primary and secondary alcohols, viz. permanganate and dichromate, but also by the very mild oxidizing agent as silver ion. Oxidation by silver ion requires an alkaline medium under which conditions it forms insoluble silver oxide, hence to dissolve this oxide a complexing agent ammonia is added, which brings silver ion as diamminosilver (I) ion, $Ag(NH_3)_2^+$. This alkaline solution of silver nitrate in presence of ammonia is commonly known as **Tollen's reagent**.

$$R-\overset{O}{\overset{\|}{C}}-H \xrightarrow[\text{or } K_2Cr_2O_7 + H_2SO_4]{KMnO_4,\ OH^-} R-\overset{O}{\overset{\|}{C}}-O^- \xrightarrow{H_3O^+} R-\overset{O}{\overset{\|}{C}}-OH$$

$$R-\overset{O}{\overset{\|}{C}}-H \xrightarrow{Ag_2O,\ OH^-} R-\overset{O}{\overset{\|}{C}}-O^- \xrightarrow{H_3O^+} R-\overset{O}{\overset{\|}{C}}-OH$$

Note that in the above reactions, aldehydes lose the hydrogen that is attached to the carbonyl carbon atom, and since ketones do not have such hydrogen, they are resistant to oxidation.

Oxidation by Tollen's reagent is accompanied by colour change (due to reduction of Ag^+ ion to metallic silver), hence the reagent is commonly used for detecting the presence of an aldehyde in laboratory.

$$\underset{\textbf{Colourless solution}}{RCHO + Ag(NH_3)_2^+} \longrightarrow RCOO^- + \underset{\textbf{Silver mirror}}{Ag}$$

Since Tollen's reagent is a mild oxidising agent, it does not attack carbon-carbon double bond, hence it is used for the synthesis of unsaturated acids from unsaturated aldehydes which are easily obtained from aldol condensation.

$$\underset{\text{Acetaldehyde}}{CH_3CHO} \xrightarrow{OH^-} \underset{\text{Aldol}}{CH_3CHOHCH_2CHO} \xrightarrow{\text{heat}} \underset{\text{Crotonaldehyde}}{CH_3CH=CHCHO} \xrightarrow{Ag(NH_3)_2^+} \underset{\text{Crotonic acid}}{CH_3CH=CHCOOH}$$

Aldehydes (except benzaldehyde) also reduce Fehling's solution (an alkaline solution of cupric ion complexed with tartarate ion) and Benedict's solution, in which complexing agent is citrate ion.

$$R-\overset{O}{\overset{\|}{C}}-H + \underset{\textbf{(deep blue colour)}}{2Cu^{2+}} + 3OH^- \longrightarrow R-\overset{O}{\overset{\|}{C}}-O^- + \underset{\textbf{(red ppt.)}}{2Cu^+\downarrow} + H_2O$$

Oxidation of ketones requires breaking of carbon-carbon bonds, and hence (**except for haloform reaction**) takes place only under vigorous conditions. It is the double bond of the enol form that is cleaved during oxidation of ketones, thus where structure permits oxidation may occur on either end of the carbonyl group to form a mixture of carboxylic acids.

$$\underset{\text{Enol}}{-\overset{H}{\underset{H}{C}}-\overset{OH}{C}=C-} \rightleftharpoons \underset{\text{Keto}}{-\underset{H}{C}-\overset{O}{\overset{\|}{C}}-\underset{H}{C}-} \rightleftharpoons \underset{\text{Enol}}{-C=\overset{OH}{C}-\overset{H}{\underset{H}{C}}-}$$

$$RCOOH + R'CH_2COOH \xleftarrow[(b\text{ route})]{\text{oxidation}} RCH_2 \overset{b}{\vdots} \overset{O}{\overset{\|}{C}} \overset{a}{\vdots} CH_2R' \xrightarrow[(a\text{ route})]{\text{oxidaton}} RCH_2COOH + R'COOH$$

Methyl ketones are oxidized smoothly by means of hypohalite (NaOH or KOH + halogen) to form carboxylate ion and haloform, and hence the reaction is commonly known as **haloform reaction**. (Details discussed earlier).

$$R-\overset{O}{\overset{\|}{C}}-CH_3 + 3X_2 + 4OH^- \longrightarrow R-\overset{O}{\overset{\|}{C}}-O^- + CHX_3 + 3X^- + 3H_2O$$

$$C_6H_5-\overset{H}{\overset{|}{C}}=\overset{CH_3}{\overset{|}{C}}-\overset{O}{\overset{\|}{C}}-CH_3 \xrightarrow{\text{Oxidation}} C_6H_5-\overset{H}{\overset{|}{C}}=\overset{CH_3}{\overset{|}{C}}-COO^- + CHX_3$$

Aldehydes and ketones having a methyl or methylene group adjacent to the carbonyl group are oxidised by selenium dioxide.

$$\underset{\text{Ethanal}}{CH_3CHO} \xrightarrow{SeO_2} \underset{\text{Glyoxal}}{CHO.CHO}\ ;\ \underset{\text{Propanone}}{CH_3COCH_3} \xrightarrow{SeO_2} \underset{\text{Methylglyoxal}}{CH_3COCHO}$$

Baeyer-Villiger oxidation. Both aldehydes and ketones are oxidised by peroxy acids. This reaction, called Baeyer-Villiger oxidation, is however especially useful with ketones, because it converts them to carboxylic esters.

$$\underset{\text{Ketone}}{R-\overset{O}{\overset{\|}{C}}-R'} + \underset{\text{Peroxy acid}}{R''-\overset{O}{\overset{\|}{C}}-O-OH} \longrightarrow \underset{\text{Ester}}{R-O-\overset{O}{\overset{\|}{C}}-R'} + \underset{\text{Carboxylic acid}}{R''-\overset{O}{\overset{\|}{C}}-OH}$$

Note that an oxygen from the peroxy acid is inserted between the carbonyl carbon and carbon atom of one the alkyl groups of the ketone. In case of mixed ketones, oxygen insertion occurs between the carbonyl carbon and the larger of the two alkyl groups of the ketone

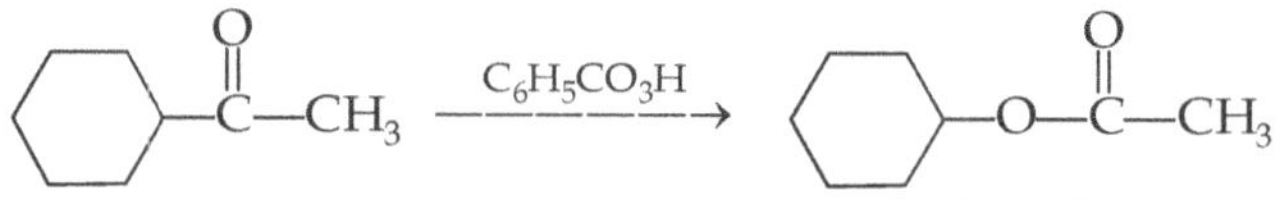

$$C_6H_{11}-\overset{O}{\overset{\|}{C}}-CH_3 \xrightarrow{C_6H_5CO_3H} \underset{\text{Cyclohexyl acetate}}{C_6H_{11}-O-\overset{O}{\overset{\|}{C}}-CH_3}$$

$$\text{Cyclopentanone} \xrightarrow{C_6H_5CO_3H} \text{δ-Valerolactone (cyclic ester)}$$

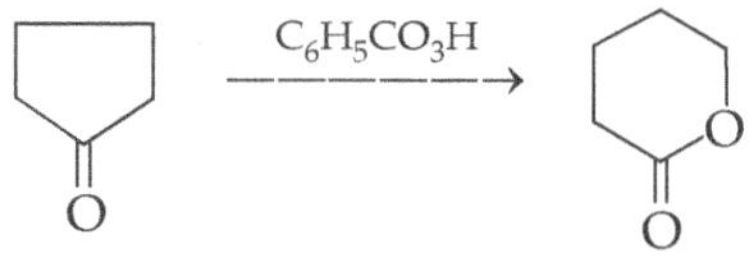

Mechanism, taking the example of cyclopentanone.

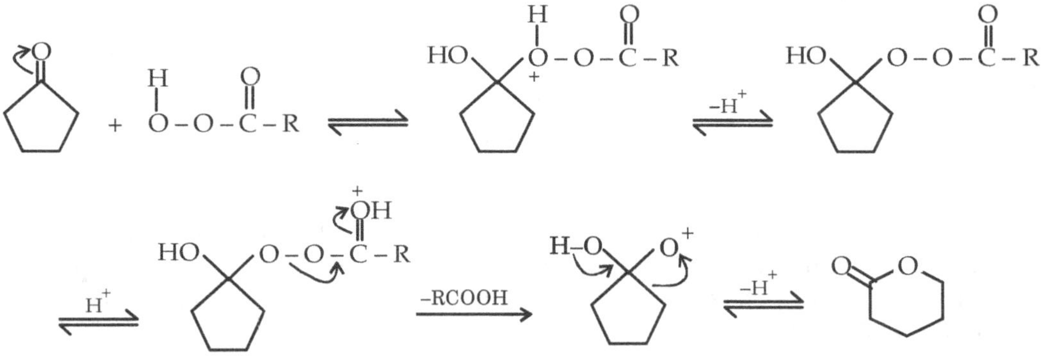

$$\text{Cyclopentanone} + H-\overset{}{O}-O-\overset{O}{\overset{\|}{C}}-R \rightleftharpoons \text{HO}-C(\text{ring})-\overset{+}{O}(H)-O-\overset{O}{\overset{\|}{C}}-R \underset{}{\overset{-H^+}{\rightleftharpoons}} \text{HO}-C(\text{ring})-O-O-\overset{O}{\overset{\|}{C}}-R$$

$$\overset{H^+}{\rightleftharpoons} \text{HO}-C(\text{ring})-O-O-\overset{+OH}{\overset{\|}{C}}-R \xrightarrow{-RCOOH} \text{H}-O-C(\text{ring})-O^+ \overset{-H^+}{\rightleftharpoons} \text{lactone}$$

The tendency of a group to migrate (migratory aptitude) in all reactions where the group migrates with its electron pairs (i.e. as anions) follows the order :

H > phenyl > 3° alkyl > 2° alkyl > 1° alkyl > methyl

TEST YOUR UNDERSTANDING - 14.15

1. Give the products of reaction for
   - (*a*) Benzaldehyde + Tollen's reagent
   - (*b*) CH_3CHO + dil. $KMnO_4$
   - (*c*) 3-Hexanone + Strong oxidant
   - (*d*) Cyclohexanone + HNO_3, heat
   - (*e*) Propanol + $Ag(NH_3)_2^+$
   - (*f*) Methyl ethyl ketone + HNO_3, heat
2. Give the products of the reaction of I_2 in KOH
   - (*i*) CH_3CH_2CHO
   - (*ii*) CH_3CH_2OH
   - (*iii*) C_6H_5CHO
   - (*iv*) $C_6H_5CH_2COCH_3$
   - (*v*) $Me_3C.COCH_3$
   - (*vi*) $CH_3CH_2COCH_2CH_2COCH_3$
   - (*vii*) $C_6H_5CH_2OH$.
3. What is the product of the reaction of each of the following ketones with peroxybenzoic acid ?
   - (*a*) $C_6H_5COC_6H_5$
   - (*b*) 2-methylcyclobutanone (structure)
   - (*c*) m-nitrobenzaldehyde (NO_2, CHO on benzene ring)
   - (*d*) cyclohexanone (=O on cyclohexane ring)

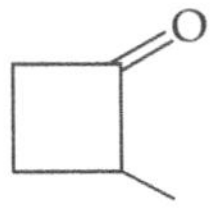

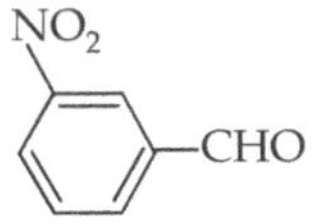

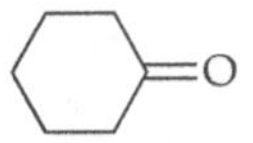

13. Reduction.

(*a*) Aldehydes and ketones can be reduced to primary and secondary alcohols respectively by a variety of reagents. Catalytic hydrogenation over a metal catalyst and reduction with lithium aluminium hydride or sodium borohydride are common methods and have been discussed in detail in the chapter on "Monohydric Alcohols". Sodium in ethanol is useful for reduction of ketones.

$$>C=O \xrightarrow[LiAlH_4 \text{ or } NaBH_4]{H_2/Ni \text{ or}} >CHOH$$

Benzaldehyde undergoes coupling reaction with Na/C_2H_5OH, so it can be reduced into alcohol by Na/C_2H_5OH.

$$CH_3CH=CHCH_2OH \xleftarrow[\text{(ii) } H^+]{\text{(i) } LiAlH_4, \text{ or } NaBH_4} CH_3CH=CHCHO \xrightarrow{H_2/Ni} CH_3CH_2CH_2CH_2OH$$

$$\text{Cyclopentanone} \xrightarrow[H^+]{LiAlH_4} \text{Cyclopentanol}$$

Cyclopentanone Cyclopentanol

Remember that reduction of carbonyl compounds to alcohols by $LiAlH_4$ or $NaBH_4$ is an example of **nucleophilic addition** reactions in which hydride ion, $H:^-$ (from $LiAlH_4$ or $NaBH_4$) is transferred from the metal to the carbonyl carbon.

$$>C=O + H—AlH_3^- \longrightarrow H—\overset{|}{\underset{|}{C}}—OAlH_3^- \xrightarrow{3 >C=O} \left(H—\overset{|}{\underset{|}{C}}—O\right)_4 Al^-$$

Tetraalkyloxyaluminate

$$\xrightarrow{4H_2O} 4\, H—\overset{|}{\underset{|}{C}}—OH + Al^-(OH)_4$$

(*b*) Aldehydes and ketones can be reduced to hydrocarbons by the action (*i*) of amalgamated zinc and concentrated hydrochloric acid (**Clemmensen reduction**), or (*b*) of hydrazine (NH_2NH_2) and a strong base like NaOH, KOH or potassium *tert*-butoxide in a high-boiling alcohol like ethylene glycol or triethylene glycol (**Wolf-Kishner reduction**).

$$>C=O \xrightarrow[\text{or } NH_2NH_2, \text{ KOH, glycol}]{Zn(Hg), \text{ HCl}} >CH_2$$

Both these methods reduce neither carboxylic acid nor the carbon-carbon double or triple bonds (however, remember that Zn and HCl reduces $—NO_2$ to $—NH_2$ group).

$$\text{Cyclopentanone} \xrightarrow[\text{base}]{NH_2NH_2} \text{Cyclopentane}$$

Cyclopentanone Cyclopentane

$$\text{Resorcinol} \xrightarrow[ZnCl_2]{CH_3(CH_2)_4COOH} \text{(4-}CO(CH_2)_4CH_3\text{ resorcinol)} \xrightarrow[HCl]{Zn(Hg)} \text{(4-}CH_2(CH_2)_4CH_3\text{ resorcinol)}$$

Resorcinol

4-*n*-Hexylresorcinol (a constituent of **dettol**)

(*c*) Aldehydes and ketones can be reduced to hydrocarbons through thioacetal formation too.

$$\underset{\text{Aldehyde or ketone}}{R(R')C{=}O} + \underset{\text{Ethanethiol}}{2CH_3CH_2SH} \xrightarrow{HA} \underset{\text{Thioacetal}}{R(R')C(S{-}CH_2CH_3)_2} + H_2O$$

$$\underset{\text{Aldehyde or ketone}}{R(R')C{=}O} + \underset{\text{Ethane-1, 2-dithiol}}{HSCH_2{-}CH_2SH} \xrightarrow{BF_3} \underset{\text{Cyclic thioacetal}}{R(R')C\langle S{-}CH_2{-}CH_2{-}S\rangle} + H_2O$$

$$R(R')C\langle S{-}CH_2{-}CH_2{-}S\rangle \xrightarrow[H_2]{\text{Raney Ni}} R(R')CH_2 + CH_3CH_3 + 2NiS$$

(*d*) Many aldehydes and ketones are converted into amines by **reductive amination** (reduction in presence of ammonia). Reduction can be done catalytically or by sodium cyanohydridoborate, $NaBH_3CN$. Reaction involves reduction of an intermediate *imine*.

$$\underset{\text{An aldehyde or ketone}}{R(R')C{=}O} + NH_3 \longrightarrow \underset{\text{An imine}}{\left[R(R')C{=}NH\right]} \xrightarrow[NaBH_3CN]{H_2,\ Ni\ or} \underset{1^\circ\ \text{Amine}}{R(R')CHNH_2}$$

(*e*) Reduction of ketones to pinacols in presence of magnesium has already been discussed in the chapter on "Polyhydric Alcohols"

$$\underset{\text{Acetone}}{2CH_3COCH_3} \xrightarrow{\text{Mg/benzene}} \underset{\text{Pinacol}}{CH_3{-}C(CH_3)(OH){-}C(CH_3)(OH){-}CH_3}$$

14. **Formation of dihalides.** Aldehydes and ketones react with PCl_5 and sulphur tetrafluoride to form corresponding dihalide.

$$\text{Cyclopentanone } (C_5H_8{=}O) \xrightarrow{PCl_5} \text{1,1-dichlorocyclopentane } (C_5H_8Cl_2) + POCl_3$$

$$\text{Cyclohexanone } (C_6H_{10}{=}O) \xrightarrow{SF_4} \text{1,1-difluorocyclohexane } (C_6H_{10}F_2) + SOF_2$$

TEST YOUR UNDERSTANDING - 14.16

1. Write down the structure and IUPAC name of the products in each of the following reactions.

(*a*) 4, 4-Dimethylcyclohexanone + NH_2NH_2, OH^- (*b*) Pent-3-enal + NH_2NH_2, OH^-

(*c*) Acetylacetic acid + Zn(Hg) and HCl (*d*) Pent-2-enal + Zn(Hg) and HCl.

2. Give structures of the compounds A to D.

(*a*) $C_6H_5CHO + HSCH_2CH_2SH \xrightarrow{\text{dry HCl}} [A] \xrightarrow[\text{Ni}]{\text{Raney}} [B]$

(*b*) $[D] \xrightarrow[\text{(ii) } H_2O_2, OH^-]{\text{(i) } BH_3/THF}$ O=⟨cyclohexane⟩=$CH_2 \xrightarrow{NaBH_4} [C]$.

3. (*a*) Write structures for the products of the reaction of PCl_5 with

(*i*) propanal (*ii*) propanone (*iii*) benzophenone

(*b*) Give the products in the following reactions :

(*i*) $C_6H_5CHO + SF_4 \xrightarrow{\text{heat}}$ (*ii*) ⟨cyclohexane⟩=O + MoF_6 ⟶

15. **Polymerisation.** Lower aldehydes undergo polymerisation to form different products under different conditions.

$$nHCHO \underset{}{\overset{\text{evaporate to dryness}}{\rightleftharpoons}} (CH_2O)_n$$
(n = 6 to 50) Paraformaldehyde

$$3HCHO \overset{\text{room temp.}}{\rightleftharpoons} (CH_2O)_3$$
Metaformaldehyde (6-membered cyclic compound)

$$3CH_3CHO \overset{\text{conc. } H_2SO_4}{\rightleftharpoons} (CH_3CHO)_3$$
Paraldehyde (6-membered cyclic compound)

$$4CH_3CHO \overset{\text{conc. } H_2SO_4,\ 0°C}{\rightleftharpoons} (CH_3CHO)_4$$
Metaldehyde (8-membered cyclic compound)

$$3CH_3COCH_3 \xrightarrow[\text{heat}]{\text{conc. } H_2SO_4}$$ 1,3,5-trimethylbenzene (CH_3, H_3C, CH_3)

Mesitylene

14.6 Special Reactions Given by Aromatic Aldehydes and Ketones

1. **Reaction with ammonia.** Benzaldehyde reacts with ammonia to form hydrobenzamide, recall that aldehydes other than formaldehyde give aldehyde ammonia, while formaldehyde forms hexamethylenetetramine, commonly known as **urotropine**, an important urinary antiseptic.

$$\begin{matrix} C_6H_5CH=O \\ C_6H_5CH=O \end{matrix} + \begin{matrix} H_2NH \\ H_2NH \end{matrix} + O=CHC_6H_5 \longrightarrow \begin{matrix} C_6H_5CH=N \\ C_6H_5CH=N \end{matrix} > CHC_6H_5$$

Hydrobenzamide

2. **Benzoin condensation.** Aromatic aldehydes, when heated with aqueous ethanolic NaCN or KCN, undergoes self condensation to form **benzoins**. For example,

$$2C_6H_5CHO \xrightarrow[C_2H_5OH]{\text{KCN, heat}} C_6H_5CHOHCOC_6H_5 \xrightarrow{\text{oxi.}} C_6H_5COCOC_6H_5 \xrightarrow[\text{rearrangement}]{\text{benzil-benzilic acid}} C_6H_5-\underset{C_6H_5}{\overset{OH}{C}}-COOH$$

Benzoin (An α-hydroxyketone) | Benzil | Benzilic acid

3. **Perkin reaction.** Condensation of an aromatic aldehyde with an acid anhydride in presence of sodium salt of the same acid to form α, β-unsaturated acid is known as Perkin reaction.

(*i*) $C_6H_5CHO + (CH_3CO)_2O \xrightarrow[(ii)\ H^+]{(i)\ CH_3COONa} C_6H_5CH = CHCOOH$

Benzaldehyde Acetic anhydride Cimmanic acid

(*ii*) $C_6H_5CHO + (CH_3CH_2CO)_2O \xrightarrow[(ii)\ H^+]{(i)\ CH_3CH_2COONa} C_6H_5CH = C(CH_3)COOH$

Benzaldehyde Propanoic anhydride α-Methylcinnamic acid

Remember that it is the α-carbon atom of the anhydride that reacts with the aldehydic group, observe (*ii*) example.

4. **Reaction with benzene nucleus.** Aromatic aldehydes and ketones undergo electrophilic substitutions in the *meta* position. However, these reactions are slow because of deactivating influence of the carbonyl group. Moreover, certain side reactions like oxidation make the yield poor.

14.7 Analysis of Aldehydes and Ketones

1. Aldehydes and ketones can be differentiated from non-carbonyl compounds through their reactions with semicarbazide, 2, 4-dinitro-phenylhydrazine, and hydroxylamine with which they form precipitates. Semicarbazones and oximes are colourless, while 2, 4-dinitrophenylhydrazones are usually orange. The melting points of these derivatives can also be used in indentifying specific aldehydes and ketones.
2. Aldehydes are differentiated from ketones through their ease of oxidation. They give a positive test with Tollen's reagent, while ketones do not. However, a positive Tollen's test is also given by few other easily oxidisable compounds, *e.g.* α-hydroxy ketones, certain phenols and hydroxylamines.
3. **Schiff's test** is a highly sensitive test for aldehydes. An aldehyde reacts with the fuchsin-aldehyde reagent to form a characteristic megenta colour.
4. Aldehydes are easily oxidised by cold, dilute, neutral $KMnO_4$ and by CrO_3 in sulphuric acid.
5. Aliphatic aldehydes and ketones having α-hydrogen react with bromine in CCl_4 (*caution* this is also a test for unsaturation).
6. Methyl ketones, acetaldehyde, ethyl alcohol and methyl secondary alcohols give positive iodoform test. In general, iodoform test is given by following groupings.

(*a*) $-\overset{O}{\overset{\|}{C}}-CH_3$ present in ethanal, $H-\overset{O}{\overset{\|}{C}}-CH_3$ and all methyl ketones

(*b*) $-\underset{H}{\overset{OH}{C}}-CH_3$ present in ethanol and all secondary methyl ketones.

(*c*) $R-\overset{O}{\overset{\|}{C}}-CH_2X$ since these products are formed during holoform reaction.

(*d*) $R-\overset{X}{CH}-CH_3$ since these on hydrolysis with aq. NaOH give 2° alcohols having methyl group.

TEST YOUR UNDERSTANDING - 14.17

1. What happens when an aldehyde or a ketone is treated with the following reagents ?
   Conc. H_2SO_4, cold dil., neutral $KMnO_4$, CrO_3 in H_2SO_4, and Br_2 in CCl_4.
2. By rapid test tube reactions distinguish between
   (*a*) 2-Pentanol and 2-pentanone
   (*b*) Pentanal and diethyl ketone
   (*c*) $C_6H_5COCH_2CH_3$ and $C_6H_5CH(OH)CH_2CH_2CH_3$
   (*d*) $C_6H_5CH = CHCH_2OH$ and $C_6H_5CH = CHCHO$.

14.8 Illustrative Examples

Example 1 :

Give various steps involved in the following conversions :

$$C_6H_5CH = CHCHO \text{ to } C_6H_5CHBrCHBrCH_2Cl.$$

Solution :

Conversion involves two main reactions, viz. addition of Br_2 on C = C and conversion of —CHO to —CH_2Cl. Since bromine oxidizes —CHO to —COOH, so —CHO first be converted to CH_2Cl before adding bromine.

$$C_6H_5CH = CHCHO \xrightarrow[\text{(ii) } H_2O]{\text{(i) } NaBH_4} C_6H_5CH = CHCH_2OH \xrightarrow{PCl_5} C_6H_5CH = CHCH_2Cl \xrightarrow{Br_2} C_6H_5CHBrCHBrCH_2Cl.$$

Example 2 :

Write structures of the compounds from A to I.

(a) $C_6H_6 + CH_2 = CHCH_2OH \xrightarrow{HF} [A] \xrightarrow[\text{(ii) } H_2O_2/OH^-]{\text{(i) } BH_3/HF} [B] \xrightarrow[\text{Pyridine}]{CrO_3} [C] \xrightarrow[\text{(ii) } H_3O^+]{\text{(i) } CN^-} [D]$

(b) 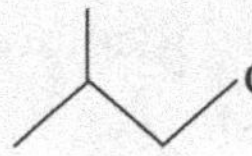 $CHO + BrCH_2COOC_2H_5 \xrightarrow{Zn} [E] \xrightarrow[\text{Pyridine}]{CrO_3} [F] \xrightarrow{HOCH_2CH_2OH} [G] \xrightarrow{LiAlH_4} [H] \xrightarrow{H_3O^+} [I].$

Solution :

(*a*) [A] is $C_6H_5CH_2CH = CH_2$, (obtained by Friedel-craft alkylation)

[B] is $C_6H_5CH_2CH_2CH_2OH$, (obtained by *anti*-Markovnikov hydration)

[C] is $C_6H_5CH_2CH_2CHO$;

[D] is $C_6H_5CH_2CH_2CHOHCOOH$

(*b*)

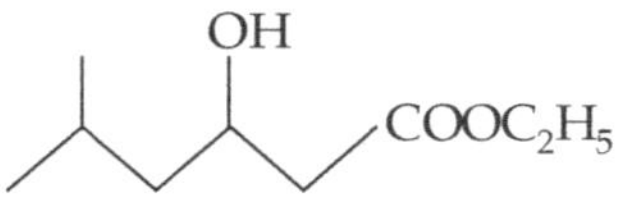

[E] (Perkin reaction)

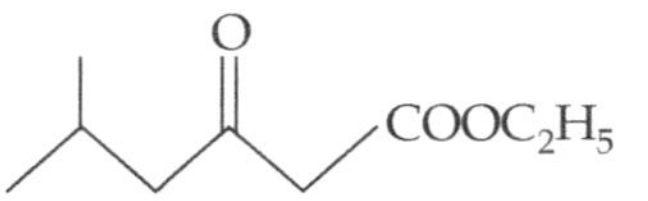

[F]

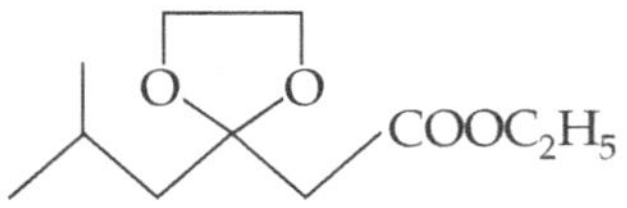

[G] (Protection of keto group)

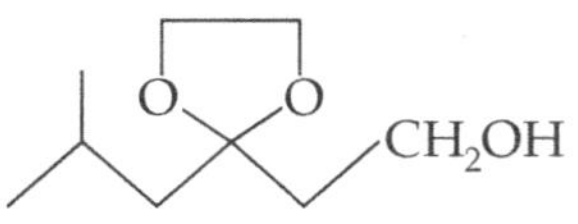

[H] (Reduction of ester)

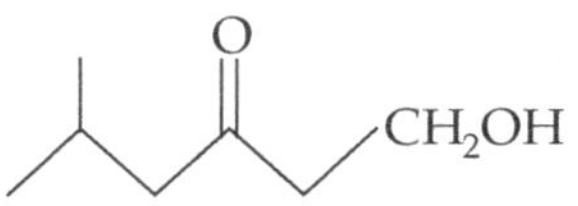

[I] (Regeneration of keto group)

Example 3 :

Write structures for A to D in the following.

$$(CH_3)_2CO \xrightarrow{CN^-} [A] \xrightarrow{H_3O^+} [B] \xrightarrow[\text{heat}]{H_2SO_4} [C] \xrightarrow[\text{(ii) } H_2O_2,\, OH^-]{\text{(i) } BH_3/THF} [D].$$

Solution :

[A] [B] [C] [D]

Example 4 :

Identify A to C in the following :

$$C_6H_5CH_2CH_3 \xrightarrow{2NBS} [A] \xrightarrow{H_3O^+} [B] \xrightarrow{NaOCl} [C] + [D]$$

Solution :

$C_6H_5CBr_2CH_3$, [A] $C_6H_5COCH_3$, [B] $C_6H_5COO^-Na^+ + CHCl_3$ [C] and [D]

Example 5 :

Identify A to C in the following reactions.

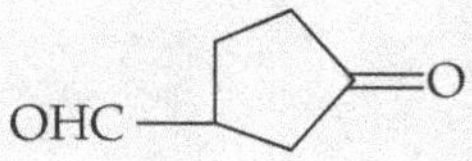 $\xrightarrow[H^+]{CH_2OHCH_2OH}$ [A] $\xrightarrow[CH_3OH]{NaBH_4}$ [B] $\xrightarrow{H_3O^+}$ [C]

Solution :

Aldehydes are more reactive than ketones, hence acetal formation at first step will be with the —CHO group ; this is done to protect the aldehydic group.

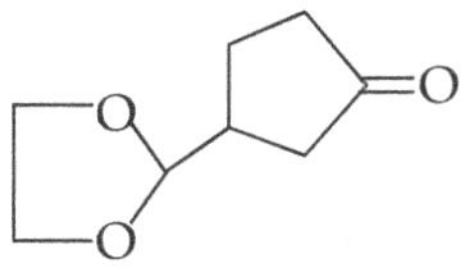

[A]

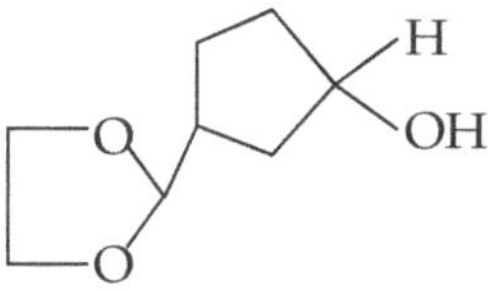

[B]

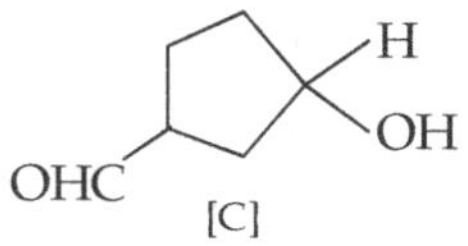

[C]

Example 6 :

Complete the following reactions.

(a) $CH \equiv CH \xrightarrow{C_2H_5MgBr} [A] \xrightarrow[\text{(ii) } H^+]{\text{(i) } CO_2} B \xrightarrow{H_2SO_4,\, Hg^{2+}} C \xrightarrow[H_2SO_4]{CrO_3} [D]$

(b) $C_6H_5CH_3 \xrightarrow{NBS} E \xrightarrow{NaCN} F \xrightarrow[\text{(ii) } H_3O^+]{\text{(i) } C_6H_{11}MgBr} G$

Solution :

(a) $CH \equiv CH \xrightarrow[(-C_2H_6)]{C_2H_5MgBr} \underset{[A]}{HC \equiv CMgBr} \xrightarrow[(ii)\ H^+]{(i)\ CO_2} \underset{[B]}{HC \equiv C \rightarrow COOH} \xrightarrow{H_2SO_4, Hg^{2+}}$

$HOCH = CHCOOH \xrightarrow{\text{tautomerises}} \underset{[C]}{OHCCH_2COOH} \xrightarrow{CrO_3} \underset{[D]}{HOOCCH_2COOH}$

anti-Markownikov hydration due to —I effect of —COOH

(b) $C_6H_5CH_3 \xrightarrow{NBS} \underset{[E]}{C_6H_5CH_2Br} \xrightarrow{NaCN} \underset{[F]}{C_6H_5CH_2CN} \xrightarrow{C_6H_{11}MgBr} \underset{[G]}{C_6H_5CH_2COC_6H_{11}}$

[G] Cyclohexyl benzyl ketone

Example 7 :

Give steps involved in the following conversions.

(a) Acetaldehyde to 2, 3-dibromopentanoic acid

(b) Acetaldehyde to α-hydroxypropanoic acid (lactic acid)

(c) Benzene to *p*-chlorobenzaldehyde

(d) Cyclopentane to cyclopentanecarbaldehyde.

Solution :

(a) $2H_3CHO \xrightarrow{OH^-} CH_3CHOHCH_2CHO \xrightarrow{heat} CH_3CH = CHCHO$

$\xrightarrow{[Ag(NH_3)_2]^+} CH_3CH = CHCOOH \xrightarrow{Br_2} CH_3\underset{Br}{CH}\underset{Br}{CH}COOH$

(b) $CH_3CHO \xrightarrow{NaCN} CH_3CHOHCN \xrightarrow{H^+} \underset{\text{Lactic acid}}{CH_3CHOHCOOH}$

(c) $C_6H_6 \xrightarrow[(ii)\ Mg,\ ether]{(i)\ Br_2, Fe} C_6H_5MgBr \xrightarrow[(ii)\ H_3O^+]{(i)\ CH_2O} C_6H_5CH_2OH \xrightarrow{Cl_2, Fe} p\text{-}Cl.C_6H_4CH_2OH$

$\xrightarrow{CrO_3,\ Pyridine} p\text{-}ClC_6H_4CHO$

(d) Cyclopentane $\xrightarrow[hv]{Cl_2}$ C₅H₉Cl $\xrightarrow{Mg,\ ether}$ $C_5H_9MgCl \xrightarrow[(ii)\ H_3O^+]{(i)\ CH_2O} C_5H_9CH_2OH \xrightarrow[Pyridine]{CrO_3} C_5H_9CHO$

Example 8 :

Perform each of the following transformations :

(a) $C_6H_5COCH_2CH_3 \longrightarrow C_6H_5C \equiv CCH_3$

(b) $p\text{-}OHCC_6H_4COOH \longrightarrow p\text{-}OHCC_6H_4CHO$

(c) 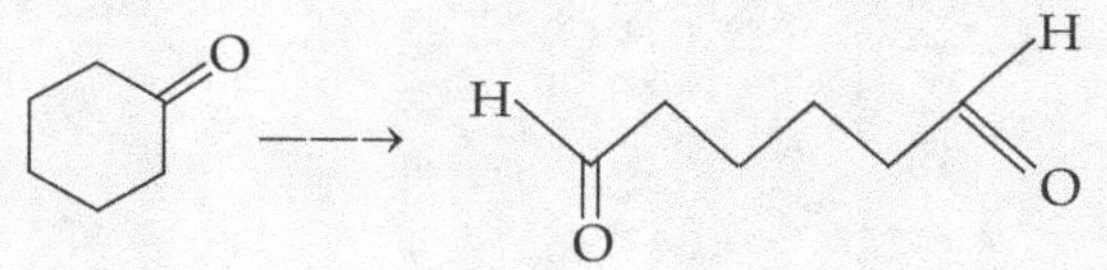 Cyclohexanone ⟶ $OHC-CH_2CH_2CH_2CH_2-CHO$

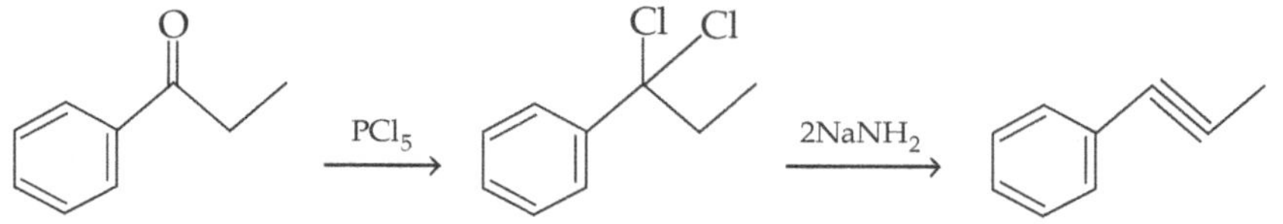

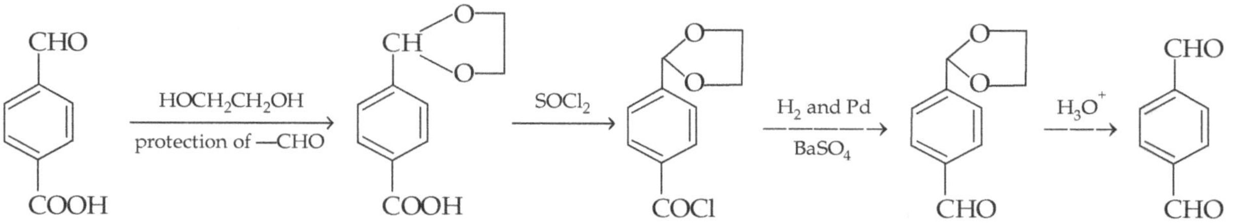

Solution:

(a) $C_6H_5COCH_2CH_3 \xrightarrow{PCl_5} C_6H_5CCl_2CH_2CH_3 \xrightarrow{2NaNH_2} C_6H_5C\equiv CCH_3$

(b) p-$OHC-C_6H_4-COOH \xrightarrow[\text{protection of —CHO}]{HOCH_2CH_2OH}$ p-(1,3-dioxolan-2-yl)$C_6H_4COOH \xrightarrow{SOCl_2}$ p-(1,3-dioxolan-2-yl)$C_6H_4COCl \xrightarrow[BaSO_4]{H_2 \text{ and Pd}}$ p-(1,3-dioxolan-2-yl)$C_6H_4CHO \xrightarrow{H_3O^+}$ p-$OHC-C_6H_4-CHO$

(c) Cyclohexanone $\xrightarrow{NaBH_4}$ Cyclohexanol $\xrightarrow[\text{heat}]{\text{conc. } H_2SO_4}$ Cyclohexene $\xrightarrow[(ii)\ Zn]{(i)\ O_3}$ $OHC(CH_2)_4CHO$

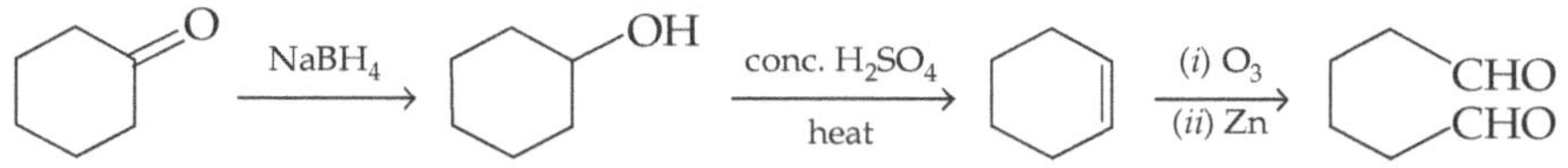

Example 9 :

Illustrate the following series of reactions by providing structure to each of the intermediate.

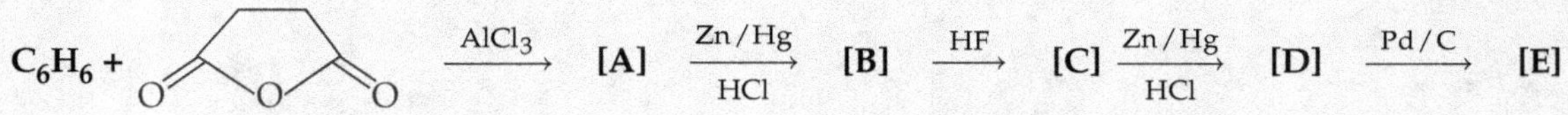

C_6H_6 + succinic anhydride $\xrightarrow{AlCl_3}$ [A] $\xrightarrow[HCl]{Zn/Hg}$ [B] $\xrightarrow{HF}$ [C] $\xrightarrow[HCl]{Zn/Hg}$ [D] $\xrightarrow{Pd/C}$ [E]

Solution:

Benzene + succinic anhydride $\xrightarrow{AlCl_3}$ $C_6H_5COCH_2CH_2COOH$ [A] $\xrightarrow[HCl]{Zn/Hg}$

$C_6H_5CH_2CH_2CH_2COOH$ [B] $\xrightarrow[(-H_2O)]{HF}$ α-Tetralone [C] $\xrightarrow[HCl]{Zn/Hg}$ Tetralin [D] $\xrightarrow{Pd/C}$ Naphthalene [E]

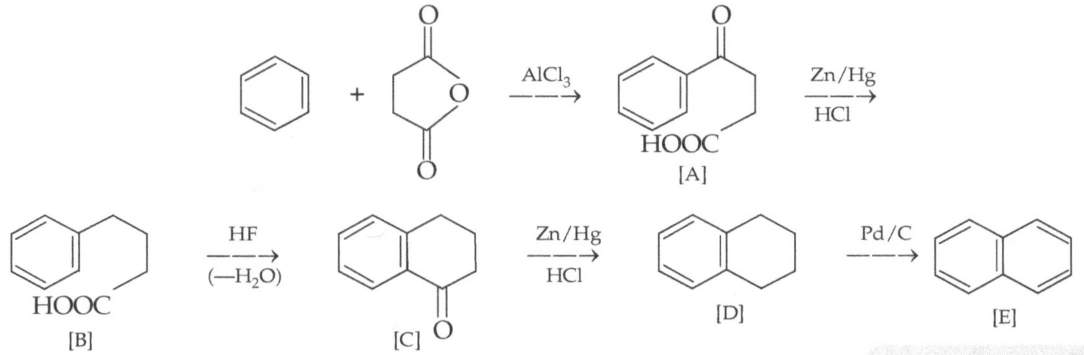

Example 10 :

Give steps involved in the following conversions.

(a) $^{14}CH_3OH$ **to** $CH_3{}^{14}CH_2OH$
(b) $^{14}CH_3OH$ **to** $^{14}CH_3CH_2OH$
(c) $^{14}CH_3CH_2OH$ **to** $^{14}CD_3CHO$
(d) $^{14}CH_3CHO$ **to** $^{14}CH_3CHDOH$.

Solution:

(a) $^{14}CH_3OH \xrightarrow[300°C]{Cu} H_2{}^{14}C=O \xrightarrow[(ii)\ H_3O^+]{(i)\ CH_3MgBr} CH_3{}^{14}CH_2OH$

(b) $^{14}CH_3OH \xrightarrow{HBr} {}^{14}CH_3Br \xrightarrow[\text{ether}]{Mg} {}^{14}CH_3MgBr \xrightarrow[\text{(ii) } H_3O^+]{\text{(i) } CH_2O} {}^{14}CH_3CH_2OH$

(c) $^{14}CH_3CH_2OH \xrightarrow{Cu} {}^{14}CH_3CHO \xrightarrow{D_2O,\ OD^-\ \text{(trace)}} {}^{14}CD_3CHO$

(d) $^{14}CH_3CHO \xrightarrow[\text{LiAlD}_4]{D_2/\text{Pt or}} {}^{14}CH_3CHDOD \xrightarrow{H_2O} {}^{14}CH_3CHDOH.$

Example 11 :

How will you carry out following transformations ?

(a)  [structure] to [structure] **(b)** 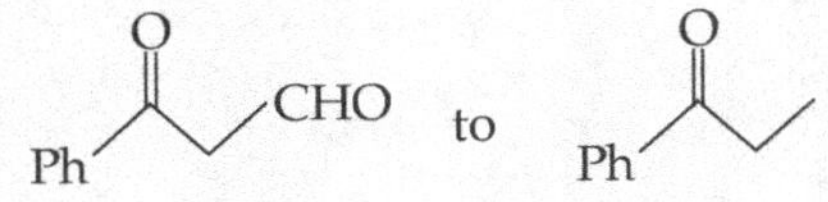 Ph–CO–CH₂–CHO to Ph–CO–CH₂CH₃

(c) 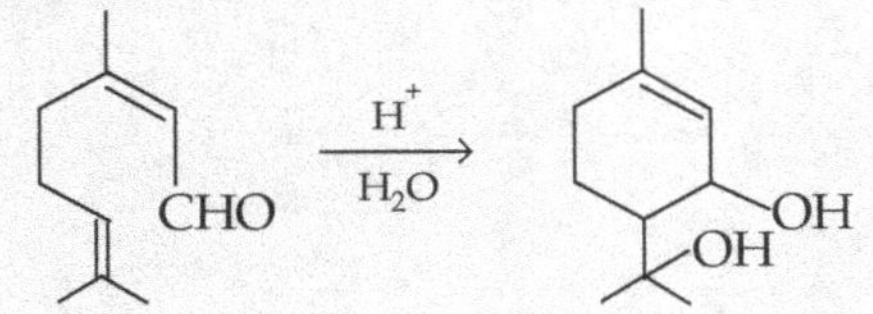 [structure: CHO] $\xrightarrow[H_2O]{H^+}$ [structure: OH, OH]

Solution :

The sterically unhindered keto group in (*a*) and the more reactive aldehyde group in (*b*) are more easily effected.

(*a*) [structure] $\xrightarrow{HSCH_2CH_2SH}$ [structure] $\xrightarrow[\text{Ni}]{\text{Raney}}$ [structure] + HS SH

(*b*) [structure: Ph, CHO] $\xrightarrow{HSCH_2CH_2SH}$ [structure: Ph, S, S] ⟶ [structure: Ph]

(*c*) [structure: H, O] $\xrightarrow{H^+}$ [structure: H, OH, +] ⟶ [structure: H, OH, ⊕] $\xrightarrow[(-H^+)]{H_2O}$ [structure: OH, OH]

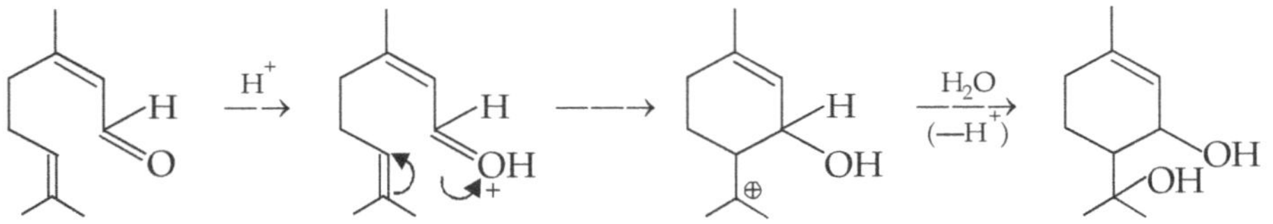

Example 12 :

Write down the steps involved in the following reactions, each involves aldol condensation.

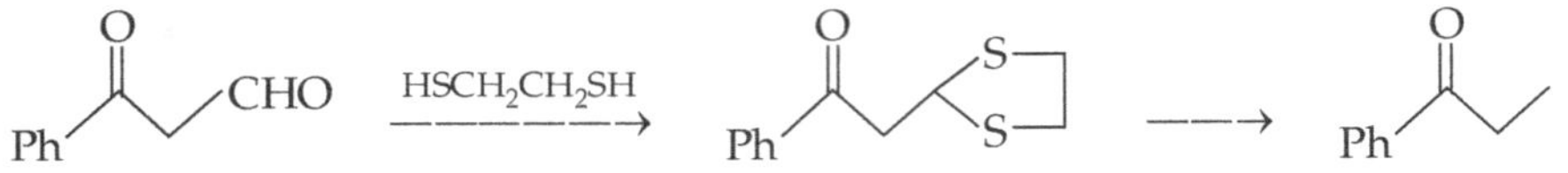

(a) 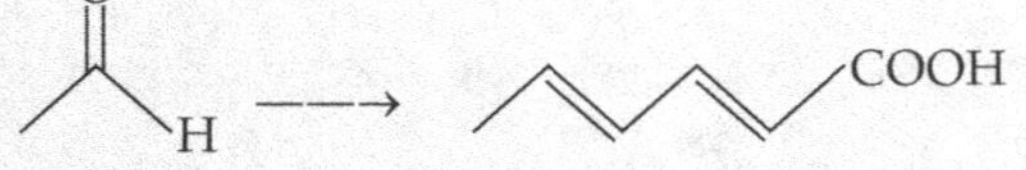 [structure: O, H] ⟶ [structure: COOH] **(b)** 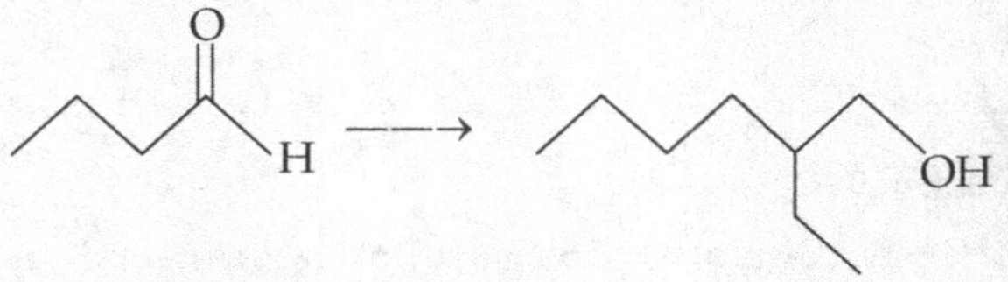 [structure: O, H] ⟶ [structure: OH]

(c) 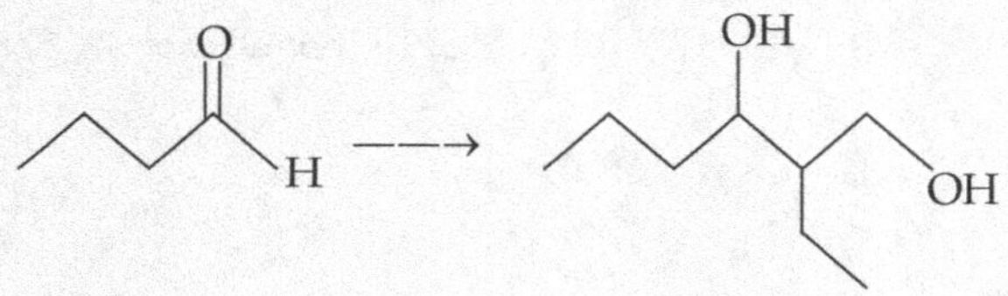 [structure: O, H] ⟶ [structure: OH, OH] **(d)** 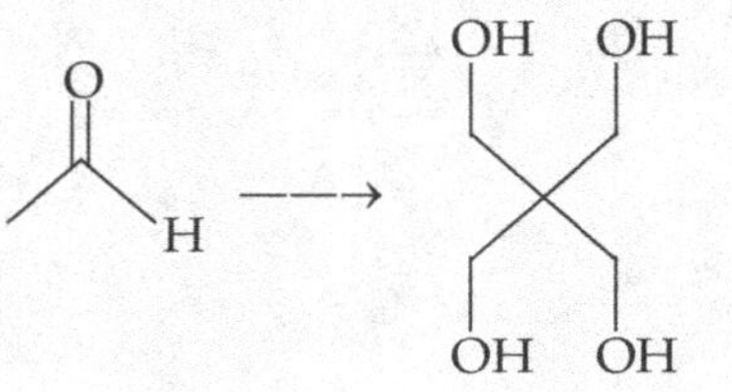 [structure: O, H] ⟶ [structure: OH, OH, OH, OH]

Solution :

(*a*) 2 CH_3CHO $\xrightarrow[(ii)\ (-H_2O)]{(i)\ OH^-}$ $CH_3CH=CHCHO$ $\xrightarrow[(ii)\ -H_2O]{(i)\ CH_3CHO}$ $CH_3CH=CHCH=CHCHO$ $\xrightarrow[[Ag(NH_3)_2]^+]{\text{mild oxidation}}$ $CH_3CH=CHCH=CHCOOH$

Sorbic acid (*food preservative*)

(*b*) 2 $CH_3CH_2CH_2CHO$ $\xrightarrow{OH^-}$ $CH_3CH_2CH_2CH(OH)CH(C_2H_5)CHO$ $\xrightarrow[(-H_2O)]{\text{heat}}$ $CH_3CH_2CH_2CH=C(C_2H_5)CHO$ $\xrightarrow{H_2/Pt}$ $CH_3CH_2CH_2CH_2CH(C_2H_5)CH_2OH$

2-Ethyl-1-hexanol

(*c*) 2 $CH_3CH_2CH_2CHO$ $\xrightarrow{OH^-}$ $CH_3CH_2CH_2CH(OH)CH(C_2H_5)CHO$ $\xrightarrow{H_2/Pt}$ $CH_3CH_2CH_2CH(OH)CH(C_2H_5)CH_2OH$

2-Ethyl-1, 3-hexanediol
(an *insect repellant*)

(*d*) $H-\underset{H}{\overset{H}{C}}-CH=O + 3CH_2=O$ $\xrightarrow[\text{(aldol condensation)}]{Ca(OH)_2}$ $HOCH_2-\underset{CH_2OH}{\overset{CH_2OH}{C}}-CHO$ $\xrightarrow[OH^-]{CH_2O}$ $HOCH_2-\underset{CH_2OH}{\overset{CH_2OH}{C}}-CH_2OH + HCOO^-$

Acetaldehyde

Pentaerythritol (a *humectant*)

Example 13 :

Give steps involved in the following conversion.

1-(1-hydroxycyclopentyl)-1-phenylethanol: $\text{(cyclopentyl-OH)}-\underset{C_6H_5}{\overset{OH}{C}}-CH_3$ $\xrightarrow{H_2SO_4}$ 2-methyl-2-phenylcyclohexanone (CH_3, C_6H_5 on C-2)

Solution :

$\text{(cyclopentyl-OH)}-\underset{C_6H_5}{\overset{OH}{C}}-CH_3$ $\xrightarrow[(-H_2O)]{H^+}$ $\text{(cyclopentyl-OH)}-\underset{C_6H_5}{\overset{+}{C}}-CH_3$ $\xrightarrow[\text{shift}]{\text{ring}:CH_2}$ 2-hydroxy-1-methyl-1-phenylcyclohexyl cation ($\overset{+}{C}$–OH; CH_3, C_6H_5) $\xrightarrow{-H^+}$ (Enol) $\rightleftharpoons$ (Keto)

3° Carbocation
(conjugated with Ar—)

(Enol)

(Keto)

Example 14 :

Identify the final product formed in each case and explain its formation.

(a) $CH_3COCH_3 + CH \equiv CH \xrightarrow[(ii)\,H^+]{(i)\,NaNH_2}$ **(b)** $(CH_3)_2C(OH)CH_2OH \xrightarrow{H^+}$

(c) Cyclohexanone $+ CH_2ClCOOCH_2CH_3 \xrightarrow{Me_3COK}$ **(d)** 3-Pentanone $+ NH_3 \xrightarrow{CN^-}$

Solution :

(*a*) $HC \equiv CH \xrightarrow{NaNH_2} :\overset{\ominus}{C} \equiv CH$

$$(CH_3)_2C=O \xrightarrow{:\overset{\ominus}{C} \equiv CH} (CH_3)_2C(O^-)C \equiv CH \xrightarrow{H^+} (CH_3)_2C(OH)C \equiv CH$$

(*b*)

$$(CH_3)_2C(OH)CH_2OH \xrightarrow{H^+} (CH_3)_2C(\overset{+}{O}H_2)CH_2OH \xrightarrow[(-H_2O)]{}$$

3° alcohol is more basic than 1°

$$(CH_3)_2\overset{+}{C}CH_2OH \xrightarrow{-H^+} [(CH_3)_2C=CHOH] \xrightarrow{\text{tautomerization}} (CH_3)_2CHCHO$$

(*c*)

$$CH_2ClCOOCH_2CH_3 \xrightarrow{Me_3CO^-} \bar{C}HClCOOCH_2CH_3$$

$$\text{Cyclohexanone} \xrightarrow{\bar{C}HClCOOC_2H_5} \text{(1-oxido-cyclohexyl)}-CHClCOOC_2H_5 \xrightarrow[(-Cl^-)]{} \text{spiro epoxide } O-CHCOOC_2H_5$$

(*d*)

$$\text{3-Pentanone} + NH_3 \longrightarrow C=NH \xrightarrow{CN^-} C(CN)NH^{\ominus} \xrightarrow{H_2O} C(CN)NH_2$$

Example 15 :

Predict the product and explain its formation in each of the following reactions.

(a) Cyclohexanone $+ CH_2=CHCN \xrightarrow{OH^-}$ **(b)** Cyclohexanone $+ CH_3CH_2NO_2 \xrightarrow{OH^-}$

Solution :

(a) Cyclohexanone $\xrightarrow{OH^-}$ carbanion $\xrightarrow[\text{(CN is —I group)}]{CH_2 = CHCN}$ 2-($CH_2\ddot{C}HCN$)cyclohexanone $\xrightarrow{H_2O}$ 2-(CH_2CH_2CN)cyclohexanone + OH^-

(b) Cyclohexanone + $H—C(H)(CH_3)—NO_2$ $\xrightarrow{OH^-}$ 1-[$CH(CH_3)NO_2$]cyclohexanol $\longrightarrow$ cyclohexylidene=$C(CH_3)NO_2$

Example 16 :

Can you suggest a proper mechanism for the following reaction ?

$$2C_6H_6 + (CH_3)_2CO \xrightarrow{H^+} (C_6H_5)_2C(CH_3)_2.$$

Solution :

$CH_3—CO—CH_3 \xrightarrow{H^+} CH_3—\overset{+}{C}(OH)—CH_3$ (An electrophile) $\xrightarrow{C_6H_6} C_6H_5—C(OH)(CH_3)—CH_3 \xrightarrow[(—H_2O)]{H^+} C_6H_5—\overset{\oplus}{C}(CH_3)—CH_3$ (Another electrophile) $\xrightarrow{C_6H_6} C_6H_5—C(CH_3)_2—C_6H_5$

Example 17 :

Semicarbazide (1 mol) is added to a mixture of cyclohexanone (1 mol) and benzaldehyde (1 mol). If the product is isolated immediately, it consists almost entirely of the semicarbazone of cyclohexanone, if the product is isolated after several hours, it consists almost entirely of the semicarbazone of benzaldehyde. Explain.

Solution :

Semicarbazone formation is reversible. Cyclohexanone reacts more rapidly because its C = O group is not sterically hindered (its R groups are tied back into a ring), but benzaldehyde gives the more stable product, $C_6H_5CH = NNHCONH_2$, because of conjugation. Hence, initially the rate controlled product (cyclohexanone semicarbazone) is formed ; later, after equilibrium is established the equilibrium controlled product (*i.e.* the more stable benzaldehyde semicarbazone) is formed.

Example 18 :

An organic compound of the formula $C_5H_8O_2$ reduces Tollen's reagent and also responds iodoform test. It reacts with hydroxylamine hydrochloride to form a dioxime and can be reduced to *n*-pentane. Deduce the structure of the compound.

Solution :

Positive test with Tollen's reagent indicates the presence of —CHO group, while positive iodoform test indicates the presence of $—COCH_3$ grouping. Two carbonyl groups is also indicated by the formation of dioxime. Reduction of the compound to *n*-pentane indicates the presence of 5 carbon atoms in a continuous chain. Hence the compound should be $CH_3—\underset{\underset{O}{\|}}{C}CH_2CH_2CHO$.

Example 19 :

Compound X, $C_9H_{10}O$, is inert to Br_2 in CCl_4. Vigorous oxidation with hot alkaline permanganate yields benzoic acid. X gives a precipitate with semicarbazide hydrochloride and with 2, 4-dinitrophenylhydrazine (DNPH). Write all possible structures for X. How can these isomers be distinguished by using simple chemical tests ?

Solution :

Formation of benzoic acid, on oxidation of the compound X, indicates that X is having only one side chain. The formula reveals five degree of unsaturation, four for the benzene ring indicated by the formation of benzoic acid and hence fifth must be present in the side chain. The side unsaturation must be due to C = O group, indicated by reaction with DNPH. Thus the possible structures for the compound X are

$$\underset{\text{I}}{C_6H_5COCH_2CH_3} \qquad \underset{\text{II}}{C_6H_5CH_2COCH_3} \qquad \underset{\text{III}}{C_6H_5CH_2CH_2CHO} \qquad \underset{\text{IV}}{C_6H_5\overset{\overset{CH_3}{|}}{C}HCHO}$$

Difference between I, II, III and IV. Aldehydes III and IV undergo oxidation by cold $KMnO_4$ and CrO_3 in H_2SO_4; while compound II undergoes iodoform reaction.

Example 20 :

The Grignard reagent of an alkyl halide (I) reacts with propanal to give a secondary alcohol (II). II is converted into another alkyl halide (III), Grignard reagent of (III) is hydrolyzed to form an alkane (IV). Compound IV can be produced by coupling alkyl halide (I). Establish the structure of I and explain the reactions involved.

Solution :

Let us translate the given description into chemical equations.

$$\underset{\text{I}}{RBr} \xrightarrow[\text{ether}]{Mg} RMgBr \xrightarrow[\text{(ii) } H_3O^+]{\text{(i) } CH_3CH_2CHO} \underset{\text{II}}{CH_3CH_2CH(OH)R} \xrightarrow{HBr} \underset{\text{III}}{CH_3CH_2\overset{\overset{R}{|}}{C}HBr}$$

$$\xrightarrow{Mg,\ ether} \underset{\text{IV}}{CH_3CH_2\overset{\overset{R}{|}}{C}HMgBr} \xrightarrow{H_2O} CH_3CH_2CH_2R$$

Since IV is formed by coupling of I, it must be symmetrical, *i.e.* R should be $CH_3CH_2CH_2$—. Hence compound I is $CH_3CH_2CH_2Br$ and thus the various reactions can be written as below.

$$\underset{\text{I}}{CH_3CH_2CH_2Br} \xrightarrow{Mg,\ ether} \underset{\text{II}}{CH_3CH_2CH_2MgBr} \xrightarrow[\text{(ii) } H_3O^+]{\text{(i) } CH_3CH_2CHO} CH_3CH_2CH_2\overset{\overset{CH_2CH_3}{|}}{C}HOH$$

$$\xrightarrow{HBr} CH_3CH_2CH_2\overset{\overset{CH_2CH_3}{|}}{C}HBr \xrightarrow{Mg,\ ether} \underset{\text{III}}{CH_3CH_2CH_2\overset{\overset{CH_2CH_3}{|}}{C}HMgBr} \xrightarrow{HOH} CH_3CH_2CH_2\overset{\overset{CH_2CH_3}{|}}{C}H_2 \xleftarrow[\text{(coupling)}]{Na} \underset{\text{I}}{2BrCH_2CH_2CH_3}$$

Example 21 :

Glycerol and ethanal are treated in equivalent amounts. Predict the number of isomeric acetals formed.

$$CH_2OHCHOHCH_2OH + CH_3CHO \longrightarrow$$

Solution :

Cyclic acetal may be formed by the reaction of CH_3CHO (a) with the 1- and 2- OH groups, and (b) with 1- and 3- OH groups. The former possibility creates two chiral centers, hence two pairs of enantiomers will be formed, one pair is the *cis-* and the other is *trans.*

$$CH_2(OH)-CH(OH)-CH_2OH + O=C(H)(CH_3) \longrightarrow$$ *cis* + *trans*

Reaction of CH_3CHO with 1- and 3- OH groups will give *cis*- and *trans*- isomers, none of which is chiral. These isomers are diastereomers.

$$HOCH_2-CHOH-CH_2OH + O=C(H)(CH_3) \longrightarrow$$ *cis* + *trans*

Thus, on the whole six isomers will be formed.

Example 22 :

The three isomeric dioxanes; 1,2-dioxane, 1,3-dioxane and 1,4-dioxane; behave differently. One of these acts like an ether and is used as an excellent solvent for Grignard reactions, the other isomer when heated explodes, and the third quickly hydrolyzes in dil. acid. Predict which one is which, and explain the difference.

Solution :

1,2-Dioxane, I — 1,3-Dioxane, II — 1,4-Dioxane, III

The isomer I has an peroxide linkage (–O–O–) which decomposes on heating to give radicals. In the presence of organic compounds, radical reactions can be explosive. The isomer II behaves like an acetal which hydrolyzes in dil. acid to alcohol and HCHO, while the III isomer behaves like a simple ether, the two oxygens are far enough apart to act independently.

Example 23 :

Acetone, when dissolved in water having labelled oxygen (O^{18}) gives $CH_3CO^{18}CH_3$, and this conversion is catalyzed by traces of strong acids and strong bases. Devise a mechanism for this.

Solution :

Acid catalyzed reaction :

$$CH_3-\overset{O}{\overset{\|}{C}}-CH_3 \underset{-H^+}{\overset{H^+}{\rightleftharpoons}} CH_3-\overset{^+OH}{\overset{\|}{C}}-CH_3 \underset{-H_2O^{18}}{\overset{H_2O^{18}}{\rightleftharpoons}} CH_3-\underset{^{18}\overset{+}{O}H_2}{\overset{OH}{C}}-CH_3 \underset{H^+}{\overset{-H^+}{\rightleftharpoons}} CH_3-\underset{^{18}OH}{\overset{OH}{C}}-CH_3$$

$$\underset{-H^+}{\overset{H^+}{\rightleftharpoons}} CH_3-\underset{^{18}OH}{\overset{^+OH_2}{C}}-CH_3 \underset{+H_2O}{\overset{-H_2O}{\rightleftharpoons}} CH_3-\underset{:\ddot{O}-H}{\overset{+}{C}}-CH_3 \longleftrightarrow CH_3-\underset{^{18}\overset{+}{O}H}{\overset{\|}{C}}-CH_3 \underset{H^+}{\overset{-H^+}{\rightleftharpoons}} CH_3-\underset{^{18}O}{\overset{\|}{C}}-CH_3$$

Base-catalyzed reaction :

$$OH^- + H_2O^{18} \rightleftharpoons H_2O + {}^{18}OH^-$$

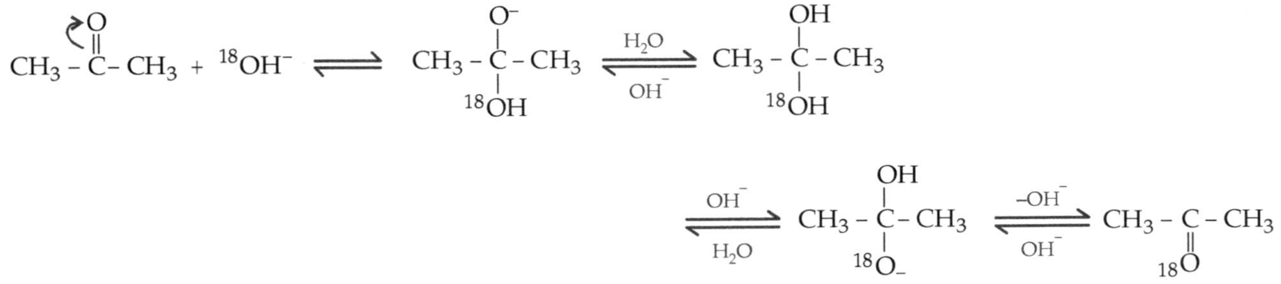

$$CH_3-\overset{O}{\overset{\|}{C}}-CH_3 + {}^{18}OH^- \rightleftharpoons CH_3-\underset{^{18}OH}{\overset{O^-}{C}}-CH_3 \underset{OH^-}{\overset{H_2O}{\rightleftharpoons}} CH_3-\underset{^{18}OH}{\overset{OH}{C}}-CH_3$$

$$\underset{H_2O}{\overset{OH^-}{\rightleftharpoons}} CH_3-\underset{^{18}O^-}{\overset{OH}{C}}-CH_3 \underset{OH^-}{\overset{-OH^-}{\rightleftharpoons}} CH_3-\underset{^{18}O}{\overset{\|}{C}}-CH_3$$

Example 24 :

Bisphenol A, an important constituent of many polymers like polyurethanes, polycarbamates, and epoxy resins, is synthesized from phenol and acetone in presence of HCl. Propose a mechanism for this reaction.

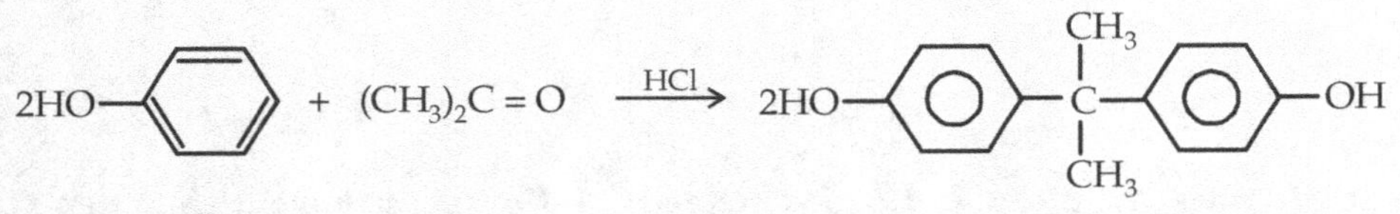

$$2HO-C_6H_5 + (CH_3)_2C=O \xrightarrow{HCl} HO-C_6H_4-\underset{CH_3}{\overset{CH_3}{C}}-C_6H_4-OH$$

Bisphenol A

Solution :

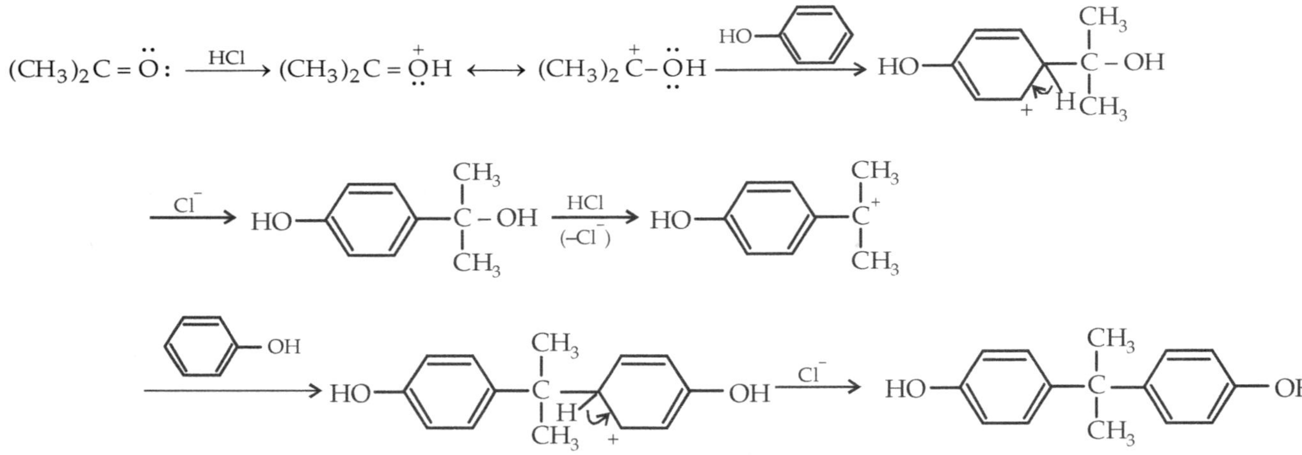

$$(CH_3)_2C=\ddot{O}: \xrightarrow{HCl} (CH_3)_2C=\overset{+}{\ddot{O}}H \longleftrightarrow (CH_3)_2\overset{+}{C}-\ddot{O}H \xrightarrow{HO-C_6H_5} HO-C_6H_4^{+}(H)-\underset{CH_3}{\overset{CH_3}{C}}-OH$$

$$\xrightarrow{Cl^-} HO-C_6H_4-\underset{CH_3}{\overset{CH_3}{C}}-OH \xrightarrow[(-Cl^-)]{HCl} HO-C_6H_4-\underset{CH_3}{\overset{CH_3}{C^+}}$$

$$\xrightarrow{C_6H_5-OH} HO-C_6H_4-\underset{CH_3}{\overset{CH_3}{C}}-C_6H_4^{+}(H)-OH \xrightarrow{Cl^-} HO-C_6H_4-\underset{CH_3}{\overset{CH_3}{C}}-C_6H_4-OH$$

Bisphenol A

Example 25 :

$$\text{2-(N(CH}_3)_2\text{)-tetrahydrofuran (2-H)} \xrightarrow{H_3O^+} HO-(CH_2)_3-CH=O + (CH_3)_2\overset{+}{N}H_2$$

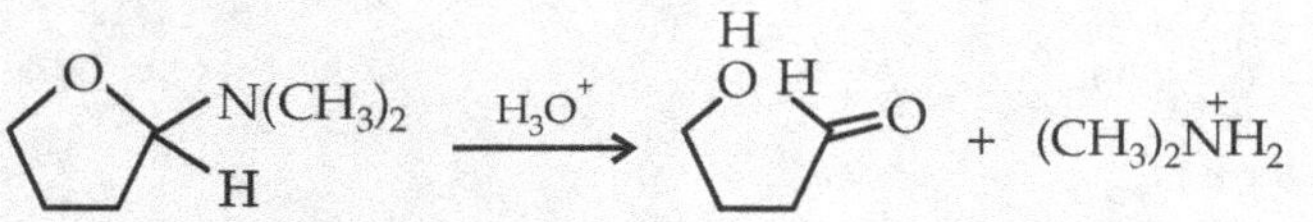

(a) **Propose a mechanism for the above hydrolysis of aminoacetals.**

(b) **Although aminoacetals are easily and quickly hydrolyzed by dilute acids, the nucleosides (having an aminoacetal functional group) which are building blocks of DNA are not easily hydrolysed. Explain.**

Solution :

(a) Tetrahydrofuranyl-$\ddot{N}Me_2$ $\xrightarrow{H_3O^+}$ protonated $\overset{+}{N}HMe_2$ $\longrightarrow$ oxocarbenium ion

Resonance stabilized carbocation

$\xrightarrow{H_2O}$ $\overset{+}{O}H_2$ adduct $\xrightarrow{-H^+}$ 2-hydroxytetrahydrofuran (–OH) $\xrightarrow{H^+}$ ring-O protonated

$\longrightarrow$ [ring-opened carbocation $\longleftrightarrow$ $=\overset{+}{O}-H$] $\xrightarrow{H_2O}$ $\equiv$ HO–$CH_2CH_2CH_2$–CHO

(b) In the nucleosides the lone pair of electrons on nitrogen (forming a part of aminoacetal functional group) is involved in aromatic sextet, hence not easily available for protonation with dilute acids. Protonation may occur with extremely strong acids.

Example 26 :

Complete the following by supplying structures to compounds A and B

$$C_6H_5CH=CHC_6H_5 \xrightarrow[KMnO_4]{\text{cold dil.}} [A] \xrightarrow{HNO_3} [B] \xrightarrow[\text{(ii) } H^+]{\text{(i) } OH^-} (C_6H_5)_2C{<}^{OH}_{COOH}$$

Propose mechanism for the conversion of compound (B) to the final product.

Solution :

(A): $C_6H_5CH(OH)-CH(OH)C_6H_5$ (B): $C_6H_5-CO-CO-C_6H_5$

$$\underset{\text{(B), Benzil}}{C_6H_5-CO-CO-C_6H_5} \xrightarrow{OH^-} C_6H_5-C(=O)-C(O^-)(OH)-C_6H_5 \xrightarrow[\text{acid rearrangement}]{\text{benzilic}} C_6H_5-C(O^-)(C_6H_5)-C(=O)-OH \xrightarrow{H^+} \underset{\text{Benzilic acid}}{(C_6H_5)_2C{<}^{OH}_{COOH}}$$

Example 27 :

Identify compounds A, B, C and D through the structure of the compound Z.

2-Methyl-1,3-dithiane $\xrightarrow[\text{(ii) A}]{\text{(i) BuLi}}$ [ ] $\xrightarrow{Hg^{2+}, H_3O^+}$ Z

[B] $\xrightarrow[\text{(ii) } (CH_3)_2S]{\text{(i) } O_3}$ Z

[E] (butyl–C(OH)(CH_3)–phenyl) $\xleftarrow[\text{(ii) } H_3O^+]{\text{(i) C}}$ Z $\xrightarrow[\text{(ii) } H_3O^+]{\text{(i) D}}$ [F] (butyl–C(OH)(CH_3)–C_6H_4–C=O ring)

Solution :

The structure of compound Z can be established with the help of the known structure of the compounds E and F with the help of following facts.

(a) Both are 3° alcohols and formed by identical reaction which seems to be Grignard reagent. Further both E and F have $CH_3CH_2CH_2CH_2$– group as common, so the compound Z can be a Grignard reagent or a ketone with *n*-butyl group as one alkyl group.

(b) Further the formation of Z from A and B suggests that Z is a ketone rather than the Grignard reagent. Thus the compound Z is hexa-2-one which explains all reactions.

Z $\xrightarrow[\text{(i) } H_3O^+]{\text{(i) } C_6H_5MgBr \text{ (C)}}$ E; Z $\xrightarrow[\text{(i) } H_3O^+]{\text{(i) D (MgBr-substituted aryl, O/O protected)}}$ F (OH, CH_3)

Formation of Z from A and B separately :

1,3-dithiane (H, CH_3) $\xrightarrow{\text{BuLi}}$ dithiane anion (CH_3) $\xrightarrow[\text{(A)}]{n\text{–}C_4H_9Br}$ dithiane (n-C_4H_9, CH_3) $\xrightarrow[H_3O^+]{Hg^{2+}}$ Z $\xleftarrow[\text{(ii) } (CH_3)_2S]{\text{(i) } O_3}$ (B) (R, R)

Example 28 :

Give steps involved in each of the following conversions.

(a) Anethole ($CH{=}CHCH_3$, OCH_3) $\longrightarrow$ Tyramine ($CH_2CH_2NH_2$, OCH_3)

(b) p-benzoquinone + butadiene $\longrightarrow$ product (OH, OH)

Solution :

(a) $CH{=}CHCH_3$ / OCH_3 $\xrightarrow[\text{(ii) } CH_3COOH]{\text{(i) } O_3, Zn}$ CHO / OCH_3 $\xrightarrow[OH^-]{CH_3NO_2}$ $CH{=}CHNO_2$ / OCH_3 $\xrightarrow{H_2 / Ni}$ $CH_2CH_2NH_2$ / OCH_3 $\xrightarrow[\text{(ii) neutralize}]{\text{(i) HI, heat}}$ $CH_2CH_2NH_2$ / OH

(b) butadiene + p-benzoquinone $\xrightarrow[\text{reaction}]{\text{Diels-Alder}}$ adduct $\xrightarrow[\text{(Diels-Alder reaction)}]{\text{butadiene}}$ diketone $\xrightarrow{NaBH_4}$ diol (OH, OH)

EXERCISE 14.1 (MCQ - ONE option correct)

1. 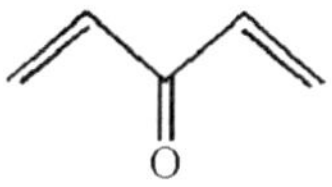 $CH_2=CH-CO-CH=CH_2$ has its IUPAC name as

(a) divinyl ketone (b) 1, 4-pentdien-3-one (c) 1, 3-penten-2-one (d) 1, 4-pentandione-3.

2. In the following reaction, the compound A is

$$[A] \xrightarrow{H_2SO_4,\ HgSO_4} CH_3CH_2COCH_3$$

(a) $HC \equiv CCH_2CH_3$ (b) $CH_3C \equiv CCH_3$
(c) Either of the two (d) $CH_3CH_2CH = CH_2$

3. $C_6H_5C \equiv CCH_3 \xrightarrow{Hg^{2+}/H^+}$ A. Here A is

(a) $C_6H_5COCH_2CH_3$ (b) $C_6H_5CH_2COCH_3$

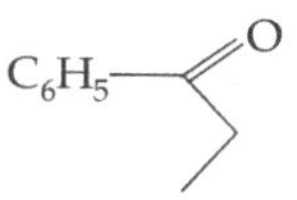

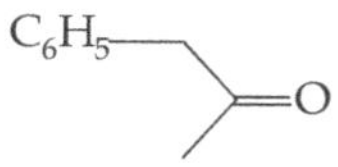

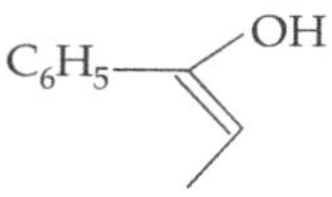

(c) $C_6H_5C(OH)=CHCH_3$ (d) $CH_3CH=C(OH)CH_3$

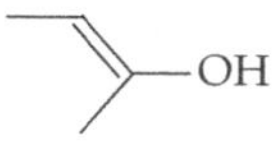

4. Carbonyl compounds show two types of important properties : nucleophilic addition and acidity of α-hydrogen atoms. Which factor is most useful in explaining these two ?

(a) Presence of carbon-oxygen double bond
(b) Resonance in carbonyl group
(c) Ability of oxygen to accommodate negative charge
(d) All are equally important.

5. Identify the end product in the following series of reactions

$$C_6H_6 + CH_3CH_2COCl \xrightarrow{AlCl_3} [B] \xrightarrow[ether]{Mg} \text{End product}$$

(a) $C_6H_5COCH_2CH_2Mg$

(b) $C_6H_5-C(OH)(CH_2CH_3)-CH_2CH_3$

(c) $CH_3CH_2-C(C_6H_5)(OH)-C(C_6H_5)(OH)-CH_2CH_3$

(d) $C_6H_5-C(OC_2H_5)_2-CH_2CH_3$

6. Identify the nature of the compound (Z).

$$\underset{\text{n-Butyl alcohol}}{CH_3CH_2CH_2CH_2OH} \xrightarrow{CrO_3/Pyridino} [X]$$

$$\xrightarrow{(CH_3)_2CHCH_2MgBr} [Y] \xrightarrow[Pyridine]{CrO_3} [Z]$$

(a) $2CH_3CH_2CH_2COOH$
(b) $CH_3CH_2CH_2COOH + (CH_3)_2CHCOOH$
(c) $CH_3CH_2CH_2COCH_2CH(CH_3)_2$
(d) $CH_3CH_2CH_2CHOHCH_2CH(CH_3)_2$.

7. An organic compound A of the molecular formula $C_5H_{10}Cl_2$ is hydrolyzed to compund B, $C_5H_{10}O$ which gives an oxime with hydroxylamine and yellow precipitate with a mixture of iodine and sodium hydroxide. The compound A should be

(a) $CH_3CH_2CCl_2CH_2CH_3$
(b) $CH_3CH_2CH_2CCl_2CH_3$
(c) $CH_3CH_2CH_2CH_2CHCl_2$
(d) $CH_3CH_2CH_2CHClCH_2Cl$.

8. Identify the nature of the reagent in the following reaction.

$$C_6H_5CH = C(CH_3)COCH_3 \xrightarrow{?} C_6H_5CH = C(CH_3)COOH$$

(a) alk. $KMnO_4$ (b) conc. HNO_3
(c) NaOI, H^+ (d) any of the three.

9. Identify the compound X in the following reaction.

$$C_6H_5COCHO \xrightarrow{OH^-} X$$

(a) $C_6H_5COCH_2OH$ (b) $C_6H_5CHOHCH_2OH$
(c) $C_6H_5CHOHCOO^-$ (d) $C_6H_5COO^- + CH_3OH$.

10. $CH_3CHO + H_2O^{18} \xrightarrow{HCl}$ Acetaldehyde. The structure of the product acetaldehyde is

(a) CH_3CHO (b) CH_3CHO^{18}
(c) A mixture of (a) & (b) (d) Reaction is not possible.

11. Observe the following two reactions, here the products (A) and (B) are

(i) $CH_3CHO + LiAlD_4 \longrightarrow [A]$

(ii) $CH_3CHO + D_2 \xrightarrow{Pt} [B]$

(a) CH_3CD_2OD (b) CH_3CHDOD
(c) CH_3CH_2OD (d) CH_3CHDOH.

12. Identify P in the reaction, 2-ethoxytetrahydropyran $\xrightarrow{H_2O,\ H^+}$ P

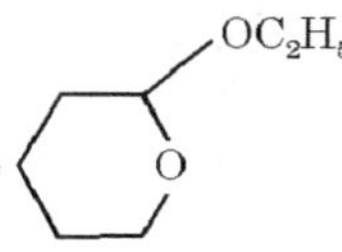

(a) $HOCH_2CH_2CH_2CH_2CH_2CH_2OH + C_2H_5OH$
(b) $OHC.CH_2CH_2CH_2CH_2CHO$
(c) $HOCH_2CH_2CH_2CH_2CHO + C_2H_5OH$
(d) No reaction.

13. Identify the product, if any, in the following chemical equation

$$\text{Cyclopentanone} + 4D_2O \xrightarrow[reflux]{KOD}$$

(a) 

(b) 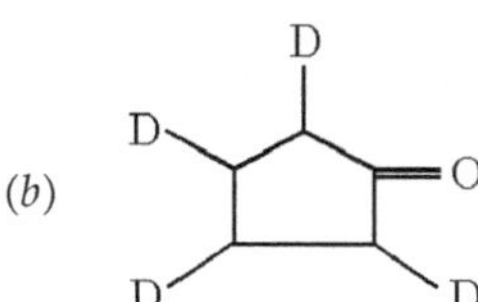

(c) 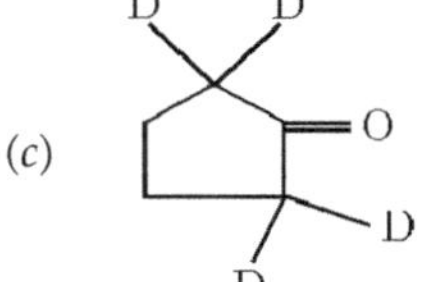

(d) No reaction takes place.

14. The most likely acid-catalysed aldol condensation products of each of the two aldehydes I and II will respectively be

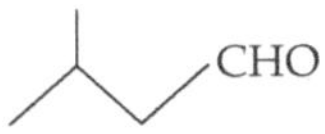

CHO (I) and CHO (II)

(*a*) OH CHO and OH CHO

(*b*) CHO and CHO

(*c*) CHO and CHO

(*d*) CHO and OH CHO

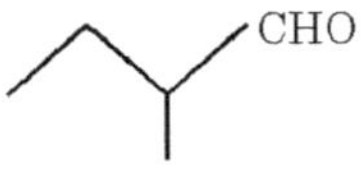

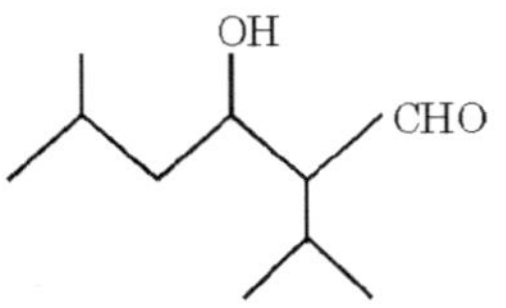

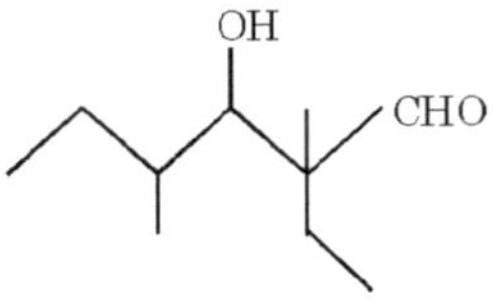

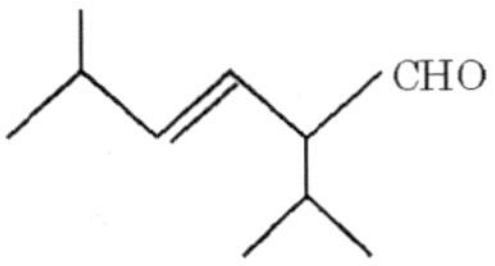

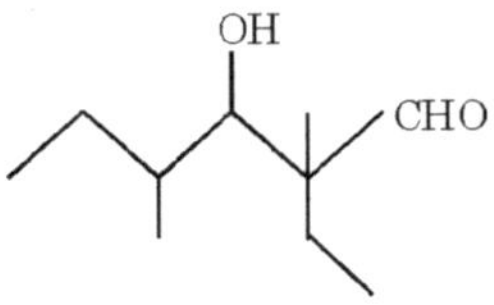

15. Identify A : O Cl $\xrightarrow{C_2H_5MgCl}$ A

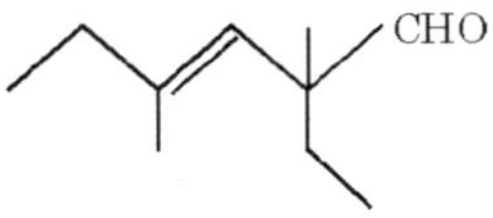

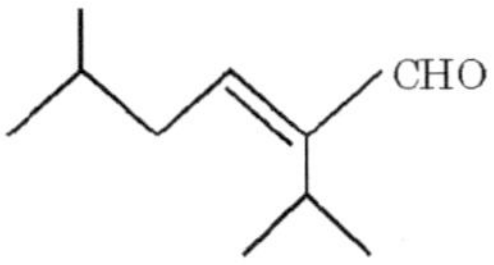

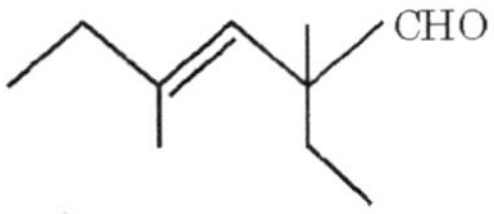

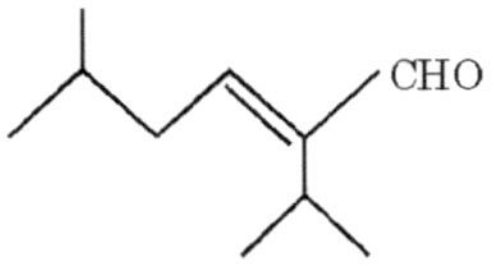

(*a*) OH Cl

(*b*) O + $MgCl_2$

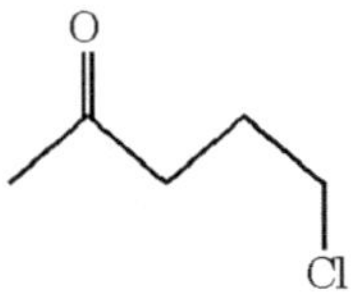

(*c*) O

(*d*) O

16. 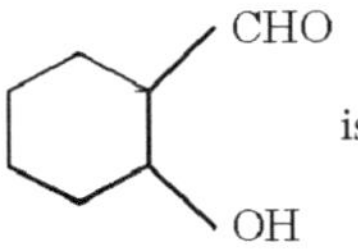 CHO OH is formed by intramolecular aldol condensation of

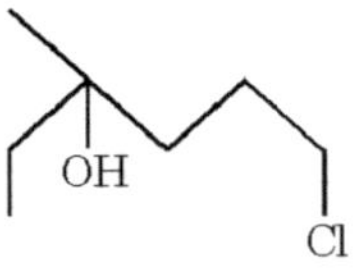

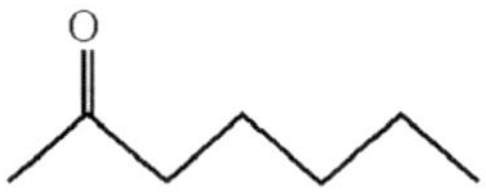

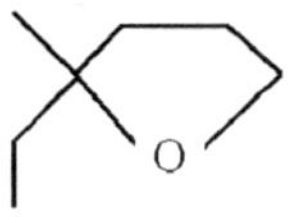

(*a*) CHO CH_2OH

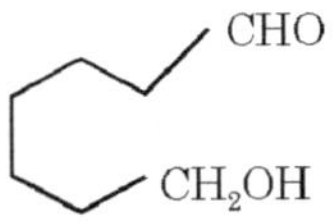

(*b*) CHO CHO

(*c*) CHO O

(*d*) O O

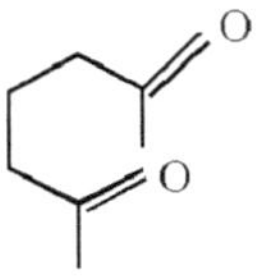

17. 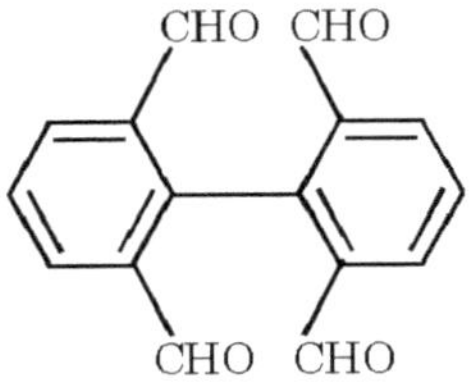 CHO CHO CHO CHO $\xrightarrow[(ii)\ H^+/H_2O]{(i)\ NaOH/100°C}$ Major product is

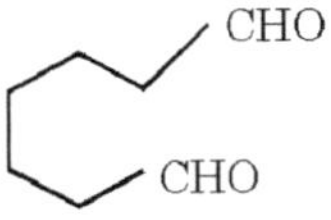

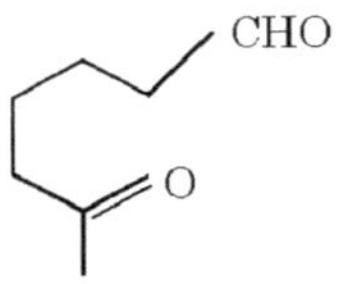

(*a*) COOH COOH COOH COOH

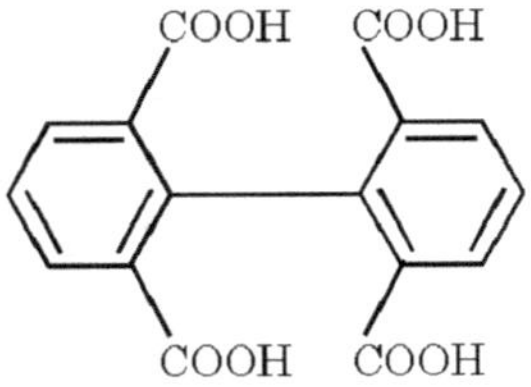

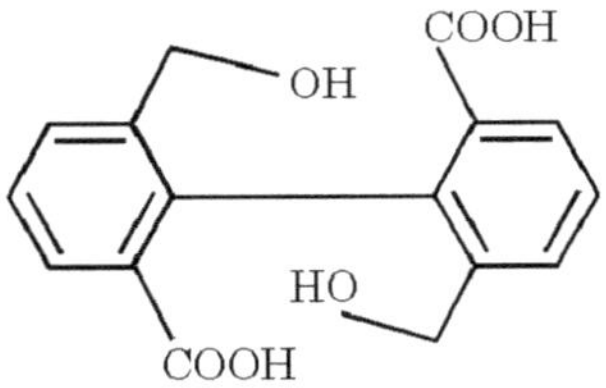

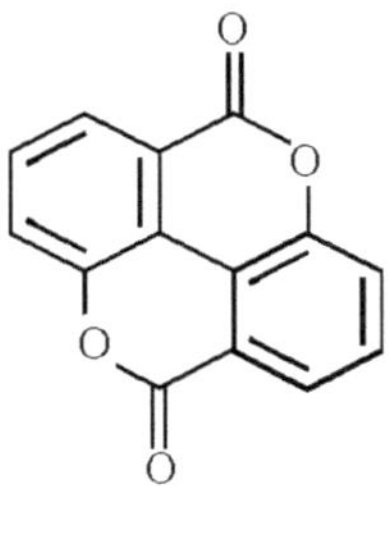

(*b*) COOH OH HO COOH

(*c*) O O O O

(*d*) CH_2OH CH_2OH CH_2OH CH_2OH

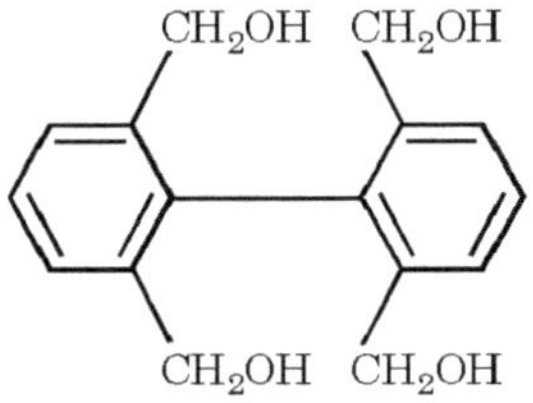

18. Which of the following will undergo hydration most readily ?

(*a*) CH_3COCH_3 (*b*) CH_3COCCl_3

(*c*) CCl_3COCCl_3 (*d*) CF_3COCF_3.

19. In the following reactions [A] and [B] respectively are

Cyclohexanone (O) $+ Cl_2 \longrightarrow$ [A] ; Cyclohexanecarbaldehyde (CHO) $+ Br_2 \xrightarrow{CHCl_3}$ [B]

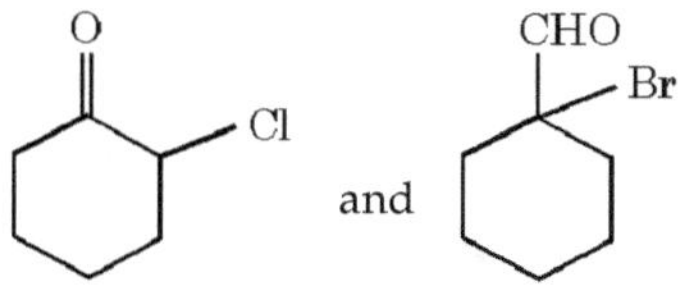

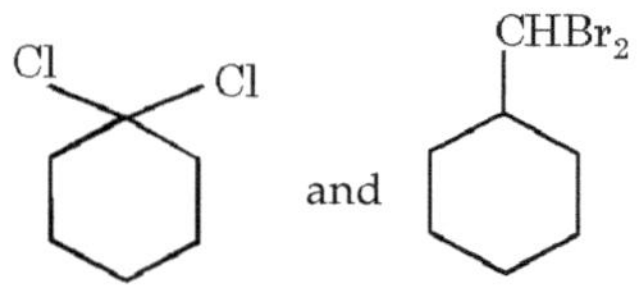

(a) O, Cl and CHO, Br

(b) O, Cl and CHO, Br

(c) Cl, Cl and $CHBr_2$

(d) O, Cl and COOH

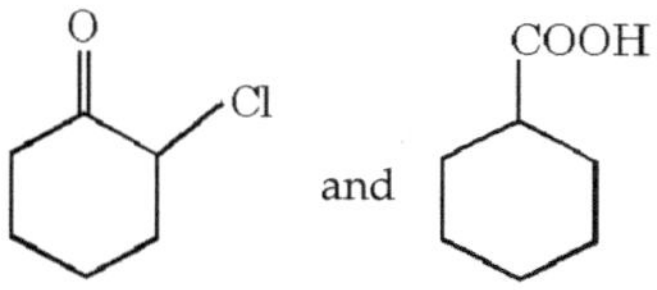

20. Acetic acid on heating gives
(a) methane (b) ethane
(c) methyl radical (d) ketene.

21. Which one is the best method for reducing 3-bromopropanal to 1-bromopropane ?

$$BrCH_2CH_2CHO \longrightarrow BrCH_2CH_2CH_3$$

(a) Wolf-Kishner reduction
(b) Clemmensen reduction
(c) Either of the two
(d) None of the two.

22. The appropriate reagent for the following transformation

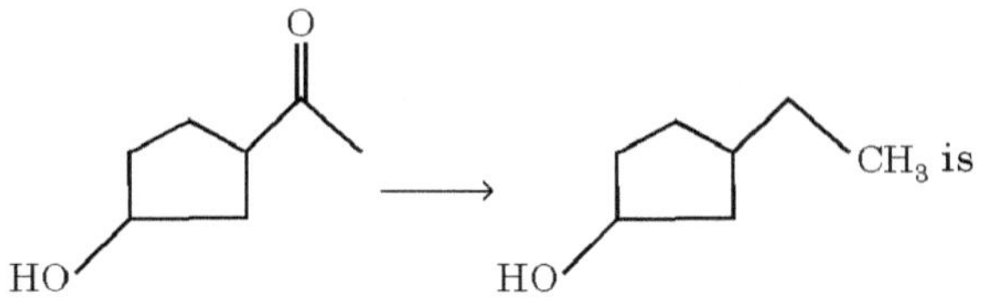

HO–cyclopentyl–C(=O)–CH$_3$ $\longrightarrow$ HO–cyclopentyl–CH$_2$–CH_3 is

(a) Zn (Hg), HCl (b) NH_2NH_2, OH^-
(c) H_2/Ni (d) $NaBH_4$.

23. Aldehydes when treated with alcohols form first hemiacetals and then acetals in the following way

$$R'-\overset{H}{\overset{|}{C}}=O + ROH \xrightarrow{H^+} R'-\overset{H}{\overset{|}{C}}-OR \xrightarrow[(-H_2O)]{H^+}$$
$$\phantom{R'-C=O+ROH \xrightarrow{H^+} R'-}\underset{|}{}\ OH$$

A hemiacetal

$$\left[R'-\overset{H}{\overset{|}{\overset{+}{C}}}-OR \longleftrightarrow R'-\overset{H}{\overset{|}{C}}=\overset{+}{O}R\right] \xrightarrow[(ii)\ -H^+]{(i)\ ROH} R'-\overset{H}{\overset{|}{C}}-OR$$
$$\qquad\text{I}\qquad\qquad\qquad\text{II}\qquad\qquad\qquad\qquad\qquad | \ OR$$

In the above reaction, which of the two cations is more stable?
(a) I (b) II
(c) Both are equally stable (d) None is stable.

24. The enol form of acetone, after treatment with D_2O gives

(a) $CH_3-\overset{OD}{\overset{|}{C}}=CH_2$ (b) $CD_3-\overset{O}{\overset{||}{C}}-CD_3$

(c) $CH_2=\overset{OH}{\overset{|}{C}}-CH_2D$ (d) $CD_2=\overset{OD}{\overset{|}{C}}-CD_3$

25. How many α hydrogens are present in benzyl methyl ketone,
(a) 3 (b) 4 (c) 5 (d) No

26. In the Cannizzaro reaction, given below,

$$2C_6H_5CHO \xrightarrow{OH^-} C_6H_5CH_2OH + C_6H_5COO^-$$

the slowest step is
(a) the attack of OH^- at the carbonyl group
(b) the transfer of hydride to the carbonyl group
(c) the abstraction of proton from the carboxylic acid
(d) the deprotonation of $C_6H_5CH_2OH$.

27. Among the following compounds, which will react with acetone to give product containing >C = N –.
(a) $C_6H_5NHCOCH_3$ (b) $(CH_3)_3N$
(c) $C_6H_5NHC_6H_5$ (d) $C_6H_5NHNH_2$.

28. $C_6H_5CH(OH)CH(OH)CH_3 \xrightarrow{H^+}$ [A]. Here [A] is
(a) $C_6H_5CH = CHCH_3$ (b) $C_6H_5CH = C(OH)CH_3$
(c) $C_6H_5COCH_2CH_3$ (d) $C_6H_5CH_2COCH_3$.

29. $C_6H_{11}Cl \xrightarrow[(ii)\ Li,\ (iii)\ CuLi]{(i)\ Mg,\ ether}$ [A] $\xrightarrow{CH_3CH_2COCl}$ [B].

The compund B is

(a) $C_6H_{11}-\underset{CH_2CH_3}{\underset{|}{\overset{OH}{\overset{|}{C}}}}-CH_2CH_3$ (b) $C_6H_{11}COCH_2CH_3$

(c) $C_6H_{11}CH_2COCH_3$ (d) $C_6H_{11}CH_2CH_2CHO$.

30. Which of the following compunds is oxidised to prepare methyl ethyl ketone ?
(a) 2-Propanol (b) 1-Butanol
(c) 2-Butanol (d) *tert*-Butyl alcohol.

31. The product formed by the reaction of chlorine with C_6H_5CHO in the absence of catalyst is
(a) chlorobenzene (b) benzyl chloride
(c) benzoyl chloride (d) *o*-chlorobenzaldehyde.

32. Which alkene is formed from the following ylide carbonyl pair ?
$CH_3CH_2CH_2CH = PPh_3$ + 2-Butanone
(a) 3-Methyl-3-heptene (b) 4-Methyl-3-heptene (c) 5-Methyl-3-heptene (d) 1-Methyl-5-heptene.

33. An organic compound A has the molecular formula C_3H_6O. It undergoes iodoform test. When saturated with HCl it gives B of molecular formula $C_9H_{14}O$; A and B respectively are
(a) propanal and mesitylene
(b) propanone and mesityl oxide
(c) propanone and 2, 6-dimethyl-2, 5-heptadien-4-one
(d) propane and mesitylene oxide.

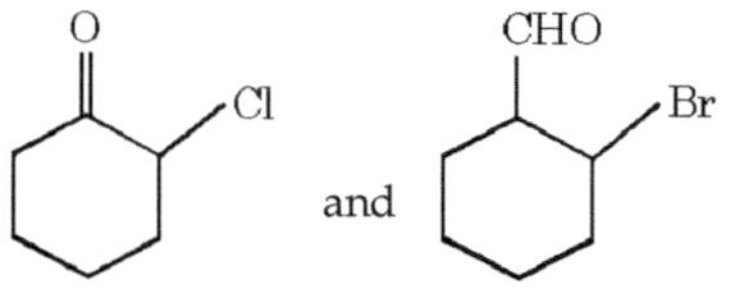

34. Compound A (molecular formula C_3H_8O) is treated with acidified dichromate to form a product B (molecular formulae C_3H_6O). B forms a shining silver mirror on warming with ammonical silver nitrate.B when treated with an aqueous solution of $H_2NCONHNH_2HCl$ and sodium acetate gives a product C. Identify the structure of C
(a) $CH_3CH_2CH = NNHCONH_2$
(b) $(CH_3)_2C = NNHCONH_2$
(c) $(CH_3)_2C = NCONHNH_2$
(d) $CH_3CH_2CH = NCONHNH_2$.

35. Identify the final product (D).

$$C_6H_5CH_3 + (CH_2CO)_2O \xrightarrow{AlCl_3} [A] \xrightarrow[HCl]{Zn/Hg} [B] \xrightarrow{HF} [C] \xrightarrow[(ii)\ H_3O^+]{(i)\ CH_3MgI} [D]$$

(a) CH_3, OH, CH_3 (b) CH_3, CH_3, OH

(c) H_3C, CH_3, OH (d) H_3C, CH_3, OH

36. Identify the final product [E]

$$C_6H_6 \xrightarrow{Br_2/Fe} [A] \xrightarrow{(CH_3CO)_2O,\ AlCl_3} [B] \xrightarrow{CH_3OH/HCl} [C] \xrightarrow[(ii)\ D_2O]{(i)\ Mg} [D] \xrightarrow{H_3O^+} [E]$$

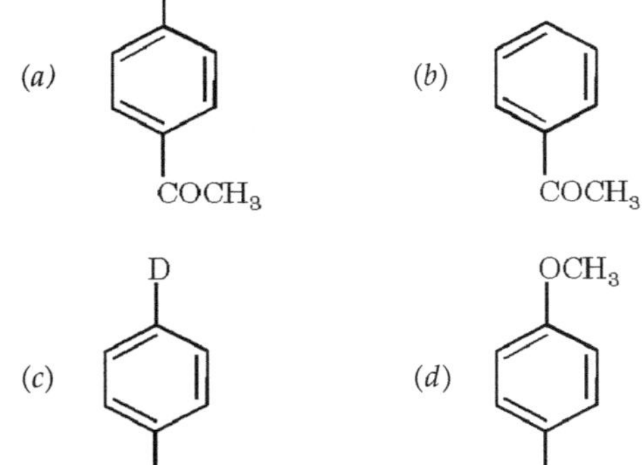

37. Identify the final product D in the following reaction.

$$\text{CH}_2\text{=CHCH}_2\text{OH} \xrightarrow{C_6H_6,\ HF} [A] \xrightarrow{H_2/Pt} [B] \xrightarrow{NBS} [C] \xrightarrow{alc.\ KOH} [D].$$

(a) (b)

(c) Both (d) None.

38. Which compound(s) does(do) not undergo **Cannizzaro condensation?**

(a) Methanal (b) Trichloroacetaldehyde
(c) Benzaldehyde (d) Ethanal

39. Treatment of propionaldehyde with dil. NaOH solution gives

(a) $CH_3CH_2COOCH_2CH_2CH_3$
(b) $CH_3CH_2CH(OH).CH(CH_3).CHO$
(c) $CH_3CH_2CHOHCH_2CH_2CHO$
(d) $CH_3CH_2COCH_2CH_2CHO$

40. Which of the following forces explain the boiling point of aldehydes and ketones?

(a) Hydrogen bonding (b) Vander waal
(c) Dipole-dipole attraction (d) Any other

41. Which of the following will give yellow precipitate with I_2/NaOH?

(a) $ICH_2COCH_2CH_3$ (b) $CH_3COOCOCH_3$
(c) CH_3CONH_2 (d) $CH_3CH(OH)CH_2CH_3$

42. Which of the following reactants on reaction with conc. NaOH followed by acidification gives adjacent lactone as the product?

(a) COOCH$_3$, COOH (b) COOH, CHO
(c) COOH, COOH (d) CHO, CHO

43. The smallest ketone and its next homologue are reacted with NH_2OH to form oxime

(a) Two different oximes are formed
(b) Three different oximes are formed
(c) Two oximes formed are optically active
(d) All oximes formed are optically active

44. Cyclohexene on ozonolysis followed by reaction with zinc dust and water gives compound **E**. Compound **E** on further treatment with aqueous KOH yields compound **F**. Compound **F** is

(a) CHO (b) CHO
(c) COOH (d) CO_2H, CO_2H

45. In the following reaction sequence, the correct structures of E, F and G are

$$\text{PhCOCH}_2\overset{*}{\text{C}}\text{OOH} \xrightarrow{Heat} [E] \xrightarrow[NaOH]{I_2} [F] + [G]$$

[* implies ^{13}C labelled carbon)

(a) E = $Ph\overset{*}{C}OCH_3$ F = $Ph\overset{*}{C}OO^{\ominus}Na^{\oplus}$ G = CHI_3
(b) E = $PhCO\overset{*}{C}H_3$ F = $Ph\overset{*}{C}OO^{\ominus}Na^{\oplus}$ G = CHI_3
(c) E = $PhCO\overset{*}{C}H_3$ F = $PhCOO^{\ominus}Na^{\oplus}$ G = $\overset{*}{C}HI_3$
(d) E = $PhCO\overset{*}{C}H_3$ F = $PhCOO^{\ominus}Na^{\oplus}$ G = $\overset{*}{C}H_3I$

46. Cyclohexanone $+ Ph_2P=CH_2 \longrightarrow (X)$

Product (X) is

(a) PPh_3 (=)cyclohexane   (b) CH_2 (=)cyclohexane

(c) 1-methylcyclohexene   (d) methylcyclohexane

47. $HC\equiv CH \xrightarrow[H_2SO_4]{HgSO_4} (A) \xrightarrow[5°C]{dil.\ \overset{\ominus}{O}H} (B)$

Give the IUPAC name of "B" is

(a) 2-butenal (b) 3-hydroxybutanal
(c) 3-formyl-2-propanol (d) 4-oxo-2-propanol

48. p-($C-Cl$ with $C=O$)-C$_6$H$_4$-CHO $\xrightarrow[(ii)\ H_2O]{(i)\ CdMe_2}$

Product is

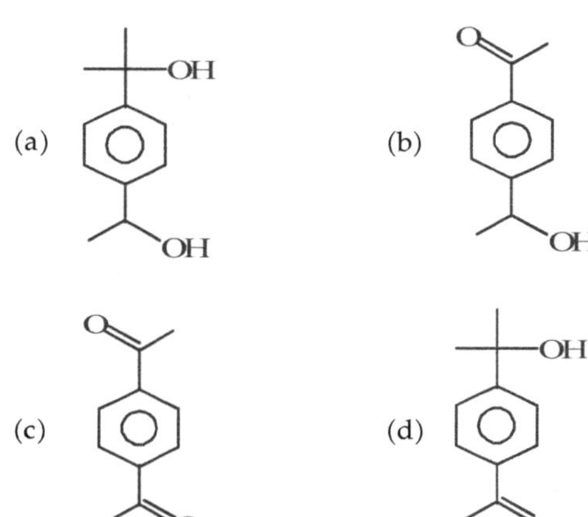

49. Cyclodecane-1,6-dione $\xrightarrow[H_2O]{Mg/Hg} A \xrightarrow[\Delta]{H_3/PO_4} B$

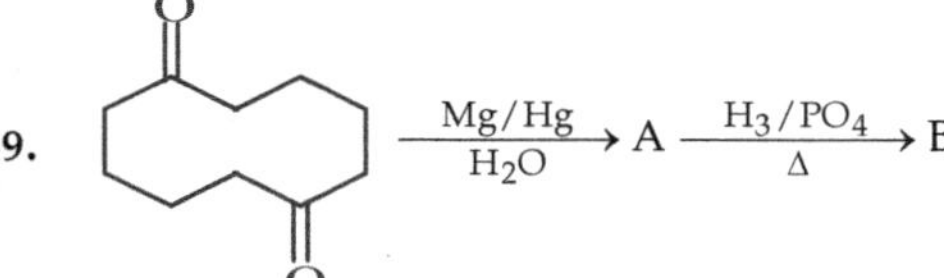

B is

(a) Bicyclo-[4, 4, 0] deca-1, 6-diene
(b) Cyclodecanone
(c) Spiro-[4, 5]-decan-6-one
(d) Bicyclo-[4, 4, 0] deca-1, 5-diene

50. 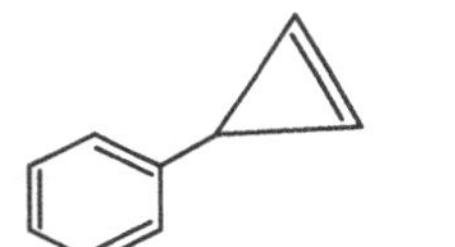 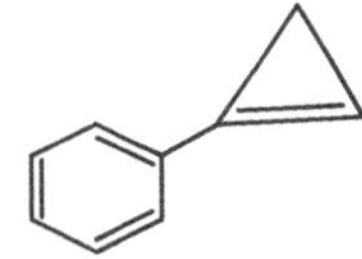

To distinguish between the above isomeric hydrocarbons molecules, which will work best ?

(a) Bromine water test
(b) O_3/H_2O, heating and passing evolved gas through lime water
(c) O_3/H_2O, Δ, $I_2/NaOH$
(d) Tollen's test

51. Which of the following sequence of reagents can best be utilized for the given transformation ?

$R-C(=O)H \longrightarrow R-C(=O)D$

(a) Cl_2, AcOH; D_2O; $LiAlH_4/H_2O$
(b) D_2O/D_3O^+, Cl_2, AcOH; $NaBH_4/H_2O$
(c) H_2C-SH / H_2C-SH, base; D_2O and then $HgCl_2/CdCO_3-H_2O$
(d) Base, H_2C-SH / H_2C-SH, $HgCl_2/CdCO_3-H_2O$ and then D_2O

52. In a Cannizzaro reaction, the intermediate that will be the best hydride donor is

(a) $C_6H_5-C(H)(OH)-O^{\ominus}$ (b) $C_6H_5-C(H)(O^{\ominus})-O^{\ominus}$

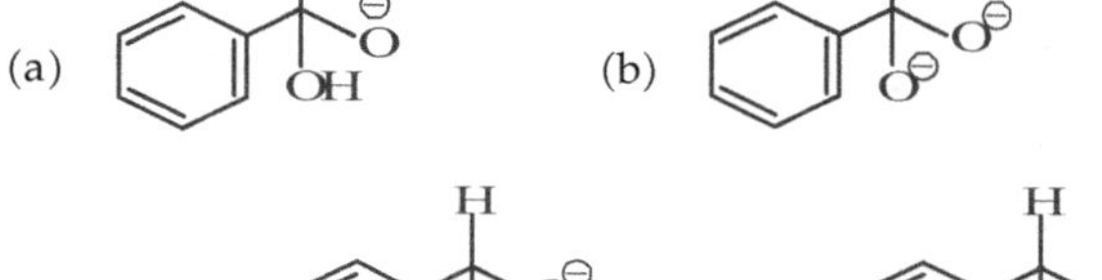

(c) H_3CO (d) O_2N

53. Which will form(s) stable gem-diol ?

I. $Ph-\underset{O}{\underset{\|}{C}}-\underset{O}{\underset{\|}{C}}-\underset{O}{\underset{\|}{C}}-Ph$ II. CCl_3CHO

III. Indane-1,2,3-trione (ninhydrin skeleton)   IV. $Ph-\underset{O}{\underset{\|}{C}}-\underset{O}{\underset{\|}{C}}-Ph$

V. $H-\overset{O}{\overset{\|}{C}}-H$

(a) I, II, III, V only (b) I, II, III, IV only
(c) II, III, IV only (d) II, III,

54. In Cannizaro reaction which species is best hydride donor (in conc. alkaline medium)

(a) $H-\overset{O}{\overset{\|}{C}}-O^-$ (b) $H-\underset{OH}{\underset{|}{\overset{O^-}{\overset{|}{C}}}}-H$

(c) $H-\underset{O^-}{\underset{|}{\overset{O^-}{\overset{|}{C}}}}-H$ (d) $H_5C_6-\underset{O^-}{\underset{|}{\overset{O^-}{\overset{|}{C}}}}-H$

55. The $K_{eq.}$ value in HCN addition to the following aldehydes are in the order :

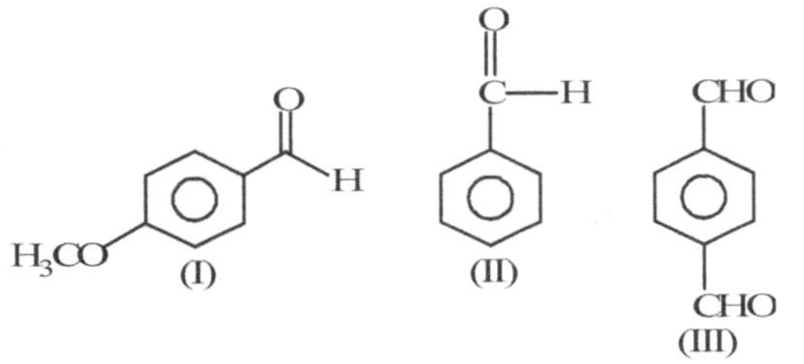

(I) H_3CO–C_6H_4–CHO (II) C_6H_5–CHO (III) OHC–C_6H_4–CHO

(a) I > II > III (b) III > II > I
(c) III > I > II (d) II < I > III

56. The major product obtained in the reaction :

$$H_5C_6-\overset{O}{\overset{\|}{C}}-\overset{CH_3}{\overset{|}{C}H}-CH_3 + D_2O \xrightarrow[\text{room temp.}]{OD^-}$$

is

(a) $H_5C_6-\overset{O}{\overset{\|}{C}}-\overset{CD_3}{\overset{|}{C}}HCH_3$ (b) $H_5C_6-\overset{O}{\overset{\|}{C}}-\overset{CD_3}{\overset{|}{C}}D-CD_3$

(c) $H_5C_6-\overset{O}{\overset{\|}{C}}-\underset{CH_3}{\underset{|}{C}}D-CH_3$ (d) None of these

57. The reacion

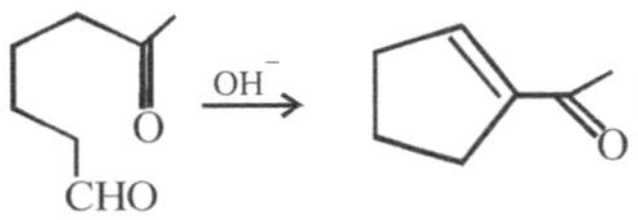

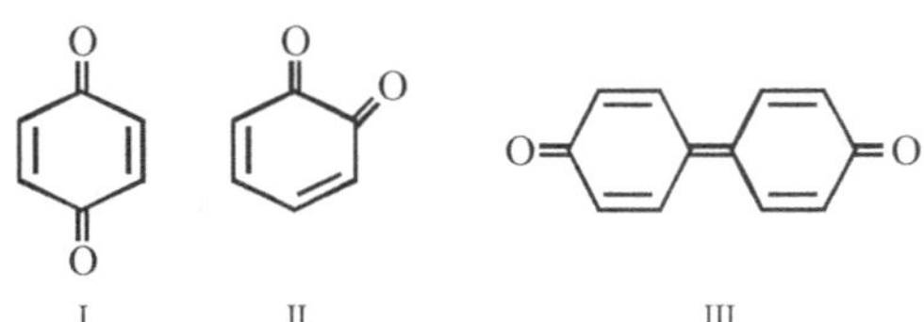

is an example of

(a) oxidation reaction (b) reduction
(c) both (d) aldol condensation

58. A new carbon - carbon bond is formed in

Aldol condensation (I) Kolbe's reaction (II)
Reimer-Tiemann reaction (III) Wurtz-Fittig reaction (IV)

(a) I, III (b) II, III
(c) I, III, IV (d) All the four

59. The correct stability order of the following three quinones is

I II III

(a) I > III > II (b) I = III > II
(c) I = II > III (d) III > I > II

60. Ninhydrin has three keto groups, which of the keto group is expected to be hydrated most easily?

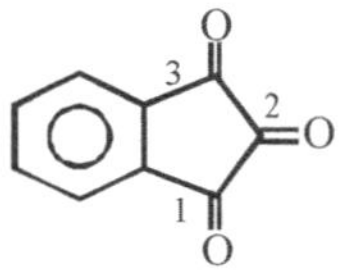

(a) 2 (b) 3
(c) 1 (d) all equal

61.
$$2\ \begin{matrix}CHO\\|\\COOH\end{matrix} \xrightarrow{OH^-} \begin{matrix}COO^-\\|\\CH_2OH\end{matrix} + \begin{matrix}COO^-\\|\\COO^-\end{matrix}$$

The above reaction can said be to an example of
(a) intramolecular Cannizzaro reaction
(b) intermolecular Cannizzaro reaction
(c) crossed Cannizzaro reaction
(d) Tischenko reaction

62. Which of the following complex hydride is a stronger reducing agent ?

(a) $Li^+[AlH_4]^-$ (b) $Li^+[Al(OCMe_3)_3H]^-$
(c) $Al(CH_2CHMe_2)_2H$ (d) All are equal

63.

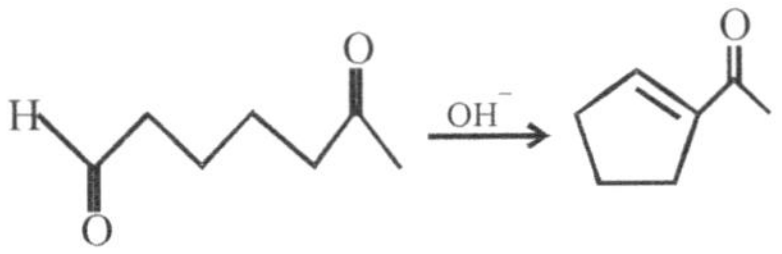

The above reaction involves

(a) 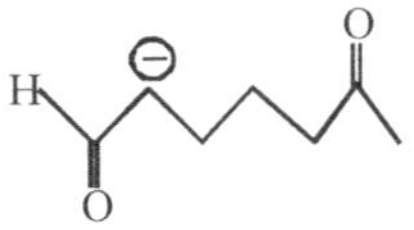 (b)

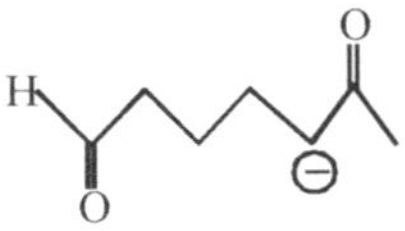

(c) 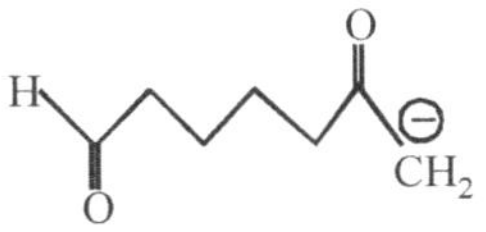 (d)

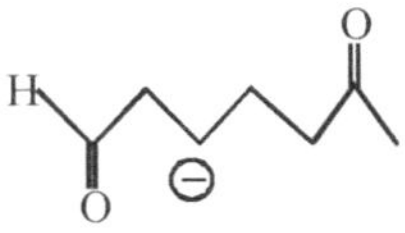

64. $CH_3CHO + 4HCHO \xrightarrow{Ca(OH)_2} C(CH_2OH)_4 + \frac{1}{2}(HCOO)_2Ca$

the above reaction is an example of
(a) aldol condensation (b) Cannizzaro reaction
(c) both (d) none

65. Which of the following can't be prepared by the direct of Reimer –Tiemann reaction ?

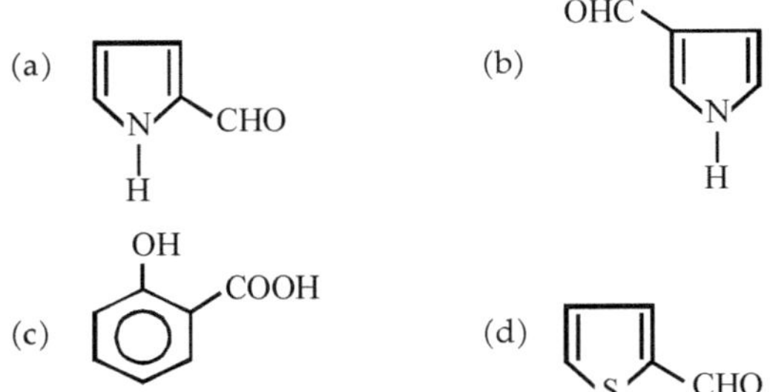

(a) (b)

(c) (d)

66. Cannizzaro reaction between formaldehyde molecules involves the formation of

(a) $H-\overset{OH}{\overset{|}{C}}-H$ with O^- below (b) $H-\overset{O^-}{\overset{|}{C}}-H$ with O^- below

(c) Both (a) and (b) (d) none

67.

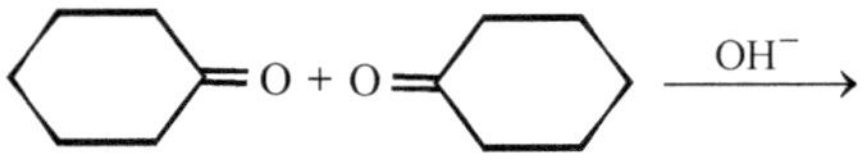

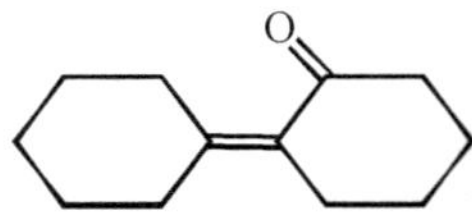

This reaction is an example of
(a) Aldol condensation (b) Cannizzaro reaction
(c) Claisen condensation (d) Wittig reaction

EXERCISE 14.2 (MCQ 1 or >1 option correct, Passage based, Matching, A/R)

DIRECTIONS for Q. 1 to Q. 50 : Multiple choice questions with one or more than one correct option(s).

1. Which of the following statement is true regarding the following chemical reaction ?

$$CH_3CHO \xrightarrow{HCN} CH_3CHOHCN$$

(*a*) The product on hydrolysis gives a mixture of two compounds :
(*b*) The product is a mixture of two compounds which can be separated by fractional distillation.
(*c*) The product is a mixture of two compounds which can't be separated by fractional distillation.
(*d*) The product on hydrolysis gives a single compound.

2. One mole of $C_6H_5COCH_2CH_3$ is treated with one mole of Br_2 in basic solution, the product(s) formed is (are)
(*a*) 1 mole of $C_6H_5COCBr_2CH_3$
(*b*) 1 mole of $C_6H_5COCHBrCH_2Br$
(*c*) 0.5 mole of $C_6H_5COCBr_2CH_3$
(*d*) 0.5 mole of unreacted $C_6H_5COCH_2CH_3$.

3. Pentaerythritol, an important industrial chemical, is prepared by the following reaction

$$4CH_2O + CH_3CHO \xrightarrow{Ca[OH]_2} CH_2OH\text{—}C(CH_2OH)_2\text{—}CH_2OH$$

Pentaerythritol

This reaction involves
(*a*) Cannizzaro reaction (*b*) aldol condensation
(*c*) Crossed Cannizzaro (*d*) crossed aldol condensation

4. A mixture of cinnamaldehyde and crotonaldehyde is treated with concentrated alkali,

$$C_6H_5\overset{\beta}{C}H = \overset{\alpha}{C}HCHO + \overset{\gamma}{C}H_3\overset{\beta}{C}H = \overset{\alpha}{C}HCHO \xrightarrow{OH^-}$$

which statement is not true about the above reaction ?
(*a*) Aldol condensation takes place and α-carbon atom of crotonaldehyde provides the carbanion,
(*b*) Aldol condensation takes place and β-carbon atom of crotonaldehyde provides the carbanion.
(*c*) Aldol condensation takes place and γ-carbon atom of crotonaldehyde provides the carbanion.
(*d*) Aldol condensation takes place and α-carbon atom of cinnamic aldehyde provides the carbanion.

5. Which of the following undergoes Cannizzaro reaction ?
(*a*) $(CH_3)_3C.CHO$ (*b*) $(CH_3)_3CCDO$
(*c*) $C_6H_5CH_2Cl$ (*d*) CH_3CHO

6. Each of the following two ketones is treated with a base (KOH)

$$(+)-C_6H_5\text{—}\overset{O}{\overset{\|}{C}}\text{—}\overset{CH_3}{\overset{|}{C}H}\text{—}C_6H_5 \xrightarrow{OH^-} P_I;$$

I

$$(+)-C_6H_5\text{—}\overset{O}{\overset{\|}{C}}\text{—}\underset{C_2H_5}{\underset{|}{\overset{CH_3}{\overset{|}{C}}}}\text{—}C_6H_5 \xrightarrow{OH^-} P_{II}$$

II

Which of the following statement is false regarding above reactions?
(*a*) Both P_I as well as P_{II} are racemic mixtures
(*b*) Both P_I as well as P_{II} are optically pure enantiomers
(*c*) P_I is optically pure while P_{II} is a racemic mixture
(*d*) P_I is a racemic mixture while P_{II} is optically pure.

7. Predict the nature of products

CHO, Cl (meta) $\xrightarrow{\text{Conc. KOH}}$ A + B

(*a*) COO^-K^+, OH (*b*) COO^-K^+, Cl

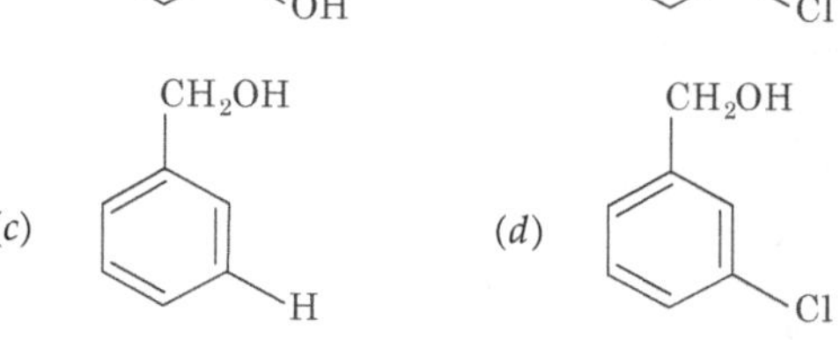

(*c*) CH_2OH, H (*d*) CH_2OH, Cl

8. Which of the following can be used for the preparation of chloroform?
(a) $C_6H_5CHCl_2$ (b) CH_3CHO
(c) CD_3COCH_3 (d) CCl_3CHO

9. The product of acid hydrolysis of P and Q can't be distinguished by

$OCOCH_3$, CH_3 (P) CH_3, $OCOCH_3$ (Q)

(*a*) Lucas reagent (*b*) 2, 4-DNP
(*c*) Fehling solution (*d*) $NaHSO_3$.

10. Acetaldehyde is obtained in the reactions

(a) $CH_2 = CH-CH_2-CH = CH_2 \xrightarrow[2.\ Zn,\ H_2O]{1.\ O_3}$

(b) $CH_3CH=$ (ring) $\xrightarrow[2.\ Zn,\ H_2O]{1.\ O_3}$

(c) $HC \equiv CH + H_2O \xrightarrow[H_2SO_4]{HgSO_4}$

(d) $CH_3COCl + H_2O \xrightarrow{Pd\text{-}BaSO_4}$

11. Which of the following statements are correct about a carbonyl group?
(a) The carbonyl carbon is sp^2–hybridized
(b) The carbonyl carbon is sp^3–hybridized
(c) The three groups attached to the carbonyl carbon lie in different planes
(d) The three groups attached to the carbonyl carbon lie in the same plane

12. Phosphorus pentachloride reacts with
(a) alcohols (b) ketones
(c) ethers (d) amines

13. Which of the following aldehydes undergo aldol condensation?
(a) CH_3CHO (b) C_6H_5CHO
(c) $C_6H_5CH_2CHO$ (d) p–ClC_6H_4CHO

14. Which of the following do not undergo base catalysed aldol condensation?
(a) Benzaldehyde
(b) 2,2, dimethyl propionaldehyde
(c) 2-methyl propionaldehyde
(d) p-methylbenzaldehyde

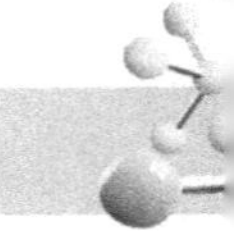

15. Which of the following statements are correct about the C = O bond?
(a) It is made up of one π-bond and one σ-bond
(b) It is used the sp^2-hybrid orbital of carbon for its formation
(c) It is planar in nature
(d) It undergoes addition reactions

16. Which compound(s) undergoes (undergo) aldol condensation?
(a) Acetaldehyde (b) Benzaldehyde
(c) Phenylacetaldehyde (d) Ethylmethyl ketone

17. Dry distillation of a mixture of calcium acetate and calcium formate can form
(a) acetone (b) formaldehyde
(c) acetaldehyde (d) propanone

18. Which of the following are generally used for preparing derivatives of aldehydes and ketones?
(a) Hydroxylamine hydrochloride
(b) 2,4-Dinitrophenylhydrazine
(c) Phenylhydrazine hydrochloride
(d) Hydrogen cyanide

19. Base catalysed aldol condensation occurs with :
(a) propionaldehyde
(b) benzaldehyde
(c) 2-Methyl propionaldehyde
(d) 2, 2-Dimethyl propionaldehyde

20. Which of the following compounds will give a yellow precipitate with iodine and alkali?
(a) 2-Hydroxy propane (b) Acetophenone
(c) Methyl acetate (d) Acetamide

21. Which of the following compounds will react with ethanolic KCN?
(a) Ethyl chloride (b) Acetyl chloride
(c) Chlorobenzene (d) Benzaldehyde

22. Keto-enol tautomerism is observed in
(a) $H_5C_6-\overset{O}{\overset{\|}{C}}-H$ (b) $H_5C_6-\overset{O}{\overset{\|}{C}}-CH_3$
(c) $H_5C_6-\overset{O}{\overset{\|}{C}}-C_6H_5$ (d) $H_5C_6-\overset{O}{\overset{\|}{C}}-CH_2-CH_2-CH_3$

23. Which of the following are the examples of aldol condensation?
(a) $2CH_3CHO \xrightarrow{\text{dil. NaOH}} CH_3CHOHCH_2CHO$
(b) $2CH_3COCH_3 \xrightarrow{\text{dil. NaOH}} (CH_3)_2COHCH_2COCH_3$
(c) $2HCHO \xrightarrow{\text{dil. NaOH}} CH_3OH$
(d) $C_6H_5CHO + HCHO \xrightarrow{\text{dil. NaOH}} C_6H_5CH_2OH$

24. A new carbon-carbon bond formation is possible in
(a) Cannizzaro reaction (b) Friedel–Crafts alkylation
(c) Clemmensen reduction (d) Reimer–Tiemann reaction

25. Which of the following will undergo aldol condensation?
(a) Acetaldehyde (b) Propanaldehyde
(c) Benzaldehyde (d) Trideuteroacetaldehyde

26. Among the following compounds, which will react with acetone to give a product containing > C = N –bond ?
(a) $C_6H_5NH_2$ (b) $(CH_3)_3N$
(c) $C_6H_5NHC_6H_5$ (d) $C_6H_5NHNH_2$.

27. Select correct statements :
(a) [benzene ring]–OH and [cyclohexene ring]–OH both give colour with neutral $FeCl_3$ solution
(b) 2-Pentanone and 3-pentanone are position isomers as well as metamers
(c) When benzaldehyde reacts with hydroxylamine product formed shows geometrical isomerism
(d) 1, 2-Dibromocyclohexane shows geometrical and optical isomerism

28. [cyclohexane]=O ⟶ [cyclohexane] ; This change can be carried out using:
(a) NH_2NH_2, glycol/OH^- (b) Sn(Hg)/conc. HCl
(c) P/HI (d) $NH_3/LiAlH_4$

29. In which cases products formed are not according to reaction?
(a) [cyclopentane]–OH + $HNO_3 \xrightarrow{H_2SO_4}$ [cyclopentane]–NO_2
(b) [cyclohexane]–OH + $HNO_3 \xrightarrow{H_2SO_4}$ [cyclohexane]–ONO_2
(c) $CH_2 = CH - CHO + LiAlH_4 \longrightarrow CH_3CH_2CH_2OH$
(d) $(CH_3)_3C$–Cl + $CH_3ONa \longrightarrow (CH_3)_3C$–O – CH_3

30. Which of the following compounds will give haloform test?

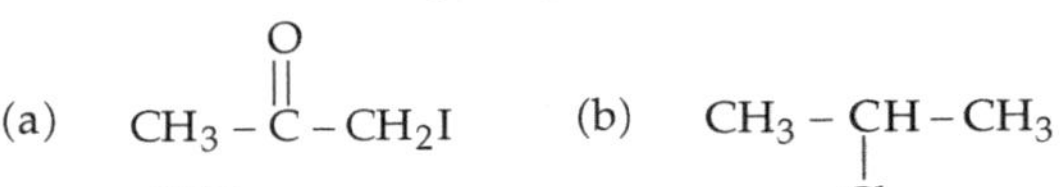

(a) $CH_3-\overset{O}{\overset{\|}{C}}-CH_2I$ (b) $CH_3-\underset{Cl}{\underset{|}{CH}}-CH_3$
(c) [benzene ring]$-\underset{O}{\underset{\|}{C}}-CH_3$ (d) CH_3CH_2Br

31. [cyclohexane]=O $\xrightarrow[\text{or reagent R}]{\text{reaction R}}$ [cyclohexane] ; R can be :

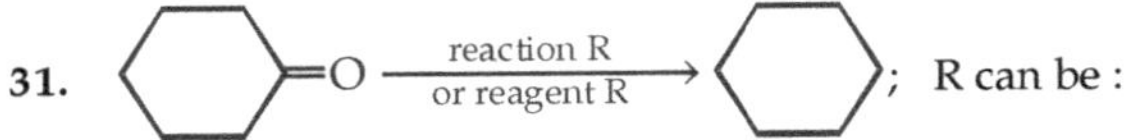

(a) Wolf Kischner reduction (b) Clemmensen reduction
(c) (P + HI) mixture (d) Rosen mund reduction

32. Cannizzaro reaction will be given by :
(a) [cyclohexane]–CHO (b) [cyclohexene]–CHO
(c) [benzene ring]–CHO (d) CCl_3CHO

33. $CH_3-\overset{O}{\overset{\|}{C}}-CH_3 \xrightarrow{SeO_2} A$; A will :
(a) reduce Tollens reagent (b) give iodoform test
(c) form dioxime (d) give Cannizzaro reaction

34. $3CH_3-\overset{O}{\overset{\|}{C}}-CH_3 \xrightarrow{\text{conc. } H_2SO_4} A$; which is/are correc statement(s) about A :
(a) A is an aromatic compound
(b) A can be oxidised to carboxylic acid
(c) A can undergo free radical as well as electrophili substitution reaction
(d) A contains two carbonyl group

35. Identify the set from the following which contains the tw compounds each of which can form acetone in a single-step reaction
(a) $CH_3CH(OH)CH_3$, $(CH_3)_2C = CH_2$
(b) $(CH_3COO)_2Ca$, $(CH_3)_2C = CH_2$
(c) $(CH_3COO)_2Ca$, $CH_3C \equiv CH$
(d) $CH_3C \equiv CH$, $CH_3C(Cl)_2CH_3$

36. $CH \equiv CH \xrightarrow{HgSO_4/H_2SO_4} B \xleftarrow{\text{reaction R}} A$. A, B an reaction R are :
(a) $CH_3-\overset{O}{\overset{\|}{C}}-Cl$, CH_3CHO, Rosenmund (Pd/$BaSO_4$, H_2)
(b) CH_3COOH, $LiAlH_4$, hydroboration oxidation
(c) CH_3CN, CH_3CHO, Stephen ($SnCl_2$ / HCl)
(d) $CH \equiv CH$, CH_3CHO, hydroboration oxidation

37. Which is/are correct statement(s)?
(a) In presence of conc. H_2SO_4, CH_3CHO changes to cyclic trimer-paraldehyde which is a *hypnotic*
(b) At room temperature, HCHO forms cyclic trimer-trioxan
(c) In presence of $Ba(OH)_2$, HCHO forms hexose
(d) Bakelite is the polymer of HCHO and urea

38. $3HCHO + CH_3CHO \xrightarrow{NaOH} A$; A formed can :
(a) reduce Tollen's reagent
(b) give Cannizzaro reaction
(c) react with Na
(d) give green colour with $Cr_2O_7^{2-} / H^+$

39. A formed in previous question further reacts with NaOH to give:
(a) $HOH_2C-C(CH_2OH)_2-CH_2OH$ by reduction (I)
(b) $HOH_2C-C(CH_2OH)_2-COONa$ by oxidation (II)
(c) only I (d) only II

40. Which are correct statements :
(a) Cannizzaro reaction is proton-hydride transfer reaction
(b) Hofmann-degradation of acid amide involves intramolecular migration of alkyl/aryl group from C to N
(c) Fries migration is intramolecular
(d) Cannizzaro reaction is disproportionation

41. m-Chlorobenzaldehyde on reaction with conc. KOH at room temperature gives
(a) potassium m-chlorobenzoate
(b) m-hydroxy benzaldehyde
(c) m-chlorobenzyl alcohol
(d) m-hydroxybenzyl alcohol

42. A mixture of benzaldehyde and formaldehyde on heating with aqueous NaOH solution gives
(a) benzyl alcohol (b) sodium benzoate
(c) sodium formate (d) methyl alcohol

43. Which of the following reactants on reaction with conc. NaOH followed by acidification gives following lactone as the product?

(phthalide: benzene ring fused with C(=O)–O–CH_2)

(a) benzene with $COOCH_3$ and $COOH$ (ortho)
(b) benzene with $COOH$ and CHO (ortho)
(c) benzene with $COOH$ and $COOH$ (ortho)
(d) benzene with CHO and CHO (ortho)

44. The smallest ketone and its next homologue are reacted with NH_2OH to form oxime
(a) Two different oximes are formed
(b) Three different oximes are formed
(c) Two oximes formed are optically active
(d) All oximes formed are optically active

45. MeCHO and PhCHO will give different type of reaction with
(a) NaOI (b) Brady's reagent
(c) MeMgBr (d) KOH, Δ

46. $HCHO \xrightarrow[\Delta]{conc.\ NaOH} MeOH + HCOONa$
True about the above reaction is/are :
(a) it is Cannizzaro reaction
(b) it is redox reaction
(c) it is a bimolecular reaction
(d) it is a disproportionation reaction

47. Which of the following will give yellow precipitate with $NaOH/I_2$
(a) $Ph-CH(OH)-Me$ (b) CH_3CHO
(c) $Me-C(=O)-C(=O)-OH$ (d) EtOH

48. HO–cyclopentanone (3-hydroxycyclopentanone) $\xrightarrow{30\% H_2SO_4}$ W (minor) + X (major); W $\xrightarrow{KMnO_4/H^-, \Delta}$ Y; X $\xrightarrow{KMnO_4/H^-, \Delta}$ Z

Of the 4 compounds listed above, more than one will :
(a) exhibit resonance due to conjugation in their structure
(b) show $NaHCO_3$ test
(c) have a cyclic structure
(d) show 2, 4-DNPH precipitation

49. Which of the following compounds will give yellow crystals of iodoform on reaction with aq. $NaOH + I_2$?
(a) $CH_3-C(=O)-CH_3$ (b) $CH_3-C(OH)(CH_3)-CH_3$
(c) $Ph-CO-CH_3$ (d) $CH_3-CH(Cl)-CH_3$

50. Compound (X), molecular formula C_8H_8O, is water insoluble and gives yellow ppt. with $I_2/NaOH$. It reacts with H_2NOH in presence of NH_4Cl/NH_4OH to give two geometrical isomers, which do not undergo dehydration but can go for rearrangement with acids. Compound (X) can be
(a) $H_5C_6-C(=O)-CH_3$ (b) $H_5C_6-CH_2-CHO$
(c) $H_5C_6-CH(OH)-CH_3$ (d) cyclopentadienyl–CH=C(CH_3)–... with C=O and H_3C

INSTRUCTION for Q. 51 to 82 : Read the passages given below and answer the questions that follow.

PASSAGE 1

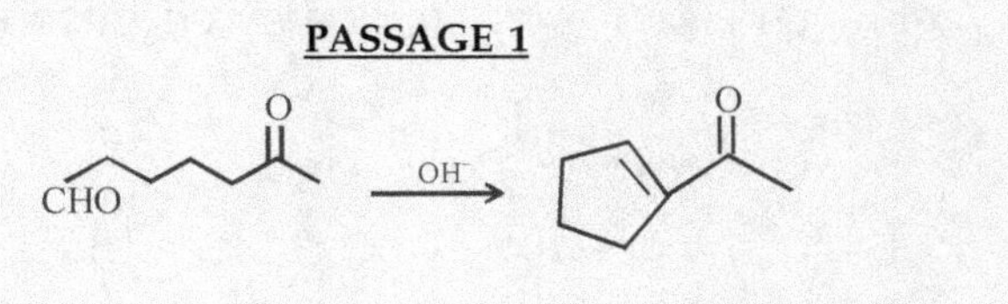

51. The reaction is an example of
(a) aldol condensation
(b) crossed aldol condensation
(c) intramolecular aldol condensation
(d) none of the three

52. How many carbanions are possible in this case ?
(a) 1 (b) 2
(c) 3 (d) 4

53. Which of the functional group is acting as nucleophile ?
(a) Aldehyde (b) Ketone
(c) Either of the two (d) None of the two

PASSAGE 2

The carbonyl group C = O governs the chemistry of aldehydes and ketones in two ways (a) : by providing a site for nucleophilic addition, and (b) by increasing the acidity of the hydrogen atoms attached to the alpha carbon.

The mobile π electrons of the carbon-oxygen double bond are pulled strongly towards oxygen, which makes carbonyl oxygen electron-rich and carbonyl carbon electron-deficient. Further, since carbonyl group is flat, it is relatively open to attack from above or below. The positive charge on the carbonyl carbon atom means that it is especially susceptible to attack by a nucleophile. On the other hand, the negative charge on the carbonyl oxygen atom means that nucleophilic addition is susceptible to acid catalysis.

In addition to nucleophilic addition reactions, carbonyl compounds exhibit the unusual acidity of alpha-hydrogen atoms. The unusual acidity of the alpha-hydrogen of carbonyl compounds is due to its strong electron-withdrawing nature which in turn makes alpha-carbon also electron-withdrawing. Hence in presence of base it easily loses hydrogen as proton and itself converted into carbanion.

54. The carbonyl carbon is more reactive toward the nucleophile
(a) in presence of acids
(b) in absence of acids
(c) equally reactive in both cases
(d) in presence of base

55. The yield of hydrate is maximum in
(a) CH_3CHO (b) HCHO
(c) O_2NCH_2CHO (d) CH_3COCH_3

56. Which of the following reactions of aldehydes is due to nucleophilic addition on carbonyl group as well as due to acidic nature of the α-carbon atom?
(a) Reformatsky reaction (b) Aldol condensation
(c) Cannizzaro reaction (d) Wittig reaction

57. The final product obtained during aldol condensation of propanal is reduced in two ways.

$$[B] \xleftarrow{H_2,\ Pd/C} CH_3CH_2CH=\underset{}{\overset{CH_3}{\overset{|}{C}}}CHO \xrightarrow{LiAlH_4} [A]$$

Which of the above reactions is a nucleophilic addition?
(a) Reaction leading to [A] (b) Reaction leading to [B]
(c) Both (d) None

58. The compounds A and B in the above question are
(a) $CH_3CH_2CH=\overset{CH_3}{\overset{|}{C}}CH_2OH$, $CH_3CH_2CH_2\overset{CH_3}{\overset{|}{C}}HCH_2OH$
(b) $CH_3CH_2CH=\overset{CH_3}{\overset{|}{C}}CH_2OH$, $CH_3CH_2CH_2\overset{CH_3}{\overset{|}{C}}HCHO$
(c) $CH_3CH_2CH=\overset{CH_3}{\overset{|}{C}}CH_2OH$, $CH_3CH_2CH=\overset{CH_3}{\overset{|}{C}}OH$
(d) $CH_3CH_2CH_2\overset{CH_3}{\overset{|}{C}}HCH_2OH$, $CH_3CH_2CH_2\overset{CH_3}{\overset{|}{C}}HCH_2OH$

PASSAGE 3

In the following reaction sequence, product I, J and L are formed. K represents a reagent.

$$\text{Hex}-3-\text{ynal} \xrightarrow[2.\ PBr_3]{1.\ NaBH_4} I \xrightarrow[3.\ H_3O^+]{1.\ Mg/ether,\ 2.\ CO_2} J \xrightarrow{K}$$

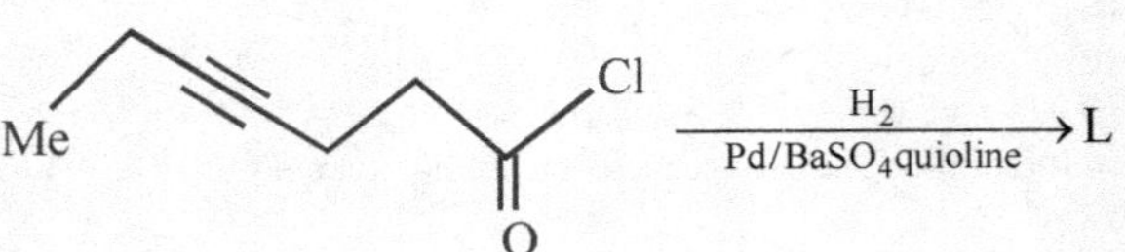

59. The structure of the product I is –
(a) Me ... Br
(b) Me ... Br
(c) Me ... Br
(d) 

60. The structures of compound J and K, respectively, are
(a) Me ... COOH and $SOCl_2$
(b) Me ... OH, O and $SOCl_2$
(c) Me ... COOH
(d) Me ... COOH and CH_3SO_2Cl

61. The structure of product L is
(a) Me ... CHO
(b) Me ... CHO
(c) Me ... CHO
(d) Me ... CHO

PASSAGE 4

A tertiary alcohol H upon acid catalysed dehydration gives a product I. Ozonolysis of I leads to compounds J and K. Compound J upon reaction with KOH gives benzyl alcohol and compound L, whereas K on reaction with KOH gives only M.

M=
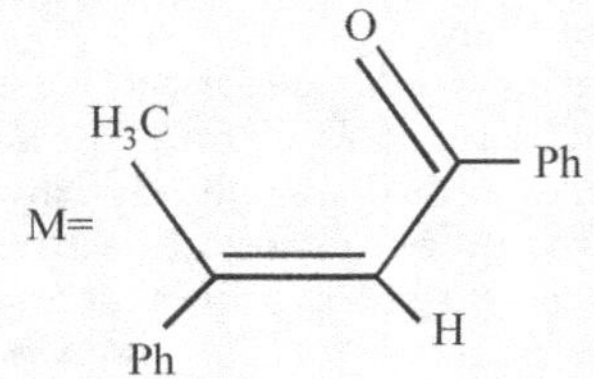

62. Compound H is formed by the reaction of

(a) 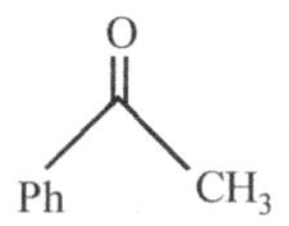 $PhCOCH_3$ + PhMgBr

(b) 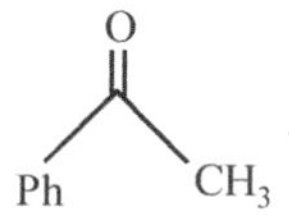 $PhCOCH_3$ + $PhCH_2MgBr$

(c) 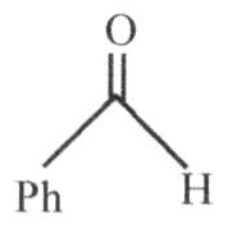 PhCHO + $PhCH_2MgBr$

(d) 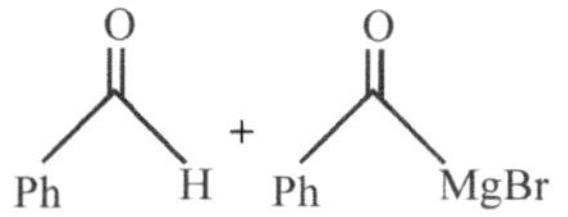 PhCHO + PhCOMgBr

63. The structure of compound I is

(a) 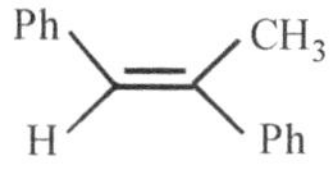 Ph, H / CH_3, Ph

(b) 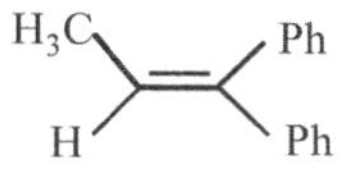 H_3C, H / Ph, Ph

(c) 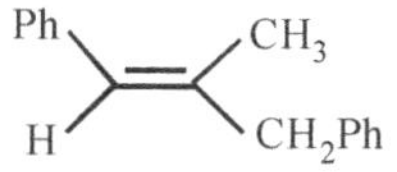 Ph, H / CH_3, CH_2Ph

(d) 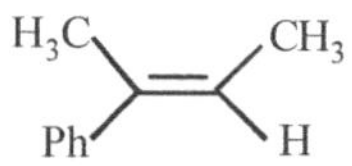 H_3C, Ph / CH_3, H

64. The structure of compounds J, K and L respecitvely, are –

(a) $PhCOCH_3$, $PhCH_2COCH_3$ and $PhCH_2COO^-K^+$
(b) PhCHO, $PhCH_2CHO$ and $PhCOO^-K^+$
(c) $PhCOCH_3$, $PhCH_2CHO$ and $CH_3COO^-K^+$
(d) PhCHO, $PhCOCH_3$ and $PhCOO^-K^+$

PASSAGE 5

A carbonyl compound **P**, which gives positive iodoform test, undergoes reaction with MeMgBr followed by dehydration to give an olefin **Q**. Ozonolysis of **Q** leads to a dicarbonyl compound **R**, which undergoes intramolecular aldol reaction to give predominantly **S**.

$$\mathbf{P}\xrightarrow[\text{2. }H^+,H_2O\text{ 3. }H_2SO_4,\Delta]{\text{1. MeMgBr}}\mathbf{Q}\xrightarrow[\text{2. Zn},H_2O]{\text{1. }O_3}\mathbf{R}\xrightarrow[\text{2. }\Delta]{\text{1. }OH^-}\mathbf{S}$$

65. The structure of the carbonyl compound **P** is

(a) 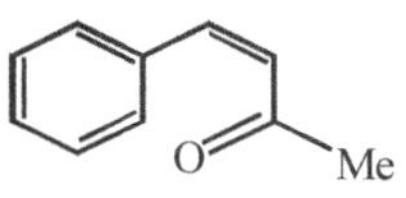 O, Me

(b) 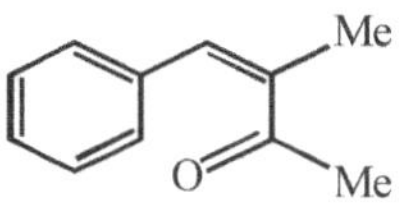 Me, O, Me

(c) 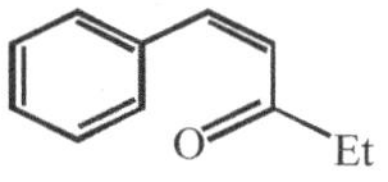 O, Et

(d) 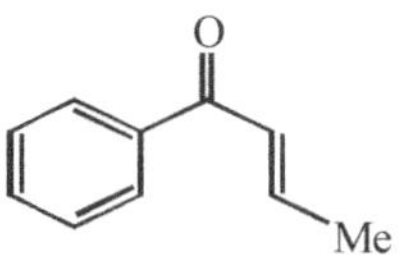 O, Me

66. The structures of the products Q and R, respectively, are

(a) 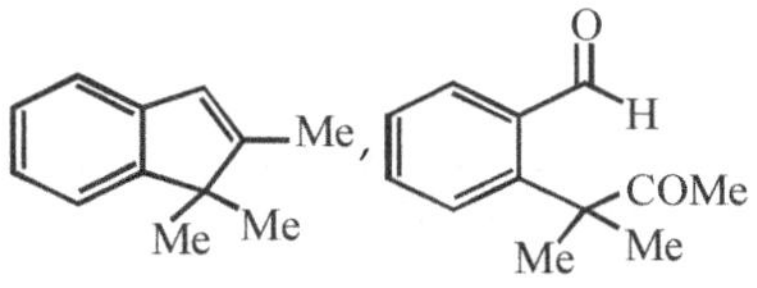 Me, Me Me ; O, H, COMe, Me Me

(b) 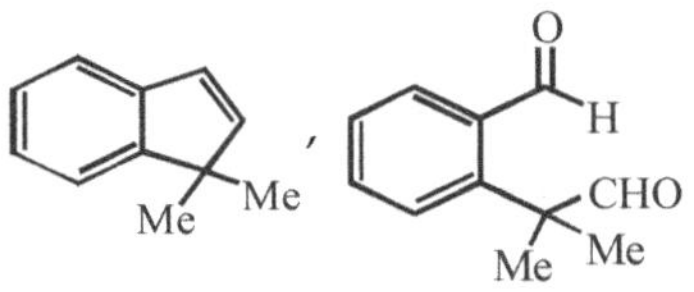 Me Me ; O, H, CHO, Me Me

(c) 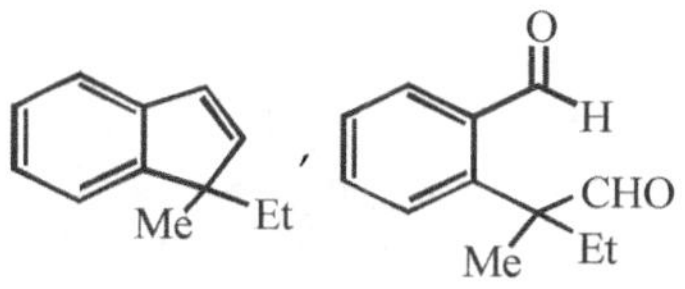 Me Et ; O, H, CHO, Me Et

(d) 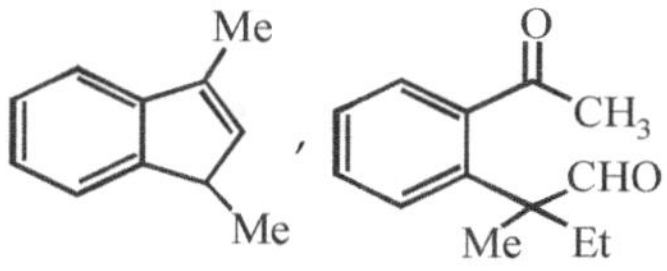 Me, Me ; O, CH_3, CHO, Me Et

67. The structure of the product **S** is

(a) 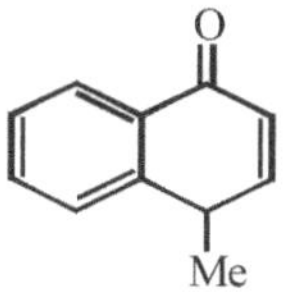 O, Me

(b) 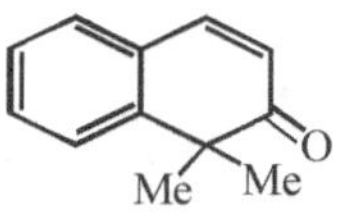 O, Me Me

(c) 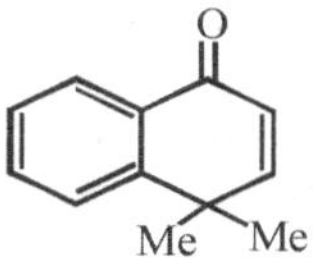 O, Me Me

(d) 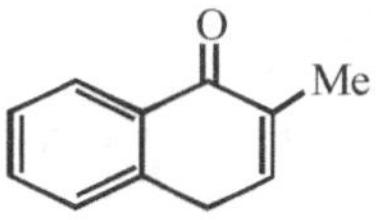 O, Me

PASSAGE 6

$$\xrightarrow[Zn/H_2O]{O_3} P_1 \xrightarrow{KOH} P_2 \xrightarrow[EtONa]{N_2H_4} P_3 \xrightarrow{CrO_3} P_4$$

$$P_1 \xrightarrow[\Delta]{KOH} P_5 \xrightarrow[\text{excess}]{H_2/Pd} P_3 \xrightarrow{HBr} P_6 \xrightarrow[\text{excess}]{NH_3} P_7$$

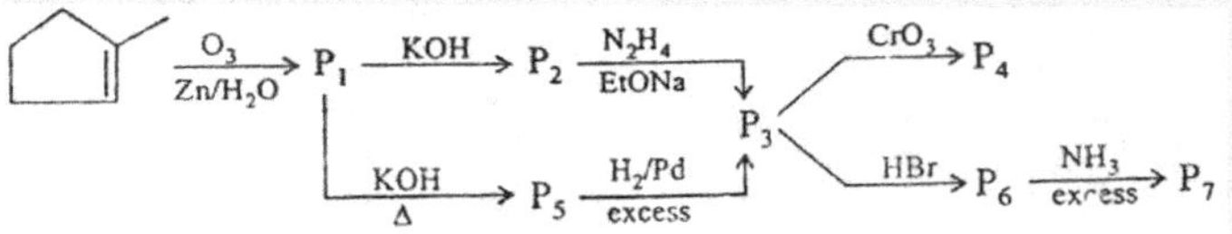

68. Which of the following statement is correct about P_4 ?
(a) It will not give yellow/orange or red colour with 2, 4-DNP
(b) It will give red colour with ceric ammonia nitrate
(c) It will not give Fehling test
(d) It will give Bielstien test

69. Which of the following statement is correct abot P_7 ?
(a) It will not give mustard oil reaction
(b) It will not give carbylamine test or isocyanide test
(c) It will decolourize bromine water
(d) It will give base soluble product with Hinsberg reagent

70. Which of the following reaction will be useful for conversion of P_3 to P_4.
(a) Clemmensen's reduction
(b) Oppenauer oxidation
(c) Meerwin Pondorff Verely reduction
(d) Tischenko reaction

PASSAGE 7

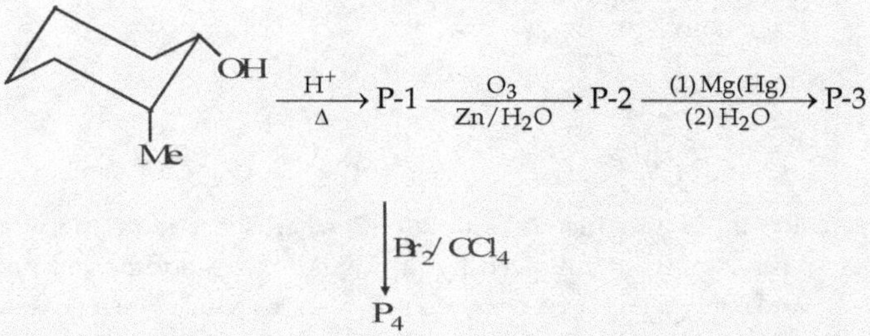

OH, Me $\xrightarrow[\Delta]{H^+}$ P-1 $\xrightarrow[Zn/H_2O]{O_3}$ P-2 $\xrightarrow[(2)\,H_2O]{(1)\,Mg(Hg)}$ P-3

P-1 $\xrightarrow{Br_2/CCl_4}$ P_4

71. If methyl group is in axial position in product (P-4), then what is the position of Br atoms on C_1 and C_2 respectively.
(a) axial, equatorial
(b) equatorial, axial
(c) axial, axial
(d) equatorial, equatorial

72. Correct sequence of reagents to convert P-4 into P-3.
(a) (i) Zn, Δ; (ii) dil. H_2SO_4
(b) (i) Na/Et_2O; (ii) B_2H_6; (iii) NaOH, H_2O_2
(c) (i) Mg (excess)/Et_2O; (ii) O_2 (excess); (iii) NH_4Cl (excess)
(d) (i) Mg (1 eq.); (ii) $Hg(OAc)_2 + H_2O$; (iii) $NaBH_4$

73. Which of the following will produce same visual change as P-1 with Br_2 water ?

(a) 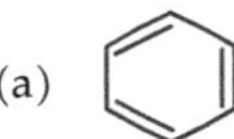 (b) 

(c) 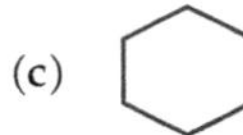 (d) None of these

PASSAGE 8

Citral or 3, 7-dimethyl-2, 6-octadienal is a mixture of a pair of terpenoids having molecular formula $C_{10}H_{16}O$. The two compounds are double bond isomers. The E-isomer is known as geranial (citral – *a*). The Z-isomer is known as neral (citral – *b*), whereas geranial has a strong lemon odour, neral enjoys a mild lemony fragrance. Citral therefore finds applications in making deodorants and soaps.

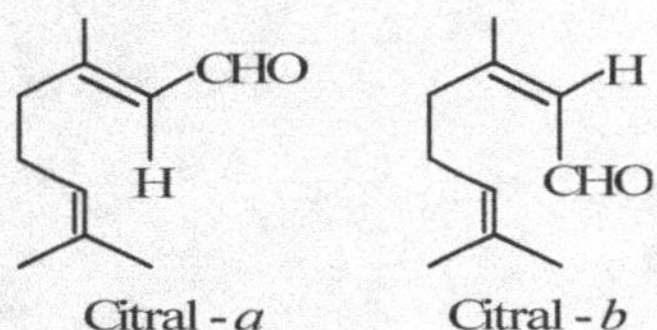

Citral - *a* Citral - *b*

Citral, when subjected to reductive ozonolysis forms three compounds – X, Y and Z (decreasing molar mass, X > Y = Z)

74. Identify the 'false' statement :
(a) Citral – *a* and *b* are diastereomers
(b) All fragments obtained on reductive ozonolysis of reduced citral (Wolf-Kishner reduction) undergo haloform reaction
(c) Y and Z cannot be distinguished by Fehling's reagent
(d) Citral is an isoprene – based natural polymer (dimer)

75. X when reacted with 5% hot and dilute baryta water will form which major product;

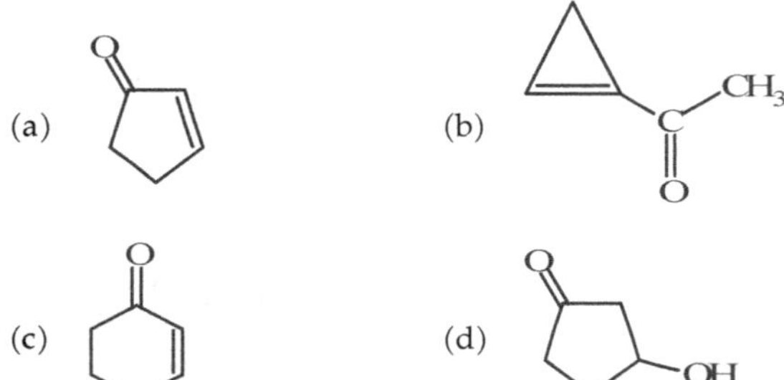

76. 100 ml of an aqueous sample of Z when successfully titrated with $Ag(NH_3)_2^+$ followed by rapid and excess addition of hot and conc. H_2SO_4 evolves a mixture of gases which when passed over red hot charcoal occupy a volume of 6.72 ml at NTP. The molarity of the initial sample is
(a) 10^{-1} (b) 10^{-2}
(c) 10^{-3} (d) 10^{-4}

PASSAGE 9

An optically active organic compound 'A' has molecular formula $C_{11}H_{16}O_2$ and it neither forms salt with NaOH nor decolourises bromine water, but evolves a gas on treatment with CH_3MgBr. A on treatment with HI gives another optically active compound $B(C_9H_{10}I_2)$. B on treatment with aqueous KOH yields another optically active compound $C(C_9H_{12}O_2)$. C on treatment with PCC yields $D(C_9H_8O_2)$ which gives positive iodoform test as well as positive Tollen's test. D is optically inactive and on treatment with $Cl_2/AlCl_3$ gives one and only one possible monochloro derivative $E(C_9H_7O_2Cl)$

Based on the above information answer the fllowing questions :

77. The compound (A) is

(a) 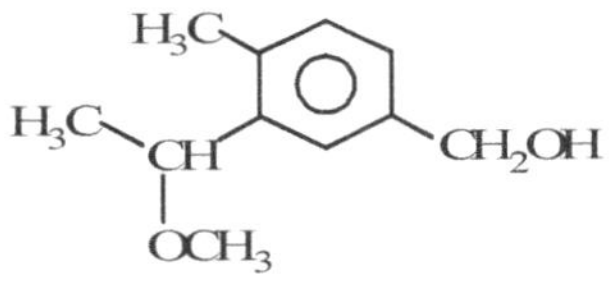 H_3C–CH(OCH_3)– ring (H_3C) –CH_2OH

(b) 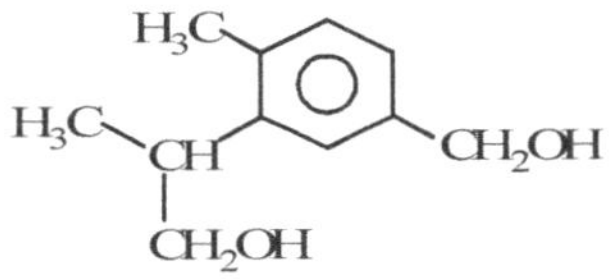 H_3C–CH(CH_2OH)– ring (H_3C) –CH_2OH

(c) 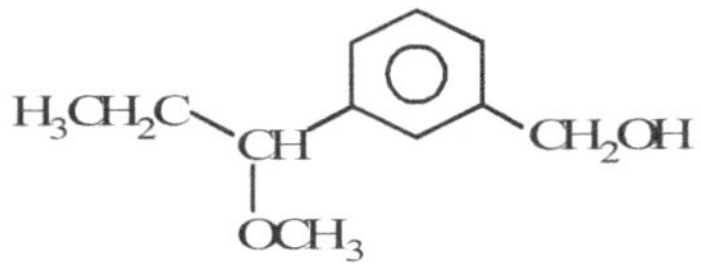 H_3CH_2C–CH(OCH_3)– ring –CH_2OH

(d) 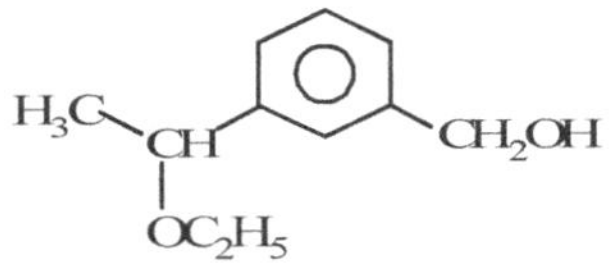 H_3C–CH(OC_2H_5)– ring –CH_2OH

78. Conversion of B into C mainly follows
(a) S_N1 mechanism only
(b) S_N2 mechanism only
(c) S_N1 at one site and S_N2 at other site
(d) $S_N{}^i$ only

79. The compound 'E' is

(a) 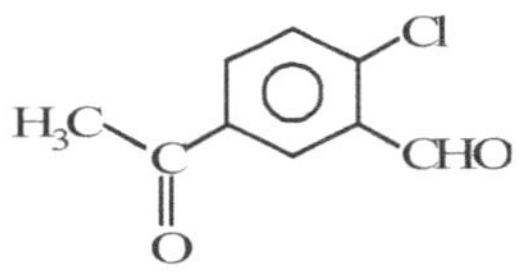 H_3C–C(=O)– ring (Cl) –CHO (b) 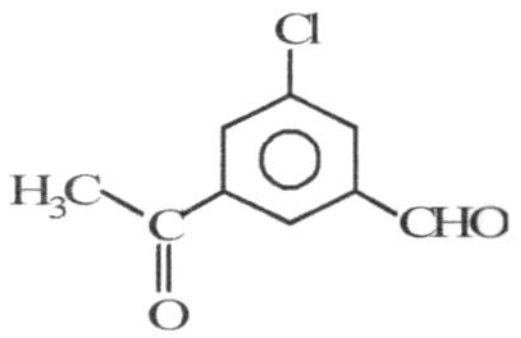 H_3C–C(=O)– ring (Cl) –CHO

(c) 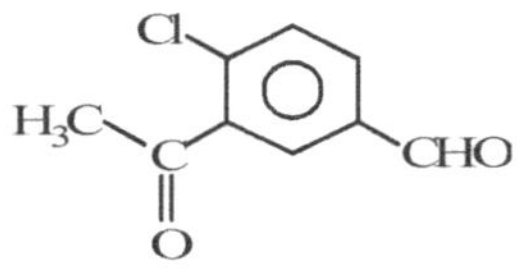 H_3C–C(=O)– ring (Cl) –CHO (d) 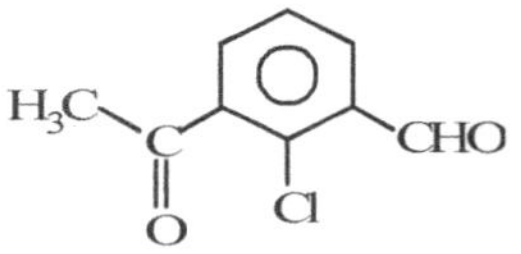 H_3C–C(=O)– ring (Cl) –CHO

PASSAGE 10

Two aliphatic aldehydes P and Q react in the presence of aqueous K_2CO_3 to give compound R, which upon treatment with HCN provides compound S. On acidification and heating, S gives the product shown below.

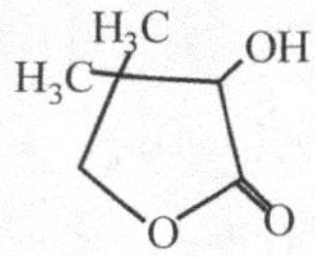

H_3C, H_3C, OH, O, O

80. The compounds P and Q respectively are :

(a) $H_3C-CH(CH_3)-CH_2-CHO$ and H_3C-CHO

(b) $H_3C-CH(CH_3)-CH_2-CHO$ and $HCHO$

(c) $H_3C-CH(CH_3)-CH_2-CHO$ and H_3C-CHO

(d) $H_3C-CH(CH_3)-CH_2-CHO$ and $HCHO$

81. The compound R is :

(a) $(H_3C)_2C(CH_2OH)-CHO$ (b) $(H_3C)_2C(CHO)-CH(OH)-CH_3$

(c) $H_3C-CH(CH_3)-CH(CH_2OH)-CHO$ (d) $H_3C-CH(CH_3)-CH(CHO)-CH(OH)-CH_3$

82. The compound S is :

(a) $H_3C-CH(CH_3)-CH(CHO)-CH_2-CN$ (b) $(H_3C)_2C(CHO)-CH_2-CN$

(c) $H_3C-CH(CH_3)-CH(CH_2OH)-CH(CN)-OH$ (d) $(H_3C)_2C(CH_2OH)-CH(CN)-OH$

Instructions for Q. 83 to Q. 88 : Following questions are Multiple Matching type Questions :

53. $—CHO > C=O$

Column I	*Column II*
(A) OHC–(CH_2)_4–CO–CH_3 + OH⁻	(a) Cyclization
(B) cyclopentanone + $C_6H_5CO_3H$	(b) Aldol condensation
(C) CHO-substituted alkene + H^+	(c) Ring expansion
(D) $HOCH_2CH_2CH_2CH_2Cl+OH^-$	(d) Williamson synthesis

84.

Column I	*Column II*
(A) 4-(2-(1-hydroxyethyl)phenyl)cyclohexanone (O=, OH)	(a) aldol condensation
(B) biphenyl-2-CHO	(b) Cannizzaro reaction
(C) OHC-phenyl–cyclohexyl-CHO	(c) haloform reaction
(D) acetophenone	(d) reaction with chlorine

85.

Column I	*Column II*
(A) Schiff's reagent	(a) Elimination reaction
(B) Alcoholic KOH	(b) colourless solution due to SO_2
(C) Ammonical $AgNO_3$	(c) Aldehydes
(D) Benedict solution	(d) Chloroform

86.

Column - I	Column - II	Column - III
A. $CH_3CHO \xrightarrow{Zn/Hg.HCl}$	p. $(CH_3)_2CH(OH)$	w. Clemmensen reduction
B. $CH_3COCH_3 \xrightarrow{[H]}$	q. $(CH_3)_2C(OH)-C(OH)(CH_3)_2$	x. $LiAlH_4$ reduction
C. $CH_3COCH_3 \xrightarrow{NH_2NH_2,\,OH^-}$	r. $CH_3CH_2CH_3$	y. Pinacol reduction
D. $CH_3COCH_3 \xrightarrow{Mg/HCl}$	s. CH_3CH_3	z. Wolf-Kishner reduction

87. Match the column :

Column-I (Reactions)	**Column-II (products)**
A. cyclopentanone $\xrightarrow[\text{trans.of KOH}]{HCN}$ (A) $\longrightarrow$ (B) $\longrightarrow$ (C)	(a) Formation of six membered ring takes place
B. cyclopentanone $\xrightarrow{NH_2OH}$ (A) $\longrightarrow$ (B)	(b) Final product is ketone or α, β-unsaturated ketone.
C. $H_3C-\overset{O}{\overset{\|}{C}}-CH_2-CH_2-CH_2-\overset{O}{\overset{\|}{C}}-H \xrightarrow[\Delta]{OH^-}$ (A)	(c) Final product formed will give positive Tollen's test.
D. 1-(1-hydroxy-1-phenylethyl)cyclopentanol (Ph, CH_3, OH, OH) $\xrightarrow[\Delta]{H^+}$ (A)	(sd) Final product formed will react with 2, 4-DNP
	(e) Ring expansion takes place

88.

	Column I	Column II
(A)	H_3C, O, O; aq. NaOH →; O	(a) Nucleophilic substitution
(B)	O, $CH_2CH_2CH_2Cl$; CH_3MgI →; O, CH_3	(b) Electrophilic substitution
(C)	O, $CH_2CH_2CH_2\overset{18}{O}H$; H_2SO_4 →; $\overset{18}{O}$	(c) Dehydration
(D)	$CH_2CH_2CH_2C(CH_3)_2$, OH; H_2SO_4 →; H_3C, CH_3	(d) Nucleophilic addition

Instructions for Q. 89 to 100 : Following questions are Assertion and Reasoning Type Questions :

Note : Each question contains STATEMENT-1 (Assertion) and STATEMENT-2 (Reason). Each question has 5 choices (a), (b), (c), (d) and (e) out of which ONLY ONE is correct.

(a) Statement-1 is True, Statement-2 is True; Statement-2 is a correct explanation for Statement-1.

(b) Statement-1 is True, Statement-2 is True; Statement-2 is NOT a correct explanation for Statement-1.

(c) Statement -1 is True, Statement-2 is False.

(d) Statement -1 is False, Statement-2 is True.

(e) Statement -1 is False, Statement-2 is False.

89. **Statement 1 :** Acetaldehyde on treatment with alkali gives aldol.
Statement 2 : Acetaldehyde molecule contains hydrogen atom.

90. **Statement 1 :** Acetylene on treatment with alkaline $KMnO_4$ produce acetaldehyde.
Statement 2 : Alkaline $KMnO_4$ is a reducing agent.

91. **Statement 1 :** Hydroxyketones are not directly used in Grignard reaction.
Statement 2 : Grignard reagents react with hydroxyl group.

92. **Statement 1 :** Isobutanal does not give iodoform test.
Statement 2 : It does not have α-hydrogen

93. **Statement 1 :** Cyclohexanone forms cyanohydrin in good yield but 2, 4, 6-trimethyl cyclohexanone does not.
Statement 2 : The formation of cyanohydrin involves the nucleophilic attack by CN^- ion on the carbonyl carbon.

94. **Statement 1 :** There are two $-NH_2$ groups in semicarbazide.
Statement 2 : One group is involved in the formation of semicarbazones.

95. **Statement-1 :** Acetoacetic ester, $CH_3-\overset{O}{\overset{\|}{C}}-CH_2\overset{O}{\overset{\|}{C}}OC_2H_5$ will give iodoform test
Statement-2 : It contains $CH_3-\overset{O}{\overset{\|}{C}}-$group.

96. **Statement-1 :** Crossed Cannizzaro reaction between formaldehyde and benzaldehyde gives benzyl alcohol and formate ion.
Statement-2 : Formaldehyde is a better hydride donor than benzaldehyde.

97. **Statement-1 :** Protonation of a carbonyl group increases its electrophilic character.
Statement-2 : Protonation of a carbonyl group involves addition of an electrophile on nucleophilic oxygen.

98. **Statement-1 :** HO–cyclopentyl–$\overset{O}{\overset{\|}{C}}-CH_3$ → HO–cyclopentyl–CH_2CH_3
This conversion is favoured with, Wolf-Kishner reduction, but unfavoured with Clemmensen's reduction.
Statement-2 : Clemmenson reduction is base sensitive reaction, whereas Wolf-Kishner reduction is acid sensitive.

99. **Statement-1 :** Formaldehyde can't be prepared by Rosenmund's reduction method.
Statement-2 : Formyl chloride is unstable

100. **Statement-1 :** The aldol condensation product is $C_6H_5-\underset{OH}{CH}-\underset{CH_3}{CH}-CHO$ whcn propanal is slowly added to excess of benzaldehyde.
Statement-2 : On slow addition self aldol condensation of propanal can be prevented.

EXERCISE 14.3 (Subjective Problems)

1. Give IUPAC names for the following :

(a) $C_6H_5CH = CHCHO$ (b) [structure: O]

(c) [structure: O] (d) [structure: O, COOH]

2. Give the structural formula of
(a) Trimethylacetaldehyde
(b) α, γ-Dimethylcaproaldehyde
(c) p, p′-Dimethylbenzophenone.

3. What are the expected H—C—O and H—C—H bond angles in CH_2O ?

4. Compare the polarities of the C = O and C = C bonds. How does this difference influence the reactivity of each bond as a nucleophilic site for reaction ?

5. Account for the following :
(a) The boiling points of 2-propanol, propanone, and 2-methylpropene differ very much, although they have approximately same molecular weight.
(b) Carbonyl compounds are more soluble in water than the corresponding alkanes but less than the corresponding alcohols.
(c) 2-Butanone has a lower $\Delta H°$ of combustion than butanol.

6. What is a ketene ? Give the structural formula and atomic orbital representation of ketene.

7. (a) How will you prepare an aldehyde by the reduction of a carboxylic acid ester ?
(b) Give the product of the reaction of *cis*-1, 2-cyclohexanediol with periodic acid. Why is the *trans*-glycol almost inert to this reagent ?

8. Give reagent(s) used for preparing $(CH_3)_2CHCH_2COCH_3$ from
(a) an alkyne (b) an alcohol
(c) an acid chloride + organocopper compound
(d) a carboxylic acid
(e) an acid chloride + organocadmium compound
(f) a nitrile.

9. Write the organometallic compound and other chemical compound (a carbonyl compound) used for preparing following alcohols.
(a) 1-Phenyl-1-propanol (b) 2-Phenyl-2-propanol
(c) 1-Phenyl-2-propanol (d) 3-Phenyl-1-propanol
(e) 1-Methylcyclohexanol (f) Cyclohexylmethanol
(g) 1-Cyclohexylethanol (h) 1-Pentyn-3-ol
(i) 3-Pentyn-2-ol (j) 1-(*p*-tolyl) ethanol.

10. Write down the structure of the compound obtained when phenyl acetaldehyde or cyclohexanone is treated with each of the following reagents ?
(a) Tollen's reagent (b) CrO_3/H_2SO_4
(c) Cold dil. $KMnO_4$ (d) Acidic $KMnO_4$, heat
(e) H_2, Ni, pressure (f) $NaBH_4$
(g) C_6H_5MgBr, H_2O (h) $Me_2CHMgCl, H_2O$
(i) $HC \equiv CLi, H_2O$ (j) Semicarbazide
(k) ethyl alcohol, dry HCl (gas) (l) *tert*-Butyl amine
(m) C_2H_5SH, H^+.

11. Convert propanal into following
(a) *n*-Propanol (b) α-Hydroxybutanoic acid
(c) *sec*-Butyl alcohol (d) 1-Phenyl-1-propanol
(e) 2-Methyl-3-pentanol.

12. Name the reagent used to convert 2-methyl-2-pentenal to
(a) 2-methyl-2-pentenol (b) 2-methylpentanol
(c) 2-methylpentane (d) 2-methylpentanal.

13. A carbonyl group can be reduced to methylene group by three methods : Clemmensen, Wolf-Kishner and Raney Ni desulphurization. How would you decide which method should be applied for a particular carbonyl compound?

14. Select the best way for reducing the carbonyl group to methylene in each of the following :
(a) $BrCH_2CH_2CHO$ (b) $(CH_3)_2C(OH)CH_2CH_2COCH_3$
(c) $C_6H_5CHOHCH_2COC_2H_5$ (d) $H_2C—CHCH_2COCH_3$ (epoxide, O bridging)

15. Identify the reduced product.
(a) (bicyclic enone) $\xrightarrow{\text{Pt, 1 eq. } H_2}$ [A]
(b) (3-formylcyclohexanone, CHO) $\xrightarrow[CH_3OH]{\text{1 eq. } NaBH_4}$ [B]

16. How will you convert $C_6H_5CH = CHCOCH_3$ to
(a) $C_6H_5CH = CHCOOH$ (b) $C_6H_5CH = CHCHOHCH_3$
(c) $C_6H_5CH_2CH_2COCH_3$ (d) $C_6H_5CH = CHCH_2CH_3$
(e) $C_6H_5CH_2CH_2CH_2CH_3$.

17. Arrange the following in decreasing ease of hydration :
(a) $CH_3CHO, (CH_3)_2CO, HCHO, CH_2ClCOCH_3, CH_2ClCHO$
(b) CHO (cyclohexanecarbaldehyde), CHO Br (1-bromocyclohexanecarbaldehyde), O (cyclohexanone), O Br (2-bromocyclohexanone)

18. (a) Write down the structure of the product(s) obtained by treating each of the following aldehyde with conc. OH^-
(i) Benzaldehyde (ii) Trimethylacetaldehyde
(iii) (pyran-CHO) (iv) Benzal chloride
(v) *tert*-Butyldichloromethane
(b) Write down the structure of the product(s) obtained by treating each of the following with conc. NaOH.
(i) $C_6H_5CH_2CHO$ (ii) $CH_3CH = CHCHO$
(iii) $C_6H_5CH = CHCHO + CH_3CH = CHCHO$
(iv) $CH_3CHO + 4\ HCHO$.

19. Identify A to D in the following series of reactions :

(cyclopentanone) $\xrightarrow[\text{(ii) } H_2O]{\text{(i) } CH_3MgI}$ [A] $\xrightarrow[\text{heat}]{H_2SO_4}$ [B] $\xrightarrow{\text{(i) } O_3/H_2O/Zn}$ [C] $\xrightarrow{OH^-}$ [D]

20. Complete the following reactions :
(a) $C_6H_5COCH_2CH_3 + SO_2Cl_2 \longrightarrow$
(b) Me_2(cyclohexanone)$=O$ + NBS $\longrightarrow$

21. Describe a simple chemical test that can be applied for distinguishing between
(a) phenylacetaldehyde and benzyl alcohol
(b) 2-pentanone and 3-pentanone
(c) cyclohexanone and cyclohexyl methyl ether
(d) diethyl acetal and *n*-valeraldehyde
(e) diethyl acetal and di-*n*-propyl ether
(f) methyl *m*-tolyl ketone and propiophenone
(g) 2-pentanone and 2-pentanol
(h) paraldehyde and diisobutyl ether
(i) dioxane and trioxane.

22. Identify compounds [A] to [D] and explain their formation.

(Ph–C(CH_3)_2–CH_2–COOH) $\xrightarrow{PCl_3}$ [A] $C_{11}H_{13}OCl$ $\xrightarrow{AlCl_3}$ [B] $C_{11}H_{12}O$ $\xrightarrow[\text{heat}]{NH_2NH_2,\ OH^-}$ [C] $C_{11}H_{14}$ $\xleftarrow[\text{or Conc. } H_2SO_4]{AlCl_3}$ [D] $C_{10}H_{13}CH_2OH$

23. Identify the compounds [A] to [E] in the following reactions.

$n\text{-}C_5H_{11}C \equiv CH \xrightarrow{LiNH_2}$ [A] $\xrightarrow{CH_2ClCH_2CH_2Br}$ [B] $\xrightarrow[\text{(ii) R'CHO}]{\text{(i) Mg}}$ [C] $\xrightarrow[\text{catalyst}]{H_2,\ \text{Lindlar}}$ [D] $\xrightarrow{CrO_3}$ [E]

24. Identify [A] in the following reaction.

$Cl-C_6H_4$ (benzene) $+ CCl_3CH(OH)_2 \xrightarrow{H^+}$ [Intermediate] $\xrightarrow[H^+]{C_6H_5Cl}$ [A]

25. Give the possible product(s) obtained in each of the following reactions.

(a) (Et-substituted bicyclic dialdehyde, CHO, CHO) $\xrightarrow{\text{base}}$ (b) (pyrazolinium, $\overset{+}{N}-CH_2COC_6H_5$, $N-CH_2COC_6H_5$) $\xrightarrow{\text{base}}$

26. Complete the following explaining each step

(a) (cyclohexanone) $\xrightarrow{CH_3OCH{=}PPh_3}$ [A] $\xrightarrow{H^+,\ H_2O}$ [B]

(b) (octahydronaphthalene) $\xrightarrow[\text{(ii) Zn, } CH_3COOH]{\text{(i) } O_3}$ [C] $\xrightarrow{\text{base}}$ [D]

SOLUTIONS

EXERCISE 14.1

6	(c)	11	(b)	16	(b)	21	(b)	26	(b)	31	(c)	36	(c)	41	(d)	46	(b)	51	(c)	56	(c)	61	(b)	66	(c)
7	(b)	12	(c)	17	(c)	22	(b)	27	(d)	32	(a)	37	(b).	42	(d)	47	(b)	52	(c)	57	(d)	62	(a)	67	(a)
8	(c)	13	(c)	18	(d)	23	(b)	28	(c)	33	(c)	38	(d)	43	(b)	48	(b)	53	(a)	58	(d)	63	(b)		
9	(c)	14	(d)	19	(b)	24	(b)	29	(b)	34	(a)	39	(b)	44	(a)	49	(c)	54	(c)	59	(d)	64	(c)		
10	(b)	15	(c)	20	(d)	25	(c)	30	(c)	35	(c)	40	(c)	45	(c)	50	(c)	55	(b)	60	(a)	65	(b)		

1. Theoretical

2. $HC \equiv CCH_2CH_3$ or $CH_3C \equiv CCH_3 \xrightarrow[Hg^{2+}]{H_2SO_4} CH_3CH_2COCH_3$

3. $C_6H_5C \equiv CCH_3 \xrightarrow{H^+} C_6H_5\overset{+}{C} = CHCH_3 \longrightarrow$
Benzylic type carbocation (more stable)

$$\underset{\substack{|\\ C_6H_5C = CHCH_3}}{{}^+OH_2} \xrightarrow{-H^+} \underset{\substack{|\\ C_6H_5\ C = CHCH_3}}{OH} \xrightarrow{\text{tautomerises}} \underset{(a)}{C_6H_5COCH_2CH_3}$$

4. Theoretical

5. $C_6H_6 + C_2H_5COCl \xrightarrow{AlCl_3} C_6H_5COC_2H_5 \xrightarrow[\text{(bimolecular reduction)}]{\text{Mg, ether}} C_2H_5-\overset{C_6H_5}{\underset{OH}{C}}-\overset{C_6H_5}{\underset{OH}{C}}-C_2H_5$

6. $n\text{-}C_3H_7CH_2OH \xrightarrow[\text{Pyridine}]{CrO_3} n\text{-}C_3H_7CHO \xrightarrow{Me_2CHCH_2MgBr} n\text{-}C_3H_7CH(OH)CH_2CHMe_2 \xrightarrow{CrO_3/\text{Pyridine}} n\text{-}C_3H_7COCH_2CHMe_2$

7. $CH_3CH_2CH_2CCl_2CH_3 \longrightarrow \underset{\text{unstable}}{[CH_3CH_2CH_2C(OH)_2CH_3]} \longrightarrow CH_3CH_2CH_2COCH_3 \xrightarrow{I_2/OH^-} \mathbf{CHI_3}\downarrow$

8. Alk. $KMnO_4$ and conc. HNO_3 can't be used because they oxidize the C = C bond too. Since the compound has —$COCH_3$ grouping, i can easily be oxidised by alkaline halogen (NaOX) ; **haloform reaction.**

9. It is an example of internal crossed—Cannizzaro reaction.

$$C_6H_5COCHO \xrightarrow{OH^-} C_6H_5CH(OH)COO^- Na^+$$

10. $CH_3CHO + H_2O^{18} \overset{H^+}{\rightleftharpoons} \underset{\text{Hydrate}}{\left[CH_3\underset{OH}{\underset{|}{C}}HO^{18}H\right]} \underset{H^+}{\rightleftharpoons} CH_3CHO^{18} + H_2O$

The unstable half-labelled hydrate loses H_2O but not H_2O^{18} because C—O^{18} bond is strong as compared to C—O^{16}, hence relativel difficult to cleave.

11. $>C = O + D_2/Pt$ (or $LiAlD_4$) $\longrightarrow >CDOD$

12. 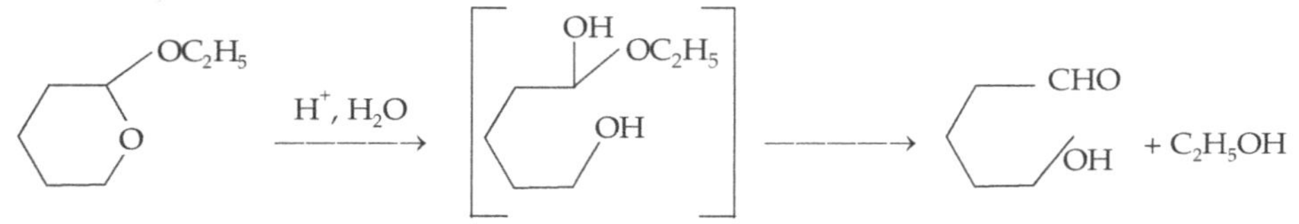

13. 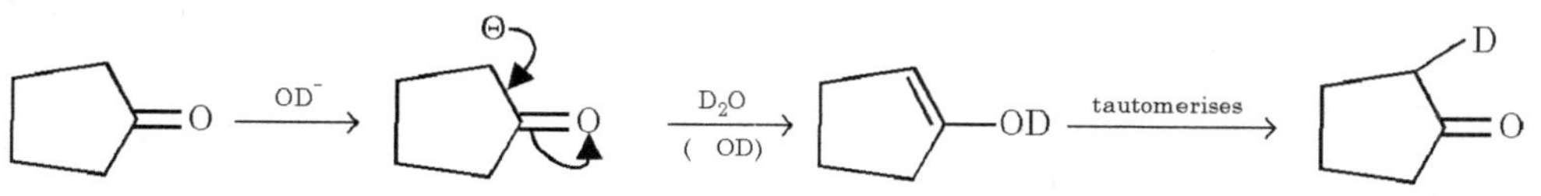 Cyclopentanone $\xrightarrow{OD^-}$ enolate $\xrightarrow[(\ OD)]{D_2O}$ enol (—OD) $\xrightarrow{\text{tautomerises}}$ 2-deuteriocyclopentanone

Reaction is repeated till all other α-hydrogen atoms are replaced.

14. 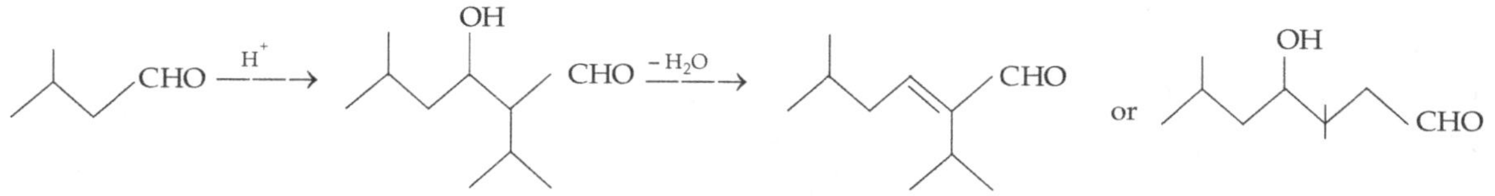 CHO (I) $\xrightarrow{H^+}$ OH, CHO $\xrightarrow{-H_2O}$ CHO or OH, CHO

I

Conjugated system (stable)

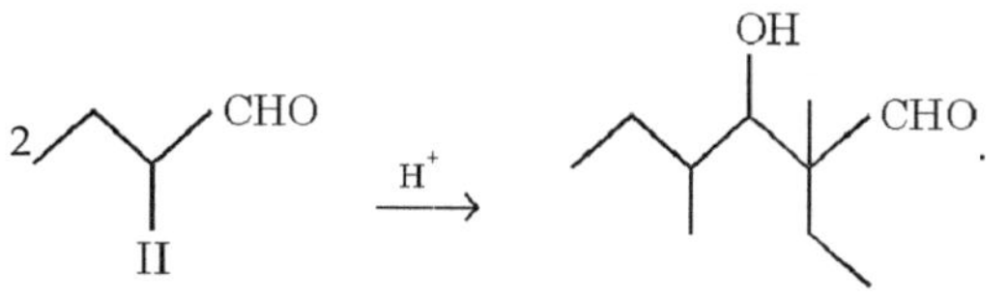

2 CHO (II) $\xrightarrow{H^+}$ OH, CHO.

It does not lose water because the double bond so formed will be isolated.

II

It does not lose water because the double bond so formed will be isolated.

15. 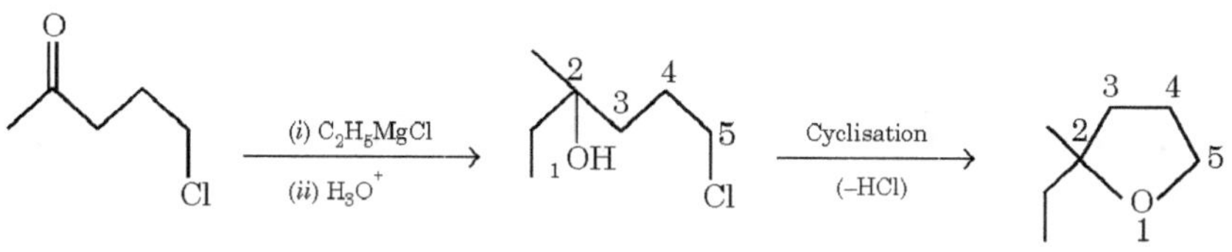 O, Cl $\xrightarrow[(ii)\ H_3O^+]{(i)\ C_2H_5MgCl}$ 1 OH, 2, 3, 4, 5 Cl $\xrightarrow[(-HCl)]{\text{Cyclisation}}$ O 1, 2, 3, 4, 5

3° alcohol

16. Since the product is having an aldehydic group, the reactant should be a dialdehyde because —CHO are more reactive than ketones so in a ketoaldehyde the final product should have a ketonic group.

17. It is an example of intramolecular Cannizzaro reaction followed by cyclization.

18. Presence of electron-withdrawing group on the carbonyl carbon atom increases nucleophilic addition.

19. Halogenation of carbonyl compounds takes place in α-position ; since aldehydes are easily oxidisable so here $CHCl_3$ is used and not water.

20. $CH_3COOH \xrightarrow{\text{heat}} CH_2 = C = O + H_2O$. This is an industrial method for the preparation of ketene, another method is

$CH_3COCH_3 \xrightarrow{700°} CH_2 = C = O + CH_4$.

21. $BrCH_2CH_2CHO \xrightarrow[HCl]{Zn\ (Hg)} BrCH_2CH_2CH_3$

Wolf-Kishner reduction will cause dehydrobromination (—HBr) because it involves alkaline conditions.

22. Zn(Hg), HCl is not used here, because the acidic medium of the reagent may cause dehydration.

23. II cation (oxonium ion) is more stable because here every atom has an octet of electrons

$$R-\overset{H}{\overset{|}{C^+}}-\ddot{O}R \longleftrightarrow R-\overset{H}{\overset{|}{C}}=\overset{+}{\ddot{O}}R$$

I (+vely charged C has six electrons) II (each atom, except H, has eight electrons)

24. Recall that α H's of carbonyl compounds are easily replaced by D of D_2O.

25. 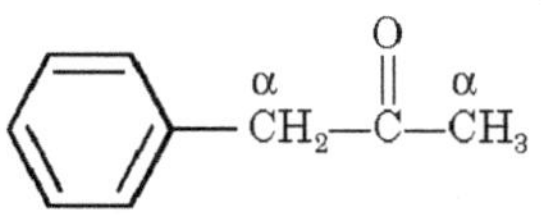 $C_6H_5-\overset{\alpha}{C}H_2-\overset{O}{\overset{||}{C}}-\overset{\alpha}{C}H_3$

26. Consult mechanism of Cannizzaro reaction.

27. Only $C_6H_5NHNH_2$ has $—NH_2$ group.

28. $C_6H_5\ \underset{OH}{\underset{|}{C}H}-\underset{OH}{\underset{|}{C}HCH_3} \xrightarrow[-H_2O]{H^+} \left[C_6H_5-\overset{+}{C}H-\underset{OH}{\underset{|}{C}HCH_3}\right] \longrightarrow C_6H_5CH_2-\underset{OH}{\underset{|}{\overset{+}{C}}}\ CH_3 \xrightarrow{-H^+} C_6H_5CH_2COCH_3$

Benzylic 2° carbocation 3° carbocation

29. $C_6H_{11}Cl \xrightarrow[(ii)\ Li,\ (iii)\ CuCl]{(i)\ Mg,\ ether} [C_6H_{11}]_2\ LiCu \xrightarrow{CH_3CH_2COCl} C_6H_{11}COCH_2CH_3$

[A] [B]

30. Methyl ethyl ketone (a C_4 compound) can't be prepared from 2-propanol (a C_3 compound) ; *tert*-butyl alcohol, being 3° alcohol, is not oxidised easily, 1-butanol, a 1° alcohol will form aldehyde. Thus 2-butanol should be the answer.

$$CH_3\underset{|}{\overset{OH}{C}}HCH_2CH_3 \xrightarrow{\text{Oxidation}} CH_3COCH_2CH_3$$

31. $C_6H_5CHO \xrightarrow{Cl_2,\ h\nu} C_6H_5COCl$

32. $CH_3CH_2CH_2CH = PPh_3 + CH_3COCH_2CH_3 \xrightarrow[\text{reaction}]{\text{Wittig}} CH_3CH_2CH_2CH = \overset{CH_3}{\overset{|}{C}}CH_2CH_3$

3-Methyl-3-heptene

33. Since the compound A has the molecular formula C_3H_6O and undergoes iodoform test, it should be CH_3COCH_3. Further reaction of A with HCl gives $C_9H_{14}O$ having three times the number of carbon atoms in A, hence B should be trimer of acetone, *i.e.*, it should be *phorone.*

$$\underset{\text{Acetone (3 moles)}}{(CH_3)_2C = O + H_3CCOCH_3 + O = C(CH_3)_2} \longrightarrow \underset{\text{2, 6-Dimethyl-2, 5-heptadien-4-one (phorone)}}{(CH_3)_2C = CHCOCH = C(CH_3)_2}$$

34.

$$\underset{(A)}{C_3H_8O} \xrightarrow[H_2SO_4]{K_2Cr_2O_7} \underset{(B)}{C_3H_6O} \xrightarrow[CH_3COONa]{H_2NCONHNH_2\ HCl} C$$

(B) $\xrightarrow{\text{Ammonical } AgNO_3}$ Silver mirror

Since B reduces ammonical silver nitrate, it should be an aldehyde and hence A is primary alcohol, which should be $C_2H_5CH_2OH$. Hence

$$\underset{(A)}{CH_3CH_2CH_2OH} \xrightarrow{K_2Cr_2O_7,\ H_2SO_4} \underset{(B)}{CH_3CH_2CHO} \xrightarrow{H_2NCONHNH_2} \underset{(C)}{CH_3CH_2CH = NNHCONH_2}$$

35. Toluene (H_3C–C_6H_5) $\xrightarrow[AlCl_3]{(CH_3CO)_2O}$ [A] H_3C–C_6H_4–CO–CH_2CH_2–$COOH$ (HOC=O) $\xrightarrow[HCl]{Zn/Hg}$ [B] H_3C–C_6H_4–$CH_2CH_2CH_2$–$COOH$ (HOC=O) $\xrightarrow{HF}$ [C] methyl-tetralone (H_3C, C=O)

[C] $\xrightarrow[(ii)\ H_3O^+]{(i)\ CH_3MgI}$ [D] (H_3C, OH, CH_3)

36. [A] Bromobenzene (Br); [B] Br–C_6H_4–$COCH_3$; [C] Br–C_6H_4–$C(OCH_3)_2CH_3$; [D] D–C_6H_4–$C(OCH_3)_2CH_3$; [E] D–C_6H_4–$COCH_3$

37. [A] $C_6H_5CH_2CH=CH_2$; [B] $C_6H_5CH_2CH_2CH_3$; [C] $C_6H_5CH(Br)CH_2CH_3$; [D] $C_6H_5CH=CHCH_3$ (conjugated)

46. (b) Cyclohexanone $+ Ph_2P = CH_2 \longrightarrow$ methylenecyclohexane (Wittig reaction)

47. (b) $CH \equiv CH \xrightarrow[H_2SO_4]{HgSO_4} CH_3-CHO \xrightarrow[5°C]{dil.NaOH}$

$CH_3-\underset{}{\overset{OH}{CH}}-CH_2-CHO$ (3-hydroxybutanal)

48. (b)

49. (c) Cyclodecane-1,6-dione $\xrightarrow[H_2O]{Mg/Hg}$ diol (OH, OH) $\xrightarrow{H^{\oplus}}$ carbocation $\longrightarrow$ spiro carbocation $\xrightarrow{-H^{\oplus}}$ spiro ketone

50. (c) Both molecules will respond to A and B; neither will respond to D.

51. (c) Aldehyde is first converted into cyclic thioacetal and then strong base like PhLi is used to generate carbanion and then treated with D_2O. Finally, the aldehyde is regenerated.

52. (c) The methoxy group being electron-releasing group makes the release of hydride group more easy.

53. (a) Ph—C(=O)—C(OH)—C(=O)—Ph with H-bonds (I); Cl—C(O)(Cl)—C(OH)—H, Cl---HO (I); (III); H—C(OH)(OH)—H (V)

(I) (I) (III) (V)

54. (c) $H—C—H$ (C=O) $\overset{\ddot{O}H^-}{\rightleftharpoons}$ $H—C(O^-)(OH)—H$ $\overset{OH^-}{\rightleftharpoons}$ $H—C(O^-)(O^-)—H$

The dianion will clearly be a much powerful hydride donor.

55. (b) III > II > I

In I, $-OCH_3$ is electron donating group (+M) so will decrease the electron deficiency of carbonyl carbon to the most.

In II, there is no electron donating group.

In III, electron withdrawing group is present which will increase electron deficiency at carbonyl carbon.

56. (c) Under basic conditions only the protons at carbon atom α to the carbonyl group are replaced by deuterium.

57. (d) It is an example of intramolecular aldol condensation. The carbon atom labelled as α acts as a nucleophile.

$\xrightarrow{OH^-}$ $\longrightarrow$ (OH) $\xrightarrow{-H_2O}$

58. (d) Aldol condensation :

$2CH_3CHO \xrightarrow{OH^-} H_3C-\underset{H}{\overset{OH}{C}}-CH_2CHO$ (New C–C bond)

Kolbe reaction :

Sodium phenoxide (ONa) $\xrightarrow[Pressure]{CO_2, 140°C}$ salicylic acid (OH, COOH) (New C–C bond)

Reimer-Tiemann reaction :

Phenol (OH) $\xrightarrow[3KOH]{CHCl_3}$ salicylaldehyde (OH, CHO) (New C–C bond) $+ 3KCl + 2H_2O$

Wurtz-Fittig reaction :

$H_3CCl + 2Na + Cl-C_6H_5 \xrightarrow{Na}$

$H_3C-C_6H_5 + 2NaCl$ (New C–C bond)

59. (d) The keto group has considerable resonance energy; hence more the number of keto groups in a compound, higher is its stability. However, here all the three compounds have same (two) number of keto groups. Compound II is least stable because two adjacent keto groups destabilize the molecule due to positive charge on the adjacent carbon atoms. Relative stability of I and III can be ascertained by the stability of their fully reduced forms (phenols), since fully reduced form of III has two benzene rings, it will be more stable than the I whose reduced form has only one benzene ring. Thus

III > I > II

60. (a) [Structure: benzene ring fused with C(=O)–C(OH)(OH)–C(=O), each C=O hydrogen-bonded O-----H to an OH]

61. (b) **Two molecules of the same aldehyde** are reacting in presence of alkali to form sodium salt of the acid and an alcohol, hence it is an example of intermolecular Cannizzaro reaction.

62. (a) Lithium tri-tert-butoxyaluminium hydride (LBAH) and diisobutyl-aluminium hydride (DBAH) are less reactive than LAH because they are much more sterically hindered and hence face difficulty in transferring their hydride ions.

63. (b) The reaction is an example of intramolecular aldol condensation. In this keto aldehyde, three different enolates are possible corresponding to the following three carbanions.

[Carbanions I, II and III of the keto aldehyde; III bears $\overset{\ominus}{C}H_2$]

However, carbanion II is formed preferentially because aldehydes are more reactive towards nucleophilic addition than the ketones due to electronic as well as steric factors.

64. (c) First three HCHO molecules react with acetaldehyde via crossed aldol condensation, while the fourth HCHO molecule reacts via crossed Cannizzaro reaction.

CH_3CHO (Ethanal, 3α-hydrogen) + $H-\overset{O}{\overset{||}{C}}-H$ (Methanal, no α-H) $\xrightarrow{Ca(OH)_2}$ (crossed aldol) condensation

$CH_2OH.CH_2CHO$ (Two α-H) $\xrightarrow[\text{(crossed aldol)}]{HCHO,\ Ca(OH)_2}$

$CH(CH_2OH)(CH_2OH)CHO$ (1 α-H) $\xrightarrow[\text{(crossed aldol)}]{HCHO,\ Ca(OH)_2}$ $HOH_2C-C(CH_2OH)(CH_2OH)-CHO$ (No α-H)

$\xrightarrow[\text{(crossed Cannizzaro)}]{HCHO,\ Ca(OH)_2} C(CH_2OH)_4 + \frac{1}{2}(HCOO)_2Ca$

65. (b) Reimer-Tiemann reaction develops – CHO or – COOH group in *ortho* position to the OH group in phenols or to the hetero atom in pyrrole and thiophene.

66. (c) Consult mechanism of Cannizzaro reaction.

67. (a) Condensation of aldehydes/ketones having $\alpha-H$ in presence of base to form α, β-unsaturated carbonyl compound (aldol condensation).

[Cyclohexanone + cyclohexanone $\xrightarrow{OH^-}$ aldol alkoxide $\xrightarrow{H_2O}$ β-hydroxy ketone (OH) $\xrightarrow[(-H_2O)]{OH^-}$ α,β-unsaturated ketone]

EXERCISE 14.2

>1 CORRECT OPTION	1	(a,c)	2	(c,d)	3	(a,b)	4	(a,b,d)	5	(a,b,c)	6	(a,b,c)	7	(b,d)	8	(b,c,d)
	9	(a,b,d)	10	(b, c, d)	11	(a, d)	12	(a, b, c)	13	(a, c)	14	(a, b, d)	15	(a,b,c,d)	16	(a, c, d)
	17	(a, b, c)	18	(a, b, c)	19	(a,c)	20	(a, b)	21	(a, b, d)	22	(b, d)	23	(a, b)	24	(b, d)
	25	(a, b, d)	26	(a, d)	27	(a,b,c,d)	28	(a, b, c)	29	(a, c, d)	30	(a,b,c,d)	31	(a, b, c)	32	(b, c, d)
	33	(a,b,c,d)	34	(a, b, c)	35	(a,b,c,d)	36	(a, c, d)	37	(a, b, c)	38	(a,b,c,d)	39	(a, b)	40	(a,b,c,d)
	41	(a, c)	42	(a, c)	43	(d)	44	(b)	45	(a, d)	46	(a, b, c, d)	47	(a, b, c, d)	48	(a, c, d)
	49	(a, c, d)	50	(a, d)												
PASSAGE 1	51	(c)	52	(c)	53	(b)										
PASSAGE 2	54	(a)	55	(b)	56	(b)	57	(a)	58	(b)						
PASSAGE 3	59	(d)	60	(a)	61	(c)										
PASSAGE 4	62	(b)	63	(a)	64	(d)										
PASSAGE 5	65	(b)	66	(a)	67	(b)										
PASSAGE 6	68	(c)	69	(d)	70	(b)										
PASSAGE 7	71	(d)	72	(c)	73	(b)										
PASSAGE 8	74	(c)	75	(a)	76	(c)										
PASSAGE 9	77	(d)	78	(a)	79	(b)										
PASSAGE 10	80	(b)	81	(a)	82	(d)										
MATCH THE FOLLOWING	83	(A)- a, b ; (B) –c ; (C) - a ; (D) - a, d														
	84	(A)-a, c, d ; (B)-b ; (C)- a, b, d ; (D)- a, c, d														
	85	(A) – b, c; (B) – a; (C) – c, d; (D) – c														
	86	(A) – s, w; (B) – p, x; (C) – r, z; (D) – q, y														
	87	(A) – a, b, d, e; (B) – a, e; (C) – a, b, d; (D) – a, b, d, e														
	88	(A) – c, d, e; (B) – a, d; (C) – c, d; (D) – b, e														
A/R	89	(a)	90	(e)	91	(e)	92	(c)	93	(a)	94	(b)				
	95	(d)	96	(a)	97	(b)	98	(a)	99	(a)	100	(d)				

1. Since the product, $CH_3CHOHCN$ has a chiral carbon and is a mixture of two enantiomers (racemic mixture) which can't be separated by fractional distillation. By fractional crystallisation from a suitable solvent they can be separated.
2. Substitution by one mole of Br gives $C_6H_5COCHBrCH_3$; the electron-withdrawing Br increases the acidity of the remaining α hydrogen which *reacts more rapidly* than the hydrogens on the unsubstituted ketones.

$$\underset{\text{0.5 mole}}{\overset{\text{Less acidic}}{C_6H_5COCH_2CH_3}} \xrightarrow[\text{OH}^-]{\text{0.5 mole Br}_2} \underset{\text{(0.5 mole, but not isolated)}}{\overset{\text{More acidic}}{[C_6H_5COCHBrCH_3]}} \xrightarrow[\text{OH}^-]{\text{0.5 mole Br}_2} \underset{\text{0.5 mole}}{C_6H_5COCBr_2CH_3}$$

3. Acetaldehyde having three α-hydrogen atoms undergo aldol condensation with three moles of CH_2O. The product formed now undergoes intermolecular Cannizzaro reaction with the fourth mole of CH_2O to form pentaerythritol.

$$H{-}C(H)(H){-}CHO + 3CH_2O \xrightarrow[\text{(aldol condensation)}]{Ca(OH)_2} CH_2OH{-}C(CH_2OH)(CH_2OH){-}CHO \xrightarrow[\text{Cannizzaro reaction}]{CH_2O,\ OH^-} CH_2OH{-}C(CH_2OH)(CH_2OH){-}CH_2OH + HCOO^-$$

4. Removal of γ-hydrogen of crotonaldehyde provides more stable allylic carbanion, hence here γ-carbon (not α) provides the carbanion (nucleophile) for carbonyl carbon of cinnamaldehyde.

$$H_2C(H){-}CH=CH{-}C(H)=O \xrightarrow{OH^-} \left[H_2\bar{C}{-}CH=CH{-}C(H)=O \longleftrightarrow H_2C=CH{-}CH=C(H){-}O^-\right]$$

5. Only the first three compounds give Cannizzaro reaction ; $C_6H_5CHCl_2$ is converted into C_6H_5CHO, under the Cannizzaro conditions, hence it also responds the reaction.
6. Carbonyl compounds having αH form carbanion on treatment with a base, carbanion being flat can be attacked by proton on either side of the face forming racemic mixture. Only ketone I has α H, so it will form carbanion while ketone II does not form such carbanion.
7. It is an example of Cannizzaro reaction.
8. Only b, c and d will undergo haloform reaction, but not a because on hydrolysis by alkali it gives C_6H_5CHO, having no αH.
9.

$$\underset{P}{CH_2=C(OCOCH_3)(CH_3)} \xrightarrow[(-CH_3COOH)]{H^+} \underset{\text{enolic form}}{CH_2=C(OH)(CH_3)} \longrightarrow \underset{\text{Acetone}}{(CH_3)_2C=O}$$

$$\underset{Q}{CH_3CH=CH{-}OCOCH_3} \xrightarrow[(-CH_3COOH)]{H^+} CH_3CH=CH{-}OH \longrightarrow \underset{\text{Propanal}}{CH_3CH_2CHO}$$

Acetone and propanal can be distinguished by Fehling solution, and not by others.

48. (a, c, d)

W (cyclopent-3-enone) $\xrightarrow[H^+]{KMnO_4}$ $(HOOCCH_2)_2C=O$ $\xrightarrow{\text{heat}}$ $(H_3C)_2C=O$ (Y)

X (cyclopent-2-enone) $\xrightarrow[H^+]{KMnO_4}$ HO–CO–CH₂CH₂–CO–COOH $\xrightarrow{\text{heat}}$ Z

49. (a, c, d)

(a) and (c) have methyl keto $\left(CH_3-\overset{O}{\overset{\|}{C}}-\right)$ group.

(d) forms $CH_3-\underset{OH}{\underset{|}{CH}}-CH_3$, on reaction with aq. NaOH, which then gives iodoform test.

50. (a, d) Compound (X) gives positive haloform test. Hence [X should be (a), (c) and (d).] However, c does not react with NH_2OH to give two oximes.

Sol. (68-70) :

1-methylcyclopentene $\xrightarrow[Zn/H_2O]{O_3}$ P_1 (keto-aldehyde, CHO) $\xrightarrow{KOH}$ P_2 (3-hydroxycyclohexanone, OH) $\xrightarrow[EtONa]{H_2N-NH_2}$ P_3 (cyclohexanol, OH) $\xrightarrow{CrO_3}$ P_4 (cyclohexanone)

P_1 $\xrightarrow[\Delta]{KOH}$ P_5 (cyclohexenone) $\xrightarrow[\text{excess}]{H_2/Pd}$ P_3 $\xrightarrow{HBr}$ P_6 (bromocyclohexane, Br) $\xrightarrow[\text{excess}]{NH_3}$ P_7 (cyclohexylamine, NH_2)

71. (d)

Chair cyclohexane with Br (eq), Br (eq) and Me.

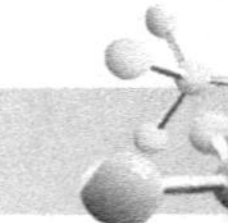

72. (c) [1,3-dibromo-2-methylcyclohexane] $\xrightarrow[Et_2O]{Mg(excess)}$ [di-MgBr] $\xrightarrow{O_2(excess)}$ [di-OMgBr] $\xrightarrow{NH_4^{\oplus}(excess)}$ [diol, –OH, –OH]

73. (b) [cyclopropane] gives addition reaction and decolourises Br_2 water.

Sol. (74-75) :

Citral $\xrightarrow{O_3}$ X (Molecular mass = 100) + Y (58) + Z (58) (CHO–CHO)

(Y and Z can be distinguished by Fehling reagent)

X $\xrightarrow{OH^-}$ 2-hydroxycyclopentanone $\xrightarrow{H_2O}$ cyclopentanone

Citral $\xrightarrow[(ii)\ O_3]{(i)\ \text{Wolf-Kishner reduction } -CHO \rightarrow -CH_3}$ [keto-aldehyde, –CHO] + acetone + CH_3–CHO

All undergo haloform reaction

76. (c) $\underset{(Z)}{\overset{CHO}{\underset{CHO}{|}}} \xrightarrow{[Ag(NH_3)_2]^+} \overset{COOH}{\underset{COOH}{|}} \xrightarrow{conc.H_2SO_4} CO + CO_2 2CO^* = 3CO(6.72\ ml)$ (C)

$$\text{Moles} = \frac{6.72}{22400} = 3\times10^{-4} \qquad \therefore \text{Moles of } \overset{CHO}{\underset{CHO}{|}} = 10^{-4} \text{ (in 100 ml)} = 10^{-3}\ M$$

Sol. (77-79) :

(A) H_3C–CH(OC_2H_5)–C_6H_4–CH_2OH $\xrightarrow{HI}$ (B) H_3C–CH(I)–C_6H_4–CH_2I $\xrightarrow{aq.\ KOH}$ (C) H_3C–CH(OH)–C_6H_4–CH_2OH $\xrightarrow{PCC}$ (D) H_3C–C(=O)–C_6H_4–CHO $\xrightarrow[AlCl_3]{Cl_2}$ (E) H_3C–C(=O)–C_6H_3(Cl)–CHO

Sol. (80- 82)

Let us summarize the given facts of the problem.

$$\underset{(2\ aldehydes)}{P + Q} \xrightarrow{aq.K_2CO_3} R \xrightarrow{HCN} S \xrightarrow[Heat]{H^+/H_2O} \text{[lactone: } H_3C, H_3C, OH]$$

Structures of P, Q, R and S can be established on going backward from the known final product.

[lactone] $\xleftarrow{-H_2O}$ (Unstable hydroxy acid: H_3C, H_3C, OH, HO, =O, OH) $\xleftarrow[Heat]{H^+/H_2O}$

(R) H_3C, H_3C, OH, CHO $\xrightarrow{HCN}$ (S) H_3C, H_3C, OH, HO, C–N

(P & Q) $(H_3C)_2CH$–CHO + H–CHO $\xrightarrow{aq.\ K_2CO_3}$ (R)

87. A - (p, q, s, t); B - (p, t); C - (p, q, s); D - (p, q, s, t)

(A) $\xrightarrow[OH^-]{HCN}$ (A) $\xrightarrow{LiAlH_4}$ (B) $\xrightarrow[HCl]{NaNO_2}$ $\xrightarrow{NaNO_2+HCl}$ ⟷ $\xrightarrow{-H^+}$ (C)

(B) $\xrightarrow{H_2NOH}$ (A) $\xrightarrow[\text{Beckmann rearrangement}]{PCl_5}$ (B)

(C) Intramolecular aldol condensation

(D) Pinacol – Pinacolone rearrangement

88. (A) – c, d, e ; (B) – a, d ; (C) - c, d; (D) – b, c

$\xrightarrow{aq/NaOH}$ (Carbanion) $\xrightarrow{H_2O}$ (Nucleophilic addition) $\xrightarrow[\text{dehydration}]{OH^-/\Delta}$

(B) $\xrightarrow[\text{Nucleophilic addition}]{CH_3MgI}$ $\xrightarrow{H_2O}$ (Nucleophilic substitution)

(C) $\xrightarrow{H_2SO_4}$ (Nucleophilic addition) $\xrightarrow[\text{dehydration}]{H_2SO_4}$

(D) $\xrightarrow[\text{dehydration}]{H_2SO_4}$ $\xrightarrow{\text{Electrophilic substitution}}$

97. (a) The given conversion is unfavoured with Clemmensen reduction because with highly acidic medium, it will attack on –OH group of the given compound.

100. (d) $C_6H_5-CH=C(CH_3)-CHO$ is the condensation product.

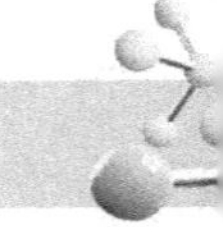

EXERCISE 14.3

1. (*i*) 3-Phenylpropenal (*ii*) 4-Methyl-3-penten-2-one (*iii*) 4-Methyl-3-hexanone
(*iv*) 4-Ketopentanoic acid (—COOH group has a higher priority over —CO group).

2. (*a*) $(CH_3)_3CCHO$ (*b*) $CH_3CH_2CH(CH_3)CH_2CH(CH_3)CHO$ (*c*) $H_3C-C_6H_4-CO-C_6H_4-CH_3$

3. $H_2C=O$ is a planar molecule, *i.e.*, its C is sp^2 hybridised (theoretically, its bond angle should be 120°). However, the H—C—O bond angle is slightly greater (121.8°) than the expected 120°, while the H—C—H angles are 116.5°, slightly less than 120°.

4. The C = O bond is polarised ($\overset{\delta+}{C}=\overset{\delta-}{O}$) due to more electronegative nature of oxygen, while the C = C bond is nearly non-polar. The π bond of C = C is an electron source, and is a nucleophilic site, while in C = O, the nucleophilic site is O.

5. (*a*) 2-Propanol has highest boiling point due to intermolecular H—bonding, since propanone and 2-methylpropene have no hydrogen on oxygen, they can't undergo association. However, the dipole-dipole attractive forces of carbonyl compounds are responsible for their higher boiling point than those of alkenes.
(*b*) Oxygen of C = O forms H—bond with the H of water making the former to dissolve in the latter (water) ; such hydrogen bond formation is not possible in an alkene as it has no oxygen. However, carbonyl group has no H atom which can form H—bond with the O of H_2O, hence these are less water soluble than alcohols.
(*c*) Alkyl substituents stabilize C = O as they do C = C by releasing electrons towards the sp^2 hybridized C. The enthalpy of the ketone is lower because it has two R groups, while the aldehydes have only one.

6. Ketenes have the general formula, $R_2C=C=O$. Structural formula for the ketene is $H_2C=C=O$,

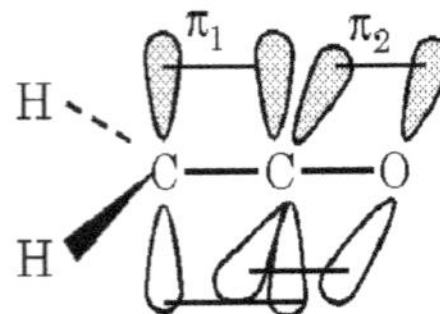

7. (*a*) Reduction of RCOOR with $LiAlH_4$ gives RCH_2OH, since the intermediate aldehyde RCHO is generally susceptible to further reduction. Hence one equivalent of the less reactive diisobutyllithium aluminium hydride (DBAH) is used at —70°C followed by hydrolysis ; when aldehyde is obtained in good yield.

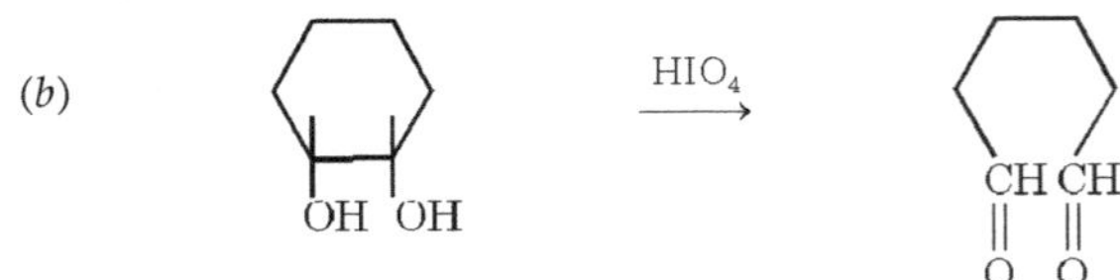

cis-1, 2-Cyclohexanediol Hexan-1, 6-dial

The corresponding *trans*-form does not form transition state easily, hence it is not oxidised by periodic acid.

8. (*a*) $(CH_3)_2CHCH_2C\equiv CH + H_2O$ in $HgSO_4$, H_2SO_4
(*b*) $(CH_3)_2CHCH_2CHOHCH_3 + KMnO_4$ or a Cr(VI) reagent
(*c*) $(CH_3)_2CHCH_2COCl + (CH_3)_2CuLi$ (from CH_3MgI + Li, then Cu)
(*d*) $(CH_3)_2CHCH_2COOH + 2CH_3Li$
(*e*) $(CH_3)_2CHCH_2COCl + (CH_3)_2Cd$ (from $CH_3MgI + CdCl_2$)
(*f*) $(CH_3)_2CHCH_2C\equiv N + CH_3MgI$ or CH_3Li.

9. In such cases, proceed backward *i.e.*, first write down the structure of the required compound and then apply your memory for getting the two required components for its preparation.

(*a*) $C_6H_5CH(OH)CH_2CH_3 \longleftarrow C_6H_5MgBr + CH_3CH_2CHO$ **or** $C_6H_5CHO + CH_3CH_2MgBr$
A 2° alcohol

(*b*) $C_6H_5-C(OH)(CH_3)-CH_3 \longleftarrow C_6H_5MgBr + (CH_3)_2CO$ **or** $C_6H_5COCH_3 + CH_3MgBr$
A 3° alcohol

(*c*) $C_6H_5CH_2CHOHCH_3 \longleftarrow C_6H_5CH_2CHO + CH_3MgBr$
1-Phenyl-2-propanol, a 2°alcohol

(*d*) $C_6H_5CH_2CH_2CH_2OH \longleftarrow C_6H_5CH_2CH_2MgBr + HCHO$
3-Phenylpropanol, a 1° alcohol

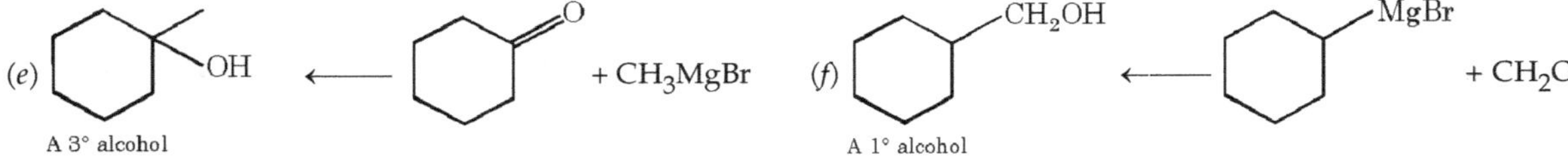

A 3° alcohol A 1° alcohol

(g) 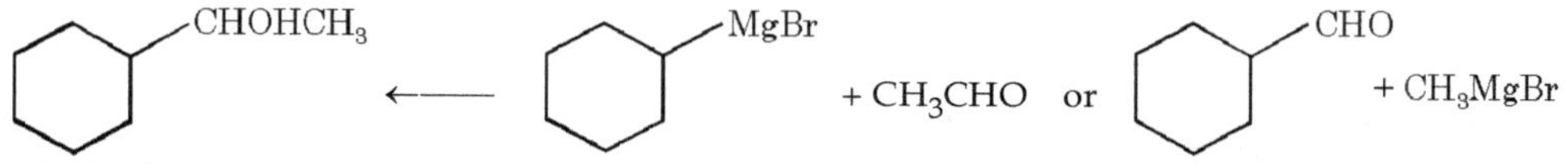 Cyclohexyl–$CHOHCH_3$ (A 2° Alcohol) $\longleftarrow$ Cyclohexyl–$MgBr$ + CH_3CHO or Cyclohexyl–CHO + CH_3MgBr

(h) $CH_3CH_2CHOHC \equiv CH$ (A 2° alcohol) $\longleftarrow$ $CH_3CH_2CHO + HC \equiv CLi$

(i) $CH_3CHOHC \equiv CCH_3$ (A 2° alcohol) $\longleftarrow$ $CH_3CHO + CH_3C \equiv CLi$

(j) p-$CH_3C_6H_4CHOHCH_3 \longleftarrow$ p-$CH_3C_6H_4MgBr + CH_3CHO$ **or** p-$CH_3C_6H_4CHO + CH_3MgBr$

10.

Reagent	Product from $C_6H_5CH_2CHO$	*Product from* 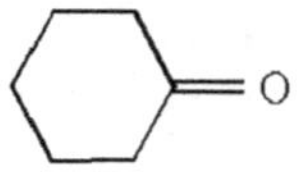 cyclohexanone (cyclohexyl=O)
(a) Tollen's reagent	$C_6H_5CH_2COO^-Ag^+$	No reaction
(b) CrO_3/H_2SO_4	$C_6H_5CH_2COOH$	No reaction
(c) Cold dil $KMnO_4$	$C_6H_5CH_2COOH$	No reaction
(d) $KMnO_4$, H^+, heat	C_6H_5COOH	$HOOC(CH_2)_4COOH$
(e) H_2, Ni, Pressure	$C_6H_5CH_2OH$	$C_6H_{11}CHOH$
(f) $NaBH_4$	$C_6H_5CH_2OH$	$C_6H_{11}CHOH$
(g) C_6H_5MgBr, H_2O	$C_6H_5CH_2CHOHC_6H_5$	$C_6H_{10}(OH)(C_6H_5)$
(h) $Me_2CHMgCl$, H_2O	$C_6H_5CH_2CHOHCHMe_2$	$C_6H_{10}(OH)(CHMe_2)$
(i) $HC \equiv CLi$, H_2O	$C_6H_5CH_2CHOHC \equiv CH$	$C_6H_{10}(OH)(C \equiv CH)$
(j) $NH_2CONHNH_2$	$C_6H_5CH_2CH = NNHCONH_2$	$C_6H_{10} = NNHCONH_2$
(k) C_2H_5OH, HCl	$C_6H_5CH_2CH(OC_2H_5)_2$	$C_6H_{10}(OC_2H_5)(OC_2H_5)$
(l) Me_3CNH_2	$C_6H_5CH = NMe_3$	$C_6H_{10} = NCMe_3$
(m) C_2H_5SH, H^+	$C_6H_5CH_2CH(OH)(SC_2H_5)$	$C_6H_{10}(OH)(SC_2H_5)$

Where C_6H_{11}— is cyclohexyl, C_6H_{10}– is cyclohexane-1,1-diyl; C_6H_{10} = is cyclohexylidene

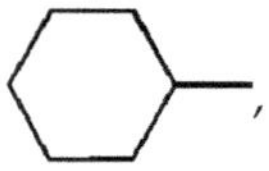

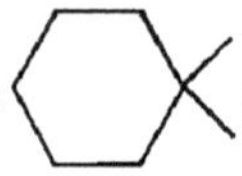

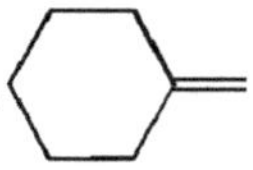

11. Write down the structure of the compound to be prepared.

(a) $CH_3CH_2CH_2OH \xleftarrow[\text{or } H_2,\, Ni]{LiAlH_4} CH_3CH_2CHO$

(b) $CH_3CH_2CH(OH)COOH \xleftarrow{H_2O,\, H^+} CH_3CH_2CH(OH)CN \xleftarrow[H^+]{CN^-} CH_3CH_2CHO$

(c) $CH_3CH_2CH(OH)CH_3 \longleftarrow CH_3CH_2CHO + CH_3MgBr$

(d) $CH_3CH_2CH(OH)C_6H_5 \longleftarrow CH_3CH_2CHO + C_6H_5MgBr$

(e) $CH_3CH_2CH(OH)CH(CH_3)_2 \longleftarrow CH_3CH_2CHO + (CH_3)_2CHMgBr$

12. 2-Methyl-2-pentenal, $CH_3CH_2CH = C(CH_3)CHO$ to

(a) $CH_3CH_2CH = C(CH_3)—CH_2OH$
(reduction of only —CHO to —CH_2OH, hence $NaBH_4$ is used)

(b) $CH_3CH_2CH_2CH(CH_3)CH_2OH$
(reduction of —CHO to —CH_2OH as well as C = C, hence H_2/Pt is used)

*(c) $CH_3CH_2CH_2CH(CH_3)CH_3$
(reduction of —CHO to >CH_2 and also of C = C)

**(d) $CH_3CH_2CH_2CH(CH_3)CHO$
(reduction of only C = C, hence —CHO must be first protected)

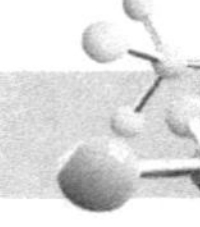

$$*(c)\ CH_3CH_2CH=\underset{}{\overset{CH_3}{\overset{|}{C}}}CHO \xrightarrow[\text{Wolf-Kishner reduction}]{NH_2NH_2,\ OH^-,\ heat} CH_3CH_2CH=\overset{CH_3}{\overset{|}{C}}CH_3 \xrightarrow{H_2/Pt} CH_3CH_2CH_2\overset{CH_3}{\overset{|}{C}}HCH_3$$

$$**(d)\ CH_3CH_2CH=\overset{CH_3}{\overset{|}{C}}CHO \xrightarrow[HCl]{CH_3OH} CH_3CH_2CH=\overset{CH_3}{\overset{|}{C}}CH(OCH_3)_2 \xrightarrow[(ii)\ HCl,\ H_2O]{(i)\ H_2/Pt} CH_3CH_2CH\overset{CH_3}{\overset{|}{C}}HCHO$$

13. If a carbonyl compound has some other functional group which is stable to acids but react with strong base, then Clemmensen method (Zn/Hg + HCl) should be used. In case, the carbonyl compound is sensitive to acid but stable in base, then Wolf-Kishner method (NH_2NH_2, OH^-) should be used. Raney Ni desulfurization occurs under neutral conditions : however it can't be used with reactants with good leaving groups because —SH is an excellent nucleophile.

14. (*a*) $BrCH_2CH_2CHO \longrightarrow BrCH_2CH_2CH_3$. It should be carried out by Clemmensen reduction because strong base (used in Wolf-Kishner method) causes dehydrohalogenation. Desulfurisation by Raney Ni can't be used because $HSCH_2CH_2SH$, used for converting C = O into thioacetal, can displace Br^- (a good leaving group), hence thioacetal will not be formed.

$$BrCH_2CH_2CHO + HSCH_2CH_2SH \longrightarrow HSCH_2CH_2SCH_2CH_2CHO + Br^-$$

(*b*) $Me_2C(OH)\ CH_2CH_2COCH_3 \longrightarrow Me_2C(OH)CH_2CH_2CH_2CH_3$. It can be carried out by Wolf-Kishner reduction or desulphurisation. Clemmensen method, using HCl, is not suitable because 3° alcohol is easily dehydrated in presence of acid.

(*c*) $C_6H_5CH(OH)CH_2COCH_2CH_3 \longrightarrow C_6H_5CH(OH)CH_2CH_2CH_2CH_3$.
Here again acid causes dehydration of an alcohol which is although 2° but produces quite stable alkene because its double bond is conjugated with the benzene. Hence either of the other two methods can be used.

(*d*) Epoxides are very reactive, hence these are opened up by the reagents used in either of the three methods used for reducing carbonyl group. Thus none of the three methods give good result for reducing a carbonyl group.

15. (*a*) [A] is ; [B] is —CHO group is reduced earlier than keto.

O
CH_2OH

16. (*a*) $C_6H_5CH=CHCOCH_3 \xrightarrow[\text{(haloform reaction)}]{Cl_2,\ OH^-} C_6H_5CH=CHCOOH$ (*b*) $C_6H_5CH=CHCOCH_3 \xrightarrow{LiAlH_4} C_6H_5CH=CHCHOHCH_3$

(*c*) $C_6H_5CH=CHCOCH_3 \xrightarrow[\text{Birch reduction}]{Li,\ liq.NH_3,\ ether} C_6H_5CH_2CH_2COCH_3$ (*d*) $C_6H_5CH=CHCOCH_3 \xrightarrow{NH_2NH_2,\ OH^-} C_6H_5CH=CHCH_2CH_3$

(*e*) $C_6H_5CH=CHCOCH_3 \xrightarrow[(ii)\ H_2/Pt]{(i)\ NH_2NH_2,\ OH^-} C_6H_5CH_2CH_2CH_2CH_3$

17. Aldehydes are more easily hydrated than ketones. Further, presence of electron–withdrawing group increases hydration.

(*a*) $HCHO > CH_2ClCHO > CH_3CHO > CH_2ClCOCH_3 > CH_3COCH_3$

(*b*) CHO, Br > CHO > O, Br > O

18. (*a*) All these compounds undergo Cannizzaro reaction (a characteristic reaction of aldehydes lacking α-hydrogen atom). Note that compounds (*iv*) and (*v*) although do not have an aldehydic group, however, in presence of OH^- these are converted into aldehydes lacking α-hydrogen atom, hence they also undergo Cannizzaro reaction.

$$C_6H_5CHCl_2 \xrightarrow{OH^-} C_6H_5CH(OH)_2 \longrightarrow C_6H_5CHO;\quad Me_3CCHCl_2 \xrightarrow{OH^-} Me_3CCH(OH)_2 \longrightarrow Me_3CCHO$$

Thus the products in these compunds will be

(*i*) and (*iv*) $C_6H_5COO^-Na^+ + C_6H_5CH_2OH$ (*iii*) O, COO^-Na^+ + O, CH_2OH

(*ii*) and (*v*) $Me_3CCOO^-Na^+ + Me_3CCH_2OH$

(*b*) All these compounds have α-hydrogen, so they will undergo aldol condensation.

$$(i)\ 2C_6H_5CH_2CHO \xrightarrow{OH^-} C_6H_5CH_2\overset{OH}{\overset{|}{C}H}\underset{C_6H_5}{\underset{|}{C}H}CHO \xrightarrow{-H_2O} C_6H_5CH_2CH=\underset{C_6H_5}{\underset{|}{C}}CHO$$

Highly conjugated system
(C = C is conjugated with —CHO
as well as benzene ring)

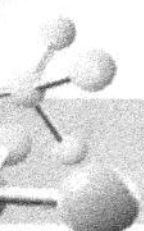

(*ii*) In $CH_3CH = CHCHO$, since the —CHO group is conjugated with the double bond, hydrogen atom of the methyl group (allylic hydrogen) becomes acidic, *i.e.*, it is the allylic carbanion that will be formed rather than vinylic, hence in such cases aldol condensation involves allylic hydrogen atom which is, of course, not the α-hydrogen atom.

$$2\,CH_3CH = CHCHO \longrightarrow CH_3CH = CH\underset{}{\overset{OH}{\overset{|}{C}}}HCH_2\,CH = CHCHO \xrightarrow[-H_2O]{} CH_3CH = CHCH = CHCH = CHCHO$$

(*iii*) $$C_6H_5CH = CHCHO + CH_3CH = CHCHO \xrightarrow{OH^-} C_6H_5CH = CH\overset{OH}{\overset{|}{C}}HCH_2\,CH = CHCHO \xrightarrow[(-H_2O)]{heat} C_6H_5CH = CHCH = CHCH = CHCHO$$

(*iv*) $$H—\overset{H}{\overset{|}{C}}=O + HCH_2CHO \longrightarrow H—\underset{OH}{\underset{|}{\overset{H}{\overset{|}{C}}}}—CH_2CHO$$

Here only CH_3CHO has α-hydrgoen atom so it will be forming carbanion which then adds on carbonyl carbon of formaldehyde. The process repeats till all the three hydrogen atoms of CH_3CHO are replaced by $—CH_2OH$ group.

$$H—\underset{OH}{\underset{|}{\overset{H}{\overset{|}{C}}}}—CHO \xrightarrow[\text{(aldol condensation)}]{CH_2O,\ OH^-} H—\underset{H}{\underset{|}{\overset{CH_2OH}{\overset{|}{C}}}}—CHO \xrightarrow[\text{(aldol condensation)}]{CH_2O} CH_2OH—\underset{H}{\underset{|}{\overset{CH_2OH}{\overset{|}{C}}}}—CHO \xrightarrow[\text{(aldol condensation)}]{CH_2O}$$

$$CH_2OH—\underset{CH_2OH}{\underset{|}{\overset{CH_2OH}{\overset{|}{C}}}}—CHO \xrightarrow[\text{(Cannizzaro reaction)}]{CH_2O} CH_2OH—\underset{CH_2OH}{\underset{|}{\overset{CH_2OH}{\overset{|}{C}}}}—CH_2OH + HCOO^-$$

19. 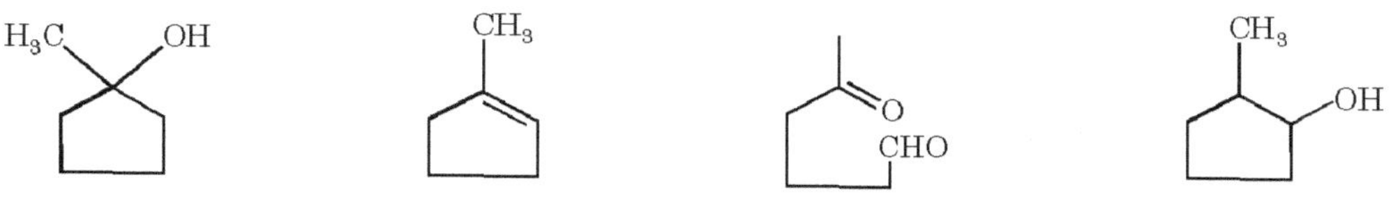

[A] [B] [C] [D]

20. (*a*) Halogenation occurs at the α-position to the C = O group under free radical conditions, hence product will be $C_6H_5COCHClCH_3$.

(*b*) 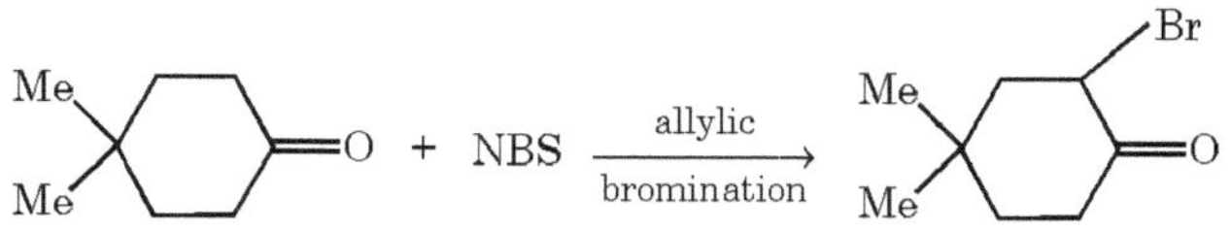

21. (*a*) Only phenylacetaldehyde, $C_6H_5CH_2CHO$ responds Tollen's reagent.
(*b*) Only 2-pentanone, $CH_3COCH_2CH_2CH_3$ responds iodoform test
(*c*) Only cyclohexanone gives crystals with 2, 4-dinitrophenylhydrazine
(*d*) Only *n*-valeraldehyde responds Tollen's reagent.
(*e*) Diethyl acetal on treatment with acid regenerates aldehyde which responds Tollen's reagent.
(*f*) Only propiophenone, $C_6H_5CH_2COCH_3$ responds iodoform test
(*g*) Only 2-pentanone responds 2, 4-dinitrophenylhydrazine, while 2-pentanol gives colour reaction with CrO_3/H_2SO_4.
(*h*) Paraldehyde, a cyclic trimer of acetaldehyde, $(CH_3CHO)_3$, on treatment with acid gives CH_3CHO which responds Tollen's or Schiff's reagent.
(*i*) Trioxane, $(CH_2O)_3$ on treatment with acid followed by heating gives CH_2O which responds Tollen's reagent or Schiff's test.

Dioxane is a cyclic ether 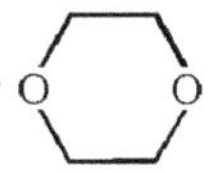

22. First step involves the conversion of —COOH to —COCl [A]. Conversion of [A] to [B] involves loss of HCl but without any change in carbon number, it indicates that the reaction is intramolecular Friedel Crafts acylation. Thus conversion of [A] to [C] can be represented as below.

$\xrightarrow{PCl_3}$ [A] $\xrightarrow[(-HCl_3)]{AlCl_3}$ [B] $\xrightarrow{NH_2NH_2, OH^-}$ [C]

[D] $\xrightarrow[\text{or } H_2SO_4]{AlCl_3}$ $\oplus CH_2$ ⟶ [C]

23. $n\text{-}C_5H_{11}C \equiv CLi$ [A] $n\text{-}C_5H_{11}C \equiv CCH_2CH_2CH_2Br$ [B] $n\text{-}C_5H_{11}C \equiv CCH_2CH_2CH_2CHR'(OH)$ [C]

$n\text{-}C_5H_{11}(H)C=C(H)(CH_2)_3CHOHR'$ [D] $n\text{-}C_5H_{11}(H)C=C(H)(CH_2)_3COR'$ [E]

24. $Cl_3CCH(OH)_2 \xrightarrow[-H_2O]{H^+} Cl_3C.\overset{+}{C}HOH \xrightarrow{C_6H_5Cl} [Cl-C_6H_4-CH(OH)CCl_3] \xrightarrow[H^+]{C_6H_5Cl} Cl-C_6H_4-CH(CCl_3)-C_6H_4-Cl$ [A] DDT

25. (a) Here either of the α-carbon can act as a nucleophile to form two possible compounds by intramolecular aldol condensation.

base, α carbon as nucleophile ← (Et, α, CHO, CHO, α') → base, α' as nucleophile

(b) Here only one product will be formed by the aldol condensation since here only one α carbon (α' carbon) can form a stable carbanion; in the second case (α carbon) +ve and –ve charges will be present an adjacent atoms causing unstability.

$\xrightarrow[\alpha' \text{ as nucleophile}]{\text{base}}$ (C_6H_5, COC_6H_5)

26. (a) cyclohexanone + $CH_3OCH = PPh_3$ $\xrightarrow[\text{reaction}]{\text{Wittig}}$ [A] ($=CH-\ddot{O}CH_3$) ⇌ ($CH=\overset{+}{O}CH_3$, H) $\xrightleftharpoons{H_2O}$ ($\overset{+}{O}H_2$, $CH-OCH_3$) $\xrightleftharpoons{-H^+}$ (OH, $CH-OCH_3$) $\xrightleftharpoons{-CH_3OH}$ CHO [B]

(b) $\xrightarrow[\text{(ii) Zn, } CH_3COOH]{\text{(i) } O_3}$ (O, O, α, α) $\xrightarrow[\text{(aldol cond.)}]{\text{base}}$ ≡

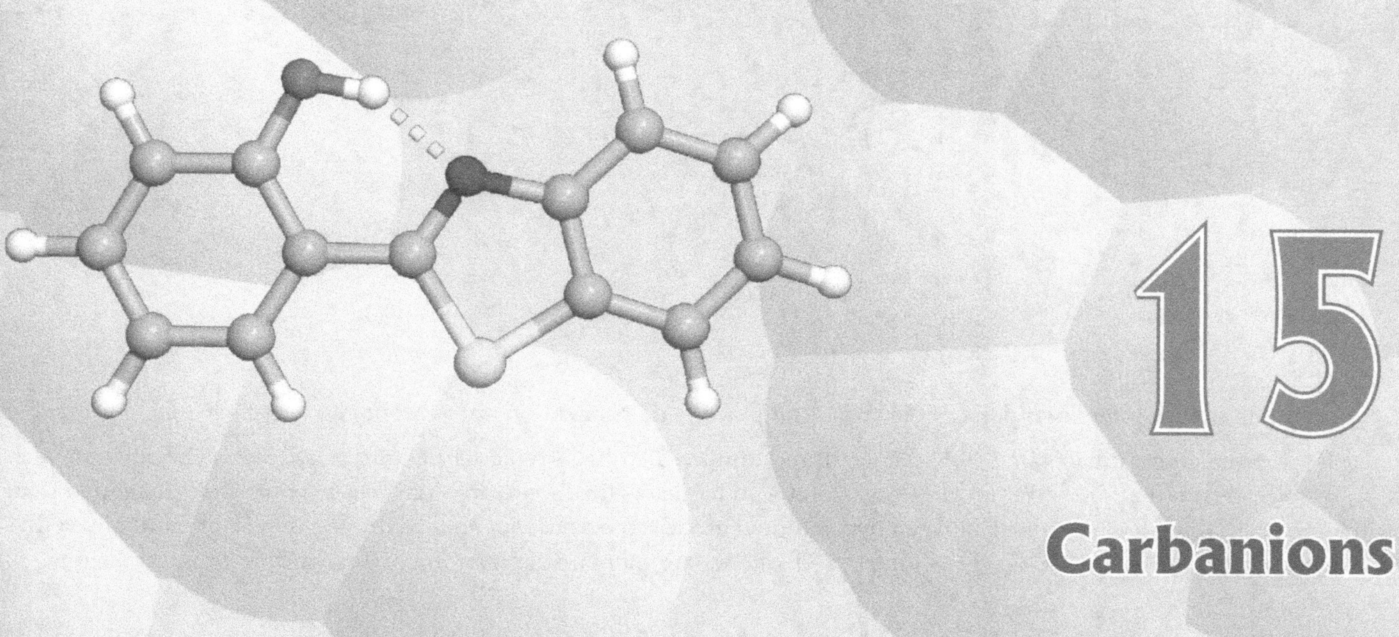

15 Carbanions

CHAPTER HIGHLIGHTS

In the preceding chapter we found nucleophilic addition to the carbonyl group as one of the important characteristics of aldehydes and ketones. However, another important characteristic of carbonyl compounds is the unusual acidity of its α hydrogen atom; i.e. such hydrogens are far more acidic than a hydrogen in an alkane. The reason for the unusual acidity of the α hydrogens of carbonyl compounds is due to stability of its corresponding enolate anion (carbanion).

$$-\overset{O}{\overset{\|}{C}}-\overset{H}{\overset{|}{\underset{|}{C}}}- \underset{}{\overset{\bar{:B}}{\rightleftharpoons}} \underbrace{-\overset{O}{\overset{\|}{C}}-\overset{\ddot{}\,-}{\underset{|}{C}}-}_{I} \longleftrightarrow \underbrace{-\overset{O^-}{\overset{|}{C}}=\underset{|}{C}-}_{II} \equiv -\overset{O^{\ominus}}{\overset{\vdots}{C}}\text{---}\underset{|}{C}-$$

Resonance-stabilized anion

Note that of the above two resonating structures, II is more stable because negative charge is present on oxygen (an electronegative element). Since the structure II (an enolate ion) makes a greater contribution to the hybrid, such carbanions are commonly known as **enolate ions** rather than carbanions.

15.1 Reactions Involving Carbanions

The carbonyl group occurs in compounds other than aldehydes and ketones and thus the α-hydrogens of such compounds should also be acidic. Such compounds (acids) in which proton is lost from carbon are called **carbon acid**, and hence the conjugate base of a carbon acid is known as carbanion. However, note that different carbon acids differ in their acidic property, e.g. aldehydes and ketones are more acidic than esters because the lone pair of electrons of the carbanions of an ester is not as readily delocalized as the carbanion of an aldehyde or ketone.

$$R-\overset{\cdot\cdot}{C}H-\overset{\overset{:\ddot{O}}{\|}}{C}-R \longleftrightarrow R-CH=\overset{\overset{:\ddot{O}:^-}{|}}{C}-R$$

Electron pair on C is delocalised

$$R-\overset{\cdot\cdot}{C}H-\overset{\overset{:\ddot{O}:^-}{|}}{C}=\overset{+}{\ddot{O}}R \longleftrightarrow R-\overset{\cdot\cdot}{C}H-\overset{\overset{:\ddot{O}}{\|}}{C}-\ddot{O}R \longleftrightarrow R-CH=\overset{\overset{:\ddot{O}:^-}{|}}{C}-\ddot{O}R$$

Electron pair on C is localised   Electron pair on C is delocalised

Note that in esters two pairs of electrons compete for delocalization onto carbonyl oxygen.

Nitroalkanes, nitriles and N,N-disubstituted amides also have relatively acidic α-hydrogens because in each case, the electrons left after the removal of the proton can be delocalized onto an atom that is more electronegative than carbon. Further, if the α-carbon is in between two carbonyl groups, the acidity of an α-hydrogen is even greater. Thus ethyl acetoacetate (a β-keto ester) and acetylacetone (a β-diketone) are more acidic than the corresponding ordinary ketone.

$$CH_3-\overset{\overset{O}{\|}}{C}-CH_2-\overset{\overset{O}{\|}}{C}-OC_2H_5 \qquad CH_3-\overset{\overset{O}{\|}}{C}-CH_2-\overset{\overset{O}{\|}}{C}-CH_3$$

Ethyl acetoacetate (Ethyl 3–oxobutyrate)   Acetylacetone (2,4-Pentanedione)

Higher acidity of α-hydrogens bonded to two electronegative groups (>C = O, $-NO_2$, –C ≡ N) is because the electrons left after the removal of proton can be delocalized onto two oxygen atoms.

$$CH_3-\overset{\overset{:\ddot{O}}{\|}}{C}-CH=\overset{\overset{:\ddot{O}:^-}{|}}{C}-CH_3 \longleftrightarrow CH_3-\overset{\overset{:\ddot{O}}{\|}}{C}-\overset{\cdot\cdot}{\underset{}{C}}H^{-}-\overset{\overset{:\ddot{O}}{\|}}{C}-CH_3 \longleftrightarrow CH_3-\overset{\overset{:\ddot{O}:^-}{|}}{C}=CH-\overset{\overset{:\ddot{O}}{\|}}{C}-CH_3$$

Resonance stabilization of 2,4-pentanedione anion

TEST YOUR UNDERSTANDING - 15.1

1. How many acidic hydrogens are present in each of the following?
   (a) 3,3-Dimethyl-2-butanone (b) Benzyl methyl ketone
   (c) 2,2-Dimethylpropanal (d) Cyclohexane-1,3-dione
2. Arrange the listed compounds in each of the following groups in order of decreasing acidity.
   (a) $CH_3\overset{\overset{O}{\|}}{C}CH_3$, $CH_3\overset{\overset{O}{\|}}{C}OH$, $CH_3\overset{\overset{O}{\|}}{C}OCH_3$, $CH\equiv CH$
   (b) $CH_3\overset{\overset{O}{\|}}{C}CH_2\overset{\overset{O}{\|}}{C}CH_3$, $H_3CO\overset{\overset{O}{\|}}{C}CH_2\overset{\overset{O}{\|}}{C}OCH_3$, $CH_3\overset{\overset{O}{\|}}{C}CH_2\overset{\overset{O}{\|}}{C}OCH_3$
   (c) cyclohexanone, N-methyl lactam (NCH_3), lactone (O)

The pK_a values of some carbon acids

	pK_a		pK_a
$CH_3C(=O)NMe_2$	30	$N\equiv CCH_2CN$	11.8
$CH_3C(=O)OCH_2CH_3$	25	$CH_3C(=O)CH_2C(=O)OC_2H_5$	10.7
$CH_3C\equiv N$	25	$C_6H_5-C(=O)CH_2C(=O)CH_3$	9.4
$CH_3C(=O)CH_3$	20	$CH_3C(=O)CH_2C(=O)CH_3$	8.9
$CH_3C(=O)H$	17	$CH_3C(=O)CH_2C(=O)H$	5.9
$CH_3CH_2NO_2$	8.6	$O_2NCH_2NO_2$	3.6

15.2 Reactions *via* Enols and Enolate Ions

Although in majority of cases, enolates are carbanions, in some cases ordinary carbanions (not enolates) serve as carbanions.

15.2.1 Racemization

When a solution of (+)-*sec*-butyl phenyl ketone in aqueous ethanol solution is treated with either acids or bases, a racemic mixture of the ketone is formed after some time.

$$(C_6H_5)(H_3C)(H)C-C(=O)-C_6H_5 \xrightarrow[H_3O^+]{OH^-\text{ or}} (C_6H_5)(H_3C)C=C(OH)(C_6H_5) \longrightarrow (\pm)\text{– Butyl phenyl ketone}$$

(R) – (+) –*sec*-Butyl phenyl ketone *(chiral)*; Enol, E or Z *(achiral)*

In the acyclic ketone, the enol or enolate anion formed can be E or Z. Protonation on one face of the E isomer and protonation on the same face of the Z isomer produces enantiomers.

Mechanism

Base-catalyzed enolization.

$$>C(H)-C(=\ddot{O}:) \underset{}{\overset{OH^-}{\rightleftharpoons}} >C^--C(=O) \leftrightarrow >C=C-\ddot{O}:^- \overset{H-OH}{\rightleftharpoons} >C=C(OH) + OH^-$$

Ketone (chiral) → Enol (achiral)

Acid-catalyzed enolization

$$>C(H)-C(=\ddot{O}:) \overset{H-\overset{+}{O}H_2}{\rightleftharpoons} >C(H)-C(H)=\overset{+}{\ddot{O}}-H \ (H-\ddot{O}-H) \rightleftharpoons >C=C(\ddot{O}-H) + H_3O^+$$

Ketone (chiral) → Enol (achiral)

TEST YOUR UNDERSTANDING - 15.2

1. What do you expect when each of the following optically active ketone is treated with a base?

(a) $CH_3(C_2H_5)(C_3H_7)C-\overset{O}{\overset{||}{C}}-C_6H_5$ (b) $C_2H_5(CH_3)(H)C-CH_2-\overset{O}{\overset{||}{C}}-C_6H_5$ (c) 2-methylcyclohexanone (H, CH_3 at the α-carbon)

2. Explain with mechanism what happens when *sec*-butyl phenyl ketone is treated with D_3O^+ in the presence of D_2O.
3. Predict which form (*keto* or *enol*) will present in the larger concentration at equilibrium in each of the following. Suggest the reason for the predominant form.

(a) 2, 4-Pentanedione (b) 2,4-Cyclohexadien-1-one

15.2.2 Formation of Lithium Enolates

The amount of carbonyl compound converted to enolate depends on the pK_a of the carbonyl compound and the base used to remove the α-hydrogen. For example, when OH^- is used to remove an α-proton from acetone (pK_a = 20), only a small amount of the carbonyl group is converted into enolate because OH^- is a weaker base than the base being formed.

$$\underset{\substack{\text{Weaker acid}\\(pK_a = 20)}}{CH_3-\overset{O}{\overset{||}{C}}-CH_3} + \underset{\text{Weaker base}}{Na^+OH^-} \rightleftharpoons \underset{\text{Stronger base}}{CH_3-\overset{O^-Na^+}{\overset{|}{C}}=CH_2} + \underset{\substack{\text{Stronger acid}\\(pK_a = 16)}}{H_2O}$$

On the other hand, if a very strong base is used, the equilibrium lies far to the right. **Lithium diisopropylamide (LDA*)** is a very strong base used for converting ketones completely to the corresponding enolate form.

$$\underset{\substack{\text{Stronger acid}\\(pK_a=20)}}{CH_3-\overset{O}{\overset{||}{C}}-CH_3} + \underset{\text{Stronger base}}{(iso\text{-}C_3H_7)_2N^-Li^+} \longrightarrow \underset{\text{Weaker base}}{CH_3-\overset{O^-Li^+}{\overset{|}{C}}=CH_2} + \underset{\substack{\text{Weaker acid}\\(pK_a=38)}}{(iso\text{-}C_3H_7)_2NH}$$

Regioselective formation of enolate anion : An unsymmetrical ketone can form two possible enolates. Which of the two enolates predominates depends upon the nature of the base used and on the conditions employed.

(a) As in the formation of alkenes, the *enolate with the more highly substituted double bond is the* ***thermodynamically more stable enolate.*** The thermodynamic enolate is formed predominantly under conditions that permit the establishment of an equilibrium i.e., by using a relatively weak base in a protic solvent.

Kinetic (less stable) enolate $\xleftarrow{\text{LDA}}$ 2-Methylcyclohexanone $\xrightleftharpoons{\text{Weak base}}$ Thermodynamic (more stable) enolate

(b) *The enolate with the less substituted double bond is usually formed faster* because here hydrogen is removed from the less sterically hindered and slightly more acidic position. This enolate, called the **kinetic enolate** is formed predominantly when the reaction is kinetically controlled (or rate controlled), i.e. by using a very strong base like LDA. LDA, being a strong and sterically hindered base rapidly removes proton from the less hindered α-carbon of the ketone. The notable feature of LDA is that although it is a strong base, it is a poor nucleophile hence it does not attack the carbonyl carbon. The poor nucleophilic character of LDA is again due to the presence of two bulky alkyl substituents on the N which make difficult for the N to come close enough to the carbonyl carbon.

* LDA is easily prepared by adding an alkyllithium to diisopropylamine in THF at –78°C.

$$\underset{\substack{\text{Stronger acid}\\(pK_a=38)}}{[(CH_3)_2CH]_2NH} + \underset{\text{Stronger base}}{C_4H_9^-Li^+} \xrightarrow{\text{THF}} \underset{\text{Weaker base}}{[(CH_3)_2CH]_2N^-Li^+} + \underset{\substack{\text{Weaker acid}\\(pK_a=50)}}{C_4H_{10}}$$

Lithium enolate in desired aldol reaction : One of the important applications of lithium enolate is to carry out (i) aldol condensation in unsymmetrical ketone, and (ii) mixed (crossed) aldol condensation between two different aldehydes/ ketones, each capable of undergoing aldol condensation itself, in a **desired direction**. For example, aldol condensation between CH_3COCH_3 and CH_3CH_2CHO gives rise to three aldol products;

$$CH_3COCH_3 + CH_3CH_2CHO \xrightarrow{OH^-} \text{Three products}$$

However, the desired aldol can be obtained by taking ketone in the form of lithium enolate and adding another aldehyde or ketone to this lithium enolate.

$$CH_3-\overset{O}{\overset{\|}{C}}-CH_3$$

The ketone is added to LDA which removes an α–H from the ketone to produce an enolate — $(Me_2CH)_2\overset{-}{N}\overset{+}{Li}$ / THF, –78°C

$$CH_3-\overset{O^-Li^+}{\overset{|}{C}}=CH_2$$

The aldehyde is added when enolate reacts with the aldehyde at its carbonyl carbon — $\overset{\displaystyle O}{\overset{\|}{C}}HCH_2CH_3$

$$CH_3-\overset{O}{\overset{\|}{C}}-CH_2-\underset{O^-Li^+}{\underset{|}{CH}}-CH_2CH_3$$

Acid-base reaction occurs when water is added — H – OH

$$CH_3-\overset{O}{\overset{\|}{C}}-CH_2-\underset{OH}{\underset{|}{CH}}-CH_2CH_3$$

TEST YOUR UNDERSTANDING - 15.3

1. Give the starting materials used for preparing following aldol products.

(a) $CH_3\overset{CH_3}{\overset{|}{C}}HCOCH_2\overset{OH}{\overset{|}{C}}HCH_2CH_3$

(b) $CH_3CH=CHCOCH_2\overset{OH}{\overset{|}{C}}HCH_3$

(c) [structure: 4-methylcyclohex-3-enyl–C(CH₃)(OH)–CH₂–CO–CH=C(CH₃)₂]

(d) [structure: p-tolyl–C(CH₃)(OH)–CH₂–CO–CH=C(CH₃)₂]

15.2.3 Alkylation of the α-Carbon of Carbonyl Compounds *via* Lithium Enolates

Alkylation of the α-carbon of carbonyl compounds (ketones*, esters and nitriles) gives us another important way to form a new carbon-carbon bond.

$$\text{Cyclopentanone} \xrightarrow{LDA\ /\ THF} \text{enolate (carbanion)} \xrightarrow{1^\circ\ RX} \text{2-R-cyclopentanone}$$

* Aldehydes are not suitable for direct alkylation because they are more reactive (strong electrophiles) than ketones, hence they will undergo aldol condensation with enolate ion (formed from another molecule of the aldehyde) very readily.

$$C_6H_5CH_2\overset{O}{\overset{\|}{C}}OCH_3 \xrightarrow[\text{(ii) 1° RX}]{\text{(i) LDA/THF}} C_6H_5\overset{R}{\overset{|}{C}}H\overset{O}{\overset{\|}{C}}OCH_3$$

$$CH_3CH_2CH_2C \equiv N \xrightarrow[\text{(ii) 1° RX}]{\text{(i) LDA/THF}} CH_3CH_2\overset{R}{\overset{|}{C}}HC \equiv N$$

Since enolate ions are strong bases, *successful alkylations occur only when primary alkyl, primary benzylic, and primary allylic halides are used;* with secondary and tetiary halides, elimination becomes the main course of the reaction.

In case the ketone is unsymmetrical, two different products can be formed.

LDA; CH_3; CH_3I; H_3C

Kinetic enolate (favoured at low temp.)

Thermodynamic enolate (favoured at high temp.)

TEST YOUR UNDERSTANDING - 15.4

1. Predict the product(s) in each of the following reactions.

(a) $CH_3COCH_3 \xrightarrow[\text{(ii) } CH_2=CHCH_2Br]{\text{(i) LDA}}$

(b) $CH_3CH_2CN \xrightarrow[\text{(ii) } C_6H_5CH_2Br]{\text{(i) LDA}}$

(c) $\xrightarrow[\text{(ii) } CH_3CH_2I]{\text{(i) LDA}}$

(d) $\xrightarrow[\text{(ii) } CH_3I]{\text{(i) LDA}}$

15.2.4 Alkylation and Acylation of the α-Carbon *via* Enamine

An *enamine* (a vinyl amine), the nitrogen analogue of an enol, is formed when an aldehyde or a ketone reacts with a secondary amine.

Pyrrolidine (a 2° amine)

An enamine

The resonance of an enamine shows that it has some carbanions character. Although, an enamine is a stronger nucleophile than an enol, it is quite selective in its alkylation reactions.

enamine (major) ⟷ iminium ion (minor)

Like enolates, enamines react with electrophiles and thus they help in introducing an electrophile to the α-carbon of an aldehyde or a ketone.

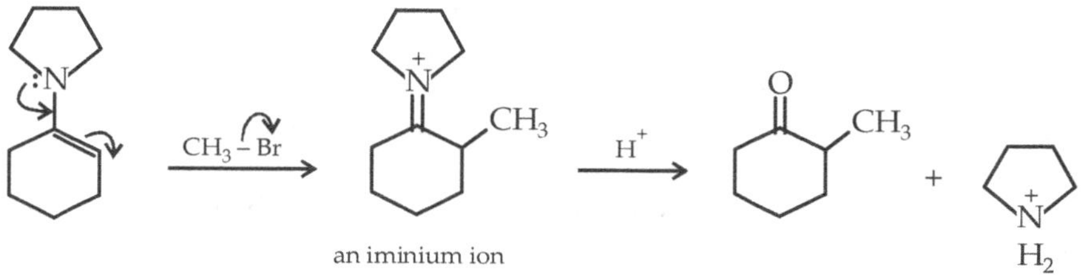

an iminium ion

Since, alkylation step is an S_N2 reaction, only primary alkyl halides or methyl halides should be used. Note that the iminium ions are unreactive toward further alkylation, so only one alkyl group can be introduced via enamine route (advantage over enolate route which may lead to monoalkylated, dialkylated and O–alkylated products).

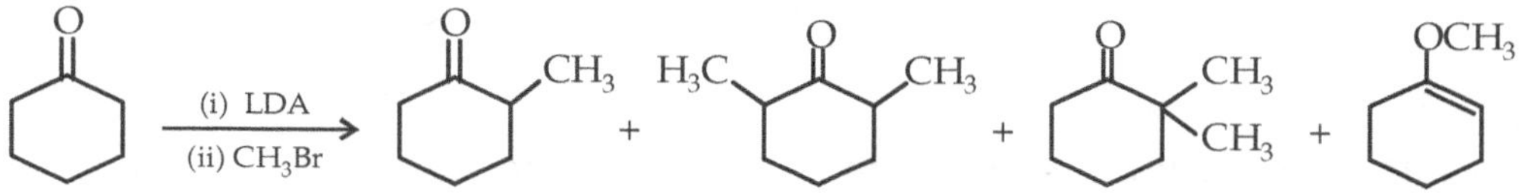

Aldehydes and ketones can also be acylated *via* an enamine intermediate.

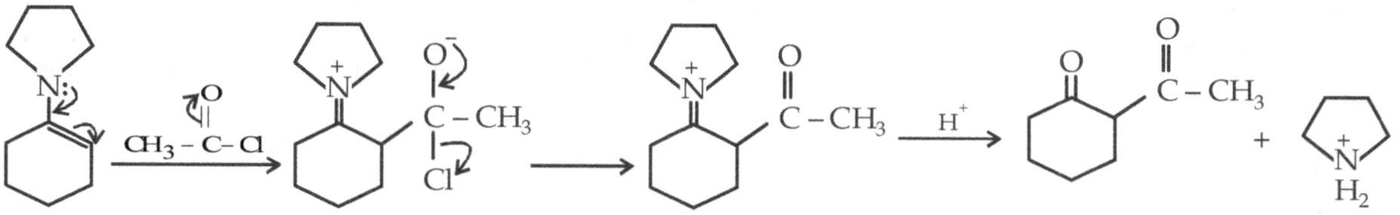

The enamine alkylation/acylation is sometimes called **Stork reaction**. Note that β-diketones are easily alkylated, hence they serve as useful intermediates in the synthesis of more complicated molecules.

TEST YOUR UNDERSTANDING - 15.5

1. Give the expected product of the following acid-catalyzed reactions.
   (a) Acetophenone + Dimethylamine
   (b) Acetophenone + Methylamine
   (c) Cyclohexanone + Aniline
   (d) Cyclohexanone + Piperidine
2. Give steps involved in the following conversions through enamine formation.
   (a) Cyclopentanone ⟶ 2-Allylcyclopentanone
   (b) 3-Pentanone ⟶ 2-Methyl-1-phenyl-3-pentanone
   (c) Acetophenone ⟶ Dibenzoylmethane

15.2.5 α-Halogenation of Aldehydes and Ketones

Discussed in the chapter on **'Aldehydes and Ketones'**.

TEST YOUR UNDERSTANDING - 15.6

1. How would you accomplish the following conversions?
   (a) $CH_3CH_2CHO \longrightarrow CH_3CH(NMe_2)CHO$
   (b) $CH_3CH_2CHO \longrightarrow CH_3CH(OH)CHO$
   (c) 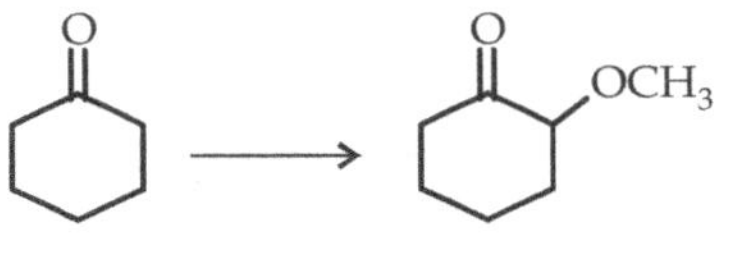
   (d)

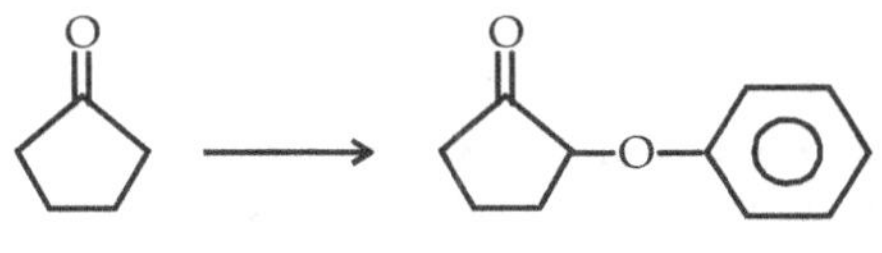

2. How will you prepare the following compounds from a carbonyl compound with no carbon-carbon double bonds?

(a) (b)

α-Brominated carbonyl compounds are useful in synthetic chemistry, because such compounds easily undergo reactions of alkyl halides.

$Br^- +$ [cyclohexenone] $\xleftarrow{tert\text{-}BuO^-}$ [2-bromocyclohexanone] $\xrightarrow{:Nu^-}$ [2-Nu-cyclohexanone] $+ Br^-$

15.2.6 α-Halogenation of Carboxylic Acids (The HVZ Reaction)

Carboxylic acids do not undergo substitution reactions at the α-carbon (of course except halogenation through the HVZ reaction) because the OH group is much more acidic than the α-carbon. However, if a carboxylic acid is treated with PBr_3 and Br_2 (or red phosphorus and excess Br_2), then bromination occurs at the α-carbon; the reason being the fact that here the α-substitution occurs on an acyl bromide rather than the parent carboxylic acid. For details, consult chapter on **'Carboxylic Acids'**.

15.2.7 Nucleophilic Addition of Enolates to Carbonyl Compounds

Under this heading following reactions are covered.

(a) **Aldol condensations :** Discussed earlier in the chapter on **'Aldehydes and Ketones'**.

(b) **Reactions related to aldol condensation :** There are other important reactions which involve the attack by a carbanion (provided by compounds other than aldehydes and ketones) on a carbonyl group. These reactions are Perkin, Knoevenagel, Claisen, Dieckmann etc. These reactions may also be grouped in **nucleophilic acyl substitution.**

(i) **Perkin reaction :**

$$C_6H_5CHO + (CH_3CO)_2O \xrightarrow{CH_3COONa} C_6H_5CH = CHCOOOH$$

Here the carbanion is provided by $(CH_3CO)_2O$.

(ii) **Knoevenagel reaction :**

$$C_6H_5CHO + H_2C(COOC_2H_5)_2 \xrightarrow{\text{piperidine}} C_6H_5CH = CHCOOH$$

Here the carbanion (nucleophile) is provided by $H_2C(COOC_2H_5)_2$.

(iii) **Claisen condensation :**

$$CH_3COOC_2H_5 + H_3CCOOC_2H_5 \xrightarrow{C_2H_5ONa} CH_3COCH_2COOC_2H_5$$

Here the carbanion is provided by $CH_3COOC_2H_5$.

(iv) **Dieckmann condensation :**

$$COOC_2H_5(CH_2)_4COOC_2H_5 \xrightarrow{C_2H_5ONa}$$ [2-oxocyclopentyl]$COOC_2H_5$

Here the carbanion is provided by α-carbon of the ester.

All these reactions are discussed in appropriate chapters on **Aldehydes and Ketones** or **Functional Derviatives of Carboxylic Acids.**

(c) Reformatsky reaction :

$$>C=O + BrCH_2COOR \xrightarrow[\text{benzene}]{Zn} >C<^{OZnBr}_{CH_2COOR}$$

Here the carbanion is provided by the carbon atom attached to halogen (Br).

$$BrCH_2COOR + Zn \longrightarrow \overset{+\delta}{BrZn}\ \overset{-\delta}{CH_2}\ COOR$$

For details, consult chapter on **"Aldehydes and Ketones"**.

(d) Addition of Grignard reagents :

$$>C=O + CH_3MgX \xrightarrow{H^+} >C<^{OH}_{CH_3}$$

$$-C\equiv N + CH_3MgX \longrightarrow -C\lessgtr^{NMgX}_{CH_3} \xrightarrow{H^+} -C\lessgtr^{O}_{CH_3}$$

Here the carbanion (nucleophile) is provided by alkyl or aryl group of the Grignard reagent. For details, consult chapter on **"Organometallic Compounds"**.

(e) Wittig reaction :

$$>C=O + Ph_3P=C<^{R}_{R'} \text{ or } Ph_3\overset{+}{P}-\overset{-}{C}<^{R}_{R'} \xrightarrow{H^+} >C=C<^{R}_{R'} + Ph_3P=O$$

Details are given in the chapter on **"Aldehydes and Ketones"**.

15.2.8 Nucleophilic Acyl Substitution

Here the nucleophilic attack finally gives substituted product (*the typical reaction of acyl compounds*), while in aldol condensation, the nucleophilic attack leads to addition (*the typical reaction of aldehydes and ketones*). Examples of this type are Claisen condensation, Dieckmann condensation (both discussed in esters) and acylation of organocopper compounds (discussed in the preparation of ketones in the chapter on **'Aldehydes and Ketones'**).

$$R'-\overset{O}{\overset{\|}{C}}-Cl + LiCu<^{R}_{R} \longrightarrow R'-\overset{O}{\overset{\|}{C}}-R + RCu + LiCl$$

Here the carbanion is provided by alkyl group.

15.2.9 Nucleophilic Aliphatic Substitution (Substitution on an sp^3 Carbon by a Nucleophile)

(a) **Coupling of alkyl halides with organometallic compounds :** Discussed in the preparation of alkanes, in the chapter on **'Aliphatic Hydrocarbons–I'**. Here, carbanion is provided by alkyl group of the organometallic compound.

(b) Alkylation of malonic ester, ethyl acetoacetate and related compounds.

15.3 ILLUSTRATIVE EXAMPLES

Example 1 :

Propose a mechanism to show how acetophenone undergoes *base-promoted* bromination to form tribromoacetophenone.

Solution :

$$C_6H_5-\overset{O}{\overset{\|}{C}}-\underset{H}{\overset{H}{C}}-H \xrightleftharpoons{OH^-} \left[C_6H_5-\overset{O}{\overset{\|}{C}}-\bar{C}H_2 \longleftrightarrow C_6H_5-\overset{O^-}{C}=CH_2\right]$$

$$\xrightarrow{Cl-Cl} C_6H_5-\overset{O}{\overset{\|}{C}}-\underset{H}{\overset{Cl}{C}}-H \xrightarrow{OH^-} \left[C_6H_5-\overset{O}{\overset{\|}{C}}-\overset{Cl}{\bar{C}H} \longleftrightarrow C_6H_5-\overset{O^-}{C}=\overset{Cl}{CH}\right]$$

$$\xrightarrow{Cl-Cl} C_6H_5-\overset{O}{\overset{\|}{C}}-\underset{H}{\overset{Cl}{C}}-Cl \xrightarrow{OH^-} \left[C_6H_5-\overset{O}{\overset{\|}{C}}-\overset{Cl}{\bar{C}}-Cl \longleftrightarrow C_6H_5-\overset{O^-}{C}=\overset{Cl}{C}-Cl\right] \xrightarrow{Cl-Cl} C_6H_5-\overset{O}{\overset{\|}{C}}-\underset{Cl}{\overset{Cl}{C}}-Cl$$

Example 2 :

Propose mechanism for the following conversion.

Cyclohexanone + pyrrolidine $\xrightarrow[\text{(ii) } C_6H_5CH_2Br,\ H_3O^+]{\text{(i) } H^+}$ 2-($CH_2C_6H_5$)cyclohexanone

Solution :

[Iminium ion ($\overset{+}{N}$=C) with H, $CH_2C_6H_5$ $\longleftrightarrow$ carbocation form with H, $CH_2C_6H_5$] $\xrightarrow{H_2O}$

$\overset{+}{O}H_2$, H, $CH_2C_6H_5$ adduct $\xrightarrow[(-H_3O^+)]{H_2O}$ OH, H, $CH_2C_6H_5$ amino alcohol $\xrightarrow{H_3O^+}$ H–$\overset{+}{N}$, OH, H, $CH_2C_6H_5$

$\longrightarrow$ pyrrolidine (N–H) + [OH, $\overset{+}{C}$, H, $CH_2C_6H_5$ $\longleftrightarrow$ $\overset{+}{O}$–H, H, $CH_2C_6H_5$] $\xrightarrow{H_2O}$ O, H, $CH_2C_6H_5$

Example 3 :

Give steps for preparing following compounds using malonic ester synthesis.

(a) **3-Phenylpropanoic acid** **(b)** **2-Benzylbutanoic acid**

(c) **Cyclopentanecarboxylic acid** **(d)** **2,2-Dimethylbutanoic acid**

Solution :

In malonic ester synthesis, the $-CH_2COOH$ or $-\overset{|}{C}HCOOH$ part of the product is coming from malonic ester itself, so the other substituent(s) should be introduced by alkylation of malonic ester before the final steps of hydrolysis and decarboxylation.

$$H_2C(COOC_2H_5)_2 \xrightarrow{H_3O^+} H_2C(COOH)_2 \xrightarrow{\text{heat}} H_3CCOOH + CO_2$$

Further note that malonic ester synthesis can be applied for synthesising carboxylic acids having either one or two substituents on the α-carbon (not three), i.e. either $-CH_2COOH$ or $-\overset{|}{C}HCOOH$ type and not R_3CCOOH type. For getting the right route for synthesis of such questions, first write down the structure of the product and know the nature of alkyl group to be introduced.

(a) $C_6H_5CH_2CH_2COOH$ (b) $CH_3CH_2CH(CH_2C_6H_5)COOH$ (c) cyclopentane–COOH (d) $CH_3CH_2C(CH_3)_2COOH$

(a) $H_2C(COOC_2H_5)_2 \xrightarrow[\text{(ii) } C_6H_5CH_2Br]{\text{(i) } C_2H_5ONa} C_6H_5CH_2CH(COOC_2H_5)_2 \xrightarrow[\text{(ii) heat}]{\text{(i) } H_3O^+} C_6H_5CH_2COOH$

(b) $C_2H_5OOCCH_2COOC_2H_5 \xrightarrow[\text{(ii) } CH_3CH_2Br]{\text{(i) } C_2H_5ONa} [\ ] \xrightarrow[\text{(ii) } C_6H_5CH_2Br]{\text{(i) } C_2H_5ONa}$

$$C_2H_5OOC-C(CH_2CH_3)(CH_2C_6H_5)-COOC_2H_5 \xrightarrow[\text{(ii) heat}]{\text{(i) } H_3O^+} CH_3CH_2CH(CH_2C_6H_5)COOH$$

(c) $C_2H_5OOCCH_2COOC_2H_5 \xrightarrow[\text{(ii) } Br(CH_2)_4Br]{\text{(i) } C_2H_5ONa}$ 1,1-cyclopentane$(COOC_2H_5)_2$ $\xrightarrow[\text{(ii) heat}]{\text{(i) } H_3O^+}$ cyclopentane–COOH

(d) 2,2-Dimethylbutanoic acid has three alkyl groups on the α-carbon atom, but malonic ester has only two α-hydrogen atoms so only two alkyl groups (sbstituents) can be introduced in malonic ester. Thus the compound (d) can't be prepared through malonic ester synthesis.

Example 4 :

Give steps involved in the conversion of ethyl acetoacetate into

(a) 3-propyl-5-hexen-2-one

(b) cyclopropyl methyl ketone

(c) 4-phenylbut-3-en-2-one

(d) benzyl *sec*-2-propenylphenyl ketone

Solution :

(a) OC_2H_5 —(i) $C_2H_5O^-$ (ii) Br→ OC_2H_5

—(i) $C_2H_5O^-$ (ii) Br→ OC_2H_5 —H^+→ OH —heat ($-CO_2$)→

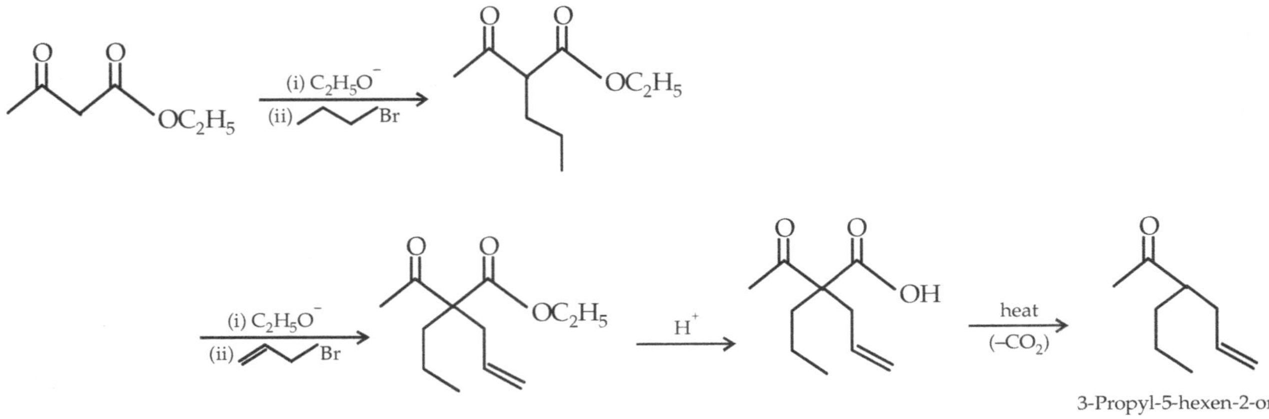

3-Propyl-5-hexen-2-one

(b) OC_2H_5 —(i) $C_2H_5O^-$ (ii) Br $(CH_2)_4$ Br→ OC_2H_5 —(i) H_3O^+ (ii) heat→

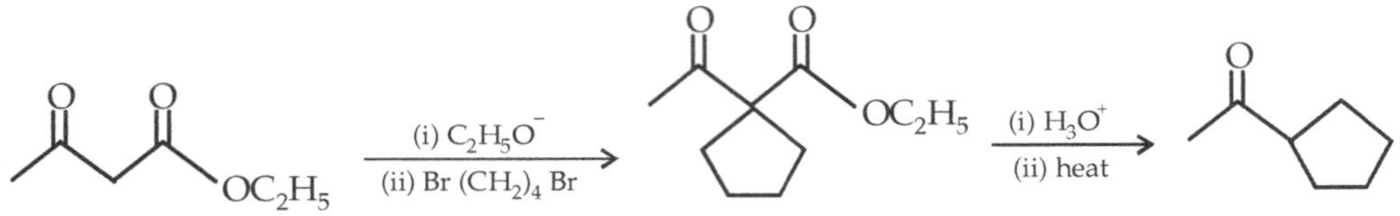

(c) $C_2H_5CH=O$ + OC_2H_5 —(Knoevenagel reaction)→ CHC_6H_5 OC_2H_5

—H_3O^+→ C_6H_5 OH —heat→ C_6H_5

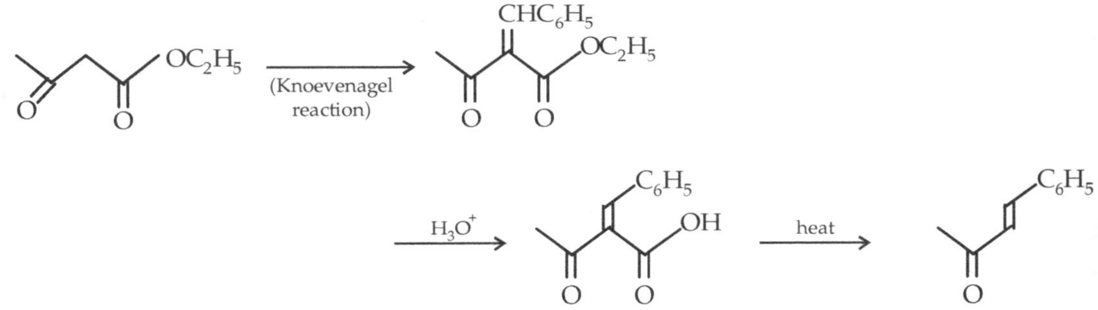

4-Phenylbut-3-en-2-one

(d)

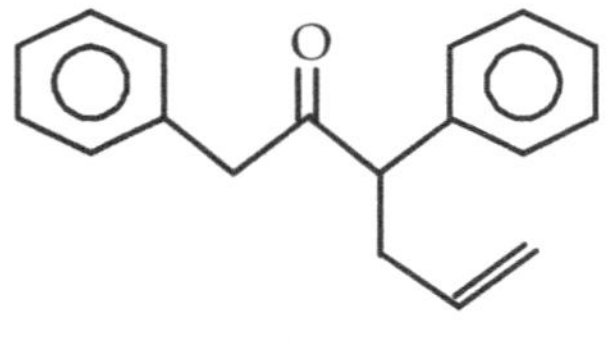

This compound can't be prepared from ethyl acetoacetate because here ketonic group is having substituents on both $-CH_2-$ groups which is not possible because in acetoacetic ester only one $-CH_2-$ is activated. However, this can be prepared from dibenzyl ketone in the following way.

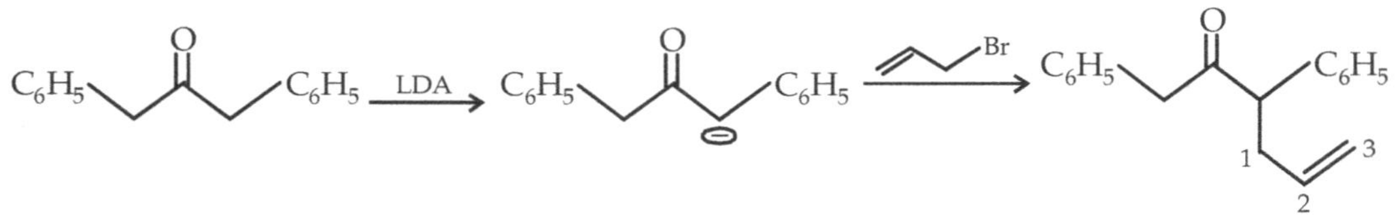

C_6H_5 C_6H_5 —LDA→ C_6H_5 C_6H_5 —Br→ C_6H_5 C_6H_5 1 2 3

Example 5 :

Perkin condensation between benzaldehyde and ethanoic anhydride in presence of sodium ethanoate leads to the more stable *trans*-cinnamic acid. Suggest a method for preparing the *cis*-cinnamic acid (*cis*-3-phenylpropenoic acid).

Solution :

Remember that a *cis*-alkene can often be prepared from an alkyne by hydrogenation of a triple bond over Lindlar's catalyst.

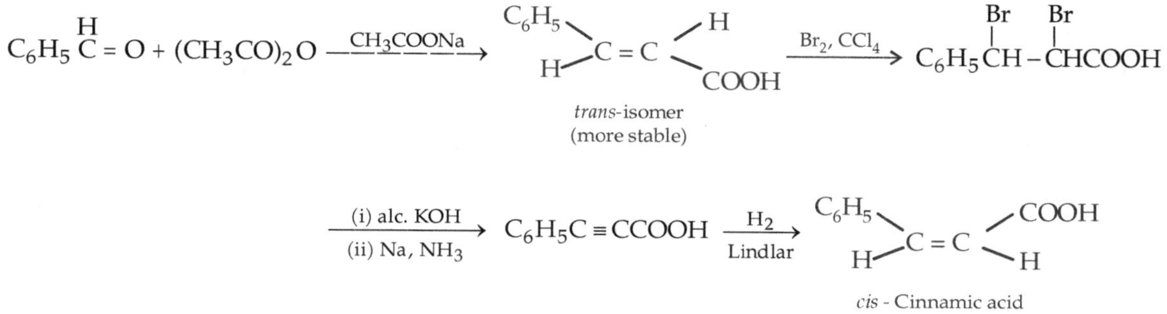
C6H5CH=O + (CH3CO)2O
CH3COONa
trans-isomer
(more stable)
Br2, CCl4
C6H5CH(Br)–CH(Br)COOH
(i) alc. KOH
(ii) Na, NH3
C6H5C≡CCOOH
H2
Lindlar
cis - Cinnamic acid

Example 6 :

Complete the following and comment on the reaction of each step.

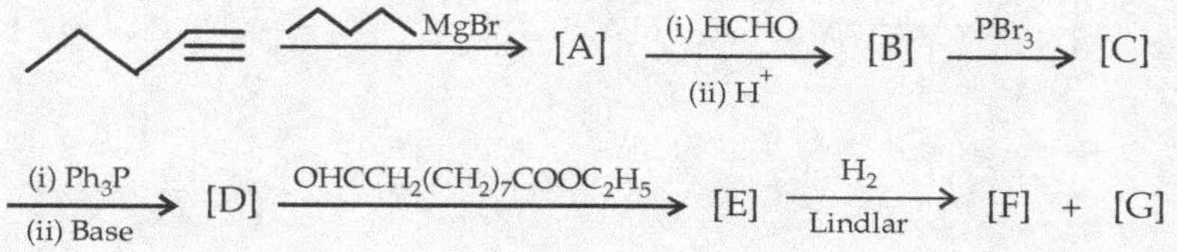
MgBr
[A]
(i) HCHO
(ii) H+
[B]
PBr3
[C]
(i) Ph3P
(ii) Base
[D]
OHCCH2(CH2)7COOC2H5
[E]
H2
Lindlar
[F] + [G]

Solution :

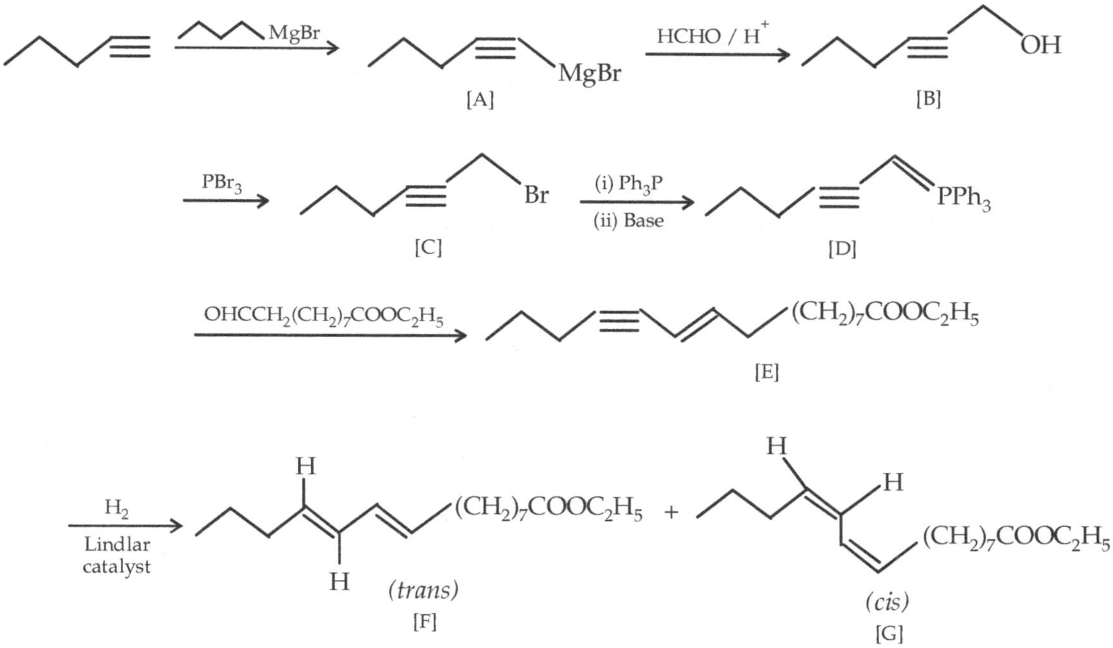
MgBr
[A]
HCHO / H+
OH
[B]
PBr3
Br
[C]
(i) Ph3P
(ii) Base
PPh3
[D]
OHCCH2(CH2)7COOC2H5
(CH2)7COOC2H5
[E]
H2
Lindlar
catalyst
(CH2)7COOC2H5
(trans)
[F]
(cis)
[G]

Example 7 :

Give steps involved in the conversion of

(a) ethyl cyanoacetate to valproic acid (2-propylpentanoic acid), an antiepileptic compound.

(b) benzaldehyde to acetophenone involving 1,3-dithiane as an intermediate.

(c) Ethyl phenyl ketone to darvone, an analgesic using $(CH_3CH_2CO)_2O$, $C_6H_5CH_2MgBr$, HCHO and $(CH_3)_2NH$ as reagents.

$$C_6H_5CH_2-\underset{OCOC_2H_5}{\overset{C_6H_5}{\overset{|}{\underset{|}{C}}}}-\overset{CH_3}{\overset{|}{C}}HCH_2NMe_2 \quad \text{(darvone)}$$

(d) $2NaCH(COOC_2H_5)_2 + BrCH_2CH_2CH_2Br \longrightarrow$ cyclopentane-1,2-dicarboxylic acid (COOH, COOH)

Solution :

(a) $NC-CH_2-COOC_2H_5 + 2CH_3CH_2CH_2Br \xrightarrow{\text{base}} (CH_3CH_2CH_2)_2C(CN)COOC_2H_5 \xrightarrow[\text{(ii) heat}]{\text{(I) } OH^-} (CH_3CH_2CH_2)_2CHCOOH$

(b) $C_6H_5\overset{O}{\overset{||}{C}}H + HS-CH_2CH_2CH_2-SH \xrightarrow{H^+}$ 2-phenyl-1,3-dithiane (H, C_6H_5) $\xrightarrow[\text{(ii) } CH_3I]{\text{(i) } C_4H_9Li}$ 2-methyl-2-phenyl-1,3-dithiane (CH_3, C_6H_5)

$\xrightarrow[CH_3OH,\ H_2O]{HgCl_2,} CH_3\overset{O}{\overset{||}{C}}C_6H_5 + HS-CH_2CH_2CH_2-SH$

(c) $C_6H_5-\underset{O}{\underset{||}{C}}-CH_2CH_3 + HCHO + HN(CH_3)_2 \xrightarrow[\text{reaction}]{\text{Mannich}} C_6H_5-\underset{O}{\underset{||}{C}}-\overset{CH_3}{\overset{|}{C}}HCH_2NMe_2$

$\xrightarrow[\text{(ii) } H_3O^+]{\text{(i) } C_6H_5CH_2MgBr} C_6H_5-\underset{OH}{\underset{|}{\overset{CH_2C_6H_5}{\overset{|}{C}}}}-\underset{CH_3}{\underset{|}{C}H}-CH_2NMe_2 \xrightarrow[\text{Acylation}]{(CH_3CH_2CO)_2O} C_6H_5-\underset{OCOCH_2CH_3}{\underset{|}{\overset{CH_2C_6H_5}{\overset{|}{C}}}}-CH(CH_3)CH_2NMe_2$

Darvone

(d) $2NaCH(COOC_2H_5)_2 + BrCH_2CH_2CH_2Br \longrightarrow (C_2H_5OOC)_2CH-CH_2CH_2CH_2-CH(COOC_2H_5)_2 \xrightarrow[\text{(ii) } Br_2]{\text{(i) } C_2H_5ONa}$

$(C_2H_5OOC)_2CH-CH_2CH_2CH_2-CBr(COOC_2H_5)_2 \xrightarrow{C_2H_5ONa}$ tetraethyl cyclopentane-1,1,2,2-tetracarboxylate $\xrightarrow[\text{(ii) } H_3O^+ \text{ (iii) heat}]{\text{(i) } OH^-}$ cyclopentane-1,2-dicarboxylic acid (COOH, COOH)

EXERCISE 15.1 (MCQ - ONE option correct)

1. Predict the product P in the following reaction

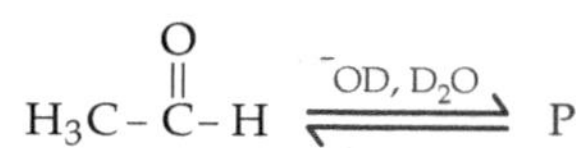

$H_3C-\overset{O}{\overset{||}{C}}-H \xrightleftharpoons{^-OD,\ D_2O} P$

(a) $D_3C-\overset{O}{\overset{||}{C}}-D$ (b) $H_3C-\overset{O}{\overset{||}{C}}-D$

(c) $D_3C-\overset{O}{\overset{||}{C}}-H$ (d) $H_3C-\overset{OH}{\overset{|}{C}H}-H$

2. Which of the following is true regarding conversion of a ketone into its enolic form by acids and bases?
   (a) In both types, the first step is the protonation of the carbonyl group
   (b) In both types, the first step is the removal of α-hydrogen
   (c) The two steps i.e. protonation and removal of α-hydrogen are reversed in the base - and acid-catalyzed reactions
   (d) None is true

3. Which of the following reactions of optically active *sec*-butyl phenyl ketone undergoes fastest?
   (a) Acid-catalyzed deuterium exchange
   (b) Base-promoted bromination
   (c) Acid-catalyzed racemization
   (d) None of these

4. $$3CH_2O + CH_3CHO \xrightarrow[40°C]{\text{dil. } Na_2CO_3} HOH_2C-\underset{CH_2OH}{\underset{|}{\overset{CH_2OH}{\overset{|}{C}}}}-CHO$$

   The above reaction involves
   (a) one aldol condensation and one Cannizzaro reaction
   (b) two aldol condensations
   (c) two aldol condensation and one Cannizzaro reaction
   (d) three aldol condensations

5. In case, there is a competition between intramolecular aldol condensation and intermolecular aldol condensation, which factor favours intramolecular aldol reaction over intermolecular?
   (a) Using excess of base
   (b) Using limited amount of base
   (c) Using high dilution technique
   (d) Using large excess of the compound

6. The compound P in the following reaction should be

$$CH_3CH_2CHO + D_2O + OD^- \longrightarrow P$$

   (a) CH_3CH_2CDO (b) CD_3CH_2CHO
   (c) CH_3CD_2CHO (d) CD_3CD_2CHO

7. Predict the nature of Z in the following reaction

$$CH_3COCH_2Br \xrightarrow{OH^-,\ Br_2} Z$$

   (a) $CH_2BrCOCH_2Br$ (b) $CH_3COCHBr_2$
   (c) $CH_2BrCOCHBr_2$ (d) No reaction

8. Predict the nature of [Y] and [Z] in the following reaction

$$\text{(1,3-dithiane, S S)} \xrightarrow[C_6H_5CH_2Br]{C_4H_9Li} [X] \xrightarrow[H_2]{\text{Raney Ni}} [Y] + [Z]$$

   (a) Y is $C_6H_5CH_2CH_2CH_2CH_3$ and Z is CH_4
   (b) Y is $CH_3\overset{CH_2C_6H_5}{\overset{|}{C}}HCH_3$ and Z is CH_4
   (c) Y is $C_6H_5CH_2CH_3 + CH_3CH_2CH_3$
   (d) Y is $C_6H_5CH_2CH_2CH_3$ and Z is NiS

9. Which of the following order is correct regarding the percentage of enolic form of 2,4-pentanedione in three solvents : H_2O (A), CH_3CN (B) and C_6H_{14} (C)?
   (a) A > B > C (b) B > A > C
   (c) C > A > B (d) C > B > A

10. Which of the following compound does not form carbanion with sodium ethoxide?
    (a) $CH_3COCH_2COOC_2H_5$ (b) $(CH_3)_3C.COOC_2H_5$
    (c) $CH_2(COOC_2H_5)_2$ (d) $CH_2\begin{matrix} \diagup CN \\ \diagdown COOC_2H_5 \end{matrix}$

11. Carbanion is
    (a) an electrophile (b) a nucleophile
    (c) a Zwitter ion (d) a free radical

12. The enol form of acetone, after treatment with D_2O, gives.
    (a) $CH_3-\overset{OD}{\overset{|}{C}}=CH_2$ (b) $CD_3-\overset{O}{\overset{||}{C}}-CD_3$
    (c) $CH_2=\overset{OH}{\overset{|}{C}}-CH_2D$ (d) $CD_2=\overset{OD}{\overset{|}{C}}-CD_3$

EXERCISE 15.2 (MCQ 1 or >1 option correct, Passage based, Matching, A/R)

DIRECTIONS for Q. 1 to Q. 7 : Multiple choice questions with one or more than one correct option(s).

1. Which of the following statement is false regarding enolization of

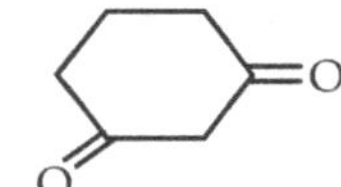

   (a) It can form two enolic forms of equal stability
   (b) It can form two enolic forms of different stability
   (c) It can form more than two enolic forms of different stability
   (d) It can form only one enolic form

2. 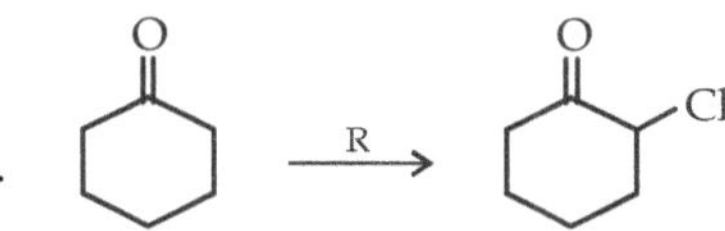

   Here the reagent R is
   (a) Cl_2 in presence of CH_3COOH
   (b) Cl_2 in presence of NaOH
   (c) Cl_2 in presence of water
   (d) Cl_2 in presence of light

3. Which statement is true about acetoacetic ester?
   (a) Its keto form boils at a higher temp. than the enolic form
   (b) Its enolic form boils at a higher temp. than the keto form
   (c) Both boil at same temperature
   (d) It discharges the colour of bromine dissolved in CCl_4

4. $2C_6H_5CHO \xrightarrow[H_2O]{OH^-} C_6H_5CH_2OH + C_6H_5COO^-$

   Which statement is correct regarding the above reduction of benzaldehyde to benzyl alcohol?
   (a) One hydrogen is coming from H_2O as H^+ and another from C_6H_5CHO as H^-
   (b) One hydrogen is coming from H_2O as H^- and another from C_6H_5CHO as H^+
   (c) One hydrogen from H_2O and another from C_6H_5CHO, both in the form of H^-
   (d) The reduction is an example of disproportionation reaction

5. A primary carbanion is
   (a) more reactive than a secondary carbanion
   (b) more stable than a secondary carbanion
   (c) less stable than a secondary carbanion
   (d) more stable than a tertiary carbanion

6. Which have active methylene group?
   (a) $CH_3-\overset{O}{\overset{||}{C}}-CH_2-\overset{O}{\overset{||}{C}}-CH_3$
   (b) $CH_3-CH_2-NO_2$
   (c) $CH_3-\overset{O}{\overset{||}{C}}-CH_2-CN$
   (d) $C_6H_5-\overset{O}{\overset{||}{C}}-CH_2-CN$

7. Which have acidic H?
   (a) CH_3COOH (b) C_6H_5-OH
   (c) $CH_3-\overset{O}{\overset{||}{C}}-CH_2-CN$ (d) $NaNH_2$

INSTRUCTION for Q. 8 to 11 : Read the passages given below and answer the questions that follow.

PASSAGE 1

Due to acidic nature of α-hydrogens, esters when treated with a strong base (generally C_2H_5ONa) undergo condensation of form β-keto ester.

$$CH_3\overset{O}{\overset{||}{C}}OC_2H_5 + CH_3\overset{O}{\overset{||}{C}}OC_2H_5 \xrightarrow[(ii)\ H_3O^+]{(i)\ C_2H_5ONa/C_2H_5OH} CH_3\overset{O}{\overset{||}{C}}CH_2COOC_2H_5 + C_2H_5OH.$$

Ethyl acetoacetate (Acetoacetic ester)

Mechanism

Step 1.

$$\underset{\text{Ethyl acetate}}{CH_3-\overset{O}{\overset{||}{C}}-OC_2H_5} + {}^-OC_2H_5 \rightleftharpoons {}^-CH_2-\overset{O}{\overset{||}{C}}-OC_2H_5$$

Step 2.

$$\underset{\text{Ethyl acetate (2nd mole)}}{CH_3-\overset{O}{\overset{||}{C}}-OC_2H_5} + {}^-CH_2-\overset{O}{\overset{||}{C}}OC_2H_5 \rightleftharpoons$$

$$CH_3-\overset{O^-}{\overset{|}{\underset{OC_2H_5}{\underset{|}{C}}}}-CH_2\overset{O}{\overset{||}{C}}OC_2H_5 \rightleftharpoons CH_3-\overset{O}{\overset{||}{C}}-CH_2\overset{O}{\overset{||}{C}}OC_2H_5 + {}^-OC_2H_5$$

Although the products at the end of the second step are acetoacetic ester and ethoxide ion, the reaction does not stop at this step ; had it so been, the yield of the β-keto ester would have been very little because the overall equilibrium upto this point is favourable to reactants and not to products.

8. The IUPAC name of ethylacetoacetate is
   (a) acetoacetic ester (b) ethyl 3-oxobutanoate
   (c) ethyl acetic ester (d) ethylacetoacetate

9. The net reaction in the step 2 of the reaction is
   (a) nucleophilic addition (b) nucleophilic substitution
   (c) both (a) and (b) (d) elimination

10. Which of the following statement is true ?
   (a) The reaction is still not complete because acetoacetic ester is a stronger acid than ethyl acetate
   (b) The reaction is still not complete because acetoacetic ester is a stronger acid than ethanol
   (c) Both (a) and (b)
   (d) The reaction stops at the given final step giving acetoacetic ester and ethoxide ion.

11. The above reaction, known as Claisen condensation involves the formation of new bond between
   (a) carbon and oxygen
   (b) the two carbonyl carbon atoms of the two components
   (c) α – carbon atoms of the two components
   (d) the α-carbon of one molecule and the carbonyl carbon of another molecule

Instructions for Q. 12 : Following questions are Multiple Matching type Questions :

12.

Column - I (Reaction)	Column - II (Carbanion provided by)
(A) Roformatsky reaction	(a) $CH_3CO\bar{C}H_2$
(B) Aldol condensation	(b) $\bar{C}H_2COOC_2H_5$
(C) Claisen condensation	(c) $\bar{C}H_2CHO$
(D) HVZ reaction	(d) $R\bar{C}H-\overset{O}{\overset{||}{C}}-Br$

EXERCISE 15.3 (Subjective Problems)

1. Give the important resonance forms for the enolate of
   (a) acetone (d) ethyl acetoacetate
   (b) cyclohexanone (e) ethyl cyanoacetate
   (c) 2,4-pentanedione (f) nitroacetone
2. What happens when cyclohexanone is treated with (a) dil. NaOH, (b) dilute HCl
3. Give steps involved in the following conversions.

(a) $C_6H_5CHO \longrightarrow C_6H_5CHO^{18}$

(b) $C_6H_5CHO \longrightarrow C_6H_5CH_2CHO$

(c) $C_6H_5CHO \longrightarrow C_6H_5CH = CH - CH = CHCHO$

(d) $C_2H_5OCOC_2H_5$ (ethyl carbonate) to PhCOCH₂COCH₂COPh

(e) $C_2H_5O-C(=O)-OC_2H_5$ (ethyl oxalate) to $(CH_3)_2CHCH_2CH(\overset{+}{N}H_3)COO^-$

(f) CH_3CHO to (lactone: 5-methyl-2-oxotetrahydrofuran-4-carboxylic acid, H_3C, COOH)

(g) C_6H_5CHO to (1-indanone)

(h) (cyclohexanone) to (D, D, D-labelled cyclohexene)

4. Is it possible to convert 4-hydroxy-4-methyl-2-pentanone to acetone?

$$CH_3COCH_2C(OH)(CH_3)_2 \xrightarrow{OH^-} CH_3COCH_3$$

5. Give steps involved in the conversion of acetone and ethanal to dehydrocitral,

(dehydrocitral structure, CHO)

SOLUTIONS

TEST YOUR UNDERSTANDING - 15.1

1. (a) $\mathbf{CH_3}-\overset{O}{\overset{\|}{C}}-C(CH_3)_2-CH_3$ (Three) (b) $C_6H_5-\overset{O}{\overset{\|}{C}}-\mathbf{CH_3}$ (Three) (c) $H_3C-C(CH_3)_2-\overset{O}{\overset{\|}{C}}H$ (Zero) (d) cyclohexane-1,3-dione with H atoms (Six)

2. Acidity of an acid follows the stability of the corresponding conjugate base. Conjugate bases of the corresponding acids are arranged in decreasing order.

(a) $CH_3-\overset{O}{\overset{\|}{C}}-O^-$ > $CH_3-\overset{O}{\overset{\|}{C}}-\overset{-}{C}H_2$ > $\overset{-}{C}H_2-\overset{O}{\overset{\|}{C}}-\ddot{O}CH_3$ > $HC\equiv C^-$ ( )

Equivalent resonating structures; –ve charge is fully delocalized onto C=O; –ve charge is partly delocalized onto C=O; –ve charge not delocalized

(c) I (cyclohexanone carbanion) > II (lactone carbanion, Ö:) > III (lactam carbanion, $\ddot{N}CH_3$)

I: –ve charge fully delocalized

II, III: –ve charge partly delocalized, O is more electronegative than N hence II is more stable than III

TEST YOUR UNDERSTANDING - 15.2

1. (a) The ketone does not have any hydrogen on its α-carbon (which is a stereocenter) and thus it will not undergo enolization.
(b) The ketone has α-hydrogen on an achiral carbon, hence it will undergo enolization but *without racemization* because the stereocenter is a β-carbon which is not involved in enolization.

(c) 2-methylcyclohexanone (chiral) $\overset{H^+}{\rightleftharpoons}$ planar enol (achiral) $\overset{H^+}{\rightleftharpoons}$ (racemic mixture)

2. $C_2H_5-C(CH_3)(H)-CO-C_6H_5 \overset{D_3O^+}{\rightleftharpoons} C_2H_5-C(CH_3)(H)-C(=\overset{+}{O}D)\,C_6H_5 \overset{-H^+}{\rightleftharpoons}$

$(CH_3)(C_2H_5)C=C(\ddot{O}D)(C_6H_5) \overset{D^+}{\rightleftharpoons} C_2H_5-C(CH_3)(D)-C(=O^+D)-C_6H_5 \overset{-D^+}{\rightleftharpoons} C_2H_5-C(CH_3)(D)-CO-C_6H_5$ + Enantiomer

3. (a) $CH_3-\overset{O}{\overset{\|}{C}}-CH_2-\overset{O}{\overset{\|}{C}}-CH_3 \rightleftharpoons CH_3-\overset{OH}{\overset{|}{C}}=CH-\overset{O}{\overset{\|}{C}}-CH_3$

Keto form (24%) 2,4-Pentanedione Enol form (76%)

The greater stability of the β-enol form is due to resonance stabilization of the conjugated double bonds and (in a cyclic form) through hydrogen bonding.

Resonance stabilization and H-bonding in the cyclic form of enol-2,4-pentanedione

(b) 2,4-Cyclohexadien-1-one (keto form) ⇌ Phenol (enol form, »100)

The stability of the enolic form is again due to high resonance energy of the benzene ring.

TEST YOUR UNDERSTANDING - 15.3

1. (a) $CH_3\overset{CH_3}{\overset{|}{C}}H\overset{O}{\overset{\|}{C}}CH_3 \xrightarrow[\text{(ii) OHCCH}_2\text{CH}_3]{\text{(i) LDA}} CH_3\overset{CH_3}{\overset{|}{C}}H\overset{O}{\overset{\|}{C}}CH_2\overset{OH}{\overset{|}{C}}HCH_2CH_3$

(b) $CH_3CH=CHCOCH_3 \xrightarrow[\text{(ii) OHCCH}_3]{\text{(i) LDA}} CH_3CH=CHCOCH_2\overset{OH}{\overset{|}{C}}HCH_3$

(c) (i) LDA (ii) [ketone]

(d) (I) LDA (ii) [ketone]

TEST YOUR UNDERSTANDING - 15.4

1. (a) [structure: hex-5-en-2-one] (b) [structure with CN and C_6H_5]

(c) [structure with O and CH_2CH_3] (Minor) + [structure with O and H_3CH_2C] (Major) (d) [structure with O and CH_3]

TEST YOUR UNDERSTANDING - 15.5

1. (a) $C_6H_5-\underset{|}{C}(N(CH_3)_2)=CH_2$ (b) $C_6H_5-C(=NCH_3)-CH_3$ (c) cyclohexylidene $=NC_6H_5$ (d) 1-piperidinocyclohexene

2. (a) Cyclopentanone + HNR_2 (Any 2° aliphatic amine) $\xrightarrow{H^+}$ enamine (NR_2) $\xrightarrow[\text{(ii) } H_3O^+]{\text{(i) Br-allyl}}$ 2-Allylcyclopentanone

(b) 3-Pentanone $\xrightarrow{(C_2H_5)_2NH}$ enamine ($N(C_2H_5)_2$) $\xrightarrow[\text{(ii) } H_3O^+]{\text{(i) } BrCH_2C_6H_5}$ product (numbered 5, 4, 3, 2, 1 with C_6H_5)

(c) $C_6H_5-\overset{O}{\overset{||}{C}}-CH_3 \xrightarrow[H^+]{HN(\text{piperidine})} C_6H_5-\underset{N(\text{piperidine})}{C}=CH_2 \xrightarrow[\text{(ii) } H_3O^+]{\text{(i) } C_6H_5COCl} C_6H_5-\overset{O}{\overset{||}{C}}-CH_2\overset{O}{\overset{||}{C}}C_6H_5$

TEST YOUR UNDERSTANDING - 15.6

. (a) $CH_3CH_2CHO + Br_2 \xrightarrow{H^+, H_2O} CH_3\underset{Br}{\underset{|}{C}}HCHO \xrightarrow{HNMe_2} CH_3\underset{NMe_2}{\underset{|}{C}}HCHO$

(b) $CH_3CH_2CHO + Br_2 \xrightarrow{H^+, H_2O} CH_3\underset{Br}{\underset{|}{C}}HCHO \xrightarrow{OH^-} CH_3\underset{OH}{\underset{|}{C}}HCHO$

(c) Cyclohexanone $\xrightarrow[H^+, H_2O]{Br_2}$ 2-bromocyclohexanone (Br) $\xrightarrow{CH_3ONa}$ 2-methoxycyclohexanone (OCH_3)

(d) Cyclopentanone $\xrightarrow[\text{(ii) } C_6H_5ONa]{\text{(i) } Br_2, H^+}$ 2-phenoxycyclopentanone (OC_6H_5)

. (a) $CH_3CH_2CH_2\overset{O}{\overset{||}{C}}CH_2CH_2CH_3 \xrightarrow[H^+, OH^-]{Br_2} CH_3CH_2\overset{Br}{\overset{|}{C}}H\overset{O}{\overset{||}{C}}CH_2CH_2CH_3 \xrightarrow{tert-BuO^-} CH_3CH=CH\overset{O}{\overset{||}{C}}CH_2CH_2CH_3$

(b) 1-methylcyclohexyl $\overset{O}{\overset{||}{C}}CH_2CH_3$ (CH_3) $\xrightarrow[H^+OH^-]{Br_2}$ 1-methylcyclohexyl $\overset{O}{\overset{||}{C}}\overset{Br}{\overset{|}{C}}HCH_3$ (CH_3) $\xrightarrow{Base}$ 1-methylcyclohexyl $\overset{O}{\overset{||}{C}}CH=CH_2$

EXERCISE 15.1

1	(c)	5	(c)	9	(d)
2	(c)	6	(c)	10	(b)
3	(d)	7	(b)	11	(b)
4	(d)	8	(c)	12	(b)

1. Only acidic hydrogens (α – to C = O) are replaced.
2. The steps in the base- and acid- catalyzed keto-enol interconversions are reversed. In the base-catalyzed reaction, the base removes the α-proton in the first step and the oxygen is protonated in the second step. In the acid-catalyzed reaction, the acid protonates the oxygen in the first step and the α-proton is removed in the second step.
3. All the three reactions proceed at about the same rate, because the rate determining step in each reaction is same (removal of a proton from the α-carbon atom).
4. $$HCHO + CH_3CHO \xrightarrow[\text{(aldol)}]{OH^-} HOCH_2-CH_2-CHO \xrightarrow[\text{(aldol)}]{HCHO} HOCH_2-CH(CH_2OH)-CHO \xrightarrow[\text{(aldol)}]{HCHO} HOCH_2-C(CH_2OH)_2-CHO$$
5. For getting good yield in intramolecular aldol condensation leading to cyclization, very dilute solution must be used. When very dilute solutions are used (high dilution technique), probability for interacting one end of a molecule with the other end of the same molecule will be more than with the other molecule.
6. Only acidic hydrogens (α-hydrogen) of an aldehyde/ketone are easily exchanged.
7. Presence of Br in $CH_3-\overset{O}{\overset{\|}{C}}-CH_2Br$ makes the carbon, to which it is attached, more acidic hence hydrogen attached to it will be first and more readily replaced by Br.
8. Carbon-2 of 1,3-dithiane is more electropositive (acidic) due to the presence of electronegative sulphur on both sides. Hence it reacts with the nucleophile (C_4H_9Li) easily.

$$\text{1,3-dithiane} \xrightarrow[(-C_4H_{10})]{C_4H_9Li} \text{2-carbanion} \xrightarrow{C_6H_5CH_2Br} \text{2-}(CH_2C_6H_5)\text{-1,3-dithiane} \xrightarrow[H_2]{\text{Raney Ni}} C_6H_5CH_2CH_3 + CH_3CH_2CH_3$$

9. In a polar solvent, such as water, the keto form is stabilized by solvation, hence it is more stable. When the interaction between solvent becomes minimal, the enol form achieves stability by internal hydrogen bonding.

EXERCISE 15.2

>1 CORRECT OPTION	1	(a,c,d)	2	(a,b)	3	(a,d)
	4	(a,d)	5	(b, d)	6	(a, b, c, d)
	7	(a, b, c)				
PASSAGE 1	8	(b)			9	(b)
	10	(c)			11	(d)
MATCH THE FOLLOWING	12	(A) - b, (B) - a, c, (C) - b, (D) - d				

1. Cyclohexane-1,3-dione ⇌ 3-hydroxycyclohex-3-enone *or* 3-hydroxycyclohex-2-enone (OH)

More stable (conjugated system)

2. 2-chlorocyclohexanone $\xleftarrow[\text{(base-promoted chlorination)}]{Cl_2 / OH^-}$ cyclohexanone $\xrightarrow[\text{(acid-catalyzed chlorination)}]{Cl_2 / CH_3COOH}$ 2-chlorocyclohexanone

3. $H_3C-\overset{\overset{O^{\delta-}}{\|\delta+}}{C}-CH_2-\overset{\overset{O^{\delta-}}{\|\delta+}}{C}-OC_2H_5 \rightleftharpoons H_3C-\overset{\overset{OH\cdots\cdots O}{|}}{C}=CH-\overset{\|}{C}-OC_2H_5$

ketonic form (higher b.p. due to dipole-dipole interaction) — enolic form (chelation lowers b.p.)

This form discharges colour of Br_2 in CCl_4.

4. The hydrogen atom that is added to the carbonyl carbon of the aldehyde in the reduction is derived directly from the other aldehyde molecule as a hydride ion. The second hydrogen that is added to the negatively charged oxygen is coming from the solvent (consult mechanism of Cannizzaro reaction). Oxidation of one molecule of the compound at the expense of other molecule of the same compound is known as disproportionation.

EXERCISE 15.3

1. (a) $CH_3-\overset{\overset{O}{\|}}{C}-\overset{..-}{C}H_2 \longleftrightarrow CH_3-\overset{\overset{O^-}{|}}{C}=CH_2$ (b)  [cyclohexanone carbanion] ⟷ [cyclohexene enolate]

(c) 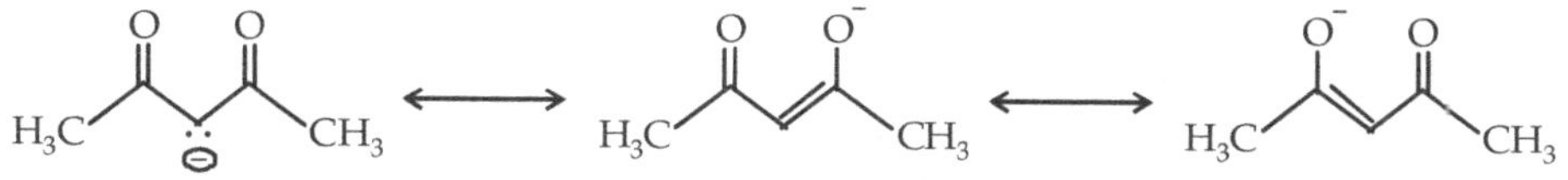 [$H_3C-CO-\overset{\ominus}{C}H-CO-CH_3$ resonance structures] ⟷ ⟷

(d) 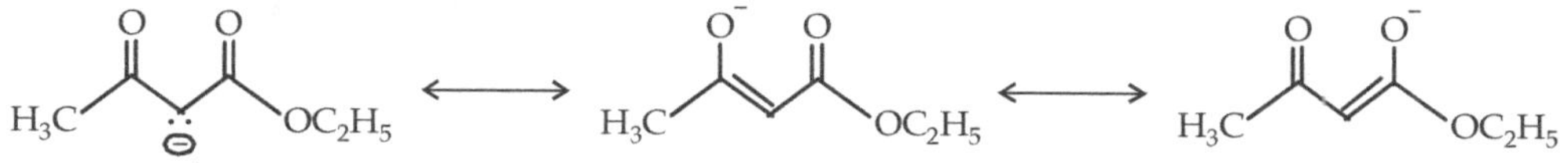 [$H_3C-CO-\overset{\ominus}{C}H-CO-OC_2H_5$ resonance structures] ⟷ ⟷

(e) $N\equiv C-\overset{\ominus}{C}H-\overset{\overset{O}{\|}}{C}-OC_2H_5 \longleftrightarrow \overset{-}{N}=C=CH-\overset{\overset{O}{\|}}{C}-OC_2H_5 \longleftrightarrow N\equiv C-CH=\overset{\overset{O^-}{|}}{C}-OC_2H_5$

(f) $^-O-\overset{\overset{O}{\|}}{\overset{+}{N}}-\overset{\ominus}{C}H-\overset{\overset{O}{\|}}{C}CH_3 \longleftrightarrow {}^-O-\overset{\overset{^-O}{|}}{\overset{+}{N}}=CH-\overset{\overset{O}{\|}}{C}-CH_3 \longleftrightarrow {}^-O-\overset{\overset{O}{\|}}{\overset{+}{N}}-CH=\overset{\overset{O^-}{|}}{C}-CH_3$

(Other resonance forms of the $-NO_2$ group are not shown)

2. (a) 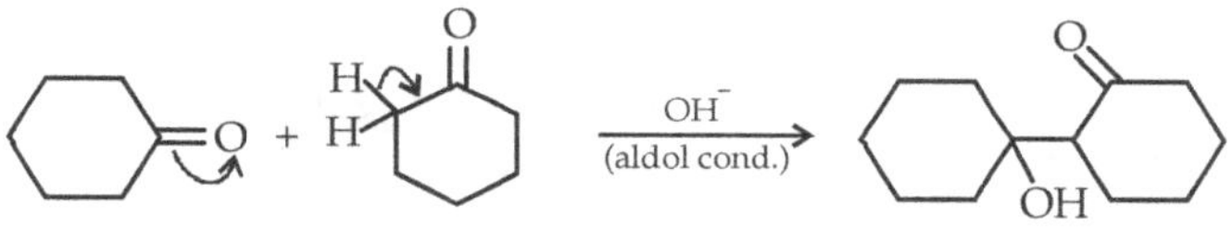 [cyclohexanone] + [cyclohexanone] $\xrightarrow[\text{(aldol cond.)}]{OH^-}$ [aldol product, OH]

as an electrophile as a nucleophile

(b) 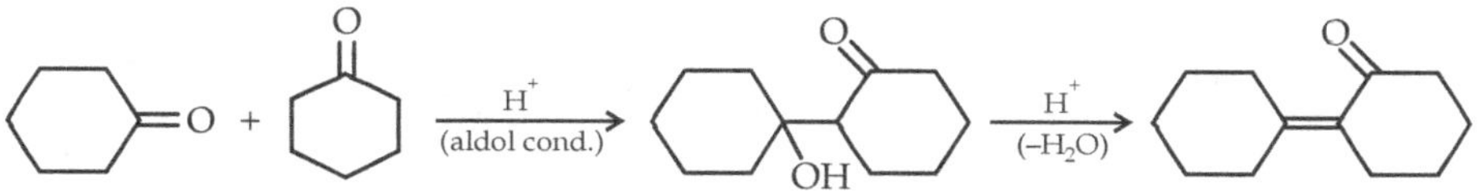 [cyclohexanone] + [cyclohexanone] $\xrightarrow[\text{(aldol cond.)}]{H^+}$ [aldol product, OH] $\xrightarrow[(-H_2O)]{H^+}$ [α,β-unsaturated ketone]

3. (a) $C_6H_5CHO + H_2O^{18} \xrightarrow{H^+} C_6H_5CHO^{18} + H_2O$

Mechanism : $C_6H_5-\overset{\overset{H}{|}}{C}=O \underset{}{\overset{H^+}{\rightleftharpoons}} C_6H_5-\overset{\overset{H}{|}}{C}=\overset{+}{O}H \overset{H_2O^{18}}{\rightleftharpoons} C_6H_5-\overset{\overset{H}{|}}{\underset{\underset{^{18}O^+H_2}{|}}{C}}-OH \overset{-H^+}{\rightleftharpoons}$

$C_6H_5-\overset{\overset{H}{|}}{\underset{\underset{^{18}OH}{|}}{C}}-OH \overset{H^+}{\rightleftharpoons} C_6H_5-\overset{\overset{H}{|}}{\underset{\underset{^{18}OH}{|}}{C}}-{}^+OH_2 \overset{-H_2O}{\rightleftharpoons} C_6H_5-\overset{\overset{H}{|}}{\underset{\underset{^{18}O^+H}{\|}}{C}} \overset{-H^+}{\rightleftharpoons} C_6H_5-\overset{\overset{H}{|}}{C}=O^{18}$

$CH_3CHO + CH_3CHO \xrightarrow{H^+} CH_3CH=CH-\overset{H}{C}=O$

(b) $C_6H_5\overset{\overset{O}{\|}}{C}H \xrightarrow{CH_3CH=CH-\overset{H}{C}=O} C_6H_5CH=CH-CH=CH\overset{\overset{O}{\|}}{C}H$

(c) $C_6H_5CH = O + Ph_3P = CH - OPh \xrightarrow[\text{reaction}]{\text{Wittig}} C_6H_5CH = CH - OPh \xrightarrow[\text{Cleavage of vinyl ether}]{H^+}$

$C_6H_5CH = CH - OH \xrightleftharpoons{\text{tantomerizes}} C_6H_5 - CH_2 - CH = O$

(d) $C_2H_5O-\overset{O}{\overset{\|}{C}}-OC_2H_5 + H_3C\overset{O}{\overset{\|}{C}}Ph \xrightarrow[\text{(Claisen cond.)}]{OC_2H_5}$ (diketo ester, Ph) $\xrightarrow[^-OC_2H_5\text{ (Claisen)}]{H_3C\overset{O}{\overset{\|}{C}}Ph}$ (triketone, Ph ... Ph)

(e) (ethyl isovalerate) + $\begin{matrix}COOC_2H_5\\ |\\ COOC_2H_5\end{matrix}$ $\xrightarrow[\text{(Crossed Claisen)}]{^-OC_2H_5}$ (a, a', b; OC_2H_5, OC_2H_5) $\xrightarrow[\text{(ii) heat (–}CO_2\text{ from b-keto acids)}]{\text{(i) }H^+}$

(keto ester, OC_2H_5) $\xrightarrow[\text{(Reductive amination)}]{NH_3, H_2/Pd}$ (NH_2, OH)

(Exists as zwitterion)

(f) Proceed backward, recall that a γ-lactone (a cyclic ester) can be easily obtained from a γ-hydroxy acid which in turn can be obtained from CH_3CHO and succinic acid by an aldol-*type* condensation.

H_3C, COOH (lactone ring) $\longleftarrow$ $H_3C-CH(OH)-CH(COOH)-CH_2-HOOC$ $\longleftarrow$ $CH_3CHO + \begin{matrix}H_2CCOOH\\ |\\ H_2CCOOH\end{matrix}$

A r-lactone

A r-hydroxy acid

(g) $C_6H_5CHO \xrightarrow[CH_3COONa]{(CH_3CO)_2O}$ (cinnamic acid, HO, O) $\xrightarrow[\text{(ii) }SOCl_2]{\text{(i) }H_2 / Ni}$ (Cl, O) $\xrightarrow{HF}$ (indanone-type ketone, O)

(h) (cyclohexanone) $\xrightarrow[D_2O]{OD^-}$ (D, D, D, D) $\xrightarrow{LiAlH_4}$ (OH; D, D, D, D) $\xrightarrow{PBr_3}$ (Br; D, D, D, D) $\xrightarrow{\text{alc. KOH}}$ (D, D, D)

1,3,3-Trideutero cyclohexene

4. The reaction is an example of reverse of the aldol condensation commonly known as *retrograde aldol* or *retro aldol*. According to the *principle of microscopic reversibility* (a reaction and its reverse follow exactly the same path but in opposite directions), all steps in the aldol condensation take place in the reverse order.

(O, OH) $\xrightleftharpoons{OH^-}$ (O, O^-) $\rightleftharpoons$ (O) + $\left[H_2C^- \text{(O)} \xrightleftharpoons{H_2O} \text{(O)} + OH^- \right]$

5. (acetone, O) + (acetaldehyde, H, O) $\xrightarrow[\text{(aldol)}]{OH^-}$ (H, O)

2 (H, O) $\xrightarrow[\text{(aldol)}]{OH^-}$ (CHO)

3-methyl-2-butenal
(α, β-unsaturated aldehyde, α-H is acidic)

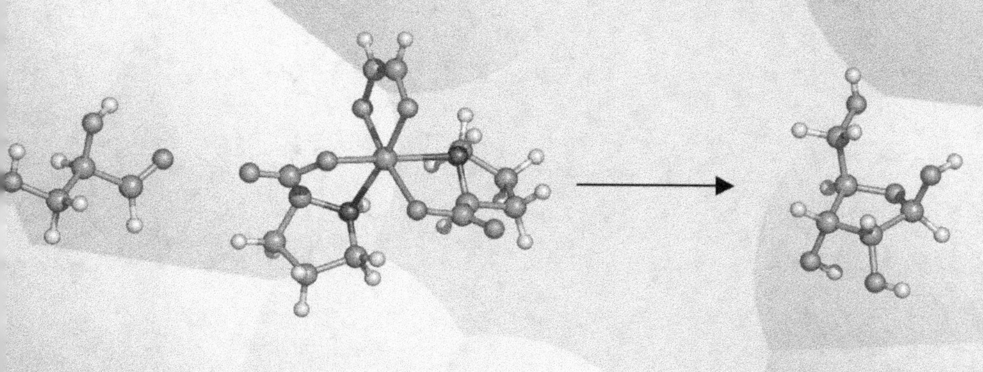

16

α,β-Unsaturated Carbonyl Compounds

CHAPTER HIGHLIGHTS

α, β-Unsaturated carbonyl compounds contain both a carbon-carbon double bond and a carbon-oxygen double bond separated by just one carbon-carbon single bond. Thus note that such compounds have a conjugated system $-\overset{|}{C}=C-\overset{|}{C}=O$.

16.1 Preparation

α, β - Unsaturated compounds are prepared by the following methods.

(i) Aldol condensation leads to α, β-unsaturated aldehydes and ketones.

(ii) Dehydrohalogenation of α-haloacids lead to α, β-unsaturated carboxylic acids.

(iii) Perkin reaction leads to α, β-unsaturated carboxylic acids.

(iv) Other methods specific for few compounds.

TEST YOUR UNDERSTANDING - 16.1

1. Give steps involved in the following preparation

(a) $CH_3CH=CH\overset{O}{\overset{||}{C}}OH$ from $CH\equiv CH$

(b) $CH_2=CH\overset{O}{\overset{||}{C}}OCH_3$ from $CH_2=CH_2$

(c) $CH_2 = C(CH_3)COOCH_3$ from CH_3COCH_3

(d) HOOC–CH=CH–CH=CH–COOH from adipic acid.

(e) $CH_3COCH=CH_2$ from CH_3COCH_3

(f) Cinnamic acid from toluene

(g) Maleic acid from succinic acid

16.2 Properties

α, β-Unsaturated compounds possess not only the properties of the individual functional groups, i.e. C = C, and $-\overset{|}{C}=O$, but also certain other properties, characteristic of the conjugated system.

However, here stress is given only those properties which are due to the presence of α,β-unsaturated carbonyl moiety.

16.2.1 Electrophilic Addition

Usually, the carbon-carbon double bond is a rich source of electrons and hence undergoes electrophilic additions easily. Further, a carbon-carbon double bond is activated by an electron-releasing substituent toward electrophilic addition because an electron-releasing substituent stabilizes the transition state leading to carbocation by dispersing the developing positive charge, conversely an electron-withdrawing substituent (e.g. C = O, –COOH, –COOR, –CN, etc.) on a carbon-carbon double bond destabilizes the transition state hence it deactivates the C = C to electrophilic addition.

$$-\overset{|}{C}=\overset{|}{C}\leftarrow G + Y^+ \longrightarrow \left[-\overset{|}{\underset{\underset{Y_{\delta^+}}{\vdots}}{C}}\cdots\overset{|}{\underset{\delta^+}{C}}\leftarrow G\right] \longrightarrow -\underset{Y}{\overset{|}{C}}-\overset{|}{C^+}\leftarrow G$$

G is an electron-releasing group; Y^+ Electrophile; Transition state (stable)

$$-\overset{|}{C}=\overset{|}{C}\rightarrow W + Y^+ \longrightarrow \left[-\overset{|}{\underset{\underset{Y_{\delta^+}}{\vdots}}{C}}\cdots\overset{|}{\underset{\delta^+}{C}}\rightarrow W\right] \longrightarrow -\underset{Y}{\overset{|}{C}}-\overset{|}{C^+}\rightarrow W$$

W is an electron-withdrawing group; Transition state (unstable)

Thus α,β-unsaturated ketones, acids, esters and nitriles are in general less reactive than simple alkenes toward reagent like Br_2 and HX. However, the groups which deactivate a C=C bond toward electrophilic reagents activate the C=C bond toward nucleophiles. Hence, unlike ordinary alkenes, the C=C of an α,β-unsaturated ketones, acids, esters, or nitriles are susceptible to nucleophiles. This reactivity towards nucleophiles is due to inductive effect of the substituent as well as to its conjugation with the carbon-carbon double bond.

In the addition of an unsymmetrical reagent to the double bond of an α,β-unsaturated carbonyl compound hydrogen (positive end of the reagent) is attached to the α-carbon and the negative end of the reagent is attached to the β-carbon.

$$CH_2=CHCHO + HCl \longrightarrow \underset{Cl}{\underset{|}{C}H_2}-\underset{H}{\underset{|}{C}}HCHO$$

$$CH_2=CHCOOH + H_2O \longrightarrow \underset{OH}{\underset{|}{C}H_2}-\underset{H}{\underset{|}{C}}HCHO$$

$$CH_3CH=CHCOOH + HBr \longrightarrow CH_3\underset{Br}{\underset{|}{C}H}\underset{H}{\underset{|}{C}H}-COOH$$

$$(CH_3)_2C=CHCOCH_3 + CH_3OH \xrightarrow{H_2SO_4} (CH_3)_2\underset{OCH_3}{\underset{|}{C}}-\underset{H}{\underset{|}{C}}HCOCH_3$$

Such additions are again in consistent with the formation of the most stable carbocation.

$$-\overset{|}{C}=\overset{|}{C}-\overset{|}{C}=O \xrightarrow{H^+} \begin{cases} -\overset{|}{C}\overset{\cdots}{=}\overset{|}{C}\overset{\cdots}{=}\overset{|}{C}-O-H & \text{More stable} \oplus \\ -\underset{H}{\overset{|}{\underset{|}{C}}}-\overset{|}{C}\overset{\cdots}{=}\overset{|}{C}\overset{\cdots}{=}O & \text{Less stable} \oplus \end{cases}$$

Positive charge on the highly electronegative oxygen

The more stable carbocation, now adds the negative ion or basic molecule in either of the two ways.

$$-\overset{|\beta}{C}\overset{\cdots}{=}\overset{|\alpha}{C}\overset{\cdots}{=}\overset{|}{C}-O-H \ (\oplus) \xrightarrow{Br^-} \begin{cases} -\underset{Br}{\overset{|}{\underset{|}{C}}}-\overset{|}{C}=\overset{|}{C}-O-H & \text{Actually formed} \\ -\overset{|}{C}=\overset{|}{C}-\underset{Br}{\overset{|}{\underset{|}{C}}}-O-H & \text{Not formed} \end{cases}$$

Of the above two possibilities, only addition to the β-carbon yields a stable product, the enol form of a saturated carbonyl compound.

$$\underset{\text{enol form}}{-\underset{Br}{\overset{|}{\underset{|}{C}}}-\overset{|}{C}=\overset{|}{C}-O-H} \rightleftharpoons \underset{\text{Keto form}}{-\underset{Br}{\overset{|}{\underset{|}{C}}}-\underset{H}{\overset{|}{\underset{|}{C}}}-\overset{|}{C}=O}$$

16.2.2 Nucleophilic Addition

α, β-Unsaturated carbonyl compounds contain two electrophilic sites, the carbonyl carbon and the carbon atom that is β to carbonyl group. Thus such compounds may react with nucleophiles in two different ways.

(a) Direct or simple addition : The nucleophile preferentially adds directly to the carbonyl group forming direct addition product, also known as 1,2-addition product (remember that the numbers 1 and 2 do not refer to IUPAC locants but are used in a manner analogous to that employed in additions on conjugated dienes). Strong but simple (not bulky) bases like organolithium and Grignard reagents and lithium aluminium hydride tend to react by simple addition.

$$CH_3\overset{4}{C}H=\overset{3}{C}H\overset{O^1}{\overset{2\|}{C}}H + CH_3MgBr \xrightarrow[\text{(ii) } H^+]{\text{(i) ethanol}} \underset{\text{Direct addition (1,2–addition) (84\%)}}{CH_3CH=CH\overset{OH}{\overset{|}{C}}HCH_3}$$

(b) Conjugate or 1,4-addition : When the nucleophiles are weak or bulky strong bases, they add preferentially to the β-carbon forming conjugated or 1,4-addition product.

$$C_6H_5CH=CH\overset{O}{\overset{\|}{C}}OH + H_2NOH \longrightarrow C_6H_5\underset{NHOH}{\underset{|}{C}}HCH_2\overset{O}{\overset{\|}{C}}OH$$

Note that in 1,4-addition, the nucleophile adds at the carbon-carbon double bond rather than at the carbon-oxygen double bond. Here the nucleophilic portion of the reagent is attached to the β carbon quite ignoring the fact that it has more or less number of hydrogen atoms.

Remember that nucleophilic addition to the usual carbon-carbon double bond is very rare. However, it occurs easily with α,β-unsaturated carbonyl compounds because here the carbanion formed is an enolate i.e. the carbanion has a conjugated system, which is more stable and formed with a lower activation energy than a simple alkyl carbanion.

Enolate anion

1,2- or 1,4-Nucleophilic addition to α,β-unsaturated carbonyl compounds may be governed by kinetic control or by thermodynamic control.

Less stable product

More stable product

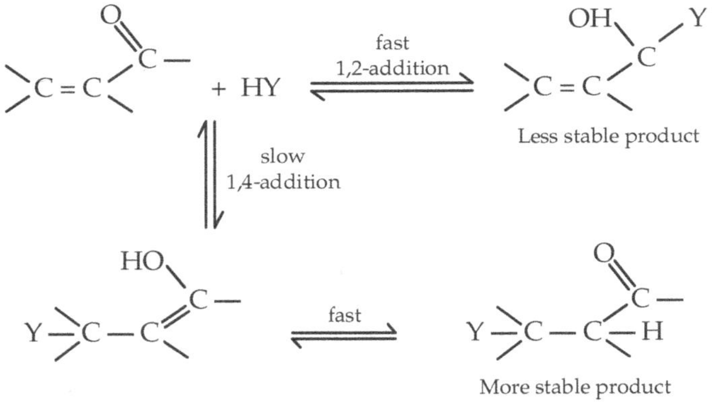

Direct addition (1,2-) occurs faster than conjugate addition (1,4-) but gives a less stable product. This kinetic control addition operates with strongly basic nucleophiles. The conjugate (1, 4-) addition gives the more stable product; recall that the carbon-oxygen double bond, in general, is a more stable structural unit than the carbon-carbon double bond. This thermodynamic control addition occurs in presence of a weakly basic nucleophile.

TEST YOUR UNDERSTANDING - 16.2

1. Write down the products in each of the following reactions :

(a) $C_6H_5CH = CHCOOC_2H_5 + OH^- \xrightarrow{\text{heat}}$

(b) $CH_3CH = CHCOCH_3 + I_2 + NaOH \longrightarrow$

(c) $CH_3CH = CHCOC_6H_5 + O_3 \longrightarrow [\quad] \xrightarrow[H_2O]{Zn}$

(d) Maleic acid + $Br_2(CCl_4) \longrightarrow$

(e) Fumaric acid + Cold alkaline $KMnO_4 \longrightarrow$

(f) $C_6H_5CH = CHCOOH + H_2 \xrightarrow[\text{pressure}]{\text{Ni, low temp.}}$

(g) $C_6H_5CH = CHCOOH + H_2 \xrightarrow[\text{pressure}]{\text{Ni, high temp.}}$

(h) $C_6H_5CH = CHCOOH + 9-BBN \longrightarrow [\quad] \xrightarrow{HOCH_2CH_2NH_2}$

(i) $CH_3CH = CHCOOC_2H_5 + (COOC_2H_5)_2 \xrightarrow{OC_2H_5^-}$

2. Compare the reaction of sodium azide in aqueous acetic acid with acrolein and propanal.

3. Give the product in each case.

(a) $CH_3CH = CHCHO + CH \equiv CMgBr \longrightarrow$

(b) $C_6H_5CH = CHCOC_6H_5 + HCN \longrightarrow$

4. Predict the nature of products in the following reactions.

(a) $CH_2 = CHCN \xrightarrow{NH_3} X + Y$

(b) $CH_2 = CHCOOCH_3 \xrightarrow{CH_3NH_2} [A] \xrightarrow{CH_2=CHCOOCH_3} [B]$

Michael reaction.

In the nucleophilic addition to α, β-unsaturated carbonyl compounds, when the nucleophile is a carbanion, the reaction is known as **Michael addition or Michael reaction**. The most common types of carbanions used are enolate ions derived from β-diketones, β-diketo esters, β-keto esters, and β-keto nitriles. Since these enolates are weak bases and quite bulky, addition occurs at the β-carbon to form 1,4-addition product.

(a) $$\underset{\text{α,β-unsaturated aldehyde}}{CH_2=CH\overset{O}{\overset{||}{C}}H} + \underset{\text{A β-diketone}}{CH_3\overset{O}{\overset{||}{C}}CH_2\overset{O}{\overset{||}{C}}CH_3} \xrightarrow{OH^-} \overset{CH_2CH_2\overset{O}{\overset{||}{C}}H}{\overset{|}{CH_3\underset{\underset{O}{||}}{C}CH\underset{\underset{O}{||}}{C}CH_3}}$$

(b) $$\underset{\text{α,β-unsaturated ketone}}{CH_3CH=CH\overset{O}{\overset{||}{C}}CH_3} + \underset{\text{A β-diketo ester}}{C_2H_5O\overset{O}{\overset{||}{C}}CH_2\overset{O}{\overset{||}{C}}OC_2H_5} \xrightarrow{C_2H_5O^-} \underset{\underset{CH(COOC_2H_5)_2}{|}}{CH_3\,CHCH_2\overset{O}{\overset{||}{C}}CH_3}$$

(c) $$\underset{\text{α,β-unsaturated amide}}{CH_3CH=CHCONH_2} + \underset{\text{a β-keto ester}}{C_2H_5COCH_2COOCH_3} \xrightarrow{CH_3O^-} \underset{\underset{C_2H_5COCHCOOCH_3}{|}}{CH_3\,CHCH_2CONH_2}$$

(d) $$\underset{\text{α,β-unsaturated ester}}{C_2H_5CH=CHCOOCH_3} + \underset{\text{a β-keto nitrile}}{CH_3\overset{O}{\overset{||}{C}}CH_2C\equiv N} \xrightarrow{^-OCH_3} \underset{\underset{CH_3COCHCN}{|}}{C_2H_5\,CHCH_2COOCH_3}$$

(e) $$\underset{\text{α,β-unsaturated ketone}}{CH_2=CHCOCH_3} + \underset{\text{a β-diketone}}{\text{2-methylcyclohexane-1,3-dione}} \xrightarrow{^-OCH_3} \text{2-methyl-2-}(CH_2CH_2COCH_3)\text{cyclohexane-1,3-dione}$$

Thus, **Michael reaction** involves addition of a stabilized enolate ion to the double bond of an α,β-unsaturated carbonyl compound. The electrophile (the α,β-unsaturated carbonyl compounds) accepts a pair of electrons, and thus called the **Michael acceptor**; while the attacking nucleophile donates a pair of electrons, hence called the **Michael donor**. A wide variety of compounds can serve as Michael acceptors and donors (Table below). Common acceptors contain a double bond conjugated with a carbonyl group, a cyano group, or a nitro group. Common donors are enolates that are stabilized by two strong electron-withdrawing groups such as carbonyl groups, cyano groups, or nitro groups.

Table : Some common Michael donors and Michael acceptors

Michael donors	(Nucleophiles)	Michael acceptors	(Electrophile)
$R-\overset{O}{\overset{\|\|}{C}}-\overset{-}{\ddot{C}H}-\overset{O}{\overset{\|\|}{C}}-R'$	β-Diketones	$CH_2=CH-\overset{O}{\overset{\|\|}{C}}-H$	Conjugated aldehydes
$R-\overset{O}{\overset{\|\|}{C}}-\overset{-}{\ddot{C}H}-\overset{O}{\overset{\|\|}{C}}-OR'$	β-Keto esters	$CH_2=CH-\overset{O}{\overset{\|\|}{C}}-R$	Conjugated ketones
$R_2Cu\ Li$	Dialkyl cuprates	$CH_2=CH-\overset{O}{\overset{\|\|}{C}}-OR$	Conjugated esters
$>\ddot{N}-\overset{\|}{C}=C<$	Enamines	$CH_2=CH-\overset{O}{\overset{\|\|}{C}}-NH_2$	Conjugated amides
$R-\overset{O}{\overset{\|\|}{C}}-\overset{-}{\ddot{C}H}-C\equiv N$	β-Keto nitriles	$CH_2=CH-C\equiv N$	Conjugated nitriles
$R-\overset{O}{\overset{\|\|}{C}}-\overset{-}{\ddot{C}H}-NO_2$	α-Nitro ketones	$CH_2=CH-NO_2$	Nitroethylene

Mechanism. The base removes a proton from α-carbon of the compound having active methylene group to form a carbanion which acts as a nucleophile. The nucleophile adds to the β-carbon of the conjugated system in the usual manner.

$$R-\overset{O}{\overset{\|}{C}}-CH_2-\overset{O}{\overset{\|}{C}}-R + :Base \longrightarrow R-\overset{O}{\overset{\|}{C}}-\ddot{C}H-\overset{O}{\overset{\|}{C}}-R + H:Base^+$$

Nucleophile

$$R-CH=CH-\overset{O}{\overset{\|}{C}}-R + R-\overset{O}{\overset{\|}{C}}-\ddot{C}H-\overset{O}{\overset{\|}{C}}-R \longrightarrow R-\underset{RCOCHCOR}{\underset{|}{C}H}-CH=\overset{O^-}{\overset{|}{C}}-R$$

$$\xrightarrow[(-:Base)]{H:Base^+} \underset{\text{Enol form}}{R-\underset{RCOCHCOR}{\underset{|}{C}H}-CH=\overset{OH}{\overset{|}{C}}-R} \rightleftharpoons \underset{\text{Keto form}}{R-\underset{RCOCHCOR}{\underset{|}{C}H}-CH_2-\overset{O}{\overset{\|}{C}}-R}$$

Note that if either of the reactant in a Michael reaction has an ester group, the base used to remove the α-proton must be the same as the leaving group of the ester. This is because the base can also act as a nucleophile and attack the carbonyl group of the ester. In case the nucleophile is different to the –OR group of the ester, the nucleophilic attack on the carbonyl group will change the reactant.

$$\underset{\text{Original reactant}}{CH_3-\overset{O}{\overset{\|}{C}}-OCH_3} + \underset{\text{(nucleophile)}}{^-OC_2H_5} \longrightarrow CH_3-\underset{OC_2H_5}{\underset{|}{\overset{O^-}{\overset{|}{C}}}}-OCH_3 \longrightarrow \underset{\text{New reactant}}{CH_3-\underset{OC_2H_5}{\underset{|}{\overset{O}{\overset{\|}{C}}}}}$$

Ammonia, primary and secondary amines are especially powerful catalysts for the Michael addition. They function not merely as a base to regenerate a carbanion but also reacts with the carbonyl groups of the substrate to form an intermedciate imine or iminium ion which is highly reactive toward nucleophilic addition. When enamines (tautomer of imines) are used in place of enolates, the reaction is called **Stork enamine reaction**. Thus reaction between cyclohexanone and acrolein in presence of pyrrolidine takes place as below.

Cyclohexanone + pyrrolidine (N–H) ⟶ enamine $\xrightarrow{CH_2=CH-\overset{O}{\overset{\|}{C}}H}$ iminium ion with $CH_2-CH=CH-O^-$ side chain

$\xrightarrow[(-OH^-)]{H_2O}$ iminium ion with $CH_2CH_2\overset{O}{\overset{\|}{C}}H$ side chain $\xrightarrow{H^+, H_2O}$ 2-($CH_2CH_2\overset{O}{\overset{\|}{C}}H$)cyclohexanone + pyrrolidinium ($\overset{+}{N}H_2$)

TEST YOUR UNDERSTANDING - 16.3

1. Write down the product obtained in the following reactions :

(a) Ethyl crotonate + Ethyl methylmalonate $\xrightarrow{^-OC_2H_5}$

(b) Ethyl α-methylacrylate + Ethyl cyanoacetate $\xrightarrow{^-OC_2H_5}$

(c) Benzalacetophenone + Acetophenone $\xrightarrow{^-OC_2H_5}$

(d) Acrylonitrile + Allyl cyanide $\xrightarrow{^-OCH_3}$

(e) $C_2H_5O_2CC \equiv CCO_2C_2H_5$ (1 mol.) + Acetoacetic ester (2 mol.) $\xrightarrow{^-OC_2H_5}$

(f) Ethyl crotonate + Malonic ester $\xrightarrow{^-OC_2H_5}$ [X] $\xrightarrow[\text{(ii) } H^+]{\text{(i) } OH^-}$ [Y] $\xrightarrow{\text{heat}}$ [Z]

2. What reagent would you use to prepare the following compounds?

(a) $CH_3COCH_2CH_2CH(COOCH_2CH_3)_2$

(b) 3-oxocyclohexyl–CH(COCH₃)(COOCH₃) [cyclohexanone ring bearing CH with COCH$_3$ and COOCH$_3$]

3. (a) Write structural formulas corresponding to the intermediates formed in the following reaction.

$$C_6H_5CH_2COCH_2C_6H_5 + CH_2=CHCOCH_3 \xrightarrow[CH_3OH]{CH_3ONa}$$ (cyclohexenone bearing C_6H_5 groups)

(b) Write down the structure of the resonance hybrid obtained by the attack of (i) an electrophile (H^+), (ii) a nucleophile on a typical α,β-unsaturated carbonyl compound, $-\overset{|}{C}=\overset{|}{C}-\overset{|}{C}=O$

16.2.3 Diels-Alder Reaction

α,β-Unsaturated carbonyl compounds undergo addition reaction with conjugated dienes in which C-1 and C-4 of the conjugated diene is attached to the doubly bonded carbons of the α,β-unsaturated carbonyl compound to form a 6-membered ring. The reaction, known as Diels-Alder reaction, is the example of *cycloaddition*.

$$CH_2=CH-CH=CH_2 + CH_2=CH-CHO \longrightarrow \text{(cyclohexene-CHO)}$$

1,3-Butadiene (Diene) + Acrolein (Dienophile) (Greek : diene-loving) → 1,2,3,6-Tetrahydrobenzaldehyde

Diels-Alder reaction, is although favoured by the presence of electron-withdrawing group in dienophile as in the case of α,β-unsaturated carbonyl compounds, it also takes place when the dienophile is a simple alkene.

$$CH_2=CH-CH=CH_2 + CH_2=CH_2 \longrightarrow \text{Cyclohexene}$$

(Diene) (Dienophile) Cyclohexene

Since Diels-Alder reaction involves a system of four π electrons (the diene) and a system of two π electrons (the dienophile), it is also known as **[4+2] cycloaddition**.

TEST YOUR UNDERSTANDING - 16.4

1. Predict the product in each of the following reactions :

(a) 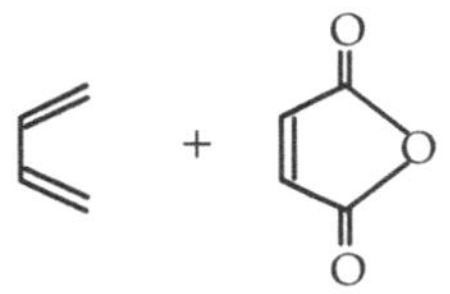 + (b) 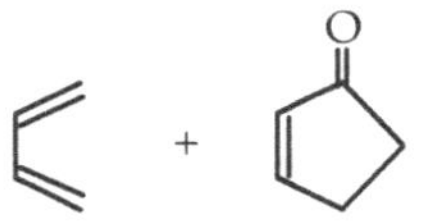 + (c)  +

2. Write down the diene and dienophile from which following products can be obtained

(a) 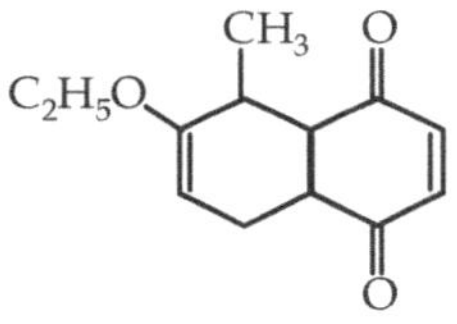 CH_3 O C_2H_5O O (b) 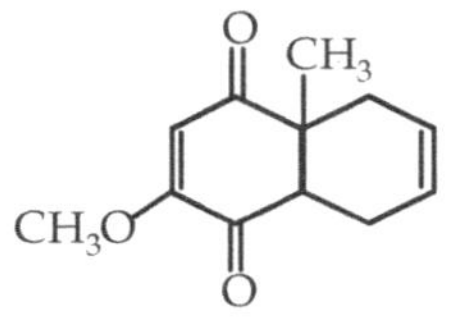 O CH_3 CH_3O O

16.3 ILLUSTRATIVE EXAMPLES

Example 1 :

Give steps involved in the following conversion.

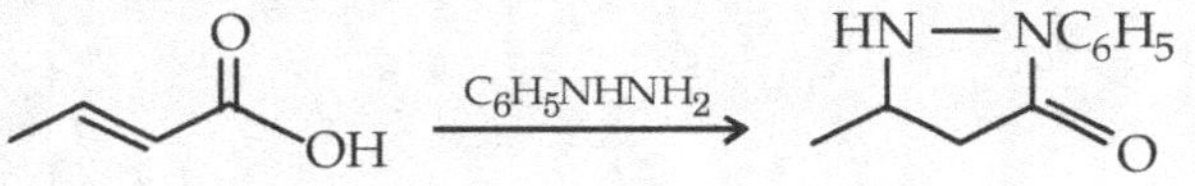

$C_6H_5NHNH_2$ → HN — NC_6H_5

Solution :

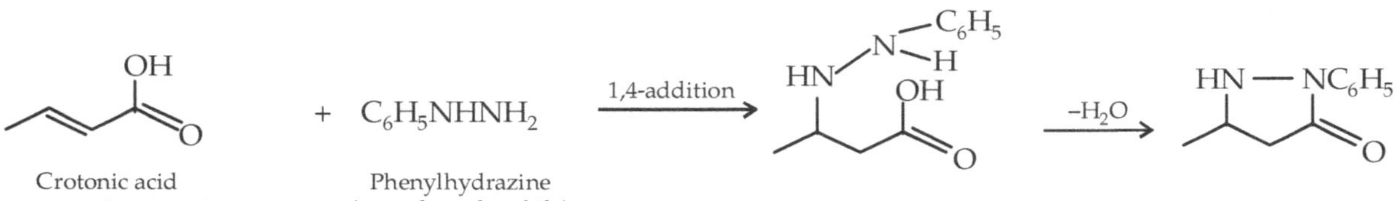

Crotonic acid (α,β-unsaturated carboxylic acid) + $C_6H_5NHNH_2$ Phenylhydrazine (a weak nucleophile) —1,4-addition→ HN–N(C_6H_5)H, OH, O —$-H_2O$→ HN — NC_6H_5, O

Example 2 :

Steps for converting cyclohexanone to each of the following

(a) 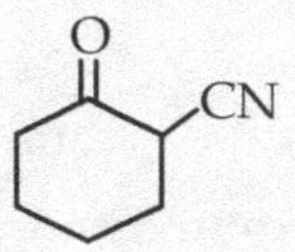 2-cyanocyclohexanone (CN) (b) 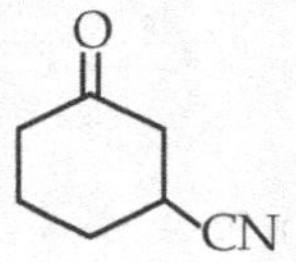 3-cyanocyclohexanone (CN)

Solution :

(a) 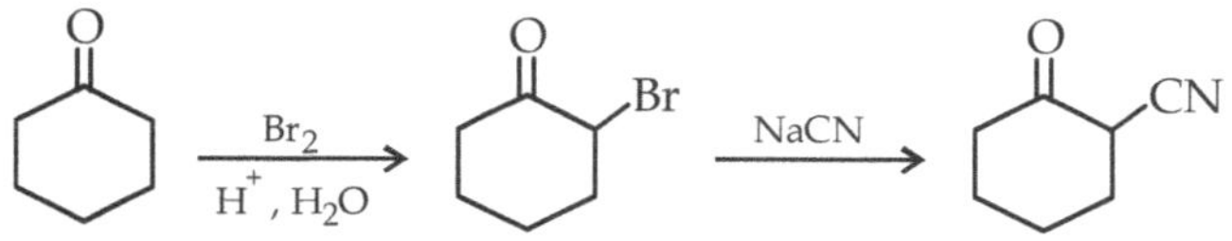 cyclohexanone —Br_2 / H^+, H_2O→ 2-bromocyclohexanone (Br) —NaCN→ 2-cyanocyclohexanone (CN)

(b) 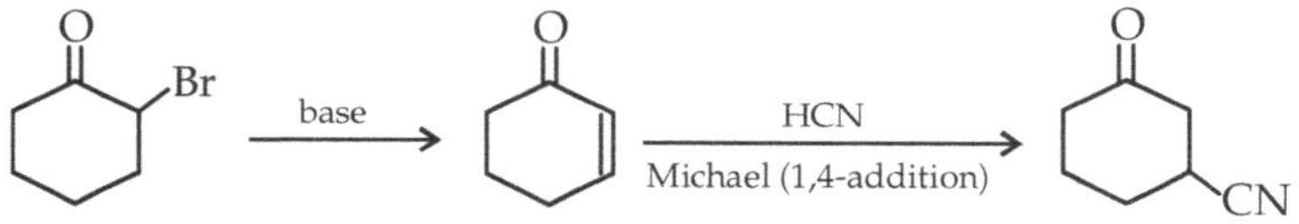 2-bromocyclohexanone (Br) —base→ cyclohex-2-enone —HCN / Michael (1,4-addition)→ 3-cyanocyclohexanone (CN)

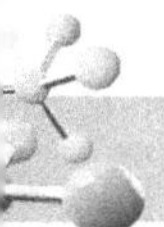

Example 3 :

Predict the final product in the following reaction and comment on the main concepts involved.

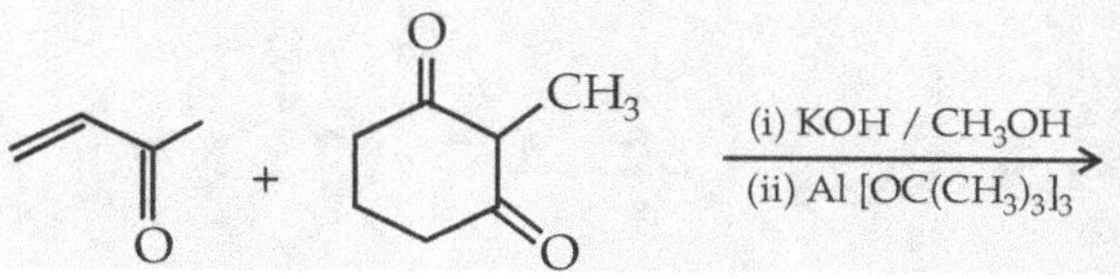

(i) KOH / CH_3OH
(ii) Al $[OC(CH_3)_3]_3$

Solution :

KOH / CH_3OH (Michael reaction)

Al *tert*-butoxide (intramolecular aldol condensation)

$-H_2O$

OH

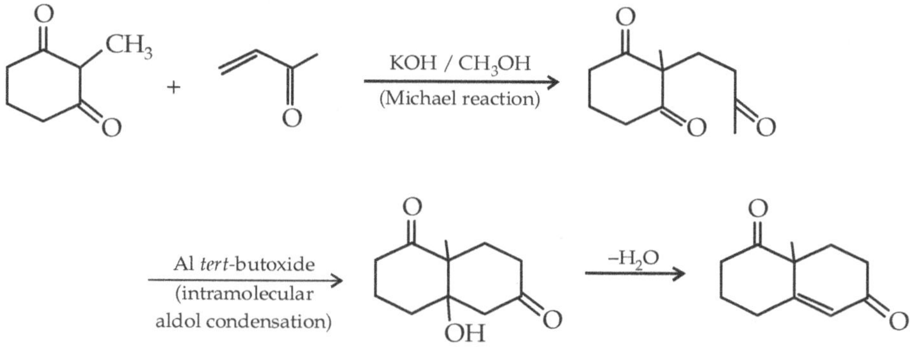

First step of the reaction involves Michael reaction. The product of Michael addition has necessary functional groups to undergo intramolecular aldol condensation to form cyclic product which undergoes dehydration to form stable α,β-unsaturated ketone. The synthesis of cyclohexanone derivatives by Michael addition followed by intramolecular aldol condensation is called **Robinson annulation.** The term **annulation or annelation** means building of a ring onto some starting molecule.

Example 4 :

Give steps involved in the following conversion.

$$HCHO \text{ (1 mol.)} + CH_2(COOC_2H_5)_2 \text{ (2 mol.)} \longrightarrow HOOC(CH_2)_3COOH$$

Solution :

The reaction involves aldol condensation followed by Michael additions.

$$H(H)C{=}O + H_2C(COOC_2H_5)_2 \xrightarrow[\text{(aldol conden.)}]{\text{base}} H_2C(OH)-CH(COOC_2H_5)_2$$

$$\xrightarrow{-H_2O} H_2C{=}C(COOC_2H_5)_2 \xrightarrow[\text{Michael addition}]{CH_2(COOC_2H_5)_2} CH_2CH(COOC_2H_5)_2 \text{ / } CH(COOC_2H_5)_2$$

$$\xrightarrow[\text{(ii) } H^+]{\text{(i) } OH^-} \xrightarrow[\text{(ii) } H^+]{\text{(i) } OH^-} CH_2CH(COOH)_2 \text{ / } CH(COOH)_2 \xrightarrow[(-2CO_2)]{\text{heat}} CH_2CH_2COOH \text{ / } CH_2COOH$$

Glutaric acid

Example 5 :

5,5-Dimethylcyclohexa-1,3-dione can be prepared from mesityl oxide, $(CH_3)_2C{=}CHCOCH_3$ and malonic ester using Michael reaction as the main rection. Give necessary steps involved in the conversion.

Solution :

Mesityl oxide + $CH_2(COOC_2H_5)_2$ $\xrightarrow{OC_2H_5^-}$ (adduct with $COOC_2H_5$ groups) $\xrightarrow[\text{Claisen condensation}]{OC_2H_5^-}$ (cyclic dione with $COOC_2H_5$) $\xrightarrow[\text{(ii) } H^+]{\text{(i) } OH^-}$ (cyclic dione with COOH) $\xrightarrow[(-CO_2)]{\text{heat}}$ 5,5-dimethylcyclohexa-1,3-dione

Example 6 :

Write steps involved in the following conversion using Diels-Alder reaction.

p-Benzoquinone $\xrightarrow{\text{benzene}}$ octahydroanthraquinone

Solution :

The conversion involves the Diels-Alder reaction between one molecule of *p*-benzoquinone and two molecules of 1,3-butadiene.

1,3-Butadiene + 1,4-Benzoquinone $\longrightarrow$ 5,8,9,10-Tetrahydro-1,4-naphthaquinone $\xrightarrow[\text{(Diels-Alder reaction)}]{\text{butadiene}}$ 1,4,5,8,11,12,13,14-Octahydro-9,10-anthraquinone

Example 6 :

Dibenzalacetone, $C_6H_5CH{=}CHCOCH{=}CHC_6H_5$, and ethyl malonate are treated in equimolar amounts to give a product (X) which does not respond to olefinic reagent. Suggest the structure for (X) and explain its formation.

Solution :

$$C_6H_5CH=CH\overset{O}{\overset{\|}{C}}\overset{\alpha}{C}H=\overset{\beta}{C}HC_6H_5 + H_2C(COOC_2H_5)_2 \xrightarrow[\text{addition}]{\text{Michael}} C_6H_5\overset{\beta}{C}H=\overset{\alpha}{C}H\overset{O}{\overset{\|}{C}}CH_2\underset{\mathbf{CH(COOC_2H_5)_2}}{\underset{|}{C}}HC_6H_5 \quad (X)$$

$$\xrightarrow[\text{Michael reaction}]{\text{internal}} C_6H_5CH-CH_2-\overset{O}{\overset{\|}{C}}CH_2CHC_6H_5 \text{ (ring closed via } C(COOC_2H_5)_2) \equiv$$

cyclohexanone ring: C=O; H_2C, CH_2; C_6H_5CH, CHC_6H_5; C bearing C_2H_5OOC and $COOC_2H_5$

Note that the compound (X) still has α,β-unsaturated carbonyl group and also a structural moiety capable of forming stable carbanion (marked by bold type), so it can undergo internal Michael reaction to form cyclic product having no carbon-carbon double bond.

EXERCISE 16.1 (MCQ - ONE option correct)

1. Which of the following is not an example of α,β-unsaturated carbonyl compound?
(a) Fumaric acid (b) *p*-Benzoquinone
(c) Mesityl oxide (d) None of these

2. Which of the following is not formed during dehydration of glycerol to prop-2-enal?

$$\underset{OH}{CH_2}-\underset{OH}{CH}-\underset{OH}{CH_2} \xrightarrow{KHSO_4} CH_2=CHCHO$$

(a) $\underset{OH}{CH_2}-CH=\underset{OH}{CH}$ (b) $CH_2=\underset{OH}{C}-\underset{OH}{CH_2}$

(c) $\underset{OH}{CH_2}CH_2CHO$ (d) None of these

3. The reactions 1 and 2 used in the preparation of the following unsaturated carbonyl compounds are

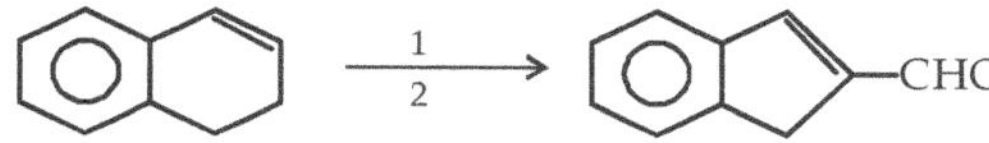

(a) Oxidation by conc. HNO_3 and intramolecular aldol condensation
(b) Oxidation by alkaline $KMnO_4$ and Michael reaction
(c) Ozonolysis and aldol condensation
(d) Ozonolysis and Michael addition

4. Which of the following carbocation is most likely to be formed during following reaction?

$$CH_2=CHCOOH + HBr \longrightarrow CH_2BrCH_2COOH$$

(a) $\overset{+}{C}H_2CH_2COOH$ (b) $CH_3\overset{+}{C}HCOOH$

(c) $CH_2=CH-\overset{OH}{\underset{+}{C}}-OH$ (d) None of these

5. (i) $CH_2=CHCOCH_3 + HBr \longrightarrow P_1$
(ii) $CH_2=CH-CH_2CHO + HBr \longrightarrow P_2$
Here P_1 and P_2 respectively are
(a) $CH_3CH(Br)COCH_3$, $CH_3CH(Br)CH_2CHO$
(b) $CH_2(Br)CH_2COCH_3$, $CH_2BrCH_2CH_2CHO$
(c) $CH_2(Br)CH_2COCH_3$, $CH_3CH(Br)CH_2CHO$
(d) P_1 and P_2 are same

6. $CH_3CH=CHCOCH_3 + CH_3MgBr \xrightarrow[\text{(ii) } H_3O^+]{\text{(i) } (C_2H_5)_2O} P$. Here P may be

(a) $CH_3CH=CH\overset{OH}{C}(CH_3)_2$

(b) $CH_3\overset{CH_3}{CH}-CH_2COCH_3$

(c) Both
(d) None

7. 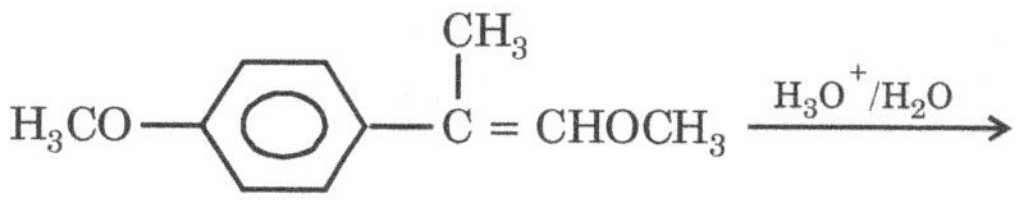 $H_3CO-C_6H_4-\overset{CH_3}{C}=CHOCH_3 \xrightarrow{H_3O^+/H_2O}$ P. Here P is

(a) 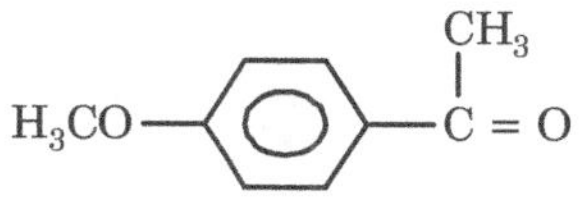 $H_3CO-C_6H_4-\overset{CH_3}{C}=O$

(b) $H_3CO-C_6H_4-\overset{CH_3}{C}HCHO$

(c) $H_3CO-C_6H_4-\overset{CH_3}{\underset{OH}{C}}-CH_2OCH_3$

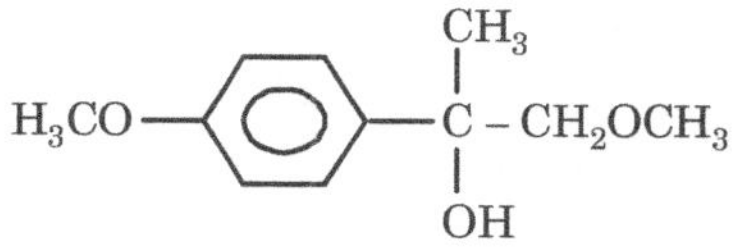

(d) None of these

8. Predict the nature of the product in the reaction

$$C_6H_5CH=CH\overset{O}{\overset{\|}{C}}C_6H_5 + NaCN(aq.) \longrightarrow$$

(a) $C_6H_5CH=CH\overset{OH}{\underset{CN}{C}}C_6H_5$

(b) $C_6H_5\underset{CN}{CH}CH_2\overset{O}{\overset{\|}{C}}C_6H_5$

(c) $C_6H_5CH_2\underset{CN}{CH}\overset{O}{\overset{\|}{C}}C_6H_5$

(d) None of these

9. Predict the major product in the following reaction

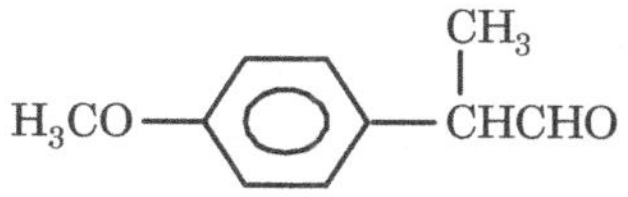

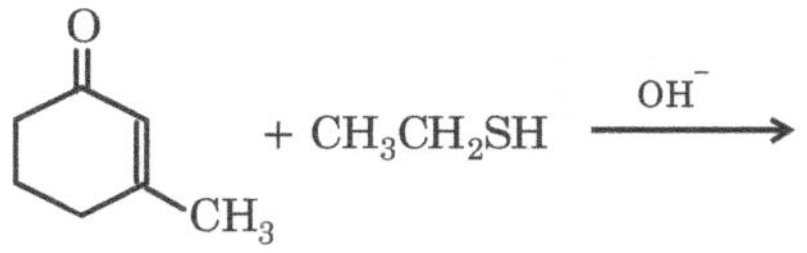

3-Methylcyclohex-2-en-1-one (C=O at C-1, CH_3 at C-3) $+ CH_3CH_2SH \xrightarrow{OH^-}$

(a) cyclohexene ring bearing HO and SCH_2CH_3 on C-1, double bond to C bearing CH_3
(b) cyclohexanone ring with SCH_2CH_3 and CH_3 on C-3
(c) cyclohexane ring with HO and SCH_2CH_3 on C-1, and SCH_2CH_3 and CH_3 on C-3
(d) None of these

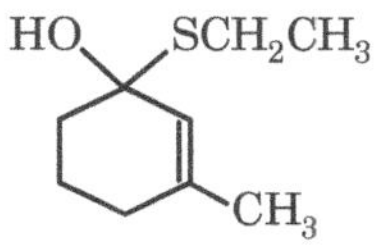

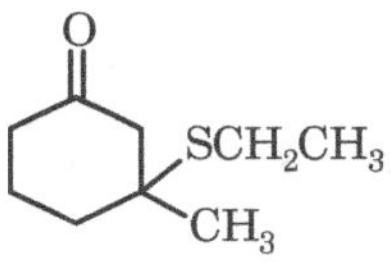

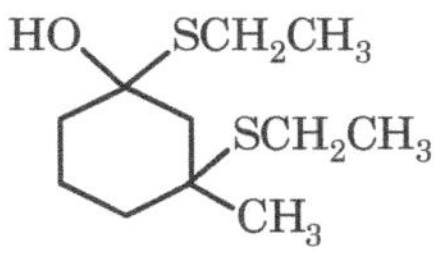

10. Predict the possible product in the following reaction :

Cyclopentadiene + Br–C₆H₄–COCH = CH–C₆H₅ $\xrightarrow{\text{piperidine}}$

(a) C₆H₅–CH(cyclopentadienyl)–CH₂–C(=O)–C₆H₄–Br

(b) Br–C₆H₄–COCHCH₂(cyclopentadienyl)–C₆H₅

(c) Both (a) and (b)
(d) No reaction

11. $\Delta^{1,9}$ - Octalone is prepared according to the following series of reactions

Cyclohexanone + methyl vinyl ketone $\xrightarrow[(1)]{^{-}OC_2H_5}$ [ ] $\xrightarrow{(2)}$ $\Delta^{1,9}$-Octalone

The reactions involved at (1) and (2) steps are
(a) conjugate addition, 1,2-addition
(b) 1,2-addition, aldol condensation
(c) 1,4-addition, aldol condensation
(d) 1,2-addition and 1,4-addition

12. In the following Michael reaction

$CH_2 = CHCHO + CH_3COCH_2COOC_3H_7-n \xrightarrow{\text{base}}$ $CH_3CO\underset{|}{C}HCOOC_3H_7-n$ with CH_2CH_2CHO on the central carbon

the best yield is obtained, when the base is
(a) OCH_3^- (b) $OC_2H_5^-$
(c) $^{-}C_3H_7-n$ (d) Equal

13. How many different products are possible by the Michael addition between following two compounds?

$CH_3CH = CHCOCH = CHCH_3 + CH_2(COOC_2H_5)_2 \xrightarrow{OC_2H_5^-}$

(a) One (b) Two
(c) Three (d) Four

14. Benzyl and dibenzyl ketone when treated in presence of a base leads to the formation of a cyclic compound, tetracyclone

$C_6H_5COCOC_6H_5$ + $C_6H_5CH_2COCH_2C_6H_5$ $\xrightarrow{\text{base}}$ Tetracyclone (tetraphenylcyclopentadienone)

The reaction involved in the conversion is
(a) Michael addition (b) Knoevenagel reaction
(c) aldol condensation (d) Both (a) and (c)

15. In Diels-Alder reaction, 1,3-butadiene can function as a
(a) diene (b) dienophile
(c) both (d) none

EXERCISE 16.2 (MCQ 1 or >1 option correct, Passage based, Matching, A/R)

DIRECTIONS for Q. 1 to 2 : Multiple choice questions with one or more than one correct option(s).

1. Which of the following does not undergo Michael addition?
(a) $C_6H_5CH = CHCOCH_3 + C_6H_5COCH_3$
(b) $C_6H_5CH = CHCH_2COC_6H_5 + CH_2(COOC_2H_5)_2$
(c) Cyclopentene + Br–C₆H₄–COCH = CH–C₆H₅
(d) $CH_2 = CHCOCH_3 + CH_3COCH_3$

2. In the absence of peroxide addition of HBr is by anti-Markownikoff rule :
(a) $CH_2 = CH - COOH$
(b) $CH_2 = CH - CHO$
(c) $CH_2 = CH - CH_2OH$
(d) $CH_2 = CH - CN$

INSTRUCTION for Q. 3 to 11 : Read the passages given below and answer the questions that follow.

PASSAGE 1

The following questions relate to the reaction sequence outlined below

1 ($CH_3COCH_2COOC_2H_5$) $\xrightarrow{EtO^-/EtOH}$ 2 (enolate) $\xrightarrow{CH_3Cl}$ 3 ($CH_3COCH(CH_3)COOC_2H_5$) $\xrightarrow{H_3O^+/\text{heat}}$ 4 ($CH_3COCH_2CH_3$) $+ CO_2$

3. Compound 1 is a/an
(a) α-keto carboxylic acid
(b) β-keto carboxylic acid
(c) α-keto ester
(d) β-keto ester

4. The first step in the sequence could be enhanced by
   (a) replacing the hydrogens at the alpha position by two alkyl groups
   (b) replacing one of the hydrogens at the alpha position by a chlorine atom
   (c) replacing one of the carbonyl groups with iodine atoms
   (d) using ethanoate/ethanoic acid instead of ethoxide/ethanol

5. Although sodium methoxide is readily available, it was not used in the first step because
   (a) it is not as strong base as ethoxide
   (b) it would cause an undesired transesterification
   (c) it would be more difficult to hydrolyze a methyl ester than an ethyl ester
   (d) a hindered base is needed to protect the carbonyl group

6. The second step is a type of reaction known as
   (a) S_N1
   (b) S_N2
   (c) electrophilic addition.
   (d) free radical substitution

7. The third step involves
   I. protonation of O in the C=O of the ester group
   II. S_N2 substitution of OC_2H_5 by OH
   III. heat-induced decarboxylation
   (a) I and II (b) I and III
   (c) II and III (d) I, II, and III

8. What type of reaction does not occur in the sequence?
   (a) Hydrolysis (b) Acid-base
   (c) Reduction (d) Decarboxylation

PASSAGE 2

A carbon-carbon double bond is a rich source of electrons and hence undergoes electrophilic additions easily. Further, a carbon-carbon double bond having an electropositive group undergoes such reactions very easily as compared to those having electronegative group.

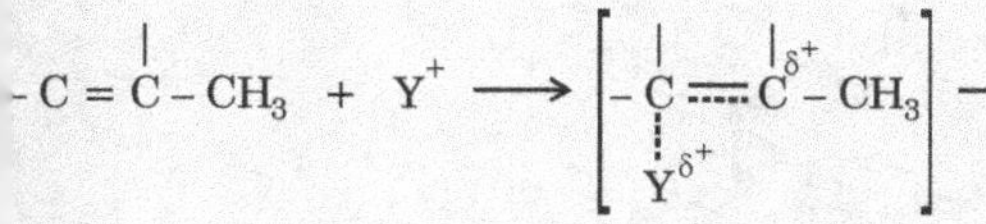

$$-C=C-CH_3 + Y^+ \longrightarrow \left[-C \overset{\delta+}{=\!=} C-CH_3 \;\; (\cdots Y^{\delta+})\right] \longrightarrow -C(Y)-\overset{+}{C}-CH_3$$

I

$$-C=C-NO_2 + Y^+ \longrightarrow \left[-C =\!= \overset{\delta+}{C}-NO_2 \;\; (\cdots Y^{\delta+})\right] \longrightarrow -C(Y)-\overset{+}{C}-NO_2$$

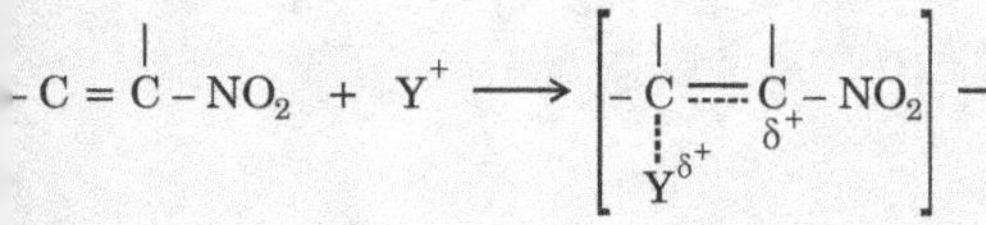

II

9. Which of the following transition state is more stable?
   (a) I (b) II
   (c) I = II (d) It can't be predicted

10. $CH_2=CHCHO + HCl \longrightarrow P$, here P should be
    (a) $CH_3CH(Cl)CHO$ (b) $ClCH_2CH_2CHO$
    (c) both (d) other product

11. $CH_2=CHCH_3 + HCl \longrightarrow P$, here P should be
    (a) $CH_3CH(Cl)CH_3$ (b) $ClCH_2CH_2CH_3$
    (c) both (d) other product

Instructions for Q. 12 to 13 : Following questions are Multiple Matching type Questions :

12.

	Column - I **(Carbon Acid)**		*Column - II* **(pK_a)**
(A)	$CH_3COCH_2COOC_2H_5$	(a)	3.6
(B)	$CH_3COOC_2H_5$	(b)	10.7
(C)	$CH_3CON(CH_3)_2$	(c)	25
(D)	$O_2NCH_2NO_2$	(d)	30

13.

	Column - I **Minimum no. of steps required**		*Column - II* **Reaction**
(A)	One	(a)	Aniline to *p*-bromoaniline
(B)	Two	(b)	Cyclohexanone → 2-cyanocyclohexanone (O, CN)
(C)	Three	(c)	Salicylic acid (OH, COOH) → 5-bromosalicylic acid (OH, COOH, Br)
		(d)	Salicylic acid (OH, COOH) → 2,4,6-tribromophenol (OH, Br, Br, Br)

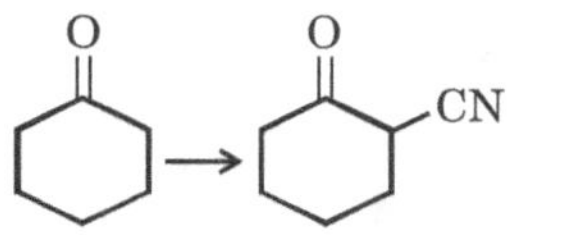

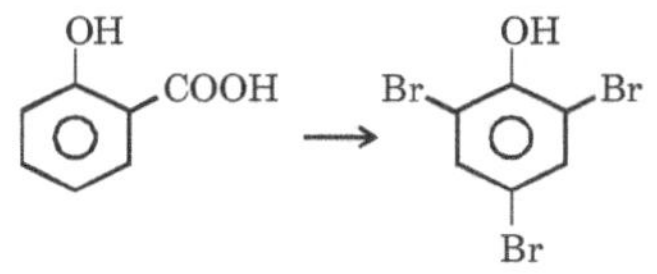

Instructions for Q. 14 : Following questions are Integer Type Questions :

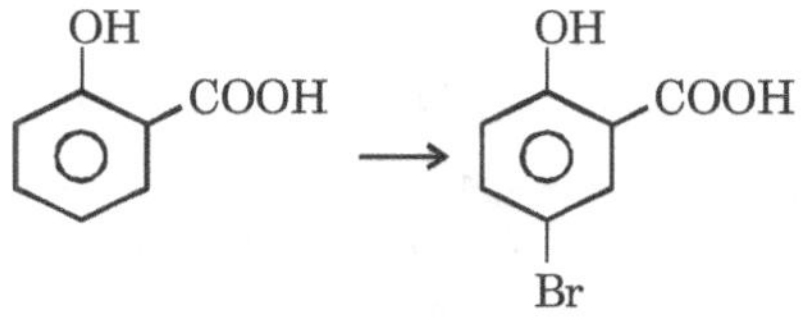

14. In the scheme given below, the total number of intramolecular aldol condensation products formed from 'Y' is

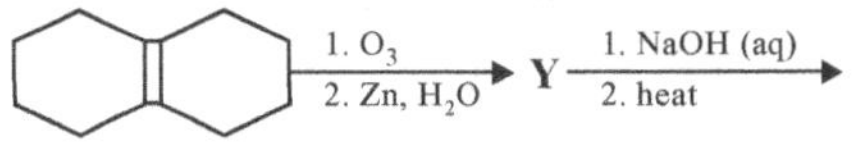

$$\text{(bicyclic alkene)} \xrightarrow[\text{2. Zn, } H_2O]{\text{1. } O_3} Y \xrightarrow[\text{2. heat}]{\text{1. NaOH (aq)}}$$

EXERCISE 16.3 (Subjective Problems)

1. Give the structures of the products obtained when benzalacetone, $C_6H_5CH{=}CHCOCH_3$ reacts with each of the following. Name the main reaction involved in each of the following
   (a) HCl
   (b) H_2O, H^+
   (c) 1,3-butadiene
   (d) Benzaldehyde in presence of a base
   (e) NH_2OH
   (f) Malonic ester
2. Give reactions involved in the conversion of ethyl 3-methylbut-2-enolate to 3,3-dimethylpentane-1,5-dioic acid using Michael addition.
3. Suggest a mechanism for the reaction between acrolein and hydrazine to form dihydropyrazole

   $CH_2{=}CH{-}CHO + H_2N-NH_2 \longrightarrow$ (dihydropyrazole, N–H)

4. Write down the final stable product obtained by the reaction of HCl on *p*-benzoquinone.
5. Give steps involved in the following conversions

   (a) $(CH_3)_2C=CHCOCH_3$ to $(CH_3)_2C(CH_2COOH)_2$

   (b) $H_2N(CH_2)_6NH_2$ to $H_2N(CH_2)_4NH(CH_2)_6NH(CH_2)_4NH_2$

6. (a) Which hydrogen of crotonaldehyde, $CH_3CH{=}CHCHO$, is acidic? Write the resonating structures of the corresponding carbanion; which resonating structure is more stable?

   (b) Give mechanism for the following reaction

   $$\text{Crotonaldehyde} + \text{Cinnamaldehyde} \xrightarrow[C_2H_5OH]{\text{base}} Ph{-}CH{=}CH{-}CH{=}CH{-}CH{=}CH{-}CHO$$

7. Propose a mechanism for the conjugate addition of a nucleophile to (a) acrylonitrile ($CH_2 = CHCN$) and to (b) nitroethylene ($CH_2 = CHNO_2$).
8. Give the suitable Michael donors and acceptors for synthesizing the following compounds by Michael reaction.

   (a) $C_6H_5CH(CH_2COC_6H_5)(C_6H_5COCH_3)$ (b) $HOOCCH_2CH_2CH_2CN$

   (c) 2-(CH_2CH_2CN)cyclopentanone (d) 2-CH_3-2-($CH_2CH_2COC_6H_5$)cyclopentanone

9. The ketone X can't be prepared in good yield by the following Michael addition between

   $$\text{cyclohexanone} + CH_2 = CHCOCH_3 \xrightarrow{OH^-} X$$

   Suggest a method for getting X in good yield from cyclohexanone and methyl vinyl ketone.
10. How the following can be prepared by using Robinson annulations?

   (a) (bicyclic enone with CH_3) (b) (bicyclic enone with angular methyl and O)

   (c) (HO, CH_3 substituted tricyclic compound with benzene ring)

SOLUTIONS

TEST YOUR UNDERSTANDING - 16.1

1. To achieve the best result and in a minimum time, carry out the conversion backwards.

(a) $\mathbf{CH_3CH=CHCOOH} \xleftarrow{Ag(NH_3)_2^+} CH_3CH=CHCHO \xleftarrow[(-H_2O)]{H^+} CH_3CH(OH)CH_2CHO$

$CH_3CH(OH)CH_2CHO \xleftarrow[\text{(aldol cond.)}]{OH^-} CH_3CHO$

$\mathbf{CH\equiv CH} \xrightarrow{H^+,\ Hg^{2+}} CH_3CHO$

(b) $\mathbf{CH_2=CHCOOCH_3} \xleftarrow[(-H_2O)]{H^+} CH_2(OH)CH_2COOCH_3 \xleftarrow{CH_3OH} CH_2(OH)CH_2COOH$

$CH_2(OH)CH_2COOH \xleftarrow{H^+} CH_2(OH)CH_2CN$

$\mathbf{CH_2=CH_2} \xrightarrow[\text{(ii) } CN^-]{\text{(i) HOCl}} CH_2(OH)CH_2CN$

(c) $\mathbf{CH_2=C(CH_3)COOCH_3} \xleftarrow[(-H_2O)]{H^+} CH_3-C(CH_3)(OH)-COOCH_3 \xleftarrow{CH_3OH} CH_3-C(CH_3)(OH)-COOH$

$CH_3-C(CH_3)(OH)-COOH \leftarrow CH_3-C(CH_3)(OH)-CN$

$\mathbf{CH_3-CO-CH_3} \longrightarrow CH_3-C(CH_3)(OH)-CN$

(d) $HOOC-CH=CH-CH=CH-COOH \xleftarrow[(-HBr)]{\text{KOH (alco.)}} HOOC-CH(Br)-CH_2CH_2-CH(Br)-COOH \xleftarrow{P,\ Br_2} HOOC(CH_2)_4COOH$

Adipic acid

(e) $CH_3COCH=CH_2 \xleftarrow[(-H_2O)]{H^+} CH_3COCH_2CH_2OH \xleftarrow[\text{(aldol cond.)}]{CH_2O,\ OH^-} CH_3COCH_3$

(f) $\mathbf{C_6H_5CH=CHCOOH} \xleftarrow[\substack{CH_3COO^- \\ \text{(Perkin reaction)}}]{(CH_3CO)_2O} C_6H_5CHO \xleftarrow[\text{(ii) } H_2O]{\text{(i) } CrO_3,\ Ac_2O} \mathbf{C_6H_5CH_3}$

(g) cis-$\mathbf{HOOCCH=CHCOOH}$ $\xleftarrow{H_2O}$ maleic anhydride $\xleftarrow{heat}$ $HOOCCH=CHCOOH$ (*cis*- and *trans*-)

$HOOCCH=CHCOOH \xleftarrow{\text{KOH (alc.)}} HOOCCH_2CH(Br)COOH$

$\mathbf{HOOCCH_2CH_2COOH} \xrightarrow{P,\ Br_2} HOOCCH_2CH(Br)COOH$

TEST YOUR UNDERSTANDING - 16.2

1.
(a) $C_6H_5CH=CHCOO^-$
(b) $CH_3CH=CHCOO^- + CHI_3$
(c) $CH_3CHO + OHCCOC_6H_5$
(d) *rac* – $HOOCCH(Br)CH(Br)COOH$
(e) *rac* – $HOOCCH(OH)CH(OH)COOH$
(f) $C_6H_5CH_2CH_2CHO$
(g) $C_6H_5CH_2CH_2CH_2OH$
(h) $C_6H_5CH=CHCH_2OH$

(i) The reaction is an example of crossed Claisen condensation. Here the carbanion is provided by γ-hydrogen due to conjugated system.

$$CH_3CH=CH\overset{O}{\overset{\|}{C}}-OC_2H_5 \xrightarrow{OC_2H_5^-} {}^-CH_2CH=CH-\overset{O}{\overset{\|}{C}}-OC_2H_5 \xrightarrow[OC_2H_5^-]{(COOC_2H_5)_2} \underset{\displaystyle COCOOC_2H_5}{\underset{|}{C}H_2CH=CHCOOC_2H_5}$$

2. Acrolein (CH_2=CHCHO) is an α,β-unsaturated aldehyde, hence it undergoes 1,4-addition reaction with sodium azide, a weak nucleophile.

$$CH_2=CHCHO \xrightarrow{NaN_3} N_3CH_2CH_2CHO$$

Propanal (CH_3CH_2CHO) does not contain any α,β-unsaturation, hence it does not undergo addition reaction with sodium azide.

3. (a) Acetylide ion is a strong base, hence it adds on α,β-unsaturated carbonyl compounds by 1,2-addition.

$$CH_3CH=CHCHO + CH\equiv CMgBr \longrightarrow CH_3CH=CH\overset{OMgBr}{\overset{|}{C}}HC\equiv CH$$

(b) CN^- is a weak base, hence it gives conjugate (1,4-)addition product.

$$C_6H_5CH=CHCOC_6H_5 + HCN \longrightarrow C_6H_5\underset{CN}{\underset{|}{C}}HCH_2COC_6H_5$$

4. (a)

$$\underset{\alpha,\beta\text{-unsaturated nitrile}}{CH_2=CHC\equiv N} + NH_3 \xrightarrow[\text{addition}]{1,4-} \underset{\substack{[X]\\ \text{(a weak nucleophile)}}}{\underset{NH_2}{\underset{|}{C}H_2CH_2CN}} \xrightarrow[\text{1,4-addition}]{CH_2=CHCN} \underset{[Y]}{\underset{\substack{NH\\|\\CH_2CH_2CN}}{\underset{|}{C}H_2CH_2CN}}$$

(b)

$$CH_2=CHCOOCH_3 \xrightarrow[\text{(conjugate addition)}]{CH_3NH_2} \underset{[A],\text{ a weak nucleophile}}{\underset{NHCH_3}{\underset{|}{C}H_2CH_2COOCH_3}} \xrightarrow[\text{conjugate addition}]{CH_2=CHCOOCH_3} \underset{[B]}{\underset{\substack{NCH_3\\|\\CH_2CH_2COOCH_3}}{\underset{|}{C}H_2CH_2COOCH_3}}$$

TEST YOUR UNDERSTANDING - 16.3

1. (a)

$$\underset{\text{Ethyl crotonate}}{CH_3CH=CHCOOC_2H_5} + \underset{\text{Ethyl methylmalonate}}{CH_3CH(COOC_2H_5)_2} \xrightarrow{^-OC_2H_5} CH_3\underset{CH_3C(COOC_2H_5)_2}{\underset{|}{C}}HCH_2COOC_2H_5$$

(b)

$$\underset{\text{Ethyl }\alpha\text{-methylacrylate}}{CH_2=\overset{CH_3}{\overset{|}{C}}COOC_2H_5} + \underset{\text{Ethyl cyanoacetate}}{CNCH_2COOC_2H_5} \xrightarrow{^-OC_2H_5} \underset{CN\underset{}{C}HCOOC_2H_5}{\underset{|}{C}H_2\overset{CH_3}{\overset{|}{C}}HCOOC_2H_5}$$

(c)

$$C_6H_5CH=CHCOC_6H_5 + \underset{\text{Acetophenone}}{C_6H_5COCH_3} \xrightarrow{^-OC_2H_5} C_6H_5\underset{CH_2COC_6H_5}{\underset{|}{C}}HCH_2COC_6H_5$$

Acetophenone forms a stable carbanion ($C_6H_5COCH_2^-$) which, being a weak base, adds to form conjugate addition.

(d)

$$\underset{\text{Acrylonitrile}}{CH_2=CHCN} + \underset{\text{Allyl cyanide}}{CH_2=CHCH_2CN} \xrightarrow{^-OC_2H_5} \underset{CH_2=CH\underset{}{C}HCN}{\underset{|}{C}H_2CH_2CN}$$

Allyl cyanide in presence of base forms a stable carbanion $CH_2=CH\bar{C}HCN$ which undergoes Michael addition.

(e) $EtOOCC \equiv CCOOEt + CH_3COCH_2COOC_2H_5 \xrightarrow{^-OC_2H_5}$

$EtOOCC(CH(COCH_3)COOC_2H_5) = CHCOOEt \xrightarrow{CH_3COCH_2COOC_2H_5} EtOOCC(CH(COCH_3)COOC_2H_5)_2CH_2COOEt$

(f) $CH_3CH = CHCOOC_2H_5 + CH_2(COOC_2H_5)_2 \longrightarrow CH_3CH(CH(COOC_2H_5)_2)CH_2COOC_2H_5$ [X]

$\xrightarrow[(ii)\ H^+]{(i)\ OH^-} CH_3CH(CH(COOH)_2)CH_2COOH$ [Y] $\xrightarrow{heat} CH_3CH(CH_2COOH)CH_2COOH$

2. (a) $CH_2 = CHCOCH_3 + CH_3CH_2OCOCH_2COCH_2CH_3$ (b) 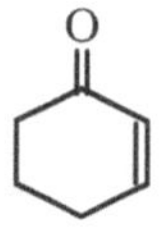 cyclohex-2-enone $+ CH_3COCH_2COCH_3$

3. (a) methyl vinyl ketone + $C_6H_5CH_2CH_2COCH_2C_6H_5$ $\xrightarrow[\text{(Michael addition)}]{CH_3ONa,\ CH_3OH}$ Michael adduct

$\xrightarrow[\text{(intramolecular aldol condensation)}]{CH_3ONa}$ β-hydroxy ketone (OH, C_6H_5, C_6H_5) $\xrightarrow{-H_2O}$ cyclohexenone product

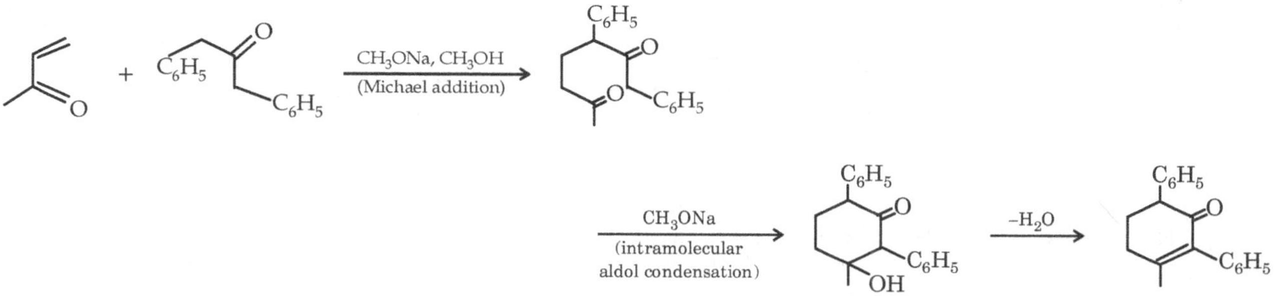

(b) (i) 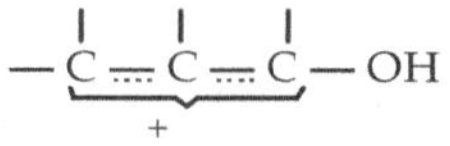 $-\overset{|}{C}\cdots\overset{|}{C}\cdots\overset{|}{C}-OH$ (+) (ii) 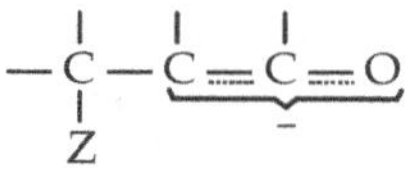 $-\overset{|}{\underset{Z}{C}}-\overset{|}{C}\cdots\overset{|}{C}\cdots O$ (−)

TEST YOUR UNDERSTANDING - 16.4

1. (a) 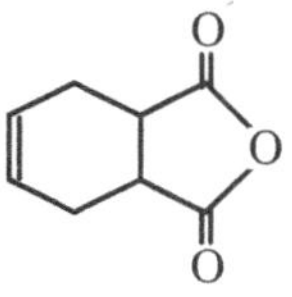 (b) 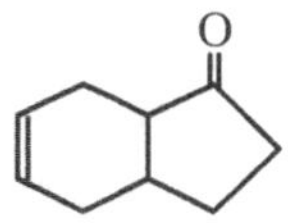 (c)

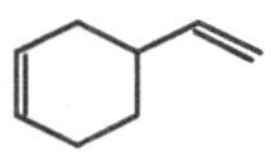

2. (a) 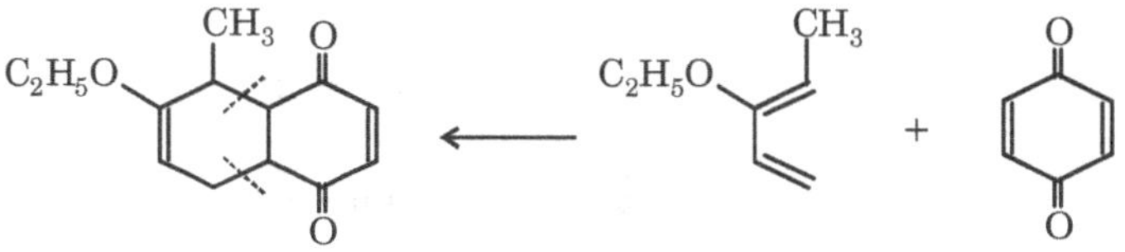 (b) Diels-Alder reaction

C_2H_5O, CH_3, CH_3O

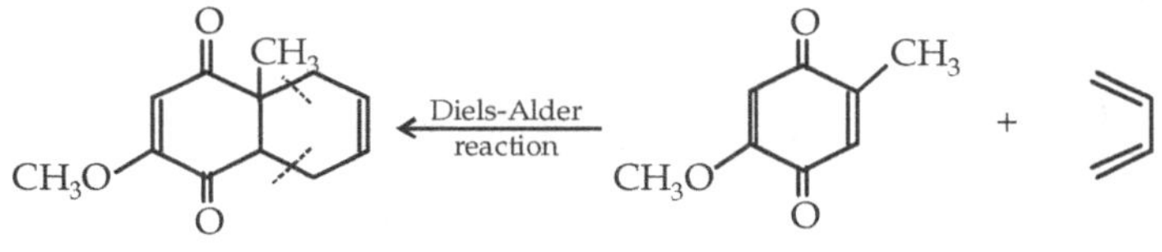

EXERCISE 16.1

1	(d)	6	(c)	11	(c)
2	(b)	7	(b)	12	(c)
3	(c)	8	(b)	13	(c)
4	(c)	9	(b)	14	(c)
5	(b)	10	(a)	15	(c)

1. All have unsaturation between α and β carbon atoms with respect to C=O linkage.

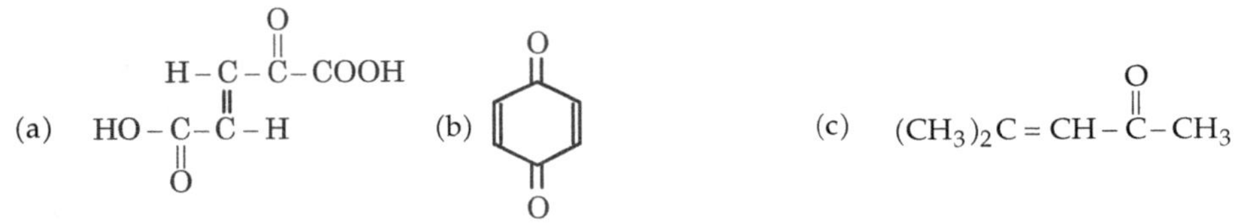

(a) $HO-\underset{\|}{\overset{}{C}}(=O)-C(-H)=C(-H)-C(=O)-COOH$ (b) (p-benzoquinone) (c) $(CH_3)_2C=CH-C(=O)-CH_3$

2. 2° Alcohol is more reactive than 1°, hence former is preferentially formed.

$$CH_2(OH)-CH(OH)-CH_2(OH) \xrightarrow{-H_2O} CH_2(OH)-CH=CH(OH) \xrightleftharpoons{\text{tantomerises}} CH_2(OH)-CH_2-CHO \xrightarrow{-H_2O} CH_2=CH-CHO$$

3. 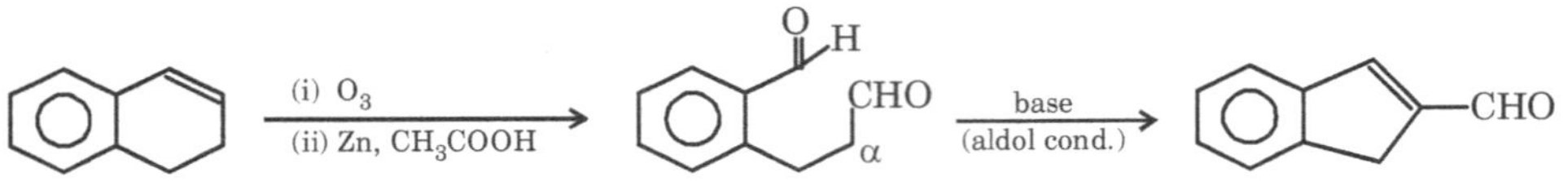 (dihydronaphthalene) $\xrightarrow[\text{(ii) Zn, } CH_3COOH]{\text{(i) } O_3}$ (dialdehyde, α-CHO) $\xrightarrow[\text{(aldol cond.)}]{\text{base}}$ (indene-CHO)

4. $\overset{+}{C}H_2-CH_2-C(=O)-OH$; +ve charge localised $\quad CH_3-\overset{+}{C}H-C(=O)-OH \quad CH_2=CH-C^+(OH)-OH$ +ve charge delocalised in both cases

5. In reaction (i), HBr undergoes conjugate addition because the compound is α,β-unsaturated ketone. In reaction (ii), HBr adds according to Markownikov's way because α,β-unsaturation is not present.

6. Grignard reagent adds on α,β-unsaturated carbonyl compounds in a simple way as well as in conjugate way. However, simple addition product dominates because CH_3MgBr is a strong nucleophile.

7. 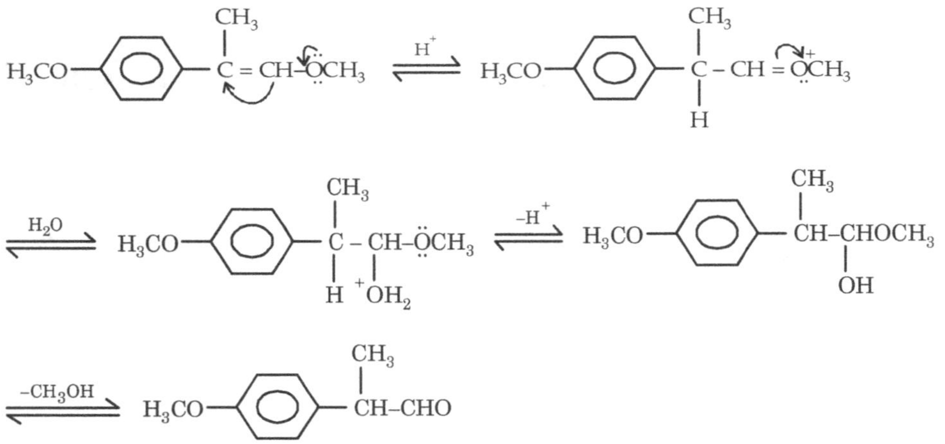 $H_3CO-C_6H_4-C(CH_3)=CH-\ddot{O}CH_3 \xrightleftharpoons{H^+} H_3CO-C_6H_4-C(CH_3)(H)-CH=\overset{+}{O}CH_3$

$$\xrightleftharpoons{H_2O} H_3CO-C_6H_4-C(CH_3)(H)-CH(\overset{+}{O}H_2)-\ddot{O}CH_3 \xrightleftharpoons{-H^+} H_3CO-C_6H_4-CH(CH_3)-CH(OH)OCH_3$$

$$\xrightleftharpoons{-CH_3OH} H_3CO-C_6H_4-CH(CH_3)-CHO$$

8. CN^-, being a weak nucleophile, adds on β-carbon w.r.t. the carbonyl group to form conjugate addition product (Michael reaction).

9. $CH_3CH_2S^-$ is a weak nucleophile, hence it adds in 1,4-addition way.

10. This is an example of Michael reaction in which nucleophile adds on β-carbon w.r.t. to carbonyl group.

11. 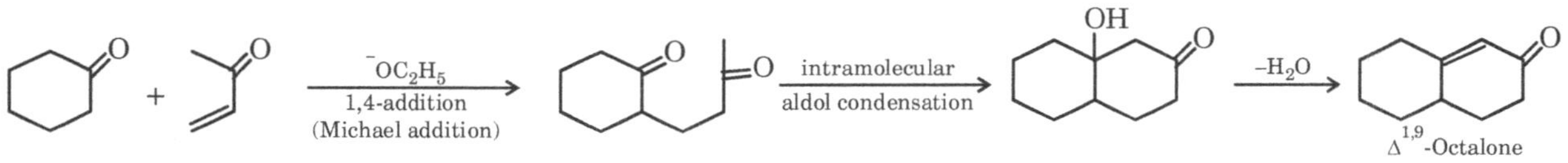 Cyclohexanone + methyl vinyl ketone $\xrightarrow[\text{1,4-addition (Michael addition)}]{^-OC_2H_5}$ (diketone) $\xrightarrow{\text{intramolecular aldol condensation}}$ (hydroxy ketone) $\xrightarrow{-H_2O}$ $\Delta^{1,9}$-Octalone

12. The base used in Michael reaction may also act as a nucleophile, so it will add to the carbonyl carbon of the ester group and change the reactant leading to low yield of the desired product.

13. (i) $2H_2C(COOC_2H_5)_2 + CH_3\overset{\beta}{C}H=\overset{\alpha}{C}H\overset{O}{\overset{\|}{C}}\overset{\alpha}{C}H=\overset{\beta}{C}HCH_3 \xrightarrow[\text{at both C=C}]{\text{Michael addition}} CH_3-CH(CH(COOC_2H_5)_2)-CH_2-\overset{O}{\overset{\|}{C}}-CH_2-CH(CH(COOC_2H_5)_2)-CH_3$

(ii) $CH_3CH=CH-\overset{O}{\overset{\|}{C}}-CH=CHCH_3 + H_2C(COOC_2H_5)_2 \xrightarrow[\text{only at one C=C}]{\text{Michael addition}} CH_3-CH(CH(COOC_2H_5)_2)-CH_2-\overset{O}{\overset{\|}{C}}-CH=CHCH_3$ (A)

(iii) (A) from (ii) $\xrightarrow{\text{internal Michael addition}}$ cyclohexanone bearing H_3C, CH_3, H_5C_2OOC, $COOC_2H_5$

14. The reaction involves *double* aldol condensation.

$C_6H_5COCOC_6H_5$ + $C_6H_5CH_2COCH_2C_6H_5$ $\xrightarrow{\text{base (double aldol condensation)}}$ (HO, OH dihydroxy cyclopentanone with four C_6H_5) $\xrightarrow{(-2H_2O)}$ tetraphenylcyclopentadienone

15. 1,3-Butadiene can function both as a diene as well as dienophile.

1,3-Butadiene (diene) + 1,3-Butadiene (dienophile) ⟶ 4-vinylcyclohexene

EXERCISE 16.2

>1 CORRECT OPTION	1	(b,d)	2	(a, d)		
PASSAGE 1	3	(d)	4	(b)	5	(b)
	6	(b)	7	(b)	8	(c)
PASSAGE 2	9	(a)	10	(b)	11	(a)
MATCH THE FOLLOWING	12	(A) - b, (B) - c, (C) - d, (D) - a				
	13	(A) – c,c; (B) – b; (C) – a				
INTEGER	14	1				

1. (b) does not have α,β-unsaturated carbonyl group, while (d) can't form stable carbanion (from acetone). Remember that cyclopentadiene is quite acidic in nature, because its carbanion is stable due to presence of conjugated system; hence it functions as the nucleophile required in Michael reaction.

14. 1

$\xrightarrow{\text{1. } O_3 \text{ 2. Zn, } H_2O}$ cyclodecane-1,6-dione $\xrightarrow{\text{NaOH(aq)}}$ (–) ⟶ OH ⟶ $\xrightarrow[-H_2O]{\text{heat}}$

The number of intra molecular aldol condensation products (α, β –unsaturated carbonyl compound formed from **Y** is 1.

EXERCISE 16.3

1. (a) $C_6H_5\underset{|}{\overset{Cl}{C}}HCH_2COCH_3$ (Cl on the benzylic carbon)
Obtained by 1,4-electrophilic addition

(b) $C_6H_5CH(OH)CH_2COCH_3$

(c) 1,3-Butadiene (a diene) + Benzalacetone (a dienophile) $\xrightarrow{\text{Diels Alder}}$ cyclohexene bearing C_6H_5 and $COCH_3$ on adjacent carbons

Benzalacetone: $C_6H_5-CH=CH-COCH_3$

(d) $C_6H_5CH=CHCOCH=CHC_6H_5$
formed by crossed aldol condensation

(e) $C_6H_5CH(NHOH)CH_2COCH_3$
formed by 1,4–nucleophilic addition

(f) $C_6H_5CH(CH(COOC_2H_5)_2)CH_2COCH_3$
formed by 1,4–nucleophilic addition

2. $CH_3-C(CH_3)=CH-C(=O)-OC_2H_5$ (Ethyl 3–methylbut–2–enoate) + $CH_2(COOC_2H_5)_2$ (Ethyl malonate) $\xrightarrow[\text{(Michael addition)}]{^{-}OC_2H_5}$ $CH_3-C(CH_3)(CH(COOC_2H_5)_2)-CH_2-C(=O)-OC_2H_5$

$\xrightarrow[\text{(ii) } H^+]{\text{(i) } OH^-}$ $CH_3-C(CH_3)(CH(COOH)_2)-CH_2COOH$ $\xrightarrow[(-CO_2)]{\text{heat}}$ $CH_3-C(CH_3)(CH_2COOH)-CH_2COOH \equiv HOOCCH_2C(CH_3)_2CH_2COOH$

3,3–Dimethylpentane–1,5–dioic acid

3. Acrolein (α,β-unsaturated ketone) (atoms numbered 1 O, 2, 3, 4; H on C-2) + $H_2N{-}NH_2$ Hydrazine (a weak base) $\xrightarrow{\text{Conjugate addition}}$ [cyclic intermediate: N–H, $\ddot{N}H_2$, C=O with H] $\rightleftharpoons$ [O^-, $\overset{+}{N}H_2$, N–H ring] $\rightleftharpoons$ [OH, NH, N–H ring] $\xrightarrow{-H_2O}$ [ring with C=N, N–H]

4. p-Benzoquinone (α,β-unsaturated ketone) + HCl $\xrightarrow{\text{1,4-addition}}$ [intermediate with Cl and H on the same carbon] $\xrightarrow{\text{tauto-merization}}$ 2-Chlorohydro-quinone (OH, Cl, OH)

5. (a) $(CH_3)_2C=CHCOCH_3 \xrightarrow[\text{(Michael addition)}]{H_2C(COO\,Et)_2} (CH_3)_2\underset{}{\overset{CH(COOEt)_2}{C}}CH_2COCH_3 \xrightarrow[\text{(ii) } OH^-]{\text{(i) NaOI}}$

$(CH_3)_2\overset{CH(COO^-)_2}{C}CH_2COO^- \xrightarrow[\text{(ii) heat}]{\text{(i) } H^+} (CH_3)_2\overset{CH_2COOH}{C}CH_2COOH$

(b) The required compound, *spermine* (a compound found in seminal fluid) can be prepared by the double nucleophilic addition of 1,4-diaminobutane (*putrescine*) on acrylonitrile.

$CH_2=CH-CN + H_2N(CH_2)_4NH_2 \xrightarrow{\text{1,4-nucleophilic addition}} H_2N(CH_2)_4NH(CH_2)_2CN$

$\xrightarrow[\text{(nucleo addn.)}]{CH_2=CH-CN} NC(CH_2)_2NH(CH_2)_4NH(CH_2)_2CN$

$\xrightarrow{H_2/\,Ni} H_2N(CH_2)_3NH(CH_2)_4NH(CH_2)_3NH_2$

Spermine

6. (a) Crotonaldehyde is an α,β-unsaturated aldehyde so here γ-hydrogens are acidic.

$$\overset{\gamma}{H_3C}-\overset{\beta}{CH}=\overset{\alpha}{CH}-\overset{O}{\overset{||}{CH}} \xrightarrow{\text{Base}} H_2\bar{C}-CH=CH-\overset{O}{\overset{||}{CH}} \longleftrightarrow CH_2=CH-\bar{C}H-\overset{O}{\overset{||}{CH}} \longleftrightarrow CH_2=CH-CH=\overset{O^-}{\overset{|}{CH}}$$

I, II, III

This structure is more stable because –ve charge in on the O atom

(b) $C_6H_5CH=CH\overset{O}{\overset{||}{C}}H + {}^-CH_2CH=CHCHO \rightleftharpoons C_6H_5CH=CH\overset{O^-}{\overset{|}{C}}HCH_2CH=CHCHO \overset{H^+}{\rightleftharpoons}$

$C_6H_5CH=CH\overset{OH}{\overset{|}{C}}HCH_2CH=CHCHO \xrightarrow{-H_2O} C_6H_5(CH=CH)_3CHO$

7. (a) $\left[CH_2=CH-C\equiv\ddot{N}: \longleftrightarrow CH_2=CH-\overset{+}{C}=\ddot{N}:^- \longleftrightarrow \overset{+}{C}H_2-CH=C=\ddot{N}:^-\right]$

Acrylonitrile

$\xrightarrow{:Nu} \left[\underset{Nu}{\underset{|}{CH_2}}-CH=C=\ddot{N}:^- \longleftrightarrow \underset{Nu}{\underset{|}{CH_2}}-\ddot{\bar{C}}H-C\equiv\ddot{N}\right] \xrightarrow{Nu:H} \underset{Nu}{\underset{|}{CH_2}}-CH_2-CN$

(b) $\left[CH_2=CH-\overset{:O:}{\overset{||}{N^+}}-\ddot{O}:^- \longleftrightarrow \overset{+}{C}H_2-CH=\underset{+}{\overset{:\ddot{O}:^-}{\overset{|}{N}}}-\ddot{O}:^-\right] \xrightarrow{:Nu}$

$\left[\underset{Nu}{\underset{|}{CH_2}}-CH=\overset{:\ddot{O}:^-}{\overset{|}{N^+}}-\ddot{O}:^- \longleftrightarrow \underset{Nu}{\underset{|}{CH_2}}-\ddot{\bar{C}}H-\overset{:O:}{\overset{||}{N^+}}-\ddot{O}:^-\right] \xrightarrow{Nu:H} \underset{Nu}{\underset{|}{CH_2}}-CH_2-\underset{+}{\overset{:O:}{\overset{||}{N}}}-\ddot{\bar{O}}:$

8. (a) $\underset{\text{acceptor}}{C_6H_5CH=CH\overset{O}{\overset{||}{C}}-C_6H_5}$, $\underset{\text{donor}}{C_6H_5\ddot{\bar{C}}H-\overset{O}{\overset{||}{C}}-CH_3}$ supplied as $C_6H_5-\underset{COOC_2H_5}{\underset{|}{CH}}-\overset{O}{\overset{||}{C}}-CH_3$

(b) $\underset{\text{acceptor}}{CH_2=CH-C\equiv N}$, $\underset{|}{\ddot{\bar{C}}HCOOH}$ supplied as $\underset{COOC_2H_5}{\underset{|}{CH_2COOC_2H_5}}$

(c) $\underset{\text{acceptor}}{CH_2=CH-C\equiv N}$; 2-(COOC₂H₅)cyclopentanone (donor)

(d) $\underset{\text{acceptor}}{CH_2=CH-\overset{O}{\overset{||}{C}}C_6H_5}$; 1-N(CH₃)₂-2-CH₃-cyclopentene (donor)

9. Although theoretically following reaction should take place

However, in such reaction, yield of the final product is very low due to following competitive reactions.

(i) The ketone enolate I can undergo self aldol condensation.

(ii) The ketone enolate I can condense with methyl vinyl ketone in aldol condensation manner.

(iii) The ketone enolate I can deprotonate the methyl vinyl ketone to form a new nucleophile.

Thus the ketone cyclohexanone must be converted into other resonance stabilized enolate, *enamine* which does not undergo any side reaction and also undergoes Michael addition smoothly.

10. Always remember that the Robinson annulation consists of a Michael addition followed by aldol cyclizaton with dehydration. In the retrosynthetic direction, perform following two disconnections.

(i) Disconnect the alkene formed in the aldol/dehydration. Since aldol condensation with dehydration forms α,β-unsaturated double bond, disconnect this double bond.

(ii) Disconnect the Michael addition to get the reactants. Since Michael addition forms a bond to the β' carbon atom, disconnect this particular β' bond.

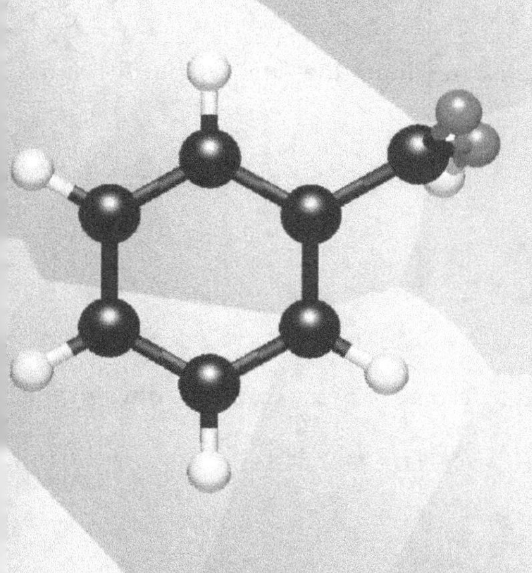

17 Carboxylic Acids

CHAPTER HIGHLIGHTS

17.1 Nomenclature

Carboxylic acids are the organic compounds having the carboxyl group, $-\overset{O}{\overset{\|}{C}}-OH$ (abbreviated as $-COOH$ or $-CO_2H$). Many of the carboxylic acids are better known by **common names** than by their systematic names. For example, formic acid (Latin : *formica,* ant), acetic acid (Latin : *acetum, vinegar*), butyric acid (Latin : *butyrum,* butter), and caproic, caprylic and capric acids (Latin : *caper,* goat) are named on their natural sources. The positions of the substituent groups are shown by Greek letters α, β, γ, δ, etc. Names of some acids are derived from acetic acid, *e.g.*

$(CH_3)_3CCOOH$
Trimethylacetic acid

$C_6H_5CH_2COOH$
Phenylacetic acid

Occasionally, they are named as carboxylic acids, *e.g.* cyclohexane carboxylic acid.

In IUPAC system, names of carboxylic acids are obtained by replacing the *-e* of the corresponding alkane with **-oic acid**. The carboxyl carbon atom is always assigned number 1.

$HCOOH$
Methanoic acid
(Formic acid)

$CH_3CH_2CH_2CH_2COOH$
Pentanoic acid
(Valeric acid)

$CH_3CH=CHCOOH$
2-Butenoic acid

$CH_3(CH_2)_4COOH$
Hexanoic acid
(Caproic acid)

$CH_3(CH_2)_6COOH$
Octanoic acid
(Caprylic acid)

$CH_3(CH_2)_8COOH$
Decanoic acid
(Capric acid)

$CH_2=\overset{CH_3}{\overset{|}{C}}COOH$
2-Methyl-2-propenoic acid
or 2-Methylpropenoic acid
(Methacrylic acid)

$\overset{H_3C}{\underset{H}{}}\!>C=C<\!\overset{H}{\underset{COOH}{}}$
trans-2-Butenoic acid
(Crotonic acid)

Common name, if any, is given in bracket.

When a carboxyl group is attached to a ring, the parent ring is named (retaining the final *-e*) and the suffix *-carboxylic acid* is added. For example,

COOH — Benzene carboxylic acid (Benzoic acid)

COOH, CH_3 — *m*-Methylbenzene carboxylic acid (*m*-Toluic acid)

In case, carboxylic is present on the side chain, compound is named as a derivative of the corresponding alkane.

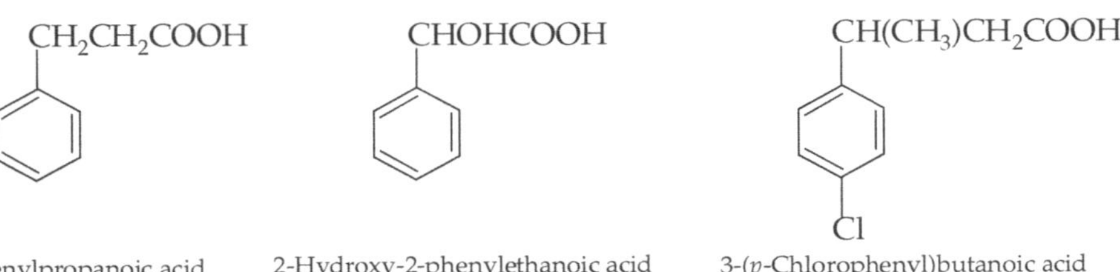

3-Phenylpropanoic acid | 2-Hydroxy-2-phenylethanoic acid (Mandelic acid) | 3-(*p*-Chlorophenyl)butanoic acid

Compounds with two carboxyl groups are designated by the suffix *-dioic acid* or *dicarboxylic acid*. The final *-e* in the base name of the alkane is retained.

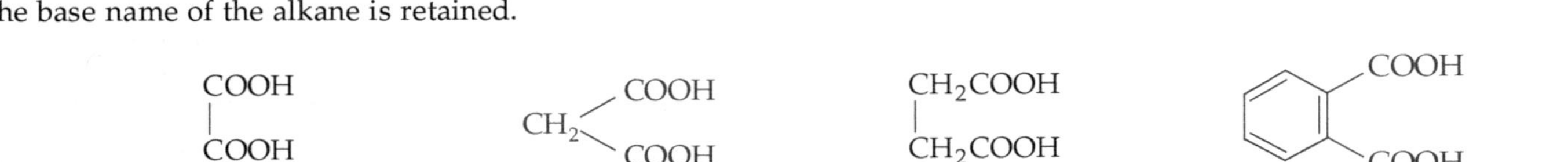

Ethanedioic acid (Oxalic acid) | Propanedioic acid (Malonic acid) | Butanedioic acid (Succinic acid) | 1, 2-Benzene dicarboxylic (Phthalic acid)

TEST YOUR UNDERSTANDING - 17.1

1. Give IUPAC name of the following compunds.

(*a*) COOH (*b*) COOH (*c*) O, H, COOH

(*d*) OH, F, COOH (*e*) OH, O, O (*f*) $CH_2 = CHCOOH$

(*g*) O, CHO OH (*h*) $CH_3(CH_2)_7CH = CH(CH_2)_7COOH$

(*i*) CH_3CH_2, H, C = C, CH_2, HH, C = C, CH_2, HH, C = C, $(CH_2)_7COOH$, H (*j*) HOOC—C_6H_4—COOH

Carboxylic acids exhibit chain, position and functional isomerism. Its functional isomers are esters, hydroxyaldehydes, hydroxyketones and hydroxyoxirane. Thus functional isomers of ethanoic acid are

$HCOOCH_3$ Methyl formate | CH_2OH–CHO Glycolaldehyde | O, OH Hydroxyoxirane

Similarly, functional isomers of propanoic acid (CH_3CH_2COOH) are

$HCOOCH_2CH_3$, CH_3COOCH_3, $CHO-CH_2CH_2OH$ (CHO above CH_2CH_2OH), $COCH_3-CH_2OH$ (COCH₃ above CH_2OH), epoxide with CH_2OH

17.2 Preparation of Carboxylic Acids

Many carboxylic acids were first isolated from natural sources, viz. formic acid was obtained by distilling ants, lactic acid from sour milk, etc. However, such methods are now only of historical importance.

1. **By oxidation of 1° alcohols and aldehydes.** Potassium permanganate (acidic or alkaline) and chromic acid convert primary alcohols to carboxylic acids through the formation of corresponding aldehydes.

$$RCH_2OH \xrightarrow[K_2Cr_2O_7,\, H_2SO_4]{KMnO_4} [RCHO] \longrightarrow RCOOH$$

Isobutyl alcohol $\xrightarrow[H_2SO_4]{KMnO_4}$ Isobutyric acid

2-*tert*-Butyl-3, 3-dimethylbutanol $\xrightarrow[H_2O,\, H_2SO_4]{H_2CrO_4}$ 2-*tert*-Butyl-3, 3-dimethylbutanoic acid

Aldehydes are very sensitive to oxidation and oxidised easily even with mild oxidising agents like Tollen's reagent, $[Ag(NH_3)_2]^+$.

$$RCHO \xrightarrow[\text{or } KMnO_4/H^+ \text{ or } K_2Cr_2O_7/H^+]{Ag_2O \text{ or } Ag(NH_3)_2^+} RCOOH$$

Ketones, although are also oxidised by strong oxidising reagents to carboxylic acids having lesser number of carbon atoms, these give poor yields. However, methyl ketones are good sources for carboxylic acids as these are quantitatively oxidised to carboxylic acids by hypohalites (haloform reaction).

$$RCOCH_3 + 3I_2 + 4NaOH \xrightarrow{heat} RCOONa + 3NaI + CHI_3 + 3H_2O$$

$$HCOOH + HOOC^{14}CH_2CH_3 \xleftarrow{[O]} CH_3C^{14}OCH_2CH_3 \xrightarrow{Oxidation} CH_3C^{14}OOH + CH_3COOH.$$

However, remember that in mixed ketones, major oxidation product is that in which carbonyl carbon (C^{14}) remains with smaller alkyl group.

2. **By oxidation of alkenes, alkynes and cycloalkenes.** These compounds can be oxidised to carboxylic acids by hot alkaline $KMnO_4$ or by ozonolysis followed by reaction with H_2O_2.

$$RCH = CHR' \xrightarrow[(ii)\ H_3O^+]{(i)\ KMnO_4,\ OH^-,\ heat} RCOOH + R'COOH$$

$$RCH = CHR' \xrightarrow[(ii)\ H_2O_2]{(i)\ O_3} RCOOH + R'COOH$$

$$RC \equiv CR' \xrightarrow[(ii)\ H_2O]{(i)\ KMnO_4 \text{ or } O_3} RCOOH + R'COOH$$

Cyclopentene $\xrightarrow[heat]{KMnO_4,\ H^+}$ Glutaric acid

TEST YOUR UNDERSTANDING - 17.2

1. From the knowledge of the chemistry so far studied, try to give steps for converting.
   (a) $CH_3CH = CH_2$ to CH_3CH_2COOH
   (b) $Me_3CCH = CH_2$ to Me_3CCOOH by four different methods.
   (c) Cyclohexenyl–CH_2OH ⟶ Cyclohexenyl–COOH (Two methods)
2. (a) Formulate the compounds from which $Me_2CHCOOH$ can be prepared by oxidation in good yield.
   (b) Give the structure of a compound that gives an equimolar amount of succinic acid on oxidative cleavage.

3. **By the carbonation of Grignard reagents.** (For details, consult chapter on "Organometallic Compounds").

$$RX + Mg \xrightarrow{\text{ether}} RMgX \xrightarrow{CO_2} R{-}\overset{\overset{O}{||}}{C}{-}O^-(MgX^+) \xrightarrow{H_3O^+} R{-}\overset{\overset{O}{||}}{C}{-}OH$$

This synthesis of carboxylic acids is applicable to 1°, 2°, 3°, allyl, benzyl and aryl halides, provided they have no groups incompatible with a Grignard reaction, such as OH, SH, NH or C = O.

$$\underset{\textit{tert}\text{-Butyl chloride}}{(CH_3)_3CCl} \xrightarrow[\text{ether}]{Mg} (CH_3)_3CMgCl \xrightarrow[\text{(ii) } H_3O^+]{\text{(i) } CO_2} \underset{\text{2, 2-Dimethylpropanoic acid}}{(CH_3)_3CCOOH}$$

$$C_6H_{11}{-}Br \xrightarrow{Mg} C_6H_{11}{-}MgBr \xrightarrow[\text{(ii) } H_3O^+]{\text{(i) } CO_2} C_6H_{11}{-}COOH$$

$$\underset{\text{Mesitylene}}{1,3,5\text{-}(CH_3)_3C_6H_3} \xrightarrow{Br_2} 2\text{-Br-}1,3,5\text{-}(CH_3)_3C_6H_2 \xrightarrow[\text{(ii) } CO_2, H^+]{\text{(i) Mg}} \underset{\text{(Mesitoic acid)}}{\underset{\text{2, 4, 6-Trimethylbenzoic acid}}{2,4,6\text{-}(CH_3)_3C_6H_2COOH}}$$

4. **By hydrolysis of nitriles.** Aliphatic nitriles, obtained by the reaction of an alkyl halide with sodium cyanide in dimethyl sulphoxide (DMSO) as solvent, are easily hydrolysed by boiling aqueous alkali or acid to corresponding carboxylic acids.

$$RCOO^- + NH_3 \xleftarrow[\text{heat}]{OH^-} \underset{\text{Alkyl nitrile}}{RC \equiv N} \xrightarrow[\text{heat}]{H^+} RCOOH + NH_4^+$$

The fact that HCN is a very weak acid tells us that CN^- ion is a strong base and hence can cause elimination as well as substitution. Indeed, with *tert*-halides elimination is the principal reaction ; even secondary halides undergo elimination reaction to some extent. Hence this synthetic method of carboxylic acids from alkyl halides is limited to the use of primary alkyl halides. Aryl halides (except for those with *o*- and *p*-nitro groups) do not react with sodium cyanide ; hence aryl nitriles are obtained from diazonium salts.

$$n\text{-}C_4H_9Br \xrightarrow{NaCN} \underset{\substack{\text{Pentanenitrile} \\ (n\text{-Valeronitrile})}}{n\text{-}C_4H_9CN} \xrightarrow[\text{(ii) } H_3O^+]{\text{(i) aq. alc. } OH^-\text{, reflux}} \underset{n\text{-Valeric acid}}{n\text{-}C_4H_9COOH}$$

$$HOCH_2CH_2Cl \xrightarrow{NaCN} \underset{\text{3-Hydroxypropanenitrile}}{HOCH_2CH_2CN} \xrightarrow[\text{(ii) } H_3O^+]{\text{(i) aq. } OH^-} \underset{\text{3-Hydroxypropanoic acid}}{HOCH_2CH_2COOH}$$

$$BrCH_2CH_2CH_2Br \xrightarrow{NaCN} \underset{\text{1, 5-Pentanedinitrile}}{NCCH_2CH_2CH_2CN} \xrightarrow{H_3O^+} \underset{\substack{\text{1, 5-Pentanedioic acid} \\ \text{(Glutaric acid)}}}{HOOCCH_2CH_2CH_2COOH}$$

Nitrile groups in cyanohydrins (aldehyde or ketone + $CN^- \rightarrow$ cyanohydrin) are hydrolyzed to corresponding α-hydroxy carboxylic acids.

2-Pentanone $\xrightarrow[(ii)\ H^+]{(i)\ NaCN}$ 2-Pentanonecyanohydrin $\xrightarrow[heat]{H_2O,\ HCl}$ 2-Hydroxy-2-methylpentanoic acid

Grignard synthesis and the **nitrile synthesis** for carboxylic acids have the advantage of increasing the length of a carbon chain by one carbon atom. Moreover, in both methods parent compounds are halides which in turn are usually prepared from alcohols, so the net result involves the conversion of an alcohol to a carboxylic acid with one more carbon atom.

5. **Malonic ester synthesis.** This is one of the most valuable methods for preparing carboxylic acids. The synthesis is based upon following two important properties of ethyl malonate (*malonic ester*), $CH_2\ (COOC_2H_5)_2$.

(*i*) High acidity of the α-hydrogens of malonic ester.

(*ii*) Extreme ease of decarboxylabion of malonic acid and substituted malonic acids.

$$HCH(COOC_2H_5)_2 + C_2H_5O^-\overset{+}{N}a \rightleftharpoons \overset{+}{Na}\overset{-}{C}H\ (COOC_2H_5)_2 + HOC_2H_5$$

Malonic ester (stronger acid) — Sodiomalonic ester — Weaker acid

$$Na^+\overset{-}{C}H\ (COOC_2H_5)_2 \xrightarrow{RX} R{-}CH(COOC_2H_5)_2 \xrightarrow{R'X} R{-}\underset{R'}{\underset{|}{C}}(COOC_2H_5)_2 + NaX$$

Ethyl alkylmalonate (An alkylmalonic ester) — A dialkylmalonic ester

The monoalkylmalonic and dialkylmalonic esters, so prepared are readily converted into monocarboxylic acids by hydrolysis, acidification, and heat

$$RCH(COOC_2H_5)_2 \xrightarrow[heat]{H_2O,\ OH^-} RCH(COO^-)_2 \xrightarrow{H^+} RCH(COOH)_2 \xrightarrow[140°C]{heat} RCH_2COOH$$

$$R_2C(COOC_2H_5)_2 \longrightarrow R_2C(COO^-)_2 \xrightarrow{H^+} R_2C(COOH)_2 \xrightarrow[140°C]{heat} R_2CHCOOH$$

Thus malonic ester provides an important method for synthesising RCH_2COOH, $R_2CHCOOH$ and RR'CHCOOH.

6. **Favorskii rearrangement.** α-Haloketones, when treated with base, are converted into carboxylic acids.

2-Bromocyclohexanone $\xrightarrow{OH^-}$ Cyclopentanecarboxylic acid (COOH)

Mechanism.

2-Bromocyclohexanone $\xrightarrow[(-H_2O)]{OH^-}$ carbanion $\xrightarrow{(-Br^-)}$ bicyclic cyclopropanone $\xrightarrow{OH^-}$ tetrahedral intermediate (–O⁻, OH) $\longrightarrow$ cyclopentane–C(=O)–O⁻ $\xrightarrow{H^+}$ cyclopentane–COOH

Industrial sources. Acetic acid is considered to be the most important carboxylic acid. Industrially, it is prepared

(*a*) By catalytic air oxidation of acetaldehyde or of various hydrocarbons.

$$CH_3CHO \xrightarrow[\text{Catalyst}]{O_2} CH_3COOH \longleftarrow \text{Hydrocarbons}$$

(*b*) From the reaction of methanol with carbon monoxide in the presence of iodine-rhodium catalyst (**Modern method**).

$$CH_3OH + CO \xrightarrow{Rh/I_2} CH_3COOH$$

(*c*) Dilute aqueous solution of acetic acid, known as *vinegar*, is prepared by air oxidation of ethyl alcohol in the presence of bacterial enzymes (*acetobacter*).

Formic acid is prepared by the reaction of carbon monoxide with sodium hydroxide followed by acidification with sulphuric acid.

$$CO + NaOH \longrightarrow HCOO^-Na^+ \xrightarrow{H_2SO_4} HCOOH$$

The important source of aliphatic carboxylic acids are the animal and vegetable fats from which straight chain carboxylic acids of even number of carbon atoms ranging from 6 to 18 are obtained in purity of over 90%. It is important to note that naturally occurring fatty acids (acids obtained from fats) always contains even number of carbon atoms because plants and animals biosynthesize fatty acids by building up CH_3COOH (a C_2 compound) units.

TEST YOUR UNDERSTANDING - 17.3

1. Which of the two methods : Grignard synthesis and nitrile synthesis ; is suitable for converting each of the halide to the corresponding carboxylic acid. Also write down the steps involved during the reaction.
   (*a*) 2-Chloroethanol to 3-hydroxypropanoic acid. (*b*) 2-Chloro-2-methylpropane to 2, 2-dimethylpropanoic acid.
   (*c*) Chlorobenzene to benzoic acid. (*d*) 1, 2-Dibromoethane to succinic acid
   (*e*) Vinyl bromide to propenoic acid.
2. (*a*) Show how you would prepare each of the following carboxylic acid through a Grignard synthesis ?
   (*i*) 2, 2-Dimethylpentanoic acid (*ii*) 3-Butenoic acid (*iii*) 4-Methylbenzoic acid.
   (*b*) Which of the above carboxylic acids can be prepared by a nitrile synthesis as well ?
3. Give the structure and name of the acids formed by a step-up reaction of the following halides.
   (*a*) C_6H_5Cl (*b*) $CH_3CHClCH_2CH_2CH_3$ (*c*) $C_6H_{11}CMe_2Cl$ (*d*) Z-MeCH = CHBr.
4. Synthesize succinic acid from $CH_2 = CH_2$.
5. Use malonic ester to prepare
   (*a*) 2-ethylbutanoic acid (*b*) 3-methylbutanoic acid
   (*c*) 2-methylbutanoic acid (*d*) trimethylacetic acid.
6. A sulphuric acid solution of each of the following compounds, when treated with carbon monoxide, gives the same acid, 2, 2-dimethylbutanoic acid. Explain.

   2-Methyl-2-butene, Neopentyl alcohol, *tert*-Pentyl alcohol

17.3 Physical Properties

(*i*) Carboxylic acids are rolar substances. Like alcohol molecules, their molecules can form hydrogen bonds with each other and also with water. As a result, low molecular weight carboxylic acids (the first four members) are miscible with water in all proportions ; water solubility decreases with increase in the length of the carbon chain.

O---H—O
R—C C—R
O—H---O

(*ii*) Carboxylic acids have higher boiling points than the corresponding alcohols. This is due to a unique hydrogen bonding arrangement in carboxylic acids ; carboxylic groups of two molecules are held together not by one but by two hydrogen bonds. This hydrogen bonding is so efficient that some carboxylic acids exist as hydrogen-bonded dimers even in the gas phase. In the pure liquid state, a mixture of hydrogen-bonded dimers and higher aggregates is present.

(iii) First two carboxylic acids have a sharp and acrid odour, while the acids with four to eight carbon atoms have unpleasant odours. These acids, formed by bacterial action, are present in trace amounts in the skin secretions of most mammals. Since metabolic processes of different persons are not exactly identical, these acids are present in different compositions on the skin of different persons which give a characteristic smell different from person to person ; this is the reason why dogs (having highly developed sense of smell) are able to differentiate one person from another.

TEST YOUR UNDERSTANDING - 17.4

1. Arrange the following compounds in order of decreasing boiling points :

(a) (i) [skeletal structure with OH], (ii) [skeletal structure], (iii) [skeletal structure with OH], (iv) [skeletal structure with OH], (v) [skeletal structure with O], (vi) [skeletal structure with O and HO]

(b) C_3H_8 (A), $CH_3CH_2CH_2OH$ (B), $CH_3CHOHCH_2OH$ (C), $CH_3OCH_2CH_3$ (D), CH_3CH_2COOH (E).

2. The true value of molecular weight of acetic acid is found to be 60, however, just above its boiling point, it is found to be 120. Explain.

3. What is glacial acetic acid and why it is so called ? What is vinegar and how is it made ?

17.4 Chemical Properties

17.4.1 Acidity of Carboxylic Acids

Carboxylic acids are the most acidic compounds that contain C, H and O. Ionization constants (K_a) of the carboxylic acid, is of the order of 10^{-5} ($pK_a \sim 5$), they are much stronger acids than water and alcohols.

The acidic character of carboxylic acids is due to resonance* in the acidic group which imparts electron deficiency (positive charge) on the oxygen atom of the hydroxyl group.

$$R-C(=\ddot{O}:)-\ddot{O}-H \longleftrightarrow R-C(-:\ddot{O}:^-)=\overset{+}{O}-H$$

Non-equivalent structures (Resonance less important)

The positive charge (electron deficiency) on oxygen atom causes a displacement of electron pair of the O—H bond towards the oxygen atom with the result the hydrogen atom of the O—H group is eliminated as proton and a carboxylate ion is formed. Once the carboxylate ion is formed, it is stabilised by means of resonance.

$$R-C(=\ddot{O}:)-\ddot{O}:^- \longleftrightarrow R-C(-\ddot{O}:^-)=\ddot{O}: \qquad R-C\left\{\begin{matrix}O\\O\end{matrix}\right\}^-$$

Resonating forms of carboxylate ion (Equivalent structures), hence resonance more important. Resonance hybrid of carboxylate ion

Due to equivalent resonating structures, resonance in carboxylate anion is more important than in the parent carboxylic acid. Hence carboxylate anion is more stabilised than the acid itself and hence the equilibrium of the ionisation of acids shifts to the right hand side.

$$RCOOH \rightleftharpoons RCOO^- + H^+$$

The existence of resonance in carboxylate ion is supported by bond lengths. For example, in formic acid, there is one C = O double bond (121 pm) and one C—O single bond. (136 pm), while in sodium formate both of the carbon-oxygen bond lengths are identical (125 pm) which is nearly intermediate between C = O and C—O bond length values. This proves resonance in carboxylate anion.

H—C(=O, 121 pm)—OH (136 pm)

Formic acid

H—C(O, 125 pm)(O, 125 pm)$^-$ Na^+

Sodium formate

Note that in resonance of carboxylic acids, —CO part of the acidic group enters into resonance with the lone pair of the —OH group and hence —COOH does not give reactions of the carbonyl group.

It is important to note that although carboxylic acids and alcohols both contain —OH group, the latter are not acidic in nature. It is due to the absence of resonance (factor responsible for acidic character of —COOH) in both the alcohols as well as in their corresponding ions (alkoxide ions).

$$\underset{\substack{\text{Alcohol}\\\text{(No resonance)}}}{R{-}O{-}H} \rightleftharpoons \underset{\substack{\text{Alkoxide ion}\\\text{(No resonance)}}}{R{-}O^-} + H^+$$

Alkoxide ions are stabilized by solvation forces, while carboxylate ions are stabilized by solvation as well as resonance and inductive effect of the carbonyl group.

Role of inductive effect of the carbonyl group. The carbonyl group is electron-withdrawing, and by attracting electrons away from the negatively charged oxygen, carboxylate anion is stabilized.

Relative acidic character of carboxylic acids with common species not having —COOH group.

$$RCOOH > HOH > ROH > HC \equiv CH > NH_3 > RH$$

Effect of substituents on acidity. We know that the carboxylic acids are acidic in nature because of stabilisation (*i.e.*, dispersal of negative charge) of carboxylate ion. So any factor which can enhance the dispersal of negative charge of the carboxylate ion will increase the acidity and *vice versa.* Thus electron-withdrawing substituents (like halogens, —NO_2, —C_6H_5 etc.) would disperse the negative charge and hence stabilise the carboxylate ion and thus increase acidity of the parent acid. On the other hand, electron-releasing substituents would intensify the negative charge, destabilise the carboxylate ion and thus decrease acidity of the parent acid.

$$G \leftarrow C\left\{\begin{matrix} O \\ O \end{matrix}\right\}^- \qquad\qquad G \rightarrow C\left\{\begin{matrix} O \\ O \end{matrix}\right\}^-$$

The substituent G withdraws electrons, stabilises anion and hence increases acidity

The substituent G releases electrons, destabilises anion and hence decreases acidity

Now since alkyl groups are electron-releasing, their presence in the molecule will decrease the acidity. In general, greater the length of the alkyl chain, lower shall be the acidity of the acid. Thus formic acid (HCOOH), having no alkyl group, is about 10 times stronger than acetic acid (CH_3COOH) which in turn is stronger than propanoic acid (CH_3CH_2COOH) and so on. Similarly, following order is observed in chloro acids.

$$\underset{\text{Trichloroacetic acid}}{Cl_3CCOOH} > \underset{\text{Dichloroacetic acid}}{Cl_2CHCOOH} > \underset{\text{Monochloroacetic acid}}{ClCH_2COOH} > \underset{\text{Acetic acid}}{CH_3COOH}$$

Trichloroacetic acid is more than 10,000 times more stronger than acetic acid, actually it is almost as strong acid as a mineral acid. For further details of the relative acidities of the carboxylic acids, consult inductive effect in Chapter on "General Organic Chemistry".

Decreasing order of aliphatic acids

(*i*) $O_2NCH_2COOH > FCH_2COOH > ClCH_2COOH > BrCH_2COOH$

(*ii*) $HCOOH > CH_3COOH > (CH_3)_2CHCOOH > (CH_3)_3\,CCOOH$

(*iii*) $CH_3CH_2CCl_2COOH > CH_3CHCl.CHCl.COOH > ClCH_2CHClCH_2COOH$

(*iv*) $F_3CCOOH > Cl_3CCOOH > Br_3CCOOH$

Benzoic acid is somewhat stronger than simple aliphatic acids. Here the carboxylate group is attached to a more electronegative carbon (sp^2 hybridised) than in aliphatic acids (sp^3 hybridised). Remember that carbon becomes more electron-withdrawing as its *s* character increases.

Acidity of dicarboxylic acids

Here two ionization constants (K_1 and K_2) characterise the two successive ionization steps of a dicaboxylic acid

$$HO{-}\overset{O}{\overset{\|}{C}}{-}\overset{O}{\overset{\|}{C}}{-}OH \overset{K_1}{\rightleftharpoons} \underset{\substack{\text{Hydrogen oxalate}\\\text{(monoanion)}}}{HO{-}\overset{O}{\overset{\|}{C}}{-}\overset{O}{\overset{\|}{C}}{-}O^-}, \quad K_1 = 6.5 \times 10^{-2}\,;\ pK_1 = 1.2$$

$$HO{-}\overset{O}{\overset{\|}{C}}{-}\overset{O}{\overset{\|}{C}}{-}O^- \overset{K_2}{\rightleftharpoons} \underset{\text{Oxalate (dianion)}}{{}^-O{-}\overset{O}{\overset{\|}{C}}{-}\overset{O}{\overset{\|}{C}}{-}O^-}, \quad K_2 = 5.3 \times 10^{-5}\,;\ pK_2 = 4.3$$

The first ionization constant of dicarboxylic acids is larger than K_a for monocarboxylic analogs. There are two reasons for this.

(*a*) Presence of two potential sites for ionization rather than one.

(*b*) One carboxyl group acts as an electron-withdrawing group to facilitate dissociation of the other. This factor is significant when two carboxyl groups are separated by only a few bonds. Thus oxalic and malonic acids are highly acidic than the corresponding monocarboxylic acids while heptanedioic acid is only slightly stronger than acetic acid.

	$HOOCCOOH$ Oxalic acid	$HOOCCH_2COOH$ Malonic acid	$HOOC(CH_2)_5COOH$ Heptanedioic acid
K_1	6.5×10^{-2}	1.4×10^{-3}	3.1×10^{-5}
pK_1	1.2	2.8	4.3

TEST YOUR UNDERSTANDING - 17.5

1. (*a*) Compare the carbon-oxygen bond length in sodium formate and sodium carbonate.
   (*b*) Compare the carbon-oxygen single bond in carboxylic acids with that in alcohols.
2. Which is the stronger acid in each of the following pairs.
   (*i*) Me_3CCH_2COOH or $Me_3\overset{+}{N}CH_2COOH$
   (*ii*) CH_3CH_2COOH or $CH_3CHOHCOOH$
   (*iii*) $CH_3COCOOH$ or $CH_2=CHCOOH$
   (*iv*) $CH_3CH_2CH_2COOH$ or $CH_3SO_2CH_2COOH$
   (*v*) Me_3CCH_2COOH or Me_3SiCH_2COOH
   (*vi*) 3-Butenoic acid or 3-Butynoic acid
3. Arrange the following in decreasing order of acidity.
   (*i*) C_2H_5OH, $HCOOH$, CH_3COOH, C_6H_5OH
   (*ii*) $HCOOH$, C_2H_5COOH, CH_3COOH, $CH_2ClCOOH$, C_6H_5COOH
   (*iii*) $CH_3CH_2CH_2COOH$, $CH_3CHClCH_2COOH$, $CH_3CH_2CHClCOOH$, $ClCH_2CH_2CH_2COOH$
   (*iv*) CH_3COOH, $CH_2ClCOOH$, $CHCl_2COOH$, CCl_3COOH
   (*v*) $CH_2BrCOOH$, $CH_2ClCOOH$, CH_2ICOOH, CH_2FCOOH
   (*vi*) $ClCH_2COOH$, CH_3CH_2COOH, $ClCH_2CH_2COOH$, $Me_2CHCOOH$, CH_3COOH
   (*vii*) $HCOOH$, C_6H_5COOH, C_6H_5OH, HCl
   (*viii*) Acetic acid, acetylene, ammonia, ethane, ethanol, sulphuric acid, water.
   (*ix*) Acetic acid, malonic acid, succinic acid.
   (*x*) α-Chlorophenylacetic acid, *p*-chlorophenylacetic acid, phenylacetic acid, α-phenylpropanoic acid.
4. Explain the following :
   (*a*) Peroxy acids are much weaker acids than carboxylic acids.
   (*b*) Highly branched acids are less acidic than unbranched acids.
   (*c*) The K_2 for fumaric acid (*trans*-butenedioic acid) is greater than for maleic acid, the *cis* isomer.

Although much weaker than the strong mineral acids (H_2SO_4, HCl, HNO_3), carboxylic acids are most acidic among organic compounds containing C, H and O. They are neutralized rapidly and quantitatively in presence of strong bases like sodium hydroxide. Aqueous mineral acids readily convert the salts back into the carboxylic acids.

$$\underset{\substack{\text{Carboxylic acid} \\ \text{(stronger acid)}}}{RCOOH} + \underset{\substack{\text{Hydroxide ion} \\ \text{(stronger base)}}}{OH^-} \underset{H^+}{\rightleftharpoons} \underset{\substack{\text{Carboxylate ion} \\ \text{(weaker base)}}}{RCOO^-} + \underset{\substack{\text{Water} \\ \text{(weaker acid)}}}{H_2O}$$

Salts of carboxylic acids are crystalline, non-volatile solids. The strong electrostatic forces holding the ions in the crystal lattice can be overcome only by heating to a high temperature, or by a very strong polar solvent. The mp of the salts are so high that before it can reach, carbon-carbon bonds break and the molecule decomposes (300° – 400°C). The alkali metal salts of carboxylic acids (sodium, potassium, ammonium) are soluble in water but insoluble in non-polar solvents ; however most of the heavy metal salts (iron, silver, copper etc.) are insoluble in water.

Except for the first four carboxylic acids, which are soluble both in water and organic solvents, **carboxylic acids and their alkali metal salts show exactly opposite solubility behaviour**. This solubility difference along with the fact that acids and their salts are readily interconvertible has been used for identifying and separation of carboxylic acids from compounds having other functional group.

(i) In case an organic compound is insoluble in water but soluble in cold dilute aqueous sodium hydroxide or aq. $NaHCO_3$, it must be an organic compound which is more acidic than water, *i.e.*, generally a carboxylic acid.

$$\underset{\substack{\text{Stronger acid}\\ \text{(insoluble in } H_2O)}}{RCOOH} + NaOH \longrightarrow \underset{\substack{\text{Weaker base}\\ \text{(soluble in } H_2O)}}{RCOONa} + \underset{\text{Weaker acid}}{H_2O}$$

$$\underset{\text{Insoluble in water}}{RCOOH} + NaHCO_3 \longrightarrow \underset{\text{Soluble in } H_2O}{RCOONa} + H_2O + CO_2\uparrow$$

(ii) A carboxylic acid can be saparated from non-acidic compounds by taking advantage of its solubility in aqueous base. The acid can be easily regenerated by acidifying the aqueous solution containing salt.

Scheme for separation of carboxylic acid from non-acidic compounds.

For solids : Mixture + *aq.* base $\xrightarrow{\text{filter}}$
- → **Insoluble**
- → Soluble $\xrightarrow{H^+}$ RCOOH

For liquids : Mixture + *aq.* base (In a separatory funnel) →
- → **Ether layer** (Non acidic component)
- → Aq. layer (—COONa component) $\xrightarrow{H^+}$ RCOOH

For complete separation, generally a water-insoluble solvent like ether is added to the acidified mixture. Since carboxylic acids are soluble in ether, ether layer containing carboxylic acid is separated, ether evaporated leaving carboxylic acids.

(iii) Salts of higher fatty acids such as palmitic acid, $C_{15}H_{31}COOH$, stearic acid, $C_{17}H_{35}COOH$, oleic acid $[C_{17}H_{33}COOH]$ are known as **soaps** ; potassium salts are soft soaps while sodium salts are hard sops.

TEST YOUR UNDERSTANDING - 17.6

1. Write an ionic equation for the reaction of acetic acid with each of the following, and specify whether the equilibrium favours starting materials or products.

(a) Sodium ethoxide	*(b)* Potassium *tert*-butoxide	*(c)* Sodium bromide
(d) Sodium acetylide	*(e)* Potassium nitrate	*(f)* Lithium amide.

17.4.2 Reactions in which —OH of —COOH Group is Replaced (*Conversion into functional derivatives*)

$$R{-}\overset{O}{\overset{\|}{C}}{-}OH \longrightarrow R{-}\overset{O}{\overset{\|}{C}}{-}Z \quad (\text{Where, } Z = {-}Cl, {-}OR', {-}NH_2)$$

1. **Conversion into acid chlorides.** Three reagents are commonly used for this purpose, namely thionyl chloride, phosphorus trichloride and phosphorus pentachloride.

$$RCOOH + SOCl_2 \longrightarrow RCOCl + HCl\uparrow + SO_2\uparrow$$

$$3RCOOH + PCl_3 \longrightarrow 3RCOCl + H_3PO_3$$

$$RCOOH + PCl_5 \longrightarrow RCOCl + HCl\uparrow + POCl_3$$

However, thionyl chloride is particularly convenient since the two gaseous products (SO_2 and HCl) are readily removed from RCOCl, any excess of the low-boiling thionyl choride (79°C) is easily removed by distillation.

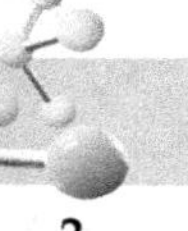

2. **Conversion into esters.** A carboxylic acid may be converted into esters in two ways ; (*i*) direct esterification with an alcohol, (*ii*) esterification through acid chlorides

$$\underset{\text{Acid}}{RCOOH} + \underset{\text{Alcohol}}{R'OH} \xrightleftharpoons{H^+} \underset{\text{Ester}}{RCOOR'} + H_2O$$

$$RCOOH \xrightarrow{SOCl_2} RCOCl \xrightarrow{R'OH} RCOOR'$$

(*i*) **Direct esterification.** A carboxyl group is converted directly into an ester when heated with an alcohol in the presence of a little mineral acid, usually conc. H_2SO_4 or dry hydrogen chloride.

$$\underset{\text{Acid}}{R{-}C(=O){-}OH} + \underset{\text{Alcohol}}{R'{-}OH} \xrightleftharpoons{H^+} \underset{\text{Ester}}{R{-}C(=O){-}OR'} + H_2O$$

This reaction is reversible and generally reaches equilibrium when appreciable quantities of both reactants and products are present. Although reversibility is a disadvantage in the direct esterification, the process has the advantage of being a single-step process and can often be made useful by application of our knowledge of equilibria. Since the position of equilibrium controls the amount of the ester formed, the use of an excess of either the carboxylic acid or the alcohol increases the yield. Just which component is used in excess depends on its availability and cost ; *e.g.*

$$\underset{\substack{\gamma\text{-Phenylbutyric acid}\\ \text{valuable, 1 mole}}}{C_6H_5CH_2CH_2CH_2COOH} + \underset{\substack{\text{Ethanol}\\ \text{cheap, 8 mole}}}{C_2H_5OH} \xrightleftharpoons{H_2SO_4,\ \text{reflux}} \underset{\text{Ethyl-}\gamma\text{-phenylbutyrate}}{C_6H_5CH_2CH_2CH_2COOC_2H_5} + H_2O$$

The yield of esterification can also be increased by removing water (one of the products) from the reaction mixture as soon as it is formed. For example, in the preparatioon of ethyl adipate, water is removed as lowest boiling point component (75°C) of the mixture in the form of azeotrope of water, ethyl alcohol, and toluene. Hence the reaction should be carried out in presence of excess of ethanol and in presence of toluene.

$$\underset{\text{Adipic acid (non-volatile)}}{HOOC(CH_2)_4COOH} + \underset{\text{(b.p.78°C)}}{2C_2H_5OH} \xrightarrow{\text{toluene, } H_2SO_4} \underset{\text{Ethyl adipate (boiling point 245°C)}}{C_2H_5OOC(CH_2)_4COOC_2H_5} + \underset{\substack{\text{Removed as}\\ \text{azeotrope,}\\ \text{boiling point 75°C}}}{2H_2O}$$

Note that it is the C—OH bond of the carboxylic acid that breaks up during esterification.

$$C_6H_5{-}C(=O){\vdots}OH + CH_3O^{18}{\vdots}H \xrightleftharpoons{H^+} C_6H_5{-}C(=O){-}O^{18}CH_3 + H_2O$$

Mechanism of esterification is necessarily the exact reverse of the mechanism of acidic ester hydrolysis that will be discussed in the chemisty of esters.

(*ii*) The presence of bulky groups near the site of reaction, whether in alcohol or in the acid, slows down esterification (as well as its reverse, hydrolysis).

Reactivity in esterification	CH_3OH	>	1°	>	2°		(>3°)
	HCOOH	>	CH_3COOH	>	RCH_2COOH	>	$R_2CHCOOH$

In some cases steric hindrance is so marked that special methods are required to prepare esters of tertiary alcohols or esters of acids like 2, 4, 6-trimethylbenzoic acid (mesitoic acid).

(*iii*) **Esterification through acid chlorides.** Since acyl chlorides are much more reactive toward nucleophilic addition-elimination than carboxylic acids, reaction of an acyl chloride and an alcohol occurs rapidly and does not require an acid catalyst. Pyridine is generally added to remove the HCl formed during reaction. Moreover, pyridine may also react with the acyl chloride to form an acylpyridinium ion, an intermediate that is even more reactive toward the nucleophile than the acyl chloride itself.

$$C_6H_5COCl + C_2H_5OH + C_5H_5N \longrightarrow \underset{\text{Ethyl benzoate}}{C_6H_5COOCH_2CH_3} + C_5H_5N^+H\ Cl^-$$

Esterification through acid chloride gives better results when *tert*-alcohols are used as one of the components because in the direct esterification, the acid used may cause dehydration by elimination reaction.

Intramolecular esterification. Hydroxy acids (compounds containing a hydroxyl and a carboxyl group in the same molecule) have the capacity to form cyclic esters called lactones. This intramolecular esterification takes place spontaneously and is especially favourable when the ring formed is either 5-membered or 6-membered. Lactones having a five membered ring are known as **γ-lactones** since they are formed from γ-hydroxy acids. The six-membered analogs are known as **δ-lactones**.

4-Hydroxybutanoic acid ⟶ 4-Butanolide (γ-Butyrolactone)

δ-Hydroxypentanoic acid ⟶ 5-Pentanolide (δ-Valerolactone)

Like other esters, lactones are hydrolyzed by aqueous base.

3. **Conversion into amides.** Acids are converted into amides by treating acid chlorides with ammonia, primary amines, and secondary amines.

$$RCOOH \xrightarrow{SOCl_2} RCOCl \xrightarrow{NH_3} RCONH_2$$

$$\underset{\text{Phenylacetic acid}}{C_6H_5CH_2COOH} \longrightarrow \underset{\substack{\text{Phenylacetyl chloride}\\\text{(Phenacyl chloride)}}}{C_6H_5CH_2COCl} \xrightarrow{NH_3} \underset{\text{Phenylacetamide}}{C_6H_5CH_2CONH_2}$$

TEST YOUR UNDERSTANDING - 17.7

1. (*a*) Which bond of carboxylic acid is broken in the formation of acid chloride, *i.e.* whether C—OH or CO—H ?
   (*b*) When benzoic acid is allowed to stand in water enriched in O^{18} in presence of acids, heavier oxygen becomes incorporated into the benzoic acid. Explain.
   (*c*) When reactive alcohols like $CH_2 = CHCH_2O^{18}H$ are esterified in acid, some H_2O^{18} is found in the product.
2. Discuss in three lines, how will you prepare ethyl acetate (an important commercial solvent) from ethanol.

4. **Formation of anhydrides.** Only one monocarboxylic acid anhydride (acetic anhydride) is important. It is prepared by the reaction of acetic acid with ketene ($CH_2 = C = O$), which in turn is prepared by high temperature dehydration of acetic acid.

$$CH_3COOH \xrightarrow[-H_2O]{AlPO_4,\,700°C} CH_2 = C = O \xrightarrow{CH_3COOH} (CH_3CO)_2O$$

Acid anhydrides, in general, can be prepared by treating acyl chloride with —COOH in the presence of pyridine or by treating sodium salts of carboxylic acids with acyl chlorides.

$$RCOCl + R'COOH \text{ (or } R'COONa) \longrightarrow RCO.O.COR' + HCl \text{ (or NaCl)}$$

17.4.3 Reduction of >C = O of –COOH to –CH₂OH

For details, consult preparation of alcohols.

$$RCOOH \xrightarrow[\text{(ii) } H_2O]{\text{(i) } LiAlH_4,\text{ ether}} RCH_2OH$$

An alternate way of reducing carboxylic acid is *via* esters.

$$RCOOH \longrightarrow RCOOR' \xrightarrow[150°C\text{ pressure}]{H_2,\text{ Copper chromite}} RCH_2OH + R'OH$$

17.4.4 Halogenation of α-Hydrogens

Aliphatic carboxylic acids react with bromine or chlorine in the persence of phosphorus (or a phosphorus halide) to give α-halo acids, the reaction as known as **Hell-Volhard-Zelinski (or HVZ) reaction.**

$$RCH_2COOH \xrightarrow{Cl_2,\,P} RCH(Cl)COOH \xrightarrow{Cl_2,\,P} RC(Cl)_2COOH$$

Halogenation occurs specifically at the α-carbon ; because of this regioselectivity and the ease with which it takes place, HVZ reaction is of considerable importance in synthesis.

The function of phosphorus is to convert a little of the acid into **acid halide which is the actual molecule on which halogenation takes place** and not on acid itself. Specific halogenation at α-position is due to formation of enols which are readily formed by acyl halides than from carboxylic acids itself.

$$RCH_2-C(=O)OH \xrightarrow[(PBr_3)]{P + Br_2} \underset{\text{Acyl bromide}}{RCH_2-C(=O)Br} \rightleftharpoons \underset{\text{Enol form}}{RCH=C(\ddot{O}H)Br}$$

$$\xrightarrow{Br-Br} RCH(Br)-C(=O)Br + HBr \xrightarrow{H_2O} RCH(Br)-C(=O)OH$$

Harpp reaction is the modification of HVZ reaction. This reaction involves α-halogenation of carboxylic acid with N-halosuccinimide in presence of HCl or HBr and $SOCl_2$.

$$RCH_2COOH \xrightarrow{SOCl_2} RCH_2COCl + \text{N-halosuccinimide (N–X)} \xrightarrow{HX} RCH(X)COCl + \text{succinimide (NH)}$$

(X = Cl or Br)

Like alkyl halides, the halogen of these halogenated acids undergoes *nucleophilic displacement* and *elimination*, hence α-halo acids are important synthetic intermediates.

(*i*) $$\underset{\text{2-Bromobutanoic acid}}{CH_3CH_2CH(Br)COOH} \xrightarrow[(ii)\,H_3O^+]{(i)\,K_2CO_3,\,H_2O,100°C} \underset{\text{2-Hydroxybutanoic acid}}{CH_3CH_2CH(OH)COOH}$$

(*ii*) $$CH_2(Br)COOH + 2NH_3 \longrightarrow \underset{\text{Aminoacetic acid (glycine)}}{CH_2(NH_3^+)COO^-} + NH_4Br$$

(*iii*) $$CH_3CH(Br)COOH \xrightarrow{\text{alc. KOH}} CH_2=CHCOO^- \xrightarrow{H^+} \underset{\text{Propenoic acid}}{CH_2=CHCOOH}$$

TEST YOUR UNDERSTANDING - 17.8

1. Give the reagent(s) required to convert the keto acid,

$CH_3CH_2COCH_2CH_2COOH$

into each of the following compunds. In case two steps are required, give the proper order.

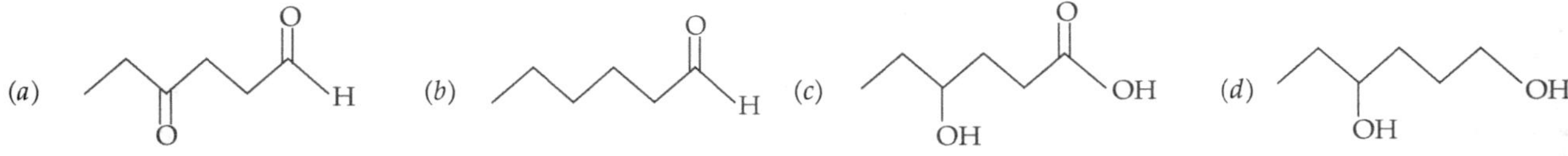

2. α-Iodo acids are not normally prepared by direct HVZ reaction. Show how you could convert octadecanoic acid to its 2-iodo derivative by efficient sequence of reactions.

3. Predict the product of each of the following reactions :

(*a*) $C_6H_5CH(OH)CH_2COOH \xrightarrow[(-H_2O)]{H^+, \text{heat}}$ (*b*) $o\text{-}HOOCC_6H_4CH_2OH \xrightarrow[(-H_2O)]{H^+, \text{heat}}$

(*c*) $CH_3CH_2CH(Br)COOH \xrightarrow{aq, NaOH}$ (*d*) $CH_3CH(Br)CH_2COOH \xrightarrow{aq, NaOH}$

4. (*a*) Convert ethanoic acid into propanedioic acid.
   (*b*) One of the steps in the above sequence involves conversion of chloroacetic acid to cyanoacetic acid ; for this step chloroacetic acid is first converted into its salt before treatment with cyanide ion. Explain.

17.4.5 Decarboxylation of Carboxylic Acids

The loss of a molecule of carbon dioxide from a carboxylic acid is known as **decarboxylation.**

$$RCOOH \longrightarrow RH + CO_2$$

Decarboxylation of simple carboxylic acids takes place with great difficulty and is rarely encountered. However, there are certain groups which if present in β-position of a carboxylic acid, decarboxylation takes place readily. Thus β-keto and β, γ-unsaturated carboxylic acids decarboxylate readily when they are heated to 100–150°C (some β-keto acids decarboxylate although slowly even at room temperature).

$$R-\overset{O}{\underset{\beta}{\overset{\|}{C}}}-\overset{\alpha}{C}H_2-\overset{O}{\overset{\|}{C}}-OH \xrightarrow{100\text{–}150°C} R-\overset{O}{\overset{\|}{C}}-CH_3 + CO_2$$

$$\overset{\gamma}{C}H_2 = \overset{\beta}{C}H\overset{\alpha}{C}H_2COOH \xrightarrow{\text{heat}} CH_2 = CHCH_3 + CO_2$$

Decarboxylation of β-keto acids takes place in the form of free acid or in the form of carboxylate ion.

(*a*) When the carboxylate anion decarboxylates, it forms a resonance stabilized enolate anion ; I.

$$R-\overset{O}{\overset{\|}{C}}-CH_2-COO^- \xrightarrow{-CO_2} \left[R-\overset{O^-}{\overset{|}{C}}=CH_2 \longleftrightarrow R-\overset{O}{\overset{\|}{C}}-\overset{-}{C}H_2 \right] \equiv R-\overset{O}{\overset{\|}{C}}\text{==}CH_2^{\ominus} \xrightarrow{H^+}$$

β-Keto acid or Malonic acid, when R = OH I_a I_b Resonance stabilized anion, I

$$R-\overset{OH}{\overset{|}{C}}=CH_2 \longrightarrow R-\overset{O}{\overset{\|}{C}}-CH_3$$

This carbanion is formed faster than the simple carbanion ($R:^-$) from a simple carboxylate ion ($RCOO^-$) because it is more stable. Recall that of the two contributing structures (I_a and I_b), I_a is more stable because here the negative charge is accommodated by oxygen (every atom has eight electrons, except hydrogen).

(b) Decarboxylation of the acid itself involves transfer of the carboxylic acidic hydrogen to the keto group, either prior to loss of carbon dioxide, or simultaneously with loss of carbon dioxide.

(i) $$R{-}\overset{O}{\overset{\|}{C}}{-}CH_2{-}\overset{O}{\overset{\|}{C}}{-}OH \rightleftharpoons R{-}\overset{\overset{+}{O}H}{\overset{\|}{C}}{-}CH_2{-}\overset{O}{\overset{\|}{C}}{-}O^- \xrightarrow[-CO_2]{} R{-}\overset{OH}{\overset{|}{C}}{=}CH_2 \xrightarrow{\text{tautomerizes}} R{-}\overset{O}{\overset{\|}{C}}{-}CH_3$$

β-Keto acid or Malonic acid, when R = OH

(ii) β-Keto acid or (Malonic acid, when R = OH) $\longrightarrow$ [Transition state] $\xrightarrow{-CO_2}$ Enol $\longrightarrow$ Keto

$$R{-}C(=O){-}CH_2{-}C(=O){-}O{-}H \longrightarrow \left[\text{cyclic transition state}\right] \xrightarrow{-CO_2} R{-}C(OH){=}CH_2 \longrightarrow R{-}C(=O){-}CH_3$$

Malonic acid and its monoanion undergo decarboxylation exactly in the same ways. Replace R— by —OH. β, γ-Unsaturated carboxylic acids also undergo decarboxylation in the same ways.

$$CH_2{=}CH{-}CH_2{-}COO^- \xrightarrow[-CO_2]{} [\bar{C}H_2{-}CH{=}CH_2 \longleftrightarrow CH_2{=}CH{-}\bar{C}H_2] \xrightarrow{H^+} CH_3{-}CH{=}CH_2$$

TEST YOUR UNDERSTANDING - 17.9

1. (a) It is difficult to decarboxylate $C_6H_5CH_2CH_2COOH$, while the corresponding phenylpropiolic acid, $C_6H_5C \equiv CCOOH$ undergoes decarboxylation in alkaline solution. Explain.
   (b) It is difficult to decarboxylate benzoic acid and phenylacetic acid, while 2, 4, 6-trinitrobenzoic acid can be decarboxylated easily by heating.
2. Give the product isolated after thermal decarboxylation of each of the following :
   (a) 1, 1-Cyclobutane dicarboxylic acid. (b) 2-Cyclopentenylmalonic acid. (c) Phenylmethylmalonic acid.
3. Give the products obtained on heating each of the following compounds.

   (a) Cyclohexane bearing COOH, COOH (on one carbon) and COOH (on the adjacent carbon)

   (b) Cyclobutane bearing COOH, COOH (on one carbon) and COOH

17.4.6 Reactions of Salts of Carboxylic Acids

(i) **Heating of sodium salts with soda lime** (NaOH + CaO) to *form alkanes.*

$$\underset{\text{Sod. acetate}}{CH_3COONa} + NaOH \xrightarrow{\text{heat}} \underset{\text{Methane}}{CH_4} \uparrow + Na_2CO_3$$

However, sodium formate on decarboxylation with soda lime gives hydrogen.

$$HCOONa \xrightarrow{NaOH} H_2 + Na_2CO_3$$

(ii) **Sodium formate on heating** gives sodium oxalate and hydrogen.

$$2HCOONa \xrightarrow{300°C} \begin{matrix} COONa \\ | \\ COONa \end{matrix} + H_2$$

(iii) Heating of sod. formate with conc. H_2SO_4.

$$2HCOONa + H_2SO_4 \longrightarrow Na_2SO_4 + 2H_2O + 2CO$$

(iv) **Electrolysis of conc. aq. solution of sod. or pot. salts gives alkanes** (*reaction is not given by sod. or pot. formate*).

$$\underset{\text{Sod. acetate}}{2CH_3COONa} + 2H_2O \xrightarrow{\text{electrolysis}} \underbrace{CH_3-CH_3 + 2CO_2}_{\text{at anode}} + \underbrace{2NaOH + H_2}_{\text{at cathode}}$$

(v) **Heating of ammonium salts** (*Formation of amides*).

$$\underset{\text{Ammo. acetate}}{CH_3COONH_4} \xrightarrow{\text{heat}} \underset{\text{Acetamide}}{CH_3CONH_2} + H_2O$$

(vi) **Dry distillation of calcium salts** (*Formation of aldehydes and ketones*).

(*a*) $$\underset{\text{Cal. formate}}{(HCOO)_2Ca} \xrightarrow{\text{heat}} \underset{\text{Formaldehyde}}{HCHO} + CaCO_3$$

(*b*) $$\underset{\text{Cal. acetate}}{(CH_3COO)_2Ca} \xrightarrow{\text{heat}} \underset{\text{Acetone}}{CH_3COCH_3} + CaCO_3$$

(*c*) $$\underset{\text{Cal. accetate}}{(CH_3COO)_2Ca} + \underset{\text{Cal. formate}}{(HCOO)_2Ca} \xrightarrow{\text{heat}} \underset{\text{Acetaldehyde}}{2CH_3CHO} + 2CaCO_3$$

(*d*) $$\begin{matrix} CH_2CH_2COO \\ | \\ CH_2CH_2COO \end{matrix}\!\!>Ca \xrightarrow{\text{heat}} \text{(cyclopentane ring)}=O + CaCO_3$$

Calcium adipate — Cyclopentanone

(vii) **Silver salt of a carboxylic acid on heating** with bromine gives alkyl halide (**Hunsdiecker reaction**).

$$RCOOAg + Br_2 \xrightarrow{CCl_4,\ \text{heat}} R\text{–}Br + CO_2 + AgBr$$

17.5 Special Properties of Formic Acid

In addition to properties discussed earlier, formic acid gives the following reactions.

1. **Action of conc. H_2SO_4** (*Dehydration*). $HCOOH \xrightarrow{H_2SO_4,\ \text{heat}} H_2O + CO$

2. **Action of heat.** $HCOOH \xrightarrow{160°C} H_2 + CO_2$

3. **Reducing agent.** (*Reactions due to —CHO group*). Like aldehydes, but unlike other acids, **formic acid reduces Tollen's reagent, Fehling solution, mercuric chloride and potassium permanganate.**

(i) $$HCOOH + \underset{\text{Tollen's reagent}}{Ag_2O} \longrightarrow CO_2 + H_2O + \underset{\text{Silver mirror}}{2Ag\downarrow}$$

(ii) $$HCOOH + \underset{\text{Fehling solution}}{2CuO} \longrightarrow CO_2 + H_2O + \underset{\text{Cuprous oxide (reddish brown)}}{Cu_2O\downarrow}$$

(iii) $$HCOOH + 2HgCl_2 \longrightarrow CO_2 + 2HCl + \underset{\text{Mercurous chloride (white)}}{Hg_2Cl_2\downarrow}$$

$$HCOOH + Hg_2Cl_2 \longrightarrow CO_2 + 2HCl + \underset{\text{Mercury (black)}}{2Hg\downarrow}$$

or $$2HCOOH + 2HgCl_2 \longrightarrow 2CO_2 + 4HCl + 2Hg\downarrow$$

(*iv*) $2KMnO_4 + 3H_2SO_4 \longrightarrow K_2SO_4 + 2MnSO_4\ 3H_2O + 5O$

$5HCOOH + 5O \longrightarrow 5CO_2 + 5H_2O$

$2KMnO_4 + 3H_2SO_4 + 5HCOOH \longrightarrow K_2SO_4 + 2MnSO_4 + 5CO_2 + 8H_2O$

However, remember that formic acid does not react with NH_2OH, semicarbazide, phenylhydrazine, etc.

17.6 Dicarboxylic Acids

Important dicarboxylic acids along with their IUPAC and common names are given below.

HOOC.COOH Ethanedioic acid (Oxalic acid)	$HOOCCH_2COOH$ Propanedioic acid (Malonic acid)	$HOOCCH_2CH_2COOH$ 1, 4-Butanedioic acid (Succinic acid)
$CH_2(CH_2COOH)_2$ 1, 5-Pentanedioic acid (Glutaric acid)	CH_2CH_2COOH – CH_2CH_2COOH 1, 6-Hexanedioic acid (Adipic acid)	$CH_2(CH_2CH_2COOH)_2$ 1, 7-Heptanedioic acid (Pimelic acid)

Dicarboxylic acids exhibit position isomerism among themselves, *e.g.*

CH_2COOH – CH_2COOH (Succinic acid) and $CH_3CH(COOH)_2$ (Methylmalonic acid)

Methods of preparation and chemical properties are similar to that of monocarboxylic acids. Two properties deserve special attention.

1. **Acidity.** Like inorganic acids containing two or more ionizable hydrogen (H_2SO_4, H_2CO_3, H_3PO_4 etc.), ionization of the second carboxyl group occurs less readily than ionization of the first, *i.e.* $K_1 > K_2$. This is because, more energy is required to separate a positive hydrogen ion from the charged anion than from the uncharged species. Dicarboxylic acids are stronger than monocarboxylic acids because one —COOH group (electron-withdrawing group) enhances the acidity of the other. This also explains that the K_1 value of dicarboxylic acids decreases with the increase in number of intervening CH_2 group(s). Thus the acidic order is

$$\underset{\text{Oxalic acid}}{HOOCCOOH} > \underset{\text{Malonic acid}}{HOOCCH_2COOH} > \underset{\text{Succinic acid}}{HOOCCH_2CH_2COOH}$$

2. **Effect of heating.** Different dicarboxylic acids on heating give different products depending upon the relative position of the two carboxyl groups.

(*i*) Dicarboxylic acids having two carboxyl groups on the same carbon atom eliminate a molecule of carbon dioxide (decarboxylation) on heating to form monocarboxylic acids.

$$\underset{\text{Oxalic acid}}{COOH\text{–}COOH} \xrightarrow{\text{heat}} \underset{\text{Formic acid}}{HCOOH} + CO_2\ ;\ \underset{\text{Malonic acid}}{HOOCCH_2COOH} \xrightarrow{\text{heat}} \underset{\text{Acetic acid}}{CH_3COOH} + CO_2$$

(*ii*) Dicarboxylic acids in which the two carboxylic groups are separated by two or three carbon atoms, *i.e.*, 1, 4- and 1, 5-dicarboxylic acids lose a molecule of water on heating or on distillation with acetic anhydride to form cyclic anhydrides. The reaction is known as **cyclodehydration.** For example,

$$\underset{\text{Succinic acid}}{CH_2COOH\text{–}CH_2COOH} \xrightarrow[(-H_2O)]{\text{heat}} \underset{\text{Succinic anhydride}}{(CH_2\text{—}CO)_2O}\ ;\ \underset{\text{Glutaric acid}}{CH_2(CH_2\text{—}COOH)_2} \xrightarrow[(-H_2O)]{\text{heat}} \underset{\text{Glutaric anhydride}}{CH_2(CH_2\text{—}CO)_2O}$$

(*iii*) Dicarboxylic acids in which the two carboxyl groups are separated by four or more carbon atoms (*i.e.* 1, 6- and 1, 7-dicarboxylic acids) when distilled with acetic anhydride form cyclic ketones. For example,

$$\begin{array}{l} CH_2-CH_2-COOH \\ | \\ CH_2-CH_2-COOH \end{array} \xrightarrow[(CH_3CO)_2O]{300°C} \begin{array}{l} CH_2-CH_2 \\ | \\ CH_2-CH_2 \end{array} \!\!> CO + CO_2 + H_2O$$

Cyclopentanone

$$H_2C \begin{array}{l} \diagup CH_2-CH_2-COOH \\ \diagdown CH_2-CH_2-COOH \end{array} \xrightarrow[(CH_3CO)_2O]{300°C} H_2C \begin{array}{l} \diagup CH_2-CH_2 \diagdown \\ \diagdown CH_2-CH_2 \diagup \end{array} CO$$

Pimelic acid — Cyclohexanone

The effect of heating on various dicarboxylic acids can be summarised in the form of **Blanc rule** according to which *dicarboxylic acids having two carboxylic groups on the same carbon atom when heated form monocarboxylic acids ; 1, 4- and 1, 5-dicarboxylic acids, on heating or on distillation with acetic anhydride form cyclic anhydrides while 1, 6- and 1, 7-dicarboxylic acids on distillation with acetic anhydride form cyclic ketones.*

TEST YOUR UNDERSTANDING - 17.10

1. Give the structure of the compound formed in each of the following reaction :

(*a*) (oxalic acid: O, OH, O, OH) + HO⁄⁄OH (ethylene glycol) ⟶ A (*b*) (succinic acid: O, OH, O, OH) $\xrightarrow{heat}$ B

2. (*a*) Give the products obtained on heating the following with conc. H_2SO_4.

(*i*) CH_3COOH (*ii*) HCOOH (*iii*) Ph_3CCOOH (*iv*) $C_6H_5COCOOH$

(*b*) Compare the reactivities of CH_3COOH and Cl_3CCOOH on heating with a base like soda lime, a mixture of NaOH and CaO.

(*c*) Give the product obtained by the oxidative cleavage of the following compounds with conc. $KMnO_4$.

(*i*) (ii)

17.7 Distinction Between α-, β-, and γ-Substituted Carboxylic Acids

1. The three halogen substituted acids (α-, β- and γ-) give different compounds with aqueous base (NaOH).

2-Bromopentanoic acid $\xrightarrow[(ii)\ H^+]{(i)\ OH^-}$ 2-Hydroxypentanoic acid

3-Bromopentanoic acid $\xrightarrow[(ii)\ H^+]{(i)\ OH^-}$ 2-Pentenoic acid (conjugated system)

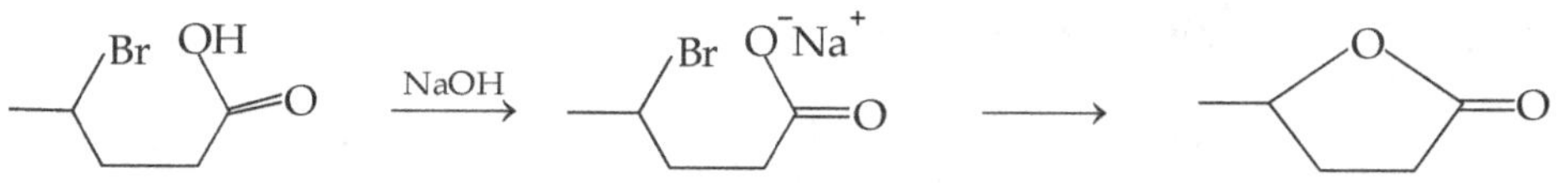

4-Bromopentanoic acid $\xrightarrow{NaOH}$ → 3-Methyl-γ- butyrolactone

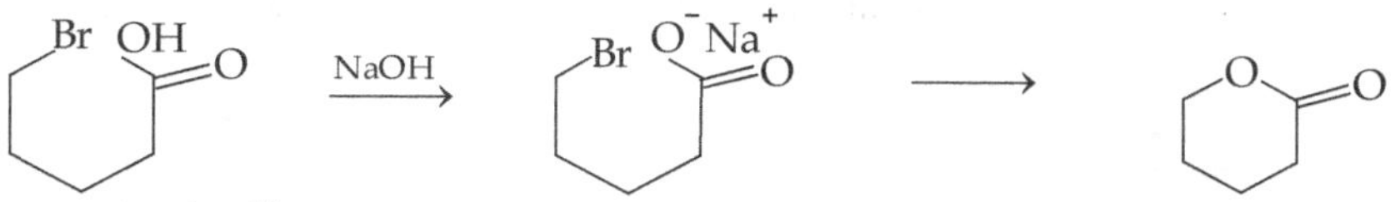

5-Bromopentanoic acid $\xrightarrow{NaOH}$ → δ-Valerolactone

2. The three (α-, β-, and γ-) hydroxy and amino acids behave differently, on heating. Hydroxy and amino acids behave in similar ways.

(a)

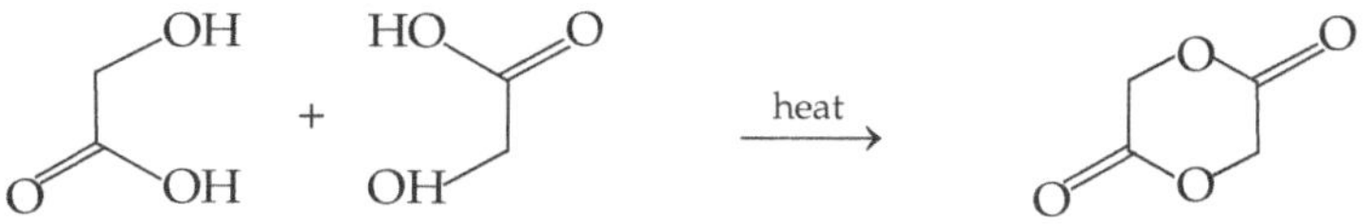

(Two molecules of α-hydroxy acids) $\xrightarrow{heat}$ Glycollide

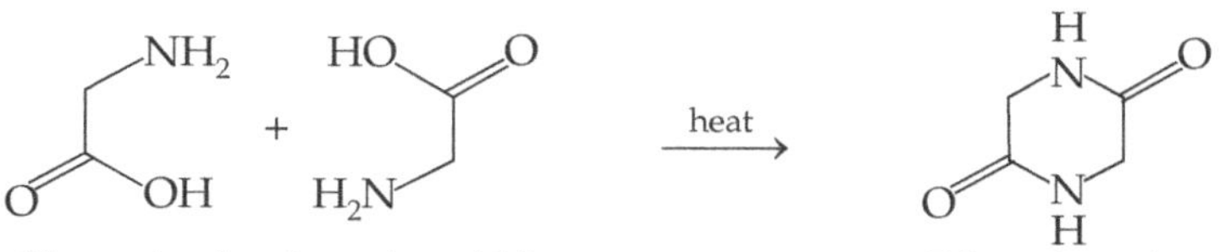

(Two molecules of α-amino acids) $\xrightarrow{heat}$ Diketopiperazine

(b)

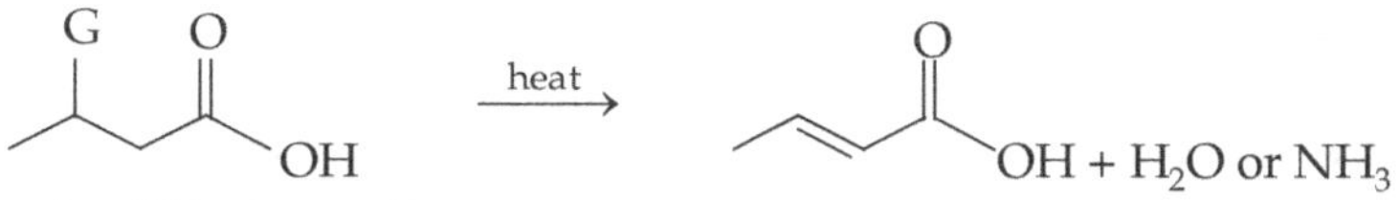

Two molecules of β-hydroxy acids or β-amino acids (G = OH or NH_2) $\xrightarrow{heat}$ $CH_3CH{=}CHCOOH$ + H_2O or NH_3

(c)

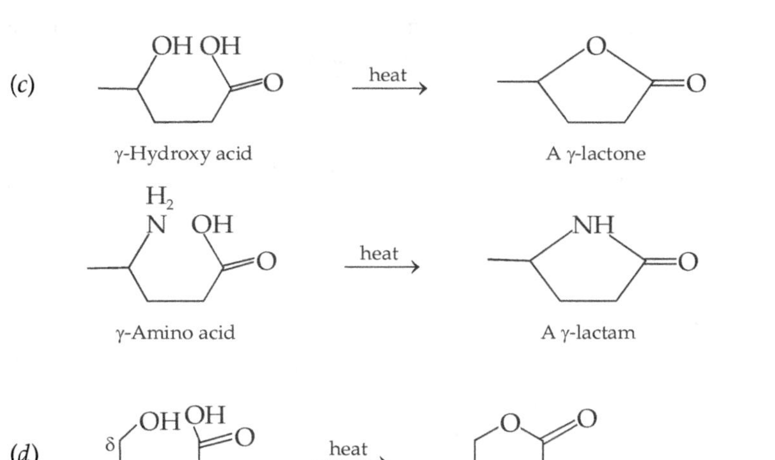

γ-Hydroxy acid $\xrightarrow{heat}$ A γ-lactone

γ-Amino acid $\xrightarrow{heat}$ A γ-lactam

(d)

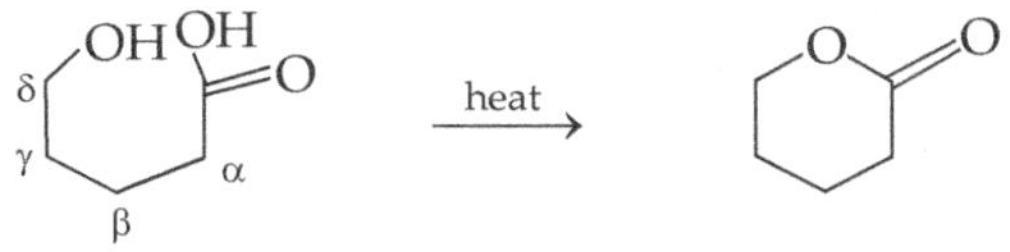

δ-Hydroxy acid $\xrightarrow{heat}$ A δ-lactone

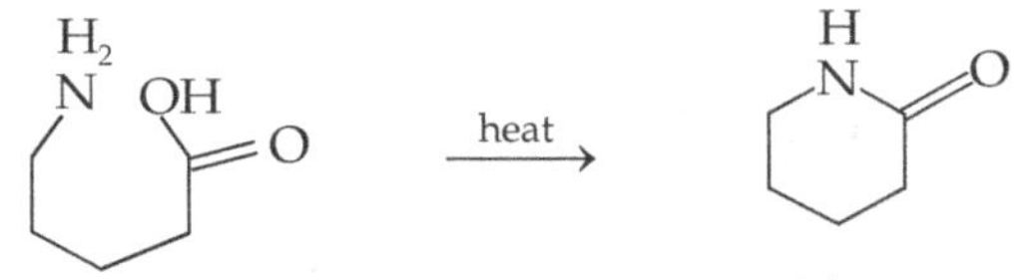

δ-Amino acid $\xrightarrow{heat}$ A δ-lactam

17.8 Additional Chemistry of Aromatic Carboxylic Acids

Preparation. Although the methods used for aliphatic carboxylic acis can be applied for preparing aromatic carboxylic acids, the most important one is due to oxidation of side chain.

Oxidation of the side chain. Generally, benzene ring is very resistant to oxidation and hence benzene homologues are oxidised in the side chain to form a carboxylic acid, the side chain is always oxidised to —COOH group, ignoring its length.

$$C_6H_5R \xrightarrow[\text{hot}]{KMnO_4} C_6H_5COOH \quad (R = —CH_3, —CH_2CH_3, -n\text{-}C_3H_7)$$

$$\text{Cyclopropylbenzene} \xrightarrow[\text{hot}]{KMnO_4} C_6H_5COOH$$

$$\text{1-Methylindane} \xrightarrow[H^+]{K_2Cr_2O_7} C_6H_4(COOH)_2 + CH_3COOH$$

(*i*) If the side chain is a *tert*-alkyl group, oxidation is difficult, but on vigorous oxidaton benzene ring in oxidised.

$$C_6H_5C(CH_3)_3 \xrightarrow[\text{heat}]{\text{alk. } KMnO_4} (CH_3)_3CCOOH$$

(*ii*) Side chain, like $—CH_2Cl$, $—CH_2OH$, and $—CH_2NH_2$, attached to benzene ring is also oxidised to —COOH group.

$$C_6H_5CH_2X \xrightarrow{KMnO_4} C_6H_5COOH$$

$$(X = —Cl, —OH, —NH_2)$$

(*iii*) Presence of electron withdrawing group like $—NO_2$ makes the ring resistant to oxidation, while presence of electron-repelling group lik $—NH_2$ makes the benzene ring susceptible to oxidation.

1-Nitronaphthalene (rings A, B) $\xrightarrow{\text{oxidaton}}$ 3-nitrophthalic acid (HOOC, HOOC on ring B, with NO_2) — Ring B containing $—NO_2$ group is retained

1-Naphthylamine (rings A, B) $\xrightarrow{\text{oxidaton}}$ phthalic acid (ring A with two COOH) — Ring B containing $—NH_2$ group is oxidised

However, oxidation of alkyl group to —COOH group in compounds containing alkyl group as well as electron-repelling group can be achieved either by carrying oxidation with a mild oxidising agent (like PbO_2) or by protecting the electron-releasing group first with tosyl chloride followed by oxidation.

$$o\text{-}CH_3C_6H_4OH \xrightarrow{PbO_2} o\text{-}HOOCC_6H_4OH$$

$$o\text{-}CH_3C_6H_4OH \xrightarrow{TsCl} o\text{-}CH_3C_6H_4OTs \xrightarrow{KMnO_4} o\text{-}HOOCC_6H_4OTs \xrightarrow{H_2O} o\text{-}HOOCC_6H_4OH$$

Acidity of aromatic acids. Benzoic acid itself is somewhat stronger acid than acetic acid. Its carboxyl group is attached to an sp^2 hybridized carbon and ionizes to a greater extent than one that is attached to an sp^3 hybridized carbon (recall that carbon becomes more electron-withdrawing as its *s* character increases).

	CH_3COOH	$CH_2 = CHCOOH$	C_6H_5—COOH
	Acetic acid	Acrylic acid	Benzoic acid
K_a	1.8×10^{-5}	5.5×10^{-5}	6.3×10^{-5}
pK_a	4.8	4.3	4.2

—COOH group attached on sp^2 C, hence more electronegative → –ve charge on O dispersesed (hence more stable) ; —COOH group on sp^3 C, hence less electronegative → –ve charge on O intensified (hence less stable)

Moreover, benzoate anion is more stable, due to presence of benzene ring, than acetate ion.

Resonance in benzoate anion due to benzene ring

Like aliphatic acids, acidity of aromatic acids is affected by substituents : electron-releasing groups like —CH_3, —OH and —NH_2 make benzoic acid weaker, while electron-withdrawing groups like —Cl, —NO_2, —CN, etc. make benzoic acid stronger.

G (—NO_2, —Cl, —CN) withdraws electrons, disperses –ve charge on O, stabilises the anion, hence strengthens acidity

G (—CH_3, —OH, —NH_2, —OCH_3) releases electrons, intensifies –ve charge on O, destabilises the anion, hence weakens acidity

Following table lists the ionization constants (acidity) of some substituted benzoic acids,

Acidity of some substituted benzoic acids, XC_6H_4COOH

$K_a(pK_a)$ for different positions of the substituent X

Value of X	*ortho*	*meta*	*para*
H	6.3×10^{-5} (4.2)	6.3×10^{-5} (4.2)	6.3×10^{-5} (4.2)
CH_3	1.2×10^{-4} (3.9)	5.3×10^{-5} (4.3)	4.2×10^{-5} (4.4)
F	5.4×10^{-4} (3.3)	1.4×10^{-4} (3.9)	7.2×10^{-5} (4.1)
Cl	1.2×10^{-3} (2.9)	1.5×10^{-4} (3.8)	1.0×10^{-4} (4.0)
Br	1.4×10^{-3} (2.8)	1.5×10^{-4} (3.8)	1.1×10^{-4} (4.0)
I	1.4×10^{-3} (2.9)	1.4×10^{-4} (3.9)	9.2×10^{-5} (4.0)
CH_3O	8.1×10^{-5} (4.1)	8.2×10^{-5} (4.1)	3.4×10^{-5} (4.5)
O_2N	6.7×10^{-3} (2.2)	3.2×10^{-4} (3.5)	3.8×10^{-4} (3.4)

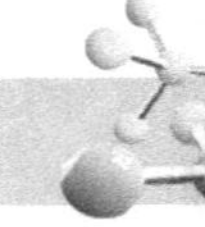

(*a*) Nearly all *ortho* substituents, whether electron-withdrawing or electron-releasing, exert an acid-strengthening effect, and the effect is unsually large. This *ortho* effect is partly due to closeness of the groups involved. Sometimes H—bonding also plays a role, *e.g.*, *o*-hydroxybenzoic acid (salicylic acid) is far stronger than the corresponding *m*- and *p*- isomers. The carboxylate ion of the *o*-isomer is stabilised by intramolecular H-bonding.

p-Hydroxybenzoate ion, I

o-Hydroxybenzoate ion, II (more stable than I)

2, 6-Dihydroxybenzoate ion, III (more stable than II)

(*b*) The —OH and —OCH_3 groups display both kinds of effect. When present in *meta* position, these groups produce electron-withdrawing acid-strengthening effect. When present in *para* position, these groups produce electron-releasing acid-weakneing resonance effect.

TEST YOUR UNDERSTANDING - 17.11

1. Discuss the resonance of the *p*-NO_2 group in *p*-$NO_2C_6H_4COO^-$.
2. Account for the following
   (*a*) *p*-Nitrobenzoic acid is more acidic than its *meta* isomer, while *p*-chlorobenzoic acid is less acidic than its *meta* isomer
   (*b*) *p*-Toluic acid is weaker than *m*-toluic acid.
   (*c*) *p*-Hydroxybenzoic acid is weaker than benzoic acid while the corresponding *m* —OH acid is stronger than benzoic acid.
3. Which of the two carboxylic acids is more stronger ?

   (*a*) *p*-$CH_3C_6H_4COOH$ or *p*-$OCH_3C_6H_4COOH$ (*b*) *p*-$NO_2C_6H_4COOH$ or *p*-$COCH_3C_6H_4COOH$ (*c*) *p*-FC_6H_4COOH or *p*-ClC_6H_4COOH
4. Arrange the following carboxylic acids in decreasing order of acidity.
   (*a*) Benzoic acid, *p*-chlorobenzoic acid, 2, 4-dichlorobenzoic acid
   (*b*) Benzoic acid, *p*-toluic acid, *p*-nitrobenzoic acid
   (*c*) *p*-Nitrobenzoic acid, *p*-nitrophenylacetic acid, β– (*p*-nitrophenyl)propanoic acid

Substitution in benzene nucleus. As described earlier, —COOH group is *m*-directing and deactivating group, so substitution takes palce in *meta*- position and require stronger conditions.

$C_6H_5COOH \xrightarrow[\text{heat}]{Br_2,\ Fe}$ *m*-BrC_6H_4COOH ; $C_6H_5COOH \xrightarrow[\text{Conc. } H_2SO_4,\ \text{heat}]{\text{Conc. } HNO_3,}$ *m*-$NO_2C_6H_4COOH$

$C_6H_5COOH \xrightarrow[\text{heat}]{\text{Conc. } H_2SO_4,}$ *m*-$HO_3SC_6H_4COOH$

When some activating group *e.g.*, —OH is present along with —COOH, substitution occurs w.r.t. —OH and —COOH group is replaced by the new group. For example,

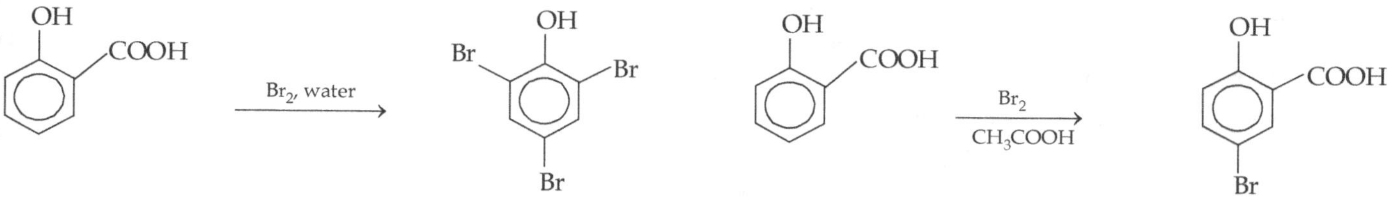

Salicylic acid (OH, COOH) $\xrightarrow{Br_2, \text{ water}}$ 2,4,6-tribromophenol (OH; Br, Br, Br)

Salicylic acid (OH, COOH) $\xrightarrow[CH_3COOH]{Br_2}$ 5-bromosalicylic acid (OH, COOH, Br)

In the second example, brominating agent is mild, hence only monobromo product will be formed. Further, bromination will be favoured at *para* position because of steric factors.

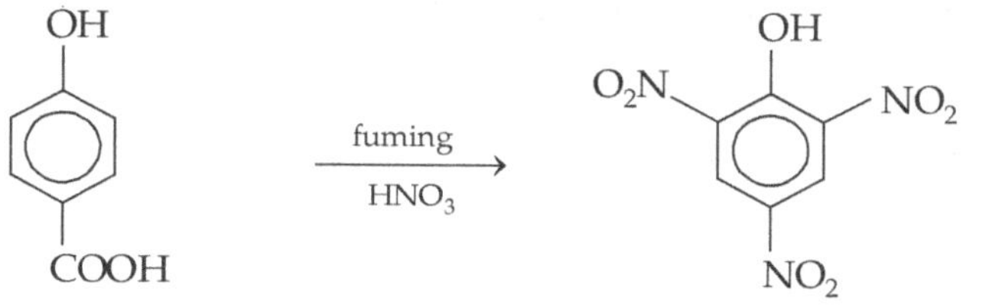

p-Hydroxybenzoic acid (OH, COOH) $\xrightarrow[HNO_3]{\text{fuming}}$ 2,4,6-trinitrophenol (OH; O_2N, NO_2, NO_2)

TEST YOUR UNDERSTANDING - 17.12

1. Identify the bracketed compounds in the following reactions.

(*a*) Benzoic acid (COOH) $\xrightarrow[\text{(ii) } H_2, Pd/BaSO_4]{\text{(i) } PCl_5}$ [A]

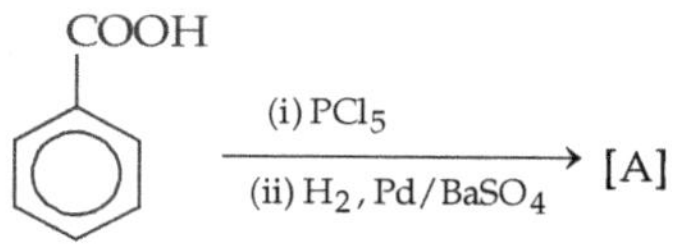

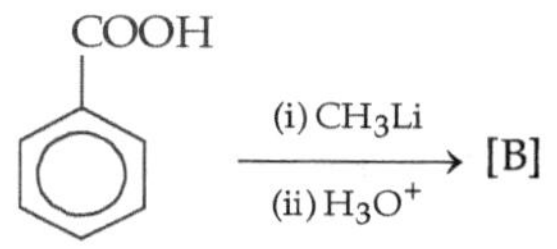

(*b*) Benzoic acid (COOH) $\xrightarrow[\text{(ii) } H_3O^+]{\text{(i) } CH_3Li}$ [B]

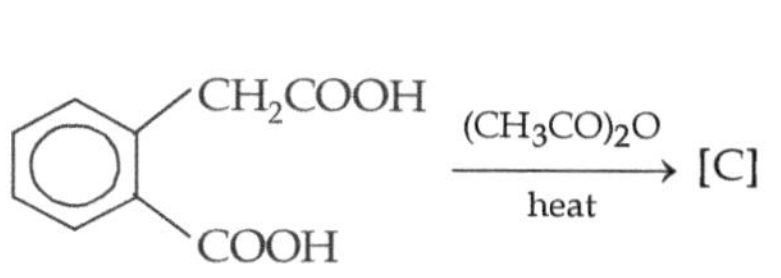

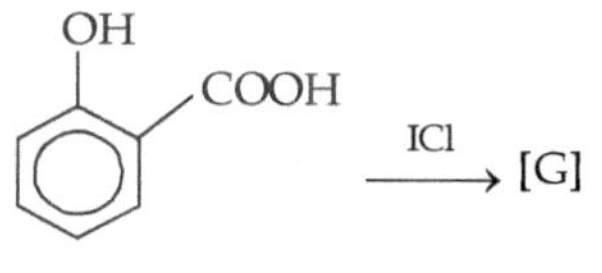

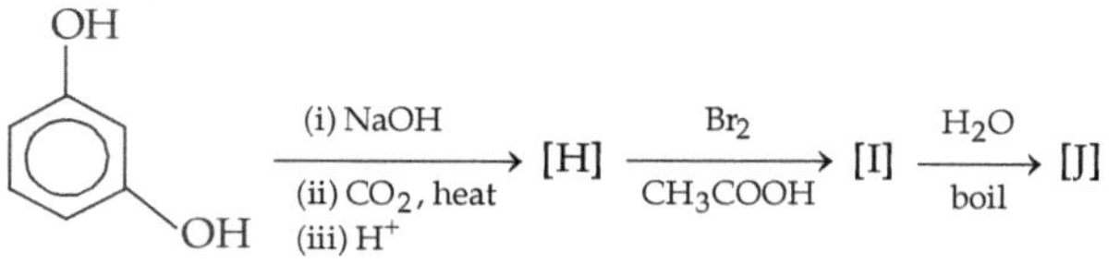

(*c*) Benzene with CH_2COOH and COOH (ortho) $\xrightarrow[\text{heat}]{(CH_3CO)_2O}$ [C]

(*d*) p-Nitrobenzoic acid (COOH, NO_2) $\xrightarrow[\text{(ii) } H_2O]{\text{(i) } B_2H_6, \text{ THF}}$ [D]

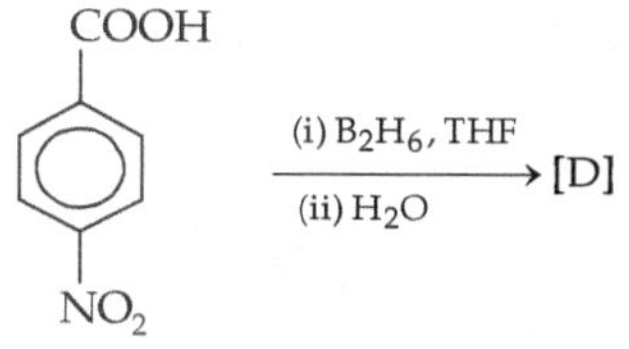

(*e*) 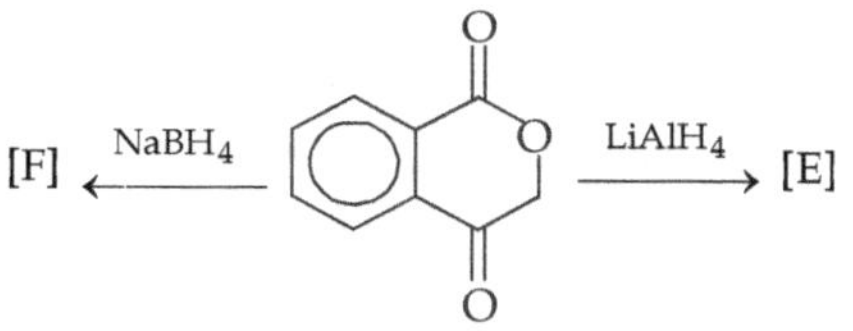 [F] $\xleftarrow{NaBH_4}$ cyclic anhydride (C=O, O, C=O fused to benzene) $\xrightarrow{LiAlH_4}$ [E]

(*f*) Salicylic acid (OH, COOH) $\xrightarrow{ICl}$ [G]

(*g*) Resorcinol (OH, OH) $\xrightarrow[\text{(ii) } CO_2, \text{ heat} \quad \text{(iii) } H^+]{\text{(i) NaOH}}$ [H] $\xrightarrow[CH_3COOH]{Br_2}$ [I] $\xrightarrow[\text{boil}]{H_2O}$ [J]

(*h*) o-Nitrobenzoic acid (COOH, NO_2) $\xrightarrow[H^+]{C_2H_5OH}$ [K] $\xrightarrow[\text{(ii) } H_3O^+]{\text{(i) excess of } C_6H_5MgBr}$ [L]

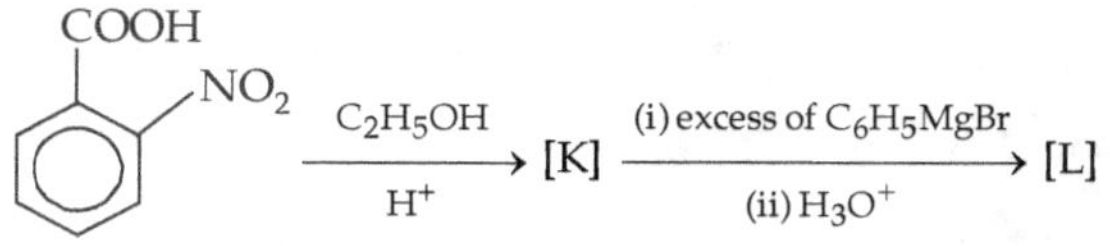

17.9 Analysis of Carboxylic Acids

(*i*) Carboxylic acids are recognized through their acidity. They dissolve in aqueous NaOH and in aqueous $NaHCO_3$; in the latter case bubbles (effervescences) of CO_2 are evolved.

NOTE.

(*a*) Phenols, with certain exceptions, are considerably weaker than carboxylic acids. Thus although they dissolve in aq. NaOH (a strong base), but not in aq. sodium bicarbonate (a weak base).

(*b*) Sulphonic acids are even more acidic than carboxylic acids, but they can be differentiated by presence of sulphur.

(*ii*) Determination of **neutralization equivalent (NE)**, *the equivalent weight of the acid as determined by titration with standard base*, is one of the characteristics of a carboxylic acid. For this, a known weight of the acid is dissolved in water or aqueous alcohol. The volume of a standard base required to neutralize the solution is measured by titration using phenolphthalein as an indicator. Suppose x g of an unknown acid requires V mL. of 1M NaOH for neutralisation. It means

Since 1000 mL of the base contains 1 equivalent of the base

V mL of the base contains $\frac{1\,M}{1000} \times V$ equivalent of base.

Since No. of eq. of base required = No. of eq. of acid present = $\frac{1\,M \times V}{1000}$

$\frac{1\,M \times V}{1000}$ eq. of acid = x g (Wt. of acid present)

$\therefore$ 1 eq. of acid = $\frac{x \times 1000}{1\,M \times V}$ g of acid

Thus by knowing the wt. of acid, and volume of standard base (known molarity), neturalization equivalent of the acid can be ascertained.

Detection of a metal salt of a carboxylic acid

(*i*) On strongly heating, it leaves a residue;

(*ii*) it decomposes at a high temperature instead of melting, and

(*iii*) it is converted into a carboxylic acid upon acidification.

TEST YOUR UNDERSTANDING - 17.13

1. (*a*) What is the relation between NE and the number of acidic hydrogens per molecule of acid?

(*b*) What is the neutralization equivalent of terephthalic acid, *p*-$HOOCC_6H_4COOH$, and melittic acid $C_6(COOH)_6$? How many moles of a base (NaOH) are needed to neutralize one mole of each of the two acids ?

2. Differentiate among 2-chloropropanoic acid ($CH_3CHClCOOH$), pyruvic acid ($CH_3COCOOH$), acrylic acid ($CH_2 = CHCOOH$ and propanoic acid (CH_3CH_2COOH).

3. Give a chemical reaction with the help of which we can distinguish among following three carboxylic acids.

n-Pentanoic acid, 2-methylbutanoic acid, and 2, 2-dimethylpropanoic acid.

17.10 ILLUSTRATIVE EXAMPLES

Example 1 :

Identify the bracketed compounds in each of the following reactions.

(i) [1,3-butadiene skeletal structure] $\xrightarrow{\text{1 mole HBr}}$ [A] $\xrightarrow[\text{(ii) } CO_2,\, H_3O^+]{\text{(i) Mg}}$ [B] $\xrightarrow{\text{heat}}$ [C]

(ii) $CH_2BrCOOC_2H_5 \xrightarrow{Zn}$ [A] $\xrightarrow[\text{(ii) } H_2O]{\text{(i) acetone}}$ [B] $\xrightarrow[\text{(ii) heat}]{\text{(i) } H_3O^+}$ [C]

(iii) Cyclohexanol $\xrightarrow[H^+]{K_2Cr_2O_7}$ [A] $\xrightarrow{C_6H_5MgBr}$ [B] $\xrightarrow[heat]{CrO_3, CH_3COOH}$ [C]

(iv) Cyclopentanol $\xrightarrow{HNO_3}$ [A] $\xrightarrow{HCN/CN^-}$ [B] $\xrightarrow[H_2SO_4]{conc.}$ [C] $\xrightarrow{H_3O^+}$ [D] $\xrightarrow{LiAlH_4}$ [E]

(v) 1-Tetralone $\xrightarrow[(ii)\,H^+]{(i)\,C_6H_5MgBr}$ [A] $\xrightarrow{S,\,heat}$ [B]

(vi) [E] $\xleftarrow[(ii)\,H^+]{(i)\,NaOH}$ [D] $\xleftarrow[excess]{P,\,Br_2}$ CH_3COOH $\xrightarrow{SOCl_2}$ [A] $\xrightarrow{[B]}$ CH_3CHO $\xrightarrow[\Delta]{dil.\,NaOH}$ [C]

(vii) Benzyl alchol $\xrightarrow[H_2SO_4]{conc.}$ A $\xrightarrow{NBS}$ B $\xrightarrow{KCN}$ C $\xrightarrow{H_3O^+}$ D

(viii) 1-Methylcyclohexene (CH_3) $\xrightarrow{O_3/H_2O}$ A $\xrightarrow[(ii)\,H^+]{(i)\,HCN}$ B $\xrightarrow{heat}$ C

Solution :

(*i*) $CH_3CH=CHCH_2Br$ — [A] obtained by 1, 4- addition; $CH_3CH=CHCH_2COOH$ — [B]; $CH_3CH=CHCH_3$ — [C]

(*ii*)

$CH_2COOC_2H_5$ | ZnBr	$(CH_3)_2CCH_2COOC_2H_5$ | OH	$(CH_3)_2C = CHCOOH$
[A]	[B]	[C]

(*iii*) Cyclohexanone [A]; 1-phenylcyclohexanol (HO, C_6H_5) — A cyclanol [B] $\xrightarrow[heat]{CrO_3}$ [1-phenylcyclohexene (C_6H_5)] $\longrightarrow$ $C_6H_5CO(CH_2)_4COOH$ — 6-Oxo-6-phenylhexanoic acid [C]

Cyclanols undergo acid catalyzed oxidative cleavage, probably *via* the alkene.

(*iv*) Cyclopentanone (O) [A]; cyclopentanone cyanohydrin (HO, CN) [B]; cyclopent-1-enecarbonitrile (CN) [C]; cyclopent-1-enecarboxylic acid (COOH) [D]; cyclopent-1-enylmethanol (CH_2OH) [E]

(*v*) 4-Phenyl-1,2-dihydronaphthalene (C_6H_5) [A] is formed via 1-phenyl-1,2,3,4-tetrahydronaphthalen-1-ol (C_6H_5, OH); 1-phenylnaphthalene (C_6H_5) [B]

(*vi*)	CH_3COCl,	$H_2/Pd/BaSO_4$,	$CH_3CH = CHCHO$,	Br_3CCOOH,	HOOC.COOH
	A	B	C	D	E

(*vii*) CH_2OH (cyclohexyl) $\xrightarrow{H^+}$ $\overset{+}{C}H_2$ (cyclohexyl) $\longrightarrow$ CH_3, $\oplus$ (cyclohexyl) $\xrightarrow{-H^+}$ CH_3 (cyclohexene) $\xrightarrow{NBS}$

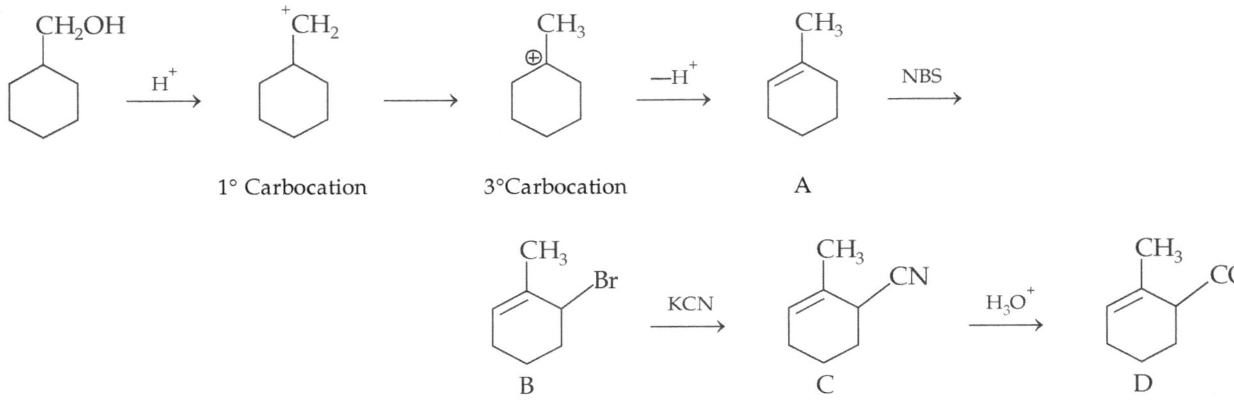

1° Carbocation 3°Carbocation A

CH_3, Br (B) $\xrightarrow{KCN}$ CH_3, CN (C) $\xrightarrow{H_3O^+}$ CH_3, COOH (D)

(*viii*) CH_3 (cyclohexene) $\xrightarrow{O_3/H_2O}$ O, COOH (A) $\xrightarrow[(ii)\ H^+]{(i)\ HCN}$ COOH, CH_3, OH, COOH (B) $\xrightarrow{heat}$ COOH, CH_3, O, O (C)

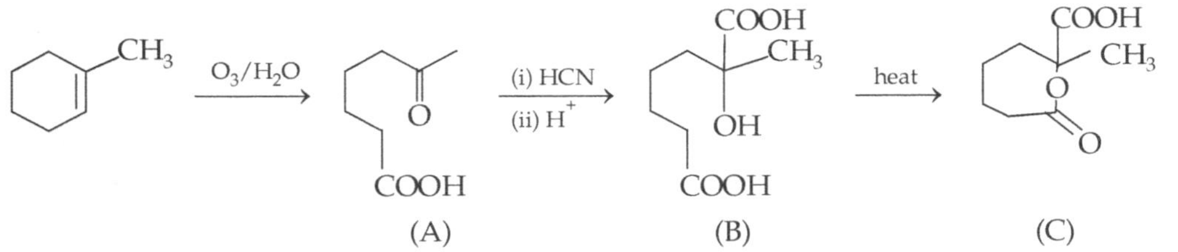

Example 2 :

Establish the structure of [X] on the basis of following reactions/facts.

$$[X] \xrightarrow{HBr} C_9H_9O_2Br \xrightarrow{KOH\ alc.} [Y] \xrightarrow{H_2/Ni} [Z]$$

(i) Compound X gives a positive test with CrO_3 in acid.

(ii) Compound Z can be obtained by the carbonation reaction of $C_6H_5CH(CH_3)$ MgBr. Is there any isomer of X ?

Solution :

Structure of Z can be ascertained by its synthesis from carbonation reaction.

$$C_6H_5CH(CH_3)\ MgBr \xrightarrow[(ii)\ H_3O^+]{(i)\ CO_2} \underset{[Z]}{C_6H_5CH(CH_3)COOH}$$

Thus going backward from Z, structure of X can be ascertained

$$\underset{Z}{C_6H_5\overset{\overset{\displaystyle CH_3}{|}}{C}HCOOH} \xleftarrow{H_2/Ni} \underset{Y}{C_6H_5\overset{\overset{\displaystyle CH_2}{||}}{C}COOH} \xleftarrow{alc.KOH} \underset{(C_9H_9O_2Br)}{C_6H_5\overset{\overset{\displaystyle CH_2Br}{|}}{C}HCOOH} \xleftarrow{HBr} \underset{X}{C_6H_5\overset{\overset{\displaystyle CH_2OH}{|}}{C}HCOOH}$$

Structure of X is confirmed by positive response with CrO_3 in acid.

Isomer of X is $C_6H_5\overset{\overset{\displaystyle OH}{|}}{C}(CH_3)COOH$; but it, being a 3°alcohol, is inert to CrO_3.

Example 3 :

Give stereochemical formulas of compounds A to G.

(a) *rac*-β-Bromobutyric acid $\xrightarrow{\text{1 mole P, Br}_2}$ A + B

(b) Maleic acid + Performic acid $\longrightarrow$ C + D

(c) 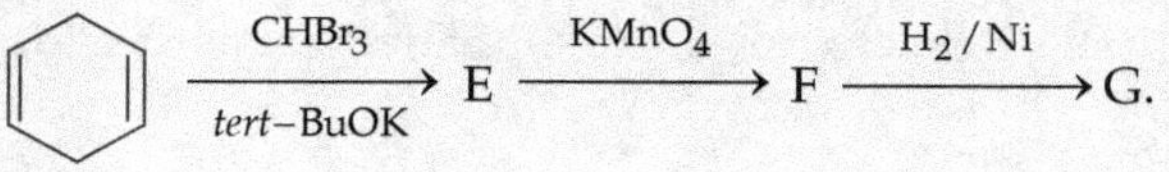 Cyclohexa-1,4-diene $\xrightarrow[\textit{tert}\text{–BuOK}]{\text{CHBr}_3}$ E $\xrightarrow{\text{KMnO}_4}$ F $\xrightarrow{\text{H}_2/\text{Ni}}$ G.

Solution :

(*a*) COOH–CH_2–C(H)(Br)–CH_3 $\xrightarrow{\text{P, Br}_2}$ I (COOH; H–C–Br; H–C–Br; CH_3) + II (COOH; Br–C–H; H–C–Br; CH_3)

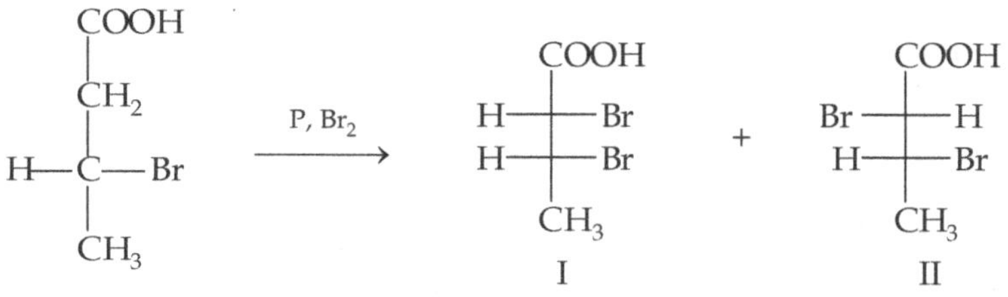

Or

COOH–CH_2–C(Br)(H)–CH_3 $\xrightarrow{\text{P, Br}_2}$ III (COOH; Br–C–H; Br–C–H; CH_3) + IV (COOH; H–C–Br; Br–C–H; CH_3)

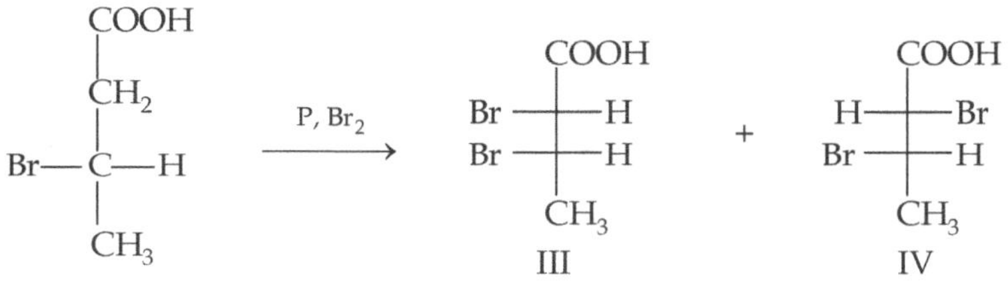

Note that I and III are enantiomers, hence they represent one racemic mixture ; similarly II and IV are enantiomers; and respresent a different racemic mixture. The two racemic mixtures are thus A and B.

(*b*) Maleic acid $\xrightarrow{\textit{anti-}\text{hydroxylation}}$ [C] (COOH; H–C–OH; HO–C–H; COOH) + [D] (COOH; HO–C–H; H–C–OH; COOH)

rac-Tartaric acid

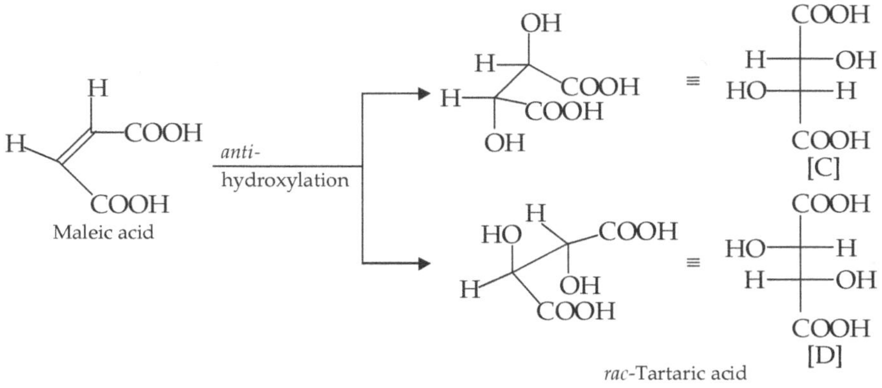

(*c*) $CHBr_3 \xrightarrow{\textit{tert}\text{-BuOK}} :CBr_2 + HBr$

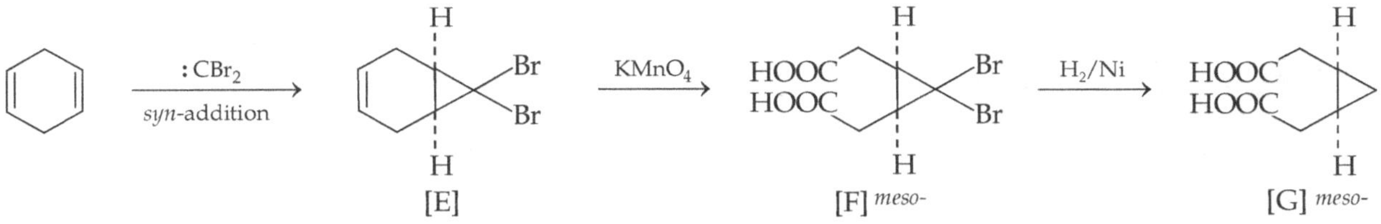

Cyclohexa-1,4-diene $\xrightarrow[\textit{syn}\text{-addition}]{:CBr_2}$ [E] $\xrightarrow{\text{KMnO}_4}$ [F] *meso-* $\xrightarrow{\text{H}_2/\text{Ni}}$ [G] *meso-*

Example 4 :

Give essential steps involved in the following conversions :

(i) Ethanol to glycine

(ii) 2-Butanol to 2-methylbutanoic acid.

(iii) 2-Chlorobutanoic acid to 3-chlorobutanoic acid.

(iv) 2-Propanol, $(CH_3)_2CHOH$ to 3-hydroxybutyric acid.

(v) Benzene to adipic acid, $HOOC.(CH_2)_4 \cdot COOH$.

(vi) Toluene to 2-methyl-5-chlorobenzoic acid.

(vii) Tetrahydrofuran to adipic acid.

(viii) Tetrahydrofuran to succinic acid.

(ix) Cyclopentanol to 2-oxocyclopentanecarboxylic acid.

(x) Benzene to 6-oxo-6-phenylhexanoic acid.

Solution :

(i) $CH_3CH_2OH \xrightarrow{MnO_4^-,\, H^+} CH_3COOH \xrightarrow{Cl_2/P} ClCH_2COOH \xrightarrow{NH_3} H_2NCH_2COOH$

(ii) The conversion involves the conversion of —OH to —COOH, which can be easily accomplished through Grignard reagent.

$$\underset{\text{2-Butanol}}{CH_3CH_2\overset{H}{\underset{OH}{C}}CH_3} \xrightarrow{SOCl_2} CH_3CH_2\overset{H}{\underset{Cl}{C}}CH_3 \xrightarrow[\text{ether}]{Mg} CH_3CH_2\overset{H}{\underset{MgCl}{C}}CH_3 \xrightarrow[\text{(ii) } H_3O^+]{\text{(i) } CO_2} CH_3CH_2\overset{H}{\underset{COOH}{C}}CH_3$$

Nitrile route should not be used because a 2° halide may undergo extensive dehydrohalogenation.

(iii)

$$\underset{\text{2-Chlorobutanoic acid}}{CH_3CH_2\overset{Cl}{C}HCOOH} \xrightarrow{\text{alc.KOH}} CH_3CH = CHCOOH \xrightarrow{H^+}$$

$$\underset{\substack{\text{An } \alpha\text{-carbocation} \\ \text{(unstable, +ve charge on adjacent C's)}}}{CH_3CH_2\overset{+}{C}H-\overset{\delta+}{\overset{O^{\delta-}}{\overset{\|}{C}}}-OH} \quad \text{or} \quad \underset{\substack{\text{A } \beta\text{-carbocation} \\ \text{(more stable)}}}{CH_3\overset{+}{C}HCH_2COOH} \xrightarrow{Cl^-} \underset{\text{3-Chlorobutanoic acid}}{CH_3\underset{Cl}{C}HCH_2COOH}$$

(iv)

$$\underset{\text{2-Propanol}}{CH_3\overset{OH}{C}HCH_3} \xrightarrow{H_2SO_4} CH_3CH = CH_2 \xrightarrow{HOCl} CH_3\overset{OH}{C}HCH_2Cl \xrightarrow{CN^-,\, H^+}$$

$$CH_3\overset{OH}{C}HCH_2CN \xrightarrow{H_3O^+} \underset{\text{3-Hydroxybutanoic acid}}{CH_3\overset{OH}{C}HCH_2COOH}$$

(v)

$$\text{Benzene} \xrightarrow{H_2/Pd} \text{Cyclohexane} \xrightarrow{Cl_2} \text{Chlorocyclohexane} \xrightarrow[\text{KOH}]{\text{alc.}} \text{Cyclohexene} \xrightarrow[H^+]{KMnO_4} \underset{\text{Adipic acid}}{HOOC(CH_2)_4COOH}$$

(vi) Toluene $\xrightarrow{Cl_2/Fe}$ p-chlorotoluene $\xrightarrow{Br_2/Fe}$ 2-bromo-4-chlorotoluene $\xrightarrow{(i)\ Mg/ether,\ (ii)\ CO_2,\ (iii)\ H^+}$ 5-chloro-2-methylbenzoic acid (CH$_3$, COOH, Cl)

Here it is advisable to introduce —COOH grop through carbonation route, because route involving the oxidation of the alkyl group gives poor yields, until a strong electron-withdrawing group like —NO_2 is present.

(vii) THF $\xrightarrow{\text{Conc. HI}}$ I(CH$_2$)$_4$I $\xrightarrow{\text{dicarbonation}}$ HOOC(CH$_2$)$_4$COOH (Adipic acid)

(viii) THF $\xrightarrow{\text{Conc. HI}}$ I(CH$_2$)$_4$I $\xrightarrow{OH^-}$ HO(CH$_2$)$_4$OH $\xrightarrow{KMnO_4}$ HOOC(CH$_2$)$_2$COOH (Succinic acid)

(ix) The required product has a keto and a carboxylic group for which CHOH and CN should be the respective precursor.

Cyclopentanol $\xrightarrow{H_2SO_4}$ Cyclopentene $\xrightarrow{HOCl}$ 2-chlorocyclopentanol $\xrightarrow{(i)\ CN^-,\ (ii)\ H_3O^+}$ 2-hydroxycyclopentanecarboxylic acid $\xrightarrow{K_2Cr_2O_7/H^+}$ 2-Oxocyclopentane carboxylic acid

(x) First write down the structure of the product and then think of its precursor, *i.e.* proceed backward. It will be very easy to write reactions.

C$_6$H$_5$CO(CH$_2$)$_4$COOH $\xleftarrow{HNO_3}$ 1-phenylcyclohexanol (HO, C$_6$H$_5$) $\xleftarrow{C_6H_5MgBr}$ Cyclohexanone $\xleftarrow{KMnO_4}$ Cyclohexanol (OH)

Benzene $\xrightarrow{H_2/Pd,\ \text{heat, high P}}$ Cyclohexane $\xrightarrow{Cl_2,\ h\nu}$ Chlorocyclohexane (Cl) $\xrightarrow{\text{(aq.)}}$ Cyclohexanol

Example 5 :

Give necessary steps (reagents) to explain the following reactions :

(a) $C_6H_5CH = CHCH_2COOH \xrightarrow{H^+}$ 5-phenyl-γ-butyrolactone (C$_6$H$_5$, O, =O)

(b) $CH_2CH_2CH_2CH_2OH$ with CHO on the first carbon $\xrightarrow{(i)\ \text{Tollen's reagent},\ (ii)\ H^+}$ δ-valerolactone

(c) $CH_3CH(OH)CH_2C\equiv CCOOH \longrightarrow$ 6-methyl-5,6-dihydro-2-pyranone (O, =O, CH$_3$)

(d) 1,1-dimethoxy-3,3-bis(COOCHMe$_2$)cyclopentane (MeO, OMe, Me$_2$HCOOC, COOCHMe$_2$) $\xrightarrow{\text{refluxed with HCl}}$ A keto acid

Solution :

(*a*) $C_6H_5CH{=}CHCH_2COOH \xrightarrow{H^+} C_6H_5\overset{+}{C}HCH_2CH_2COOH$ (Benzyl carbocation) $\equiv$ [cyclic intermediate] $\xrightarrow{-H^+}$ C_6H_5-substituted γ-lactone

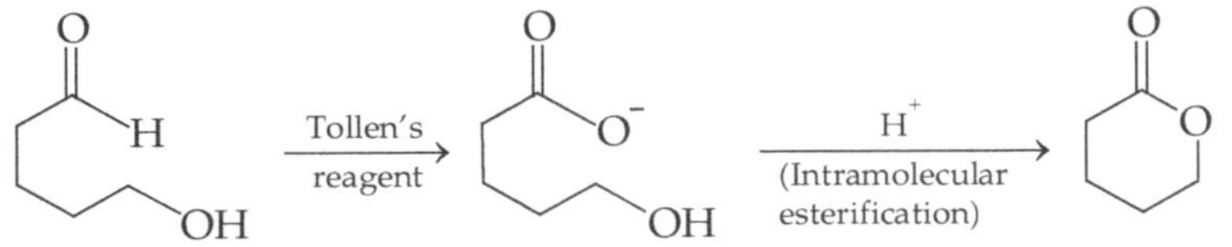

(*b*) 5-hydroxypentanal $\xrightarrow{\text{Tollen's reagent}}$ 5-hydroxypentanoate $\xrightarrow[\text{(Intramolecular esterification)}]{H^+}$ δ-valerolactone

(*c*) $\xrightarrow{H_2,\ \text{Lindlar catalyst}}$ *cis*-isomer $\xrightarrow[\text{(intramolecular esterification)}]{H^+}$ lactone (CH_3)

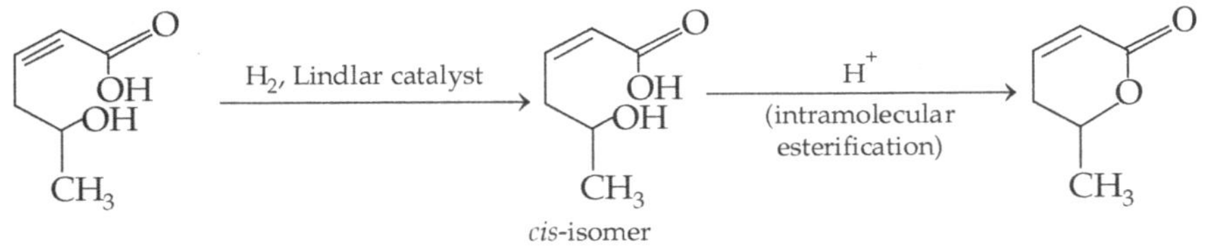

(*d*) The given compound has two types of functional groups (acetal and ester) both of which are hydrolysed by HCl.

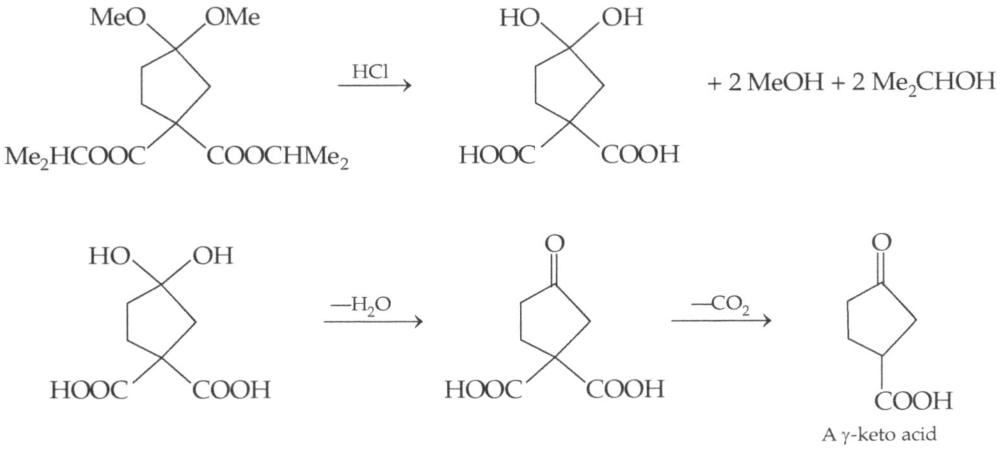

MeO, OMe / Me_2HCOOC, $COOCHMe_2$ $\xrightarrow{HCl}$ HO, OH / HOOC, COOH $+ 2\,MeOH + 2\,Me_2CHOH$

HO, OH / HOOC, COOH $\xrightarrow{-H_2O}$ O / HOOC, COOH $\xrightarrow{-CO_2}$ O / COOH

A γ-keto acid

Example 6 :

A sulphuric acid solution of each of the compounds namely tert -pentyl alcohol, neopentyl alcohol and 2-methyl-2-butene when treated with carbon monoxide gives 2, 2-dimethylbutanoic acid. Explain with mechanism.

Solution :

Each of the three compound gives *tert*-pentyl cation in presence of sulphuric acid.

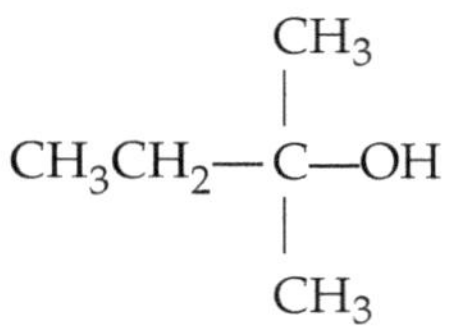

$$CH_3CH_2-\underset{CH_3}{\overset{CH_3}{\underset{|}{\overset{|}{C}}}}-OH$$

tert-Pentyl alcohol

$$\downarrow H^+, (-H_2O)$$

$$CH_3CH = \underset{}{\overset{CH_3}{\overset{|}{C}}} - CH_3 \xrightarrow{H^+} CH_3CH_2 - \overset{CH_3}{\overset{|}{\underset{CH_3}{\underset{|}{C^{\oplus}}}}} \xrightarrow[H_2O]{CO} CH_3CH_2 - \overset{CH_3}{\overset{|}{\underset{CH_3}{\underset{|}{C}}}} - COOH$$

2-Methyl-2-butene — *tert*-Pentyl cation — 2, 2-Dimethylbutanoic acid

↑ rearrangement

$$CH_3 - \overset{CH_3}{\overset{|}{\underset{CH_3}{\underset{|}{C}}}} - CH_2OH \longrightarrow CH_3 - \overset{CH_3}{\overset{|}{\underset{CH_3}{\underset{|}{C}}}} - \overset{\oplus}{C}H_2$$

Neopentyl alcohol — 1° Carbocation

Mechanism of conversion of R⁺ to RCOOH by means of CO

$$R^+ + :\overset{-}{C} \equiv \overset{+}{O}: \longrightarrow R - C \equiv \overset{+}{O}: \xrightarrow[-H^+]{H_2O} R - \underset{OH}{\underset{|}{C}} = O$$

Acylium ion (every atom has octet) — Carboxylic acid

Example 7 :

Outline a typical method for resolving *rac*-(R,S)—RCOOH.

Solution :

Racemic mixture of carboxylic acids are best separated by using optically active (R)- or (S)- naturally occurring base like quinine.

$$\text{(R, S)-RCOOH + (R)-base} \longrightarrow \underset{\substack{[A] \\ \text{Insoluble}}}{[\text{(R)-RCOO}^- \text{(R)-base H}^+]} + \underset{\substack{[B] \\ \text{Diastereomeric salts}}}{[\text{(S)-RCOO}^- \text{(R)-base H}^+]}$$

Due to difference in solubilities, [A] and [B] are separated by fractional crystallization and then hydrolysed to give back the corresponding acid and the (R)-base.

$$A \xrightarrow{HX} \text{(R)-RCOOH + (R)-base H}^+ X^- \qquad B \xrightarrow{HX} \text{(S)-RCOOH + (R)-base H}^+ X^-$$

Example 8 :

Write down the structures of the various isomers of the formula $C_4H_4O_4$, corresponding to following reaction.

(a) A dibasic acid which on heating gives propenoic acid.

(b) An unsaturated dibasic acid which gives a meso compound on reaction with alkaline $KMnO_4$.

(c) An unsaturated dibasic acid which gives a racemic mixture on reaction with alkaline $KMnO_4$.

(d) A cyclic ester that on hydrolysis gives glycol and oxalic acid.

Solution :

Write down the structure of the product and proceed backward keeping in mind the type of reaction that can give the desired product.

(*a*) $CH_2 = CHCOOH \xleftarrow{-CO_2} CH_2 = C(COOH)_2$

(*b*) Recall that alk. $KMnO_4$ is a hydroxylating reagent and causes hydroxylation in *syn*- manner. Thus *meso* product is obtained from *cis*-isomer, while *rac*-from *trans*-.

(*b*)

```
    COOH
     |                          COOH
  H—C—OH                         |
     |          ←——           H—C
  H—C—OH                         ||
     |                        H—C
    COOH                         |
                                COOH
   meso-                  Maleic acid (cis)
```

(*c*)

```
    COOH           COOH
     |              |                        COOH
 HO—C—H         H—C—OH                        |
     |      +       |          ←——         H—C
  H—C—OH       OH—C—H                         ||
     |              |                          C—H
    COOH           COOH                       |
                                             COOH
             rac-                     Fumaric acid (trans)
```

(*d*) Glycol + Oxalic acid $\xleftarrow{\text{hydrolysis}}$ Glycol oxalate

Glycol   Oxalic acid   Glycol oxalate

Example 9 :

There are four isomeric hydrocarbons corresponding to molecular formula C_8H_{14}. On ozonolysis, different isomers give different products, assign the structure to each.

(a) Isomer A gives isobutyric acid.

(b) Isomer B gives α, α′- dimethyladipic acid.

(c) Isomer C gives β, β- dimethyladipic acid.

(d) Isomer D gives diketone giving iodoform test at both ends of the molecule.

Assign structure to A, B, C and D.

Solution :

Molecular formula C_8H_{14} suggests that the compounds have 2° of unsaturation ; which means they may contain (*i*) a triple bond, or (*ii*) two double bonds, or (*iii*) a double bond and a ring. Nature of unsaturation and structure of various isomers can be ascertained by their ozonolysis products :

(*a*) $(CH_3)_2CHCOOH \xleftarrow{\text{Ozonolysis}} (CH_3)_2CHC \equiv CCH(CH_3)_2$

Isobutyric acid   [A]

(*b*) α, α′-Dimethyladipic acid $\xleftarrow{\text{Ozonolysis}}$ [B] [1,4-dimethylcyclohexene]

(*c*) β, β-Dimethyladipic acid ⟵ [C] [4,4-dimethylcyclohexene]

(*d*) $CH_3-\overset{O}{\overset{||}{C}}\cdots\cdots\overset{O}{\overset{||}{C}}-CH_3$ or $CH_3\overset{O}{\overset{||}{C}}(CH_2)_4\overset{O}{\overset{||}{C}}CH_3$ ⟵ [D] [1,2-dimethylcyclohexene]

Example 10 :

Assign structure to each isomer of the formula $C_4H_8O_2$ corresponding to the following reaction.

(a) The isomer (A) that can be hydrolysed to form ethanoic acid and alcohol.

(b) The isomer (B) that can reduce Tollen's reagent due to —CHO group and also responds haloform test.

(c) The isomer (C) that can reduce Tollen's reagent but does not respond haloform best.

(d) The isomer (D) that gives haloform test due to —$COCH_3$ group and also reduces Tollen's reagent

(e) The isomer (E) that gives haloform test due to —$COCH_3$ group and also gives turbidity with Lucas reagent.

Solution :

(a) $CH_3COOH + C_2H_5OH \xleftarrow{\text{hydrolysis}} CH_3COOC_2H_5$ (A)

(b) Molecular formula $C_4H_8O_2$ indicates that all isomers, including (B) has 1° of unsaturation which is present in the form of —CHO group. Hence the positive haloform reaction must be due to CH_3CHOH– grouping (presence of CH_3CO— grouping is discarded due to fact that the compound has only 1° of unsaturation which is in the form of —CHO group). Thus the isomer B should be $CH_3CH(OH)CH_2CHO$.

(c) $HOCH_2CH_2CH_2CHO$ (C)

(d) Since the compound D has —$COCH_3$, it can't have —CHO group (note that 1° of unsaturation is present in $C_4H_8O_2$). Hence the positive reaction with Tollen's reagent is due to α-hydroxy ketone. Thus D should be as shown below.

(e) Since the compound gives turbidity with Lucas reagent, it must have 1° aloholic group.

$$CH_3-\overset{\overset{O}{||}}{C}-\overset{\overset{OH}{|}}{CH}-CH_3 \qquad CH_3-\overset{\overset{O}{||}}{C}-CH_2-CH_2OH$$

(D) (E)

Example 11 :

Sodium salt of a carboxylic acid on ignition gives a white residue. The residue is soluble in water, reacts with hydrochloric acid with the evolution of bubbles, and turns moist litmus blue. Give the probable chemical structure of the residue and explain its formation.

Solution :

The residue should be Na_2CO_3

$$2H-\overset{\overset{O}{||}}{C}-ONa \longrightarrow HCHO + Na_2CO_3$$

Example 12 :

A hydrocarbon of the molecular formula C_6H_{10} has two isomers ; X and Y. On oxidation X gives butanoic acid and ethanoic acid, while Y gives 1, 6-hexanedioic acid Assign structure to X and Y.

Solution :

Molecular formula C_6H_{10} indicates that it has two degree of unsaturation which may be in the form of a triple bond or one double bond and one ring. Proceed backward from the oxidation product(s) in each case.

$$n\text{-}C_3H_7COOH + CH_3COOH \xleftarrow{\text{oxidation}} n\text{-}C_3H_7C \equiv CCH_3$$

[X]

COOH
COOH ⟵

1, 6-Hexanedioic acid

Cyclohexene
[Y]

Example 13 :

(i) An alkyl halide A of the formula C_3H_5Br reacts with Mg in presence of ether of form Grignard reagent which, on reaction with dry ice followed by acidification, is converted into a carboxylic acid B.

(ii) Two molecules of B are also formed by the ozonolysis of a compound C, C_8H_{10}.

Assign structures to A, B and C. Is there any isomer of A, if yes give its structure and ozonolysis.

Solution :

Alkyl halide has one degree of unsaturation ; which may be in the form of ring or a double bond. So three possible structures for A are

$CH_2 = CHCH_2Br$, $CH_3CH = CHBr$ [Not possible]

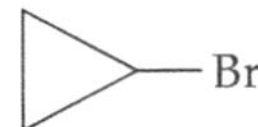

However, $CH_3CH = CHBr$, being vinylic halide does not form Grignard reagent under given conditions. So the two possible carboxylic acids (B) from the remaining alkyl halides will be $CH_2 = CHCH_2COOH$ and (cyclopropyl)—COOH.

Two molecules of B are formed from C (C_8H_{10}) by ozonolysis, so corresponding C should be either

$CH_2 = CHCH_2—C \equiv C—CH_2CH = CH_2$ or (cyclopropyl)—C ≡ C—(cyclopropyl)

↓ ozonolysis ↓ ozonolysis

$2CH_2O + 2OHCCH_2COOH$ 2 (cyclopropyl)—COOH

It is not [B] [B]

So, compounds A, B, C and isomer of A are

(cyclopropyl)—Br ; (cyclopropyl)—COOH ; (cyclopropyl)—C ≡ C—(cyclopropyl) ; $CH_2 = CHCH_2C \equiv C\,CH_2CH = CH_2$

[A] [B] [C] Isomer of [A]

Example 14 :

Give structures of the four optically acitve structural isomers A to D for $C_4H_8O_3$ that evolve CO_2 with aqueous $NaHCO_3$.

One of the isomers (say A) reacts with $LiAlH_4$ to give an achiral product. Assign the structure to A, B, C and D. Give chemical reactions to distinguish among B, C and D.

Solution :

(*i*) The molecular formula $C_4H_8O_3$ suggests that the isomers have 1° of unsaturation that must be due to —COOH, indicated by their reaction with aq. $NaHCO_3$. Hence the third oxygen may be present either as —OH or —OR.

(*ii*) Since A on reduction with $LiAlH_4$ (—COOH ⟶ —CH_2OH) gives an achiral product, a —CH_2OH group should already be is present in A . Hence the structure of A is

$$\underset{\text{[A], Chiral}}{H-\overset{\overset{CH_3}{|}}{\underset{\underset{CH_2OH}{|}}{C}}-COOH} \xrightarrow{LiAlH_4} \underset{\text{Achiral}}{H-\overset{\overset{CH_3}{|}}{\underset{\underset{CH_2OH}{|}}{C}}-CH_2OH}$$

Thus the three other isomers may be written as below.

$$\underset{[B]}{CH_3\underset{\underset{OH}{|}}{CH}CH_2COOH} \qquad \underset{[C]}{CH_3CH_2\underset{\underset{OH}{|}}{CH}COOH} \qquad \underset{[D]}{CH_3\underset{\underset{OCH_3}{|}}{CH}COOH}$$

Differentiation between B, C and D. B and C are oxidisable by $KMnO_4$ or CrO_3, while D (an ether) is inert. Further, B gives a positive haloform test, while C does not respond to it.

Example 15 :

Two isomeric carboxylic acids (A and B) of the formula $C_9H_8O_2$, on oxidation, give benzoic acid. Acid A takes up one mole of hydrogen to form resolvable carboxylic acid, while acid B on similar treatment gives non-resolvable carboxylic acid. Assign structures to A and B and their corresponding hydrogenated products.

Solution :

The given statements indicate tht A and B have a C = C linkage and a phenyl group. Since the hydrogenated product from A is resolvable, it must have four different groups to the central carbon atom, two of which are —COOH and —C_6H_5. The remaining fragment (CH_4) can be present only as H and CH_3. Hence the complete structure of the resolvable product and its precursor, A can be drawn as below.

$$C_6H_5-\overset{\overset{CH_3}{|}}{\underset{\underset{H}{|}}{C}}-COOH \xleftarrow[Pd]{H_2} \underset{[A](C_9H_8O_2)}{C_6H_5-\overset{\overset{CH_2}{||}}{C}-COOH}$$

Thus the isomeric carboxylic acid B and its hydrogenated product (non-resolvable) should have following structure.

$$\underset{B\,(C_9H_8O_2)}{C_6H_5CH=CHCOOH} \xrightarrow{H_2/Pd} \underset{\text{Non-resolvable}}{C_6H_5CH_2CH_2COOH}$$

Example 16 :

Write the structural formula for a chiral hydrocarbon, $C_{11}H_{16}$, which on oxidaton affords terephthalic acid.

Solution :

Oxidaton of the hydrocarbon ($C_{11}H_{16}$) to terephthalic acid indicates that the hydrocarbon is 1, 4-dialkylsubstituted benzene.

$$R-C_6H_4-R \xrightarrow{\text{oxidation}} HOOC-C_6H_4-COOH$$

tere-Phthalic acid

Thus the two alkyl groups of the hydrocarbon should have five carbon atoms. The smallest alkyl group with a chiral carbon is *sec*-butyl, hence the other alkyl group should be methyl.

$$H_3C-C_6H_4-\overset{*}{C}H(CH_3)C_2H_5 \xrightarrow{\text{oxidation}} HOOC-C_6H_4-COOH$$

Example 17 :

Assign structure to the compound A, C_8H_9Br which responds following series of reactions.

$$[A] \xrightarrow[\text{(ii) } CO_2,\text{ (iii) } H_3O^+]{\text{(i) Mg, ether}} [B] \xrightarrow{KMnO_4,\, OH^-} \text{Phthalic acid}$$

Solution :

Reaction of compound A with Mg in ether followed by CO_2 points out the conversion of Br to MgBr which reacts with CO_2 to form —COOH.

$$C_8H_9-Br \xrightarrow{\text{Mg, ether}} -MgBr \xrightarrow[\text{(ii) } H_3O^+]{\text{(i) } CO_2} -COOH$$

Since the final product has two —COOH groups, the second must have been introduced through the oxidation of the side chain, which should be $-CH_2CH_3$. Hence A is *o*-bromoethylbenzene.

$$o\text{-}Br-C_6H_4-CH_2CH_3 \xrightarrow[\text{(ii) } CO_2,\ (ii) H_3O^+]{\text{(i) Mg, ether}} o\text{-}HOOC-C_6H_4-CH_2CH_3 \xrightarrow{KMnO_4,\, \overset{-}{O}H} o\text{-}HOOC-C_6H_4-COOH$$

Example 18 :

Give structure of a hydrocarbon ($C_{12}H_{20}$) which gives two diastereomeric aliphatic dicarboxylic acids on oxidation

Solution :

(*i*) Molecular formula of the hydrocarbon indicates that it has 3° of unsaturation ; two of which must be present in the form of double bonds (indicated by the formation of two dicarboxylic acids) ; the third degree of unsaturation should be present in the form of ring.

(*ii*) The two diastereomeric dicarboxylic acids must be meso and recemic which is possible for the following cyclo-octadiene derivative.

[Structure: cyclo-octadiene ring with CH₃/H substituents: CH₃, H (top left); CH₃, H (top right); H₃C, H (bottom left); H, CH₃ (bottom right)]

One half of the molecule with the *cis* Me's gives the *meso* diacid and the other half with the *trans* Me's gives the racemic diacid.

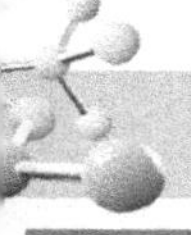

EXERCISE 17.1 (MCQ - ONE option correct)

1. The systematic name of $CH_2 = C(CH_3)$ COOH is
   (*a*) 2-methyl-2-propenoic acid
   (*b*) 2-methylpropenoic acid
   (*c*) both (*a*) and (*b*)
   (*d*) Methacrylic acid.

2. 

   Above reaction can be achieved satisfactorily by which set of reagents ?
   (*a*) NaCN, H^+, heat (*b*) Mg + ether, CO_2, H_3O^+
   (*c*) Both (*a*) and (*b*) (*d*) Oxidation.

3. Which method is expected to give good result for following reaction ?
   $HOCH_2CH_2CMe_2Cl \longrightarrow HOCH_2CH_2C(Me_2)COOH$
   (*a*) Grignard synthesis (*b*) Nitrile synthesis
   (*c*) Either of the two (*d*) None of the two.

4. 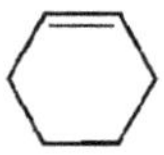 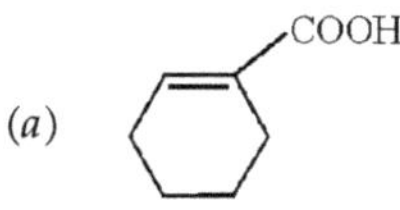 $\xrightarrow{NBS}$ [A] $\xrightarrow[(ii)\ CO_2,\ H_3^+O]{(i)\ Mg/ether}$ [B]. Here [B] is

   (*a*) COOH (*b*) COOH
   (*c*) Br, COOH (*d*) COOH

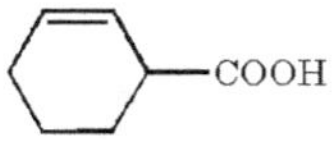

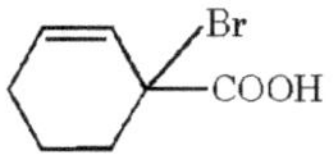

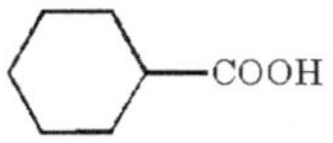

5. $CH_3CH_2CH_2CH_2OH \xrightarrow{CO,\ H_2SO_4}$ A ; $CH_3CH_2CH(OH)\ CH_3 \xrightarrow[H_2SO_4]{CO}$ B. Predict the nature of A and B.
   (*a*) A is $CH_3CH_2CH_2CH_2COOH$ and B is $CH_3CH_2CH(CH_3)COOH$
   (*b*) A and B both are $CH_3CH_2CH(CH_3)COOH$
   (*c*) A is $CH_3CH_2CH = CH_2$ and B is $CH_3CH = CHCH_3$
   (*d*) Reaction is not possible.

6. Sodium malonate having one labelled oxygen is decarboxylated to form monocarboxylic acid. Predict the final products.

   $$HOOC—CH_2—COO^{18}H \xrightarrow{1.NaOH} HOOC—CH_2—C\overset{18}{O}O^-\ Na^+ \xrightarrow{heat}$$

   (*a*) $CH_3COOH + O = C = O^{18}$
   (*b*) $CH_3COOH + O^{18} = C = O^{18}$
   (*c*) $CH_3COO^{18}H + O = C = O^{18}$
   (*d*) $CH_3COO^{18}H + O = C = O$

7. Which of the following is most difficult to decarboxylate ?
   (*a*) 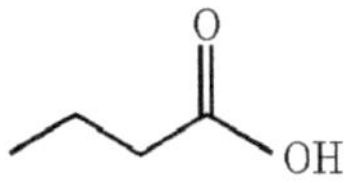 O, OH (*b*) O, O, OH
   (*c*) O, OH (*d*) HO, OH, O, O

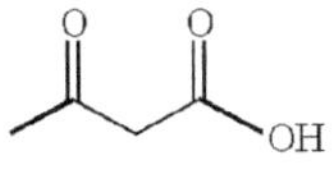

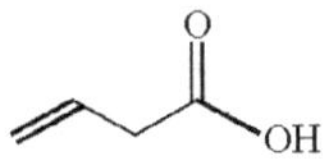

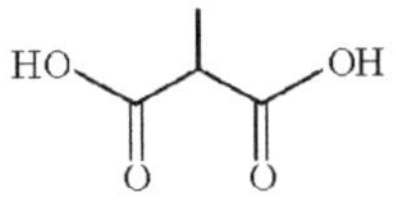

8. Which of the following carboxylic acids is decarboxylated easily?
   (*a*) 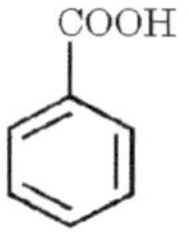 COOH (*b*) CH_2COOH
   (*c*) COOH, O_2N, NO_2, NO_2 (*d*) n-C_4H_9COOH.

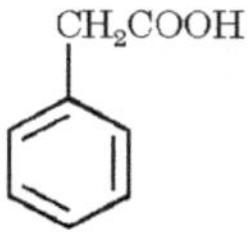

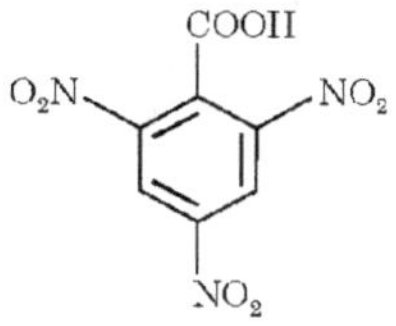

9. 0.187 g of an acid required 18.7 mL of 0.0972 M NaOH for neutralisation. The acid should be
   (*a*) methoxyacetic acid
   (*b*) ethoxyacetic acid
   (*c*) caproic acid, $C_5H_{11}COOH$
   (*d*) datas are insufficient.

10. Which type of halogen containing compound could react with OH^- to give a carboxylic acid ?
    (*a*) $RCH_2\ X$ (*b*) $RCHX_2$
    (*c*) RCX_3 (*d*) None.

11. Identify the nature of reducing agent in the following reaction.
    $BrCH_2CH_2COOH \xrightarrow{?} Br\ CH_2CH_2CH_2OH$
    (*a*) $LiAlH_4$ (*b*) BH_3/THF followed by H_3O^+
    (*c*) Both (*d*) None.

12. Identify the respective final products in the following two reactions.
    (*i*) $CH_3CH_2COOH \xrightarrow{Br_2/PCl_3} [A] \xrightarrow{Br_2} [B] \xrightarrow{H_2O} [C]$
    (*ii*) $CH_3CH_2COOH \xrightarrow{Cl_2/PBr_3} [D] \xrightarrow{Cl_2} [E] \xrightarrow{H_2O} [F]$
    (*a*) $CH_3CHOHCOOH$ and $CH_3CHOHCOOH$
    (*b*) $CH_3CHOHCOCl$ and $CH_3CHOHCOBr$
    (*c*) $CH_3CHBrCOOH$ and $CH_3CHClCOOH$
    (*d*) $CH_3CHClCOOH$ and $CH_3CHBrCOOH$.

13. Both propanoic acid, CH_3CH_2COOH as well as 2-chloropropanoic acid give precipitate with aq. $AgNO_3$. How you distinguish the precepitates in the two ?
    (*a*) By aq. NH_4OH (*b*) By aq. HNO_3
    (*c*) By either of the two (*d*) By none of the two.

14. Identify the product A
    $HC \equiv CH \xrightarrow[(ii)\ 2CO_2]{(i)\ 2Na}$ [Intermediate] $\xrightarrow{Na/C_2H_5OH}$ [A]
    (*a*) Maleic acid (*b*) Fumaric acid
    (*c*) Both (*a*) and (*b*) (*d*) Succinic acid.

15. 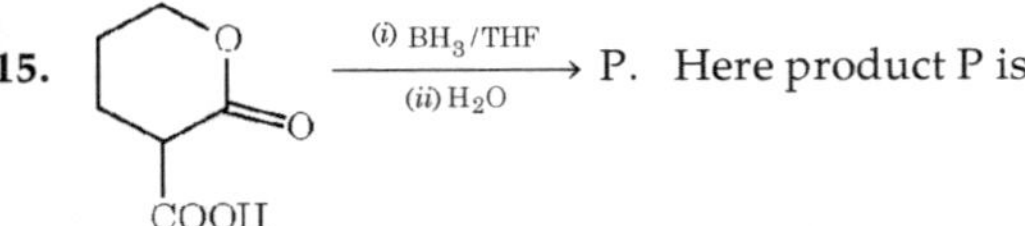 P. Here product P is

(a) (b) (c) 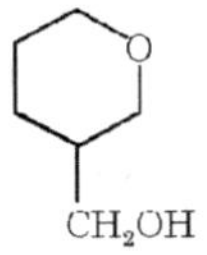 (d)

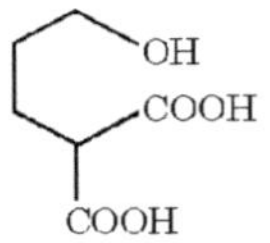

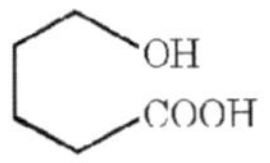

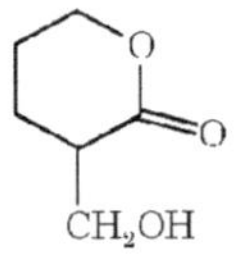

16. Predict the nature of P

$$CH_3CH_2CH_2CH_2OH + CO \xrightarrow{H_2SO_4} P$$

(a) $CH_3CH_2CH = CH_2$
(b) $CH_3CH = CHCH_3$
(c) $CH_3CH_2CH_2CH_2COOH$
(d) $CH_3CH_2CH(CH_3)COOH$.

17. On vigorous oxidation by permanganate solution, 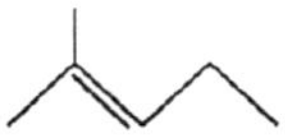 gives

(a) (b)  (c)  (d)

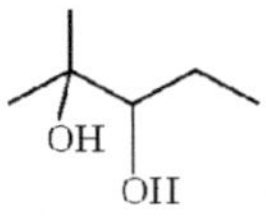

18. Identify the correct order of boiling points of the following compounds.

$CH_3CH_2CH_2CH_2OH$ **(1)** ; $CH_3CH_2CH_2CHO$ **(2)** ;
$CH_3CH_2CH_2COOH$ **(3)**

(a) 1 > 2 > 3 (b) 3 > 1 > 2
(c) 1 > 3 > 2 (d) 3 > 2 > 1.

19. Which of the following acids has smallest dissociation constant?

(a) $CH_3CHFCOOH$ (b) FCH_2CH_2COOH
(c) $BrCH_2CH_2COOH$ (d) $CH_3CHBrCOOH$.

20. Dimerisation of carboxylic acids is due to

(a) ionic bond
(b) covalent bond
(c) coordinate bond
(d) intermolecular hydrogen bond.

21. When propionic acid is treated with aqueous sodium bicarbonate, CO_2 is liberated. The carbon of CO_2 comes from

(a) methyl group (b) carboxyl group
(c) methylene group (d) bicarbonate.

22. 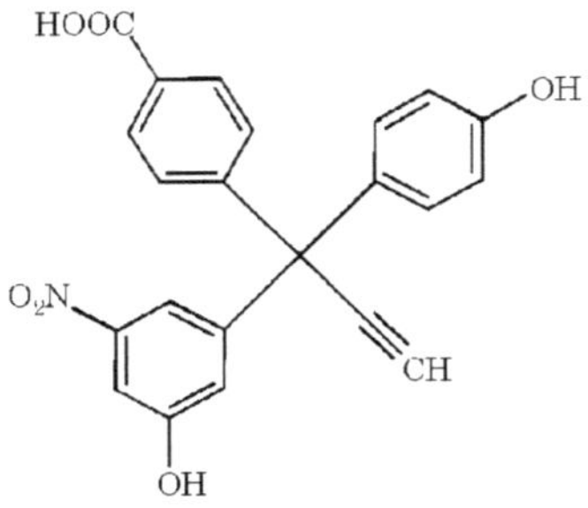 $\xrightarrow{\text{2 moles } NaNH_2}$ A

The product A will be

(a) (b) 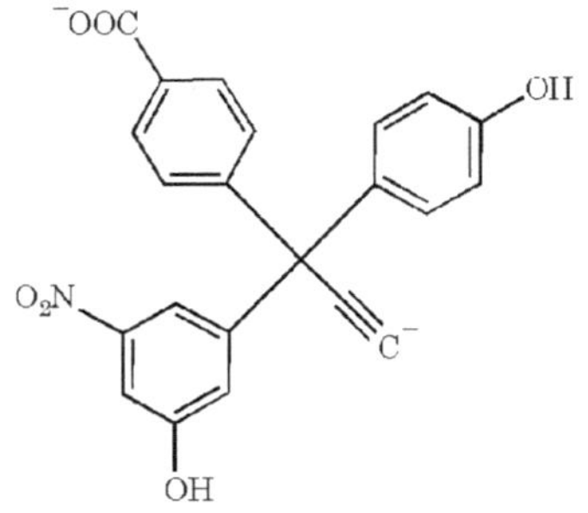 (c) 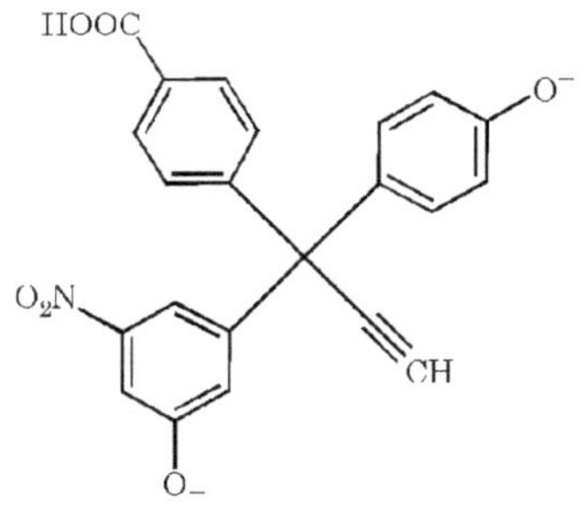 (d)

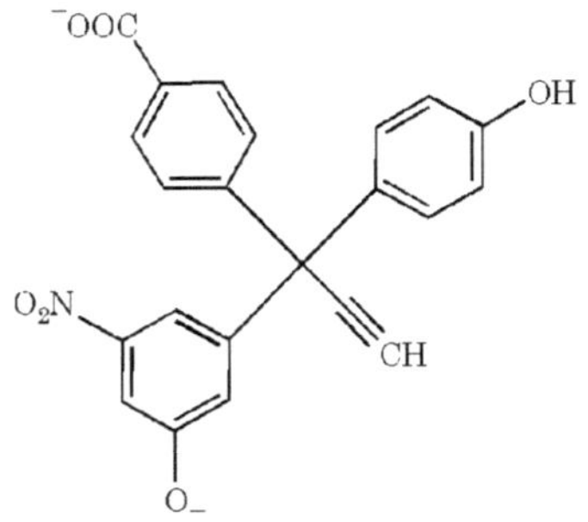

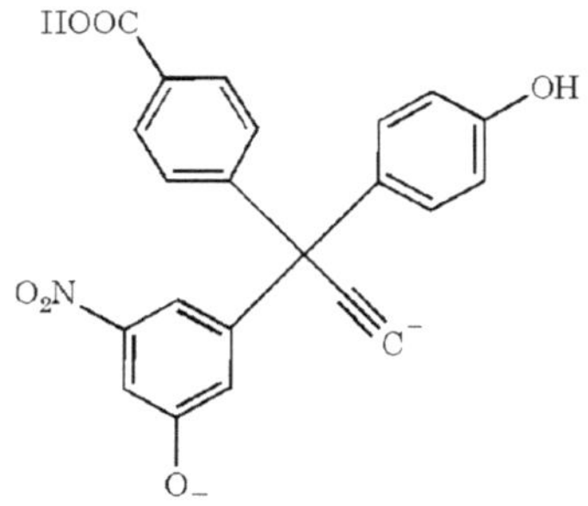

23. Two moles of acetic acid are heated with P_2O_5. The product formed is
(*a*) 2 moles of ethyl alcohol
(*b*) formic anhydride
(*c*) ethanoic anhydride
(*d*) 2 moles of methyl cyanide.

24. $CH_3CH_2COOH \xrightarrow{Cl_2, \text{red P}} A \xrightarrow{\text{alc. KOH}} B$; B is
(*a*) CH_3CH_2COCl (*b*) CH_3CH_2CHO
(*c*) $CH_2 = CHCOOH$ (*d*) $ClCH_2CH_2COOH$.

25. Lactic acid, $CH_3CHOHCOOH$, on oxidation by alkaline $KMnO_4$ gives.
(*a*) tartaric acid (*b*) pyruvic acid
(*c*) cinnamic acid (*d*) propionic acid.

26. An enantiomerically pure acid is treated with racemic mixture of an alcohol having one chiral carbon. The ester formed will be
(*a*) optically active mixture
(*b*) pure enantiomer
(*c*) meso compound
(*d*) racemic mixture.

27. Arrange the following alcohols in increasing order of acid-catalyzed esterification by ethanol.

HO (A) ; OH (B) ; OH (C)

(*a*) A < B < C (*b*) C < B < A
(*c*) B < C < A (*d*) C < A < B.

28. Identify the final porduct, P.

$CH_3CH_2MgBr + \overset{O}{CH_2 - CH_2} \xrightarrow{H^+} [\text{Intermediate}] \xrightarrow{KMnO_4} P$

(*a*) CH_3CH_2CHO (*b*) $CH_3CH_2CH_2CHO$
(*c*) CH_3CH_2COOH (*d*) $CH_3CH_2CH_2COOH$.

29. $HC \equiv CH \xrightarrow[(ii)\ CH_3I]{(i)\ 2NaNH_2} [X] \xrightarrow{H_2SO_4/Hg^{2+}} [Y] \xrightarrow{OH^-/Br_2} [Z]$

Here Z is
(*a*) CH_3CH_2COOH (*b*) $CH_3CHBrCOOH$
(*c*) CH_3COOH (*d*) $CH_2BrCOOH$.

30. Which of the following reactions yields acetic acid as the final product ?

(*i*) $CH_3CCl_3 \xrightarrow{OH^-}$

(*ii*) $CH_3COOC_2H_5 \xrightarrow{OH^-}$

(*iii*) $CH_3CHO \xrightarrow[(ii)\ H^+]{(i)\ \text{Tollen's regent}}$

(*a*) Only (*i*) (*b*) Only (*ii*)
(*c*) Only (*iii*) (*d*) All the three.

31. Identify the main product in the following reaction.

$$CH_2\,(COOH)_2 \xrightarrow{P_2O_5,\ \text{heat}} X$$

(*a*) CH_3COOH (*b*) $CO_2 + H_2O$
(*c*) C_3O_2 (*d*) COOH.COOH.

32. Identify the product Z in the following series of reactions.

$\begin{matrix} CH_2COOH \\ | \\ CH_2COOH \end{matrix} \xrightarrow{P/Br_2} X \xrightarrow{\text{alc. KOH}} Y \xrightarrow{CF_3COOH} Z$

(*a*) Maleic anhydride (*b*) Maleic acid
(*c*) *meso*-Tartaric acid (*d*) *rac*-Tartaric acid.

33. Which of the following acids has the least pK_a value ?
(*a*) CH_3COOH (*b*) C_6H_5COOH
(*c*) $CH_2 = CHOOH$ (*d*) All have same pK_a

34. Arrange the following in increasing order of their pK_a values.
CH_3COOH (**1**) ; Me_3CCH_2COOH (**2**) ; $Me_3N^+ CH_2COOH$ (**3**)
(*a*) 1 < 2 < 3 (*b*) 2 < 1 < 3
(*c*) 3 < 2 < 1 (*d*) 3 < 1 < 2.

35. Acetic acid reacts with ketene to form
(*a*) ethyl acetate (*b*) propanoic acid
(*c*) acetic anhydride (*d*) methyl acetate

36. Predict the structure of the product in the following reaction.

O COOH $\xrightarrow[(ii)\ H_3O^+]{(i)\ NaBH_4}$

(*a*) OH COOH (*b*) OH CH_2OH

(*c*) O O (*d*) O O

37. Identify Z in the reaction OH O $\xrightarrow[CCl_4]{Br_2}$ Z

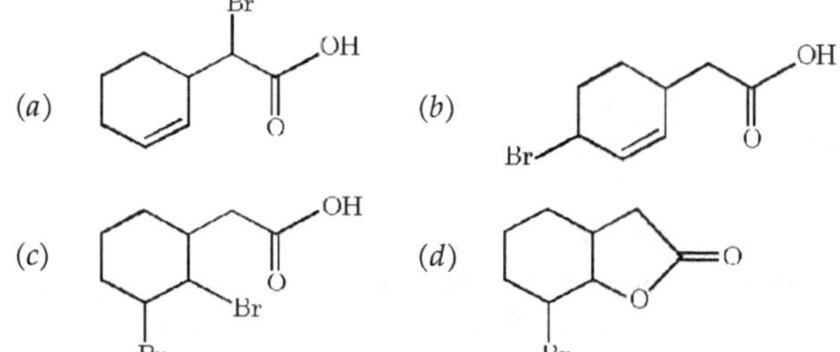

38. The possible structure for Z in the following reaction is

O $\xrightarrow[(ii)\ H_2O_2,\ OH^-]{(i)\ BH_3/THF}$ [X] $\xrightarrow[H^+]{Cl_2/NaOH}$ [Y] $\xrightarrow{\text{heat}}$ [Z]

(*a*) O COOH (*b*) O CHO

(*c*) O (*d*) COOH COOH

39. Which of the following set of reactants does not form phthalic acid on oxidation ?

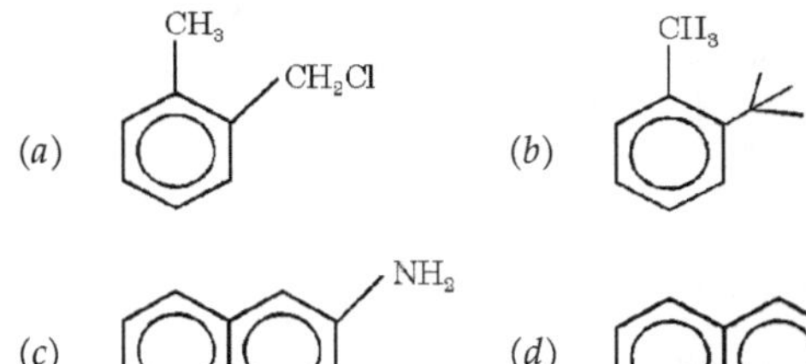

40. Which of the following has minimum pK_a value ?

(a) FCH_2COOH (b) Cl_3CCOOH

(c) 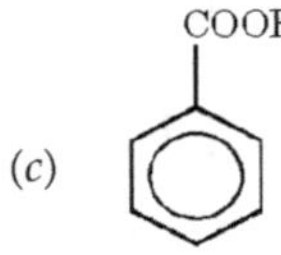

(d) OH, O_2N, NO_2, NO_2 (2,4,6-trinitrophenol)

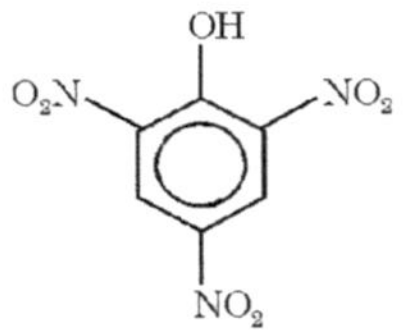

41. The correct decreasing order of pK_a values of the o-, m-, and p-nitrobenzoic acids is

(a) $o > m > p$ (b) $m > p > o$

(c) $p > m > o$ (d) $o > p > m$

42. The correct order of decreasing acidity of the three acids is

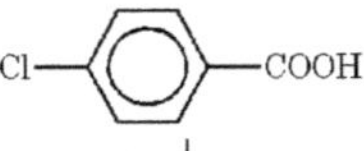

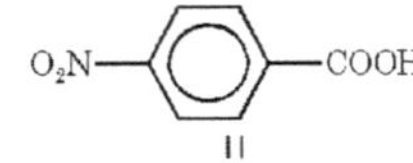

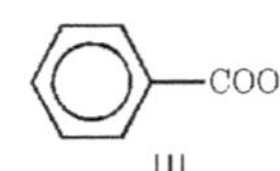

(a) III > II > I (b) II > I > III

(c) II > III > I (d) I > II > III

43. Which of the following carboxylic acids undergoes decarboxylation easily ?

(a) $C_6H_5CHOHCOOH$ (b) $C_6H_5COCOOH$

(c) $C_6H_5COCH_2COOH$ (d) $C_6H_5COCH_2CH_2COOH$

44. Predict the nature of P in the following reaction.

$$C_6H_5COCH(CH_3)COOH \xrightarrow{\text{heat}} P$$

(a) $C_6H_5COCH_3$ (b) $C_6H_5COCH_2CH_3$

(c) C_6H_5COOH (d) No action

45. 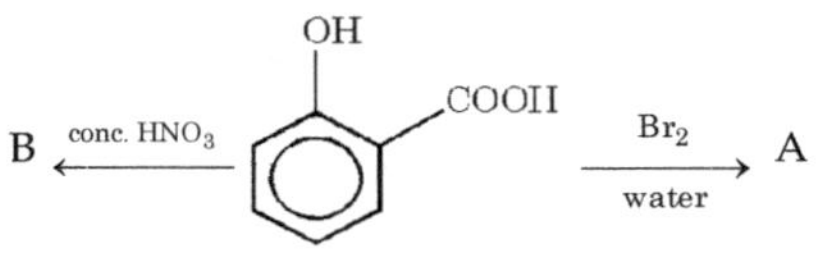 B $\xleftarrow{\text{conc. HNO}_3}$ (salicylic acid: OH, COOH) $\xrightarrow[\text{water}]{Br_2}$ A

Here A and B are ... and ... respectively

(a) o-bromophenol, o-nitrophenol

(b) 3-bromosalicylic acid, 3-nitrosalicylic acid

(c) 2, 4, 6-tribromophenol, picric acid

(d) 4-bromosalicylic acid, 4-nitrosalicylic acid

46. 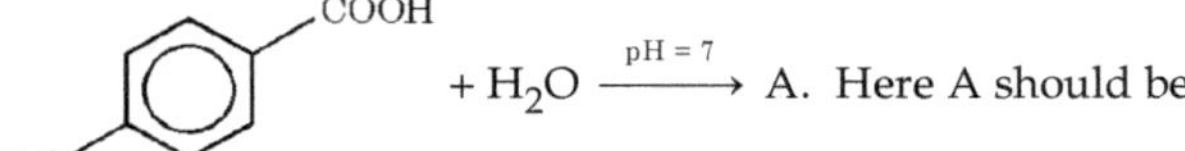

(a) HO–C_6H_4–COOH

(b) HO–C_6H_4–COO^-

(c) ^-O–C_6H_4–COO^-

(d) $H_2\overset{\oplus}{O}$–C_6H_4–COOH

47. (o-bromotoluene: CH_3, Br) $\xrightarrow[\text{(iii) KMnO}_4,\ OH^-,\ \text{(iv) H}^+]{\text{(i) Mg, THF, (ii) H}_2O}$ X. Here X is

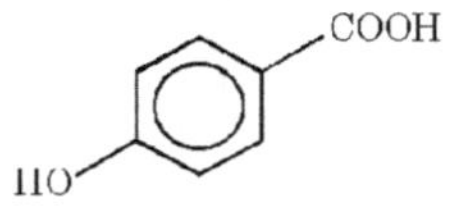

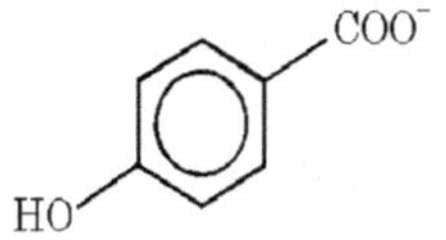

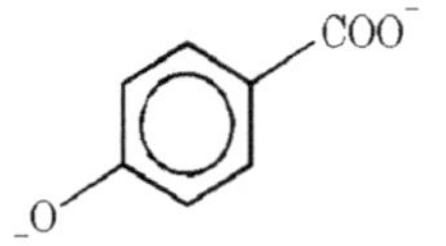

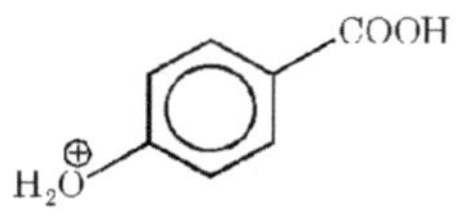

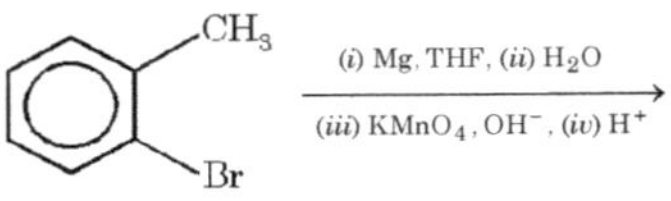

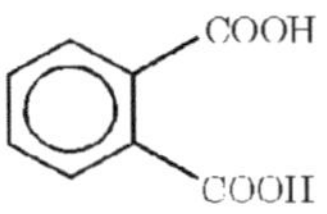

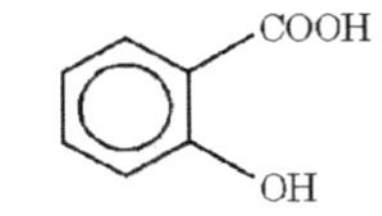

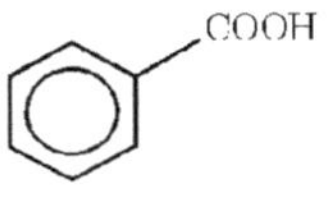

(a) (phthalic acid: COOH, COOH) (b) (COOH, OH)

(c) (COOH) (d) (benzene)

48. Predict the nature of the final product Z in the following series of reactions.

$$C_6H_5COOH \xrightarrow{PCl_5} [X] \xrightarrow[AlCl_3]{C_6H_6} [Y] \xrightarrow{C_6H_5CO_3H} [Z]$$

(a) $C_6H_5COOC_2H_5$ (b) C_6H_5COOH

(c) $C_6H_5COOC_6H_5$ (d) C_6H_5OH

49. Pick up the major product in the following reaction.

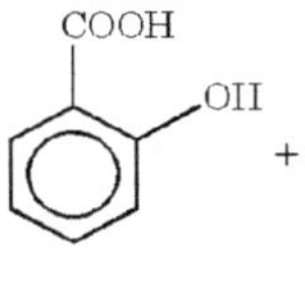

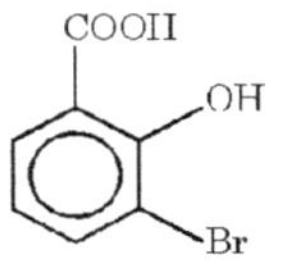

(COOH, OH) + Br_2 (in CH_3COOH) $\longrightarrow$

(a) (COOH, OH, Br) (b) 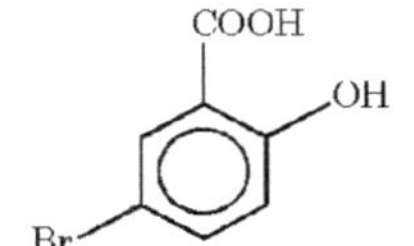

(c) both (a) and (b) (d) (COOH, OH, Br, Br)

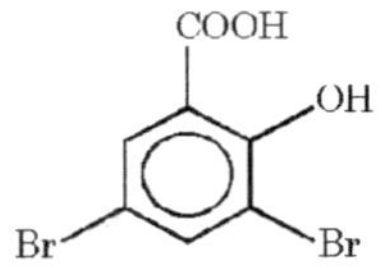

50. The organic product(s) formed in the reaction

$$C_6H_5COOH \xrightarrow[\text{II } H_2O^+]{\text{I } LiAlH_4}$$

(a) $C_6H_5CH_2OH$ (b) C_6H_5COOH

(c) $C_6H_5CH_3$ (d) CH_4

51. Which of the following gives effervescences of CO_2 with $NaHCO_3$ solution ?

(a) HCOOH (b) 2, 4, 6-Trinitrophenol

(c) Both (d) None

52. H. V. Z reaction involves the use of P and Cl_2

$$CH_3CH_2COOH \xrightarrow{P,\ Cl_2} CH_3CHClCOOH$$

The function of phosphorus is

(a) as a catalyst.

(b) in the formation of PCl_3 which carries out halogenation at the α-carbon atom.

(c) in the formation of PCl_3 which converts –COOH into –COCl.

(d) none of the three.

53. What is the main product when 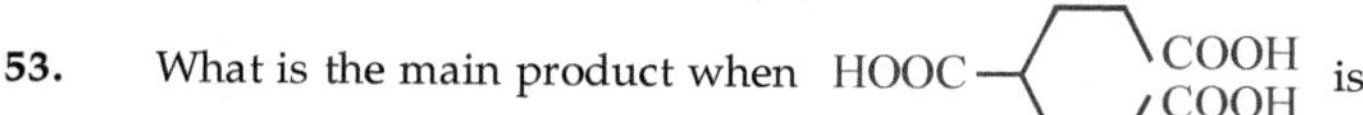 is heated ?

(a)  COOH COOH (b) 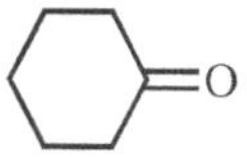 =O

(c) 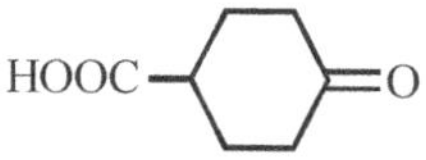 HOOC— =O (d) 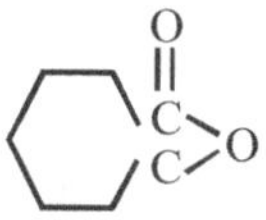 O C C O

54. The correct order of decarboxylation of the three acids is

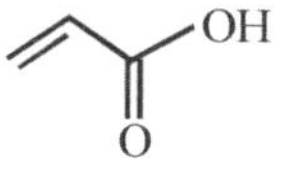

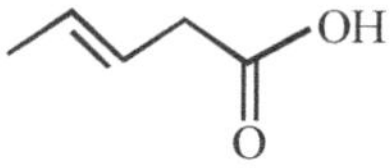

OH O I; OH O II; O O OH III

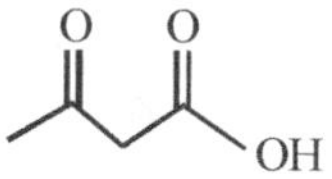

(a) III > II > I (b) III = II > I
(c) III > II = I (d) III = II = I

55. Which statement is true regarding oxidation of the following two compounds

(a) Both are oxidisable to benzoic acid under similar conditions
(b) It is very difficult to oxidise either of the two
(c) Compound I is oxidisable to benzoic acid easily while compound II is oxidisable only under vigorous conditions to benzoic acid
(d) Compound I is oxidisable to benzoic acid, while II is oxidisable only under vigorous conditions to 2, 2-dimethylpropanoic acid.

56. Predict the nature of end product in the following reaction.

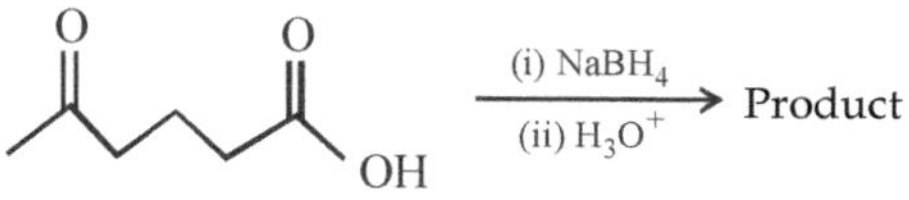

O O OH $\xrightarrow[\text{(ii) } H_3O^+]{\text{(i) } NaBH_4}$ Product

(a) 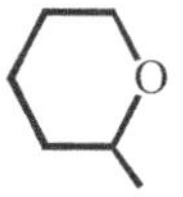 O (b) 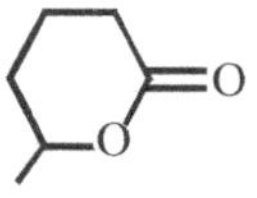 =O O

(c) 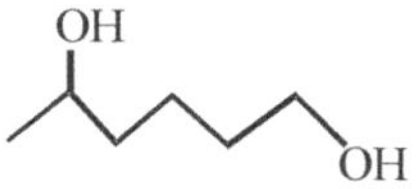 OH OH (d) 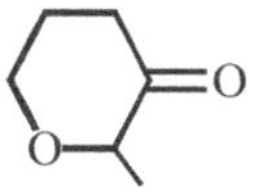 =O O

57. The correct order for the acidic character of the following carboxylic acids is

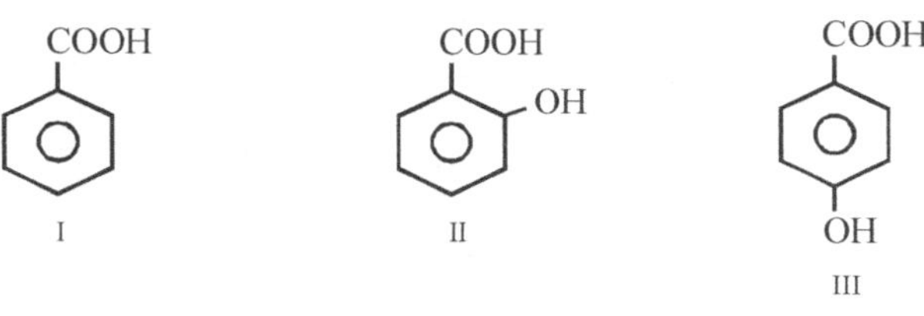

COOH OCH$_3$ IV; COOH HO OH V

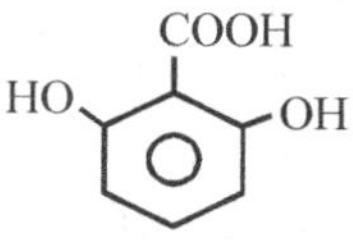

(a) IV > I > II > III > V (b) V > II > III > I > IV
(c) V > II > IV > III > I (d) V > II > IV > I > III

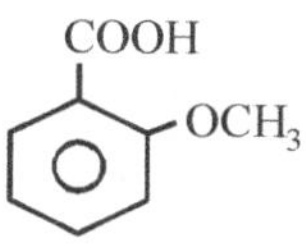

58. Salicylic acid is treated with bromine under two different conditions.

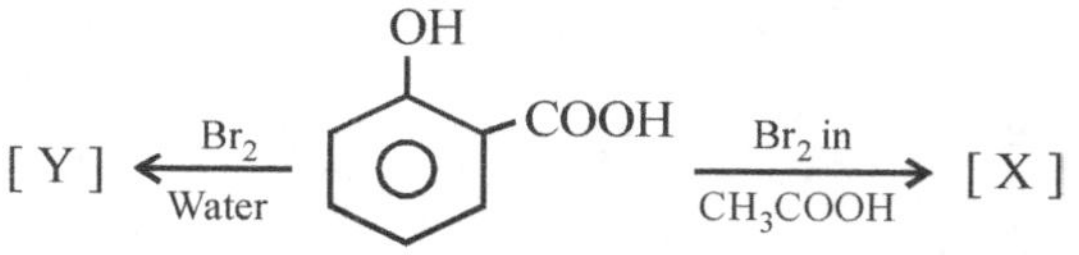

[Y] $\xleftarrow[\text{Water}]{Br_2}$ (OH, COOH) $\xrightarrow[CH_3COOH]{Br_2 \text{ in}}$ [X]

Predict the nature of [X] and [Y] in the above reactions

(a) 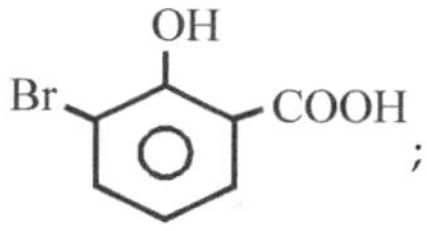 [X]: OH, Br, COOH ; [Y]: OH, COOH, Br

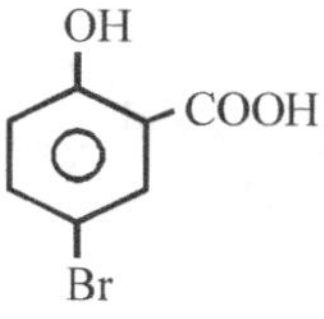

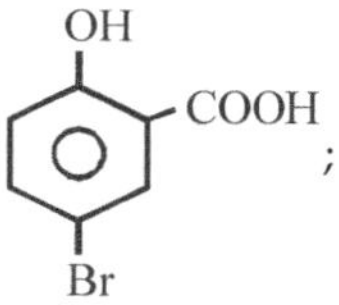

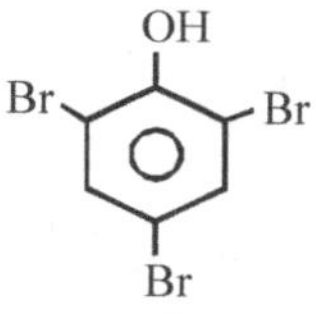

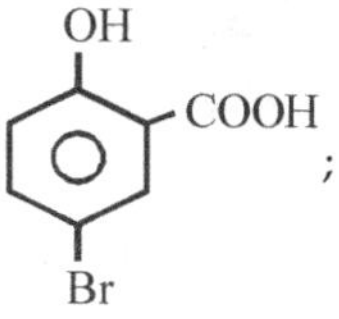

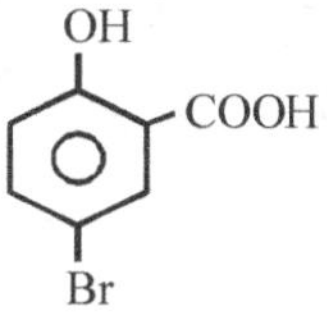

(b) [X]: OH, COOH, Br ; [Y]: OH, Br, Br, Br

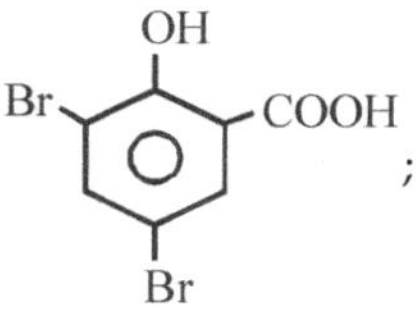

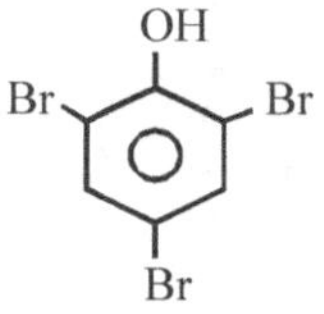

(c) [X]: OH, COOH, Br ; [Y]: OH, COOH, Br

(d) [X]: OH, Br, COOH, Br ; [Y]: OH, Br, Br, Br

59. Choose the correct statement regarding acidic character of acetic acid, CH_3COOH and peroxyacetic acid, CH_3COOOH.

(a) Peroxyacetic acid is stronger acid than acetic acid since the former has one extra oxygen, an electronegative element
(b) Peroxyacetic acid is stronger than acetic acid because its conjugate base is a weaker base than acetate
(c) Peroxyacetic acid is weaker than acetic acid because its conjugate base is less stable than that of acetate ion.
(d) Both are equally strong

60. β-Keto acids on heating easily undergo decarboxylation because
(a) it is a very storng acid
(b) it is a very weak acid
(c) its carboxylate ion is highly stable.
(d) it involves the formation of a cyclic six-membered transition state.

61. The products X and Y are respectively

$$Y \xleftarrow[\text{heat}]{NaBH_4,\ H_3O^+} CH_3COCH_2CH_2COOH \xrightarrow[\text{heat}]{LAH,\ H_3O^+} X$$

(a) [lactone with =O] and [lactone with =O]
(b) [cyclic ether] and [cyclic ether]
(c) [lactone with =O] and [cyclic ether]
(d) [cyclic ether] and [lactone with =O]

62. $C_6H_5CHO + CH_2(CN)_2 \xrightarrow[\text{(ii) } H_3O^+ \text{ (iii) heat}]{\text{(i) Pyridine}}$ Z, Z is
(a) C_6H_5–CH=CH COOH
(b) C_6H_5–CH(OH)–CH_2–COOH
(c) C_6H_4(CHO)(CH_2COOH) (ortho)
(d) C_6H_4(CHO)(CH_2 COOH) (para)

63. Which of the following is least acidic in nature ?
(a) CH_3COOH (b) $CH_2(COOH)_2$
(c) CH_3CH_2COOH
(d) $Me_3N^+CH_2CH_2CH_2COOH$

64. Arrange the following four acids in their decreasing order of acidity

I: C_6H_5COOH; II: o-$CH_3C_6H_4COOH$; III: o-$CMe_3C_6H_4COOH$; IV: 2,6-$(CH_3)_2C_6H_3COOH$

(a) I > II > III > IV (b) IV > III > II > I
(c) II > IV > III > I (d) III > IV > II > I

65. Which of the following is the correct order of decarboxylation of β-keto carboxylate anion ?

I: $RCOCH(F)COO^-$; II: $RCOCH(NO_2)COO^-$; III: $RCOCH(CN)COO^-$; IV: $RCOCH(Cl)COO^-$

(a) I > II > III > IV (b) II > I > III > IV
(c) II > III > IV > I (d) I > IV > II > III

66. 2-Acetylcyclohexanone $\xrightarrow[\text{(ii) } H^+ \text{ (iii) heat}]{\text{(i) NaIO}}$ P. The product P should be

(a) 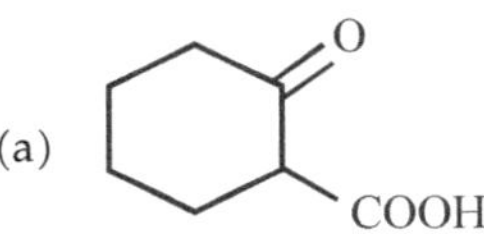 (b) 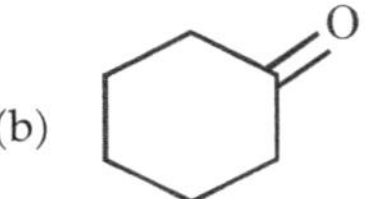
(c) HOOC–$(CH_2)_4$–COOH (d) A mixture of (a), (b) and (c)

67. Among the following compounds, the most acidic is
(a) p-nitrophenol (b) p-hydroxybenzoic acid
(c) o-hydroxybenzoic acid (d) p-toluic acid

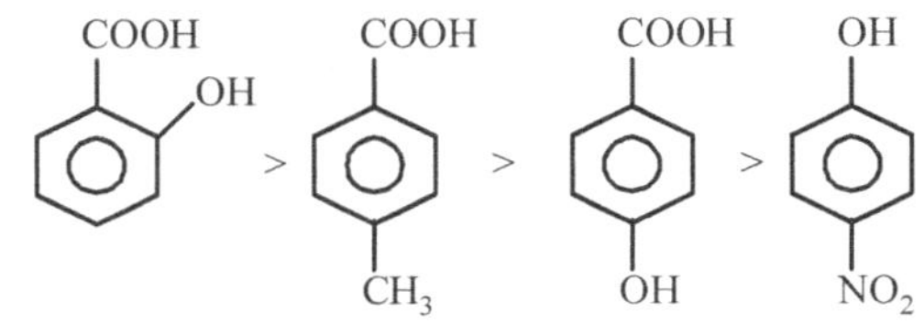

EXERCISE 17.2 (MCQ 1 or >1 option correct, Passage based, Matching, A/R)

DIRECTIONS for Q. 1 to Q. 22 : Multiple choice questions with one or more than one correct option(s).

1. $C_6H_5-\overset{O}{\overset{||}{C}}-OH + H_2O^{18} \xrightarrow{H^+}$ Product

Here the product may be

(*a*) $C_6H_5CO^{18}OH$ (*b*) $C_6H_5COO^{18}H$

(*c*) $C_6H_5COOO^{18}H$ (*d*) $C_6H_5C^{18}OOOH$.

2. RCOOH can be reduced to RCH_2OH by

(*a*) $NaBH_4$ (*b*) $LiAlH_4$

(*c*) Na/C_2H_5OH (*d*) H_2/Catalyst

3. Which of the following statement is true for the following reaction ?

$$RCOOH + LiAlH_4 \longrightarrow RCH_2OH$$

(*a*) The first step of the reaction is the formation of AlH_3 and H_2.

(*b*) A hydride ion is transferred from AlH_3 to the carboxylate carbon.

(*c*) An aldehyde is formed as an intermediate.

(*d*) Aldehyde is not the intermediate in this reaction

4. Which of the following statement is not true ?

(*a*) Maleic acid and fumaric acid are similar in their acidic strength, same is true for their corresponding monoanions.

(*b*) Maleic acid is a stronger acid than fumaric acid, similarly maleate monoanion is a stronger acid than fumarate monoanion.

(*c*) Maleic acid is a stronger acid than fumaric acid, but maleate monoanion is a weaker acid than fumarate monoanion.

(*d*) Maleic acid is a stronger acid than fumaric acid, but the corresponding monoanions have similar acidic strength.

5. Which of the following compound can be methylated by diazomethane ?

(a) C_2H_5COOH (b) $C_2H_5NH_2$

(c) C_6H_5OH (d) $CH_3COCH_2COOC_2H_5$

6. Which of the following compound is decarboxylated on heating ?

(a) $\begin{matrix} CH_2COOH \\ | \\ CH_2COOH \end{matrix}$ (b) $C_2H_5CH(COOH)_2$

(c) CH_3COCH_2COOH (d) 2-oxocyclohexane with COOH (O on ring carbon, COOH on adjacent carbon)

7. Anthranilic acid can exist in the form of following structures?

I: benzene ring with COO^- and NH_3^+ (ortho) II: benzene ring with COO^- and NH_2 (ortho) III: benzene ring with COOH and $NH_3^{\oplus}$ (ortho)

Which of the following statement is not correct regarding anthranilic acid structure ?

(*a*) Structure I exists in neutral solution (pH = 7), structure II in acidic solution (pH < 7) and structure III exists in alkaline solution (pH > 7).

(*b*) Structure II exists when pH > 7 and structure III exists when pH < 7.

(*c*) Structures I and II exist when pH > 7 and structures I and III exist when pH < 7.

(*d*) All the thre structures exist in all the three mediums.

8. Which of the following exhibit hydrogen bonding?

(a) Chloroform (b) Ethyl alcohol

(c) Acetic acid (d) Dimethyl ether

9. Which of the following statements are correct?

(a) Carboxylic acids have higher boiling points than those of alcohols of similar molecular weight

(b) Carboxylic acids have lower boiling points than those of alcohols of similar molecular weight

(c) Carboxylic acids (C_1 to C_4) are soluble in water

(d) The melting points of carboxylic acids increase or decrease in irregular manner

10. Which of the following statements are correct?

(a) The two carbon-oxygen bond lengths in formic acid are different

(b) The two carbon-oxygen bond lengths in sodium formate are equal

(c) The carbon-oxygen bond length in formic acid is less than that in sodium formate

(d) The carbon-oxygen bond length in formic acid is greater than that in sodium formate

11. Tollen's reagent reacts with

(a) formaldehyde (b) acetaldehyde

(c) acetone (d) formic acid

12. Pyroligneous acid, obtained by destructive distillation of wood, can be used for the manufacture of

(a) methyl alcohol (b) acetaldehyde

(c) acetic acid (d) propanol

13. Which are correct statements?

(a) Methyl malonic acid is converted into propanoic acid on heating

(b) Succinic acid forms succinic anhydride on heating

(c) 3-Hydroxy propanoic acid forms acrylic acid on heating

(d) $CH_3-\overset{O}{\overset{||}{C}}-CH_2COOH$ forms acetone on heating

14. Which can be used as fire-extinguisher?

(a) $CH_3COOH + NaHCO_3$

(b) Pyrene

(c) Formalin

(d) Dry ice

15. CH_3COOH can be obtained by

(a) $CH_3Br \xrightarrow{Mg/ether} \xrightarrow{CO_2/H_3O^+}$

(b) $CH_3Br \xrightarrow{AgCN} \xrightarrow{H_3O^+}$

(c) $CH_3CH = CHCH_3 \xrightarrow{KMnO_4}$

(d) $CH_3CCl_3 \xrightarrow{aq.\ KOH}, \xrightarrow{H_3O^+}$

16. Decarboxylation will take place on heating :

(a) methyl malonic acid

(b) succinic acid

(c) 2, 2-dimethyl acetoacetic acid

(d) Glutaric acid

17. Which of the following will liberate CO_2 on reaction with $NaHCO_3$:

(a) 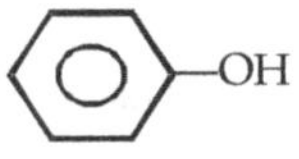

(b) CH_3COOH

(c) 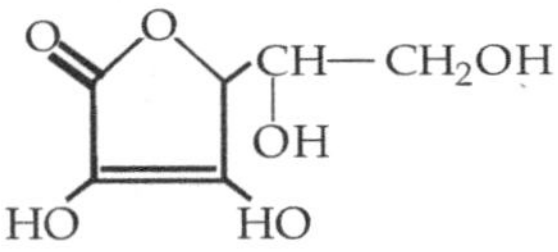

(d) CH_2OH–CH_2OH

18. Which of the following compounds can be used as an acylating agent ?

(*a*) CH_3COCl (*b*) $(CH_3CO)_2O$

(*c*) CH_3COOH (*d*) CH_3CH_2COCl.

19. Which of the following statement is true for the following reaction ?

$$RCOOH + LiAlH_4 \longrightarrow RCH_2OH$$

(a) The first step of the reaction is the formation of AlH_3 and H_2.

(b) A hydride ion is transferred from AlH_3 to the carboxylate carbon.

(c) An aldehyde is formed as an intermediate.

(d) Aldehyde is not the intermediate in this reaction

20. 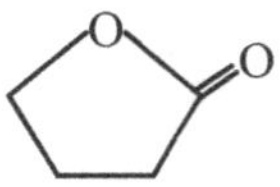 $\xrightarrow[\text{(ii) } H_3O^+]{\text{(i) } CH_3MgBr}$ Z, Z may be

(a) 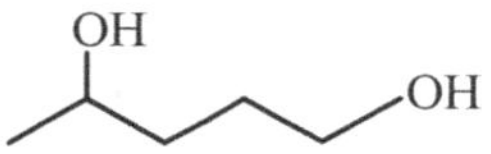

(b) 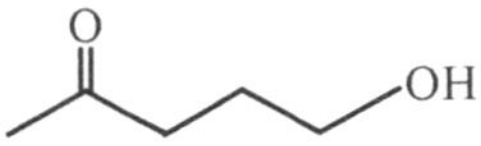

(c) 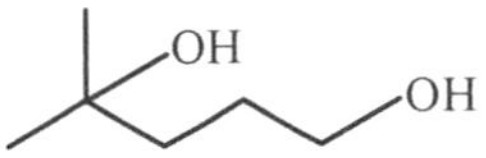

(d) 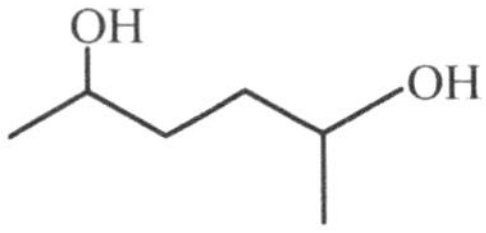

21. Formic acid and acetic acid can be distinguished by the action of

(a) conc. H_2SO_4

(b) Tollen's reagent

(c) Fehling solution

(d) heating of sodium salt

22. $C_6H_5-\overset{O}{\overset{\|}{C}}-OH + H_2O^{18} \xrightarrow{H^+}$ Product

Here the product may be

(a) $C_6H_5CO^{18}OH$ (b) $C_6H_5COO^{18}H$

(c) $C_6H_5COOO^{18}H$ (d) $C_6H_5CO^{18}OOH$

INSTRUCTION for Q. 23 to 34 : Read the passages given below and answer the questions that follow.

PASSAGE 1

Alkyl halides can be converted easily into carboxylic acids through two routes,

(i) through Grignard reagent formation, and

(ii) through hydrolysis of nitriles.

(i) $CH_3Br + Mg \longrightarrow CH_3MgBr \xrightarrow[\text{(ii) } H_3O^+]{\text{(i) } CO_2} CH_3COOH$

(ii) $CH_3CH_2Br \xrightarrow{NaCN} CH_3CH_2CN \xrightarrow{\text{(i) } H^+} CH_3COOH + NH_4^+$

Other methods, generally opted in laboratory are oxidation of alcohols. 1° alcohols give carboxylic acids with same number of carbon, while 2° alcohols give acids with lesser number of C atoms.

23. Dimethyl propanoic acid can be prepared easily from 2-chloro-2-methylpropane through

(a) Grignard reagent route

(b) nitrile route

(c) both routes

(d) none of the two

24. [skeletal structure] $\xrightarrow{\text{chromic acid}}$ Carboxylic acid

The carboxylic acid formed in the above reaction is

(a) 2-tert-butyl-3, 3-dimethylbutanoic acid

(b) 2-(1, 1′-dimethylethyl)-3, 3-dimethylbutanoic acid

(c) Methanoic acid

(d) Tricarballylic acid

25. During oxidation of $CH_3\overset{*}{C}OCH_2CH_2CH_3$, labelled carbon is mainly found in

(a) $CH_3\overset{*}{C}OOH$ (b) $CH_3CH_2CH_2\overset{*}{C}OOH$

(c) $H\overset{*}{C}OOH$ (d) $CH_3CH_2\overset{*}{C}OOH$

PASSAGE 2

Although the carboxyl group consists of C=O and – OH, it is the – OH that undergoes change, either loss of H^+ or replacement by another group takes place. However, the carbonyl group markedly influences the reactions of carboxylic acids. The presence of the C = O part is also responsible for nucleophilic substitution reactions in acid derivatives.

Presence of an electron withdrawing group increases the acidity of aliphatic as well as aromatic acids. On the other hand, electron releasing groups imparts opposite effect.

26. The marked acidity of RCOOH over ROH is due to the presence of

(a) – OH (b) C = O

(c) Both (d) None

27. Chloroacetic acid is more acidic than acetic acid because

(a) electron withdrawing group destabilizes the acid

(b) electron donating group stabilizes the acid

(c) electron withdrawing group stabilizes the carboxylate ion

(d) all the three

28. Which statement is correct when an acid weakening group is present in benzoic acid?

(a) Acid weakening groups activate the ring towards electrophilic substitution

(b) Acid weakening groups deactivate the ring towards electrophilic substitution

(c) Acid weakening groups activate the ring toward nucleophilic substitution

(d) None of the above

29. The C = O part in carboxylic acids and their derivatives make acyl compounds more reactive than alkyl compounds toward nucleophilic attack because

(a) The carbonyl group is electron donating

(b) The alkyl group is electron donating

(c) Attack of a nucleophile on a flat acyl compound is less sterically hindered

(d) Tetrahedral carbon atoms cannot have pentavalent transition states

30. Aldehydes and ketones react with nucleophiles to give addition product rather substituion because

(a) They are more acidic

(b) They are less acidic

(c) They are sterically hindered

(d) The C – H & C – C bonds do not break easily

PASSAGE 3

Hell-Volhard-Zelinsky (HVZ) reaction involves the reaction of aliphatic carboxylic acid with bromine in the presence a trace of PBr_3 to form α-bromocarboxylic acid.

$$CH_3CH_2COOH \xrightarrow{Br_2/PBr_3} CH_3CH_2COBr$$

$$\longrightarrow CH_3CHBrCOBr \xrightarrow{H_2O} CH_3CHBrCOOH$$

31. When two equivalents of the reagent are used, the product formed in the above reaction will be

(a) $CH_3CHBrCOBr$ (b) $CH_2BrCHBrCOOH$

(c) CH_3CBr_2COOH (d) both (b) and (c)

32. What will be the product when three equivalent of Br_2 is treated with 2,2-dimethylbutanoic acid?

(a) $CH_2Br-\underset{CH_2Br}{\overset{CH_2Br}{C}}-COOH$ (b) $Br_2CH-\underset{CH_3}{\overset{CH_2Br}{C}}-COOH$

(c) $Br_3C-\underset{CH_3}{\overset{CH_3}{C}}-COOH$ (d) No reaction

33. What product will be formed when PBr_3 in the given set of reactions is replaced by PCl_3?

(a) $CH_3-\overset{Cl}{C}HCOOH$ (b) $CH_3-\overset{Br}{C}H-COOH$

(c) Both (d) Reaction not possible

34. When Br_2 in the above given set of reactions is replaced by Cl_2, the product formed will be

(a) $CH_3-CH(Cl)-COOH$ (b) $CH_3-CH(Br)-COOH$

(c) $CH_3-CH(Cl)-COCl$ (d) $CH_3-CH(Cl)-COBr$

Instructions for Q. 35 : Following questions are Multiple Matching type Questions :

35.

	Column - I **(Compound)**		*Column - II* **(Oxidation product)**
(A)	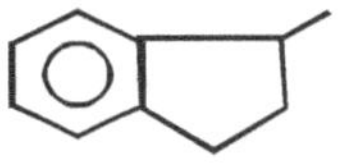 [structure]	(a)	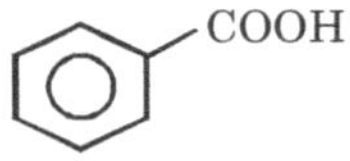 C_6H_5COOH
(B)	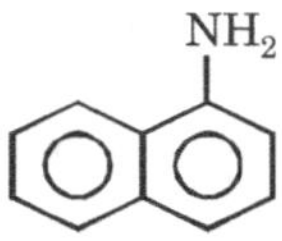 [structure: NH_2 on naphthalene]	(b)	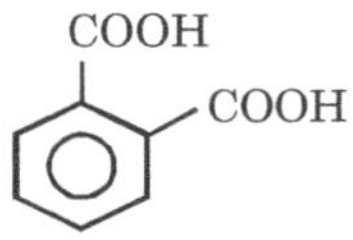 [structure: benzene with COOH, COOH]
(C)	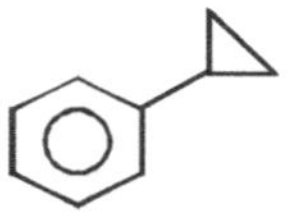 [structure]	(c)	Oxidation difficult
(D)	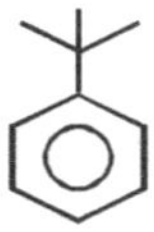 [structure]	(d)	$(CH_3)_3CCOOH$

Instructions for Q. 36 to 43 : Following questions are Assertion and Reasoning Type Questions :

Note : Each question contains STATEMENT-1 (Assertion) and STATEMENT-2 (Reason). Each question has 5 choices (a), (b), (c), (d) and (e) out of which ONLY ONE is correct.

(a) Statement-1 is True, Statement-2 is True; Statement-2 is a correct explanation for Statement-1.

(b) Statement-1 is True, Statement-2 is True; Statement-2 is NOT a correct explanation for Statement-1.

(c) Statement -1 is True, Statement-2 is False.

(d) Statement -1 is False, Statement-2 is True.

(e) Statement -1 is False, Statement-2 is False.

36. **Statement 1 :** The pK_a of acetic acid is lower than that of phenol.

Statement 2 : Phenoxide ion is more resonance stabilised.

37. **Statement 1 :** During the preparation of esters from a carboxylic acid and an alcohol in the presence of an acid catalyst, the water or the ester should be removed as fast as it is formed.

Statement 2 : The reaction between an acid and an alcohol in the presence of an acid catalyst is a reversible reaction.

38. **Statement 1 :** A carboxylic acid is a stronger acid than phenol

Statement 2 : The conjugate base of carboxylic acid, a carboxylate ion, is stabilised by two equivalent resonance structures in which the negative charge is at the more electronegative oxygen atom.

39. **Statement 1 :** C_6H_5COOH is stronger than CH_3COOH.

Statement 2 : C_6H_5COOH is weaker than HCOOH.

40. **Statement 1 :** Dichloro and trichloro acids are stronger than monochloroacetic acid.

Statement 2 : An increase in the number of electronegative groups on the alkyl chain increases the strength of the acid.

41. **Statement-1** : The pK_a value of acetic acid is lower than that of phenol.

Statement-2 : Phenoxide ion is more resonance stabilized

42. **Statement-1** : Nitration of benzoic acid gives *m*-nitrobenzoic acid.

Statement-2 : Carboxyl group increases the electron-density at *meta*-position.

43. **Statement-1** : RCOCl, $(RCO)_2O$ and RCOOR′ all react with Grignard reagents to form 3° alcohols.

Statement-2 : RCOCl reacts with R_2Cd to form ketones but $(RCO)_2O$ and RCOOR' do not react at all.

Instructions for Q. 44 : Following questions are Integer Type Questions :

44. Amongst the following, the total number of compounds soluble in aqueous NaOH is

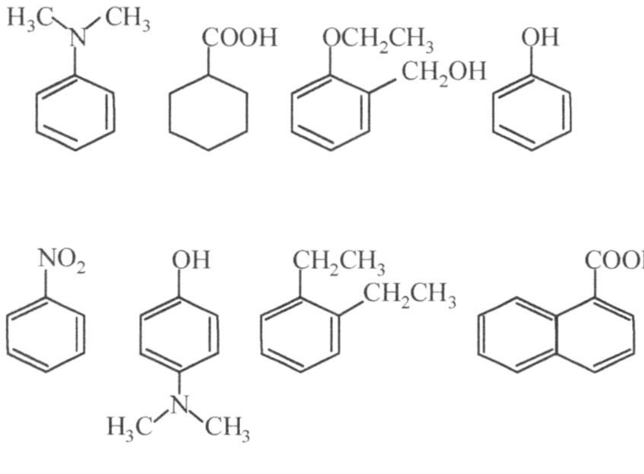

[structures: $C_6H_5N(CH_3)_2$; cyclohexane-COOH; benzene with OCH_2CH_3 and CH_2OH; phenol (OH); nitrobenzene (NO_2); 4-(dimethylamino)phenol (OH, $N(CH_3)_2$); benzene with CH_2CH_3 and CH_2CH_3; naphthalene-COOH]

EXERCISE 17.3 (Subjective Problems)

1. (*a*) Give the common and IUPAC names for the straight chain saturated carboxylic acids containing 5, 6, 8, 10 and 12 carbon atoms.

   (*b*) Give the structural formula and IUPAC name for each of the following :

   (*i*) Isovaleric acid

   (*ii*) Trimethylacetic acid

   (*iii*) α, β-Dimethylcaproic acid

   (*iv*) α-Methyl-γ-ethyloctanoic acid.

2. Write equations to obtain *n*-butanoic acid from (*a*) *n*-propanol (two different methods), and (*b*) 2-pentanone.

3. Write the products obtained from the reaction of *n*-valeric acid with

   (*a*) Al (*b*) CaO

   (*c*) $NH_3(aq)$ (*d*) H_2, Ni, 20°C, 1 atm

   (*e*) $LiAlH_4$ (*f*) hot $KMnO_4$

   (*g*) Br_2/P (*h*) Br_2/Fe

   (*i*) fuming H_2SO_4 (*j*) HNO_3/H_2SO_4

   (*k*) *n*-Valeryl alcohol.

4. Give balanced equations for the reaction of each of the following reagents with phenylacetic acid.

   (*i*) $SOCl_2$ (*ii*) PCl_3

   (*iii*) PCl_5 (*iv*) $(CH_3CO)_2O$

   (*v*) CH_3OH/H_2SO_4 (*vi*) NH_3 followed by heat.

5. Write the equations for converting isobutyric acid into each of the following.

   (*a*) Isobutyramide (*b*) Isobutyl alcohol

   (*c*) Butane (*d*) Magnesium isobutyrate.

6. Give steps involved in the following conversions :

   (*a*) $^{14}CO_2 \longrightarrow CH_3CH_2CH_2{}^{14}COOH$

   (*b*) $^{14}CO_2 \longrightarrow CH_3CH_2{}^{14}CH_2COOH$

   (*c*) $^{14}CO_2 \longrightarrow CH_3{}^{14}CH_2CH_2COOH$

   (*d*) $^{14}CH_3OH \longrightarrow {}^{14}CH_3CH_2CH_2CH_2COOH$

7. Give steps involved in the following transformations :

   (*a*) Toluene to α-bromophenylacetic acid

   (*b*) Benzene to α-methylphenylacetic acid.

   (*c*) *n*-Butanol to 2-pentenoic acid.

8. (*a*) Arrange the following in order of decreasing acidic character.

   (*i*) $CH_3COOH, CH\equiv CH, NH_3, C_2H_6, C_2H_5OH, H_2SO_4, H_2O$

   (*ii*) Acetic acid, malonic acid, succinic acid

   (*b*) Arrange the monosodium salts of the acids given in (*a*) (*i*) in order of decreasing basicity.

9. Complete the following reactions :

   (*a*) $CH\equiv CH \xrightarrow{CH_3MgBr} A \xrightarrow[(ii)\ H^+]{(i)\ CO_2}$

   $B \xrightarrow{H_2SO_4/HgSO_4} C \xrightarrow{KMnO_4} CH_2(COOH)_2$

   (*b*) $CH_3COOH \xrightarrow{LiAlH_4} A \xrightarrow{HBr} B \xrightarrow[(ii)\ CO_2]{(i)\ Mg}$

   $C \xrightarrow{Ag_2O} D \xrightarrow{Br_2} E$

10. Compare the reaction of CH_3CH_2COOH with excess of (*i*) CH_3MgBr and (*ii*) CH_3Li.

11. (*a*) Use simple chemical tests to differentiate among the following dry compounds. *n*-Butanol, *n*-butanoic acid, butane, butanal and ethyl methyl ether.

    (*b*) Differentiate between (*i*) CH_3COOH and HCOOH, (*ii*) oxalic acid and malonic acid ; and (*iii*) CH_3CH_2COCl and CH_3CH_2COOH.

    (*c*) Name the reagent or test that can be used for distinguishing between the members of each of the following pairs.

    (*i*) Acrylic acid, $CH_2{=}CHCOOH$ and propionic acid, CH_3CH_2COOH.

    (*ii*) Mandelic acid, $C_6H_5CHOHCOOH$ and benzoic acid, C_6H_5COOH.

    (*iii*) Mesotartaric acid and *o*-chlorobenzoic acid.

12. (*a*) Define the term neutralization equivalent of an acid. How many equivalents of NaOH would be neutralized by one mole of a polycarboxylic acid whose MW is 210 g/mol and NE is 70 g/eq. ?

(*b*) Can you predict the NE of melittic acid, $C_6\,(COOH)_6$?

13. Compare acetic acid and sodium acetate with respect to following properties.

(*a*) m.p. (*b*) b.p.

(*c*) Solubility in water and ether

(*d*) acidity and basicity.

14. Give schematic pathways for separation for each of the following mixtures.

(*a*) Caproic acid and ethyl carproate (*both liquids*).

(*b*) *n*-Butanoic acid and 1-hexanol (*both liquids*).

(*c*) Sodium benzoate and triphenylmethanol (*both solids*).

15. Benzoic acid and *o*-chlorobenzoic acid, both are water insoluble solids, and are separated by treatment with an aqueous solution of sodium formate. Explain.

SOLUTIONS

EXERCISE 17.1

1	(c)	6	(a)	11	(b)	16	(d)	21	(d)	26	(a)	31	(c)	36	(c)	41	(b)	46	(b)	51	(c)	56	(b)	61	(d)	66	(b)
2	(b)	7	(a)	12	(c)	17	(d)	22	(b)	27	(a)	32	(d)	37	(d)	42	(b)	47	(c)	52	(c)	57	(d)	62	(b)	67	(c)
3	(d)	8	(c)	13	(b)	18	(b)	23	(c)	28	(d)	33	(b)	38	(c)	43	(c)	48	(c)	53	(c)	58	(b)	63	(b)		
4	(b)	9	(b)	14	(b)	19	(c)	24	(c)	29	(a)	34	(d)	39	(b)	44	(b)	49	(b).	54	(b).	59	(c)	64	(b)		
5	(b)	10	(c)	15	(d)	20	(d)	25	(b)	30	(c)	35	(c)	40	(d)	45	(c)	50	(a)	55	(d)	60	(d)	65	(c)		

1. Here it is not essential to indicate the position (2) of the double bond, because no other position for the double bond is possible.
2. Since chloride is 3°, it will undergo elimination reaction with CN^- ion, hence route (*a*) can't be applied. Route (*b*) is a successful Grignard synthsis.
3. Neither method can be used because the halide is 3° and undergoes elimination reaction rather than substitution. Further, the presence of —OH group in the compound prevents the preparation of organometallic compound. A successful synthesis can be achieved by first protecting the OH group and then carrying carbonation.
4. $\xrightarrow[\text{Allylic bromination}]{\text{NBS}}$ —Br $\xrightarrow[(ii)\ CO_2]{(i)\ Mg}$ —COOH
5. $CH_3CH_2CH_2CH_2OH$ or $CH_3CH_2CH(CH_3)\,OH \xrightarrow{H^+} CH_3CH_2\overset{CH_3}{\overset{|}{C}H^{\ominus}}$ (*sec*-Butyl cation) $\xrightarrow[H_2O]{CO} CH_3CH_2\overset{CH_3}{\overset{|}{C}}HCOOH$ (2–Methylbutanoic acid)
6. The charged end loses CO_2 (for details, see mechanism in text).
7. Carbanion formed from simple carboxylate anions can't be stabilized, while other carbanions are quite stable.

$$CH_3CH_2CH_2COOH \rightleftharpoons CH_3CH_2CH_2COO^- \xrightarrow[-CO_2]{} CH_3CH_2\bar{C}H_2$$

Not stable, hence not formed

8. Higher the stability of the carbanion formed after loss of CO_2, more will be the ease of decarboxylation. Carbanion from 2, 4, 6-trinitrobenzoic acid is stabilised by the dispersal of charge due to strong–I effect of the three —NO_2 groups

NO_2, O_2N, $:\ominus$, NO_2

9. $$\text{N.E. of acid} = \frac{\text{Wt. of acid} \times 1000}{\text{Molarity of NaOH} \times \text{Vol. of NaOH}} = \frac{0.187 \times 1000}{0.972 \times 18.7} = 103 \text{ g}$$

Thus the equivalent wt. of the acid is 103 which coincides with the molecular/wt. (and eq. wt.) of ethoxyacetic acid, $C_2H_5OCH_2COOH$ (Mol. wt. and eq. wt. = 104).

10. $RCX_3 \xrightarrow{OH^-} RC(OH)_3 \xrightarrow[-H_2O]{} RCOOH$
11. $LiAlH_4$ reduces halides to alkanes.
12. (*i*) $CH_3CH_2COOH \xrightarrow[PCl_3]{Br_2} CH_3CH_2COCl \xrightarrow{Br_2} CH_3CH(Br)\,COCl \xrightarrow{H_2O} CH_3CH(Br)\,COOH.$

(*ii*) $CH_3CH_2COOH \xrightarrow[PBr_3]{Cl_2} CH_3CH_2COBr \xrightarrow{Cl_2} CH_2CHClCOBr \xrightarrow{H_2O} CH_3CH(Cl)COOH.$

13. Precipitates in two cases is due to different compounds.

$CH_3CH_2CH_2COO^-Ag^+$ (Soluble in HNO_3) — From propanoic acid; $AgCl$ (Insoluble in HNO_3) — From chloropropanoic acid

14. Reduction of alkynes by Na-C_2H_5OH occurs in *trans*-manner.
15. B_2H_6 selectively reduces a carboxylic group in presence of an ester.
16. $CH_3CH_2CH_2CH_2OH \xrightarrow[-H_2O]{H^+} CH_3CH_2CH_2\overset{+}{C}H_2$ (1° Carbocation) $\xrightarrow{\text{rearranges}} CH_3CH_2\overset{CH_3}{\overset{|}{C}H^{\oplus}}$ (2° Carbocation) $\xrightarrow{CO} CH_3CH_2\overset{CH_3}{\overset{|}{C}}HCOOH$.
17. $\xrightarrow{KMnO_4}$ O + HOOC

18. Hydrogen bonding is maximum in acids, and minimum in aldehydes.
19. In (*c*), weaker electron-withdrawing group (Br) is present maximum away from —COOH group.
20. Theoretical.

21. $CH_3CH_2\overset{O}{\overset{\|}{C}}—OH + NaH\overset{14}{C}O_3 \longrightarrow CH_3CH_2\overset{O}{\overset{\|}{C}}—O^-Na^+ + H_2O + {}^{14}CO_2$.
22. —COOH and —C ≡ CH are more acidic than enolic group = C(OH).
23. $CH_3COOH + HOOCCH_3 \xrightarrow{P_2O_5} CH_3COOCOCH_3 + H_2O$
24. $CH_3CH_2COOH \xrightarrow{\text{red P/Cl}_2} CH_3CHClCOOH \xrightarrow{\text{alc. KOH}} CH_2 = CHCOOH.$
25. $CH_3CHOH\,COOH \xrightarrow{KMnO_4/OH^-} CH_3COCOOH.$
26. An optically active reagent reacts with different rate with the two enantiomers, with the result the products formed will be unequal in amounts and hence mixture (product) will be optically active.
27. Steric factor is responsible for relative esterification.
28. $\underset{\text{Intermediate}}{CH_3CH_2CH_2CH_2OH} \xrightarrow{KMnO_4} \underset{P}{CH_3CH_2CH_2COOH}$
29. $\underset{[X]}{CH_3C \equiv CCH_3}$; $\underset{[Y]}{CH_3CH_2COCH_3}$; $\underset{[Z]}{CH_3CH_2COOH}$
30. Option (*i*) and (*ii*) will form CH_3COO^- ions, not free CH_3COOH.
31. $CH_2(COOH)_2 + P_2O_5 \xrightarrow{\text{heat}} \underset{\text{Carbon suboxide}}{O = C = C = C = O} + H_3PO_4$
32. $\begin{matrix} CH_2COOH \\ | \\ CH_2COOH \end{matrix} \xrightarrow[\text{HVZ reaction}]{P/Br_2} \begin{matrix} CH_2COOH \\ | \\ BrCHCOOH \end{matrix} \xrightarrow{\text{alc. KOH}} \underset{\text{Maleic acid}}{\begin{matrix} CHCOOH \\ \| \\ CHCOOH \end{matrix}} \xrightarrow[\textit{anti}\text{-hydroxylation}]{CF_3CO_3H}$ *rac*-Tartaric acid.
33. Lesser the pK_a value, stronger is the acid. Benzoic acid is strongest because benzoate ion is highly stabilized by resonance.
34. $Me_3\overset{+}{N}CH_2COOH$ is strongest acid, because of powerful – I effect of the $Me_3\overset{+}{N}$— group, while Me_3CCH_2COOH is the least acidic because of powerful + I effect of the Me_3C — group.
35. $CH_3COOH + O = C = CH_2 \longrightarrow CH_3COOCOCH_3$.
36. $NaBH_4$ reduces only C = O group and not —COOH group. The product formed undergoes cyclization to form γ-lactone (six-membered rings are formed easily).

[5-oxohexanoic acid] $\xrightarrow[(ii)\ H_3O^+]{(i)\ NaBH_4}$ [5-hydroxyhexanoic acid, carbons numbered 1–5] $\xrightarrow[(-H_2O)]{\text{Cyclises}}$ [six-membered lactone, ring positions numbered 1–5]

37. [cyclohex-2-enylacetic acid] $\xrightarrow[CCl_4]{Br_2}$ [(2,3-dibromocyclohexyl)acetic acid] $\xrightarrow[(-HBr)]{\text{Cyclization}}$ [bromo-substituted bicyclic lactone]

38. [X]: 2-acetylcyclohexanone; [Y], A β-keto acid: 2-oxocyclohexanecarboxylic acid $\xrightarrow{\text{heat}}$ [Z]: cyclohexanone

39. *tert*-Alkyl groups are resistant to oxidation.
40. The three —NO_2 (electron-withdrawing) groups in *o*- and *p*-positions make phenolic —OH group highly acidic. Moreover, the corresponding phenoxide is highly stable.
41. Lower the pK_a value higher is the acidity. The acidity of the three isomeric nitrobenzoic acids follows the order :

o-nitrobenzoic acid > p-nitrobenzoic acid > m-nitrobenzoic acid

o-nitrobenzoic acid	p-nitrobenzoic acid	m-nitrobenzoic acid
Due to ortho effect, –M effect, –I effect	Due to –M effect, –I effect	Only due to –I effect

42. p-Nitrobenzoic acid (COOH, NO_2) > p-chlorobenzoic acid (COOH, Cl) > benzoic acid (COOH)

43. β-Keto carboxylic acids undergo decarboxylation very easily.

44. $C_6H_5COCH(CH_3)COOH \xrightarrow{heat} C_6H_5COCH_2CH_3$

β-keto acid

45. —COOH group when present along with activating group like —OH is easily eliminated as CO_2.

46. $HO{-}C_6H_4{-}COOH + H_2O \xrightarrow{pH = 7} HO{-}C_6H_4{-}COO^- + H_3O^+$

(—COOH is more acidic than phenolic group)

47. o-Bromotoluene (CH_3, Br) $\xrightarrow{Mg,\ THF}$ o-tolylmagnesium bromide (CH_3, MgBr) $\xrightarrow{H_2O}$ toluene (CH_3) $\xrightarrow{oxi}$ benzoic acid (COOH)

48. $C_6H_5COOH \xrightarrow{PCl_5} C_6H_5COCl \xrightarrow[AlCl_3]{C_6H_6} C_6H_5COC_6H_5 \xrightarrow[\text{Baeyer-Villiger oxidation}]{C_6H_5CO_3H} C_6H_5OCOC_6H_5$

49. —OH group is activating, hence electrophilic substitution will be taking place w.r.t. —OH. Future, bromine in CH_3COOH is a mild brominating agent, hence only monobromo product will be the main product. *p*-Substituted is major product due to steric factor.

51. (c) Conjugate bases of both of the compounds, formic acid and 2, 4, 6-trinitrophenol, are highly stable.

$H{-}\overset{O}{\overset{||}{C}}{-}O^-$

formate ion
(–ve charge dispersed due to resonance)

2,4,6-trinitrophenoxide ion (O^-, O_2N, NO_2, NO_2)

(–ve charge dispersed due to three electron-withdrawing $-NO_2$ groups)

52. (c) Phosphorus converts a little of the acid into acid chloride which is more reactive than the parent carboxylic acid. Thus it is the acid chloride, not the acid itself, that undergoes chlorination on the α-carbon.

$$CH_3CH_2COOH \xrightarrow{PCl_3 \text{ from } P+Cl_2} CH_3CH_2COCl \xrightarrow{Cl_2}$$

$$CH_3CH(Cl)COCl \xrightarrow{H_2O} CH_3CH(Cl)COOH$$

53. (c) 1, 6- and 1, 7-dicarboxylic acids on heating form cyclic ketones (Blanc rule)

54. (b) β-Keto carboxylic acids and β, γ-unsaturated carboxylic acids undergo decarboxylation easily because the corresponding carbanion is quite stable due to resonance.

$$\underset{III}{CH_3-\overset{O}{\overset{||}{C}}-CH_2-COOH} \xrightarrow{-H^+} CH_3-\overset{O}{\overset{||}{C}}-CH_2-\overset{O}{\overset{||}{C}}-O^- \xrightarrow{-CO_2}$$

$$\left[CH_3-\overset{O}{\overset{||}{C}}-\overset{-}{C}H_2 \longleftrightarrow CH_3-\overset{O^-}{\overset{|}{C}}=CH_2\right] \xrightarrow{H^+}$$

$$CH_3-\overset{OH}{\overset{|}{C}}=CH_2 \rightleftharpoons CH_3-\overset{O}{\overset{||}{C}}-CH_3$$

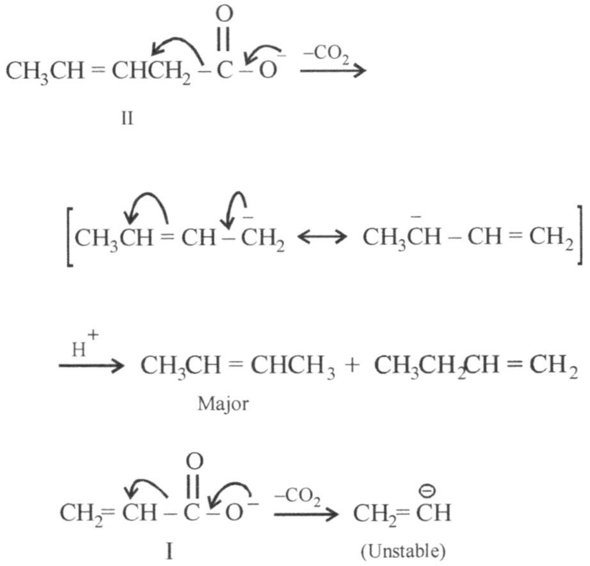

$$CH_3CH=CHCH_2-\overset{O}{\overset{||}{C}}-O^- \xrightarrow{-CO_2}$$

II

$$\left[CH_3CH=CH-\bar{C}H_2 \longleftrightarrow CH_3\bar{C}H-CH=CH_2\right]$$

$$\xrightarrow{H^+} \underset{\text{Major}}{CH_3CH=CHCH_3} + CH_3CH_2CH=CH_2$$

$$\underset{\text{I}}{CH_2=CH-\overset{O}{\overset{||}{C}}-O^-} \xrightarrow{-CO_2} \underset{\text{(Unstable)}}{CH_2=\overset{\ominus}{C}H}$$

55. **(d)** If the key atom of the side chain of a benzene ring is 1° or 2°, it is oxidised to –COOH irrespective of its nature.

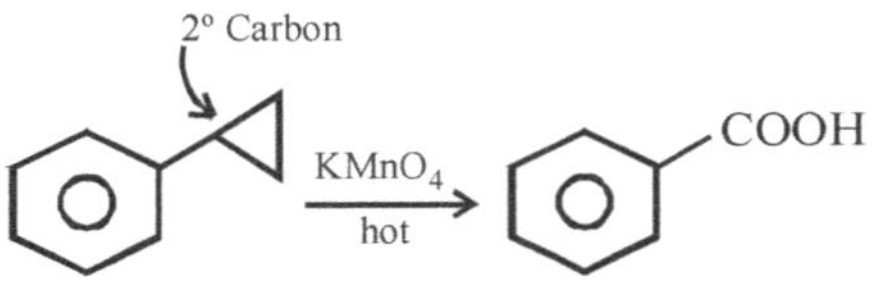

2° Carbon

Cyclopropylbenzene $\xrightarrow[\text{hot}]{KMnO_4}$ C_6H_5COOH

In case the key atom of the side chain is 3°, i.e. when it is not having any H, oxidation is very difficult. However, on vigorous oxidation, benzene ring is oxidised instead of side chain.

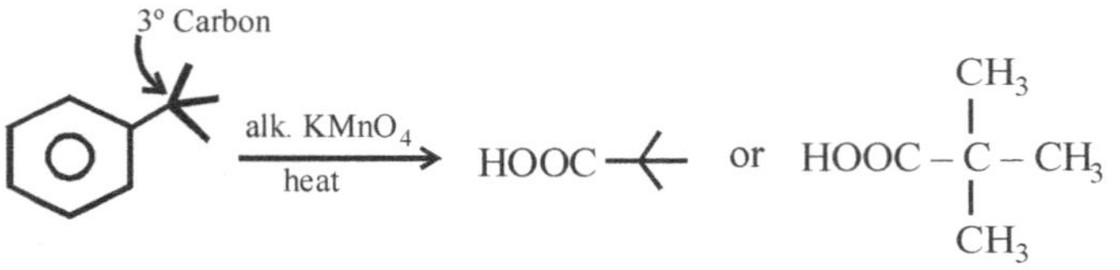

3° Carbon

tert-Butylbenzene $\xrightarrow[\text{heat}]{\text{alk. }KMnO_4}$ HOOC–C(CH$_3$)$_3$ or $HOOC-\underset{CH_3}{\underset{|}{\overset{CH_3}{\overset{|}{C}}}}-CH_3$

56. **(b)** $CH_3COCH_2CH_2CH_2COOH \xrightarrow[\text{does not reduce –COOH group}]{NaBH_4} \overset{6}{C}H_3\overset{5}{C}H(OH)\overset{4}{C}H_2\overset{3}{C}H_2\overset{2}{C}H_2\overset{1}{C}OOH$

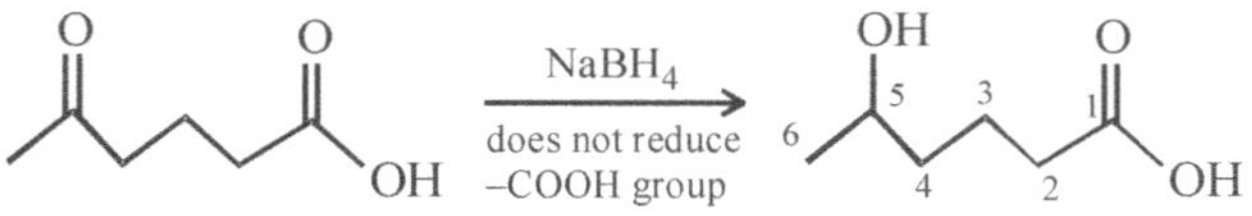

or

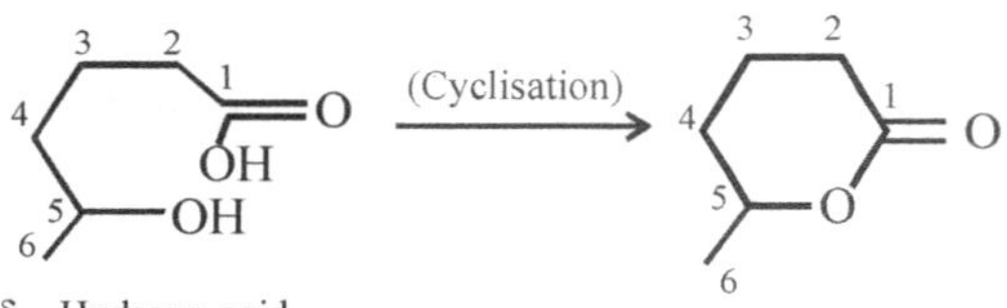

δ - Hydroxy acid $\xrightarrow{\text{(Cyclisation)}}$ δ - Lactone

57. **(d)** V is most stable because its anion is stabilized to a greater extent through H – bonding with H atom of OH present on both *ortho* positions ; followed by II in which one OH group is present. Compound IV comes next to II because here $-OCH_3$ group is present in *ortho* position which although is not capable of forming H–bonding yet more acidic than p-HOC_6H_4COOH (III) due to ortho effect. Compound III is less acidic than benzoic acid because of electron-releasing group in the para position. Thus

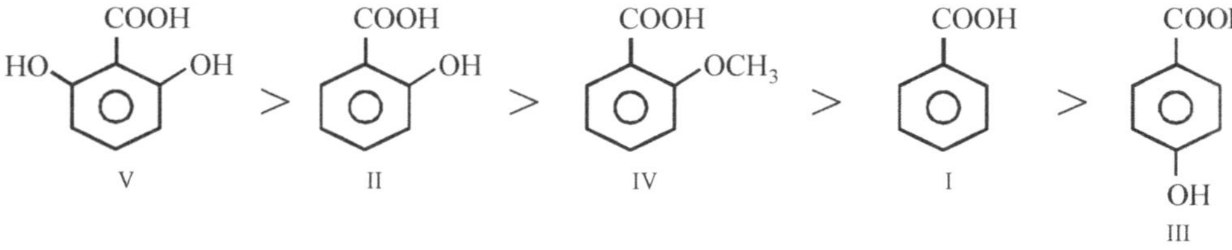

2,6-dihydroxybenzoic acid (V) > 2-hydroxybenzoic acid (II) > 2-methoxybenzoic acid (IV) > benzoic acid (I) > 4-hydroxybenzoic acid (III)

58. (b) Note that when some activating group, e.g. –OH is present along with –COOH in ortho or para position substitution occurs with respect to –OH preferably at para position due to steric factors. In case the reagent used is strong, electrophile enters at all possible positions even with the replacement of –COOH group.

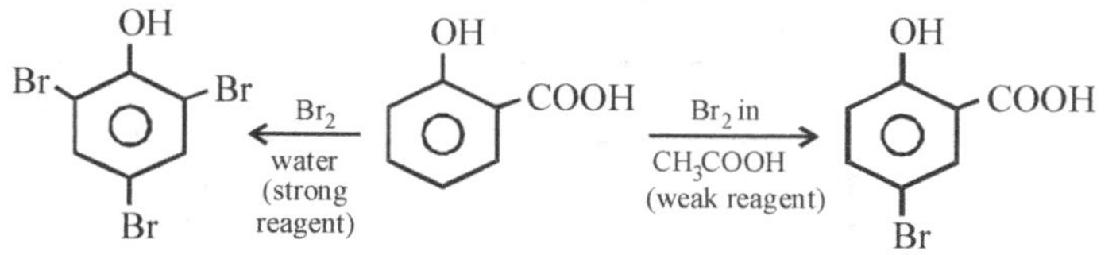

[Y] (2,4,6-tribromophenol) $\xleftarrow[\text{water (strong reagent)}]{Br_2}$ salicylic acid $\xrightarrow[\text{CH}_3\text{COOH (weak reagent)}]{Br_2 \text{ in}}$ [X] (5-bromosalicylic acid)

59. (c) $CH_3-\overset{O}{\overset{\|}{C}}-O-H \longrightarrow CH_3-\overset{O}{\overset{\|}{C}}-O^- + H^+$; $CH_3-\overset{O}{\overset{\|}{C}}-O-O-H \longrightarrow CH_3-\overset{O}{\overset{\|}{C}}-O-O^-$

Acetic acid → Conjugate base (Resonance possible, hence stable and weak base); Peroxyacetic acid → Conjugate base (Resonance not possible, hence unstable and strong base)

60. (d) Decarboxylation of β-keto acids involves transfer of the acidic hydrogen to the group followed by loss of CO_2 via a cylic six-membered transition state.

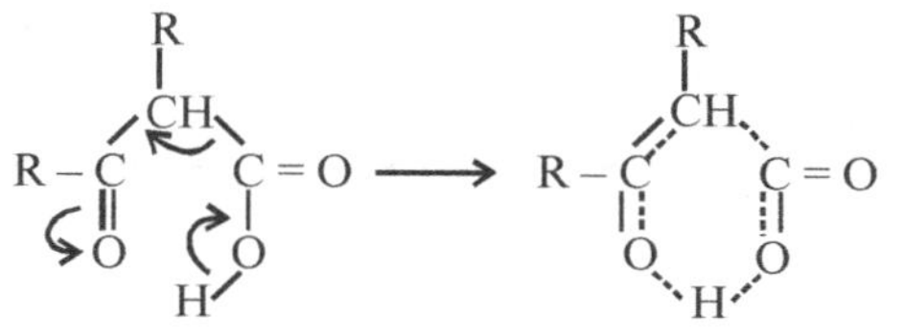

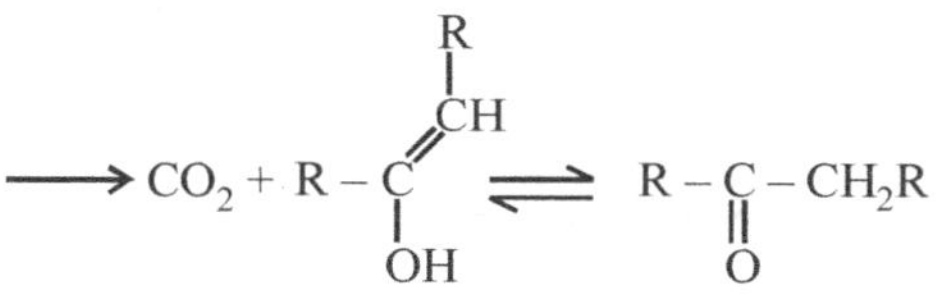

$\longrightarrow CO_2 + R-C(OH)=CHR \rightleftharpoons R-\overset{O}{\overset{\|}{C}}-CH_2R$

(enol) (keto)

61. (d) Remember that $LiAlH_4$ reduces both >C = O as well as –COOH to alcohols, while $NaBH_4$ reduces only >C = O without affecting –COOH.

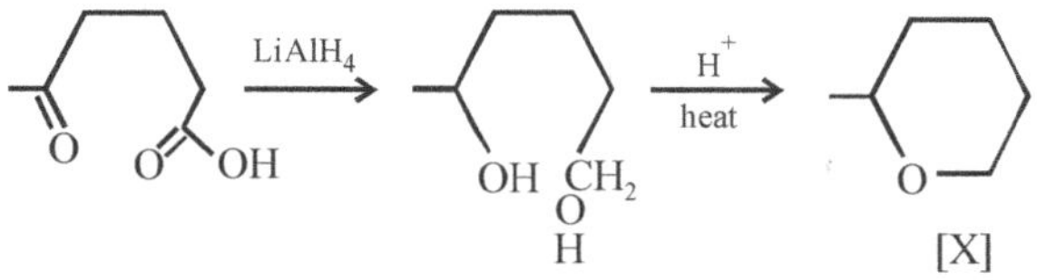

$\xrightarrow{LiAlH_4}$ $\xrightarrow[\text{heat}]{H^+}$ [X]

$\xrightarrow{NaBH_4}$ $\xrightarrow[\text{heat}]{H^+}$ [Y]

66. (b) $\xrightarrow[\text{(haloform reaction)}]{\text{(i) NaIO, H}^+}$ (COOH) $\xrightarrow{\text{heat}}$ cyclohexanone $+ CO_2$

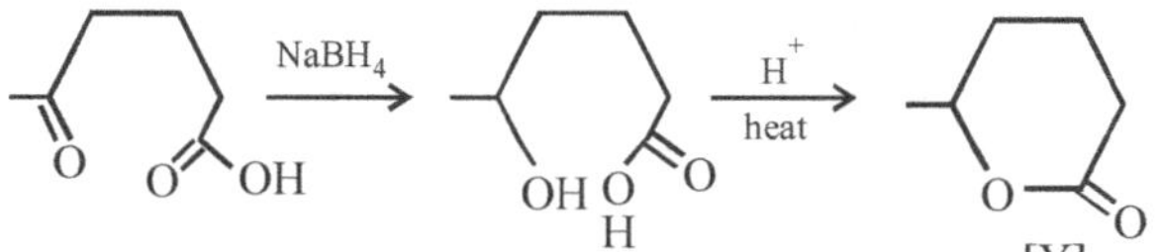

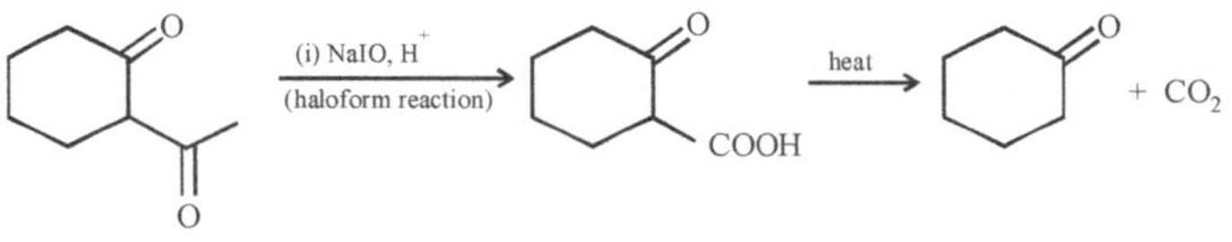

β-keto acid

67. (c) *o* - hydroxybenzoic acid is strongest acid and the decreasing order of acidity is

EXERCISE 17.2

>1 CORRECT OPTION	1	(a,b)	2	(b, d)	3	(a,b,c)	4	(a,b,d)	5	(a,c,d)
	6	(b,c,d)	7	(a,c,d)	8	(b, c)	9	(a, c, d)	10	(a, b, d)
	11	(a, b, d)	12	(a, c)	13	(a, b, c, d)	14	(a, b, d)	15	(a, c, d)
	16	(a, c)	17	(b, c)	18	(a, b, d)	19	(a, b, c)	20	(b, c)
	21	(a, b, c, d)	22	(a, b)						
PASSAGE 1	23	(a)	24	(b)	25	(a)				
PASSAGE 2	26	(b)	27	(d)	28	(a)	29	(c)	30	(d)
PASSAGE 3	31	(c)	32	(d)	33	(b, a)	34	(b, a)		
MATCH THE FOLLOWING	35	(A) - b, (B) - b, (C) - a, (D) - c, d								
A/R	36	(b)	37	(a)	38	(a)	39	(b)	40	(a)
	41	(b)	42	(c)	43	(b)				
INTEGER	44	4								

1. $$C_6H_5-\overset{O}{\overset{\|}{C}}-OH \xrightarrow{H^+} C_6H_5-\overset{OH}{\overset{|}{\underset{\oplus}{C}}}-OH \xrightarrow{H_2O^{18}} C_6H_5-\overset{OH}{\overset{|}{\underset{{}_{18}\overset{\oplus}{O}H_2}{\underset{|}{C}}}}-OH \xrightarrow{-H^+} C_6H_5-\overset{OH}{\overset{|}{\underset{{}_{18}OH}{\underset{|}{C}}}}-OH \longrightarrow C_6H_5-\underset{{}_{18}O}{\underset{\|}{C}}-OH + C_6H_5-\underset{{}_{18}OH}{\underset{|}{C}}=O$$

Remember that C—O^{18} bond is difficult to break than the C—O bond.

2. Theoretical.

3. Consult mechanism of the reaction in text.

4. Maleic acid is stronger because its monoanion is stabilized due to H-bonding between the *cis* COOH and COO^- ; while there is no such stabilization factor in fumarate monoanion (*trans* isomer), hence its formaton, *i.e.* dissociation of fumaric acid is less than that of maleic acid.

Maleic acid $\longrightarrow$ Maleate monoanion $\xrightarrow[\text{(difficult)}]{-H^+}$

Maleic acid

Maleate monoanion; (H-bonding makes its formation easier, however its deprotonation difficult)

Fumaric acid $\longrightarrow$ Fumarate monoanion $\xrightarrow[\text{(easy)}]{-H^+}$

Fumaric acid

Fumarate monoanion ; (H-bonding not possible hence its formation is difficult). However, it undergoes deprotonation easily because COOH is not involved in H-bonding

5. Diazomethane is used for methylating acidic groups ; compound (c) has enolic —OH group, hence it can also be methylated by CH_2N_2.

5. Dicarboxylic acids having two —COOH groups on the same carbon atom ; and β-keto acids are easily decarboxylated on heating.

7. When pH is greater than seven, medium is alkaline hence the Zwitterion of anthranilic acid is converted to an anion.

$$\underset{\text{Cation, III}}{C_6H_4(COOH)(\overset{\oplus}{N}H_3)} \xleftarrow[(pH<7)]{H^+} \underset{\text{Zwitterion, I (when pH = 7)}}{C_6H_4(COO^-)(\overset{+}{N}H_3)} \xrightarrow[(pH>7)]{OH^-} \underset{\text{Anion, II}}{C_6H_4(COO^-)(NH_2)}$$

18. **(a,b,d)** Stronger the basic nature of the leaving group, weaker will be its leavability. In CH_3COOH, OH^- is a strong base so it can't be removed easily to form $CH_3\overset{+}{C}O$ required for acetylation (acylation).

19. **(a,b,c)** Consult mechanism of the reaction in text.

20. (b,c)

1. **(a,b,c,d)**

2. **(a,b)** $$C_6H_5-\overset{O}{\overset{\|}{C}}-OH \xrightarrow{H^+} C_6H_5-\underset{\oplus}{\overset{OH}{\overset{|}{C}}}-OH \xrightarrow{H_2O^{18}} C_6H_5-\underset{\underset{\oplus}{_{18}OH_2}}{\overset{OH}{\overset{|}{C}}}-OH \xrightarrow{-H^+} C_6H_5-\underset{_{18}OH}{\overset{OH}{\overset{|}{C}}}-OH$$

$$\longrightarrow C_6H_5-\underset{_{18}O}{\underset{\|}{C}}-OH + C_6H_5-\underset{_{18}OH}{\underset{|}{C}}=O$$

Remember that C—O^{18} bond is difficult to break than the C—O bond.

1. **(c)** The HVZ reaction brings about halogenation only at the α-carbon of the fatty acid. In case the acid has two α-H's, α-dihalo product will be formed when 2 equivalents of halogen are used.

2. **(d)** The acid does not have an α–H, necessary for the reaction.

3–34. **(b, a)**

The α-halogen comes from halogen (Cl_2 or Br_2) whatever might the nature of PX_3 which is used for converting acid to acid halide.

1. (b)

2. **(c)** **The correct reason :** Carboxyl group only marginally decreases the electron density at *m*-position relative to *o*- and *p*-positions.

3. **(b)** **The correct explanation :** RCOCl, $(RCO)_2O$ and RCOOR' all add two molecules of Grignard reagents to give 3° alcohols.

4. **4.**

All carboxylic acids and phenols are soluble in aqueous NaOH. Four compounds are soluble in aqueous NaOH.

EXERCISE 17.3

1. (a) C-5 : n-Valeric, pentanoic C-6 : n-Caproic, hexanoic C-8 : n-Caprylic, octanoic
C-10 : *n*-Capric, decanoic C-12 : Lauric, dodecanoic.

(*b*) (*i*) 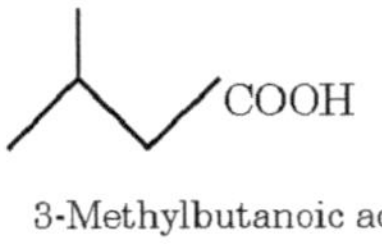 COOH
3-Methylbutanoic acid

(*ii*) 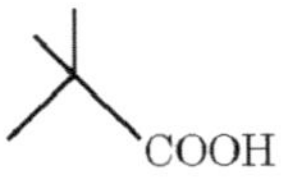 COOH
2, 2-Dimethylpropanoic acid

(*iii*) 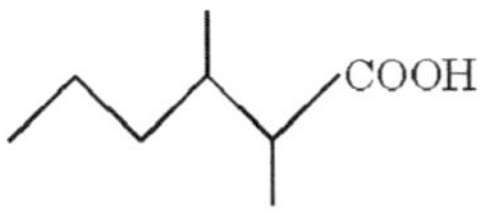 COOH
2, 3-Dimethylhexanoic acid

(*iv*) 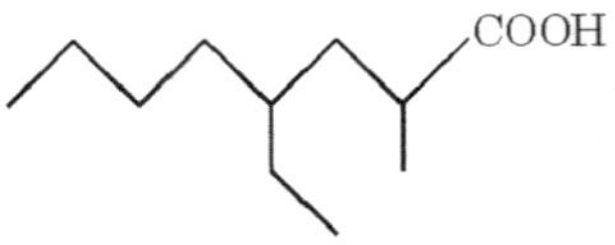 COOH
2-Methyl-4-ethyloctanoic acid

2. (*a*) $n\text{-}C_3H_7OH \xrightarrow{PBr_3} n\text{-}C_3H_7Br \xrightarrow[(ii)\ H^+]{(i)\ CN^-} n\text{-}C_3H_7COOH$

or (*i*) Mg/ether, (*ii*) CO_2

(*b*) $CH_3COCH_2CH_2CH_3 \xrightarrow[\text{(haloform raction)}]{(i)\ NaOI^-,(ii)\ H^+} CHI_3 + CH_3CH_2COOH$

3. (*a*) $(n\text{-}C_4H_9COO)_3$ Al (*b*) $(n\text{-}C_4H_9COO)_2Ca$
(*c*) $n\text{-}C_4H_9COONH_4$ (*d*), (*f*), (*h*), (*i*) and (*j*) no reaction.
(*e*) $n\text{-}C_4H_9CH_2OH$ (*g*) $n\text{-}C_3H_7CHBrCOOH$
(*k*) $n\text{-}C_4H_9COOCH_2C_4H_9\text{-}n$.

4. (*i*) $C_6H_5CH_2COOH + SOCl_2 \longrightarrow C_6H_5CH_2COCl + SO_2\uparrow + HCl\uparrow$
(*ii*) $3C_6H_5CH_2COOH + PCl_3 \longrightarrow 3C_6H_5CH_2COCl + H_3PO_3$
(*iii*) $C_6H_5CH_2COOH + PCl_5 \longrightarrow C_6H_5CH_2COCl + POCl_3 + HCl$
(*iv*) $2C_6H_5CH_2COOH + (CH_3CO)_2O \longrightarrow C_6H_5CH_2COOCOCH_2C_6H_5 + 2CH_3COOH$
(*v*) $C_6H_5CH_2COOH + CH_3OH \xrightarrow{H_2SO_4} C_6H_5CH_2COOCH_3 + H_2O$
(*vi*) $C_6H_5CH_2COOH + NH_3 \longrightarrow C_6H_5CH_2COONH_4 \xrightarrow{\Delta} C_6H_5CH_2CONH_2 + H_2O$.

5. (*a*) $Me_2CHCOOH \xrightarrow{SOCl_2} Me_2CHCOCl \xrightarrow{NH_3} Me_2CHCONH_2$
(*b*) $Me_2CHCOOH \xrightarrow{LiAlH_4} Me_2CHCH_2OH$
(*c*) $Me_2CHCOOH + n\text{-}C_4H_9MgBr \longrightarrow n\text{-}C_4H_{10}$
(*d*) $Me_2CHCOOH \xrightarrow{Mg} (Me_2CHCOO)_2\,Mg$.

6. (*a*) $\overset{14}{C}O_2 + CH_3CH_2CH_2MgBr \longrightarrow CH_3CH_2CH_2\overset{14}{C}OOH$

(*b*) $\overset{14}{C}O_2 + C_2H_5MgBr \longrightarrow C_2H_5\overset{14}{C}OOH \xrightarrow{LiAlH_4} C_2H_5\overset{14}{C}H_2OH \xrightarrow{SOCl_2} C_2H_5\overset{14}{C}H_2Cl \xrightarrow[(i)\ H^+]{(i)\ CN^-} C_2H_5\overset{14}{C}H_2COOH$

(*c*) $\overset{14}{C}O_2 + CH_3MgBr \rightarrow CH_3\overset{14}{C}OOH \xrightarrow{LiAlH_4} CH_3\overset{14}{C}H_2OH \xrightarrow[(ii)\ Mg]{(i)\ PBr_3} CH_3\overset{14}{C}H_2MgBr \xrightarrow[\text{oxide}]{\text{ethylene}} CH_3\overset{14}{C}H_2CH_2CH_2OH$

$\xrightarrow{KMnO_4} CH_3\overset{14}{C}H_2CH_2COOH$

(*d*) $\overset{14}{C}H_3OH \xrightarrow[(ii)\ Mg]{(i)\ PBr_3} \overset{14}{C}H_3MgBr \xrightarrow{HCHO} \overset{14}{C}H_3CH_2OH \xrightarrow[(ii)\ Mg]{(i)\ PBr_3} \overset{14}{C}H_3CH_2MgBr \xrightarrow[\text{oxide}]{\text{ethylene}} \overset{14}{C}H_3CH_2CH_2CH_2OH$

$\xrightarrow{KMnO_4} \overset{14}{C}H_3CH_2CH_2COOH$

7. It is advisable to proceed backward.

(*a*) $C_6H_5\underset{\displaystyle Br}{\underset{|}{C}H}COOH \xleftarrow{P, Br_2} C_6H_5CH_2COOH \xleftarrow[(ii)\ H_3O^+]{(i)\ CN^-} C_6H_5CH_2Cl \xleftarrow{Cl_2,\ heat} C_6H_5CH_3$

(b) 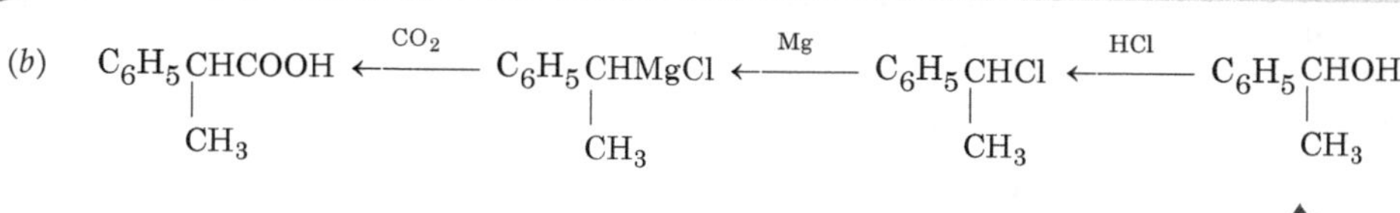

$$C_6H_6 \xrightarrow[FeCl_3]{Br_2} C_6H_5Br \xrightarrow{Mg} C_6H_5MgBr \xrightarrow{CH_3CHO} \uparrow$$

(c) $$CH_3CH_2CH=CHCOOH \xleftarrow{\text{alc. KOH}} CH_3CH_2CH_2\underset{\underset{\displaystyle Br}{|}}{C}HCOOH \xleftarrow{P,\ Br_2} CH_3CH_2CH_2CH_2COOH$$

$$CH_3CH_2CH_2CH_2OH \xrightarrow[(ii)\ Mg]{(i)\ P\,Br_3} CH_3CH_2CH_2CH_2MgBr \xrightarrow{CO_2} \uparrow$$

8. (a) (i) $H_2SO_4 > CH_3COOH > H_2O > C_2H_5OH > CH\equiv CH > NH_3 > C_2H_6$

(ii) $HOOCCH_2COOH > HOOCCH_2CH_2COOH > CH_3COOH$

(b) The weaker the acid, the more basic will be its anion.

$NaC_2H_5 > NaNH_2 > NaC\equiv CH > NaOC_2H_5 > NaOH > NaOOCCH_3 > NaHSO_4$

9. (a) $$CH\equiv CH \xrightarrow{CH_3MgBr} \underset{A}{HC\equiv CMgBr} \xrightarrow[(ii)\ H^+]{(i)\ CO_2} \underset{B}{HC\equiv CCOOH} \xrightarrow{H_2SO_4/HgSO_4}$$

$$\underset{\displaystyle OH}{HC=CHCOOH} \xrightarrow{\text{tautomerises}} \underset{\underset{\displaystyle O}{\|}}{HC}-CH_2-COOH \xrightarrow{KMnO_4} \underset{C}{CH_2(COOH)_2}$$

Note that compound B on hydration may also give ketone but it will not be oxidised to malonic acid, C.

$$HC\equiv CCOOH \xrightarrow{H_2SO_4/HgSO_4} H_2C=\underset{\underset{\displaystyle OH}{|}}{C}COOH \xrightarrow{\text{tautomerises}} H_3C-\underset{\underset{\displaystyle O}{\|}}{C}-COOH \xrightarrow{KMnO_4} CH_3COOH$$

(b) $$CH_3COOH \xrightarrow{LiAlH_4} \underset{A}{CH_3CH_2OH} \xrightarrow{HBr} \underset{B}{CH_3CH_2Br} \xrightarrow[(ii)\ CO_2]{(i)\ Mg} \underset{C}{CH_3CH_2COOH} \longrightarrow \underset{D}{CH_3CH_2COOAg} \xrightarrow{Br_2} \underset{E}{CH_3CH_2Br}$$

10. Excess or limited amount of CH_3MgBr forms CH_4, while excess of CH_3Li forms ketone.

(i) $CH_3CH_2COOH + CH_3MgBr \longrightarrow CH_4\uparrow + CH_3CH_2COO^-(MgBr)^+$

(ii) $CH_3CH_2COOH + CH_3Li \longrightarrow CH_4\uparrow + CH_3CH_2COO^-Li^+$

Since Li is more electropositive than Mg, R from R—Li will bear a more negative charge than R from R—MgX, hence RLi is a stronger nucleophile and capable of adding to the C = O of —COO⁻.

$$CH_3CH_2\overset{\overset{\displaystyle O}{\|}}{C}-O^-Li^+ \xrightarrow{CH_3Li} CH_3CH_2\overset{\overset{\displaystyle \bar{O}Li^+}{|}}{\underset{\underset{\displaystyle CH_3}{|}}{C}}-O^-Li^+ \xrightarrow{H_2O} CH_3CH_2\overset{\overset{\displaystyle OH}{|}}{\underset{\underset{\displaystyle CH_3}{|}}{C}}-OH \xrightarrow{-H_2O} CH_3CH_2\underset{\underset{\displaystyle CH_3}{|}}{C}=O$$

11. (a) (i) n-Butanoic acid gives effervescences of CO_2 with aq. $NaHCO_3$ solution.

(ii) Butanal gives a silver mirror on addition of Tollen's reagent, $[Ag(NH_3)_2]^{2+}$ (a solution of $AgNO_3$ in aq. NH_3).

(iii) n-Butanol evolves H_2 with metallic sodium.

(iv) Ether (methyl ethyl ether) dissolves in conc. H_2SO_4 with the evolution of heat.

(v) Alkane (butane) remains inert to all tests.

(b) (i) Formic acid (HCOOH) has an aldehydic type of hydrogen, hence it is readily oxidized by acidified $KMnO_4$ (indicated by decolourization of purple colour), and Tollen's reagent (indicated by formation of silver mirror).

(ii) Oxalic acid (HOOCCOOH) is oxidized by acidic $KMnO_4$, again indicated by decolourization of purple colour. Malonic acid loses CO_2 (g), on heating.

(iii) Here aq. $NaHCO_3$ solution will give CO_2 with both (acid chlorides are readily hydrolysed in alkaline as well as acidic medium), hence $AgNO_3$ solution in presence of HNO_3 should be used which will give white precipitate of AgCl with CH_3CH_2COCl insoluble in HNO_3.

(c) (i) $KMnO_4$ or Br_2/CCl_4 (ii) CrO_3/H_2SO_4 (positive for mandelic acid)

(iii) Hot $KMnO_4$ (positive for mesotartaric acid) ; elemental analysis for chlorine (positive for o-chlorobenzoic acid).

12. (*a*) Neutralization equivalent (NE) is the equivalent weight (g/eq.) of an acid as determined by titration with standard NaOH solution.

No. of eq of NaOH = No. of ionizable H's (No. of eq of acid)

$$= \frac{MW}{NE} \quad (\because \quad NE = ME/\text{No. of ionizable H's})$$

$$= \frac{210 \text{ g / mol}}{70 \text{ g / eq}} = \mathbf{3\ eq\ /\ mol}$$

(*b*)

$$NE = \frac{MW}{\text{No. of ionizable H'S}} = \frac{342 \text{ g / mol}}{6 \text{ eq / mol}} = \mathbf{57\ g/eq}$$

13. **Acetic acid.** Low m.p. ; low b.p. , soluble in water as well as in ether, stronger acid and weaker base.

Sodium acetate. High m.p. (decomposes), high b. p. (*d*), soluble in water, insoluble in ether, weaker acid and stonger base.

14. (*a*)

RCOOH, RCOOR′

↓ aq. $NaHCO_3$

org. layer → RCOOR′

aq. layer → RCOONa + H_2O $\xrightarrow{\text{HCl (aq.)}}$ RCOOH

(*b*)

C_3H_7COOH, ROH

↓ aq. $NaHCO_3$

ROH (organic layer)

aq. layer → $C_3H_7COONa + H_2O$ (Aqueous layer) $\xrightarrow[\text{to dryness}]{\text{evaporate}}$ C_3H_7COONa $\xrightarrow[H_2SO_4]{\text{Conc.}}$ C_3H_7COONa

Butyric acid is very much soluble in water, hence water should be evaporated from the aqueous solution.

(*c*)

RCOONa, Ph_3COH

↓ ether, filter

Insoluble → RCOONa (Insoluble)

Soluble → Ph_3COH + Ether $\xrightarrow[\text{ether}]{\text{evaporate}}$ Ph_3COH

15. Separation by sodium formate is similar like that by sodium bicarbonate ; sodium formate is so selected because formic acid is stronger than benzoic acid and weaker than *o*-chlorobenzoic acid.

$$\underset{\text{Weaker acid}}{C_6H_5COOH} + \underset{\text{Weaker base}}{HCOO^-} \rightleftarrows \underset{\text{Stronger base}}{C_6H_5COO^-} + \underset{\text{Stronger acid}}{HCOOH}$$

$$\underset{\text{Stronger acid}}{o\text{-}ClC_6H_4COOH} + \underset{\text{Stronger base}}{HCOO^-} \rightleftarrows \underset{\text{Weaker base}}{o\text{-}ClC_6H_4COO^-} + \underset{\text{Weaker acid}}{HCOOH}$$

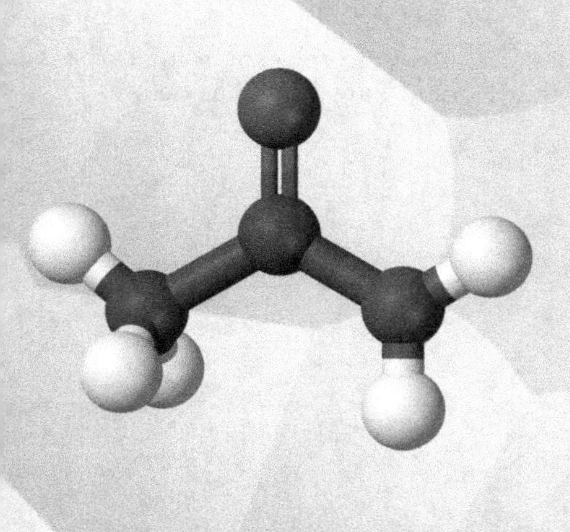

18

Functional Derivatives of Carboxylic Acids

CHAPTER HIGHLIGHTS

Four closely related functional derivatives of carboxylic acids are obtained by replacing —OH of the carboxylic group by —Cl, —OCOR, —NH_2, or —OR.

$$R-\overset{\overset{O}{\|}}{C}-Cl \qquad R-\overset{\overset{O}{\|}}{C}-O-\overset{\overset{O}{\|}}{C}-R \qquad R-\overset{\overset{O}{\|}}{C}-NH_2 \qquad R-\overset{\overset{O}{\|}}{C}-OR$$

Acid chloride | Acid anhydride | Amide | Ester

They all contain the **acyl group** $\left[R-\overset{\overset{O}{\|}}{C}-\right]$, and may be hydrolyzed to the parent acid using dilute OH^- or H_3O^+

$$R-\overset{\overset{O}{\|}}{C}- \;;\quad R-\overset{\overset{O}{\|}}{C}-X + H_2O \xrightarrow{H^+ \text{ or } OH^-} R-\overset{\overset{O}{\|}}{C}-OH + HX$$

Acyl group | Carboxylic acid derivative | Water | Carboxylic acid | Conjugate acid of leaving group

Acid derivatives are named from either the common name or the IUPAC name of the corresponding carboxylic acid. For example, four derivatives of acetic acid, CH_3COOH (IUPAC name : ethanoic acid) are named as below.

(*a*) **Acid chlorides.** Change *–ic acid* to *–yl chloride.*

(*b*) **Acid anhydrides.** Change *acid* to *anhydride.*

(*c*) **Acid amides.** Change *–ic acid* of common name (or *–oic acid* of IUPCA name) to *–amide.*

(*d*) **Esters.** Change *–ic acid* to *–ate,* preceded by name of alcohol or phenol group.

(*a*) $CH_3-C(=O)-Cl$
Acetyl chloride
(Ethanoyl chloride)

(*b*) $CH_3-C(=O)-O-C(=O)-CH_3$
Acetic anhydride
(Ethanoic anhydride)

(*c*) $CH_3-C(=O)-NH_2$
Acetamide
Ethanamide

(*d*) $CH_3-C(=O)-OC_2H_5$
Ethyl acetate
Ethyl ethanoate

TEST YOUR UNDERSTANDING - 18.1

1. Write IUPAC names of the following :

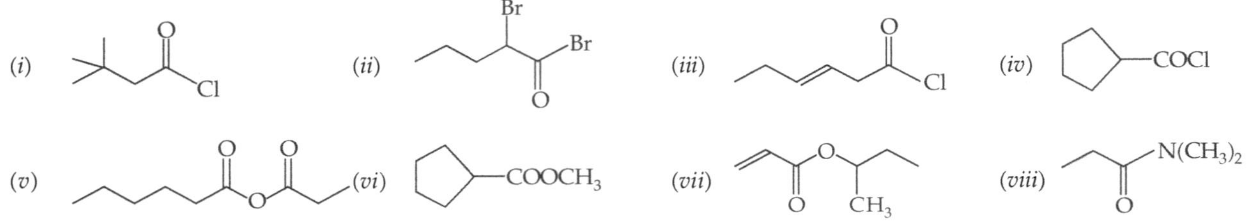

(*ix*) $CH_3NHCONHCH_3$ (*x*) $(CH_3)_2NCONH_2$

2. Write structural formula for each of the two following compounds.

(*i*) 2-Phenylbutanoyl chloride (*ii*) 2-Phenylbutanamide (*iii*) 2-Phenylbutanoic anhydride

(*iv*) N-Ethyl-2-phenylbutanamide (*v*) Butyl-2-phenylbutanoate (*vi*) 2-Phenylbutyl butanoate.

3. Why nitriles are often classified as acid derivatives ?

18.1 Structure of Carboxylic Acid Derivatives

Like other carbonyl containing compounds (aldehydes, ketones and carboxylic acids), derivatives of carboxylic acids have a planar arrangement of bonds to their carbonyl group. An important structural feature of these derivatives is that the atom attached to the acyl carbon bears an unshared pair of electrons that is capable of interacting with the carbonyl π system.

$$R-C(=\ddot{O}:)-\ddot{X}: \longleftrightarrow R-\overset{+}{C}(-\ddot{O}:^-)-\ddot{X}: \longleftrightarrow R-C(-\ddot{O}:^-)=\overset{+}{X}:$$

I II III

This interaction of the unshared electron pair (structures II and III) stabilizes the carbonyl group and decrease its electrophilic character. The extent of this electron delocalization due to X dependes upon the nature of the substituent X. More is the electronegativity of X, lesser is the electron donation to the carbonyl group and thus lesser will be the stabilizing effect ; consequently more will be electrophilic character of the carbonyl group and hence higher will be the reactivity of the derivative toward nucleophiles.

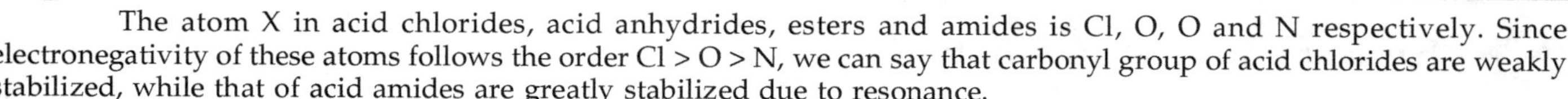

The atom X in acid chlorides, acid anhydrides, esters and amides is Cl, O, O and N respectively. Since electronegativity of these atoms follows the order Cl > O > N, we can say that carbonyl group of acid chlorides are weakly stabilized, while that of acid amides are greatly stabilized due to resonance.

Acid chloride

Weak resonance stabilization due to —I effect of chlorine as well as poor overlaping of 3*p* orbital of Cl with the *p* orbital of the carbonyl carbon.

Acid amide

Very effective resonance stabilization due to least —I effect of N as well as better overlaping of 2*p* orbital of N with *p* orbital of carbonyl carbon

As far as acid anhydrides and esters are concerned, carbonyl group of an ester is stabilized more than that of an acid anhydride because in acid anhydride there is a competition between two acyl groups for the oxygen lone pair, with the result each carbonyl group is stabilized less than the single carbonyl group of an ester.

Acid anhydride
(Each carbonyl group is less stabilized than that of an ester)

Ester
(Carbonyl group is more stable)

Thus the relative stability of the carbonyl group of the four acid derivatives follows the order.

Acid chloride < Acid anhydride < Ester < Amide

Hence electrophilic character of the carbonyl group of these derivatives will be

Acid chloride > Acid anhydride > Ester > Amide

(Decreasing electrophilic character (and hence reactivity toward nucleophiles of the carbonyl group)

Carbonyl group of carboxylate anion is extremely stabilized because the negatively charged oxygen (substituent X) is a powerful electron donor to the carbonyl group, hence carboxylates do not react with nucleophiles.

Relative stability and reactivity of carboxylic acid derivatives.

Derivative	*Formula*	*Stabilization*	*Relative Rate of hydrolysis*
Acid chloride	RCOCl	Very Small	10^{11}
Anhydride	$(RCO)_2O$	Small	10^{7}
Ester	RCOOR	Moderate	1.0
Amide	$RCONH_2$	Large	$< 10^{-2}$
Carboxylate anion	$RCOO^-$	Very large	

Rates are relative to ester as standard substrate at pH 7.

18.2 Nucleophilic Acyl Substitution

As in aldehydes and ketones, the carbonyl group in carboxylic acids and their derivatives performs two functions.

(*i*) It provides a site for nucleophilic attack.

(*ii*) It increases the acidity of α-hydrogens. This aspect is partly discussed in carboxylic acids and will be further discussed at a later stage.

Acyl compounds (carboxylic acids and their derivatives) typically undergo nucleophilic substitution in which —OH, —Cl, —OCOR, —OR, or —NH_2 is replaced by some other basic group, of course stronger than the group to be removed. Substitution at acyl carbon takes place much more readily than at a saturated carbon atom, *i.e.* at alkyl carbon in alkyl halides, R—X. Greater reactivity of carbonyl group toward nucleophiles is due to both electronic and steric factors : (*a*) the capability of oxygen to acquire electrons, and (*b*) the relatively unhindered transition state leading to tetrahedral intermediate from the trigonal reactant.

Trigonal C attack relatively unhindered

Tetrahedral C (Stable) (negative charge on O)

Acyl nucleophilic substitution

Tetrahedral C attack relatively hindered

Pentavalent C (unstable)

Alkyl nucleophilic substitution.

Thus toward nucleophiles, acid chlorides are more reactive than alkyl chlorides, amides are more reactive than amines, and esters are more reactive than ethers. Nucleophilic substitution at acyl carbon (nucleophilic addition-elimination) is similar to some extent (first step or initial step) to the nucleophilic addition to aldehydes and ketones. The two reactions differ in the second step. The tetrahedral intermediate from an aldehyde or ketone accepts a proton to form a stable **addition product**. In contrast, the tetrahedral intermediate from an acyl compound eliminates a leaving group leading to regeneration of the carbon oxygen double bond (a trigonal compound) and thus the net result is a **substitution product**. Therefore, the overall process in the case of acyl substitution occurs by a **nucleophilic addition-elimination** mechanism.

Reactant (Trigonal) — Transition state (Becoming tetrahedral) — Intermediate (Tetrahedral) — Addition product

Nucleophilic addition on aldehydes and ketones

Reactant (Trigonal) — Intermediate — Product (Trigonal) — Leaving group

Nucleophilic addition-elimination on acyl compounds.

Now the question arises why the two classes of compounds differ in their reaction toward nucleophiles. The difference lies in the nature of the substituent present on acyl carbon ; in aldehydes and ketones, this substituent (R′) is either H or an alkyl group while in acyl compounds, it (X) is OH (in carboxylic acids), Cl (in acid chlorides), OCOR, COR, or NH_2. The ease with which, :X is lost depends upons its basicity ; *the weaker the base, the better the leaving group.* For acid chloride, acid anhydrides, esters, and amides, :X is respectively

$$\underset{\text{very weak base}}{Cl^-}, \quad \underset{\text{moderately weak base}}{^-OOCR}, \quad \underset{\text{strong base}}{^-OR} \quad \text{and} \quad \underset{\text{stronger base}}{^-NH_2}$$

Hence Cl^- is lost with maximum ease and hence acid chlorides are the most reactive, while NH_2^- is lost with the most difficulty hence acid amides are the least reactive toward nucleophilic substitution. In general, the overall order of reactivity is

$$\underset{\text{Acid chloride}}{RCOCl} > \underset{\text{Acid anhydride}}{RCOOCOR} > \underset{\text{Ester}}{RCOOR'} > \underset{\text{Amide}}{RCONH_2}$$

For an aldehyde or ketone to react by nucleophilic addition-eliminiation way, their intermediate would have to eliminate a hydride ion (H:⁻) or an alkanide ion (R:⁻), both of which are the strongest bases of all and hence very poor leaving groups. Thus the intermediates of aldehydes and ketones undergo addition reaction. Remember that alkanide ion from the haloform reaction behaves as a good leaving group, this is because here the leaving group is a weakly basic trihalomethyl anion, $X_3C:^-$.

Thus nucleophilic acyl substitution proceeds by two steps. Generally, the overall rate is affected by the rate of both steps, but the first step (formation of tetrahedral intermediate) is more important. As in nucleophilic additions on aldehydes and ketones, here also the first step is (*a*) favoured by electron withdrawal, which stabilizes the developing negative charge in the transition state, and (*b*) hindered by the presence of bulky groups, which become crowded together in the transition state. The second step depends on the basicity of the leaving group, :X (weaker a base, more readily it will be lost).

Acyl nucleophilic substitution takes place readily and even by weaker nucleophiles in presence of acid because protonation of carbonyl oxygen makes carbonyl carbon more electrophilic and hence more reactive toward nucleophile. Futher, here oxygen can now acquire π electrons without having a negative charge.

$$\underset{X}{\overset{R}{>}}C=O \underset{}{\overset{H^+}{\rightleftharpoons}} \underset{X}{\overset{R}{>}}C=\overset{+}{O}H \xrightarrow{:Nu} \left[R-\overset{Nu}{\underset{X}{C}}\cdots\overset{\delta+}{OH} \right] \longrightarrow R-\overset{Nu}{\underset{X}{C}}-OH \longrightarrow \underset{Nu}{\overset{R}{>}}C=O + H:X$$

Undergoes nucleophilic attack more readily

Thus we can explain why acid derivatives are hydrolyzed more readily in acidic solution (here : Nu is H_2O:) than in neutral medium. Acid derivatives are also more readily hydrolyzed in alkaline medium than in neutral medium. Here the reason being the fact that the alkaline solutions provide a strong nucleophile (OH^-).

$$\underset{X}{\overset{R}{>}}C=O + \underset{\text{A strong nucleophile}}{:OH^-} \longrightarrow R-\overset{O^-}{\underset{X}{C}}-OH \xrightarrow[(-:X^-)]{} R-C\overset{O}{\underset{OH}{\lessgtr}} \xrightarrow{OH^-} R-C\overset{O}{\underset{O^-}{\lessgtr}}$$

TEST YOUR UNDERSTANDING - 18.2

1. Which of the compound of each pair undergoes hydrolysis rapidly ?

(*i*) Cl_3CCOCl and F_3CCOCl.

(*ii*) CH_3COOCH_3 and $C_6H_5-COOCH_3$

(*iii*) Methyl benzoate ($C_6H_5COOCH_3$) and methyl 4-nitrobenzoate (p-$O_2NC_6H_4COOCH_3$)

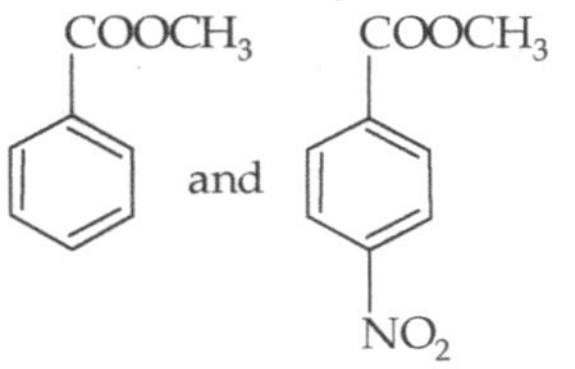

(*iv*) Methyl benzoate ($C_6H_5COOCH_3$) and methyl 2,4,6-trimethylbenzoate

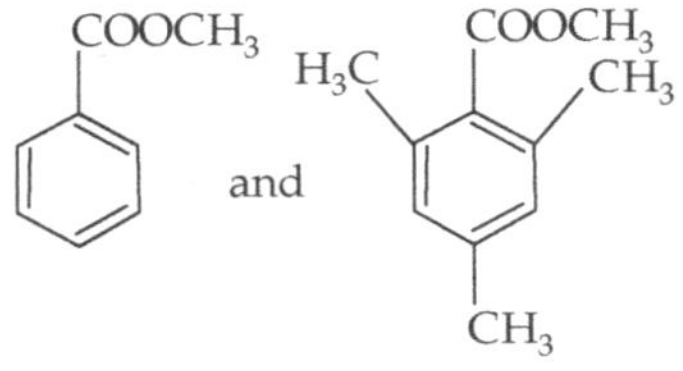

(*v*) CH_3COOCH_3 and $CH_3CONHCH_3$.

2. Give the structure of the product obtained when each of the following compound is treated with ammonia.

(*i*) $CH_3CHClCOOH$ (*ii*) $ClCH_2COCl$ (*iii*) 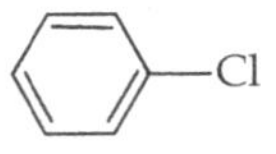 C_6H_5Cl (*iv*) o-HOC_6H_4COOH

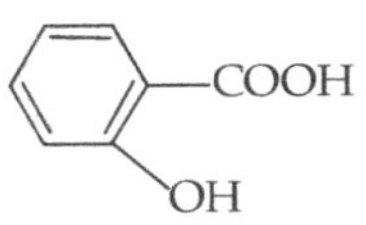

3. Although ketones do not undergo nucleophilic substitution, following reactions occur. Explain.

(*i*) $RCOCCl_3 \xrightarrow{OH^-} RCOOH + CHCl_3$

(*ii*) 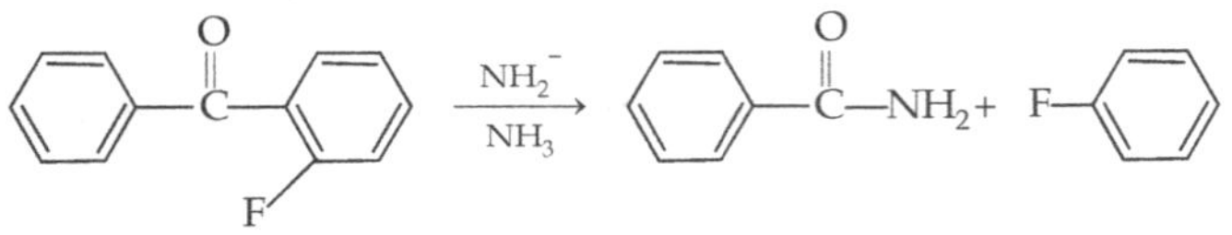 $C_6H_5COC_6H_4F$ (o-F) $\xrightarrow[NH_3]{NH_2^-} C_6H_5CONH_2 + F{-}C_6H_5$

18.3 Preparation of Acid Derivatives

We will come across many instances where one acid derivative is converted into other. The order of reactivity (or the stabilization order) of acid derivatives given earlier gives us a clue as to which syntheses are practical and which are not. In general, **a more stable (less reactive) acyl compound can be synthesised from less stable (more reactive), but the reverse is usually difficult** *and, when possible, requires special reagents.* For example, an ester can be made from the corresponding acid chloride or anhydride, but not from amide. In general, for synthesis of acid derivatives by acyl transfer the reactant must have a better leaving group at the acyl carbon than the product.

(*a*) **Preparation of acid chlorides**. Since acyl chlorides are the most reactive of the acid derivatives, we must use special reagents to prepare them. We use acid chlorides of inorganic acids, *viz* PCl_5 (an acid chloride of phosphoric acid), PCl_3 (an acid chloride of phosphorous acid), and thionyl chloride (an acid chloride of sulphurous acid). Reactions have already been given in properties of carboxylic acids. All of these reactions are examples of acyl nucleophilic substitution reactions.

(*b*) **Preparation of acid anhydrides.** Of the four carboxylic acid derivatives, acid anhydrides are less reactive (*i.e.* more stable) only from acid chlorides ; hence acid anhydrides can be prepared only from acid chlorides.

$$R{-}\overset{O}{\overset{\|}{C}}{-}Cl + HO{-}\overset{O}{\overset{\|}{C}}{-}R' \xrightarrow{\text{Pyridine}} R{-}\overset{O}{\overset{\|}{C}}{-}O{-}\overset{O}{\overset{\|}{C}}{-}R' + HCl$$

This method is applicable to the preparation of both symmetrical (R and R′ are same) and mixed anhydrides.

Sodium salts of carboxylic acids also react with acyl chlorides to give anhydrides.

$$R{-}\overset{O}{\overset{\|}{C}}{-}Cl + Na^+\bar{O}{-}\overset{O}{\overset{\|}{C}}{-}R' \longrightarrow R{-}\overset{O}{\overset{\|}{C}}{-}O{-}\overset{O}{\overset{\|}{C}}{-}R' + NaCl$$

In this reaction a carboxylate anion acts as a nucleophile and brings about nucleophilic substitution at the acyl carbon of the chloride.

Cyclic anhydrides can sometimes be prepared by simply heating the appropriate dicarboxylic acid. However this method succeeds, only when anhydride formation leads to a five- or six -membered ring.

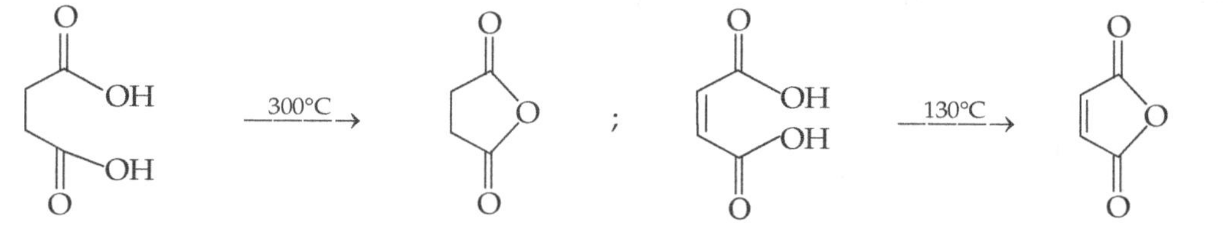

$$\text{Succinic acid} \xrightarrow{300°C} \text{Succinic anhydride} \quad ; \quad \text{Maleic acid} \xrightarrow{130°C} \text{Maleic anhydride}$$

$$\text{Phthalic acid} \xrightarrow{230°C} \text{Phthalic anhydride}$$

TEST YOUR UNDERSTANDING - 18.3

1. Explain the following.

(*a*) Adipic acid (1, 6-hexanedioic) does not form a cyclic anhydride on heating, but forms a cyclic ketone ; while suberic acid (1, 8-octanedioic acid) does not form a cyclic ketone.

(*b*) Benzoic anhydride is formed in excellent yield by adding one molar equivalent of water to two molar equivalents of benzoyl chloride.

The most important member of acid anhydrides, **acetic anhydride**, is prepared by the reaction of acetic acid with **ketene**, $CH_2 = C = O$, which itself is prepared by high temperature dehydration of acetic acid.

$$CH_3COOH \xrightarrow[(-H_2O)]{AlPO_4,\,700°C} CH_2 = C = O \xrightarrow{CH_3COOH} \underset{\text{Acetic anhydride}}{(CH_3CO)_2O}$$

(c) **Preparation of esters.** Esters are usually prepared by the reaction of alcohols (or phenols) with acids or acid chlorides.

1. **From carboxylic acids** (*esterification*). Carboxylic acids react with alcohols to form esters through a condensation reaction known as **esterification,** or **Fischer esterification.**

$$R{-}\overset{\overset{\displaystyle O}{\|}}{C}{-}OH + R'{-}OH \underset{}{\overset{HA}{\rightleftharpoons}} R{-}\overset{\overset{\displaystyle O}{\|}}{C}{-}OR' + H_2O$$

Esterifications are acid catalyzed (conc. H_2SO_4 or HCl), and proceed very slowly in the absence of strong acids. Since the reaction is reversible, the yield of ester can be increased in two manners. (For details, consult chapter on "Carboxylic Acids").

(*a*) By using excess of either the carboxylic acid or the alcohol depending on the availability and cost.

(*b*) By removing water from the reaction mixture as soon as it is formed .

Mechanism of esterification. This is a typical mechanism of acid-catalyzed nucleophilic addition-elimination at acyl carbon atom.

An important question about the mechanism of acid-catalyzed esterification is the origin of alkoxy oxygen of the ester, *i.e.* whether it is coming from carboxylic acid or alcohol. In other words whether it is the C—O bond of the alcohol or of the carboxylic acid that is broken during esterification. It has been proved by isotopically labelled experiment that the C—O bond of the carboxylic acid is broken .

$$C_6H_5{-}\overset{\overset{\displaystyle O}{\|}}{C}{-}OH + CH_3{-}\overset{18}{O}{-}H \overset{HA}{\rightleftharpoons} C_6H_5{-}\overset{\overset{\displaystyle O}{\|}}{C}{-}\overset{18}{O}{-}CH_3 + H_2O$$

The essential steps of the mechanisum are summarised below

$$R\text{—}\overset{\overset{\ddot{O}:}{\|}}{C}\text{—}\ddot{O}H + H^+ \rightleftharpoons R\text{—}\overset{\overset{+\ddot{O}H}{\|}}{C}\text{—}\ddot{O}H \;+\; R'OH \rightleftharpoons R\text{—}\underset{:\ddot{O}H}{\overset{:\ddot{O}H}{C}}\text{—}\overset{\oplus}{\ddot{O}}R'(H)$$

Carboxylic acid accepts proton from strong acid catalyst

Alcohol attacks the protonated carbonyl group to give a tetrahedral intermediate

A proton is lost at one oxygen and gained at another

$$\rightleftharpoons R\text{—}\underset{\oplus\ddot{O}H_2}{\overset{:\ddot{O}H}{C}}\text{—}OR' \rightleftharpoons R\text{—}\overset{\overset{\oplus :O\text{—}H}{\|}}{C}\text{—}OR' + H_2\ddot{O}: \rightleftharpoons R\text{—}\overset{\overset{\ddot{O}:}{\|}}{C}\text{—}\ddot{O}R' + H_3\overset{+}{O}:$$

Loss of a molecule of water gives a protonated ester

Transfer of a proton to a base (water)

Ester is formed

Salient features of acid-catalyed esterification

(*i*) All steps of the reaction are reversible, so steps leading to forward reaction constitute mechanism of *acid-catalyzed esterification of an acid*. However, the reverse steps of the reaction constitute the *mechanism of acid catalyzed hydrolysis of an ester.*

(*ii*) The reaction can be forced to proceed in a particular direction by changing the conditions. The reaction can be forced to esterification by taking excess of alcohol and removing water (product) as soon as it is formed. On the other hand, for carrying out the reverse reaction (*i.e.* for acidic hydrolysis of an ester), large excess of water should be used, *i.e.* the ester is refluxed with dilute aqueous HCl or dil. aqueous H_2SO_4.

(*iii*) Both reactions *i.e.* acid-catalyzed esterification of an acid as well as acid-catalyzed hydrolysis of an ester are affected by steric factors.

(*iv*) Mineral acid speeds up both processes by protonating carbonyl oxygen and thus rendering carbonyl carbon more susceptible to nucleophilic attack. In esterification, the nucleophile is an alcohol molecule and the leaving group is a water molecule ; in acidic hydrolysis, the roles are exactly reversed.

(*v*) Both processes involve similar type of C—O cleavage (*acyl-oxygen cleavage*).

Esterification. $$C_6H_5\text{—}\overset{\overset{O}{\|}}{C}\,\vdots\,O\text{—}H + CH_3\text{—}\overset{18}{O}\,\vdots\,H \xrightleftharpoons{H^+} C_6H_5\text{—}\overset{\overset{O}{\|}}{C}\text{—}\overset{18}{O}CH_3 + H_2O$$

Hydrolysis. $$C_6H_5\text{—}\overset{\overset{O}{\|}}{C}\,\vdots\,OCH_3 + H\text{—}\overset{18}{O}\,\vdots\,H \xrightleftharpoons{H^+} C_6H_5\text{—}\overset{\overset{O}{\|}}{C}\text{—}\overset{18}{O}H + CH_3OH$$

2. **Esters from acid chlorides and acid anhydrides.** Since acid chlorides and acid anhydrides are more reactive toward nucleophilic substitution than carboxylic acids, the reaction of an acyl chloride with an alcohol occurs rapidly in an irreversible manner and in absence of an acid catalyst. However, pyridine is often added to the reaction mixture to remove HCl (pyridine may also react with the acyl chloride to form an acylpyridinium ion which is more reactive toward the nucleophile even than the acyl chloride).

$$R\text{—}\overset{\overset{O}{\|}}{C}\text{—}Cl + R'OH + C_5H_5\ddot{N} \longrightarrow R\text{—}\overset{\overset{O}{\|}}{C}\text{—}OR' + C_5H_5\overset{+}{N}H\;Cl^-$$

Aromatic acid chlorides (ArCOCl) are considerably less reactive than the aliphatic acid chlorides.

$$(RCO)_2O + R'OH \longrightarrow RCOOR' + RCOOH$$

Cyclic anhydrides react with one molar equivalent of an alcohol to form compounds that are both esters and acids.

$$\text{Phthalic anhydride} + CH_3\underset{OH}{CH}CH_2CH_3 \xrightarrow{110°C} C_6H_4(COOH)(COOCH(CH_3)CH_2CH_3)$$

Phthalic anhydride — *sec*-Butyl hydrogen phthalate

3. **Transesterification.** When an ester is treated with an alcohol in presence of acid (H_2SO_4 or dry HCl) or base (usually alkoxide ion), alcoholysis (cleavage by an alcohol) of an ester takes place to form new ester.

$$\underset{\text{High boiling}}{R{-}\overset{O}{\overset{\|}{C}}{-}OR'} + \underset{\text{High boiling}}{R''OH} \overset{\overset{+}{H}\text{ or }\overset{-}{OR}}{\rightleftharpoons} \underset{\text{Higher boiling}}{R{-}\overset{O}{\overset{\|}{C}}{-}OR''} + \underset{\text{Lower boiling alcohol}}{R'OH}$$

Since the reaction is reversible, to carry out the reaction toward completion, it is necessary either to use a large excess of the alcohol or to remove one of the products from the reaction mixture (when the alcohol formed has low boiling point).

$$\underset{\text{Methyl acrylate}}{CH_2=CHCOOCH_3} + \underset{\text{Butyl alcohol}}{CH_3CH_2CH_2CH_2OH} \overset{HA}{\rightleftharpoons} \underset{\text{Butyl acrylate}}{CH_2=CHCOOCH_2CH_2CH_2CH_3} + CH_3OH$$

(*d*) **Preparation of amides.** Among the four acid derivatives, amides are the least reactive, hence these can be prepared by treating acyl chlorides, anhydrides, or esters with ammonia or amines (acylation of amines or ammonia). As expected, acid chlorides are the most reactive and carboxylate ions are the least.

$$\underbrace{RCOCl + 2NH_3}_{1:2\text{ molar ratio}} \longrightarrow RCONH_2 + NH_4Cl$$

$$\underbrace{(RCO)_2O + 2R'NH_2}_{1:2\text{ molar ratio}} \longrightarrow RCONHR' + RCOO^-H_3\overset{+}{N}R'$$

$$\underbrace{RCOOR' + R''_2NH}_{1:1\text{ molar ratio}} \longrightarrow RCONR_2'' + R'OH$$

Note that two molar equivalents of amine are required in the reaction with acyl chlorides and acid anhydrides ; one molecule of amine acts as a nucleophile while the other as a Bronsted base to remove the acid formed during these reactions. In case the amine used is costly or available only in small quantities, the reaction is carried out successfully using one molar equivalent of amine in presence of some other base like NaOH to react with the acid (HCl or RCOOH) formed. In case acid chloride (or acid anhydride) and ammonia are taken in 1 : 1 molar ratio, whole of the reactant will not be converted into product as is evident by following example.

$$RCOCl + NH_3 \longrightarrow \frac{1}{2}RCONH_2 + \frac{1}{2}NH_4Cl + \frac{1}{2}RCOCl$$

In industry, amides are more often made by heating ammonium salts of carboxylic acids.

$$RCOOH \xrightarrow{NH_3} RCOO^- NH_4 \xrightarrow{\text{evaporate to dryness}} RCONH_2 + H_2O$$

Since carboxylate ion has low reactivity toward nucleophilic addition-elimination, further reaction does not take place in aqueous solution. However, if the dry ammonium salt is heated, dehydration takes place forming amide.

TEST YOUR UNDERSTANDING - 18.4

1. (*a*) Predict which of the reaction takes place easily.

(*i*) $CH_3COCl + H_2O \longrightarrow CH_3COOH + HCl$

(*ii*) $CH_3COOH + NH_3 \longrightarrow CH_3CONH_2 + H_2O$

(*iii*) $(CH_3CO)_2O + NaOH \longrightarrow CH_3COOH + CH_3COONa$

(*iv*) $CH_3COBr + C_2H_5OH \longrightarrow CH_3COOC_2H_5 + HBr$

(*v*) $CH_3CONH_2 + NaOH \longrightarrow CH_3COONa + NH_3$

(*vi*) $CH_3COOCH_3 + Br^- \longrightarrow CH_3COBr + OCH_3^-$

(*b*) Give chemical reaction used for preparing *ter*-butyl acetate from acetic acid.

(*c*) RCOCl cannot be perpared by the reaction of HCl with RCOOH. Explain.

18.4 Properties of Acid Derivatives

1. The presence of the C = O group in acid derivatives makes them polar and thus these compounds have definite dipole moments. Dipole-dipole interactions contribute to the intermolecular attractive forces and hence these compounds have higher boiling points than hydrocarbons of similar shape and molecular weight. Further, they lack a hydrogen attached to electronegative oxygen (except amides in which H is attached to N), their molecules cannot form strong hydrogen bonds to each other ; hence their boiling points are lower than those of acids and alcohols of comparable molecular weight. The boiling points of these derivatives (except amides) are about the same as those of comparable aldehydes and ketones. However, amides have quite high boiling points because they are capable of forming strong intermolecular hydrogen bonding. Since N, N-disubstituted amides cannot form hydrogen bonds to each other, they have lower melting and boiling points.

$$R-C(=O)-N(H)-H\cdots O=C(R)-N(H)-H\cdots$$

2. Lower esters and amides are soluble in water as these are capable of forming hydrogen bonding with water.

3. Acid chlorides have sharp, irritating odors, at least partly due to their ready hydrolysis to HCl and carboxylic acids. Low molecular weight esters are fairly volatile and have pleasant odors ; hence these are often used in the preparation of perfumes and artificial flavourings.

(A) Reactions of Acyl Chlorides

(*i*) Since acyl chlorides are the most reactive of the acyl derivatives, they are easily converted to less reactive ones, *viz.* anhydrides, esters, and amides and also acids very easily (Reactions discussed earlier).

$$R-\overset{O}{\overset{\|}{C}}-O^- + Cl^- \xleftarrow[H_2O]{OH^-} R-\overset{O}{\overset{\|}{C}}-Cl \xrightarrow{H_2O} R-\overset{O}{\overset{\|}{C}}-OH + HCl$$

$$R-\overset{O}{\overset{\|}{C}}-OR' \xleftarrow[base]{R'OH} R-\overset{O}{\overset{\|}{C}}-Cl \xrightarrow{NaOOCR'} R-\overset{O}{\overset{\|}{C}}-O-\overset{O}{\overset{\|}{C}}-R' + NaCl$$

$$R-\overset{O}{\overset{\|}{C}}-NR_2 \textbf{ or } R-\overset{O}{\overset{\|}{C}}-NHR \xleftarrow[or\ R_2NH]{RNH_2} R-\overset{O}{\overset{\|}{C}}-Cl \xrightarrow{2NH_3} R-\overset{O}{\overset{\|}{C}}-NH_2 + NH_4Cl$$

In the laboratory, amides and esters are usually prepared from the acid chloride rather than from the acid itself since both the steps (preparation of acid chloride and its reactions with ammonia or an alcohol) are rapid and irreversible.

$$R—\overset{O}{\overset{\|}{C}}—OH \xrightarrow[\text{heat}]{SOCl_2} R—\overset{O}{\overset{\|}{C}}—Cl \xrightarrow[\text{or R'OH/pyridine}]{NH_3,\text{ cold}} R—\overset{O}{\overset{\|}{C}}—NH_2 \textbf{ or } R—\overset{O}{\overset{\|}{C}}—OR'$$

Acetyl chloride is frequently used in **acetylation (acylation, in general)** ; a reaction in which hydrogen of alcoholic, phenolic, amino, or imino group is replaced by acetyl (CH_3CO –) group.

(*ii*) **Friedel-Carft acylation.**

$$R—\overset{O}{\overset{\|}{C}}—Cl + ArH \xrightarrow[\text{Lewis acid}]{AlCl_3\text{ or other}} \underset{\text{A ketone}}{R—\overset{O}{\overset{\|}{C}}—Ar} + HCl$$

(*iii*) **Reaction of organometallic compounds.** Recall that ketones are formed with Grignard reagents, organolithium compounds, and organocopper compounds ; however the latter are preferred because organocopper reagents do not react with many of the functional groups with which Grignard reagents and organolithiums do react, *viz.*, —NO_2, —CN, —CO—, —COOR, etc.

$$R'—Li \xrightarrow{CuX} R'—\overset{R'}{\overset{|}{Cu}}Li \xrightarrow{RCOCl} R'—\overset{O}{\overset{\|}{C}}—R$$

(*iv*) **Reduction**

$$R—CH_2OH \xleftarrow{LiAlH_4} R—\overset{O}{\overset{\|}{C}}—Cl \xrightarrow[\text{or Rosenmund reduction}]{LiAlH(OBu\text{-}t)_3} R—\overset{O}{\overset{\|}{C}}—H$$

TEST YOUR UNDERSTANDING - 18.5

1. Write the structure of the tetrahedral intermediate formed in the reaction of benzoyl choride with each of the following :
 (*a*) CH_3COOH (*b*) C_2H_5OH (*c*) $(CH_3)_2NH$ (*d*) H_2O.
2. The values of K_a for hydrazoic acid (HN_3) and acetic acid (CH_3COOH) are 2.6×10^{-5} and 1.8×10^{-5} respectively. Place the acyl azides ($RCON_3$) at proper place regarding reactivity of acyl derivatives.
3. List the reagent for converting benzoyl chloride to
 (*a*) benzaldehyde (*b*) benzamide (*c*) benzyl alcohol (*d*) benzyl benzoate
 (*e*) benzoic anhydride (*f*) N-benzylbenzamide (*g*) benzoyl azide, $C_6H_5CON_3$.
4. Give the products of reaction of Me_2CuLi followed by hydrolysis with each of the following
 (*a*) NC $(CH_2)_4COCl$ (*b*) $CH_3CO—C_6H_4—COCl$ (*c*) $H_5C_2O_2C(CH_2)_4COCl$.

(B) Reactions of Acid Anhydrides.

(*i*) Acid anhydrides undergo the same reactions as acid chlorides, but a little more slowly. Compounds containing acetyl group are often prepared from acetic anhydride because it is cheap, readily available, less volatile and more easily handled than acetyl chloride and it does not form corrosive hydrogen chloride.

$$R—\overset{O}{\overset{\|}{C}}—OCH_3 + RCOOH \xleftarrow{CH_3OH} \mathbf{R—\overset{O}{\overset{\|}{C}}—OCOR} \xrightarrow{NH_3} R—\overset{O}{\overset{\|}{C}}—NH_2 + RCOONH_4$$

$$RCOO^- + R—\overset{O}{\overset{\|}{C}}—O^- \xleftarrow[H_2O]{OH^-} \mathbf{R—\overset{O}{\overset{\|}{C}}—OCOR} \xrightarrow{H_2O} R—\overset{O}{\overset{\|}{C}}—OH + RCOOH$$

Like acetyl chloride, acetic anhydride is used in acetylation (acylation) of alcohols, phenols, amines and imines.

(*ii*) **Friedel-Craft acylation.**

$$(RCO)_2O + ArH \xrightarrow{AlCl_3} Ar-\overset{O}{\overset{||}{C}}-R + RCOOH$$

Phthalic anhydride + Benzene $\xrightarrow[\text{Friedel-Craft acylation}]{AlCl_3}$ *o*-Benzoylbenzoic acid $\xrightarrow[\text{Cyclisation}]{\text{Conc. } H_2SO_4}$ 9, 10-Anthraquinone

TEST YOUR UNDERSTANDING - 18.6

1. Write down the structures of the major organic product of each of the following reactions.

(*a*) Acetic anhydride + $CH_3OH \xrightarrow{H^+}$

(*b*) Acetic anhydride + $2CH_3OH \xrightarrow{H^+}$

(*c*) Acetic anhydride + NH_3 (1 mol) $\longrightarrow$

(*d*) Succinic anhydride + $(CH_3)_2NH$ (2 mol) $\longrightarrow$

(*e*) Succinic anhydride + NaOH (2 mol) $\longrightarrow$

(*f*) Acetic anhydride + $2CH_3MgBr \xrightarrow{H_3O^+}$

(*g*) Succinic anhydride + Benzene $\xrightarrow{AlCl_3}$

2. (*a*) Give the possible ways for preparing following anhydrides :

(*i*) $CH_3\overset{O}{\overset{||}{C}}-O-\overset{O}{\overset{||}{C}}CH_2CH_3$

(*ii*) $H-\overset{O}{\overset{||}{C}}-O-\overset{O}{\overset{||}{C}}-CH_3$

(*b*) Can formic anhydride be prepared by heating formic acid ?

3. Predict the products of the following reactions :

$$\text{Toluene + Phthalic anhydride} \xrightarrow{AlCl_3} [A] \xrightarrow[\text{heat}]{\text{Conc. } H_2SO_4} [B]$$

(C) Reactions of Esters.

Esters are less reactive than acyl chlorides and acid anhydrides toward nucleophilic substitution. The three important reactions are conversion to amides, other esters (*transesterification or alcoholysis*) and hydrolysis.

(*i*) $CH_3COOC_2H_5 + NH_3 \longrightarrow CH_3CONH_2 + C_2H_5OH$

(*ii*) $CH_3COOC_2H_5 + CH_3OH \longrightarrow CH_3COOCH_3 + C_2H_5OH$

(*iii*) $CH_3COOC_2H_5 + H_2O \xrightarrow{H^+ \text{ or } OH^-} CH_3COOH \text{ (or } CH_3COO^-) + C_2H_5OH$

Since acid catalyzed esterification and acid hydrolysis of esters are reversible, if we reverse the mechanism of esterification (discussed earlier), we get the mechanism of acid catalyzed ester hydrolysis.

Mechanism of base promoted ester hydrolysis. Unlike acid catalyzed, base promoted hydrolysis of ester, also known as **saponification**, forms an alcohol and sodium salt of the acid.

$$R-\overset{O}{\overset{||}{C}}-OR' + OH^- \longrightarrow R-\overset{O}{\overset{||}{C}}-O^- + R'OH$$

The carboxylate ion is very unreactive toward nucleophilic substitution because it is quite stable and negatively charged, hence base-catalyzed hydrolysis of ester is an irreversible reaction. Since base is consumed in the reaction, we generally speak *base-promoted rather than base-catalyzed.* The base-promoted hydrolysis of an ester is also an example of nucleophilic addition-elimination at the acyl carbon

$$R(R'O)C{=}O + {:}\ddot{O}H^- \underset{}{\overset{slow}{\rightleftharpoons}} R{-}C(O^-)(OR'){-}\ddot{O}{-}H \rightleftharpoons$$

OH⁻ attacks the carbonyl carbon

The tetrahedral intermediate expels an alkoxide ion (acyl-oxygen fission)

$$R{-}\overset{O}{\overset{\|}{C}}{-}\ddot{O}{-}H + {:}\ddot{O}{-}R'^{-} \longrightarrow R{-}\overset{O}{\overset{\|}{C}}{-}\ddot{O}{:}^- + H{-}\ddot{O}{-}R'$$

Transfer of a proton leads to more stable carboxylate ion

Evidence for the above acyl-oxygen fission.

(*a*) **Istotopically labelled experiment.** When ethyl propanoate labelled with ^{18}O in the ether type oxygen of the ester is subjected to hydrolysis with aqueous base, all of the ^{18}O is found to be present in ethanol, and none in the propanoate ion. This indicates that the bond between acyl group and oxygen is cleaved during hydrolysis.

Acyl-oxygen fission / Alkyl-oxygen fission

$$C_2H_5{-}\overset{O}{\overset{\|}{C}}{-}{}^{18}O{-}C_2H_5 \xrightarrow[\text{(acyl-oxygen fission)}]{OH^-} C_2H_5{-}\overset{O}{\overset{\|}{C}}{-}O^- + HO^{18}C_2H_5 \quad \text{(Products formed)}$$

$$\xrightarrow[\text{alkyl-oxygen fission}]{OH^-} C_2H_5{-}\overset{O}{\overset{\|}{C}}{-}{}^{18}O^- + HOC_2H_5 \quad \text{(Not isolated)}$$

(*b*) **Stereochemical evidence.** Saponification of esters of optically active alcohols proceeds with **retention of configuration.**

$$CH_3{-}\overset{O}{\overset{\|}{C}}{-}O{-}C(H)(C_6H_5)(CH_3) \xrightarrow{OH^-} CH_3COO^- + HO{-}C(H)(C_6H_5)(CH_3)$$

Acyl

(R)-(+)-1-Phenylethyl acetate

(R)-(+)-Phenylethyl alcohol (same optical purity as ester)

Retention in configuration in the chiral alcohol indicates that none of the bonds to the stereogenic center are broken which is possible when acyl-oxygen fission takes place. Had alkyl-oxygen fission occurred, it would have been accompanied by inversion of configuration since bond to the stereogenic carbon is cleaved to form carbocation, and the product would have been (S)-(–)-1-phenylethyl alcohol.

(*iv*) **Reaction with Grignard reagents.** Esters react with two equivalents of a Grignard reagent to produce tertiary alcohols. Since two of the three alkyl groups of the tertiary alcohol come from the Grignard reagent, hence these must be identical.

$$R-\overset{O}{\overset{\|}{C}}-OR' + 2R''MgX \xrightarrow[\text{(ii) } H_3O^+]{\text{(i) diethyl ether}} R-\underset{R''}{\overset{OH}{C}}-R'' + R'OH$$

$$\triangleright\!-COOC_2H_5 + 2\,CH_3MgI \xrightarrow[\text{(ii) } H_3O^+]{\text{(i) ether}} \triangleright\!-\underset{CH_3}{\overset{OH}{C}}-CH_3 + C_2H_5OH$$

Ethyl cyclopropanecarboxylate

(*v*) **Reduction.** $RCOOR' \xrightarrow[\text{H}_2\text{, Copper chromite, high pressure, 150°C}]{\text{Na/C}_2\text{H}_5\text{OH, or LiAlH}_4\text{, or}} RCH_2OH + R'OH$

Hydrogenolysis (cleavage by hydrogen) of esters may also be carried out by heating ester with H_2 in presence of Pd/C.

$$C_6H_5COOCH_2C_6H_5 + H_2 \xrightarrow{Pd/C} C_6H_5COOH + CH_3C_6H_5$$

Note that here acidic part of the ester is not reduced, hence this type of hydrogenolysis is used for regenerating the protected acidic group.

$$-COOH \xrightarrow{SOCl_2} -COCl \xrightarrow{C_6H_5CH_2OH} -COOCH_2C_6H_5 \xrightarrow{H_2\,;\,Pd/C} -COOH + CH_3C_6H_5$$

TEST YOUR UNDERSTANDING - 18.7

1. (*a*) An ester has two oxygen atoms, carbonyl oxygen and carboxyl oxygen, which of the two is more basic?

   (*b*) An ester group has three carbon-oxygen bonds, can you think about their relative bond lengths ?

$$R-\overset{O}{\overset{\|z}{C}}\overset{y}{-}O\overset{x}{-}R'$$

2. How we can explain the lower rate of esterification and hydrolysis of esters when the alcohol, the acid, or both are highly branched

3. (*a*) Predict the relative rate of alkaline hydrolysis of following esters.

   Ethyl acetate, I; isopropyl acetate, II; methyl acetate, III; *ter*-butyl acetate IV

   What two factors are responsible for their relative rate of hydrolysis ?

   (*b*) Predict the order of reactivity toward alkaline hydrolysis of methyl acetate (I), methyl formate (II), methyl isobutyrate (III) methyl propionate (IV), and methyl trimethylacetate (V).

4. Arrange the following esters in decreasing ease of alkaline hydroysis.

(*a*) p-$CH_3C_6H_4COOC_2H_5$ (I); p-$OCH_3C_6H_4COOC_2H_5$ (II); p-$ClC_6H_4COOC_2H_5$ (III); $C_6H_5COOC_2H_5$ (IV); p-$NO_2C_6H_4COOC_2H_5$ (V)

(*b*) p-$NH_2C_6H_4CH_2COOCH_3$ (I); p-$CH_3C_6H_4CH_2COOCH_3$ (II); p-$NO_2C_6H_4CH_2COOCH_3$ (III); $C_6H_5CH_2COOCH_3$ (IV)

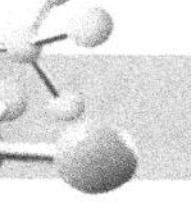

5. (*a*) Give the structural formula for the products in each of the following reaction.

(*i*) $CH_3CH_2COOCH_3 + 2C_6H_5MgBr$

(*ii*) (γ-butyrolactone) + $2CH_3MgBr$

(*iii*) (γ-butyrolactone) + CH_3NH_2

(*iv*) $CH_3COOC_2H_5 + H_2NNH_2$

(*v*) $C_6H_5COOC_2H_5 + NH_2OH$.

(*b*) Write down structure of the products formed in the following reaction.

$$CH_3CH = CHCH_2COOCH_2CH_2Br + NaOH \xrightarrow[\text{(ii) }H^+]{\text{(i) heat}}$$

(*c*) Give the structure of the product obtained by hydrogenolysis of *n*-butyl oleate over copper chromite.

6. Esters of which acid would give secondary alcohols on reaction with Grignard reagents ? Give chemical reaction involved in the preparation of 4-heptanol by the reaction of an ester with a Grignard reagent.

7. Explain the following anamoly in the acid-catalyzed hydrolysis of the following two esters.

(*a*)
$$\underset{(+)-}{CH_3-\overset{O}{\overset{\|}{C}}-O-\underset{C_6H_5}{\overset{CH_3}{C}}-C_2H_5} \xrightarrow{H_2O^{18},\,H^+} \underset{(\pm)-}{HO^{18}-\underset{C_6H_5}{\overset{CH_3}{C}}-C_2H_5} + CH_3COOH$$

(*b*)
$$\underset{(+)-}{CH_3-\overset{O}{\overset{\|}{C}}-O-\underset{H}{\overset{CH_3}{C}}-C_2H_5} \xrightarrow{H_2O^{18},\,H^+} \underset{(+)-}{HO-\underset{H}{\overset{CH_3}{C}}-C_2H_5} + CH_3COO^{18}H$$

(*vi*) **Claisen condensation.** An α-hydrogen in an ester is weakly acidic (similarity to aldehydes and ketones) and again like aldehydes and ketones the negative charge of the carbanion of esters is dispersed to the carbonyl group through resonance.

$$\overset{\ominus}{H_2C}\text{---}\overset{O}{\overset{\|}{C}}-R \qquad\qquad \overset{\ominus}{H_2C}\text{---}\overset{O}{\overset{\|}{C}}-OR$$

Carbanion of aldehyde / ketone — Carbanion of an ester

Due to acidic nature of α-hydrogens, esters when treated with a strong base (generally C_2H_5ONa) undergo condensation to form β-keto ester.

$$CH_3\overset{O}{\overset{\|}{C}}OC_2H_5 + CH_3\overset{O}{\overset{\|}{C}}OC_2H_5 \xrightarrow[\text{(ii) }H_3O^+]{\text{(i) }C_2H_5ONa/C_2H_5OH} CH_3\overset{O}{\overset{\|}{C}}CH_2COOC_2H_5 + C_2H_5OH.$$

Ethyl acetoacetate*
(Acetoacetic ester)

The reaction, known as **Claisen condensation**, is related to aldol condensation given by aldehydes and ketones : *both reactions involve the attack of a carbanion (a nucleophile) on an electron deficient carbonyl carbon.* However, the two reactions differ in the next step : in the *aldol condensation, nucleophilic attack leads to addition,* the typical reaction of aldehydes and ketones, *while in the Claisen condensation, nucleophilic attack leads to substitution,* the typical reaction of acyl compounds.

Mechanism.

Step 1. $$\underset{\text{Ethyl acetate}}{CH_3-\overset{O}{\overset{\|}{C}}-OC_2H_5} + {}^-OC_2H_5 \rightleftharpoons {}^-CH_2-\overset{O}{\overset{\|}{C}}-OC_2H_5$$

* The systematic name of ethylacetoacetate is *ethyl 3-oxobutanoate.*

Step 2.

$$CH_3-\overset{O}{\overset{\|}{C}}-OC_2H_5 + {}^{-}CH_2-\overset{O}{\overset{\|}{C}}OC_2H_5 \rightleftharpoons CH_3-\overset{O^-}{\overset{|}{\underset{OC_2H_5}{\underset{|}{C}}}}-CH_2\overset{O}{\overset{\|}{C}}OC_2H_5$$

Ethyl acetate (2nd mole)

$$\rightleftharpoons CH_3-\overset{O}{\overset{\|}{C}}-CH_2\overset{O}{\overset{\|}{C}}OC_2H_5 + {}^{-}OC_2H_5$$

Although the products at the end of the second step are acetoacetic ester and ethoxide ion, the reaction does not stop at this step ; had it so been, the yield of the β-keto ester would have been very little because the overall equilibrium upto this point is favourable to reactants and not to products.

In β-keto esters (*e.g.* acetoacetic ester), α-hydrogens are surrounded at both ends by carbonyl groups, hence such compounds are much stronger acids than ordinary esters because the negative charge can be delocalised into two carbonyl groups instead of one in ordinary esters. Due to stronger acidic nature than ethyl alcohol, the β-keto ester formed at step 2 reacts with ethoxide ion to form ethyl alcohol and an anion.

Step 3.

$$CH_3-\overset{O}{\overset{\|}{C}}-CH_2-\overset{O}{\overset{\|}{C}}OC_2H_5 + {}^{-}OC_2H_5 \rightleftharpoons CH_3-\overset{O}{\overset{\|}{C}}-\overset{-}{C}H-\overset{O}{\overset{\|}{C}}OC_2H_5 + C_2H_5OH$$

Stronger acid ($pK_a = 11$) — Anion of acetoacetic ester — Weaker acid ($pK_a = 16$)

Note that the position of equilibrium for this step is favourable, and can be made more favourable by distilling ethanol from the reaction mixture. Although, the reaction is complete at step 3, an acid is added to the reaction mixture to obtain the product in its neutral form.

$$CH_3-\overset{O}{\overset{\|}{C}}-\overset{-}{C}H-\overset{O}{\overset{\|}{C}}OC_2H_5 \xrightarrow{H_3O^+} CH_3-\overset{O}{\overset{\|}{C}}-CH_2-\overset{O}{\overset{\|}{C}}OC_2H_5 + H_2O$$

Acetoacetic ester

Like aldol condensation, Claisen condensation always involves bond formation between the α-carbon atom of one molecule and the carbonyl carbon of another.

$$2CH_3CH_2\overset{O}{\overset{\|}{C}}O\overset{\alpha}{C}H_2\overset{\beta}{C}H_3 \xrightarrow[(ii)\ H_3O^+]{(i)\ C_2H_5ONa} CH_3CH_2\overset{O}{\overset{\|}{C}}-\underset{CH_3}{\underset{|}{C}}H\overset{O}{\overset{\|}{C}}OC_2H_5 + CH_3CH_2OH$$

Ethyl propanoate — Ethyl 2-methyl-3-oxopentanoate

Unlike aldol condensation, Claisen condensation is possible only for esters having **two α hydrogen atoms;** *i.e.* for the type RCH_2COOR', but neither for $R_2CHCOOR'$ nor for R_3CCOOR'.

Intramolecular Claisen condensation (Dieckmann reaction). Esters of dicarboxylic acids undergo intramolecular Claisen condensation, provided a five or six-membered ring can be formed

$$C_2H_5O\overset{O}{\overset{\|}{C}}(CH_2)_4\overset{O}{\overset{\|}{C}}OC_2H_5 \text{ or (cyclic form: } \overset{O}{\overset{\|}{C}}-OC_2H_5,\ H_2CCOOC_2H_5) \xrightarrow[(ii)\ H_3O^+]{(i)\ C_2H_5ONa} \text{2-oxocyclopentane with } \overset{O}{\overset{\|}{C}}OC_2H_5$$

Diethyl hexanedioate (Diethyl adipate) — Ethyl 2-oxocyclopentanecarboxylate

Note that the α hydrogen atom and the ester group for the condensation are coming from the same molecule.

Crossed Claisen condensation. Like a crossed aldol condensation, a crossed Claisen condensation is possible **when one of the reactants has no α-hydrogen** and thus is incapable of undergoing self-condensation ; this component acts as an *acylating agent.*

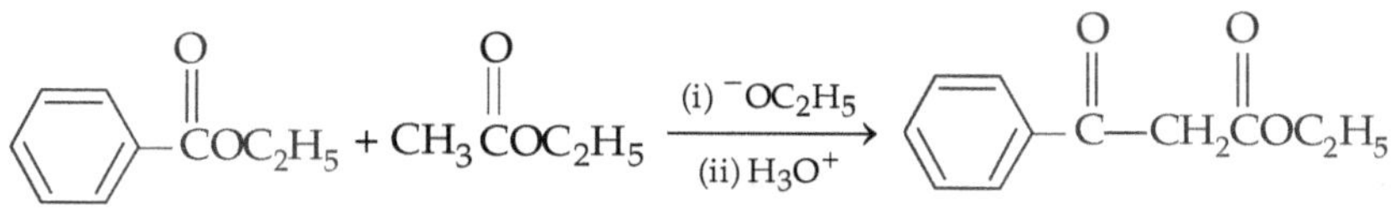

$$C_6H_5COOC_2H_5 + CH_3COOC_2H_5 \xrightarrow[\text{(ii) } H_3O^+]{\text{(i) } ^-OC_2H_5} C_6H_5COCH_2COOC_2H_5$$

Ethyl benzoate (**no α hydrogen**) + Ethyl acetate → Ethyl benzoylacetate

$$C_6H_5CH_2COOC_2H_5 + C_2H_5OCOOC_2H_5 \xrightarrow[\text{(ii) } H_3O^+]{\text{(i) } C_2H_5ONa} C_6H_5CH(COOC_2H_5)COOC_2H_5$$

Ethyl phenylacetate + Diethyl carbonate (no α carbon) → Diethyl phenylmalonate (Phenylmalonic ester)

In such cases, an ester without an α-hydrogen is mixed with the base, and then ester carrying α-hydrogen is added.

TEST YOUR UNDERSTANDING - 18.8

1. (*a*) Write structural formulas for the Claisen condensation products of each of the following.

(*i*) $CH_3CH_2CH_2CH_2COOCH_2CH_3$ (*ii*) $C_6H_5COOCH_2CH_3$ (*iii*) $C_6H_5CH_2COOCH_2CH_3$

(*b*) Give the structure of the product obtained when ethyl phenylacetate ($C_6H_5CH_2COOCH_2CH_3$) is treated with each of the following esters in presence of sodium ethoxide.

(*i*) ethyl formate (*ii*) diethyl oxalate (*iii*) ethyl phenylacetate (*iv*) ethyl benzoate.

2. Can we replace C_2H_5ONa by other base like CH_3ONa or NaOH in the following reaction?

$$2CH_3COOC_2H_5 \xrightarrow{C_2H_5ONa} CH_3COCH_2COOC_2H_5$$

3. Although ethyl propanoate gives good yield in the Claisen condensation, ethyl-2-methylpropanoate gives poor yield. Explain.

4. Name the starting material used for getting following product by Claisen condensation.

(i) 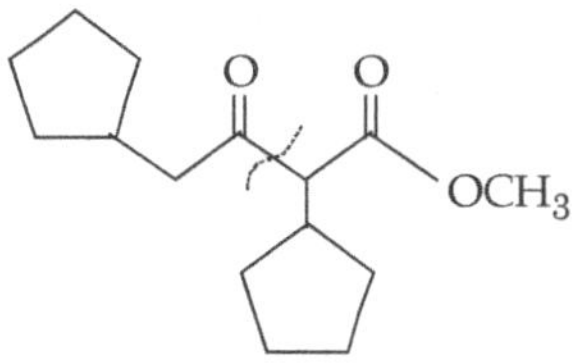 [structure: cyclopentyl–CH₂–CO–CH(cyclopentyl)–CO–OCH₃]

(ii) 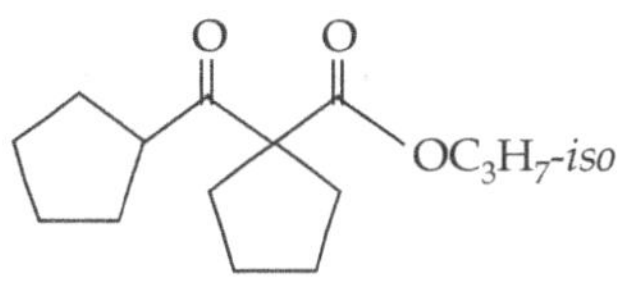 [structure: cyclopentyl–CO–C(cyclopentane ring)–CO–OC_3H_7-*iso*]

5. Following β-keto esters are formed by crossed Claisen condensation, write down the structure of the two components in each of the following.

(*i*) $C_6H_5COCH(C_6H_5)COOC_2H_5$ (*ii*) [structure: cyclopentane-1,2-dione bearing $H_5C_2O_2C$ and $COOC_2H_5$] (*iii*) [structure: indane-1,3-dione with $-COOC_2H_5$ at C-2]

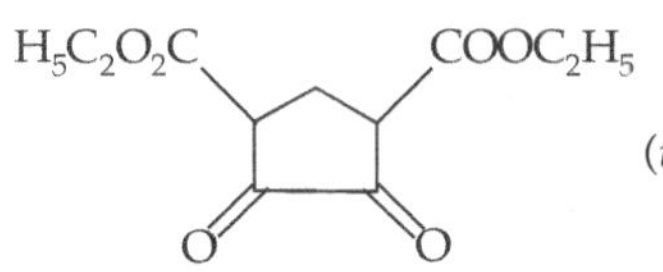

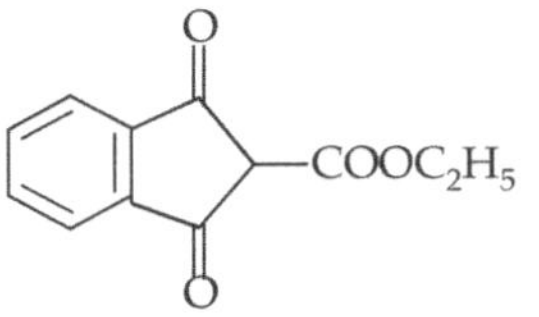

6. Give the different possible reactant(s) from which each of the following can be prepared using Claisen condensation.

(a) 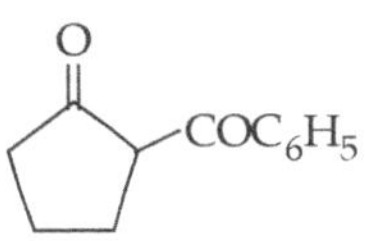 [structure: 2-(benzoyl, COC_6H_5)cyclopentanone] (b) 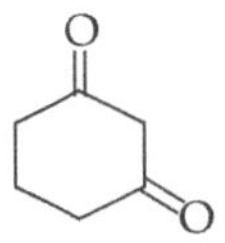 [structure: cyclohexane-1,3-dione] (c) 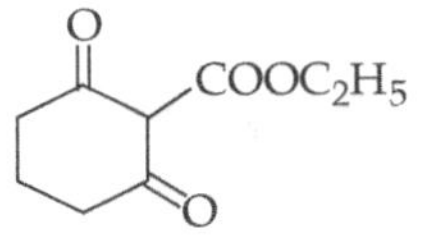 [structure: 2-($COOC_2H_5$)cyclohexane-1,3-dione]

7. (*a*) Write the structure of the Dieckmann cyclization product formed on treatment of each of the following diesters with sodium ethoxide followed by acidification.

(*i*) $CH_3CH_2OOC(CH_2)_5COOC_2H_5$

(*ii*) $C_2H_5O_2CCH_2CH_2CH(CH_3)CH_2CH_2COOC_2H_5$

(*iii*) $C_2H_5O_2CCH(CH_3)CH_2CH_2CH_2COOC_2H_5$

(*b*) Do you expect Dieckmann condensation when ethyl succinate or ethyl glutarate is treated with sodium ethoxide ?

8. Draw the structures of the starting diesters from which the following keto esters can be prepared using Dieckmann condensation.

(a) COOCH$_3$ (b) COOCH$_3$ (c) OC_2H_5 (d) $C-OCH_3$

9. Give the product(s) in the following reaction.

$\xrightarrow[CH_3COOH]{BF_3}$

(D) Reactions of amides

1. Amides are slowly hydrolyzed when heated under either acidic or basic conditions.

$$RCOO^- + NH_3 \xleftarrow[heat]{OH^-} RCONH_2 + H_2O \xrightarrow[heat]{H^+} RCOOH + NH_4^+$$

The mechanism for acid hydrolysis of an amide is similar to that for acid hydrolysis of an ester. Water acts as a nucleophile and attacks the protonated amide ; the leaving group is ammonia (or an amine). In **basic hydrolysis** of amides, hydroxide ion acts as nucleophile as well as base.

2. Unsubstituted amides are converted to RCOOH with HNO_2, and are dehydrated to RCN with P_2O_5, $SOCl_2$, $POCl_3$ or PCl_5.

$$RCONH_2 + HONO \longrightarrow RCOOH + N_2 + H_2O$$

$$RCONH_2 \xrightarrow[Heat]{P_2O_5} RCN + H_2O$$

3. **Hofmann degradation of amides.** On treatment with bromine in basic solution, unsubstituted amides are degraded to amines with one carbon atom less. This is a useful method for the preparation of 1° amines and discussed in detail in amines.

$$RCONH_2 + Br_2 + 4OH^- \longrightarrow RNH_2 + 2Br^- + CO_3^{2-} + 2H_2O$$

4. **Conversion to imides.** Compounds containing acidic as well as amide group in the same molecule at the two ends when heated, lose a molecule of water and produce a cyclic compound in which two acyl groups have become attached to nitrogen ; such compounds are called **imides.**

Phthalic anhydride $\xrightarrow{2NH_3}$ (CONH$_2$, COO$^-$NH$_4^+$) $\xrightarrow{H^+}$ (CONH$_2$, COOH) Phthalamic acid

Phthalic anhydride $\xrightarrow{NH_3,\ heat}$ Phthalimide; (CONH$_2$, COO$^-$NH$_4^+$) $\xrightarrow{heat,\ 300°C}$ Phthalimide; Phthalamic acid $\xrightarrow{heat}$ Phthalimide

NH

Phthalimide

TEST YOUR UNDERSTANDING - 18.9

1. (*a*) Outline all steps in the synthesis of succinimide from succinic acid.
   (*b*) Outline an efficient synthesis of 1-propanamine from butanoic acid.
2. Arrange the following in decreasing order of acidity : Benzamide, phthalimide and ammonia.
3. Give structure of the product obtained by acidic hydrolysis of each of the following amides.

   (*a*) N, N-Dimethylacetamide (*b*) HOOC.CHNHCOCHNH$_2$ (with CH_3 and C_2H_5 substituents) (*c*) [cyclic lactam: NH, =O] (*d*) [piperazine-2,3-dione: H–N, N–H, =O, =O]

4. Arrange the following amides in increasing ease of base-promoted hydrolysis.

   I: $NHCOCH_3$ on benzene; II: $NHCOCH_3$ on cyclohexane; III: $NHCOCH_3$ on benzene with para-NO_2; IV: $NHCOCH_3$ on benzene with meta-NO_2

5. How do amides (1°, 2° and 3°) react (*a*) with organometallic reagents ; and (*b*) with nitrous acid.
6. Give the products of reactions of $LiAlH_4$ with

   (*i*) $C_6H_5CH_2COOCH_3$ (*ii*) $(CH_3CO)_2O$ (*iii*) C_6H_5COCl (*iv*) $CH_3CH = CHCH_2CONHC_6H_5$

   (*v*) [H_3C-substituted γ-lactone, =O] (*vi*) [cyclopentyl]–$NHCOCH_3$ (*vii*) [phthalic anhydride]

18.5 Cyclic Esters or Lactones

Certain hydroxy acids have the capacity to form cyclic esters, also known as **lactones**. This intramolecular esterification takes place spontaneously and is especially favourable when the ring formed is 5- or 6-membered. Lactones containing 5- and 6-membered cyclic esters are referred to as γ-lactones and δ-lactones respectively, because these are derived from the corresponding (γ- or δ-) hydroxy carboxylic acids.

γ-Hydroxybutyric acid (OH OH, =O) $\xrightarrow{H^+}$ γ-Butyrolactone + H_2O

δ-Hydroxyvaleric acid (OH, OH, =O) $\xrightarrow{H^+}$ γ-Valerolactone + H_2O

A lactone is named by replacing the *-oic acid* ending of the parent carboxylic acid by *-olide* and identifying its oxygenated carbon by number. Thus γ-butyrolactone and δ-valerolactone may be named as 4-butanolide and 5-pentanolide, respectively.

Reactions that are expected to produce hydroxy acids often yield the derived lactones provided a 5- or 6-membered ring can be formed, *e.g.*

(*a*) $CH_3COCH_2CH_2CH_2COOH$ (5-Oxohexanoic acid) $\xrightarrow[\text{(ii) } H_3O^+]{\text{(i) } NaBH_4}$ [$CH_3CH(OH)CH_2CH_2CH_2COOH$] (5-Hydroxyhexanoic acid (δ-Hydroxy carboxylic acid)) ⟶ A 5-hexanolide

(*b*) $CH_3COCH_2CH_2COOH \xrightarrow[200°C]{Ni/H_2}$ [$CH_3CH(OH)CH_2CH_2COOH$] (A γ-hydroxy carboxylic acid) ⟶ (γ-lactone with CH_3)

(*c*) $CH_3CH(OH)CH_2C \equiv CCOOH \xrightarrow[\text{catalyst}]{H_2/\text{Lindlar}}$ [$CH_3CH(OH)CH_2CH = CHCOOH$] (cis-Alkene; A δ-hydroxy carboxylic acid) $\xrightarrow{H_3O^+}$ (unsaturated δ-lactone with CH_3)

(*d*) $CH_3COCH_2CH_2COOCH_3 \xrightarrow[\text{(ii) } H_3O^+]{\text{(i) 1 } CH_3MgBr}$ [$(CH_3)_2C(OH)CH_2CH_2COOH$] (A γ−hydroxy acid) $\xrightarrow{-CH_3OH}$ (γ-lactone with H_3C, H_3C)

Remember that a ketonic group is more reactive than an ester toward Grignard reagent.

Lactones whose rings are 3- or 4-membered (α-lactones and β-lactones) are very reactive, making their isolation difficult. However, if attempt is made to prepare a β-lactone from a β-hydroxy acid, β-elimination usually occurs forming α, β-unsaturated acid.

$$RCH(OH)CH_2COOH \xrightarrow{H^+ \text{ or heat}} RCH = CHCOOH + H_2O$$

Similarly, when α-hydroxy acids are heated, they form *cyclic diesters* called **lactides**.

$$2RCH(OH)COOH \xrightarrow{\text{heat}} \text{lactide}$$

α-Hydroxy acid

A lactide (cyclic diester)

Lactones react nearly in the same way as ester, *e.g.*

(*i*) δ-Valerolactone $\underset{H^+}{\overset{OH^-}{\rightleftharpoons}}$ δ-Hydroxypentanoate (COO^-, OH)

(*ii*) δ-Valerolactone $\xrightarrow{NH_3}$ $HOCH_2CH_2CH_2CH_2CONH_2$

(*iii*) δ-Valerolactone $\xrightarrow{CH_3OH/H_2SO_4}$ $HOCH_2CH_2CH_2CH_2COOCH_3$

(*iv*) δ-Valerolactone $\xrightarrow[\text{(ii) } H_2O]{\text{(i) } LiAlH_4}$ $HOCH_2CH_2CH_2CH_2CH_2OH$

Like esters, lactones (cyclic esters) are inert to $NaBH_4$

(*v*) (δ-valerolactone, ring =O, ring O) + $BrMg(CH_2)_3MgBr$ $\xrightarrow[\text{(ii) } H_3O^+]{\text{(i) THF}}$ (cyclohexane ring bearing OH and CH_2CH_2OH on the same carbon)

OH CH_2CH_2OH

Ester group reacts with both parts of Grignard reagent forming a diol.

18.6 Analysis of Carboxylic Acid Derivatives

1. Carboxylic acid derivatives are recognized by their hydrolysis products. We know that the ease of hydrolysis of the four products follows the following order.

Acid chlorides	>	Acid anhydrides	>	Esters	>	Amides
(hydrolyzed by water)		(hydrolyzed when heated briefly with NaOH)				(hydrolyzed when refluxed with NaOH)

2. **Saponification equivalent of ester.** An ester is hydrolyzed with excess, but known amount of base, and the amount of base used is measured and used to give the **saponification equivalent** ; the equivalent weight of the ester, which is similar to the neutralization equivalent of an acid.

$$\underset{\text{One equivalent}}{RCOOR'} + \underset{\text{One equivalent}}{OH^-} \longrightarrow RCOO^- + R'OH$$

However, unlike neutralization equivalent, saponification equivalent of esters is less useful in identification of esters because of great number of possible combinations of the two alkyl groups present in an ester, RCOOR′.

TEST YOUR UNDERSTANDING - 18.10

1. Identify each type of acid derivative which responds following test :
   (*a*) gives white precipitate insoluble in nitric acid, on treatment with alcoholic silver nitrate.
   (*b*) gives ethyl alcohol when heated with acid or base.
   (*c*) gives only propanoic acid on hydrolysis.
   (*d*) reacts immediately with cold NaOH to liberate a gas that turns moist litmus paper blue.
   (*e*) reacts with boiling NaOH and produce a gas that turns moist red litmus paper blue.
2. What is the saponification equivalent of *n*-propyl acetate ? Is this equivalent possible for any other ester or carboxylic acid ? Give their structures.
3. (*a*) What is the saponification equivalent of methyl phthalate ?
   (*b*) What is the relation between saponification equivalent and the number of ester groups per molecule ?

18.7 Illustrative Examples

Example 1 :

Identify the braketed compound(s) in the following reactions :

(i) Benzene + $\begin{matrix} CH_2CO \\ | \\ CH_2CO \end{matrix}\!\!>O$ $\xrightarrow{AlCl_3}$ [A] $\xrightarrow[HCl]{Zn(Hg)}$ [B] $\xrightarrow{SOCl_2}$ [C] $\xrightarrow{AlCl_3}$ [D] $\xrightarrow{H_2/Pt}$ [E] $\xrightarrow{H_2SO_4,\ heat}$ [F] $\xrightarrow{Pt,\ heat}$ [G] + H_2

(ii) Cyclohexane bearing COOH, COOH (on one carbon) and COOH (on adjacent carbon) $\xrightarrow{heat}$ [A] + [B]

(iii) Cyclobutane bearing COOH, COOH (on one carbon) and COOH (on adjacent carbon) $\xrightarrow{heat}$ [A] + [B]

(iv) $CH_3CO(CH_2)_3COOH$ $\xrightarrow{NaBH_4}$ [A] $\xrightarrow[heat]{H_2SO_4}$ [B]

(v) **Calcium adipate** $\xrightarrow{heat}$ [A] $\xrightarrow{C_6H_5CO_3H}$ [B]

(vi) Succinic anhydride $\xrightarrow{CH_3OH}$ [A] $\xrightarrow{PCl_5}$ [B] $\xrightarrow{CH_3NH_2}$ [C]

(vii) **Phthalic acid** $\xrightarrow{NH_3}$ [A] $\xrightarrow[300°C]{heat}$ [B]

(viii) $CH\equiv CH$ $\xrightarrow{2CH_3COOH}$ [A] $\xrightarrow{heat}$ [B]

(ix) [A] $\xrightarrow[(ii)\ H_3O^+]{(i)\ excess\ of\ CH_3MgBr}$ **2, 3-Dimethyl-2-butanol**

(x) $CH\equiv CH$ $\xrightarrow{Hg^{2+}/H_2SO_4}$ [A] $\xrightarrow{Al(OC_2H_5)_3}$ [B] $\xrightarrow{C_2H_5ONa}$ [C]

Solution :

(*i*) HOOC ; HOOC ; ClOC ; O

[A] [B] [C] [D]

H OH ; ;

[E] [F] [G]

(*ii*) $\xrightarrow[(-CO_2)]{heat}$ $\xrightarrow[(-H_2O)]{heat}$

cis- and *trans*-Cyclohexane-1, 2-dicarboxylic acid

cis- and *trans*-Anhydride

[A] and [B]

(iii) [Cyclobutane with COOH, COOH] → [Cyclobutane fused anhydride: C=O, O, C=O]

trans-1, 2-Cyclobutane-dicarboxylic acid [A] *cis*-Anhydride [B]

Remember that unlike above reaction, *trans*-dicarboxylic acid cannot form the anhydride because a 5- and 4-membered ring cannot be fused *trans*.

(iv) [A]: OH, O, OH (5-hydroxyhexanoic acid skeleton) [B]: cyclic lactone (O, O)

(v) [A]: cyclopentanone (=O) [B]: δ-valerolactone (O, O) (through Baeyer-Villeger reaction)

(vi) [A]: O, OCH_3, OH, O [B]: O, OCH_3, Cl, O [C]: O, OCH_3, $NHCH_3$, O

(vii) [A]: benzene ring with $COONH_4$, $COONH_4$ [B]: phthalimide (O, NH, O)

(viii) $CH_3CH(OCOCH_3)_2$ [A] CH_3CHO [B]

(ix) Recall that *tert*-alcohols (2, 3-dimethyl-2-butanol) are formed by the action of excess of Grignard reagents on esters. Hence the compound A should be an ester. Now further recall that in the *tert*-alcohol, two identical alkyl groups are introduced by the alkyl group of the RMgX, so the third alkyl group (which may be different or identical) is coming from the acidic moiety to the ester. So here first examine the structure of the *tert*-alcohol and then write down the structure of the ester.

$$CH_3-\underset{CH_3}{\overset{OH}{C}}-\underset{CH_3}{CH}-CH_3 \xleftarrow[\text{(ii) } H_3O^+]{\text{(i) } 2CH_3MgBr} RO-\overset{O}{\overset{\|}{C}}-\underset{CH_3}{CH}-CH_3$$

2, 3-Dimethylbutanol-2 [A]

(x) CH_3CHO [A] $\xrightarrow[\text{reaction}]{\text{Tischenko}}$ $CH_3COOC_2H_5$ [B] $\xrightarrow[\text{condensation}]{\text{Claisen}}$ $CH_3COCH_2COOC_2H_5$ [C].

Example 2 :

Give steps involved in the following reactions :

(i) C_2H_5OH **to** CH_3CN

(ii) $C_6H_5CH_3$ **to** $p\text{-}NO_2C_6H_4CN$

(iii) $C_6H_5CH_3$ **to** $p\text{-}NO_2.C_6H_4.CH_2CN$

(iv) $C_6H_5CH_3$ **to** $C_6H_5CH_2CN$

(v) $C_6H_5CH_2CH_2COOH$ **to 1-Phenylpropane.**

Solution :

(i) $$C_2H_5OH \xrightarrow{Cr_2O_7^{2-}/H^+} CH_3COOH \xrightarrow{PCl_5} CH_3COCl \xrightarrow[\text{(ii) } P_2O_5]{\text{(i) } NH_3} CH_3CN$$

(ii) $$C_6H_5CH_3 \xrightarrow[\text{Conc. } H_2SO_4]{\text{Conc. } HNO_3} p\text{-}NO_2C_6H_4CH_3 \xrightarrow[H^+]{MnO_4^-} p\text{-}NO_2C_6H_4COOH \xrightarrow[\text{(ii) } NH_3]{\text{(i) } SOCl_2} p\text{-}NO_2C_6H_4CONH_2 \xrightarrow{P_2O_5} p\text{-}NO_2C_6H_4CN$$

(iii) $$C_6H_5CH_3 \xrightarrow{\text{Nitration}} p\text{-}NO_2C_6H_4CH_3 \xrightarrow{NBS} p\text{-}NO_2C_6H_4CH_2Br \xrightarrow{CN^-} p\text{-}NO_2C_6H_4CH_2CN$$

(iv) $$C_6H_5CH_3 \xrightarrow{NBS} C_6H_5CH_2Br \xrightarrow{CN^-} C_6H_5CH_2CN$$

(v) $$C_6H_5CH_2CH_2COOH \xrightarrow{LiAlH_4} C_6H_5CH_2CH_2CH_2OH \xrightarrow[(-H_2O)]{H_2SO_4} C_6H_5CH_2CH = CH_2 \xrightarrow{H_2/Pt} \underset{\text{1-Phenylpropane}}{C_6H_5CH_2CH_2CH_3}$$

Example 3 :

Prepare 2-methylbutanoic acid from ethanol as the only organic compound, of course you can use inorganic reagents; you require.

Solution :

$$CH_3CH_2OH \xrightarrow{\text{Oxidation}} CH_3CHO$$

$$C_2H_5OH \xrightarrow{PBr_3} C_2H_5Br \xrightarrow[\text{ether}]{\text{Mg in}} C_2H_5MgBr \xrightarrow[\text{(ii) } H_3O^+]{\text{(i) } CH_3CHO} \underset{\displaystyle OH}{C_2H_5\underset{|}{C}HCH_3}$$

$$\xrightarrow{PCl_3} \underset{\displaystyle Cl}{C_2H_5\underset{|}{C}HCH_3} \xrightarrow{Mg} \underset{\displaystyle MgCl}{C_2H_5\underset{|}{C}HCH_3} \xrightarrow[\text{(ii) } H_3O^+]{\text{(i) } CO_2} \underset{\displaystyle COOH}{C_2H_5\underset{|}{C}HCH_3}$$

Example 4 :

Give all steps involved in the following conversions.

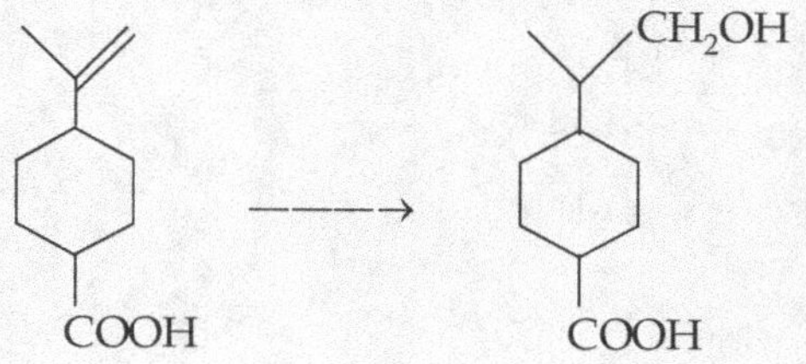

COOH → COOH (with CH_2OH)

Solution :

The conversion involves simply addition of water molecule in anti-Markovnikov way which can best be achieved by the use of BH_3. THF. However, this reagent also reacts with —COOH group so the latter must first be protected which is done by converting it into $—COOCH_2C_6H_5$.

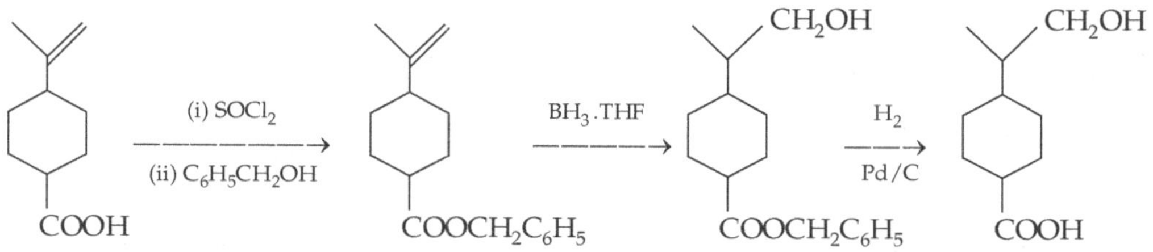

COOH $\xrightarrow[\text{(ii) } C_6H_5CH_2OH]{\text{(i) } SOCl_2}$ $COOCH_2C_6H_5$ $\xrightarrow{BH_3.THF}$ $COOCH_2C_6H_5$ (CH_2OH) $\xrightarrow[Pd/C]{H_2}$ COOH (CH_2OH)

Note that *tert*-butyl group can't be used as a protective group in place of $—CH_2C_6H_5$ group because its removal as isobutene requires H^+ which would dehydrate the $—CH_2OH$ group giving back the starting material.

Example 5 :

Give reaction(s) involved in the conversion of $(CH_3)_3CCHOHCH_3$ to $(CH_3)_3$ $CCH = CH_2$.

Solution :

Although the reaction seems to be achieved simply by dehydration, but in such case a 2° carbocation would be formed as an intermediate which will rearrange to 3° carbocation and thus the major product would be $(CH_3)_2$ $C = C(CH_3)_2$. To avoid this, pyrolyze the acetate ester of the given alcohol.

$$(CH_3)_3CCHOHCH_3 \xrightarrow{CH_3COCl} (CH_3)_3C\underset{\displaystyle OCOCH_3}{\underset{|}{C}}HCH_3 \xrightarrow[(-CH_3COOH)]{\text{heat}} (CH_3)_3CCH = CH_2$$

Example 6 :

Give steps involved in the following conversion :

O, OC_2H_5, O → OH, O

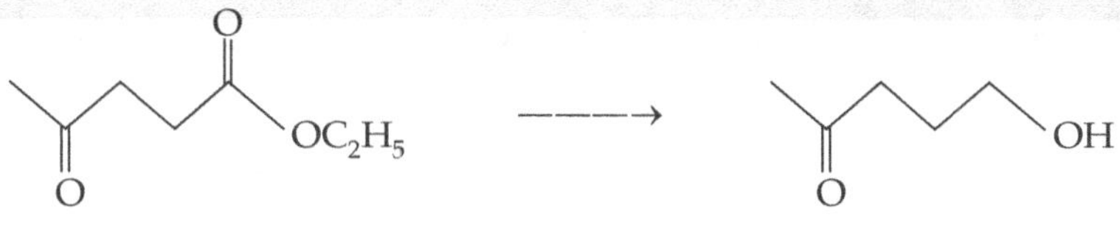

Solution :

The reaction involves simply conversion of $—COOC_2H_5$ to $—CH_2OH$, which can be easily accompanied by reducing either $—COOC_2H_5$ or —COOH to $—CH_2OH$ by means of $LiAlH_4$. However, since $LiAlH_4$ also reduces ketonic group so it should first be protected. Hence the various steps are as follows.

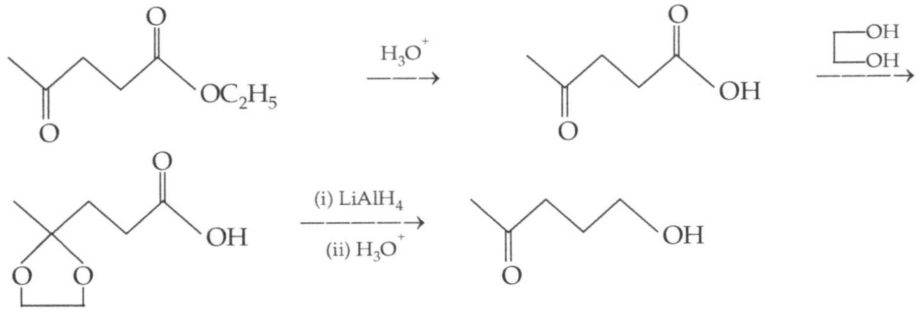

$\xrightarrow{H_3O^+}$ $\xrightarrow{CH_2OH.CH_2OH}$

$\xrightarrow[(ii)\ H_3O^+]{(i)\ LiAlH_4}$

Example 7 :

Give steps involved in the following conversion :

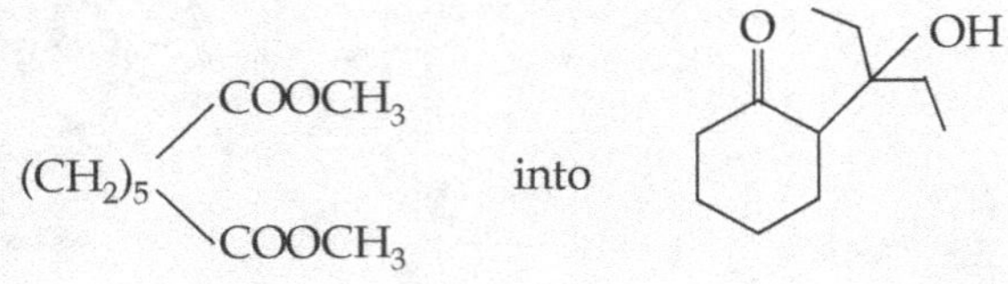

$(CH_2)_5(COOCH_3)_2$ into

Solution :

Note that the product is a *tert*-alcohol which is prepared by the interaction of an ester with excess of RMgX which here must be CH_3CH_2MgX because the *tert*-alcohol has two CH_3CH_2— groups ; the third alkyl group here is substituted cyclohexyl. Further, recall that esters of dicarboxylic acids can be converted into cyclic β-keto esters by means of Dieckmann reaction (*intramolecular Claisen condensation*). Thus the various steps can be written as below.

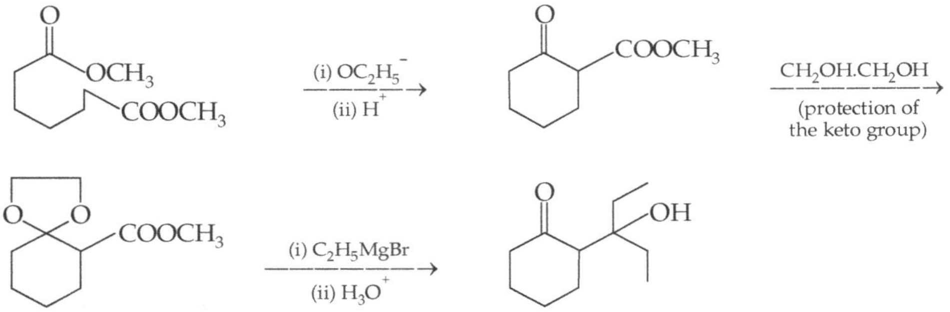

$\xrightarrow[(ii)\ H^+]{(i)\ OC_2H_5^-}$ $\xrightarrow[\text{(protection of the keto group)}]{CH_2OH.CH_2OH}$

$\xrightarrow[(ii)\ H_3O^+]{(i)\ C_2H_5MgBr}$

Example 8 :

Explain the products formed by the pyrolysis of

(a) $CH_3CH_2COOCH_2CH_2CH_2CH_3$ **(b) $CH_3COOCH(CH_3)CH_2CH_3$**

Solution :

The reaction is believed to proceed through a cyclic six-centre transition state, and involves simultaneous *syn*-elimination of a β hydrogen of the alcohol and the acetoxy group.

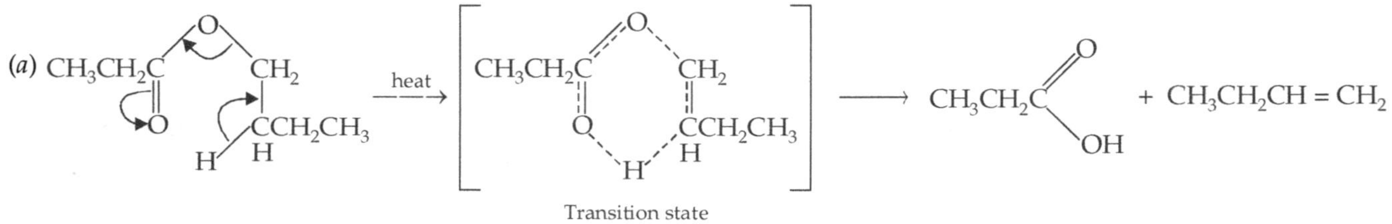

(*a*) $CH_3CH_2C(=O)-O-CH_2-CH(H)CH_2CH_3 \xrightarrow{heat}$ [Transition state] $\longrightarrow CH_3CH_2COOH + CH_3CH_2CH=CH_2$

Transition state

(*b*)

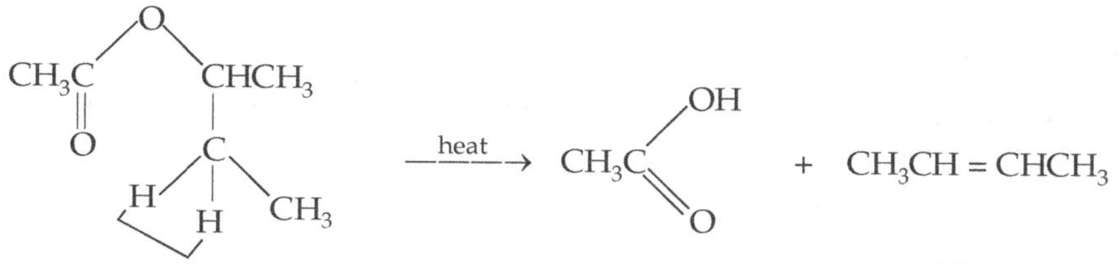

$$CH_3C(=O)-O-CH(CH_3)-CH_2CH_3 \text{ (Two } \beta\text{-H's are present)} \xrightarrow{\text{heat}} CH_3C(=O)OH + CH_3CH=CHCH_3 \text{ (2-Butene)}$$

(OR)

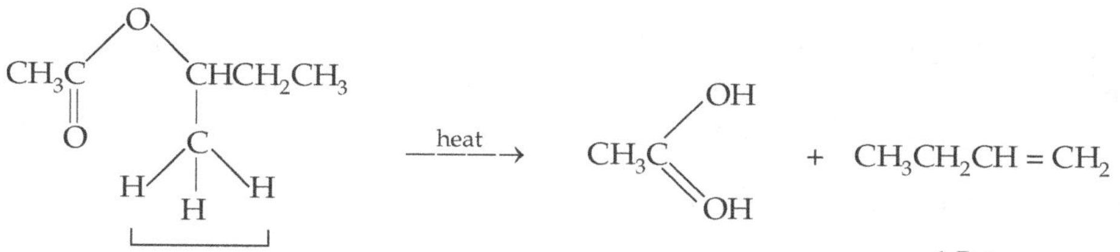

$$CH_3C(=O)-O-CH(CH_2CH_3)-CH_3 \text{ (Three } \beta\text{-H's are present)} \xrightarrow{\text{heat}} CH_3C(=O)OH + CH_3CH_2CH=CH_2 \text{ (1-Butene)}$$

Since there are two β-hydrogens that may be eliminated to give 2-butene and there are three β-hydrogens which may lead to 1-butene, hence 2-butene and 1-butene are formed in 2 : 3 ratio.

Example 9 :

Trimyristin ($C_{45}H_{86}O_6$), obtained from coconut oil, when heated with aqueous sodium hydroxide followed by acidification, gives glycerol and tetradecanoic acid as the only products. Can you assign a structure to trimyristin?

Solution :

Molecular formula and hydrolysis products of trimyristin indicate that it is a triester of glycerol with tetradecanoic acid, $CH_3(CH_2)_{12}COOH$.

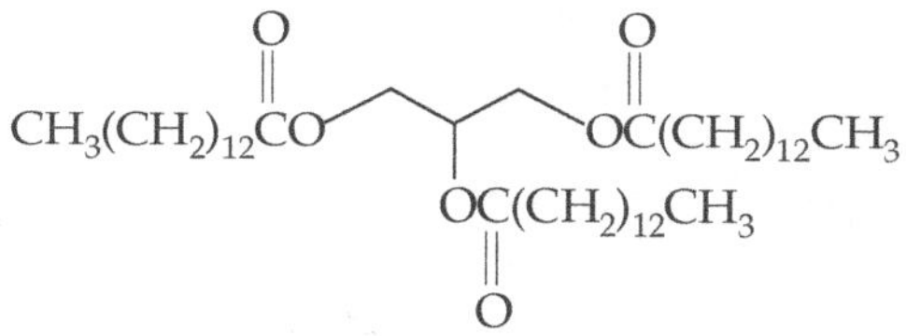

$$CH_3(CH_2)_{12}C(=O)O-CH_2-CH(OC(=O)(CH_2)_{12}CH_3)-CH_2-OC(=O)(CH_2)_{12}CH_3$$

Example 10 :

Alar ($C_6H_{12}O_3N_2$), a growth regulator for apples, itself is harmless but on hydrolysis it gives a dicarboxylic acid [X] of molecular formula $C_4H_6O_4$ and a carcinogenic compound, unsymmeterical dimethylhydrazine (UDMH). Compound X on heating yields an anhydride. Assign structure to alar.

Solution :

$$\underset{C_6H_{12}O_3N_2}{\text{Alar}} \xrightarrow{H_2O} \underset{X}{C_4H_6O_4} + \underset{\text{UDMH}}{H_2NN(CH_3)_2}$$

(*i*) Since alar, on hydrolysis, gives a carboxylic acid and a substituted amine, it must be an amide.

(*ii*) The dicarboxylic acid (X), $C_4H_6O_4$ on heating gives an anhydride, the two —COOH groups must be present on different carbon atoms, so X should be succinic acid. Hence alar should be an amide of succinic acid and UDMH.

$$\underset{\text{Succinic acid, X}}{HOOCCH_2CH_2COOH} + \underset{\text{UDMH}}{H_2NN(CH_3)_2} \xleftarrow{H_2O} \underset{\text{Alar}}{HOOCCH_2CH_2CONHN(CH_3)_2}$$

Example 11 :

An organic compound (A) of the formula $C_5H_{10}O$ is treated with perbenzoic acid to form compound (B) of the formula $C_5H_{10}O_2$. Compound (B) on acidic hydrolysis gives acetic acid and an alcohol (C) which responds haloform tert. Identify compounds (A) to (C).

Solution :

$$\underset{[A]}{C_5H_{10}O} \xrightarrow{C_6H_5CO_3H} \underset{[B]}{C_5H_{10}O_2} \xrightarrow{H^+} CH_3COOH + RCHOHCH_3$$

Given reactions indicate that compound [B] is an ester of acetic acid and the alcohol $RCHOHCH_3$, so B ($C_5H_{10}O_2$) should be an ester of the formula $CH_3COO\underset{|\atop R}{CH}CH_3$ or $CH_3COO\underset{|\atop CH_3}{CH}CH_3$; hence [A] should be a ketone. Recall that ketones when treated with per acids give esters (Baeyer-Villeger oxidation).

$$\underset{[A],\ C_5H_{10}O}{CH_3COCH(CH_3)_2} \xrightarrow{RCO_3H} \underset{[B],\ C_5H_{10}O_2}{CH_3COOCH(CH_3)_2} \longrightarrow CH_3COOH + \underset{\text{[C], responds haloform test}}{HOCH(CH_3)_2}$$

Example 12 :

An organic ester (A) of the formula $C_8H_{16}O_2$ reacts with phosphorus pentachloride and gives two compounds (B) and (C) . When (B) is treated with palladised-hydrogen supported over barium sulphate, it gives another compound (D) which on reduction with $LiAlH_4$ forms a primary alcohol (E) of the formula $C_4H_{10}O$; E can also be produced from (C), which has a branched alkyl group, by reaction with aqueous sodium hydroxide. Identify compounds (A) to (E) and explain the reactions involved.

Solution :

Let us summarise the given facts

$$\underset{\text{Ester, } C_8H_{16}O_2}{(A)} \xrightarrow{PCl_5} (B) + (C)$$

$$(B) \xrightarrow{H_2/Pd,\ BaSO_4} (D) \xrightarrow{LiAlH_4} (E) \qquad (C) \xrightarrow{\text{aq. NaOH}} (E)$$

(*i*) Since the given compound (A) is an ester, with PCl_5 it will form an acid chloride and alkyl halides which are (B) and (C).

$$\underset{A}{R-\overset{O}{\overset{\|}{C}}-O-R'} + PCl_5 \longrightarrow \underset{\text{B and C}}{R-\overset{O}{\overset{\|}{C}}-Cl + R'-Cl} + POCl_3$$

(*ii*) The given statement indicates that the compound (B) is reduced by Rosenmund reduction (specific reduction for acid chloride), so (B) should be acid chloride and (C) should be alkyl chloride. Now let us write down the given reactions of (B).

$$\underset{(B)}{R-\overset{O}{\overset{\|}{C}}-Cl} \xrightarrow[BaSO_4]{H_2/Pd} \underset{(D)}{R-\overset{O}{\overset{\|}{C}}-H} \xrightarrow{LiAlH_4} \underset{(E),\ C_4H_{10}O}{RCH_2OH}$$

So (E) can now be written as $C_3H_7CH_2OH$.

(*iii*) Nature of (C) as an alkyl halide is confirmed by its conversion to (E), a primary alcohol by reaction with aq. NaOH.

$$(C) \xrightarrow{\text{aq. NaOH}} \underset{(E),\ C_4H_{10}O}{RCH_2OH}$$

Hence the structure of (C) can be expanded as RCH_2Cl or $C_3H_7CH_2Cl$. Since (C) has a branched alkyl group, it should be $(CH_3)_2CHCH_2Cl$ and thus (E) as $(CH_3)_2CHCH_2OH$.

(*iv*) Now going backward, we can write the structure of (D), (B) and hence (A).

$$\underset{(E)}{(CH_3)_2CHCH_2OH} \xleftarrow{LiAlH_4} \underset{(D)}{(CH_3)_2CH.CHO} \xleftarrow[BaSO_4]{H_2/Pd} \underset{(B)}{(CH_3)_2CHCOCl}$$

$$\underset{(B)}{2(CH_3)_2CHCOCl} + \underset{(C)}{ClCH_2CH(CH_3)_2} \xleftarrow{PCl_5} \underset{A,\ C_8H_{16}O_2}{(CH_3)_2CH\overset{O}{\overset{\|}{C}}OCH_2CH(CH_3)_2}$$

Example 13 :

A reaction mixture of (±)-2-phenylpropanoic acid on esterification with (+) -2-butanol gives two esters. Mention the stereochemistry of the two esters produced.

Solution :

Fischer projections of 2-Phenylpropanoic acid: COOH (top), H (left), C_6H_5 (right), CH_3 (bottom) + COOH (top), C_6H_5 (left), H (right), CH_3 (bottom) — **Enantiomers**

2-Phenylpropanoic acid

$\downarrow$ (+) – $CH_3\underset{OH}{CH}CH_2CH_3$

$COO\underset{CH_3}{CH}CH_2CH_3$ (top), H (left), C_6H_5 (right), CH_3 (bottom) + $COO\underset{CH_3}{CH}CH_2CH_3$ (top), C_6H_5 (left), H (right), CH_3 (bottom) — **Diastereomers**

(+)-(+)-Ester (–)-(+)-Ester

Example 14 :

Although alcohols are neither acidic enough nor basic enough to form stable salts, these are frequently resolved. Outline the steps used for resolving racemic mixture of sec-butyl alcohol using (+)-base as a resolving agent.

Solution :

Although alcohols, themselves, are not strong acids or bases, these are converted into acidic compounds (alkyl hydrogen phthalate) on reaction with phthalic anhydride. The enantiomers of the racemic modification of alkyl hydrogen phthalate, being acidic, react with an optically active base to form diastereomeric salts which can be separated by fractional crystallisation (remember that enantiomers have similar solubility while diastereomers have different solubilities). The two separated diastereomers are then hydrolyzed to give optically active alcohols. Since hydrolysis of a carboxylic ester does not usually involve cleavage of the alkyl-oxygen bond, there is no loss of optical activity in the hydrolysis step.

Phthalic anhydride + (±) – ROH

↓

o-C_6H_4(COOR(+))(COOH) + o-C_6H_4(COOR(–))(COOH) — **Enantiomers**

↓ (+) – B (An optically active base)

o-C_6H_4(COOR(+))(COO^-(+) – BH^+) + o-C_6H_4(COOR(–))(COO^-(+) – BH^+) — **Diastereomers** (separable by fractional crystallisation)

↓ Resolve by fractional crystallisation

↓ OH^- ↓ OH^-

o-$C_6H_4(COO^-)_2$ + (+) – **ROH** ; o-$C_6H_4(COO^-)_2$ + (–) – **ROH**

Example 15 :

When benzoic acid is esterified by methanol in presence of a little sulphuric acid, the final reaction mixture contains five substances : benzoic acid, methanol, water, methyl benzoate and sulphuric acid. Outline a procedure used for the separation of the pure ester (methyl benzoate).

Solution :

$$C_6H_5COOH + CH_3OH \xrightarrow{H_2SO_4} C_6H_5COOCH_3 + H_2O$$

(*i*) The mixture containing five substances, *viz.* $C_6H_5COOCH_3$, H_2O (formed as products), C_6H_5COOH, CH_3OH and H_2SO_4 (left as residual amounts) is shaken with benzene which dissolves only methyl benzoate and benzoic acid ; while the other three substance (CH_3OH, H_2O and H_2SO_4) remain in water layer.

(*ii*) Benzene extract is now treated with aq. Na_2CO_3 which converts benzoic acid to water soluble sodium benzoate which is thus removed as water layer.

(*iii*) Benzene layer containing methyl benzoate and some residual water is distilled when benzene and water distils over first, followed by distillation of methyl benzoate at high temperature (200°C).

Example 16 :

Identify the bracketed compounds from [A] to [D] in the following sereies of reactions.

$$Me_2CHCHO + HCHO \xrightarrow{K_2CO_3\ aq.} [A] \xrightarrow[(ii)\ H_3O^+]{(i)\ HCN} [B] \xrightarrow{-H_2O} [C]$$

$$\xrightarrow{H_2NCH_2CH_2CONHCH_2CH_2SH} [D] \xrightarrow[heat]{aq.\ NaOH} \text{Products}$$

Solution :

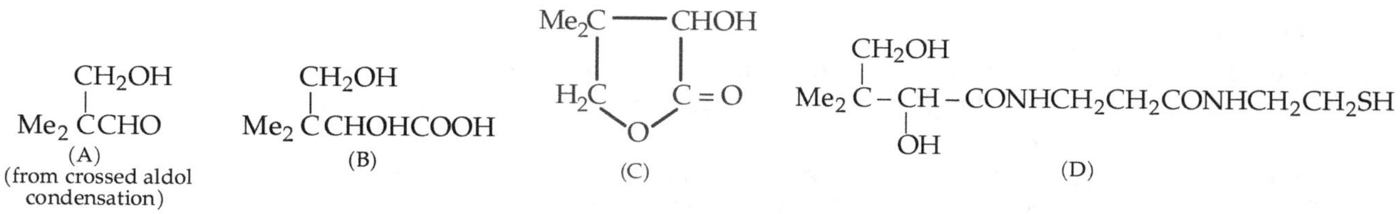

(A) $Me_2C(CH_2OH)CHO$ (from crossed aldol condensation)

(B) $Me_2C(CH_2OH)CHOHCOOH$

(C) lactone: Me_2C—CHOH, H_2C, C=O, O (ring)

(D) $Me_2C(CH_2OH)-CH(OH)-CONHCH_2CH_2CONHCH_2CH_2SH$

$Me_2C(CH_2OH)-CH(OH)COO^- + H_2NCH_2CH_2COO^- + H_2NCH_2CH_2S^-$

Products

Example 17 :

Write stereochemical formulas for the compounds A to G.

(a) ***cis*-3-Methylcyclopentanol +** $C_6H_5COCl \longrightarrow [A] \xrightarrow[\text{reflux}]{OH^-} [B]$

(b) ***cis*-3-Methylcyclopentanol +** $C_6H_5SO_2Cl \longrightarrow [C] \xrightarrow[\text{heat}]{OH^-} [D]$

(c) **(*R*)-2-Bromoheptane + OH⁻** $\xrightarrow{\text{acetone}} [E]$

(d) **(*R*)-2-Bromoheptane +** $CH_3COONa \longrightarrow [F] \xrightarrow[\text{reflux}]{OH^-,\ H_2O} [G]$

Solution :

(a) *cis*-(A): cyclopentane with H, H; H_3C, $OCOC_6H_5$ — *cis*-(B): H, H; H_3C, OH

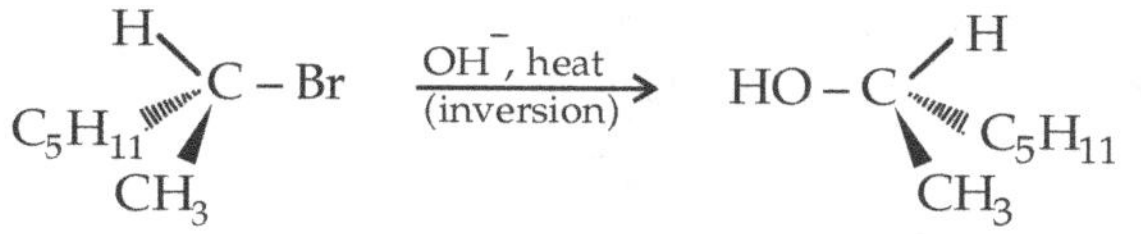

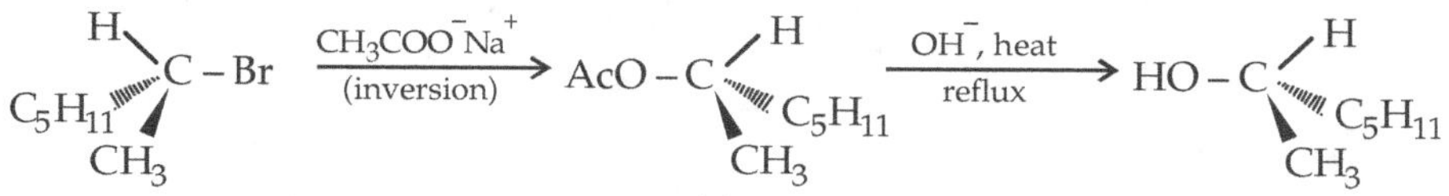

(b) *cis*-(C): H, H; H_3C, $OSO_2C_6H_5$ — *trans*-(D): H, OH; CH_3, H

(c) H, C_5H_{11}, CH_3 C–Br $\xrightarrow[\text{(inversion)}]{\bar{O}H,\ heat}$ HO–C (H, C_5H_{11}, CH_3) (E)

(d) H, C_5H_{11}, CH_3 C–Br $\xrightarrow[\text{(inversion)}]{CH_3CO\bar{O}\ \overset{+}{Na}}$ AcO–C (H, C_5H_{11}, CH_3) (F) $\xrightarrow[\text{reflux}]{\bar{O}H,\ heat}$ HO–C (H, C_5H_{11}, CH_3) (G)

Example 18 :

Esters (or carboxylic acids), and amides have two major resonance contributors, one of which involves charged structures.

$R-C(=\ddot{O}:)-\ddot{O}CH_3 \longleftrightarrow R-C(-\ddot{O}:^-)=\overset{+}{O}CH_3$ $\quad$ $R-C(=\ddot{O}:)-\ddot{N}H_2 \longleftrightarrow R-C(-\ddot{O}:^-)=\overset{+}{N}H_2$

Account for the fact that the charged structure in amides has a significant contribution than in esters or in carboxylic acids.

Solution :

In amides, positive charge resides on a lesser electronegative element (N) than that in esters or carboxylic acids where positive charge is present on a more electronegative element (oxygen).

Example 19 :

Arrange the following compounds in order of their decreasing boiling points.

Carboxylic acids, alcohols, esters, amides, nitriles

Solution :

For knowing the relative boiling point of different compounds of comparable molecular weights, consider following factors, dipole-dipole interaction, hydrogen bonding, van der Waal forces, etc. Here no specific compounds are given, so it is assumed that the vander waal forces are nearly similar in each case, hence other two factors are responsible for their following relative boiling points.

Amides > carboxylic acids > alcohols ≈ nitriles >>> esters.

(i) Boiling points of esters are lower than the boiling points of alcohols because their molecules can't form hydrogen bonds with each other. However, boiling points of esters (also for acyl chlorides, aldehydes, and ketones) are higher than those of ethers because of polar carbonyl group. Further, due to resonance polarity is less than in nitriles.

(ii) Boiling point of nitriles are similar to that of alcohols becasue the former have a strong dipole-dipole interactions, while alcohols have strong hydrogen bonds.

(iii) Carboxylic acids have relatively high boiling points than alcohols because they can form hydrogen-bonded dimers, giving them larger effective molecular weight.

(iv) Amides have the highest boiling points, because here the dipole-dipole interactions are strong than in nitriles because here dipole-dipole interaction involves separated complete charges (recall that in an amide resonating structure having separated charges contribute *significantly* to the hybrid).

Nitriles, RC≡N Carboxylic acids, RCOOH Amides, $RCONR_2$

Further if an amide has a hydrogen, bonded to nitrogen as in $RCONH_2$ or RCONHR, the molecules also form intermolecular hydrogen bonds.

Example 20 :

Predict the products in the following reaction with proper explanation.

Methyl mesitoate

Solution :

Although base promoted hydrolysis of an ester involves the attack of $^-$OH on the carbonyl carbon to form a tetrahedral intermediate which is then converted to carboxylic acid and alcohol. Here it is not so, steric hindrance due to two *ortho*-methyl groups prevents formation of the tetrahedral intermediate; and thus the nucleophile attacks on the alkyl carbon of the alcoholic portion instead of the acyl carbon of the acidic portion leading to alcohol having –OH provided by nucleophile.

EXERCISE 18.1 (MCQ - ONE option correct)

1. Bouvealt-Blanc reduction of an ester ($CH_3COOC_2H_5 \xrightarrow{Na/C_2H_5OH} C_2H_5OH$) involves
   (*a*) reduction by H_2
   (*b*) reduction by nascent H
   (*c*) electron transfer from Na to C = O
   (*d*) none of the three.

2. Benzoic anhydride is formed according to following reaction
   $C_6H_5COCl + C_6H_5COONa \longrightarrow C_6H_5COOCOC_6H_5 + NaCl$
   Here the nucleophile is provided by
   (*a*) C_6H_5COCl
   (*b*) C_6H_5COONa
   (*c*) either of the two
   (*d*) It is not an example of nucleophilic substitution.

3. Which of the following is different regarding nucleophilic substitution ?
   (*a*) $CH_3COCl + CH_3COONa \longrightarrow CH_3COOCOCH_3$
   (*b*) $CH_3COONa + CH_3CH_2Br \longrightarrow CH_3COOCH_2CH_3$
   (*c*) $CH_3COOC_2H_5 \xrightarrow{H^+} CH_3COOH + C_2H_5OH$
   (*d*) $CH_3COOCOCH_3 + CH_3OH \longrightarrow CH_3COOCH_3 + CH_3COOH$

4. Which of the following ester can be used as acylating agent in mixed Claisen condensation ?
   (*a*) $H-\overset{O}{\overset{\|}{C}}-OCH_3$
   (*b*) $C_6H_5-\overset{O}{\overset{\|}{C}}-OCH_3$
   (*c*) $C_2H_5O-\overset{O}{\overset{\|}{C}}-\overset{O}{\overset{\|}{C}}-OC_2H_5$
   (*d*) All

5. The product P in the following reaction will be
   $$\text{Ethyl ester} \xrightarrow{CH_3MgBr\ (excess)} P$$
   (*a*) OH
   (*b*) OH
   (*c*) OH
   (*d*) OH

6. Predict the nature of B.
   $$H_2NCH_2CH_2CH_2COOH \xrightarrow{heat} A \xrightarrow{LiAlH_4} B$$
   (*a*) $H_2NCH_2CH_2CH_2CH_2OH$
   (*b*) $CH_2 = CHCH_2CH_2OH$
   (*c*) $CH_3CH_2CH_2CH_2OH$
   (*d*) N H

7. Predict the nature of the product P in the following reaction:
   $$(+)\text{-}C_6H_5\underset{OCOC_2H_5}{\underset{|}{C}H}CH = CHCH_3 \xrightarrow{dil.\ NaOH} P$$
   (*a*) $(+) - C_6H_5\overset{OH}{\overset{|}{C}H}CH = CHCH_3$
   (*b*) $(\pm) - C_6H_5\overset{OH}{\overset{|}{C}H}CH = CHCH_3$
   (*c*) $(+) - C_6H_5CH{=}CH\overset{OH}{\overset{|}{C}H}CH_3$
   (*d*) $(\pm) - C_6H_5CH = CH\overset{OH}{\overset{|}{C}H}CH_3$.

8. Aspartame, an artificial sweetening agent, has following structure
   $$C_6H_5CH_2\underset{}{\overset{COOCH_3}{\overset{|}{C}H}}NHCO\overset{\overset{\oplus}{N}H_3}{\overset{|}{C}H}CH_2CO\overset{\ominus}{O}.$$
   On hydrolysis with dil. HCl, it will give
   (*a*) three neutral molecules.
   (*b*) one neutral molecule and two molecules as cations
   (*c*) two neutral molecules and one molecule as cation.
   (*d*) three molecules, all in the form of cations.

9. Unlabelled 4-butanolide is allowed to stand in an acidic solution in which water has been labelled with O^{18}. When the lactone is extracted from the solution after 4 days, what will you expect ?
   (*a*) Both oxygen of 4-butanolide should have O^{18}
   (*b*) Only carbonyl oxygen should have O^{18}
   (*c*) Oxygen other than carbonyl group should be O^{18}
   (*d*) Both oxygen should have O^{16}.

10. An ester molecule reacts with two eq. of a Grignard reagent and forms
    (*a*) a 3° alcohol having at least two identical alkyl groups.
    (*b*) a 3° alcohol having all the three identical alkyl groups.
    (*c*) a 2° alcohol having both identical alkyl groups.
    (*d*) both (*a*) and (*c*).

11. Hydrolysis of an ester may be achived under acidic as well as basic conditions. Pick up the correct statement regarding this
    (*a*) Acidic hydrolysis is faster than alkaline hydrolysis.
    (*b*) Alkaline hydrolysis is faster than acidic hydrolysis.
    (*c*) Both occur at the same rate.
    (*d*) In both, the first step is protonation of the —OH part of the —COOH group.

12. In an ester molecule there are three C—O bonds, $R-\overset{O}{\overset{\gamma\,\|}{C}}\overset{\beta}{-}O\overset{\alpha}{-}R'$. What do you expect regarding their relative bond lengths ?
    (*a*) $\alpha > \beta > \gamma$
    (*b*) $\beta = \gamma > \alpha$
    (*c*) $\gamma > \beta > \alpha$
    (*d*) $\alpha = \beta = \gamma$.

13. $C_2H_5COOCH_3 + {}^{18}OH^- \longrightarrow A + B$

In the above reaction, products A and B respectively are

(a) $C_2H_5\overset{O}{\overset{||}{C}}—O^- + CH_3\overset{18}{O}H$

(b) $C_2H_5—\overset{O^{18}}{\overset{||}{C}}—\overset{18}{O}^- + CH_3OH$

(c) $C_2H_5—\overset{O}{\overset{||}{C}}—\overset{18}{O}^- + CH_3OH$

(d) $C_2H_5—\overset{O^{18}}{\overset{||}{C}}—O^- + CH_3OH$

14. In the following reactions, X and Y are

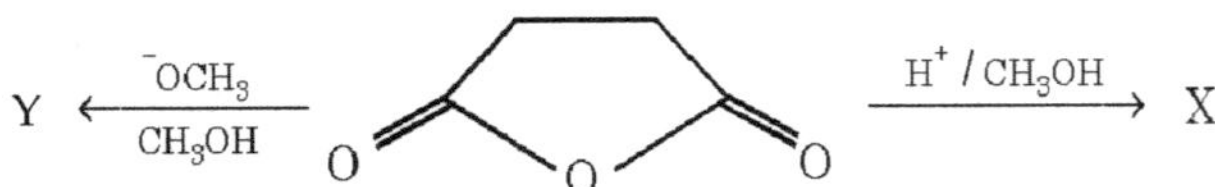

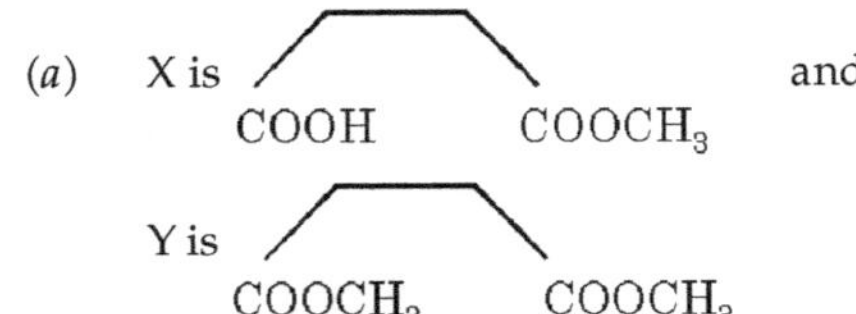

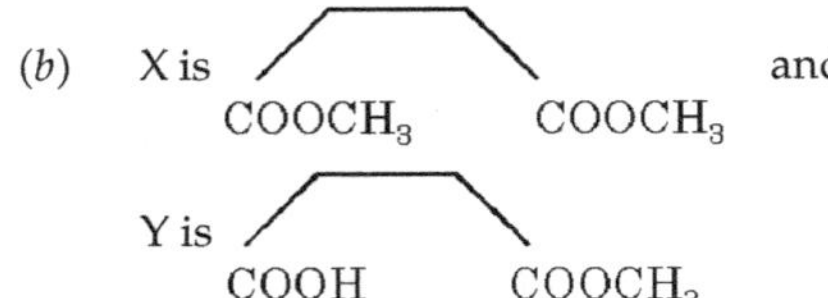

(d) Both are
$COOCH_3$ $COOCH_3$

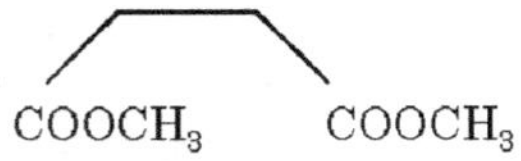

15. Acetic acid is dissolved in water having oxygen as O^{18}, What do you expect about the resulting acetic acid ? It should be

(a) $CH_3\overset{O}{\overset{||}{C}}—OH$ (b) $CH_3—\overset{O}{\overset{||}{C}}—O^{18}H$

(c) $CH_3—\overset{O^{18}}{\overset{||}{C}}—OH$ (d) $CH_3—\overset{O^{18}}{\overset{||}{C}}—O^{18}H$.

16. When butyramide is boiled with aqueous NaOH and then acidified, the resulting product contains

(a) $CH_3CH_2CH_2COO^- + NH_3$
(b) $CH_3CH_2CH_2COO^- + NH_4^+ + Cl^-$
(c) $CH_3CH_2CH_2COONa + NH_3$
(d) $CH_3CH_2CH_2COOH + Na^+ + Cl^-$.

17. The product of acid hydrolysis of P and Q can be distinguished by

(a) Lucas reagent (b) 2, 4-DNP
(c) Fehling solution (d) $NaHSO_3$.

18. An enantiomerically pure acid is treated with racemic mixture of an alcohol having one chiral carbon. The ester formed will be

(a) optically active mixture
(b) pure enantiomer
(c) meso compound
(d) racemic mixture.

19. Reactivity order of different nucleophiles (OH^-, $\bar{O}COCH_3$ and NH_2^-) toward $RCOCl + :Z \longrightarrow RCOZ + Cl^-$ is

(a) $OH^- > {}^-OCOCH_3 > NH_2^-$
(b) ${}^-OCOCH_3 > OH^- > NH_2^-$
(c) $NH_2^- > OH^- > {}^-OCOCH_3$
(d) $OH^- > NH_2^- > {}^-OCOCH_3$.

20. Acidic hydrolysis is minimum in

(a) OCOR (b) OCOR, NO_2

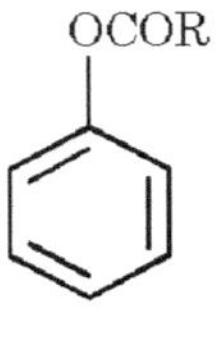

(c) OCOR, NO_2 (d) OCOR, OC_2H_5

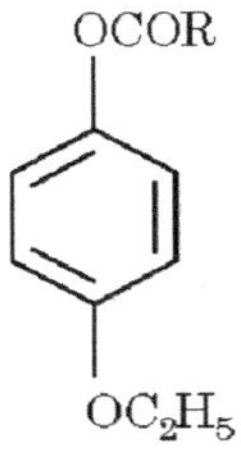

21. Which of the following amide undergoes alkaline hydrolysis most easily ?

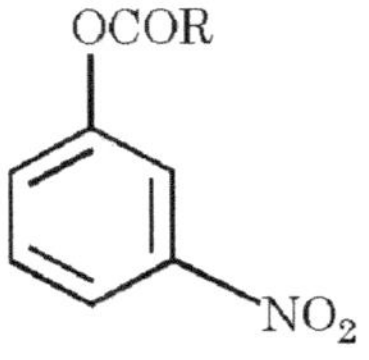

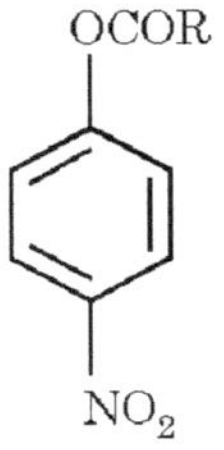

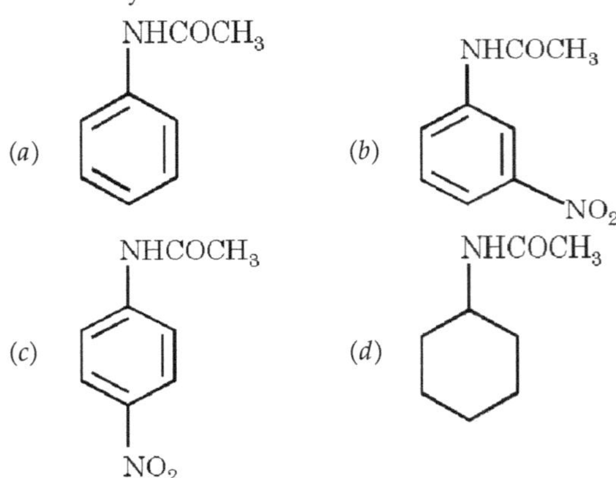

22. A keto lactone is reduced by different reagents to give A and B

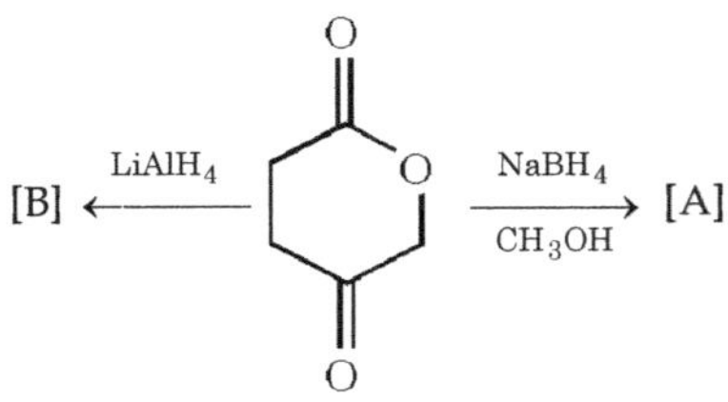

Here [A] and [B] respectively are

(a) O, O, O and OH, O, OH

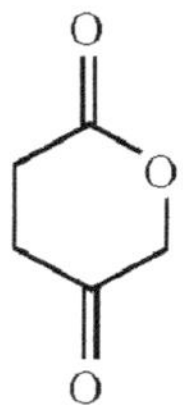

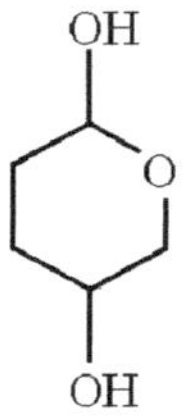

(b) 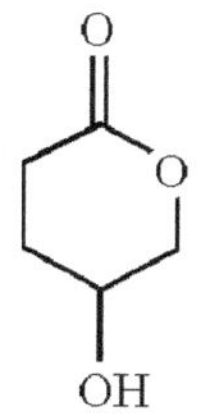 and

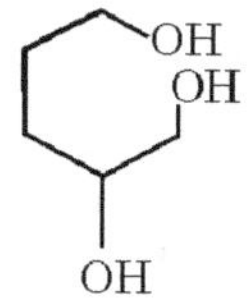

(c) 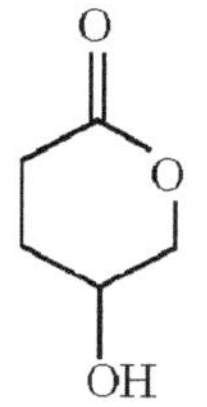 and

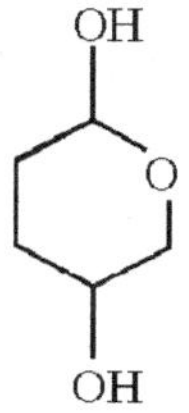

(d) 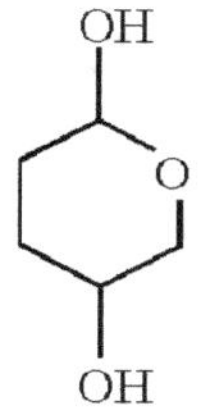 in both cases

23. 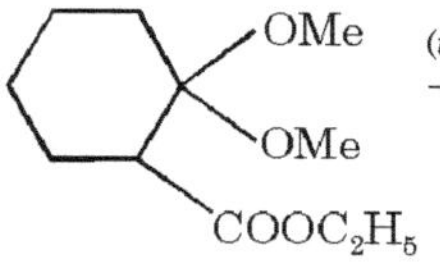 (i) H^+/H_2O, (ii) heat → Z. Here Z is

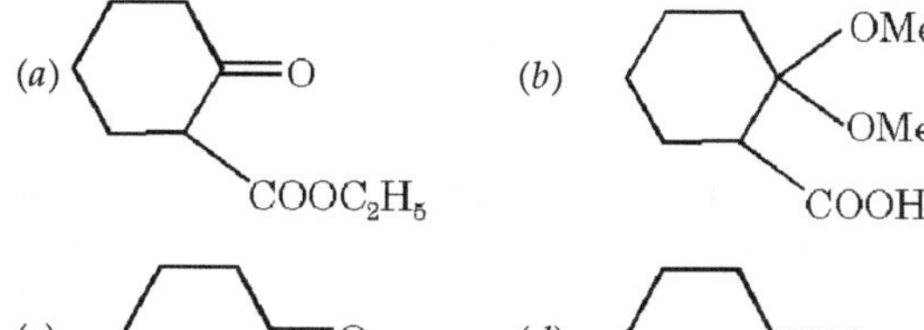

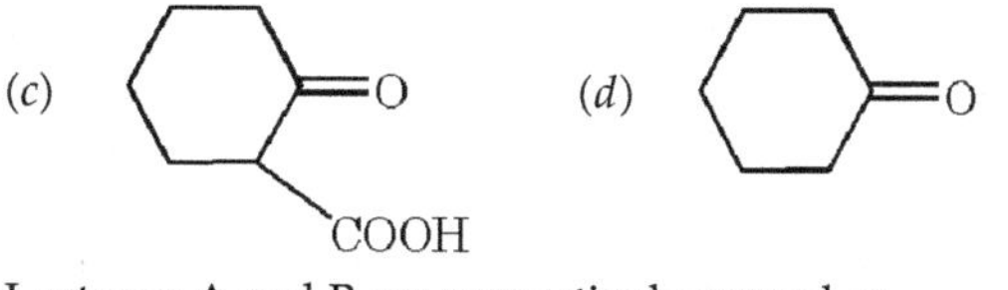

24. Lactones A and B are respectively named as

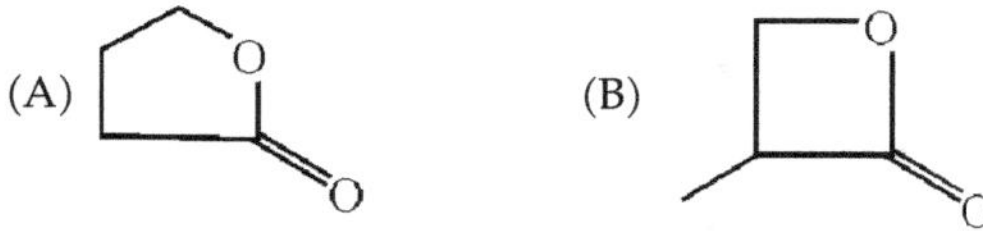

(a) γ-Pentanolactone, 2-methylbutyrolactone
(b) γ-Butyrolactone, 2-methyl-γ-butyrolactone
(c) γ-Butyrolactone, β-Butyrolactone
(d) α-Pentanolactone, 2-methyl α-butyrolactone.

25. Which of the following represents the structure of γ-pentanolactone ?

(a) 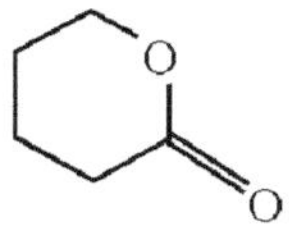 (b)

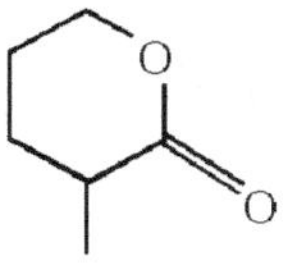

(c) 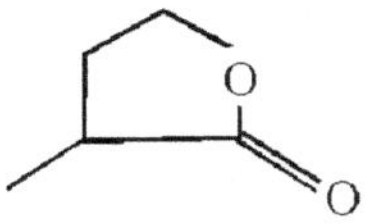 (d)

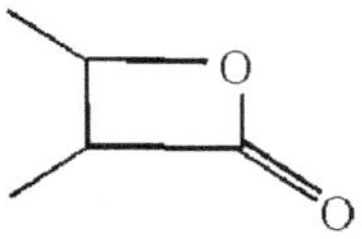

26. Predict the nature of the product P in the following reaction.

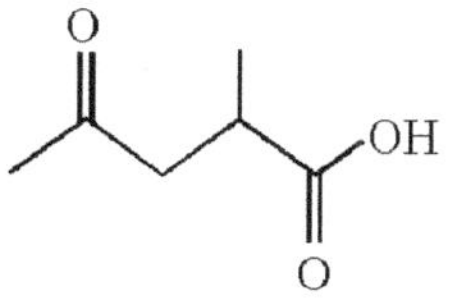

(i) $NaBH_4$, (ii) H_3O^+ → P

(a) 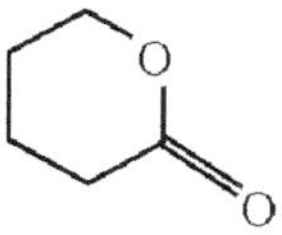 (b)

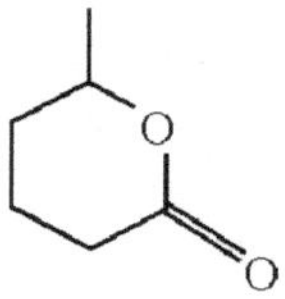

(c) 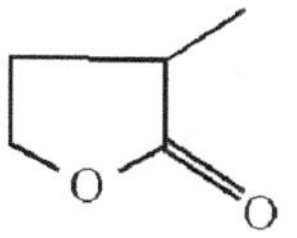 (d)

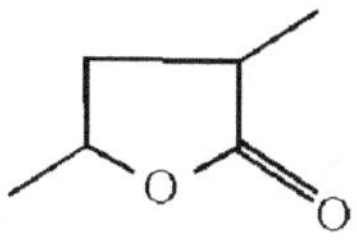

27. Give the structure of the compound A formed in the following reaction.

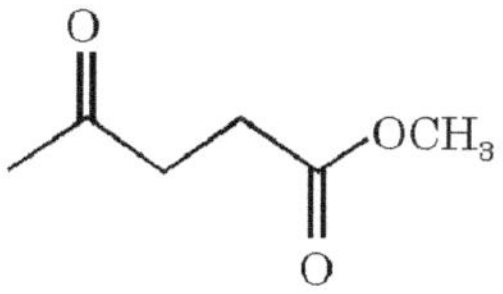

(i) 1 CH_3CH_2MgI, (ii) H_3O^+ → A

(a)

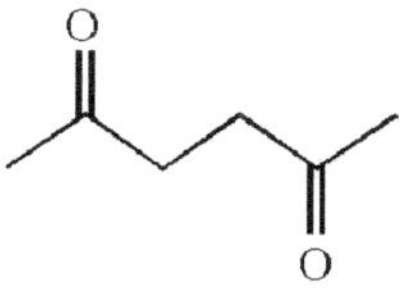

(b)

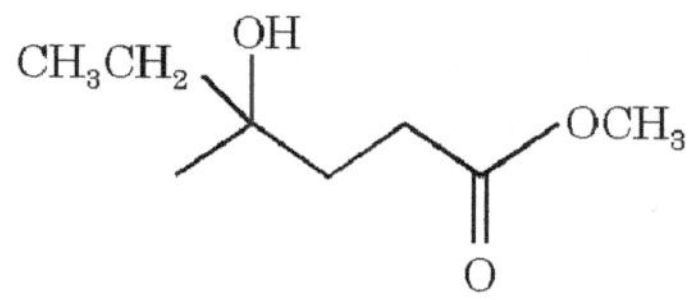

(c)

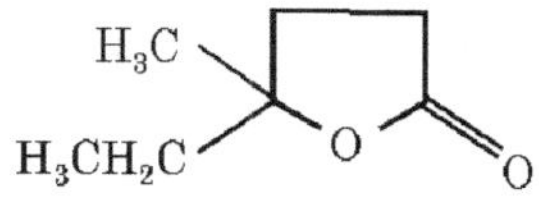

(d)

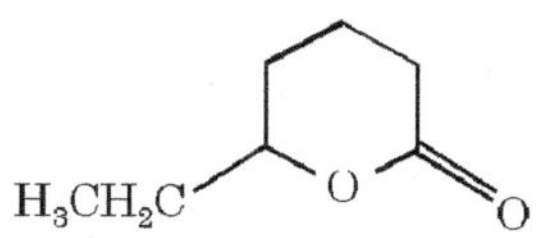

28. 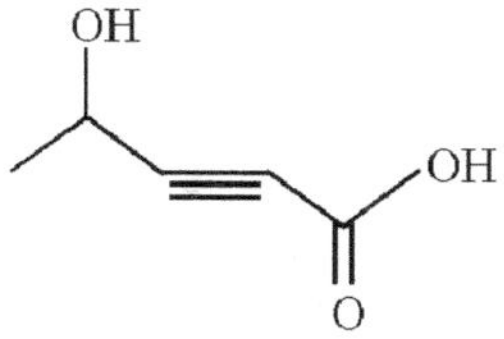 Reagent R → [ ]

Reagent R′ →

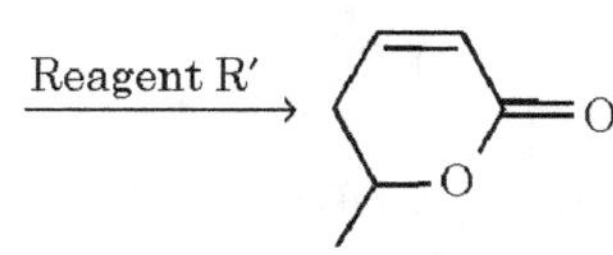

Here R and R′ respectively are

(a) Pt/ H_2, H_3O^+ (b) H_2/Pd, H_3O^+
(c) Li/NH_3, H_3O^+ (d) Ni/H_2.

29. Predict the respective compounds A and B in the following reaction :

$$CH_3CH_2COCH_3 \xrightarrow{C_6H_5CO_3H} [\quad] \xrightarrow{H_3O^+} A + B$$

(*a*) CH_3CH_2COOH, CH_3OH
(*b*) CH_3CH_2COOH, CH_3COOH
(*c*) CH_3CH_2OH, CH_3COOH
(*d*) $CH_3CH_2COCH_3, C_6H_5COOH$.]

30. In the given series of reactions, the final product D is

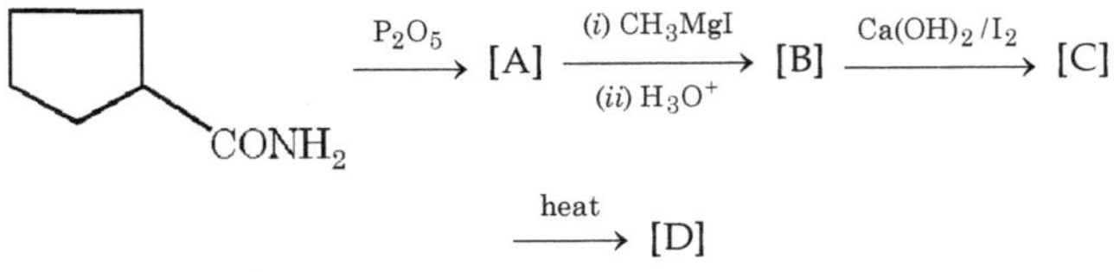

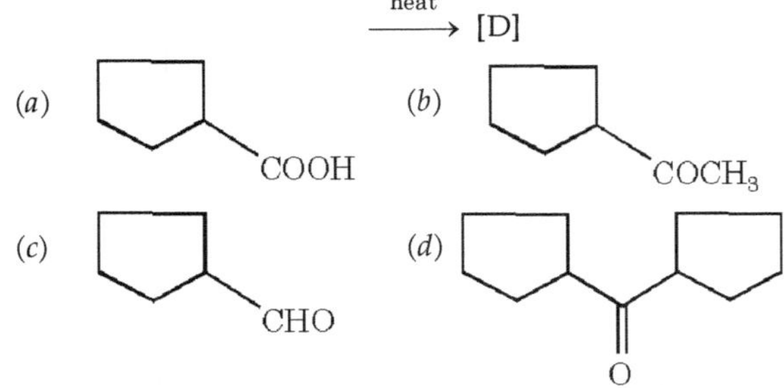

31. $C_2H_5O-\overset{O}{\overset{||}{C}}-OC_2H_5 + 2CH_3MgBr \longrightarrow A$; A is

(a) $(CH_3)_2\overset{OH}{\overset{|}{C}}-C_2H_5$ (b) $C_2H_5-\overset{OH}{\overset{|}{C}}(C_2H_5)-CH_3$

(c) CH_3COOH (d) CH_3COCH_3

32. Which of the following reagent can be used for carrying out the reaction outlined below?

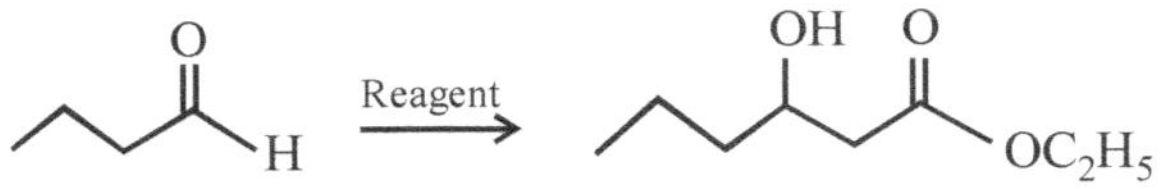

Reagent

(a) $BrMgCH_2COOC_2H_5$ (b) $BrZnCH_2COOC_2H_5$
(c) $LiCH_2COOC_2H_5$ (d) Any of the three

33.

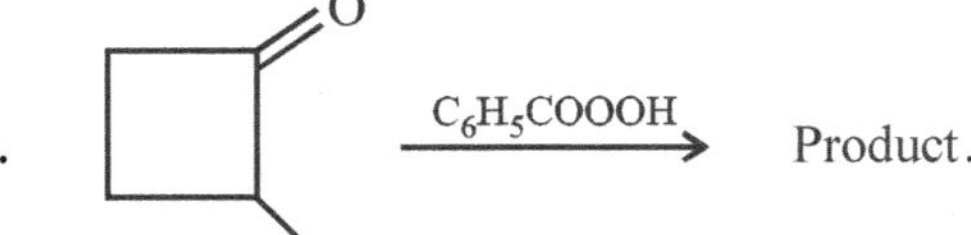

Here the product is

(a) (b)

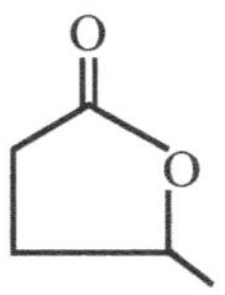

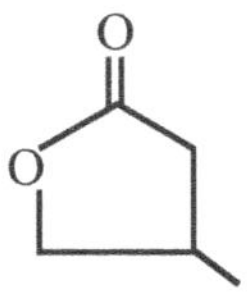

(c) COOH (d) COOH COOH

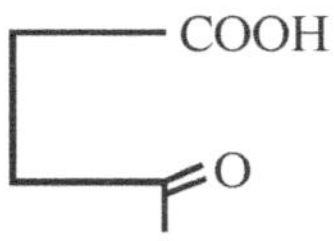

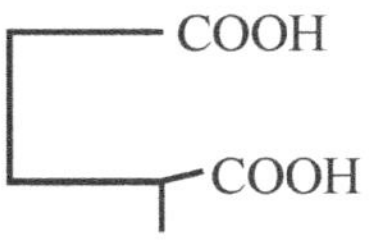

34. Acetyl chloride does not react with
(a) Water
(b) Sodium acetate
(c) 2-methylpropene
(d) It reacts with all the three

35. Which of the following reaction is possible ?

(i) $CH_3COCl + H_2O \rightarrow CH_3COOH + HCl$

(ii) $CH_3COOCH_3 + HBr \rightarrow CH_3COBr + CH_3OH$

(iii) $CH_3CONH_2 + HBr \rightarrow CH_3COBr + NH_3$

(iv) $CH_3COOCOCH_3 + H_2O \rightarrow 2CH_3COOH$

(a) (i) and (iv) (b) (i), (iii) and (iv)
(c) (i), (ii) and (iv) (d) All the four

36. Acid amides do not undergo the usual properties of carbonyl, C = O group because
(a) it is a weak base
(b) it is a weak acid
(c) it is amphoteric
(d) its carbonyl carbon is not electron deficient

37. Which of the following will undergo alkaline hydrolysis most rapidly ?

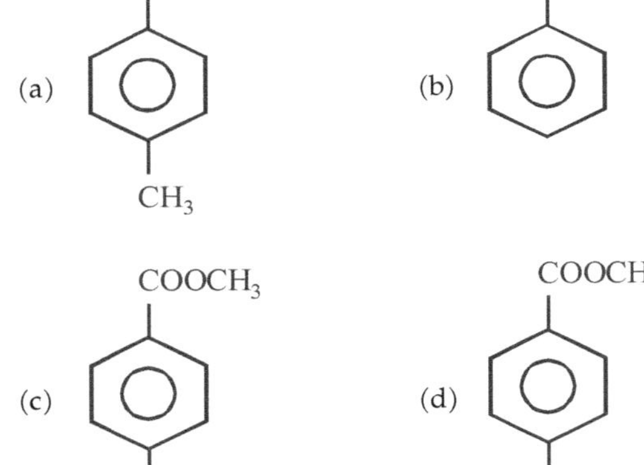

38. Hydrolysis of esters in presence of an acid is a reversible reaction, what is true about ester hydrolysis in presence of a base?
(a) It is irreversible because salts of carboxylic acids are insoluble.
(b) It is irreversible because salts of carboxylic acids have high melting points.
(c) It is irreversible because carboxylate ion is resonance stabilized.
(d) It is reversible reaction.

39. Compound A is formed by the interaction of

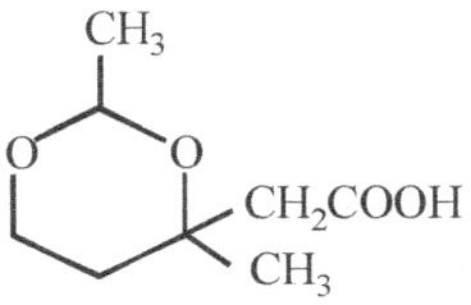

CH_3, O, O, CH_2COOH, CH_3 [A]

(a) CH_3COOH and HO CHO

(b) CH_3CHO and HO COOH OH

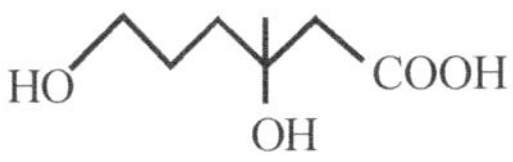

(c) CH_3COCH_2COOH and HO CHO OH

(d) CH_3CHO and HO OH COOH

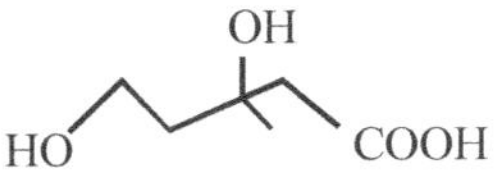

40. The yield of ester in esterification can be increased by
$CH_3CH_2OH + CH_3COOH \rightleftharpoons CH_3COOCH_2CH_3 + H_2O$
(a) removing water
(b) taking ethanol in excess
(c) taking acetic acid in excess
(d) all the above factors

41. The yield of acid amide in the reaction, $RCOCl + NH_3 \rightarrow RCONH_2$, is maximum when
(a) acid chloride and ammonia are treated in equimolar ratio
(b) acid chloride and ammonia are treated in 1 : 2 molar ratio
(c) acid chloride and ammonia are treated in 2 : 1 molar ratio
(d) All the three gives nearly similar result

42.  $COOC_2H_5$–(chain)–$COOC_2H_5$ $\xrightarrow{C_2H_5ONa}$ Z. Here Z is

(a) 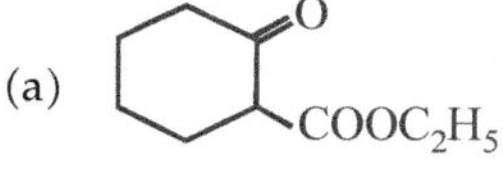
(b) 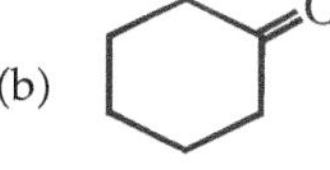
(c) 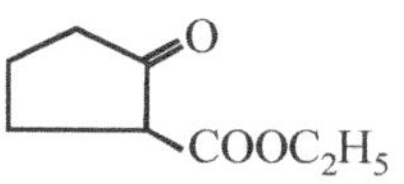 cyclopentanone with $COOC_2H_5$ (2-position)
(d) 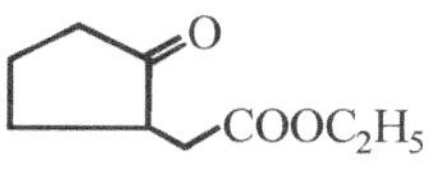 cyclopentanone with $CH_2COOC_2H_5$

43. Both aldol and Claisen condensations are given by compounds having α-hydrogen atom to a C = O group. Pick up the compound which responds aldol condensation but not Claisen condensation.

$CH_3CH_2COOC_2H_5$ (I)

$(CH_3)_2CHCOOC_2H_5$ (II) $(CH_3)_3CCOOC_2H_5$ (III)

(a) II (b) III
(c) II and III (d) None of the three

44.  BrMg–(chain)–MgBr

$+ CH_3COOC_2H_5 \rightarrow [\ ] \xrightarrow{H_3O^+} A$. Compound A is

(a)  CH_3CO–(chain)–OH
(b)  $CH_3CH(OH)$–(chain)–OH
(c) 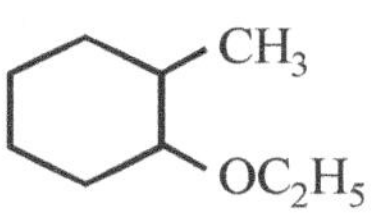 cyclohexane with CH_3 and OC_2H_5
(d) 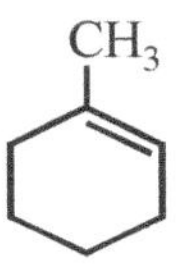 1-methylcyclohexene (CH_3)

45. Which of the following can be used for introducing a ketonic group in the compound ?
(a) Claisen rearrangement (b) Claisen reaction
(c) Pinacol rerarrangement (d) All the three

46. Which statement is true regarding reaction of an acid chloride (RCOCl) and ammonia when taken in 1 : 1 molar ratio?
(a) Whole of acid chloride is converted into $RCONH_2$
(b) One-half of acid chloride is converted into $RCONH_2$ and the other half into $RCOONH_4$
(c) One-half of acid chloride is converted into $RCONH_2$ and the remaining half remains unreacted
(d) None of the three is correct

47. Esterification of acid chloride with ethanol is usually carried out in the presence of pyridine. The function of pyridine is
(a) to remove HCl formed in the reaction
(b) to react with acid chloride to form an acylpyridinium ion
(c) both (a) and (b)
(d) as a catalyst

48. 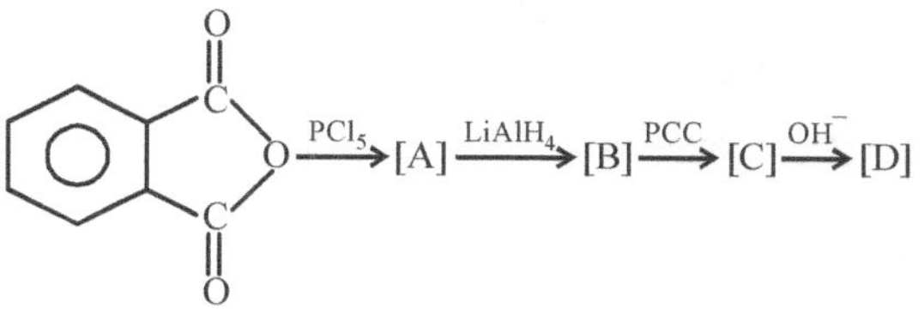 Phthalic anhydride $\xrightarrow{PCl_5} [A] \xrightarrow{LiAlH_4} [B] \xrightarrow{PCC} [C] \xrightarrow{OH^-} [D]$

Compound D is

(a) 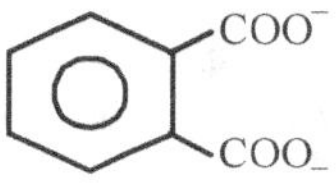 benzene with COO^- and COO^- (b) 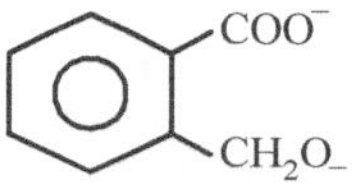 benzene with COO^- and CH_2O^-
(c) 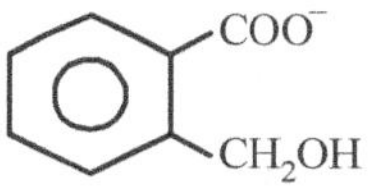 benzene with COO^- and CH_2OH (d) 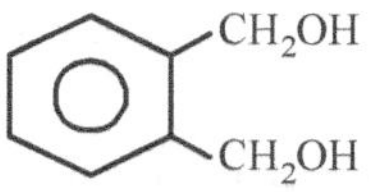 benzene with CH_2OH and CH_2OH

49. The product of acid hydrolysis of P and Q can be distinguished by

P = $H_2C{=}C(OCOCH_3)(CH_3)$, Q = H_3C–$CH{=}CH$–$OCOCH_3$

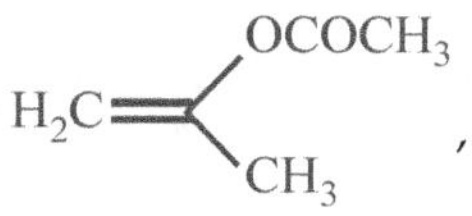

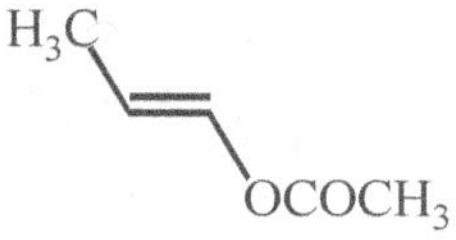

(a) Lucas Reagent (b) 2,4–DNP
(c) Fehling's Solution (d) $NaHSO_3$

50. Ethyl ester $\xrightarrow[\text{excess}]{CH_3MgBr}$ P. The product P will be

(a) 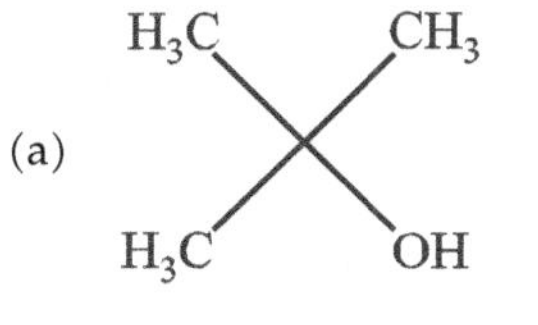

(b) 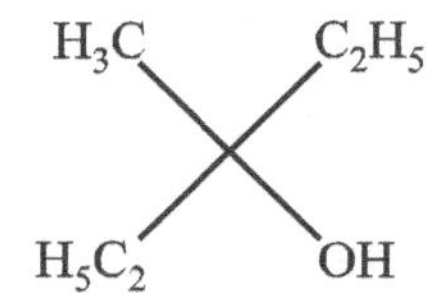

(c) 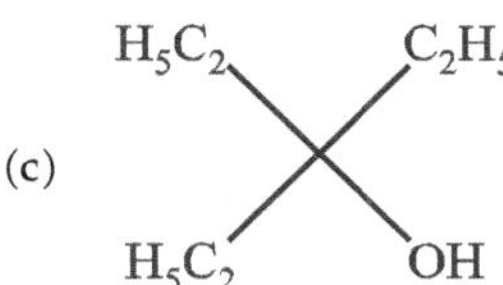

(d) 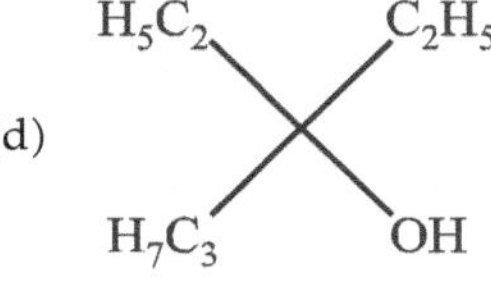

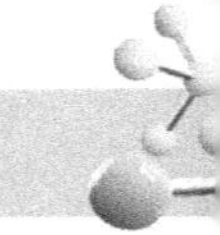

51. An enantiomerically pure acid is treated with a racemic mixture of an alcohol having one chiral carbon. The ester formed will be
(a) Optically active mixture (b) Pure enantiomer
(c) Meso compound (d) Racemic mixture

52. Which of the following statement is not upto the mark?
(a) $R-\overset{O}{\overset{||}{C}}-OR' \xrightarrow{OH^-} R-\overset{O}{\overset{||}{C}}-O^- + R'OH$
(A base-catalysed reaction)
(b) $CH_3COOC_2H_5 \xrightarrow{OH^-} CH_3COOH + C_2H_5OH$
(reaction involves acyl-oxygen fission)
(c) $C_6H_5COOH + CH_3OH \xrightarrow{H^+} C_6H_5COOCH_3 + H_2O$
(reaction involves acyl-oxygen fision)
(d) $CH_3COOCH(CH_3)C_2H_5 \xrightarrow{OH^-} CH_3COO^- + HOCH(CH_3)C_2H_5$
(configuration of the reactant is retained)

53. The products in the following reaction are
$C_6H_5COOCH_2C_6H_5 \xrightarrow{H_2-Pd/C}$
(a) $C_6H_5CH_2OH + C_6H_5CH_2OH$
(b) $C_6H_5CH_3 + C_6H_5CH_3$
(c) $C_6H_5CH_2OH + C_6H_5CH_3$
(d) $C_6H_5COOH + C_6H_5CH_3$

54. Pyrolysis of $CH_3COO\overset{CH_3}{\overset{|}{C}}HCH_2CH_3$ gives
(a) 1-butene and 2-butene in equimolar ratio
(b) 1-butene and 2-butene in 1 : 2 molar ratio
(c) 1-butene and 2-butene in 3 : 2 molar ratio
(d) 1-butene and 2-butene in 2 : 3 molar ratio

55. The relative stability of the four acid derivatives towards nucleophiles is
(a) Amide > Ester > Acid anhydride > Acid chloride
(b) Amide > Acid anhydride > Ester > Acid chloride
(c) Acid Chloride > Acid anhydride > Ester > Amide
(d) Acid Chloride > Ester > Acid anhydride > Amide

56. Which of the following statement is true about the hydrolysis of acetic anhydride ?
(i) It is more easily hydrolysed in acidic medium than in neutral
(ii) It is more easily hydrolysed in alkaline medium than in neutral
(iii) It is equally hydrolysed in all the three medium
(iv) It is more easily hydrolysed in neutral than in acidic medium
(v) It is more easily hydrolysed in neutral than in alkaline medium
(a) (i) and (ii) (b) (iii)
(c) (iv) and (v) (d) (i) and (v)

57. Which of the following compounds can undergo nucleophilic substitution easily ?

I: $C_6H_5-\overset{O}{\overset{||}{C}}-C_6H_5$
II: $C_6H_5-\overset{O}{\overset{||}{C}}-O-\overset{O}{\overset{||}{C}}-C_6H_5$
III: $C_6H_5-\overset{O}{\overset{||}{C}}-CCl_3$
IV: $C_6H_5-\overset{O}{\overset{||}{C}}-C_6H_4-F$
V: $C_6H_5-\overset{O}{\overset{||}{C}}-C_6H_4F$ (ortho F)

(a) Only II (b) I, II, III and IV
(c) II, III and V (d) II, III and IV

58. The reason for greater reactivity of acetyl chloride for nucleophilic substitution than methyl chloride is due to
(i) capability of oxygen to acquire electrons
(ii) difference in the nature of carbon of the intermediate: a tetrahedral in case of acetyl chloride and a pentavalent in case of methyl chloride
(iii) difference in attack of nucleophile on the compound
(iv) better leavability of –COCl than –Cl
(a) (i) and (ii) (b) (i) and (iii)
(c) (i), (ii) and (iii) (d) (iv)

59. The driving force for the completion of Claisen condensation between ethyl acetate and sodium ethoxide to ethyl acetoacetate is
(a) the presence of reactive methylene group in ethyl acetoacetate
(b) the phenomenon of keto enol tautomerism
(c) the presence of at least α-hydrogen atom in ester
(d) all the three factors

60. Which of the following compound undergoes Claisen condensation in presence of C_2H_5ONa ?
(i) $CH_3CH_2COOC_2H_5$
(ii) $(CH_3)_2CHCOOC_2H_5$ (iii) $ClCH_2COOC_2H_5$
(a) only (i) (b) (i) and (ii)
(c) (i) and (iii) (d) all of the three

61. Ester + CH_3MgBr (excess) $\xrightarrow{H_3O^+}$ $C_4H_{10}O$ (Alcohol)
The alcohol formed gives white ppt. with $ZnCl_2/HCl$ immediately, the ester may be
$HCOOC_3H_7$ (I) $CH_3COOC_5H_{11}$ (II)
CH_3COOCH_3 (III) $C_2H_5COOCH_3$ (IV)
(a) II (b) II and III
(c) II and IV (d) I

62. In the reaction
$H_3C-C_6H_4-\overset{O}{\overset{||}{C}}-NH_2 \xrightarrow[(2)\ C_6H_5COCl]{(1)\ NaOH/Br_2} T$
the structure of the product **T** is :
(a) $H_3C-C_6H_4-\overset{O}{\overset{||}{C}}-O-\overset{O}{\overset{||}{C}}-C_6H_5$
(b) $C_6H_5-NH-\overset{O}{\overset{||}{C}}-C_6H_4-CH_3$
(c) $H_3C-C_6H_4-NH-\overset{O}{\overset{||}{C}}-C_6H_5$
(d) $H_3C-C_6H_4-\overset{O}{\overset{||}{C}}-NH-\overset{O}{\overset{||}{C}}-C_6H_5$

(iii)

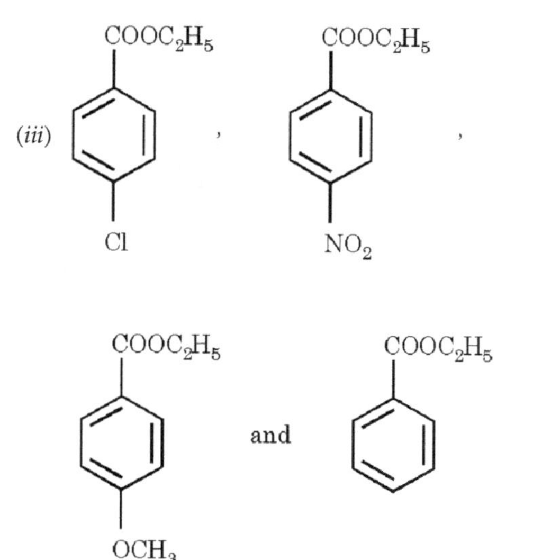

(iv) $CH_3COOC_2H_5$, CH_3COCl, $(CH_3CO)_2O$ and CH_3CONH_2.

(c) Compare the reactivity of benzoyl chloride with cyclohexanecarboxyl chloride.

8. Predict the product of the reaction of γ-butyrolactone with
   (a) ammonia (b) $LiAlH_4$ (c) $C_2H_5OH + H_2SO_4$.

9. Describe simple chemical tests that would serve to distinguish between
   (a) Acetyl chloride and acetic anhydride.
   (b) *n*-Butyryl chloride and *n*-butyl chloride.
   (c) Benzoyl bromide and *p*-bromobenzoic acid.
   (d) Propanoic acid and ethyl acetate.
   (e) Acetic anhydride and *n*-butyl alcohol.
   (f) Ammonium benzoate and benzamide.
   (g) Glyceryl monopalmitate and glyceryl tripalmitate.

10. (a) Write an equation for the reaction of $CH_3COOC_2H_5$ with CH_3MgI.
   (b) Why a ketone is not isolated from the reaction of an ester with one equivalent of CH_3MgI ?
   (c) Can you prepare a 2° alcohol from an ester and an organometallic reagent ?

11. (a) What is an ortho ester, give its general formula ? Give the product obtained by the mild hydrolysis of ethyl orthoformate.
   (b) Write down the steps involved in the preparation of ethyl orthoformate by the reaction of chloroform with sodium ethoxide.

12. Give the ester or combination of esters required to prepare the following products by a Claisen condensation.

   (a) $C_6H_5CH_2CH_2\overset{\overset{\Large O}{\|}}{C}\,\overset{\overset{\Large CH_2C_6H_5}{|}}{C}HCOOCH_3$

   (b) $C_2H_5COO.CO.\overset{\overset{\Large CH_3}{|}}{C}HCOOC_2H_5$

   (c) $OHC\overset{\overset{\Large C_6H_5}{|}}{C}HCOOCH_3$

13. Compare the reactants, conditions, and products of the Hofmann, Lossen, Curtius and Schmidt reactions.

14. Compare the acidity of the N—H in
   (a) an acid amide (*e.g.*, CH_3CONH_2) and a sulphonamide (*e.g.*, $CH_3SO_2NH_2$).
   (b) benzamide ($C_6H_5CONH_2$),a phthalimide and ammonia.

15. Explain the following :
   (a) Dimethyl sulphate is a good methylating agent.
   (b) An acyl chloride undergoes nucleophilic attack more rapidly than does an alkyl chloride.
   (c) Trialkyl phosphates are readily hydrolyzed with OH^- to dialkyl phosphate salts, while the hydrolysis of dialkyl hydrogen phosphates and alkyl dihydrogen phosphates with OH^- becomes increasingly more difficult.
   (d) Hydrolysis of the ester (A) with 5 M NaOH gives optically active alcohol, C_6H_5 while hydrolysis with dil. NaOH gives optically inactive alcohol.
   (e) The reaction '$CH_3COOC_2H_5 + H_2O \longrightarrow CH_3COOH + C_2H_5OH$' is slow in the beginning, but fast subsequently.

16. An ester (A) of the formula $C_5H_8O_2$ on acidic hydrolysis gives an acid (B) which reduces Tollen's regent and an alcohol (C) which gives iodoform test. Ester (A) can also be converted into alcohol (B) by reaction with excess of Grignard reagent (D). Identify (A) to (D).

SOLUTIONS

TEST YOUR UNDERSTANDING - 18.1

1. (*i*) 3, 3-Dimethylbutanoyl chloride (*ii*) 2-Bromopentanoyl bromide (*iii*) 3-Hexenoyl chloride
   (*iv*) Cyclopentyl methanoyl chloride (*v*) Propanoic hexanoic anhydride (*vi*) Methyl cyclopentanecarboxylate
   (*vii*) 1-Methylpropyl propenoate (*viii*) N, N-Dimethylpropanamide (*ix*) N, N′-Dimethylurea
   (*x*) N, N-Dimethylurea.

2. (*i*) O, Cl, C_6H_5 (*ii*) O, NH_2, C_6H_5 (*iii*) O, O, C_6H_5, C_6H_5

   (*iv*) O, N H, CH_3, C_6H_5 (*v*) O, O, C_6H_5 (*vi*) O, O, C_6H_5

3. Nitriles are hydrolyzed by H^+ or OH^- to acids.

TEST YOUR UNDERSTANDING - 18.2

1. Recall that the first step in nucleophilic substitution at acyl carbon is the addition of a nucleophile at acyl carbon which is facilitated by (*a*) any factor that increases the electrophilic character of the acyl carbon ; and (*b*) less steric hindrance at carbonyl carbon. Thus
   (*i*) F_3CCOCl is more reactive due to strong electron-withdrawing nature of F.
   (*ii*) CH_3COOCH_3 is more reactive because the other compound has benzene ring which decreases the electrophilic character of carbonyl carbon by supplying electrons due to resonance,
   (*iii*) $O_2N-C_6H_4-COOCH_3$ is more reactive due to electron-withdrawing nature of the —NO_2 group.
   (*iv*) $C_6H_5-COOCH_3$ is more reactive due to less steric hindrance.
   (*v*) An ester is more reactive (less stable) than an amide.
2. (*i*) $CH_3CH(Cl)\,COO^-NH_4^+$. Here addition of nucleophile takes place on —COOH. Recall that alkyl halides (CH_3CHCl—) react very slowly with nucleophiles than acyl compounds.
   (*ii*) $ClCH_2CONH_2$ (Acyl nucleophilic substitution is very fast than alkyl nucleophilic substitution).
   (*iii*) C_6H_5Cl does not react with NH_3 at room temperature.
   (*iv*) o-$HOC_6H_4-CO\bar{O}\overset{+}{N}H_4$
3. Aldehydes and ketones do not undergo nucleophilic substitution (nucleophilic addition-elemination) because generally the eliminated anions (H:⁻ or R:⁻) are strongly basic and hence poor leaving groups. In the two given cases, the leaving anions are stabilized by powerful electron withdrawing groups ; hence these are weak bases and behave as good leaving groups.

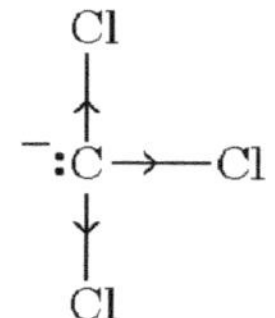

Stabilized by three electron-withdrawing groups

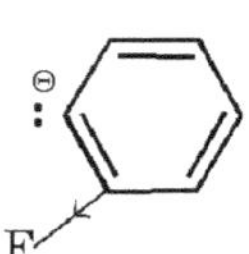

Stabilized by powerful electron withdrawing *ortho* F

TEST YOUR UNDERSTANDING - 18.3

1. (a) Formation of anhydride from adipic acid would produce a seven-membered ring which is too difficult to be formed. Instead, it loses a molecule of CO_2 and converted into a cyclic ketone with five-membered ring.

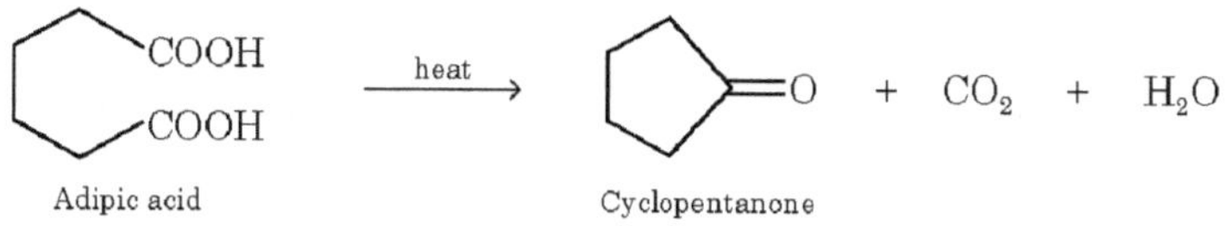

$$\text{Adipic acid (cyclic diagram, COOH, COOH)} \xrightarrow{\text{heat}} \text{Cyclopentanone} + CO_2 + H_2O$$

Suberic acid (1, 8-octanedioic acid) does not form cyclic ketone because again here seven-membered ring would be formed which is too difficult to be formed.

(b) $C_6H_5-\overset{O}{\overset{\|}{C}}-Cl + H_2O \longrightarrow C_6H_5-\overset{O}{\overset{\|}{C}}-OH + HCl$

$C_6H_5-\overset{O}{\overset{\|}{C}}-Cl + HO-\overset{O}{\overset{\|}{C}}-C_6H_5 \longrightarrow C_6H_5-\overset{O}{\overset{\|}{C}}-O-\overset{O}{\overset{\|}{C}}-C_6H_5 + HCl$

TEST YOUR UNDERSTANDING - 18.4

1. (a) Nucleophilic substitution of acyl compounds takes place readily (*i*) if the final product is more resonance stabilized than the reactant or (*ii*) if the incoming group (nucleophile) is a stronger base than the leaving group.
   (*i*) Yes. CH_3COOH is more resonance stabilized than CH_3COCl ; also OH^- is a stronger base than Cl^-.
   (*ii*) No. CH_3CONH_2 is lesser resonance stabilized than CH_3COOH. NH_3 reacts with RCOOH to form $RCOO^-NH_4^+$ which does not react. Amides are prepared from RCOOH by strongly heating dry $RCOO^-NH_4^+$ because now reaction is catalysed by acid (NH_4^+).
   (*iii*) Yes. CH_3COO^- is more stabilized than $(CH_3CO)_2O$; also the leaving group $RCOO^-$ is a weaker base than OH^-.
   (*iv*) Yes. $CH_3COOC_2H_5$ is more stabilized than CH_3COBr, and also Br^- is a much weaker base than HOC_2H_5.
   (*v*) Yes. CH_3COO^- is highly stable than CH_3CONH_2 ; although NH_2^- (the leaving group) is a stronger base than OH^- (the nucleophile).
   (*vi*) No. CH_3COBr is less stable than CH_3COOCH_3 (ester) ; also Br^- is a weaker base than OCH_3^-.

(b) $CH_3COOH \xrightarrow{NaOH} CH_3COO^-Na^+ \xrightarrow{(CH_3)_3CBr}$ Elimination reaction.

Hence $CH_3COO^-Na^+ + (CH_3)_2C=CH_2 \xrightarrow{\text{Conc. } H_2SO_4} CH_3COOC(CH_3)_3$

(c) Since acyl chloride is more reactive than the carboxylic acid, it will react with water rapidly to give the starting material

$RCOOH + HCl \rightleftharpoons RCOCl + H_2O$

Water (one of the products) cannot be removed as it is formed because here HCl (being gas) would escape.

TEST YOUR UNDERSTANDING - 18.5

. (a) $C_6H_5-\overset{OH}{\overset{|}{\underset{Cl}{\underset{|}{C}}}}-OCOCH_3$ (b) $C_6H_5-\overset{OH}{\overset{|}{\underset{Cl}{\underset{|}{C}}}}-OC_2H_5$ (c) $C_6H_5-\overset{OH}{\overset{|}{\underset{Cl}{\underset{|}{C}}}}-N(CH_3)_2$ (d) $C_6H_5-\overset{OH}{\overset{|}{\underset{Cl}{\underset{|}{C}}}}-OH$

. Since hydrazoic acid (HN_3) is slightly more acidic than acetic acid (CH_3COOH), the azide ion (N_3^-) is slightly less basic than the acetate ion (CH_3COO^-). Thus azide ion will be slightly better leaving group than the acetate ion ; hence acyl azide ($RCON_3$) will be a little more reactive than the anhydride (RCOOCOR). Thus the position of acyl azide in the order of reactivity of various acyl derivatives will be between acyl chlorides and acid anhydrides.

$$RCOCl > RCON_3 > (RCO)_2O$$

. (a) Pd/C, poisoned with quinolione and S or LBAH (b) NH_3 (c) $LiAlH_4$ (d) $C_6H_5CH_2OH + H^+$
(e) $C_6H_5COO^-Na^+$ or heat with $(CH_3CO)_2O$ (f) $C_6H_5CH_2NH_2$ (g) NaN_3 (sodium azide).

. In each case, the less reactive organometallic Me_2CuLi reacts with the more reactive —COCl group to form methyl ketone.

(a) $NC(CH_2)_4COCH_3$ (b) $2CH_3CO-C_6H_4-COCH_3$ (c) $H_5C_2OOC(CH_2)_4COCH_3$.

TEST YOUR UNDERSTANDING - 18.6

1. (a) $CH_3COOCH_3 + CH_3COOH$ (b) $2CH_3COOCH_3$

(c) $\frac{1}{2} CH_3CONH_2 + \frac{1}{2} CH_3COO^-NH_4^+ + \frac{1}{2} (CH_3CO)_2O$

(d) $CH_2CON(CH_3)_2$ | $CH_2COO^- \ H_2N^+(CH_3)_2$

(e) $CH_2COO^-Na^+$ | $CH_2COO^-Na^+$

(f) $(CH_3)_3COH$

(g) C_6H_5—CO—CH_2CH_2—COOH

2. (a) Mixed anhydrides are prepared by reacting the acid chloride of one of the acids with the carboxylic salt of the other. Thus

(i) $CH_3—\overset{O}{\overset{\|}{C}}—Cl + Na^{+-}O—\overset{O}{\overset{\|}{C}}—CH_2CH_3$

or

$CH_3CH_2—\overset{O}{\overset{\|}{C}}—Cl + Na^{+-}O—\overset{O}{\overset{\|}{C}}—CH_3 \longrightarrow CH_3—\overset{O}{\overset{\|}{C}}—O—\overset{O}{\overset{\|}{C}}—CH_2CH_3$

(ii) $CH_3—\overset{O}{\overset{\|}{C}}—Cl + Na^+ \ ^-O—\overset{O}{\overset{\|}{C}}—H \longrightarrow CH_3—\overset{O}{\overset{\|}{C}}—O—\overset{O}{\overset{\|}{C}}—H$

Acetic formic anhydride

Since HCOCl is not stable, HCOCl + CH_3 COO^-Na^- does not constitute the alternate pair for preparing acetic formic anhydride.

(b) No. On heating, formic acid undergoes dehydration intramolecularly rather than intermolecularly.

$$HCOOH \longrightarrow CO + H_2O$$

3. o-(p-Tolyl)benzoic acid [A] — 2-Methyl-9, 10-anthraquinone [B]

TEST YOUR UNDERSTANDING - 18.7

1. (a) $R—\overset{\ddot{O}:}{\overset{\|}{C}}—\ddot{\underset{\cdot\cdot}{O}}—R'$. The π electrons of the C = O bond are more easily displaced than the σ electrons of the C—O bond with the result the carbonyl oxygen acquires negative charge, hence acyl oxygen (or carbonyl oxygen) is more basic.

(b) The three C—O bonds have different bond lengths, because of relative displacement of electrons along their bonds ;

$$R—\overset{O}{\overset{z\|}{C}}\overset{y}{—}O\overset{x}{—}R'$$

The relative value of bond lengths is $x > y > z$.

2. The carbonyl carbon of RCOOH and RCOOR' is trigonal sp^2 hybridised, while that of the intermediate is tetrahedral sp^3 hybridised. If alkyl group in alcohol or in acid is extensively branched, transition state will be crowded leading to slow reaction and with difficulty too

3. (a) $\underset{III}{CH_3COOCH_3} > \underset{I}{CH_3COOC_2H_5} > \underset{II}{CH_3COOCHMe_2} > \underset{IV}{CH_3COOCMe_3}$

Steric effect, and relative basic character of the leaving groups. Basic character of the leaving groups is

$$Me_3CO^- > Me_2CHO^- > C_2H_5O^- > CH_3O^-$$

(b) $HCOOCH_3$ (II) > CH_3COOCH_3 (I) > $CH_3CH_2COOCH_3$ (IV) > $Me_2CHCOOCH_3$ (III) > $Me_3CCOOCH_3$ (V)

Remember that an alkyl group releases electrons, and thus destabilizes the transition state by intensifying the negative charge developing on oxygen. Thus lesser is electron releasing character of an alkyl group, more will be the stability of the transition state.

4. Presence of electron-withdrawing group speeds up the reaction since it helps to disperse the negative charge developing on oxygen.

(a) V > III > IV > I > II (b) III > IV > II > I.

5. (a) (i) $CH_3CH_2C(C_6H_5)_2OH$

(ii) δ-valerolactone + CH_3MgI $\xrightarrow[(ii)\ H_3O^+]{(i)\ \text{ether}}$ 2-methyltetrahydropyran-2-ol (CH₃, OH) $\xrightarrow{CH_3MgI}$ $HOCH_2CH_2CH_2CH_2C(CH_3)_2OH$

(iii) $HOCH_2CH_2CH_2CH_2CONHCH_3$ (iv) $CH_3CONHNH_2$ Acetyl hydrazide (v) $C_6H_5CONHOH$ Benzoylhydroxamic acid

(b) $CH_3CH{=}CHCH_2COOCH_2CH_2CH_2Br$ $\xrightarrow[(ii)\ H^+]{(i)\ \text{NaOH, heat}}$ $CH_3CH{=}CHCH_2COOH$ + oxetane

(c) $CH_3(CH_2)_7CH = CH(CH_2)_7COOC_4H_9\text{-}n \longrightarrow CH_3(CH_2)_{16}CH_2OH + n\text{-}C_4H_9OH$

1-Octadecanol

6. Esters of formic acid, when treated with excess of Grignard reagents, give secondary alcohols having similar alkyl groups.

$$H{-}\overset{O}{\overset{\|}{C}}{-}OC_2H_5 + 2\,n\text{-}C_3H_7MgBr \longrightarrow n\text{-}C_3H_7{-}\underset{OH}{\underset{|}{CH}}{-}C_3H_7\text{-}n$$

4-Heptanol

7. (a) However, with 3° alcohols, ester hydrolysis occurs by alkyl-oxygen cleavage leading to a 3° carbocation which being planar gives racemic product.

$$R{-}\overset{O}{\overset{\|}{C}}{-}O{-}C(CH_3)(C_6H_5){-}C_2H_5\ (+)\text{-} \xrightarrow{H^+} R{-}\overset{O}{\overset{\|}{C}}{-}OH + \overset{\oplus}{C}(CH_3)(C_6H_5){-}C_2H_5 \xrightarrow[(-H^+)]{H_2O^{18}} H\overset{18}{O}{-}C(CH_3)(C_6H_5){-}C_2H_5\ (\pm)\text{-}$$

(b) Hydrolysis of esters having 2° or 1° alcohol occur by acyl-oxygen cleavage. Since no bond to chiral carbon is broken, configuration is retained and O^{18} from water appears in acidic part.

$$CH_3{-}\overset{O}{\overset{\|}{C}}{-}O{-}C(CH_3)(H){-}C_2H_5\ (+)\text{-} \xrightarrow{H^+,\ H_2O^{18}} CH_3{-}\overset{O}{\overset{\|}{C}}{-}O^{18}H + HO{-}C(CH_3)(H){-}C_2H_5\ (+)\text{-}$$

TEST YOUR UNDERSTANDING - 18.8

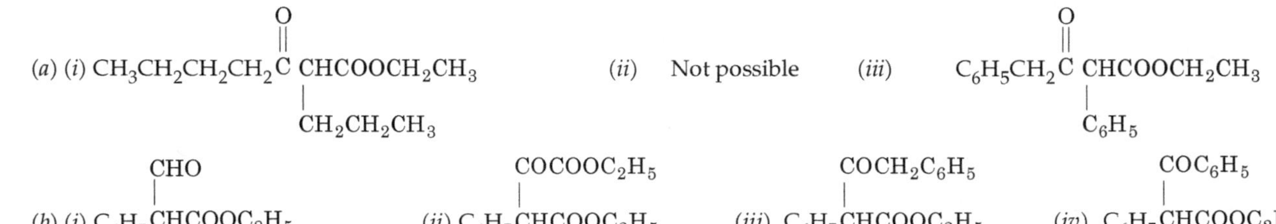

1. (a) (i) $CH_3CH_2CH_2CH_2\overset{O}{\overset{\|}{C}}\,\underset{CH_2CH_2CH_3}{\underset{|}{C}H}COOCH_2CH_3$ (ii) Not possible (iii) $C_6H_5CH_2\overset{O}{\overset{\|}{C}}\,\underset{C_6H_5}{\underset{|}{C}H}COOCH_2CH_3$

(b) (i) $C_6H_5\overset{CHO}{\overset{|}{C}H}COOC_2H_5$ (ii) $C_6H_5\overset{COCOOC_2H_5}{\overset{|}{C}H}COOC_2H_5$ (iii) $C_6H_5\overset{COCH_2C_6H_5}{\overset{|}{C}H}COOC_2H_5$ (iv) $C_6H_5\overset{COC_6H_5}{\overset{|}{C}H}COOC_2H_5$.

2. The side reaction with sodium methoxide is transesterification. The starting material, and therefore the product, would be a mixture of methyl and ethyl esters. Sodium hydroxide would irreversibly saponify the ester, completely stopping the claisen condensation as the carbonyl no longer has a leaving group attached to it.

3. $$CH_3-\underset{CH_3}{CH}-\overset{O}{\overset{\|}{C}}OC_2H_5 \xrightarrow{^-OC_2H_5} \left[CH_3-\underset{..}{\overset{CH_3}{C^-}}-\overset{O}{\overset{\|}{C}}OC_2H_5 \longleftrightarrow CH_3-\overset{CH_3}{C}=\overset{O^-}{C}OC_2H_5\right]$$

$$\xrightarrow{(CH_3)_2CH\overset{O}{\overset{\|}{C}}OC_2H_5} (CH_3)_2CH-\overset{O^-}{\underset{OC_2H_5}{C}}-\overset{CH_3}{\underset{CH_3}{C}}-\overset{O}{\overset{\|}{C}}-OC_2H_5 \xrightarrow{-C_2H_5O^-} (CH_3)_2CH-\overset{O}{\overset{\|}{C}}-\overset{CH_3}{\underset{CH_3}{C}}-\overset{O}{\overset{\|}{C}}OC_2H_5$$

The two reasons for the poor yield in this reaction are

(i) The nucleophilic carbon in the enolate is 3° and attack is hindered.

(ii) More important, the final product has no hydrogen on the α-carbon, so the deprotonation by base which is the driving force in Claisen condensation can't occur. Thus, the product will be an equilibrium mixture of product (minor) and starting materials (major).

4. Dissect the α,β-bond of the β-keto ester. Add the appropriate alcohol (ROH) to the two carbon atoms (RO^- to the carbonyl carbon and H^+ to other carbon).

(i) cyclopentyl–CH_2–C(=O)–OCH_3 (ii) cyclopentyl–C(=O)–OC_3H_7-*iso*

Note that in (b) the product of Claisen condensation would be formed in low yield because it does not have acidic hydrogen between two C = O groups to be removed to form the stable carbanion (driving force for the reaction).

5. Remove the acyl group of the product in the form of an ester.

(*i*) $$C_6H_5\overset{O}{\overset{\|}{C}}-\overset{C_6H_5}{CH}-COOC_2H_5 \longleftarrow C_6H_5COOC_2H_5 + H_2\overset{C_6H_5}{C}COOC_2H_5$$

(*ii*) H_5C_2OOC / $COOC_2H_5$ substituted cyclopentane-dione $\longleftarrow$ $\underset{COOC_2H_5}{COOC_2H_5}$ + $CH_2COOC_2H_5$–CH_2–$CH_2COOC_2H_5$

(*iii*) indanedione–$COOC_2H_5$ $\longleftarrow$ benzene-1,2-di($COOC_2H_5$) + $H_3CCOOC_2H_5$

6. (a) cyclopentanone + $CH_3O-\overset{O}{\overset{\|}{C}}-C_6H_5$ *or* OCH_3 … C_6H_5 keto ester (intramolecular)

Crossed Claisen — Intramolecular Claisen

(b) cyclohexanone with $C(=O)OC_2H_5$

(c) cyclohexane-1,3-dione + $C_2H_5O-\overset{O}{\overset{\|}{C}}-OC_2H_5$ *or* keto ester with $C(=O)(OC_2H_5)$ and OC_2H_5

7. (*a*) (*i*) 2-($COOC_2H_5$)cyclohexanone (*ii*) 4-CH_3-2-($COOC_2H_5$)cyclohexanone (*iii*) H_3C–cyclopentanone–$COOC_2H_5$

(*b*) Since three and four membered rings are difficult to form, ethyl succinate and ethyl glutarate do not undergo Dieckmann reaction. However, ethyl succinate on prolonged treatment with sodium ethoxide undergoes double Claisen condensation to form six-membered cyclic compound.

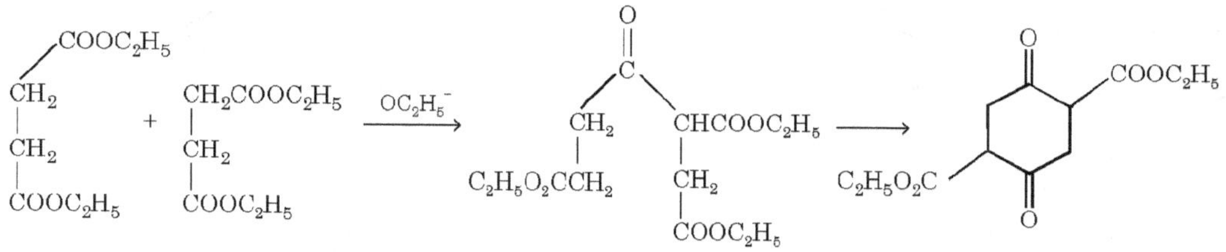

$$\begin{array}{l} CH_2COOC_2H_5 \\ | \\ CH_2COOC_2H_5 \end{array} + \begin{array}{l} CH_2COOC_2H_5 \\ | \\ CH_2COOC_2H_5 \end{array} \xrightarrow{OC_2H_5^-} C_2H_5O_2CCH_2CH_2-\overset{O}{\overset{\|}{C}}-\begin{array}{l} CHCOOC_2H_5 \\ | \\ CH_2COOC_2H_5 \end{array} \longrightarrow$$

(cyclohexane-1,4-dione bearing two $COOC_2H_5$ groups; $C_2H_5O_2C$ and $COOC_2H_5$)

8. (a) 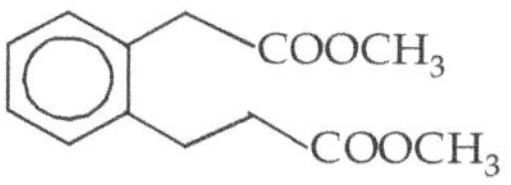 (benzene ring with CH_2COOCH_3 and CH_2COOCH_3 ortho substituents)

(b) It is a γ-keto ester, hence can't be prepared by Dieckmann condensation.

(c) 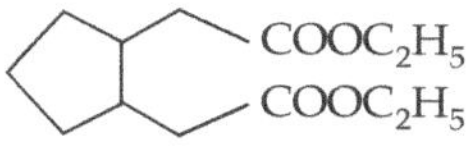 (cyclopentane with $CH_2COOC_2H_5$ and $CH_2COOC_2H_5$ substituents)

(d) 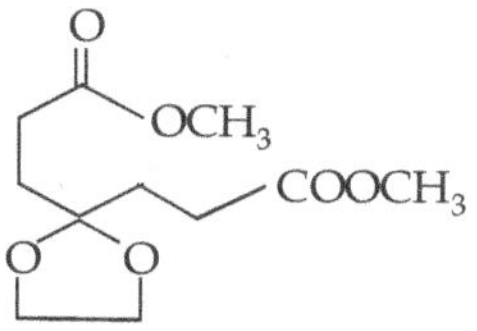 (ethylene ketal bearing $CH_2CH_2COOCH_3$ chains; OCH_3, $COOCH_3$)

Ketonic group is protected to avoid aldol condensation.

9. $CH_3COOH + BF_3 \rightleftharpoons CH_3COOBF_3^- + H^+$

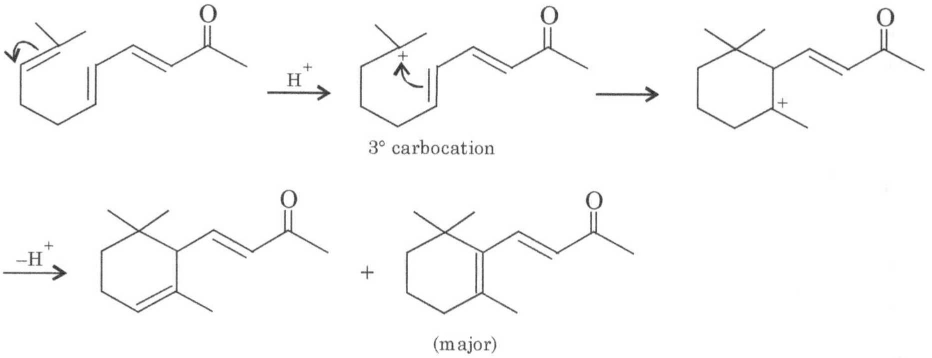

$\xrightarrow{H^+}$ (3° carbocation) $\longrightarrow$ (cyclized carbocation)

3° carbocation

$\xrightarrow{-H^+}$ (α-ionone) + (β-ionone)

(major)

TEST YOUR UNDERSTANDING - 18.9

(*a*) Succinic acid $\xrightarrow{heat}$ Succinic anhydride $\xrightarrow{2\,NH_3}$ ($CONH_2$ / $COO^-NH_4^+$) $\xrightarrow{H^+}$ Succinamic acid $\xrightarrow{heat}$ Succinimide

Succinic acid, Succinic anhydride, Succinamic acid, Succinimide

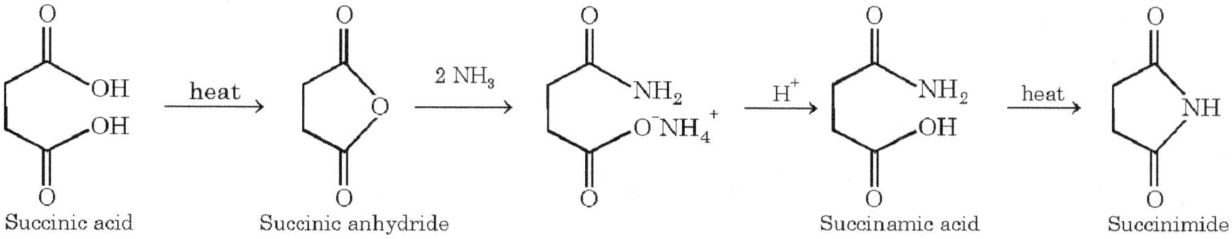

(*b*) $CH_3CH_2CH_2COOH \xrightarrow{SOCl_2} CH_3CH_2CH_2COCl \xrightarrow{NH_3} CH_3CH_2CH_2CONH_2 \xrightarrow{Br_2/NaOH} CH_3CH_2CH_2NH_2$

Butanoic acid; 1-Propanamine

Let us draw the structure of the conjugate base and study their relative basicity.

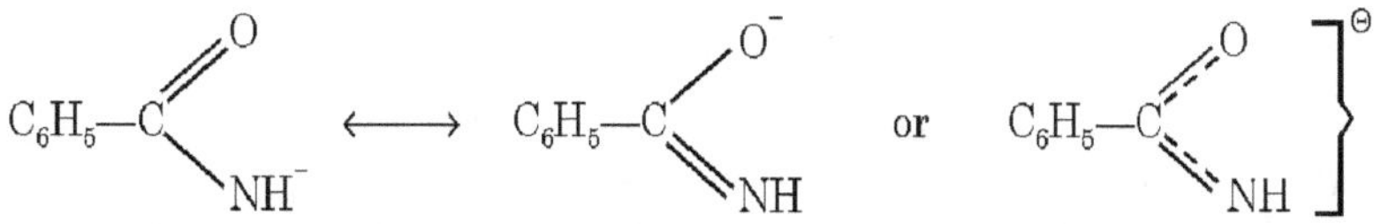

$$C_6H_5-C(=O)-NH^- \longleftrightarrow C_6H_5-C(-O^-)=NH \quad \text{or} \quad \left[C_6H_5-C\overset{\cdots O}{\underset{\cdots NH}{}}\right]^{\ominus}$$

Resonance in conjugate base of benzamide.

In conjugate base of NH_3, *i.e.* NH_2^-, the negative charge is localised. Thus the order of basic character of the three conjugate bases is

$NH_2^- > C_6H_5CONH^- >$ Conjugate base of phthalimide

Acidity order is Phthalimide > Benzamide > NH_3

3. (*a*) $CH_3COOH + Me_2\overset{+}{N}H_2$ (*b*) $COOH.CH(CH_3)NH_3^+ + COOHCH(C_2H_5)NH_3^+$

(*c*) (*d*)

4. Hydrolysis of amides is an example of nucleophilic addition-elimination reaction which is enhanced in presence of electron-withdrawing group. Thus II < I < IV < III

5. (*a*) $RCONH_2 + R'Li \longrightarrow RCONH^-Li^+ + R'H$

1° amide metal salt

$RCONHR' + R''Li \longrightarrow RCON^-R'Li^+ \downarrow + R''H$

2° amide

$RCONR_2' + R''Li \longrightarrow RCOR'' + R_2'NLi$

3° amide

(*b*) $RCONH_2 + HONO \longrightarrow RCOOH + N_2 + H_2O$

1° amide

$RCONHR' + HONO \longrightarrow RCON(R')-N=O$

N-Nitrosoamide

$RCONR_2'$ (3° amide) does not react with nitrous acid.

6. (*i*) $C_6H_5CH_2CH_2OH + CH_3OH$ (*ii*) $2CH_3CH_2OH$

(*iii*) $C_6H_5CH_2OH$ (*iv*) $CH_3CH = CHCH_2CH_2NHC_6H_5$

(*v*) $HOCH_2CH(CH_3)CH_2CH_2OH$ (*vi*) cyclopentyl–$NHCH_2CH_3$ (*vii*)

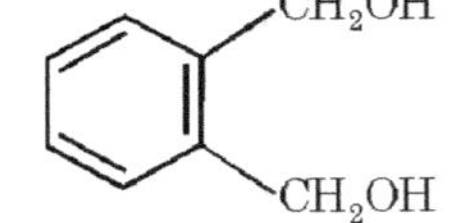

TEST YOUR UNDERSTANDING - 18.10

1. (*a*) $RCOCl$ (*b*) $RCOOC_2H_5$ (c) $(CH_3CH_2CO)_2O$

(*d*) $RCOO^-NH_4^+$ (*e*) $RCOO^-NH_4^+$, $RCONH_2$, or RCN.

2. $CH_3COOC_3H_7\text{-}n + OH^- \longrightarrow CH_3COO^- + n\text{-}C_3H_7OH$

n-Propyl acetate

One mole of the ester requires one mole of OH^- for hydrolysis (saponification), thus Saponification equivalent (SE) = M.W. of ester = 10[illegible] ($C_5H_{10}O_2$).

Number of esters (RCOOR') having $C_5H_{10}O_2$ as the molecular formula can be ascertained by taking different possibilities for R and R' (total number of C in R and R' should be 4). Since R' is coming from alcohol part, it can CH_3, C_2H_5, *n*-C_3H_7, *iso*-C_3H_7, *n*-C_4H_9, *iso*-C_4H_9, *sec*-C_4H_9, or *tert*-C_4H_9 ; while R (coming from acidic part) can be *n*-C_3H_7, *iso*-C_3H_7, C_2H_5, CH_3, or H. Thus nine different esters are possible, including *n*-propyl acetate.

(i) $HCOOC_4H_9$-*n* (ii) $HCOOC_4H_9$-*iso* (iii) $HCOOC_4H_9$-*sec* (iv) $HCOOC_4H_9$-*tert*
(v) $CH_3COOC_3H_7$-*n* (vi) $CH_3COOC_3H_7$-*iso* (vii) $C_2H_5COOC_2H_5$ (viii) *n*-$C_3H_7COOCH_3$
(ix) *iso*-$C_3H_7COOCH_3$.

Number of carboxylic acids (RCOOH) having $C_5H_{10}O_2$ as molecular formula. Since here one carbon atom is present as —COOH, so the remaining four carbon atoms must be present as butyl group, *i.e.*

$CH_3CH_2CH_2CH_2COOH$ (Butanoic acid); $(CH_3)_2CHCH_2COOH$ (Isobutanoic acid); $C_2H_5CH(CH_3)COOH$ (sec. Butanoic acid); $(CH_3)_3C.COOH$ (*tert*-Butanoic acid)

3. (*a*) $C_6H_4(COOCH_3)_2 + 2OH^- \longrightarrow C_6H_4(COO^-)_2 + 2CH_3OH$

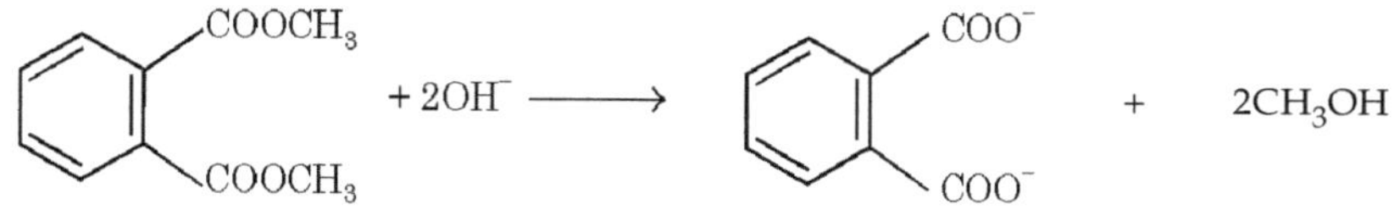

Methyl phthalate (M.W. = 194) → Phthalate anion

Since 1 mole of phthalate used 2 moles of OH^-; S. E. = M.W./2 = 194/2 = 97

(*b*) S.E. = M.W./No. of ester groups per molecule.

EXERCISE 18.1

1	(c)	6	(d)	11	(b)	16	(d)	21	(c)	26	(d)
2	(b)	7	(d)	12	(a)	17	(c)	22	(b)	27	(c)
3	(b)	8	(b)	13	(c)	18	(a)	23	(d)	28	(b)
4	(d)	9	(b)	14	(a)	19	(c)	24	(c)	29	(c)
5	(a)	10	(d)	15	(d)	20	(d)	25	(c)	30	(d)

1. In Bouvealt-Blanc reduction, reduction involves the transfer of electron from metal (Na or Li).
2. $C_6H_5-\overset{O}{\overset{\|}{C}}-O^-$ is a nucleophile, while $C_6H_5-\overset{O^{\delta-}}{\overset{\|}{C}}{}^{\delta+}-Cl$ acts as an electrophile.
3. Only reaction (*b*) is S_N2 while the others are acyl bimolecular nucleophilic substitution.
4. In mixed condensation, an ester not having any α-hydrogen atom acts as acylating agent because it does not form enolate ion.
5. Esters (other than formates) react with excess of RMgX forming 3° alcohols having two alkyl groups corresponding to alkyl part of the RMgX. Since here RMgX is CH_3MgBr, so the 3° alcohol formed should have at least two methyl groups which is only option (*a*).
6. Like γ- and δ-hydroxy acids, γ- and δ- amino carboxylic acids form corresponding lactam.

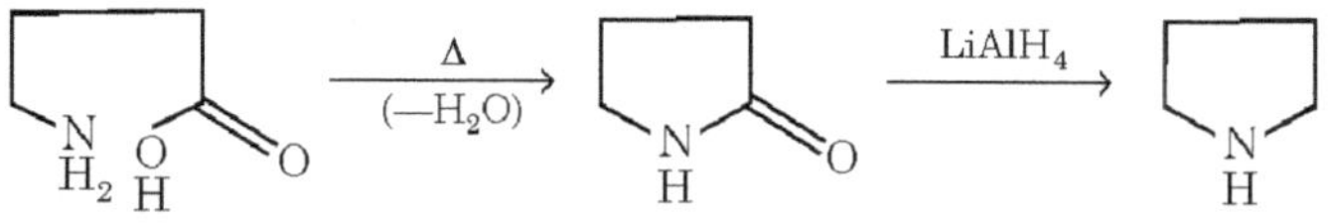

$$H_2N(CH_2)_3COOH \xrightarrow[(-H_2O)]{\Delta} \text{[A] (pyrrolidin-2-one)} \xrightarrow{LiAlH_4} \text{[B] (pyrrolidine)}$$

7. In presence of dil. NaOH, esters are hydrolysed *via* S_N1 mechanism which involves the formation of carbocation, hence the product (alcohol) will be optically inactive, provided chiral carbon is present in the parent ester. Further, carbocation is formed as an intermediate which rearranges to the more stable carbocation, thus the rearranged product is formed as the final product.

$$C_6H_5CH(OCOC_2H_5)CH=CHCH_3 \xrightarrow{\text{dil. NaOH}} C_6H_5\overset{+}{C}HCH=CHCH_3 \longleftrightarrow \underset{\text{More Stable}}{C_6H_5CH=CH\overset{+}{C}HCH_3} \xrightarrow{OH^-} \underset{(\pm)-\text{Alcohol}}{C_6H_5CH=CHCH(OH)CH_3}$$

8. $$C_6H_5CH_2CH(COOCH_3)-NH-\overset{O}{\overset{\|}{C}}-CH(\overset{\oplus}{N}H_3)CH_2COO^{\ominus} \xrightarrow{H_3O^{\oplus}} C_6H_5CH_2CH(COOH)\overset{\oplus}{N}H_3 + HOOC.CH(\overset{\oplus}{N}H_3)CH_2COOH + CH_3OH$$

9. Consult mechanism of lactone (or ester) hydrolysis by acids.
10. $$HCOOR + R'MgX\ (\text{excess}) \longrightarrow \underset{\text{A 2° alcohol}}{H-C(OH)(R')-R'}\ ;\ RCOOR'' + R'MgX\ (\text{excess}) \longrightarrow \underset{\text{(A 3° alcohol)}}{R-C(OH)(R')-R''}$$

11. Alkaline hydrolysis is irreversible because here $RCOO^-$ is isolated ; moreover the product $RCOO^-$ stabilizes itself due to resonance.
12. The γ-carbon-oxygen bond is shortest because it has double bond character. The β-C—O bond is shorter because it also has some double bond character due to resonance. The α-C—O bond is longest because it is always a single bond.

$$R—\overset{\overset{\ddot{O}:}{\|\gamma}}{C}\underset{\beta}{—}\ddot{O}\underset{\alpha}{—}R' \longleftrightarrow R—\overset{\overset{:\ddot{O}:^-}{|}}{C}=\overset{+}{O}—R'$$

I (More important) II (Less important)

13. Esters undergo acyl-oxygen cleavage during hydrolysis.

$$C_2H_5—\overset{\overset{O}{\|}}{C}—O—CH_3 + {}^{18}OH^- \longrightarrow C_2H_5—\overset{\overset{O}{\|}}{C}—{}^{18}O^- + CH_3OH$$

acyl-O alkyl-O

14. $\underset{COOCH_3\quad COOCH_3}{}$ $\xleftarrow[CH_3OH]{^-OCH_3}$ (succinic anhydride) $\xrightarrow{H^+, CH_3OH}$ $\underset{COOH\quad COOCH_3}{}$

15. $CH_3—\overset{\overset{O}{\|}}{C}—OH \xrightarrow{H_2O^{18}} CH_3—\underset{{}^{18}\overset{+}{O}H_2}{\overset{O^-}{|}C}—OH \longrightarrow \left[CH_3—\underset{{}^{18}OH}{\overset{OH}{|}C}—OH\right] \longrightarrow$

$$CH_3—\underset{{}^{18}OH}{C}=O \xrightarrow{H_2O^{18}} CH_3—\underset{{}^{18}OH}{\overset{{}^{18}OH}{|}C}—OH \longrightarrow CH_3—\overset{\overset{O^{18}}{\|}}{C}—{}^{18}OH$$

16. $CH_3CH_2CH_2CONH_2 \xrightarrow[(-NH_3)]{OH^-} CH_3CH_2CH_2COO^- Na^+ \xrightarrow{HCl} CH_3CH_2CH_2COOH + Na^+ + Cl^-$

17. $CH_2=C(CH_3)—OCOCH_3 \xrightarrow{H^+} CH_2=C(CH_3)—OH \xrightleftharpoons{\text{tautomerism}} CH_3COCH_3$ or CH_3COCH_3
Acetone

$CH_3CH=CH—OCOCH_3 \xrightarrow{H^+} CH_3CH=CH—OH \xrightleftharpoons{\text{tautomerism}} CH_3CH_2CHO$ or CH_3CH_2CHO
Propanal

Acetone and propanal can be distinguished by Fehling solution.
18. Remember that the two enantiomers react differently *i.e.* at different rate with an optically active reagent leading to the formation of two isomers (diastereomers) in different amounts, hence the resulting mixture will be optically active.
19. Stronger a nucleophile, more will be its reactivity toward nucleophilic substitution.
20,21. Recall that presence of electron-withdrawing group in *p*- or *o*-position increases nucleophilic substitution, while electron-releasing group decreases the reactivity.
22. Only ketonic group is reduced by $NaBH_4$, while $LiAlH_4$ reduces both ketonic as well as lactone group to the —OH groups.

23. (cyclohexane with OMe, OMe, $COOC_2H_5$) $\xrightarrow{H^+/H_2O}$ (cyclohexane with OH, OH, COOH) $\longrightarrow$ (cyclohexanone with COOH) $\xrightarrow{heat}$ (cyclohexanone)
β-Keto acid

Remember that β-keto acids undergo decarboxylation on heating.
24,25. In lactones, the root word is derived from the name of the parent carboxylic acid prefix α, β or γ- is inserted on the basis of relative positions of the —OH and —COOH groups in the parent hydroxy acid.

26. 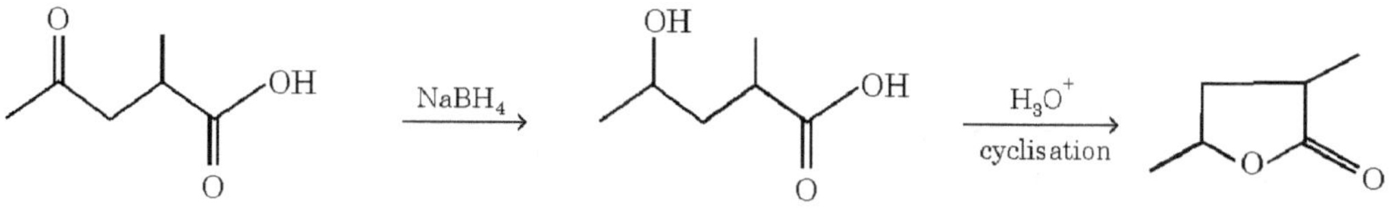 $CH_3COCH_2CH(CH_3)COOH \xrightarrow{NaBH_4} CH_3CH(OH)CH_2CH(CH_3)COOH$ (A γ-hydroxy acid) $\xrightarrow[\text{cyclisation}]{H_3O^+}$ γ-lactone (5-methyl-3-methyl-oxolan-2-one)

27. 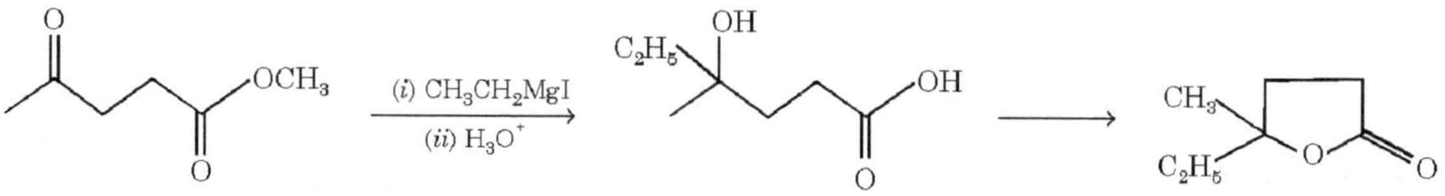 $CH_3COCH_2CH_2COOCH_3$ (A keto ester (ketonic gp. is more reactive toward RMgX)) $\xrightarrow[(ii)\ H_3O^+]{(i)\ CH_3CH_2MgI}$ $CH_3C(OH)(C_2H_5)CH_2CH_2COOH$ (A γ-hydroxy acid) $\longrightarrow$ γ-lactone with CH_3 and C_2H_5 on C-5

28. (*i*) Since the product has a C = C bond, so C ≡ C should be partially reduced to C = C.
(*ii*) Since the final prouct is a cyclic, the intermediate should be *cis*- or *syn*- alkene, because *anti*-alkene will not be able to undergo cyclisation. Hence the reagent R should be H_2/Pd (Lindlar catalyst) which gives *syn*-alkene. The second reagent R′ is H_3O^+.

29. In Baeyer Villeger oxidation (conversion of ketones to esters by per acids), oxygen is introduced between the larger alkyl group and the C = O carbon.

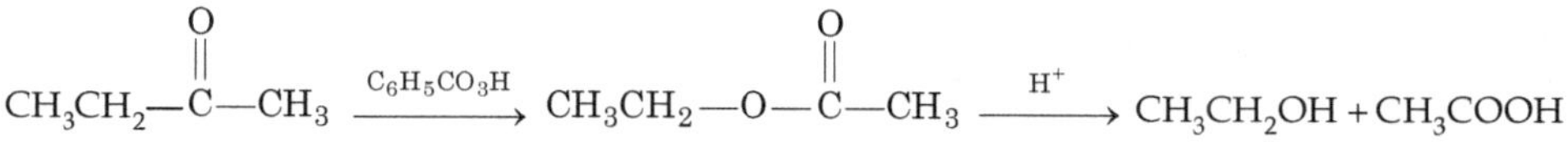

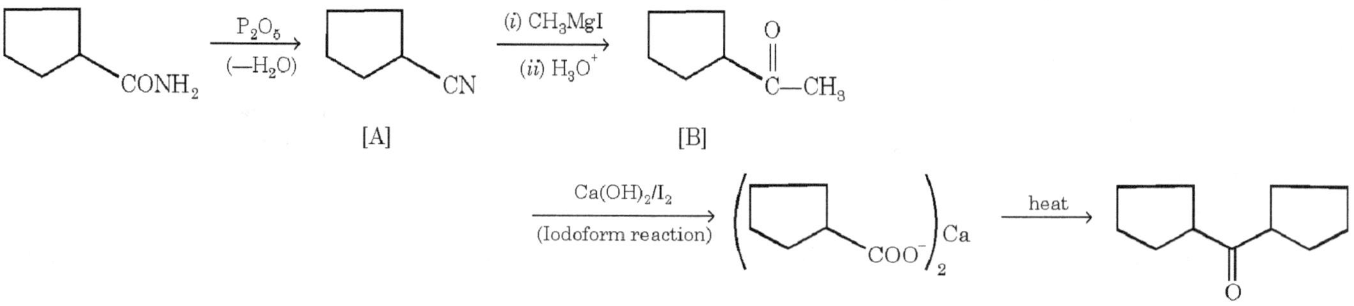

$$CH_3CH_2-\overset{O}{\overset{||}{C}}-CH_3 \xrightarrow{C_6H_5CO_3H} CH_3CH_2-O-\overset{O}{\overset{||}{C}}-CH_3 \xrightarrow{H^+} CH_3CH_2OH + CH_3COOH$$

30. Cyclopentyl-$CONH_2$ $\xrightarrow[(-H_2O)]{P_2O_5}$ Cyclopentyl-CN [A] $\xrightarrow[(ii)\ H_3O^+]{(i)\ CH_3MgI}$ Cyclopentyl-$\overset{O}{\overset{||}{C}}-CH_3$ [B] $\xrightarrow[\text{(Iodoform reaction)}]{Ca(OH)_2/I_2}$ $(\text{Cyclopentyl-}COO^-)_2Ca$ [C] $\xrightarrow{\text{heat}}$ Dicyclopentyl ketone [D]

EXERCISE 18.2

MCQ > 1 CORRECT OPTION	1	(a,b,c)	2	(a,b,c)	3	(a,c,d)	4	(c,d)
	5	(a,b,d)	6	(a, b, c, d)	7	(a, b, c, d)	8	(a, b, c)
	9	(a, c)	10	(a, b, c, d)	11	(a, d)		
PASSAGE 1	12	(c)	13	(c)	14	(b)		
Match the following	15	(A) - (b, c), (B) - (d), (C) - (a), (D) - (a)						
	16	(A) – b; (B) – d; (C) – c; (D) – a						
	17	(A) - a, b; (B) - a, b; (C) - c; (D) - d						
A/R	18	(c)	19	(a)	20	(c)	21	(c)

. Alkyl isonitriles are not hydrolysed to acids, all others give carboxylic acids on hydrolysis.

.. The first three are examples of nucleophilic addition elimination reaction, option (*c*) is although ketone, it undergoes acyl type of nucleophilic substitution, *i.e.* nucleophilic addition elimination because the leaving group here is an aryl anion having electron withdrawing F in the *o*-position making the carbanion stable.

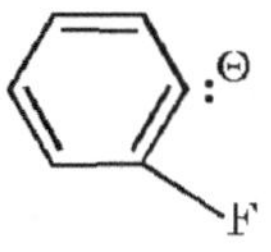

Thus it is a weaker base and better leaving group than the ordinary Ar^-. In (d) –OH is a poor leaving group.

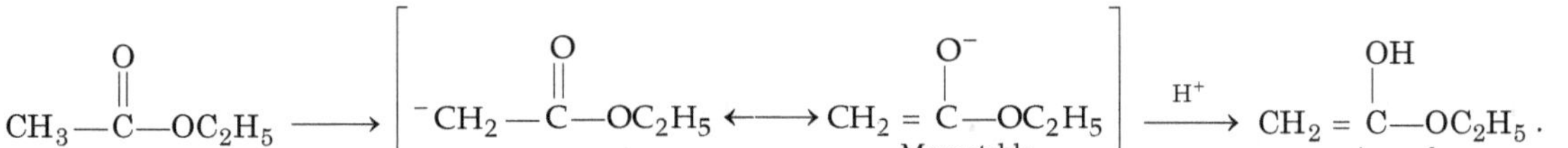

(o-fluorophenyl carbanion, :⊖, F)

. $$CH_3-\overset{O}{\overset{||}{C}}-OC_2H_5 \longrightarrow \left[{}^-CH_2-\overset{O}{\overset{||}{C}}-OC_2H_5 \longleftrightarrow \underset{\text{More stable}}{CH_2=\overset{O^-}{\overset{|}{C}}-OC_2H_5}\right] \xrightarrow{H^+} \underset{\text{An enol}}{CH_2=\overset{OH}{\overset{|}{C}}-OC_2H_5}.$$

. Nature of the final products indicate that Q is an ester, and hydrolysed by alkali. Thus P must be $(CH_3)_2CHCHO$ which undergoes Tischenko reaction.

. Stronger the basic nature of the leaving group, weaker will be its leavability. In CH_3COOH, OH^- is a strong base so it can't be removed easily to form $CH_3\overset{+}{C}O$ required for acetylation (acylation).

EXERCISE 18.3

1. (a) $C_6H_5COCH_2CH_3$ Propiophenone (Ethyl phenyl ketone) (b) $CH_3CH_2CONHOH$ Propanehydroxamic acid (c) $CH_3CH_2CONHCH_3$ N-Methylpropanamide (d) $CH_3CH_2COC_3H_7$-*n* 3-Hexonone

(e) CH_3CH_2CHO Propanal (f) $CH_3CH_2\overset{O}{\overset{\|}{C}}—O—O—\overset{O}{\overset{\|}{C}}CH_2CH_3$ Propionyl peroxide

2. (a) $CH_3(CH_2)_3NH_2$ (b) $CH_3(CH_2)_3NH_2$ (c) No reaction (d) $CH_3(CH_2)_2COOC_2H_5$

3. (a) The hydrolysis involves *O*-acyl cleavage and hence configuration of the alcohol is retained. The products formed are

$$CH_3COO^-Na^+ + (R) - HO\overset{CH_3}{\overset{|}{C}}HCH_2CH_3$$

(b) Here also *O*-acyl cleavage occurs. $CH_3COOH + (R) - HO\overset{CH_3}{\overset{|}{C}}HCH_2CH_3$

(c) In presence of a high concentration of nucleophile (5 M NaOH), the ester undergoes bimolecular nucleophilic acyl substitution, with the *O*-acyl cleavage. Further since the bond to the chiral carbon is not broken, configuration of the alcohol is retained.

$$(R)—C_6H_5\overset{O+COR}{\overset{|}{C}}HCH = CHCH_3 \xrightarrow{5MNaOH} (R)—C_6H_5\overset{OH}{\overset{|}{C}}HCH = CHCH_3 + RCOOH$$

(d) In presence of a low concentration of nucleophile (dil. NaOH), ester undergoes S_N1 reaction involving alkyl-oxygen fission. Further note that carbocation is formed as an intermediate, so it stabilizes to the more stable benzylic- allylic cation having double bond in conjugation with the ring. Since carbocation is planar, the product formed will be racemic mixture.

$$(R)–C_6H_5\overset{OCOR}{\overset{|}{C}}HCH = CHCH_3 \xrightarrow{\text{dil. NaOH}} C_6H_5—\overset{+}{C}H—CH = CHCH_3 \longleftrightarrow \underset{\text{More stable}}{C_6H_5CH = CH—\overset{\oplus}{C}HCH_3} \xrightarrow{OH^-} \underset{\text{racemic mixture}}{C_6H_5CH = CH—\overset{OH}{\overset{|}{C}}HCH_3}$$

(e) $C_6H_5CH_2OH + C_2H_5OH$ (f) $C_6H_5\overset{O}{\overset{\|}{C}}—O—O^-Na^+ + C_6H_5COOCH_3$ Sod. peroxybenzoate (g) I—C_6H_4—CH_2OCOCH_3

(h) $C_6H_5—\overset{O}{\overset{\|}{C}}—O—C_6H_5$ (deactivated benzene ring; activated benzene ring) $\xrightarrow[\text{nitration}]{\text{mono-}}$ $C_6H_5—\overset{O}{\overset{\|}{C}}—O—C_6H_4—NO_2$

4. (a) $C_6H_5—\overset{OH}{\overset{|}{\underset{n\text{-}C_3H_7}{\underset{|}{C}}}}—C_3H_7\text{-}n$ 4-Phenyl-4-heptanol (b) $C_6H_5COOCH_2CH(CH_3)_2$ Isobutyl benzoate

(c) $HCONH_2 + HOCH_2(CH_2)_3CH_3$ Formamide 1-Pentanol (d) $CH_3CH_2CH_2—\overset{O}{\overset{\|}{C}}—O—\overset{O}{\overset{\|}{C}}—CH_2CH_3$. Butyric propionic anhydride

5. (a) $CH_3CH_2CH_2COOH + C_6H_5CH_2OH$ (b) *m*-$ClC_6H_4COOH + CH_3OH$

(c) $HOCH_2CH_2CH(CH_3)COOH$ (d) $CH_3CH = CHCH_2COOH$ + $H_2C—CH_2$ (epoxide, bridged by O)

6. (*a*) $(CH_3)_2CHCH_2CuLi$ [A], $C_6H_5COCH_2CH(CH_3)_2$ [B] (*b*) $C_6H_5CH_2C(OH)(n\text{-}C_4H_9)_2$ [C]

(*c*) $CH_2=CHCH_2COC_6H_5$ [D]

(*d*) $BrCH_2COOH$ [E] $BrZnCH_2COOC_2H_5$ [F] $(CH_3)_2C(OH)CH_2COOC_2H_5$ [G] $(CH_3)_2C=CHCOOH$ [H] $(CH_3)_2C=CHCH_2OH$ [I]

7. (*a*) $p\text{-}NO_2C_6H_4COCl > C_6H_5COCl > p\text{-}CH_3OC_6H_4COCl$

Greater the partial +ve charge on carbonyl carbon, higher is the reactivity of carbonyl group towards nucleophilic substitution.

(*b*) (*i*) $CH_3COO\mathbf{CH_3} > CH_3COO\mathbf{CH_2CH_3} > CH_3COO\mathbf{CH(CH_3)_2} > CH_3COO\mathbf{C(CH_3)_3}$

Size of the alkyl group of the alcoholic part increases from left to right, steric hindrance increases, and hence rate of hydrolysis decreases.

(*ii*) $\mathbf{H}COOCH_3 > \mathbf{CH_3}COOCH_3 > \mathbf{(CH_3)_2CH}COOCH_3 > \mathbf{(CH_3)_3C}COOCH_3$

Size of the alkyl group of the acidic part increases from left to right.

(*iii*) – I group disperses negative charge in transition state and thus increases reactivity of ester for hydrolysis. Thus the relative order of ester hydrolysis is

$p\text{-}NO_2C_6H_4COOC_2H_5 > p\text{-}ClC_6H_4COOC_2H_5 > C_6H_5COOC_2H_5 > p\text{-}CH_3OC_6H_4COOC_2H_5$

(*iv*) Lesser the basic character of the leaving group ($Cl^- < \bar{O}COCH_3 < {}^-OC_2H_5 < NH_2^-$), more easily it is removed.

$$CH_3COCl > (CH_3CO)_2O > CH_3COOC_2H_5 > CH_3CONH_2$$

(*c*) Cyclohexanecarboxyl chloride reacts faster than benzoyl chloride.

8. (*a*) $HOCH_2CH_2CH_2CONH_2$ (*b*) $HOCH_2CH_2CH_2CH_2OH$ (*c*) $HOCH_2CH_2CH_2COOC_2H_5$.

9. (*a*) On reaction with water, acetyl chloride reacts with water and liberates HCl which is detected by giving a white precipitate of AgCl on adding $AgNO_3$. Acetic anhydride on reaction with water liberates only acetic acid and no HCl.

(*b*) *n*-Butyryl chloride ($n\text{-}C_3H_7COCl$) gives pleasant smelling ester with ethyl alcohol.

(*c*) Only benzoyl bromide (C_6H_5COBr) gives yellow precipitate of AgBr with alcoholic $AgNO_3$.

(*d*) Only propanoic acid gives CO_2 with aqueous $NaHCO_3$ solution.

(*e*) Only acetic anhydride reacts with aq. $NaHCO_3$ solution and evolve CO_2.

(*f*) Ammonium benzoate evolves ammonia immediately on treatment with *cold* aq. NaOH.

(*g*) Glyceryl monopalmitate has two free alcoholic groups ; hence it is oxidised by CrO_3 / H_2SO_4.

10. (*a*)

$$CH_3-\overset{O}{\overset{\|}{C}}-OC_2H_5 \xrightarrow{CH_3MgI} CH_3-\underset{CH_3}{\overset{OMgI}{C}}-OC_2H_5 \xrightarrow{-MgI(OC_2H_5)} \underset{\text{Acetone (as intermediate)}}{CH_3-\underset{CH_3}{C}=O} \xrightarrow{CH_3MgI} CH_3-\underset{CH_3}{\overset{CH_3}{C}}-OMgI \xrightarrow{H^+} \underset{tert\text{-Butanol}}{CH_3-\underset{CH_3}{\overset{CH_3}{C}}-OH}$$

(*b*) Ketones are more reactive than esters towards RMgX.

(*c*) A formate ester when treated with 2 eq. of Grignard reagent gives 2° alcohol with identical alkyl groups.

$$H-\overset{O}{\overset{\|}{C}}-OC_2H_5 \xrightarrow[(ii)\ H_3O^+]{(i)\ 2RMgBr} H-\underset{R}{\overset{OH}{C}}-R$$

A 2° alcohol

11. (*a*) An *ortho ester* has three alkoxy groups (– OR) attached to the same carbon atom ; thus the general formula for ortho esters is $RC(OR')_3$; where R = H or an alkyl group, while R′ = an alkyl group.

$$\underset{\text{Ethyl orthoformate}}{HC(OC_2H_5)_3} \xrightarrow{\text{mild hydrolysis}} \underset{\text{Ethyl formate}}{HCOOC_2H_5} + 2C_2H_5OH$$

(*b*)

$$CHCl_3 + 3C_2H_5ONa \xrightarrow{C_2H_5O^-} HC(OC_2H_5)_3 + 3NaCl$$

Mechanism. Dichlorocarbene, formed from chloroform, inserts between H and O of C_2H_5OH to form α, α-dichloromethyl ethyl ether which solvolyses rapidly *via* S_N1 in ethyl alcohol.

$$HCCl_3 \xrightarrow{C_2H_5O^-} :CCl_2 \xrightarrow{C_2H_5O—H} C_2H_5O—CHCl_2 \xrightarrow{-Cl^-}$$

$$\left[C_2H_5\ddot{O}—\overset{+}{C}HCl \longleftrightarrow C_2H_5\overset{+}{O}=CHCl\right] \xrightarrow{C_2H_5OH} C_2H_5O—\overset{OC_2H_5}{\overset{|}{C}}HCl \xrightarrow[(-\,HCl)]{C_2H_5OH} HC\,(OC_2H_5)_3$$

12. In the Claisen condensation, the bond formed is between the carbonyl carbon of one ester and the carbon which is α to the —COOR group of the ester molecule. Thus work backward by breaking this C—C bond and adding OR to the carbonyl carbon and H to the other carbon. Mixed Claisen condensations are practical, when one ester has α H.

(*a*)
$$C_6H_5CH_2CH_2\overset{O}{\overset{\|}{C}}—\overset{CH_2C_6H_5}{\overset{|}{C}}HCOOCH_3 \xleftarrow[(ii)\ -\ C_2H_5OH]{(i)\ C_2H_5ONa} C_6H_5CH_2CH_2\overset{O}{\overset{\|}{C}}—OC_2H_5 + \overset{CH_2C_6H_5}{\overset{|}{C}}H_2COOCH_3$$

C_2H_5O H

(*b*)
$$C_2H_5OOC—\overset{O}{\overset{\|}{C}}—\overset{CH_3}{\overset{|}{C}}HCOOC_2H_5 \xleftarrow[(ii)\ -\ C_2H_5OH]{(i)\ C_2H_5ONa} C_2H_5OOC—\overset{O}{\overset{\|}{C}}—OC_2H_5 + \overset{CH_3}{\overset{|}{C}}H_2COOC_2H_5$$

(*c*)
$$H—\overset{O}{\overset{\|}{C}}—\overset{C_6H_5}{\overset{|}{C}}HCOOCH_3 \xleftarrow[(ii)\ -\ C_2H_5OH]{(i)\ C_2H_5ONa} H—\overset{O}{\overset{\|}{C}}—OC_2H_5 + \overset{C_6H_5}{\overset{|}{C}}H_2COOCH_3$$

13.

Reaction	*Reactant*	*Reagents/Conditions*	*Product*
Hofmann	$RCONH_2$ (Amides)	Br_2, OH^-	RNH_2
Lossen	RCONHOH Hydroxyamic acids	OH^-	$RNCO \xrightarrow{H_2O} RNH_2$
Curtius	$RCON_3$ Acid azides	(*i*) heat in benzene (*ii*) heat in H_2O or R′OH	(*i*) RNCO (*ii*) RNH_2 or RNHCOOR′
Schmidt	RCOOH Carboxylic acids	HN_3, H_2SO_4, OH^-	RNH_2

14. More stable a conjugate base of an acid, higher will be its acidic character.

(*a*) Since the conjugate base of the sulphonamide is stabilized by delocalization of the negative charge to two oxygens, the parent compound sulphonamide will be more acidic than the acid amide, CH_3CONH_2, where delocalization is possible to only one oxygen.

$$R—\overset{:O:}{\overset{\|}{\underset{:O:}{\underset{\|}{S}}}}—\ddot{N}H_2 \xrightarrow{B^-} \left[R—\overset{:O:}{\overset{\|}{\underset{:O:}{\underset{\|}{S}}}}—\ddot{N}H^- \longleftrightarrow R—\overset{:\ddot{O}:^-}{\overset{|}{\underset{:O:}{\underset{\|}{S}}}}=\ddot{N}H \longleftrightarrow R—\overset{:O:}{\overset{\|}{\underset{:\ddot{O}:^-}{\underset{|}{S}}}}=\ddot{N}H\right]$$

$$R—\overset{:O:}{\overset{\|}{C}}—\ddot{N}H_2 \xrightarrow{B^-} \left[R—\overset{:O:}{\overset{\|}{C}}—\ddot{N}H^- \longleftrightarrow R—\overset{:\ddot{O}:^-}{\overset{|}{C}}=\ddot{N}H\right]$$

(*b*) Amides are much more acidic than NH_3 because the negative charge on $:NH_2^-$ from ammonia is localised, while in amides it is delocalized to the oxygen of C = O. Since phthalimide has two C = O's, while benzamide has only one, the imide anion from phthalimide is more stabilized than the amide anion from benzamide.

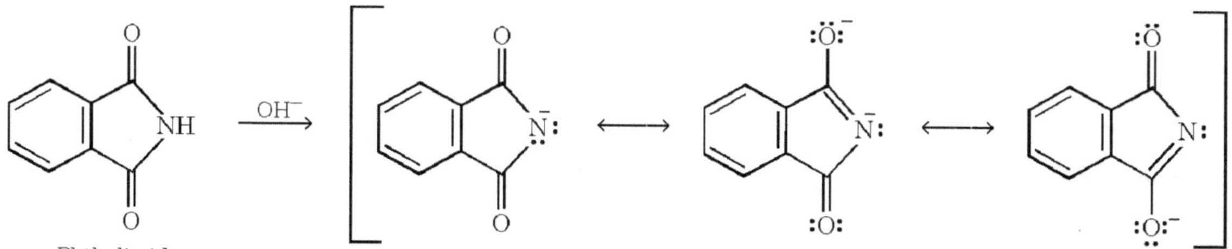

Phthalimide $\xrightarrow{OH^-}$ [resonance structures] Phthalimide anion

$$C_6H_5-\overset{\overset{:O:}{\|}}{C}-\ddot{N}H_2 \xrightarrow{OH^-} \left[C_6H_5-\overset{\overset{:O:}{\|}}{C}-\ddot{N}H^- \longleftrightarrow C_6H_5-\overset{\overset{:\ddot{O}:^-}{|}}{C}=\ddot{N}H\right]$$

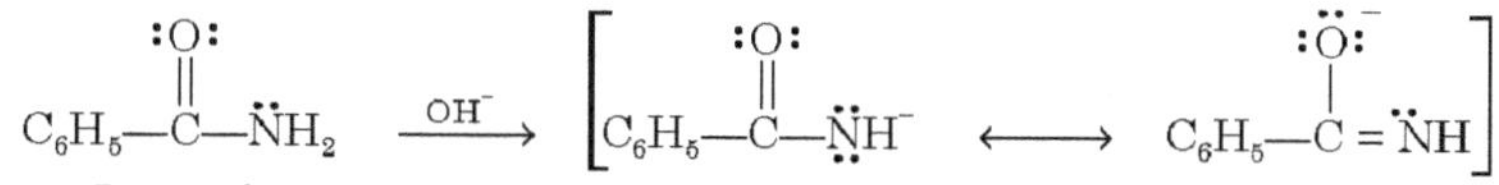

Benzamide

Thus the acidic character of the three compounds follows the order :

Phthalimide > Benzamide >>> NH_3.

15. (*a*) Dialkyl sulphates, in general, are good alkylating agents, because the alkyl sulphate anion, *e.g.* $CH_3OSO_3^-$ is the conjugate base of a strong acid, methyl sulphuric acid, CH_3OSO_3H. Thus due to very weak basic nature of the methyl sulphate anion, it is a good leaving group.

$$\underset{\text{Phenol}}{C_6H_5OH} \xrightarrow{OH^-} C_6H_5O^- \xrightarrow{CH_3-OSO_2OCH_3} C_6H_5OCH_3 + \underset{\text{Methyl sulphate anion}}{{}^-OSO_2OCH_3}$$

(*b*) Acyl chlorides are more reactive than alkyl chlorides due to following factors.

(*i*) Presence of C = O in acid chlorides makes the acyl carbon more electrophilic by attracting electrons.

(*ii*) The transition state of the acyl chloride leading to tetrahedral intermediate is less sterically hindered than the transition state with the petavalent carbon in the S_N2 reaction of RX.

(*iii*) In the formation of an alkyl transition state, a stronger σ-bond must be partially broken, while a weaker π-bond is broken in the acyl case.

(*c*) In the hydrolysis of trialkyl phosphates, OH^- attacks on the neutral molecule (having no charge), while in the dialkyl and monoalkyl phosphates the substrates have –1 and –2 charges which make the attack of OH^- progressively more difficult.

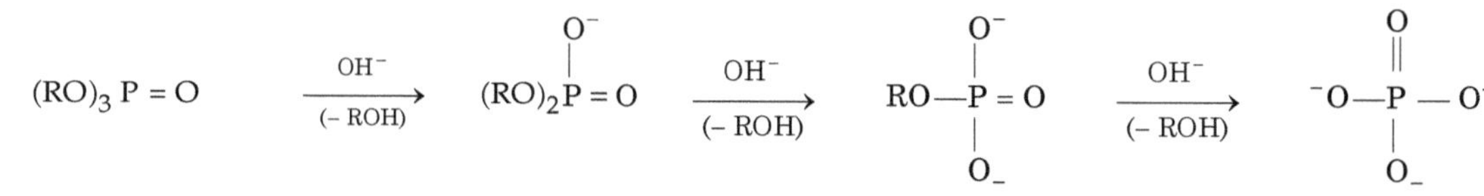

$$\underset{\substack{\text{Trialkyl phosphate}\\ \text{(neutral)}}}{(RO)_3P=O} \xrightarrow[(-\,ROH)]{OH^-} \underset{\substack{\text{Dialkyl phosphate}\\ \text{(carries –1 charge)}}}{(RO)_2\overset{\overset{O^-}{|}}{P}=O} \xrightarrow[(-\,ROH)]{OH^-} \underset{\substack{\text{Monoalkyl phosphate}\\ \text{(carries –2 charge)}}}{RO-\overset{\overset{O^-}{|}}{\underset{\underset{O^-}{|}}{P}}=O} \xrightarrow[(-\,ROH)]{OH^-} \underset{\text{Phosphate ion}}{{}^-O-\overset{\overset{O}{\|}}{\underset{\underset{O^-}{|}}{P}}-O^-}$$

(*d*) Recall that concentration of the reagent affects the kinetics of the S_N reaction. In presence of high concentration of nucleophile, reaction opts S_N2 mechanism, while in low concentration (dil. NaOH) S_N1 mechnism is followed. Since in S_N2 reaction configuration is retained, so the optically active ester will be hydrolysed to optically active alcohol.

$$\underset{\text{Optically active}}{C_6H_5\overset{*}{C}HCH=CHC_2H_5 \atop \quad|\atop \quad OCOCH_3} \xrightarrow[(S_N2)]{5\text{ M NaOH}} \underset{\text{Optically acitve}}{C_6H_5\overset{*}{C}HCH=CHC_2H_5 \atop \quad|\atop \quad OH}$$

However, in S_N1 reaction since carbocations are formed as intermediate which may rearrange, if possible, to the more stable carbocation. Thus rearranged product may be formed. Further, carbocation being planar, may be attacked on either side of the face forming racemic mixture.

$$\underset{\displaystyle \mathrm{OCOCH_3}}{\mathrm{C_6H_5\underset{|}{C}H{-}CH{=}CHC_2H_5}} \xrightarrow[S_{N^1}]{\text{dil. NaOH}} \left[\mathrm{C_6H_5\overset{+}{C}H{-}CH{=}CHC_2H_5} \longleftrightarrow \underset{\text{More stable}}{\mathrm{C_6H_5CH{=}CH{-}\overset{+}{C}HC_2H_5}} \right]$$

$$\xrightarrow{OH^-} \mathrm{C_6H_5CH{=}CH{-}\underset{\underset{\displaystyle OH}{|}}{C}HCH_3}$$

Rearranged (optically inactive) alcohol

(*e*) Acetic acid formed in the reaction, catalyses the hydrolysis of ester by providing H^+.

16. $\mathrm{H{-}\overset{\overset{\displaystyle O}{||}}{C}{-}OCH(CH_3)_2}$ [A] $\mathrm{H{-}\overset{\overset{\displaystyle O}{||}}{C}{-}OH}$ [B] $\mathrm{HOCH\,(CH_3)_2}$ [C] $\mathrm{CH_3MgI}$ [D]

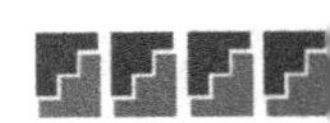

CARBONYL COMPOUNDS

PAST YEAR QUESTIONS JEE ADVANCED/IIT-JEE (2013 - 2017)

MCQs with One Correct Answer

1. The compound that does **NOT** liberate CO_2, on treatment with aqueous sodium bicarbonate solution, is **[JEE Adv. 2013]**

(a) Benzoic acid (b) Benzenesulphonic acid
(c) Salicylic acid (d) Carbolic acid (Phenol)

2. The major product in the following reaction is

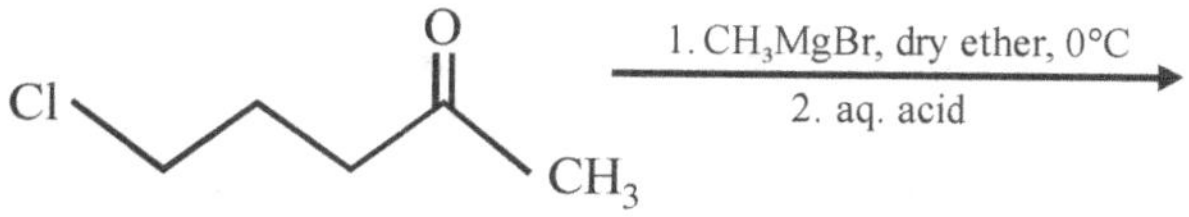

Cl–CH$_2$CH$_2$CH$_2$–C(=O)–CH$_3$ $\xrightarrow[\text{2. aq. acid}]{\text{1. } CH_3MgBr\text{, dry ether, 0°C}}$

[JEE Adv. 2014]

(a) 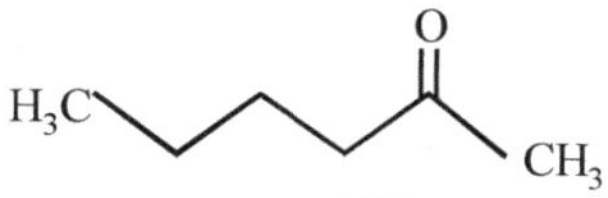 H_3C, O, CH_3

(b) 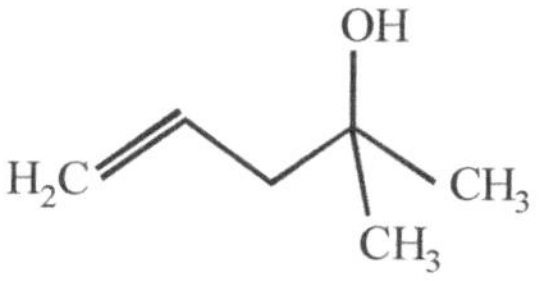 OH, H_2C, CH_3, CH_3

(c) 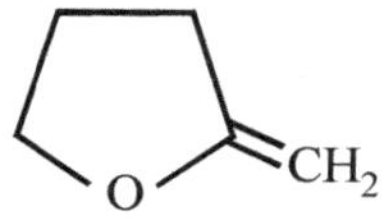 O, CH_2

(d) 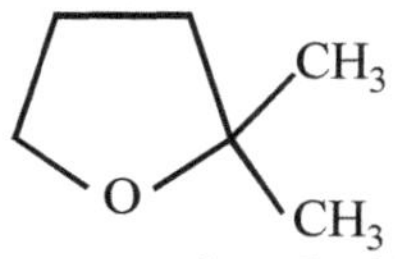 O, CH_3, CH_3

3. The correct order of acidity for the following compounds is

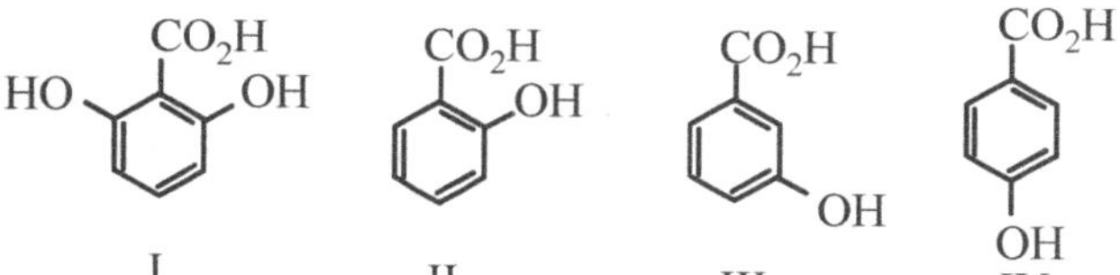

I: CO_2H, HO, OH
II: CO_2H, OH
III: CO_2H, OH
IV: CO_2H, OH

[JEE Adv. 2016]

(a) I > II > III > IV (b) III > I > II > IV
(c) III > IV > II > I (d) I > III > IV > II

4. The major product of the following reaction sequence is **[JEE Adv. 2016]**

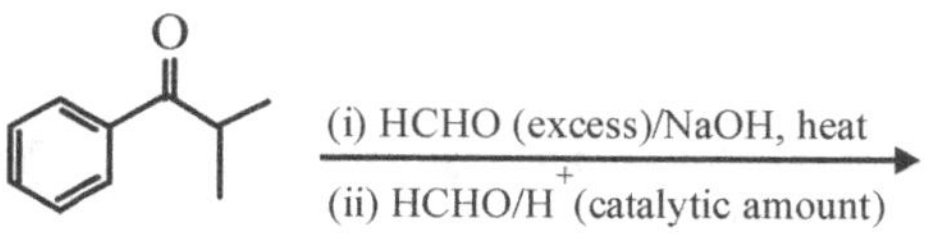

$\xrightarrow[\text{(ii) HCHO/}\overset{+}{H}\text{ (catalytic amount)}]{\text{(i) HCHO (excess)/NaOH, heat}}$

(a) 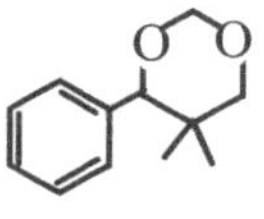 O, O
(b) 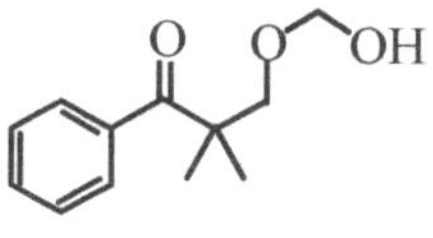 O, O, OH
(c) 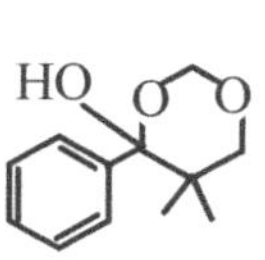 HO, O, O
(d) 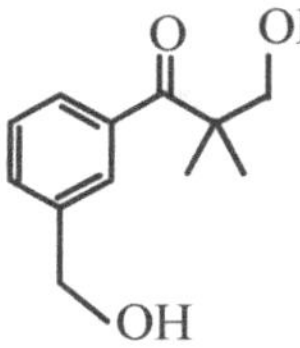 O, OH, OH

MCQs with One or More Than One Correct

1. In the following reaction, the product(s) formed is(are) **[JEE Adv. 2013]**

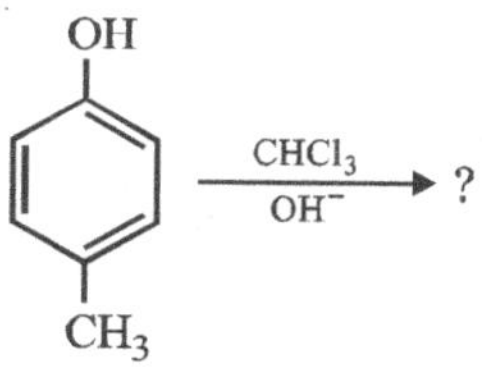

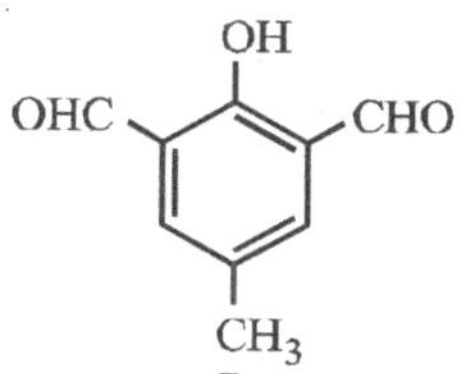

OH, CH_3 $\xrightarrow[OH^-]{CHCl_3}$?

P: OH, OHC, CHO, CH_3
Q: O, H_3C, $CHCl_2$
R: OH, H_3C, $CHCl_2$
S: OH, CHO, CH_3

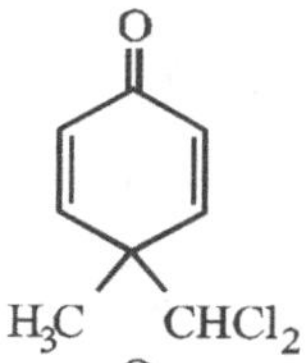

(a) P (major) (b) Q (minor)
(c) R (minor) (d) S (major)

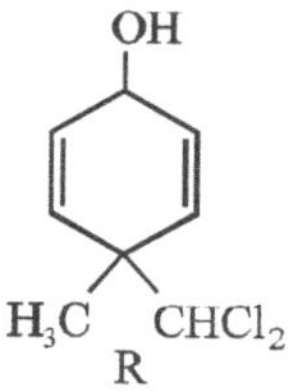

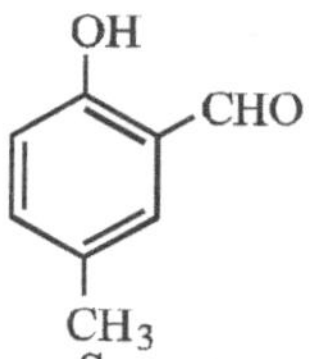

2. After completion of the reactions (I and II), the organic compound(s) in the reaction mixtures is(are) **[JEE Adv. 2013]**

Reaction I : H_3C–C(=O)–CH_3 (1.0 mol) $\xrightarrow[\text{aqueous NaOH}]{Br_2\text{ (1.0 mol)}}$

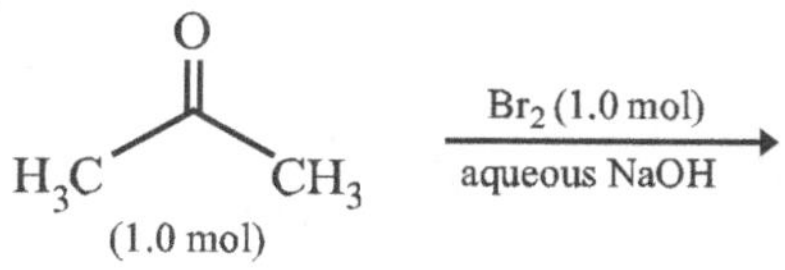

Reaction II : H_3C–C(=O)–CH_3 (1.0 mol) $\xrightarrow[CH_3COOH]{Br_2\text{ (1.0 mol)}}$

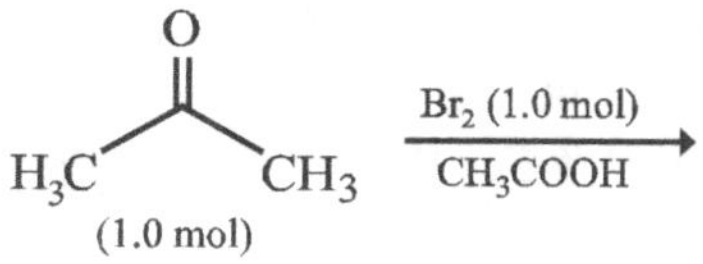

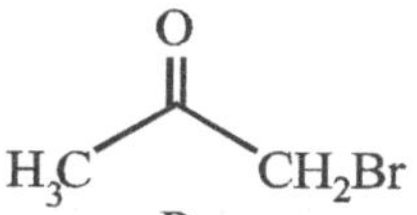

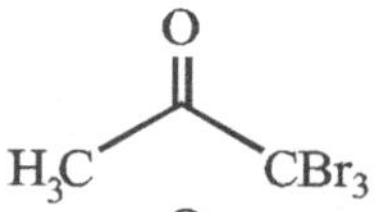

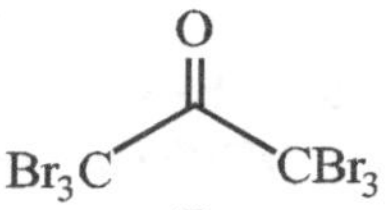

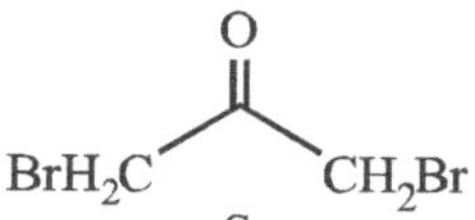

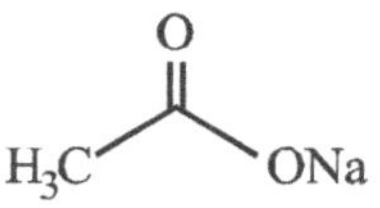

P: H_3C–C(=O)–CH_2Br
Q: H_3C–C(=O)–CBr_3
R: Br_3C–C(=O)–CBr_3
S: BrH_2C–C(=O)–CH_2Br
T: H_3C–C(=O)–ONa
U: $CHBr_3$

(a) Reaction I : P and Reaction II : P
(b) Reaction I : U, acetone and Reaction II : Q, acetone
(c) Reaction I : T, U, acetone and Reaction II : P
(d) Reaction I : R, acetone and Reaction II : S, acetone

3. The major product of the following reaction is **[JEE Adv. 2015]**

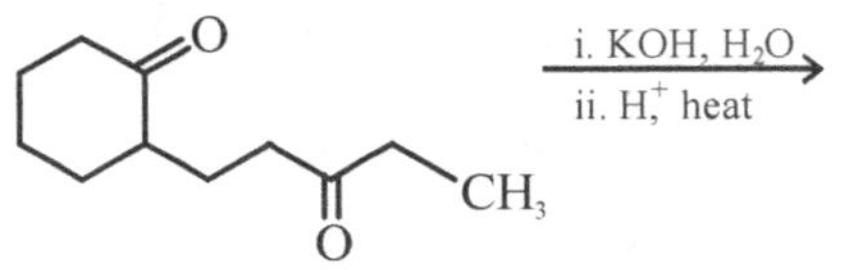

i. KOH, H_2O; ii. H^+, heat

(a) 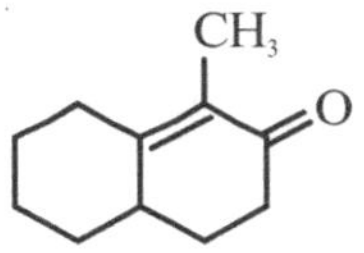 (b)

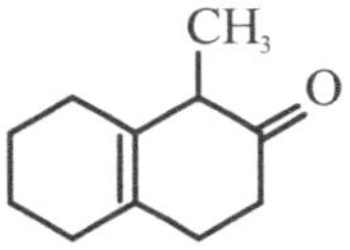

(c) 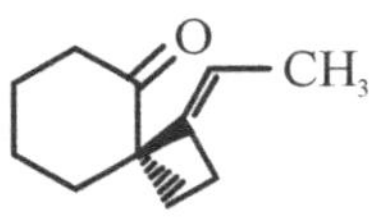 (d)

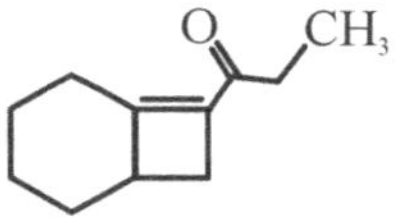

4. Positive Tollen's test is observed for **[JEE Adv. 2016]**

(a) 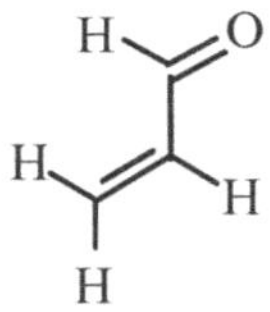 (b)

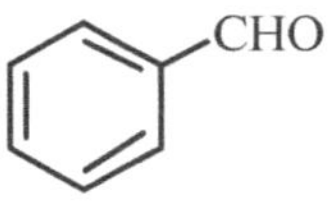

(c) 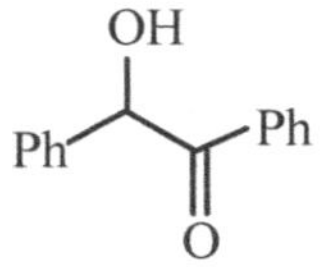 (d)

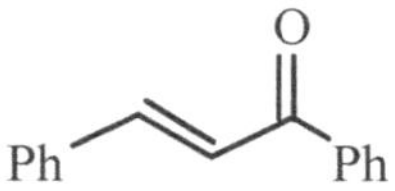

5. The correct statement(s) about the following reaction sequence is(are) **[JEE Adv. 2016]**

$$\text{Cumene}(C_9H_{12}) \xrightarrow[\text{(ii)}H_3O^+]{\text{(i)}O_2} \mathbf{P} \xrightarrow{CHCl_3/NaOH} \mathbf{Q}\text{ (major)} + \mathbf{R}\text{ (minor)}$$

$$\mathbf{Q} \xrightarrow[PhCH_2Br]{NaOH} \mathbf{S}$$

(a) **R** is steam Volatile
(b) **Q** gives dark violet coloration with 1% aqueous $FeCl_3$ solution
(c) **S** gives yellow precipitate with 2, 4–dinitrophenylhydrazine
(d) **S** gives dark violet coloration with 1% aqueous $FeCl_3$ solution

6. Reagent(s) which can be used to bring about the following transformation is (are) **[JEE Adv. 2016]**

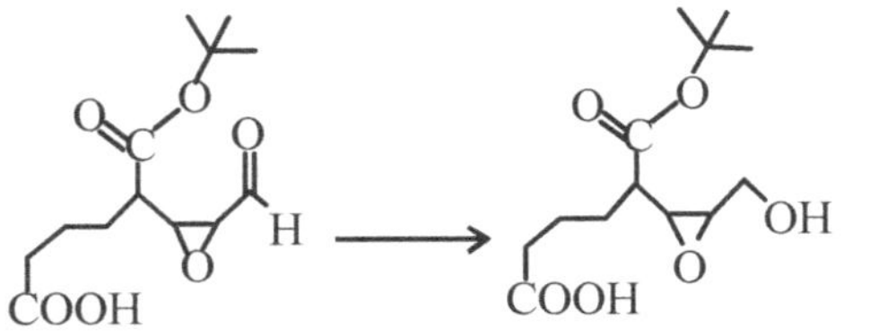

(a) $LiAlH_4$ in $(C_2H_5)_2O$ (b) BH_3 in THF
(c) $NaBH_4$ in C_2H_5OH (d) Raney Ni/H_2 in THF

7. Compounds P and R upon ozonolysis produce Q and S, respectively. The molecular formula of Q and S is C_8H_8O. Q undergoes Cannizzaro reaction but not haloform reaction, whereas S undergoes haloform reaction but not Cannizzaro reaction **[JEE Adv. 2017]**

(i) $P \xrightarrow[\text{ii) }Zn/H_2O]{\text{i) }O_3/CH_2Cl_2} \underset{(C_8H_8O)}{Q}$

(ii) $R \xrightarrow[\text{ii) }Zn/H_2O]{\text{i) }O_3/CH_2Cl_2} \underset{(C_8H_8O)}{S}$

The option(s) with suitable combination of P and R, respectively, is(are)

(a) 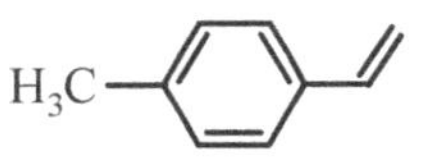 and

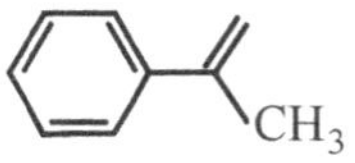

(b) 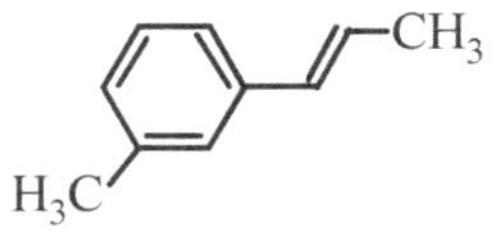 and

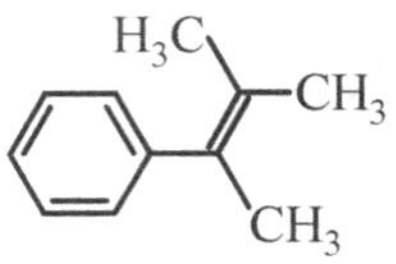

(c) 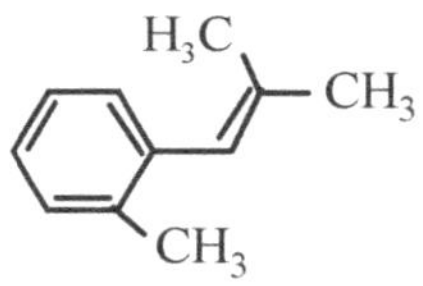 and

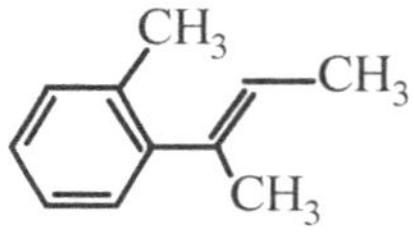

(d) 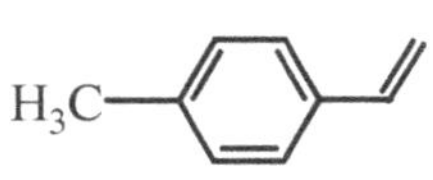 and

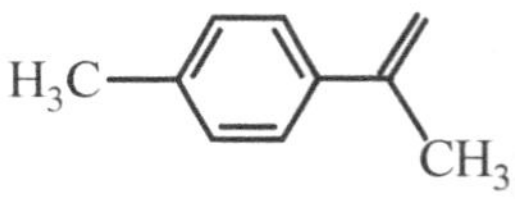

Match the Following

1. Different possible **thermal** decomposition pathways for peroxyesters are shown below. Match each pathway from **List-I** with an appropriate structure from **List-II** and select the correct answer using the code given below the lists. **[JEE Adv. 2014]**

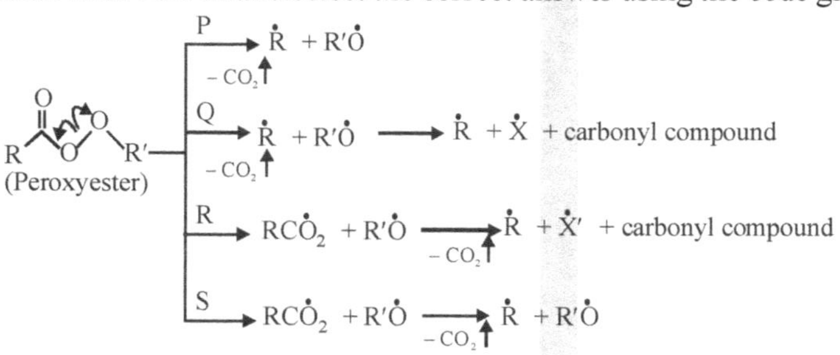

(Peroxyester)

P: $\xrightarrow{-CO_2\uparrow} \dot{R} + R'\dot{O}$

Q: $\xrightarrow{-CO_2\uparrow} \dot{R} + R'\dot{O} \longrightarrow \dot{R} + \dot{X}$ + carbonyl compound

R: $\longrightarrow R\dot{C}O_2 + R'\dot{O} \xrightarrow{-CO_2\uparrow} \dot{R} + \dot{X}'$ + carbonyl compound

S: $\longrightarrow R\dot{C}O_2 + R'\dot{O} \xrightarrow{-CO_2\uparrow} \dot{R} + R'\dot{O}$

List-I	List-II
P. Pathway P	**1.** $C_6H_5CH_2C(=O)O\text{–}O\text{–}CH_3$
Q. Pathway Q	**2.** $C_6H_5C(=O)O\text{–}O\text{–}CH_3$
R. Pathway R	**3.** $C_6H_5CH_2C(=O)O\text{–}O\text{–}C(CH_3)_2CH_2C_6H_5$
S. Pathway S	**4.** $C_6H_5C(=O)O\text{–}O\text{–}C(CH_3)_2C_6H_5$

Code :

	P	Q	R	S
(a)	1	3	4	2
(b)	2	4	3	1
(c)	4	1	2	3
(d)	3	2	1	4

Comprehension Based Questions

PASSAGE-1

P and Q are isomers of dicarboxylic acid $C_4H_4O_4$. Both decolorize Br_2/H_2O. On heating, P forms the cyclic anhydride. Upon treatment with dilute alkaline $KMnO_4$, P as well as Q could produce one or more than one from S, T and U.

S: COOH / H–C–OH / H–C–OH / COOH

T: COOH / H–C–OH / HO–C–H / COOH

U: COOH / HO–C–H / H–C–OH / COOH

[JEE Adv. 2013]

1. Compounds formed from P and Q are, respectively
   - (a) Optically active S and optically active pair (T, U)
   - (b) Optically inactive S and optically inactive pair (T, U)
   - (c) Optically active pair (T, U) and optically active S
   - (d) Optically inactive pair (T, U)) and optically inactive S

2. In the following reaction sequences V and W are respectively

$$Q \xrightarrow[\Delta]{H_2/Ni} V$$

$$\text{Benzene} + V \xrightarrow{AlCl_3\,(\text{anhydrous})} \xrightarrow[2.\ H_3PO_4]{1.\ Zn\text{-}Hg/HCl} W$$

   - (a) V: succinic anhydride (cyclic) and W: 1-tetralone (tetralin ring with C=O)
   - (b) V: $HOH_2C\text{–}CH{=}CH\text{–}CH_2OH$ (cis) and W: 1,2-dihydronaphthalene
   - (c) V: succinic anhydride (cyclic) and W: tetralin
   - (d) V: $HOH_2C\text{–}CH{=}CH\text{–}CH_2OH$ (trans) and W: $C_6H_5CH_2CH{=}CHCH_2OH$

PASSAGE-2

In the following reactions

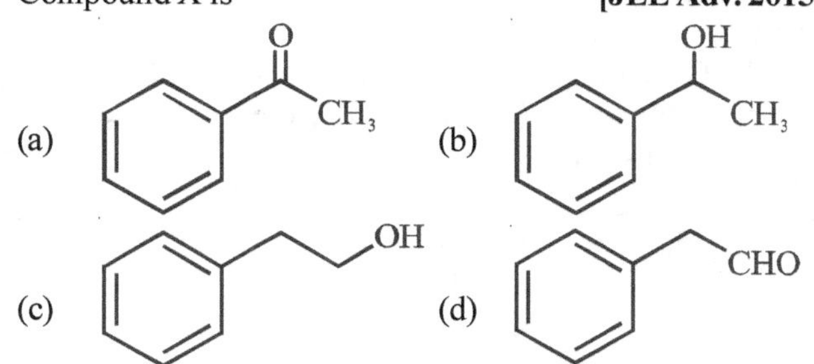

$$C_8H_6 \xrightarrow[H_2]{Pd-BaSO_4} C_8H_8 \xrightarrow[(ii)\,H_2O_2,\ NaOH,\ H_2O]{(i)\,B_2H_6} X$$

$$C_8H_6 \xrightarrow{H_2O,\ HgSO_4,\ H_2SO_4} C_8H_8O \xrightarrow[(ii)\,H^+,\ heat]{(i)\,EtMgBr,\ H_2O} Y$$

3. Compound X is **[JEE Adv. 2015]**
   - (a) $C_6H_5COCH_3$
   - (b) $C_6H_5CH(OH)CH_3$
   - (c) $C_6H_5CH_2CH_2OH$
   - (d) $C_6H_5CH_2CHO$

4. The major compound Y is [JEE Adv. 2015]

(a) 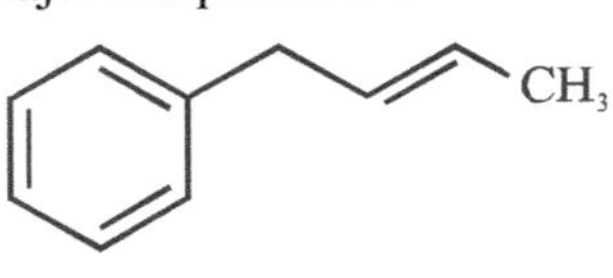 CH3
(b) 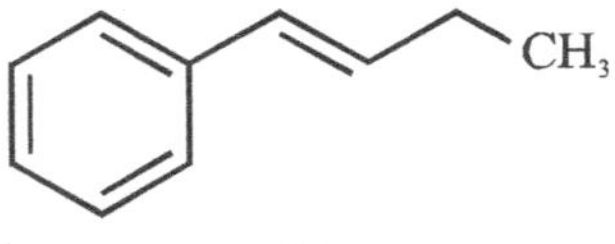 CH3
(c) 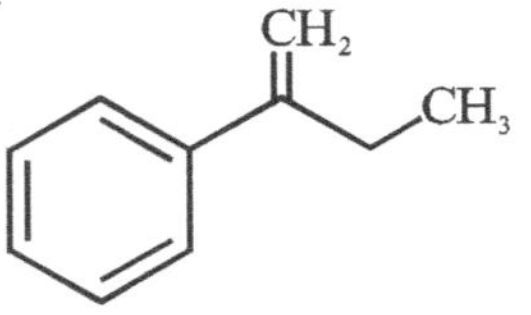 CH2 CH3
(d) 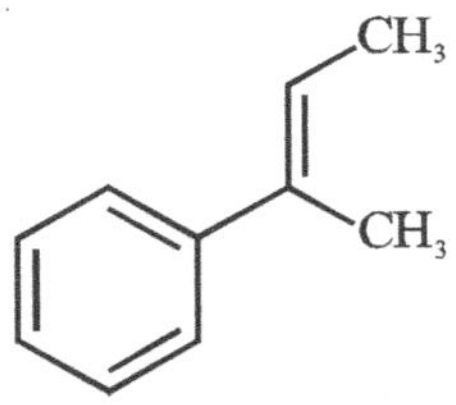 CH3 CH3

PASSAGE-3

By appropriately matching the information given in the three columns of the following table. [JEE Adv. 2017]
Columns 1, 2 and 3 contain starting materials, reaction conditions, and type of reactions, respectively.

	Column 1		Column 2		Column 3
(I)	Toluene	(i)	NaOH/Br_2	(P)	Condensation
(II)	Acetophenone	(ii)	Br_2/hv	(Q)	Carboxylation
(III)	Benzaldehyde	(iii)	$(CH_3CO)_2O$/ CH_3COOK	(R)	Substitution
(IV)	Phenol	(iv)	NaOH/CO_2	(S)	Haloform

5. For the synthesis of benzoic acid, the only CORRECT combination is
(a) (II) (i) (S) (b) (IV) (ii) (P)
(c) (I) (iv) (Q) (d) (III) (iv) (R)

6. The only CORRECT combination that gives two different carboxylic acids is
(a) (II) (iv) (R) (b) (IV) (iii) (Q)
(c) (III) (iii) (P) (d) (I) (i) (S)

7. The only CORRECT combination in which the reaction proceeds through radical mechanism is
(a) (III) (ii) (P) (b) (IV) (i) (Q)
(c) (II) (iii) (R) (d) (I) (ii) (R)

PASSAGE-4

The reaction of compound P with CH_3MgBr (excess) in $(C_2H_5)_2O$ followed by addition of H_2O gives Q. The compound Q on treatment with H_2SO_4 at 0°C gives R. The reaction of R with CH_3COCl in the presence of anhydrous $AlCl_3$ in CH_2Cl_2 followed by treatment with H_2O produces compound S. [Et in compound P is ethyl group]

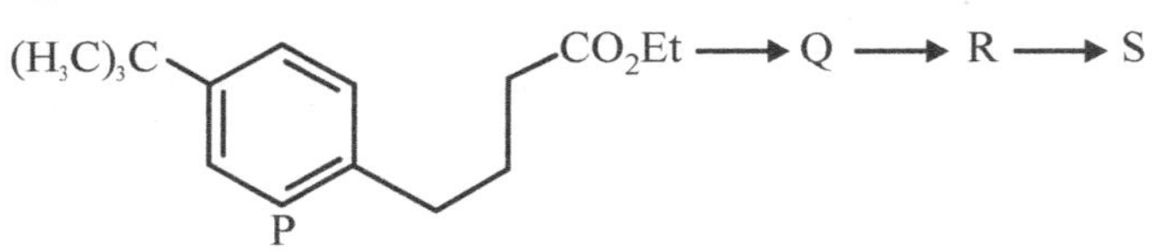

$(H_3C)_3C$ — CO_2Et ⟶ Q ⟶ R ⟶ S
P

8. The product S is [JEE Adv. 2017]

(a) 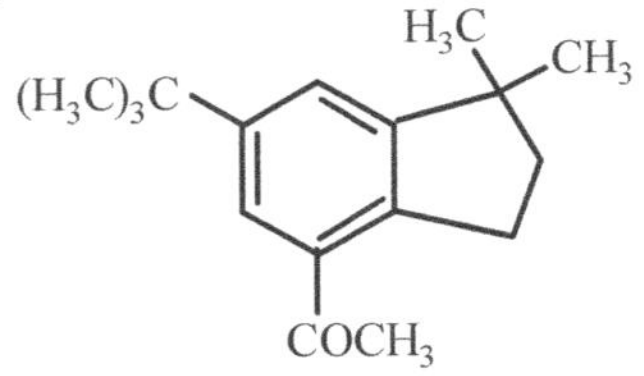 H_3C CH_3 $(H_3C)_3C$ $COCH_3$
(b) 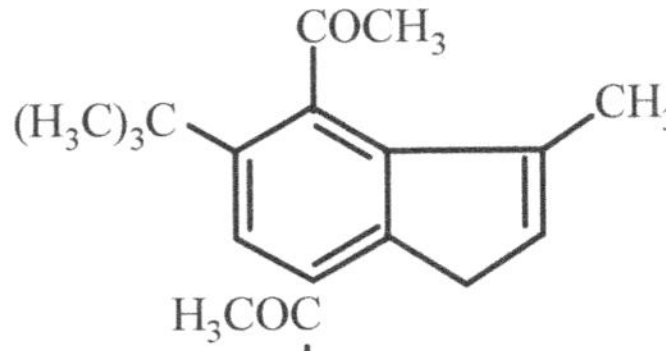 $COCH_3$ $(H_3C)_3C$ CH_3
(c) 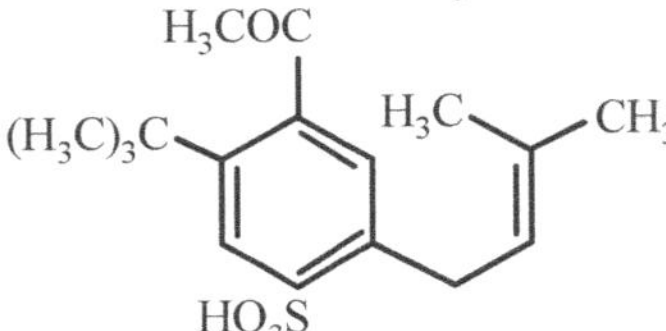 H_3COC $(H_3C)_3C$ H_3C CH_3
(d) 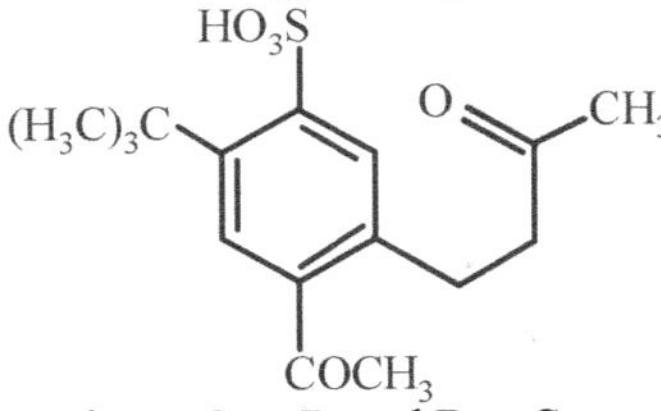 HO_3S $(H_3C)_3C$ O CH_3 $COCH_3$

9. The reactions, Q to R and R to S, are [JEE Adv. 2017]
(a) Dehydration and Friedel–Crafts acylation
(b) Aromatic sulfonation and Friedel–Crafts acylation
(c) Friedel–Crafts alkylation, dehydration and Friedel–Crafts acylation
(d) Friedel–Crafts alkylation and Friedel–Crafts acylation

Integer Value Correct Type

1. The total number of carboxylic acid groups in the product P is [JEE Adv. 2013]

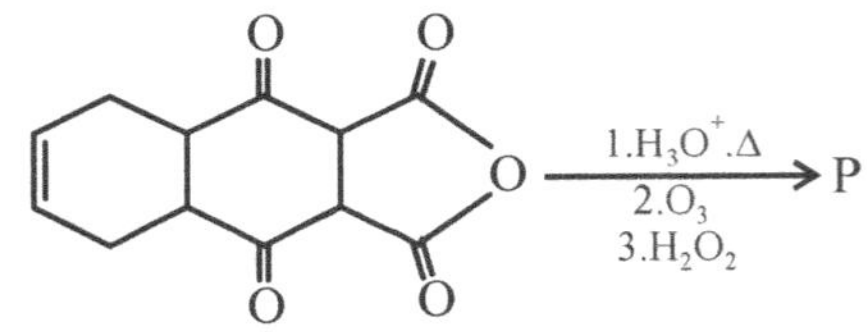

O O O O O ⟶ P (1. H_3O^+, Δ; 2. O_3; 3. H_2O_2)

2. Consider all possible isomeric ketones, including stereoisomers of MW = 100. All these isomers are independently reacted with $NaBH_4$ (**NOTE:** stereoisomers are also reacted separately). The total number of ketones that give a racemic product(s) is/are [JEE Adv. 2014]

3. Among the following, the number of reaction(s) that produce(s) benzaldehyde is [JEE Adv. 2015]

I. 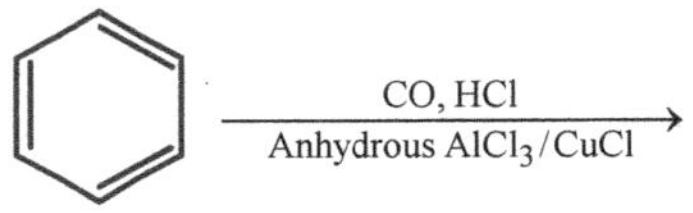 (benzene) $\xrightarrow[\text{Anhydrous } AlCl_3/CuCl]{CO, HCl}$

II. 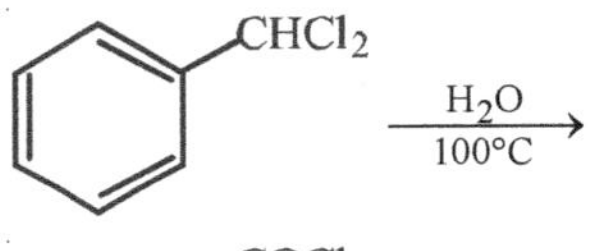 (benzene)–$CHCl_2$ $\xrightarrow[100°C]{H_2O}$

III. 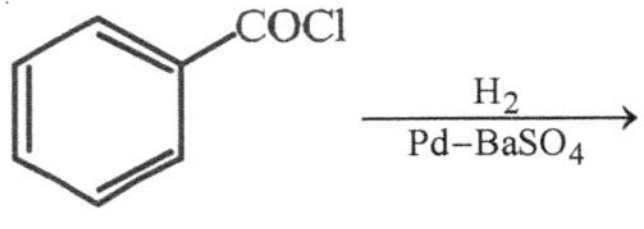 (benzene)–COCl $\xrightarrow[Pd–BaSO_4]{H_2}$

IV. 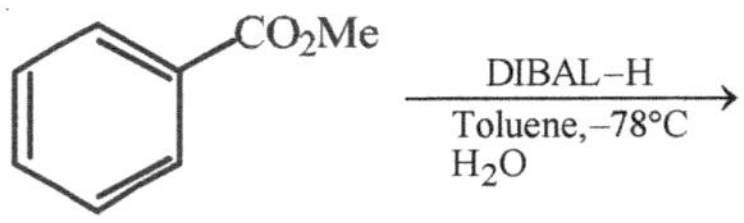 (benzene)–CO_2Me $\xrightarrow[\text{Toluene, –78°C}, H_2O]{DIBAL–H}$

PAST YEAR QUESTIONS JEE MAIN/AIEEE (2013 - 2017)

1. The most suitable reagent for the conversion of $R-CH_2-OH \rightarrow R-CHO$ is: **[JEE M 2014]**
(a) $KMnO_4$
(b) $K_2Cr_2O_7$
(c) CrO_3
(d) PCC (Pyridinium Chlorochromate)

2. In the reaction,

$$CH_3COOH \xrightarrow{LiAH_4} A \xrightarrow{PCl_5} B \xrightarrow{Alc.KOH} C,$$

the product C is: **[JEE M 2014]**
(a) Acetaldehyde (b) Acetylene
(c) Ethylene (d) Acetyl chloride

3. In the following sequence of reactions : **[JEE M 2015]**

$$\text{Toluene} \xrightarrow{KMnO_4} A \xrightarrow{SOCl_2} B \xrightarrow[BaSO_4]{H_2/Pd} C$$

the product C is :
(a) $C_6H_5CH_2OH$ (b) C_6H_5CHO
(c) C_6H_5COOH (d) $C_6H_5CH_3$

4. The correct sequence of reagents for the following conversion will be : **[JEE M 2017]**

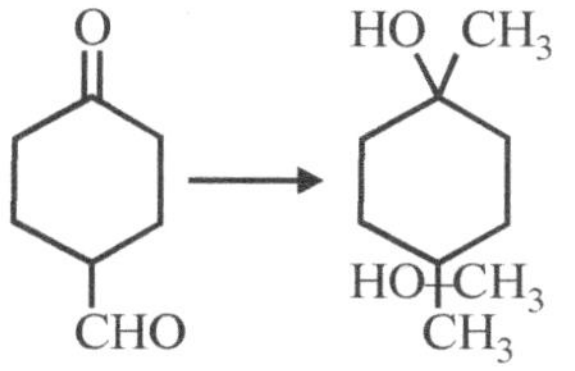

O, CHO → HO CH$_3$, HO CH$_3$ CH$_3$

(a) $[Ag(NH_3)_2]^+ OH^-, H^+/CH_3OH, CH_3MgBr$
(b) $CH_3MgBr, H^+/CH_3OH, [Ag(NH_3)_2]^+ OH^-$
(c) $CH_3MgBr, [Ag(NH_3)_2]^+ OH^-, H^+/CH_3OH$
(d) $[Ag(NH_3)_2]^+ OH^-, CH_3MgBr, H^+/CH_3OH$

5. The major product obtained in the following reaction is : **[JEE M 2017]**

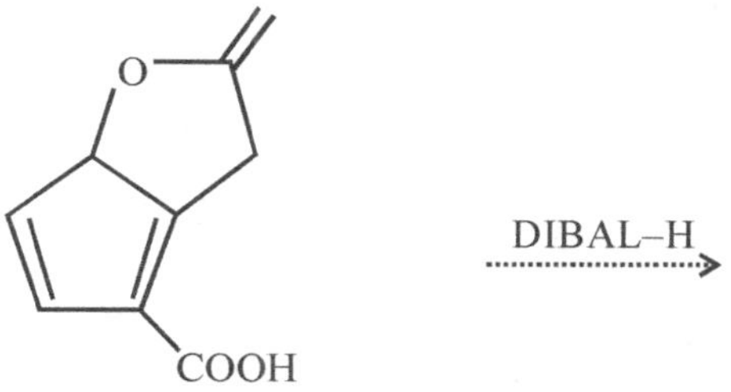

O, COOH —DIBAL–H→

(a) 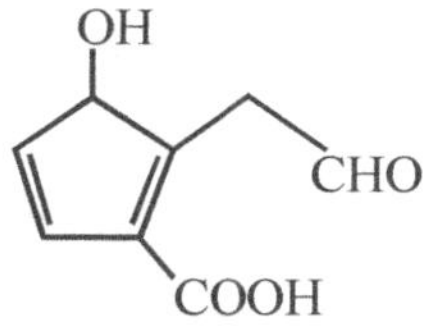 OH, CHO, COOH (b) 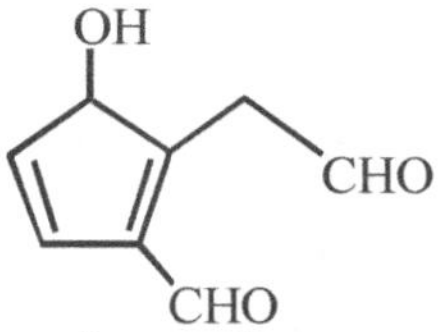 OH, CHO, CHO
(c) 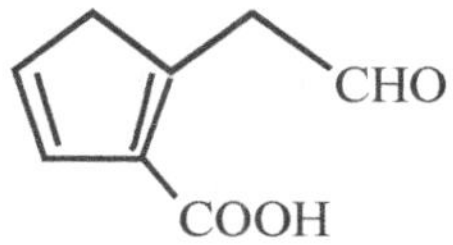 CHO, COOH (d) 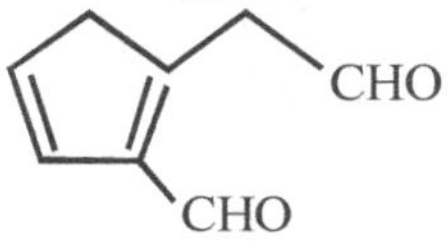 CHO, CHO

6. Sodium salt of an organic acid 'X' produces effervescence with conc. H_2SO_4. 'X' reacts with the acidified aqueous $CaCl_2$ solution to give a white precipitate which decolourises acidic solution of $KMnO_4$. 'X' is : **[JEE M 2017]**
(a) C_6H_5COONa (b) HCOONa
(c) CH_3COONa (d) $Na_2C_2O_4$

SOLUTIONS

PAST YEAR QUESTIONS JEE ADVANCED/IIT-JEE (2013 - 2017)

MCQs with One Correct Answer

1. **(d)** Carbolic acid (Phenol) is weaker acid than carbonic acid and hence does not liberate CO_2 on treatment with aq. $NaHCO_3$ solution.

2. **(d)**

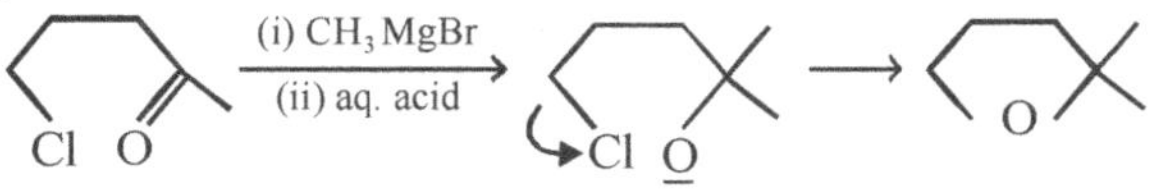

Cl O —(i) CH_3MgBr (ii) aq. acid→ Cl O → O

3. **(a)**

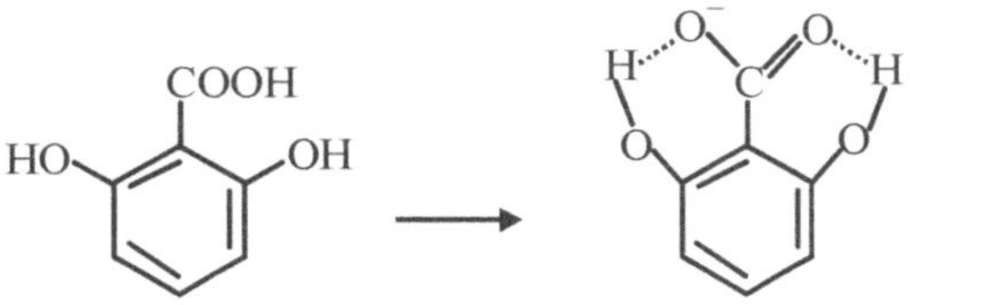

COOH, HO, OH (I) → H, O$^-$, C, O, H, O, O (stabilizes by more H-bonding)

COOH, OH (II) → O, O$^-$, H, O (stabilizes by H-bonding)

COOH, OH (III) → COO$^-$, OH (stabilizes by –I effect)

COOH, OH (IV) → COO$^-$, OH (destabilizes by +M effect)

∴ acidity order is I > II > III > IV

4. **(a)**

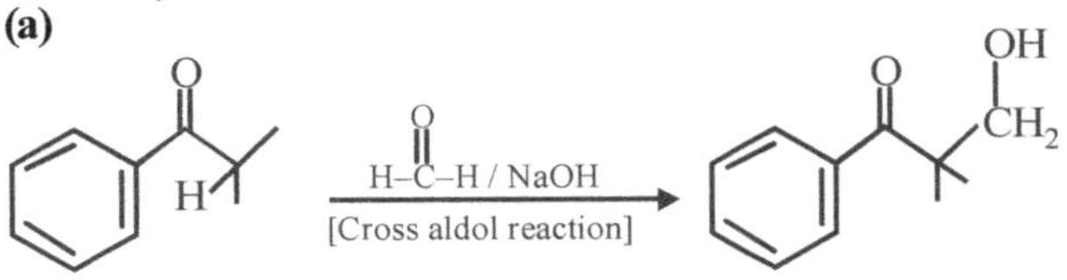

O, H —H–C(=O)–H / NaOH [Cross aldol reaction]→ O, OH, CH_2

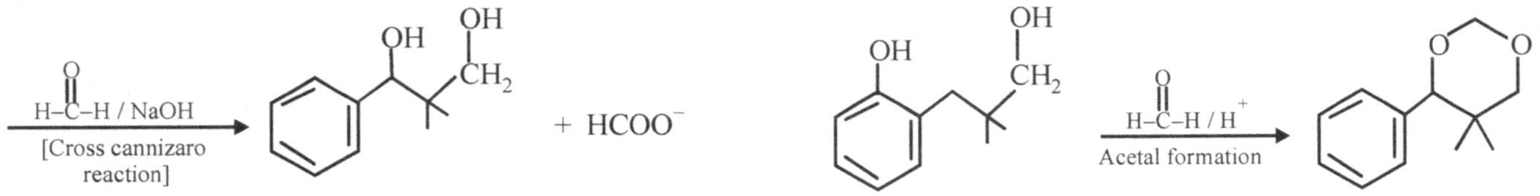

H–C(=O)–H / NaOH [Cross cannizaro reaction] → + $HCOO^-$

H–C(=O)–H / H^+ Acetal formation →

MCQs with One or More Than One Correct

1. **(b, d)**

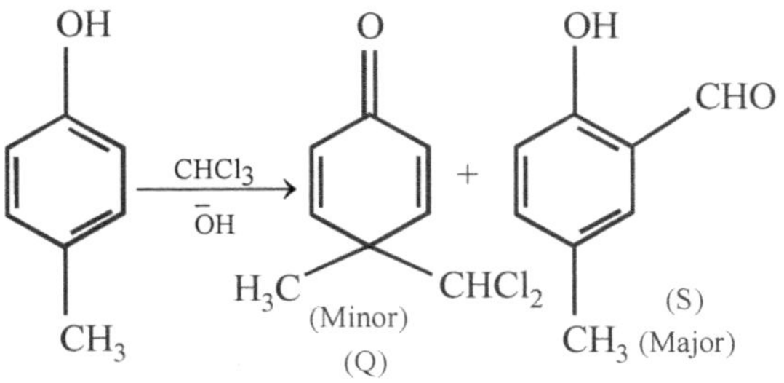

$\xrightarrow[\bar{O}H]{CHCl_3}$ (Minor) (Q) + (S) CH_3 (Major)

$$CHCl_3 + \bar{O}H \longrightarrow :CCl_2 + H_2O + Cl^-$$

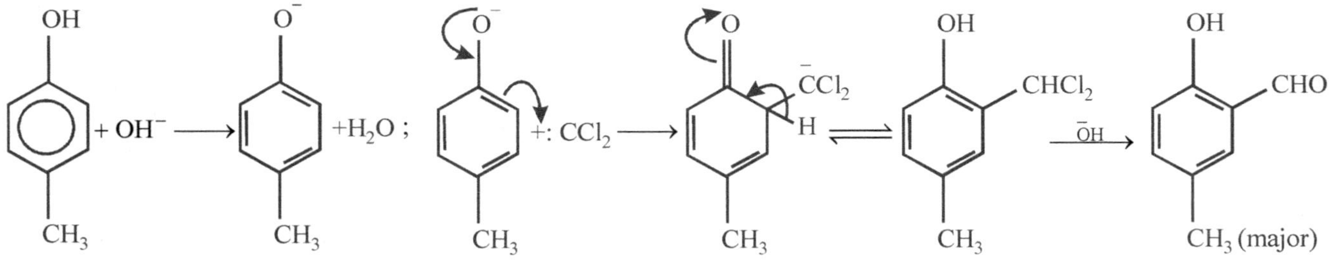

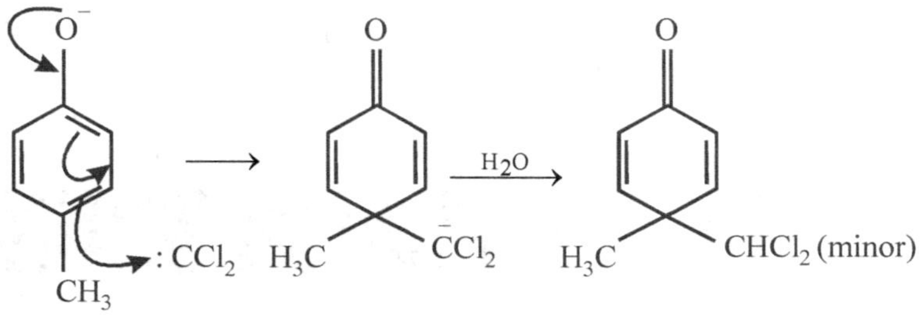

$+ OH^- \longrightarrow$ $+H_2O$; $+: CCl_2 \longrightarrow$ $\rightleftharpoons$ $\xrightarrow{\bar{O}H}$ CH_3 (major)

$\longrightarrow$ $\xrightarrow{H_2O}$ H_3C $CHCl_2$ (minor)

2. **(c)** Reaction I : CH_3COCH_3 (1.0 mol) $\xrightarrow[Na^{\oplus}OH^{\varepsilon}]{Br_2\,(1.0\,mol)}$ CH_3COONa (T) + $CHBr_3$ (U) + CH_3COCH_3 (unreacted)

Reaction II : CH_3COCH_3 (1.0 mol) $\xrightarrow[CH_3COOH]{Br_2\,(1.0\,mol)}$ CH_3COCH_2Br (P)

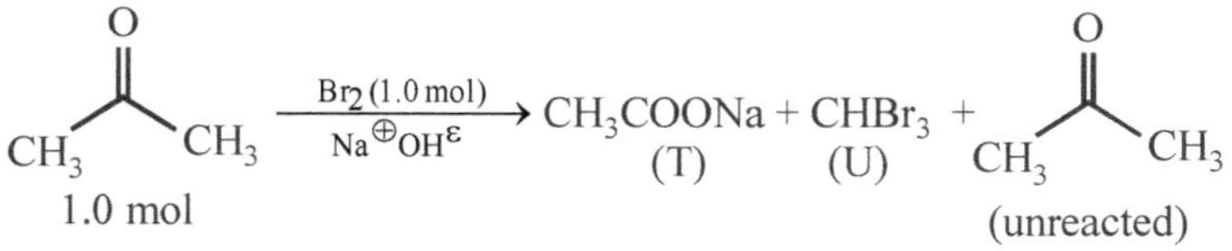

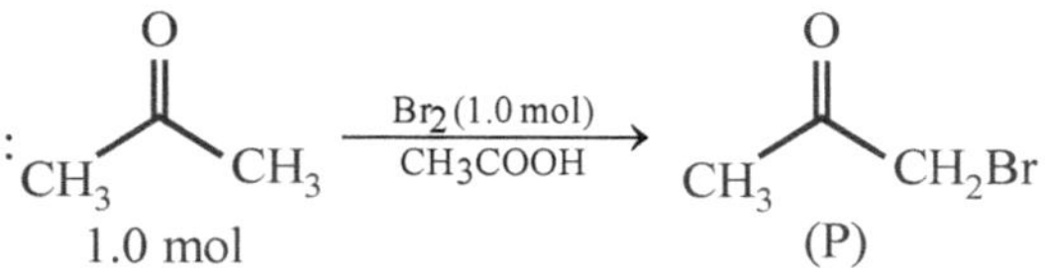

3. **(a)** $\xrightarrow{KOH,\,H_2O}$ $\longrightarrow$ $\xrightarrow{H^+}$

(Minor) + (Major)

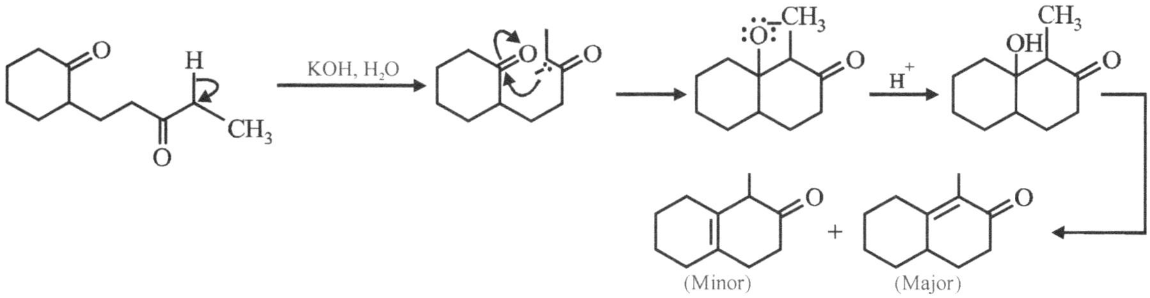

4. **(a, b, c)** Aldehydes and α-Hydroxyketones show positive Tollen's test.

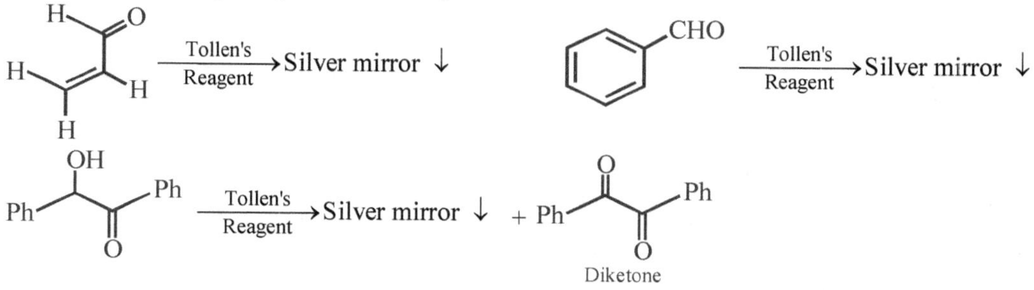

$CH_2=CH-CHO \xrightarrow[\text{Reagent}]{\text{Tollen's}}$ Silver mirror ↓ $\qquad C_6H_5CHO \xrightarrow[\text{Reagent}]{\text{Tollen's}}$ Silver mirror ↓

$Ph-CH(OH)-CO-Ph \xrightarrow[\text{Reagent}]{\text{Tollen's}}$ Silver mirror ↓ + $Ph-CO-CO-Ph$

Diketone

5. **(b, c)** Cumene $\xrightarrow[\text{(ii) } H_3O^+]{\text{(i) } O_2}$ Phenol (P) $\xrightarrow{CHCl_3/NaOH}$ o-hydroxybenzaldehyde Q (Major) + p-hydroxybenzaldehyde R (Minor)

o-hydroxybenzaldehyde $\xrightarrow[PhCH_2Br]{NaOH}$ $o-(PhCH_2O)C_6H_4CHO$ (S)

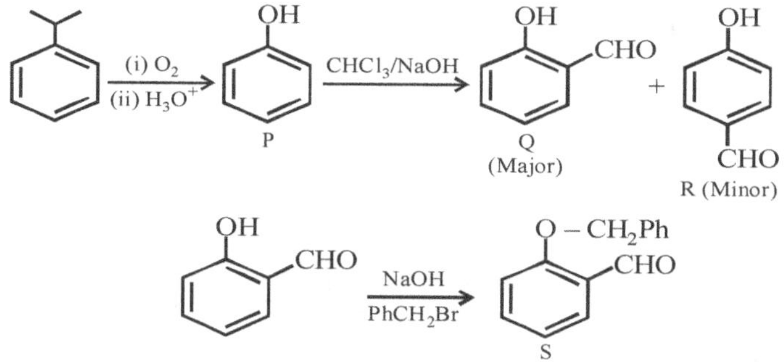

Q is steam volatile not R.
Q and R show positive test with 1% aqueous $FeCl_3$ solution.
Q, R, S give yellow precipitate with 2, 4-dinitrophenyl hydrazine.

6. **(c, d)**

$LiAlH_4/(C_2H_5)_2O$: Reduces to esters, carboxylic acid, epoxides and aldehydes and ketones.
BH_3 in T.H.F : Reduces to –COOH and aldehydes into alcohols but do not reduce to esters and epoxides.
$NaBH_4$ in C_2H_5OH : Reduces only aldehydes and ketones into alcohols but not to others.
Raney Ni in T.H.F. : Do not reduce to –COOH, –COOR and epoxide but it can reduce aldehyde into alcohols.

7. **(a, b)**

(c) $CH_3-C_6H_4-CH=CH_2$ (P) $\xrightarrow[\text{(ii) Zn, } H_2O]{\text{(i) } O_3, CH_2Cl_2}$ Q (C_8H_8O), i.e., $CH_3-C_6H_4-CHO$ (Q) $+ H-\overset{O}{\overset{\|}{C}}-H$

(+ve cannizaro reaction)

$C_6H_5-C(CH_3)=CH_2$ (R) $\xrightarrow[\text{(ii) Zn, } H_2O]{\text{(i) } O_3, CH_2Cl_2}$ $C_6H_5-CO-CH_3$ $+ H-\overset{O}{\overset{\|}{C}}-H$

(S) (+ve haloform reaction)

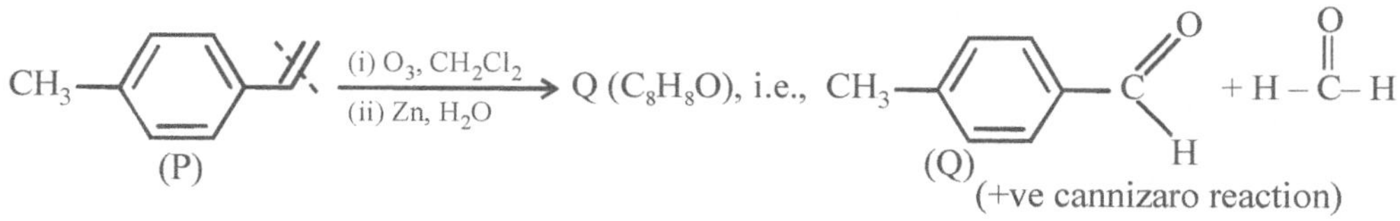

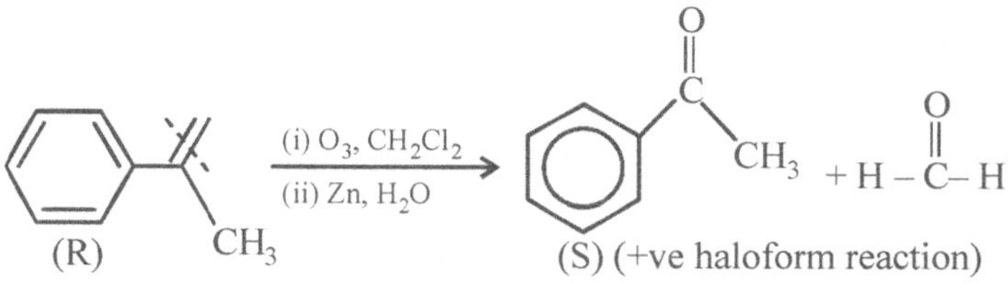

(d) $m-CH_3-C_6H_4-CH=CH-CH_3$ (P) $\xrightarrow[Zn, H_2O]{O_3, CH_2Cl_2}$ $m-CH_3-C_6H_4-CHO$ $+ CH_3-\overset{O}{\overset{\|}{C}}-H$

(+ve cannizaro reaction)

(Q)

$m-CH_3-C_6H_4-C(CH_3)=C(CH_3)-CH_3$ (R) $\xrightarrow[Zn, H_2O]{O_3, CH_2Cl_2}$ $m-CH_3-C_6H_4-CO-CH_3$ $+ CH_3-\overset{O}{\overset{\|}{C}}-CH_3$

(+ve haloform reaction)

(S)

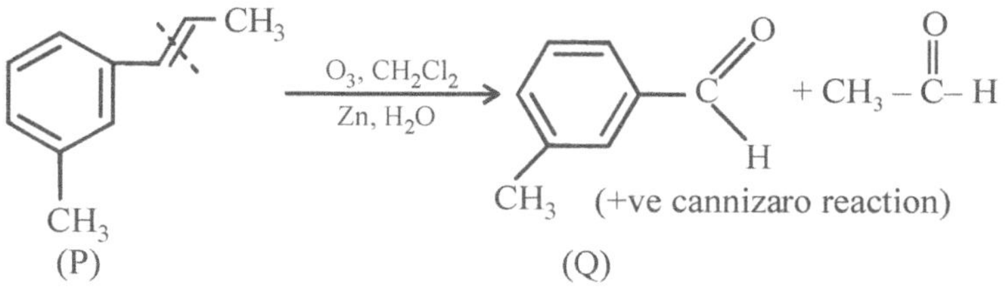

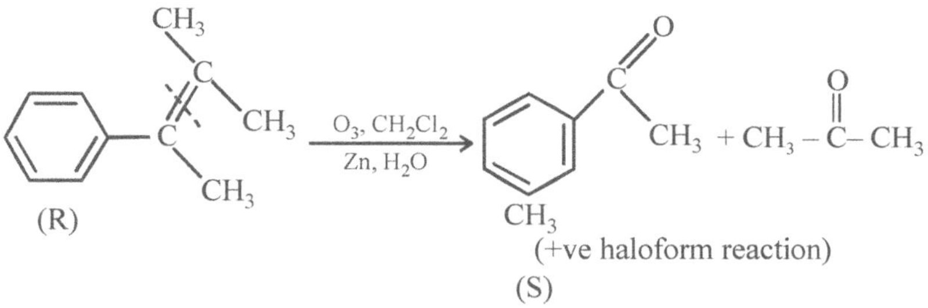

Match the Following

1. (a)

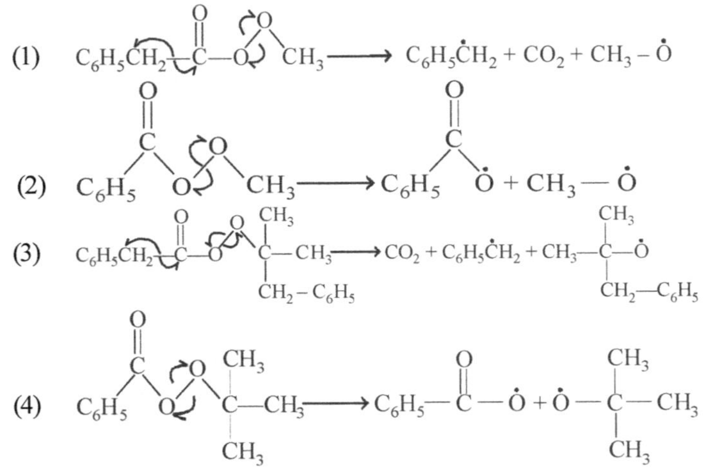

(1) $C_6H_5CH_2-C(=O)-O-O-CH_3 \longrightarrow C_6H_5\dot{C}H_2 + CO_2 + CH_3-\dot{O}$

(2) $C_6H_5-C(=O)-O-O-CH_3 \longrightarrow C_6H_5-C(=O)-\dot{O} + CH_3-\dot{O}$

(3) $C_6H_5CH_2-C(=O)-O-O-C(CH_3)(CH_2-C_6H_5)-CH_3 \longrightarrow CO_2 + C_6H_5\dot{C}H_2 + CH_3-C(CH_3)(CH_2-C_6H_5)-\dot{O}$

(4) $C_6H_5-C(=O)-O-O-C(CH_3)_2-CH_3 \longrightarrow C_6H_5-C(=O)-\dot{O} + \dot{O}-C(CH_3)_2-CH_3$

Comprehension Based Questions

1. (b) HOOC(H)C=C(H)COOH 'P' (Cis) $\xrightarrow[\text{(Syn addition)}]{\text{Cold alk. } KMnO_4}$ COOH, H–C–OH, H–C–OH, COOH

Meso (S), optically inactive

H(HOOC)C=C(H)COOH 'Q' (trans) $\xrightarrow[\text{(Syn addition)}]{\text{Cold alk. } KMnO_4}$ COOH, H–C–OH, OH–C–H, COOH (T) + COOH, OH–C–H, H–C–OH, COOH (U)

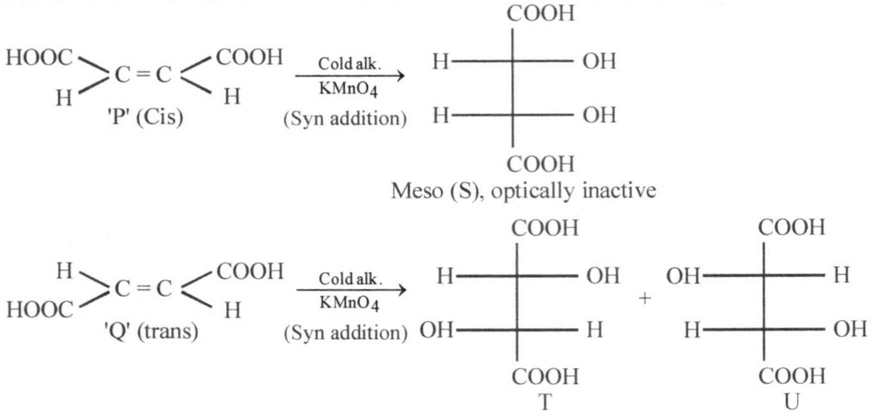

(Racemic Mixture), optically inactive

2. (a) HOOC–CH=CH–COOH (Q) $\xrightarrow[\Delta]{H_2 / Ni}$ succinic anhydride (V)

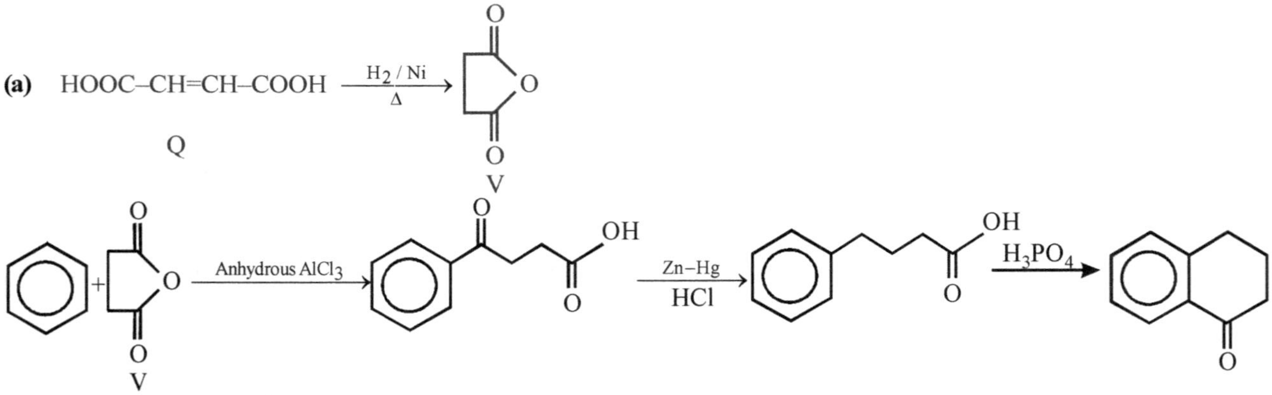

Benzene + V (anhydride) $\xrightarrow{\text{Anhydrous } AlCl_3}$ $C_6H_5-CO-CH_2-CH_2-COOH$ $\xrightarrow[HCl]{Zn-Hg}$ $C_6H_5-CH_2CH_2CH_2-COOH$ $\xrightarrow{H_3PO_4}$ α-tetralone

3. (c) $C_8H_6 \xrightarrow[H_2]{Pd\text{-}BaSO_4}$ styrene $\xrightarrow[\text{ii. } H_2O_2,\ NaOH,\ H_2O]{\text{i. } B_2H_6}$ $C_6H_5CH_2CH_2OH$ (X)

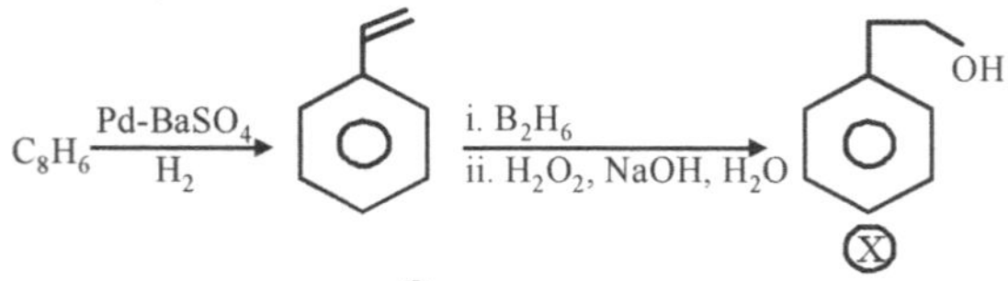

4. (d) $C_8H_6 \xrightarrow[HgSO_4,\ H_2SO_4]{H_2O}$ $C_6H_5COCH_3$ $\xrightarrow[\text{ii. } H^+,\ \text{Heat}]{\text{i. Et MgBr, } H_2O}$ $C_6H_5C(CH_3)=CHCH_3$ (Y)

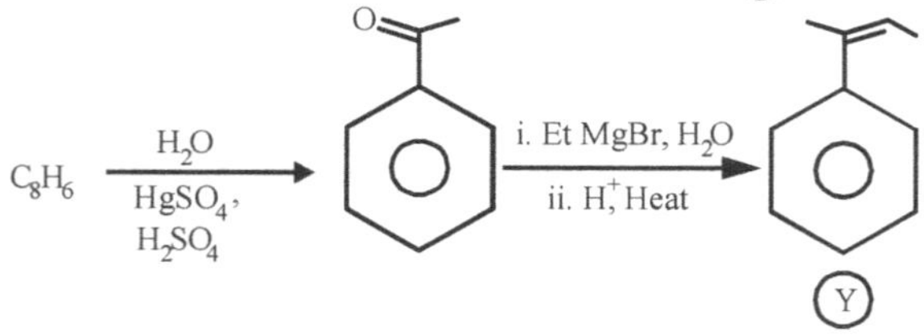

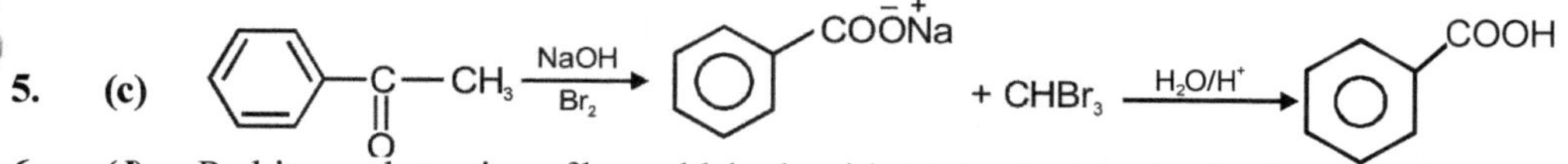

5. (c) $C_6H_5COCH_3 \xrightarrow[Br_2]{NaOH} C_6H_5COO^-Na^+ + CHBr_3 \xrightarrow{H_2O/H^+} C_6H_5COOH$

6. (d) Perkin condensation of benzaldehyde with $(CH_3CO)_2O/CH_3COOK$ yields cis and trans form of cinnamic acid.

$$\underset{\text{Benzaldehyde}}{C_6H_5CHO} + \underset{\text{Acetic anhydride}}{(CH_3CO)_2O} \xrightarrow[(ii)\,H^+]{(i)\,CH_3COONa} \underset{\substack{\text{Cinnamic acid}\\ \text{cis and trans}}}{C_6H_5CH=CHCOOH}$$

7. (a) Alkylbenzenes when treated with Br_2 at high temperature, in the presence of sunlight and absence of halogen carrier undergo **halogenation in the side chain.** Thus

$$\underset{\text{Toluene}}{C_6H_5CH_3} \xrightarrow[\text{light}]{Br_2/\text{heat}} \underset{\text{Benzyl chloride}}{C_6H_5CH_2Br} \xrightarrow[\text{heat, light}]{Br_2} \underset{\text{Benzyl chloride}}{C_6H_5CHBr_2} \xrightarrow[\text{heat, light}]{Br_2} \underset{\text{Benzo trichloride}}{C_6H_5CBr_3}$$

8. (a) & 9. (d)

$(CH_3)_3C$–C_6H_4–CH_2CH_2–$COOEt$ (P) $\xrightarrow{CH_3MgBr(excess)/(C_2H_5)_2O}$ $(CH_3)_3C$–C_6H_4–CH_2CH_2–$C(CH_3)_2\overset{-}{O}\overset{+}{Mg}Br$ $\xrightarrow{H_2O}$ $(CH_3)_3C$–C_6H_4–CH_2CH_2–$C(CH_3)_2$–O–H (Q)

(Q) $\xrightarrow[0°C]{H_2SO_4}$ $(CH_3)_3C$–C_6H_4–CH_2CH_2–$C(CH_3)_2$–$\overset{\oplus}{O}H_2$ $\xrightarrow{-H_2O}$ $(CH_3)_3C$–C_6H_4–CH_2CH_2–$\overset{\oplus}{C}(CH_3)_2$ $\xrightarrow{\text{(Friedel Craft alkylation)}}$ (R) $\xrightarrow[\text{(Friedel Craft Acylation)}]{CH_3-\overset{O}{\overset{||}{C}}-Cl/AlCl_3}$ (S), which carries CH_3, CH_3, $(CH_3)_3C$ and $COCH_3$ groups

Integer Value Correct Type

1. (2) The anhydride $\xrightarrow{H_3O^{\oplus}}$ the dicarboxylic acid (COOH, COOH) $\xrightarrow[-2CO_2]{\Delta}$ the diketone $\xrightarrow{O_3/H_2O_2}$ the diacid with HOOC and HOOC groups

No. of –COOH group is '2'

2. (5) General molecular formula for ketones is $C_nH_{2n}O$ $\therefore$ $C_nH_{2n}O = 100$ or $12n + 2n + 16 = 100, n = 6$

Possible isomeric ketones with 6 carbon atoms are

(I) $CH_3CH_2CH_2CH_2-\overset{O}{\overset{||}{C}}-CH_3$

(II) $CH_3CH_2CH_2-\overset{O}{\overset{||}{C}}-CH_2CH_3$

(III) $CH_3CH_2\overset{*}{C}H(CH_3)-\overset{O}{\overset{||}{C}}-CH_3$

(IV) $CH_3-CH(CH_3)-CH_2-\overset{O}{\overset{||}{C}}-CH_3$

(V) $CH_3-CH(CH_3)-\overset{O}{\overset{||}{C}}-CH_2CH_3$

(VI) $CH_3-C(CH_3)_2-\overset{O}{\overset{||}{C}}-CH_3$

Note that only isomer III has a chiral carbon so on reduction with $NaBH_4$ it will give diastereomeric alcohols, while all other five isomers will give racemic mixture.

3. (4) $C_6H_6 \xrightarrow[\text{Anhyd } AlCl_3/CuCl]{CO,\ HCl} C_6H_5CHO$ (Gatterman Koch Reaction)

$C_6H_5CHCl_2 \xrightarrow[100°C]{H_2O} C_6H_5CH(OH)_2 \xrightarrow{-H_2O} C_6H_5CHO$

$C_6H_5COCl \xrightarrow[Pd\text{–}BaSO_4]{H_2} C_6H_5CHO$ (Rosenmund Reduction)

$C_6H_5COOMe \xrightarrow[\text{Toluene, } -78°C\ H_2O]{DIBAL\text{–}H} C_6H_5CHO$

PAST YEAR QUESTIONS JEE MAIN/AIEEE (2013 - 2017)

1. (d) An excellent reagent for oxidation of 1° alcohols to aldehydes is PCC.

$R-CH_2-OH \xrightarrow{PCC} R-CHO$

2. (c) $\underset{}{CH_3COOH} \xrightarrow{LiAlH_4} \underset{(A)}{CH_3CH_2OH} \xrightarrow{PCl_5} \underset{(B)}{CH_3CH_2Cl} \xrightarrow{Alc.\ KOH} \underset{(C)}{CH_2=CH_2}$

Hence the product (C) is ethylene.

3. (b) $C_6H_5CH_3 \xrightarrow{KMnO_4} \underset{(A)}{C_6H_5COOH} \xrightarrow{SOCl_2} \underset{(B)}{C_6H_5COCl} \xrightarrow[BaSO_4]{H_2/Pd} \underset{(C)}{C_6H_5CHO}$

(B) → (C): Rosenmund's reaction

4. (a) 4-oxocyclohexane-CHO $\xrightarrow[\text{Tollens reagent}]{[Ag(NH_3)_2]OH}$ 4-oxocyclohexane-CO_2H $\xrightarrow[\text{(esterification)}]{H^+/CH_3OH}$ 4-oxocyclohexane-$C(=O)OCH_3$ $\xrightarrow{CH_3MgBr}$ 1,1-dimethylcyclohexane with 4-$C(OH)(CH_3)_2$ ($H_3C-C(OH)-CH_3$)

5. (b) DIBAL-H is an electrophilic reducing agent. It reduces both ester and carboxylic group into an aldehyde at low temperature.

Bicyclic lactone with CO_2H $\xrightarrow{DIBAL\text{–}H}$ cyclopentene with OH, CH_2CHO and CHO

6. (d) $\underset{'x'}{Na_2C_2O_4} + \underset{(conc.)}{H_2SO_4} \rightarrow Na_2SO_4 + CO\uparrow + CO_2\uparrow + H_2O$

$\underset{x'}{Na_2C_2O_4} + CaCl_2 \rightarrow \underset{\text{(white ppt.)}}{CaC_2O_4\downarrow} + 2NaCl$

$5CaC_2O_4\downarrow + \underset{\text{(purple)}}{2KMnO_4} + 8H_2SO_4 \longrightarrow K_2SO_4 + 5CaSO_4 + \underset{\text{(colourless)}}{2MnSO_4} + 10CO_2 + 8H_2O$

www.ingramcontent.com/pod-product-compliance
Lightning Source LLC
LaVergne TN
LVHW080054160726
843469LV00047B/1815